WESTWARD EXPANSION

AN EYEWITNESS HISTORY

WESTWARD EXPANSION

An Eyewitness History

Sanford Wexler

 Facts On File

New York • Oxford

For my mother and father

Westward Expansion: An Eyewitness History

Copyright © 1991 by Sanford Wexler

Facts On File, Inc.   Facts On File Limited
460 Park Avenue South   Collins Street
New York, NY 10016   Oxford OX4 1XJ
USA   United Kingdom

Library of Congress Cataloging-in-Publication Data
Westward expansion : an eyewitness history / [edited by] Sanford
   Wexler.
         p.   cm.—(The Eyewitness history series)
   Includes bibliographical references and index.
   ISBN 0-8160-2407-3
   1. United States—Territorial expansion.   2. Frontier and pioneer
life—United States.   3. Pioneers—United States—Biography.
4. Explorers—United States—Biography.   5. West (U.S.)—Description
and travel.   I. Wexler, Sanford.   II. Series.
E179.W47   1991
973—dc20   90-42599

British CIP data available on request from Facts On File.

Facts On File books are available at special discounts when purchased in bulk quantities for businesses, associations, institutions or sales promotions. Please contact the Special Sales Department of our New York office at 212/683-2244 (dial 800/322-8755 except in NY, AK or HI).

Jacket design by Keith Lovell
Composition by Maple-Vail Composition Services
Manufactured by The Maple-Vail Book Manufacturing Group
Printed in the United States of America

10 9 8 7 6 5 4 3 2 1

This is book is printed on acid-free paper.

Contents

Acknowledgments

Special thanks to Gerard Helferich, vice president and associate publisher at Facts On File, for originating the idea for this volume; Carl Waldman and Molly Braun, for providing indispensable background material on Native American figures and tribes; Alan, Cliff and Gloria Wexler, for their encouragement and invaluable research advice; Gary Krebs, assistant editor at Facts On File, for keeping all of the many pieces together; Paul Scaramazza, for copyediting the text; Kathy Ishizuka at Facts On File; Maja Felaco at the Library of Congress; Fred Pernell at the National Archives; Gene Michael at the New York Public Library Picture Collection; the librarians at the New York Public Library; and the many archivists, researchers and scholars whose earlier efforts paved the way for this book.

The Eyewitness History Series

Historians have long recognized that to truly understand the past we must relive it. We can see past eras and events clearly only when we free our minds from the knowledge of what unfolded between then and now and permit ourselves to experience events with the fresh vision of a contemporary participant or observer.

To stimulate our powers of historical imagination we must begin by immersing ourselves in the documents of the period, so that we can view events as eyewitnesses. The Eyewitness History Series offers readers and students the opportunity to exercise their historical imaginations by providing in a single volume a large collection of excerpts from what historians call "primary sources," the memoirs, diaries, letters, journalism and official documents of the period.

To give these historical raw materials a framework, each chapter begins with a brief summary of the "Historical Context" followed by a detailed "Chronicle of Events." However, the bulk of each chapter consists of a large selection of quotations from eyewitness accounts of the events of the time. These have been selected to give the reader the widest range of views possible. Each has a specific source in the Bibliography to facilitate further study. To further stimulate the reader's historical imagination, a selection of contemporary illustrations is included in each chapter. Modern maps have been included in an appendix for the convenience of readers.

Rather than interrupt the main text with lengthy official documents, we have included them in an appendix. Another appendix includes brief biographies of the major personalities referred to in the text.

Eyewitness Histories are intended to encourage students and readers to discover the powers and the pleasures of historical imagination, while also providing them with comprehensive and self-contained works of reference to significant historical periods.

Preface

Selecting the firsthand accounts for this book was at first fairly straightforward. Most of the prominent figures would of course be quoted, such as Daniel Boone, Lewis and Clark, Stephen F. Austin, Thomas Hart Benton and John C. Fremont. Also deserving attention were the thousands of emigrants who in the early 1800s forsaked the security of their homes in the East and loaded their meager belongings onto flatboats bound for such frontier outposts as Cincinnati and Columbus, and who, a few decades later, braved the Oregon Trail for destinations in California and the Pacific Northwest. But did these less-celebrated pioneers leave behind written accounts, and if so, how available are these records?

When driving cross-country today one is unlikely to find any sign of those sprawling wagon trains that transported scores of Americans across the continent in the mid-1800s. But by visiting the American western history section of any major research library one may find the legacy these resilient pioneers left behind. Their myriad stories are found in the form of published diaries, letters, reminiscences and illustrations. Some have happy endings, while others tell of terrible hardships that resulted in failure and defeat. All of them describe the experiences of those who participated in expanding the western frontier. Unfortunately, we have been able to excerpt here only a cross section of these thrilling firsthand accounts.

In these pages, you will see the western frontier through the eyes of the Pennsylvania farmer crossing the Appalachians; the settler tracing the Wilderness Road across Kentucky to the Ohio Valley; the cotton planter rafting down the Mississippi River to the Gulf; the fur trapper hunting along the Upper Missouri; the gold miner scurrying for the "diggings" in California; the New England woman following the Oregon Trail; the homesteader establishing a claim in Nebraska; and the Texas cowboy driving his herd to the cattle town of Abilene, Kansas.

Although many of these firsthand accounts are personal, they reveal much about the period of westward expansion as well as about the rugged individualism integral to shaping the American West. While some emigrants moved westward for a new start in life and a chance to acquire virgin land, others were attracted by the opportunity to find their fortunes in fur trading, mining or cattle raising. Still others traveled westward simply for adventure and freedom. Whatever their motives, all were responsible for settling a vast continent.

The period of westward expansion was also filled with bloody conflicts. Disputes between nations over borders and territorial rights often escalated into full-scale wars. In the French and Indian War, the British pushed the French out of North America; the American Revolution dissolved Britain's colonial American empire; and the Mexican War virtually doubled the size of the United States. These wars, and others, are included in the chapter essays, and quotations from participants on both sides are included with the eyewitness accounts.

Native Americans were also targets of warfare, as they were compelled to surrender their ancestral lands. Alongside quotations from military officers, politicians and government commissioners are excerpts from speeches by tribal chiefs, demonstrating that leaders such as Tecumseh and Sitting Bull were not only great warriors, but also eloquent orators.

This book is arranged chronologically, starting with the French and Indian War, then following with the settlement of the trans-Appalachian frontier, the trans-Mississippi West, the Pacific Northwest, the Far West and, finally, the Great Plains. Thematically, it embraces the related stories of North American exploration; Indian-white relations; the wars and diplomacy of American expansion; and the settlers' experiences. It encompasses the eras of the fur trader, the miner, the cowboy and the Prairie farmer.

As you read through the text you may wish to refer to the appendices. Appendix B provides brief biographies of major personalities. Appendix C offers maps that may serve as a guide to following the rivers, trails, railroad routes and territories referred to in the historical essays and the quotations.

Every effort has been made in the editing process to retain the full meaning and flavor of the original, firsthand accounts. In most cases, spelling and grammar have been left unchanged, but obvious typographical errors have been corrected. The position of each historical figure quoted is the one he or she held at that time. For example, Andrew Jackson, the nation's seventh president, is referred to as a U.S. Army general during the War of 1812.

Although many selections are fragmentary or brief, they may lead you to explore the rich store of primary source material. Below every quotation is a source reference. Full bibliographic citations are given at the end of the book. (Some of the longer titles have been slightly abridged in the text.)

Whether you read *Westward Expansion* from beginning to end or only browse through it, you will witness some of the most exciting moments in American history. I hope that this book will serve as a gateway through which readers will be drawn to explore more deeply the vast and compelling story of westward expansion.

Introduction

The western frontier usually calls to mind romantic images of the cowboy rounding up cattle on the Great Plains or the town sheriff shooting it out with a gang of outlaws. But before there were towns with names like Deadwood, Dodge City and Tombstone, there were the settlements of Jamestown, Plymouth and Quebec—the frontier outposts of the 16th and 17th centuries. Even though the Spanish, French and British settlers who established these villages wore armor and ruffled collars, rather than buckskin, they were the first true frontiersmen.

It took a century and a half for the early pioneers to reach the crest of the Appalachian Mountains—only a few hundred miles from the Atlantic Coast. In another 50 years the eastern half of the Mississippi Valley was settled, and by 1850 that entire region had been divided into states. By 1890 the director of the census could announce: "Up to and including 1880 the country had a frontier settlement, but at present the unsettled area has been so broken into by isolated bodies of settlement that there can hardly be said to be a frontier line."

Generations of scholars, writers and students, American and foreign, have asked, "What was the West?" There is no absolute answer, because the American West was an area with shifting boundaries from colonial times through the first half of the 19th century, and even today it has some characteristics of the frontier. If Alaska and Hawaii are considered as having a part in westward expansion, then western settlement is still not complete, although their boundaries are definite. In 1888, British historian Lord Bryce, author of *The American Commonwealth,* wrote that "the West is the most American part of America . . . . What England is to the rest of Europe, what America is to England, that the Western States and Territories are to the Atlantic States."

The most influential treatise on the West is Frederick Jackson Turner's famous 1893 essay, *The Significance of the Frontier in American History.* Although through the years it has been criticized by some historians and scholars, it remains the basic doctrine on westward expansion. "The existence of an area of free land," Turner stated, "its continuous recession, and the advance of American settlement westward, explain American development." He described the frontier experience as one that repeated itself in a series of "Wests" stretching from the Appalachians to the Pacific Coast. Turner believed that American democracy and, indeed, the American character, were products of this unique confrontation of man and wilderness.

Turner's thesis does not sound novel today, but in 1893 it was a polemic directed against two dominant schools of historians: one group interpreted American history in terms of the slavery controversy and was led by Hermann Edouard von Holt; the other, headed by Turner's former teacher, Herbert B. Adams of Johns Hopkins University, explained American institutions as the outgrowth of English, or rather ancient Teutonic, germs planted in the New World. Turner argued that the West, not the proslavery South or the antislavery North, was the most influential among American sections, and that the unique attitudes and institutions produced by the frontier, especially through its encouragement of democracy, had been more significant than the imported European heritage in shaping American society.

Gradually, Turner's "frontier hypothesis" was accepted by most historians, as well as by a good portion of the general public. Within a decade after its appearance, students were flocking to Turner's seminars at the University of Wisconsin, and he was lecturing throughout the nation. American history textbooks began to cover the westward movement and enlivened their political narratives with thrilling tales of frontier life.

The standard work in their field, *Westward Expansion: A History of the American Frontier* by Ray Allen Billington and Martin Ridge (1960), is based on Turner's frontier thesis. It follows in detail the advance of the frontier through a series of successive Wests: the first one occupied by the fur trader, then the cattle rancher, followed by the miner and the pioneer farmer. "The history of the American West," Billington and Ridge declare, "is, almost by definition, a triumphant narrative for it traces virtually unbroken chains of successes in national experience."

Recent critics of Turner, Billington and Ridge argue that they present the frontier only as a golden land of opportunity, but in reality, it was a desolate place where pioneers were subject to starvation, ferocious blizzards, epidemics, droughts and bankruptcy. Moreover, they fault traditional western histories for failing to consider either the tragedy of the Native Americans or the contribution of frontier women and blacks and other minorities in taming the West.

Debunking the myth of the heroic West began as early as the 1920s, when historian Charles C. Beard charged that the frontier thesis explained the American past less accurately than such economic forces as capitalism, the slave system and labor conflicts. During the 1940s other aspects of the Turner thesis came under attack. He was faulted, for example, for explaining migration solely in geographic terms, rather than as a complex social phenomenon. Other historians have turned to comparative studies to test the frontier hypothesis, rather than belabor its merits. For example, the Turner thesis is applied to world history in Walter P. Webb's *The Great Frontier* (1952).

More recent historians of the West, such as William H. Goetzman, Howard R. Lamar, Gerald D. Nash and Earl Pomeroy, have described the destruction of both people and nature that resulted from the march across the continent. Nevertheless, even among these historians, who acknowledge the darker side of the Old West, it is agreed that the American frontier experience was an important phase in the nation's history, and one that had a positive impact on millions of people.

Frontier hypotheses, like all theories of history, can neither be proved nor disproved, categorically. Efforts to prove or disprove a theory can, indeed, uncover and reconstruct more eyewitness accounts by the very people who lived during the period of westward expansion, especially those omitted from previous histories. However, emphasizing *only* neglected figures and negative aspects of the American West would also result in a history shaded with bias. Why not concentrate our efforts on revealing the many aspects of the frontier experience? As you will discover in this volume, there is an abundance of primary source material available.

Here the westering movement is told in terms of individuals: explorers, fur trappers, soldiers, Indians, politicians, homesteaders, women pioneers, missionaries, miners, cattle ranchers and many others. From these varied eyewitness accounts the reader can draw his own conclusions about the significance of the frontier in American history.

1. The Colonial Frontier: 1754–1794

THE FRENCH AND INDIAN WAR

While the British colonies in America expanded and grew more independent during the early and mid-1700s, they also became involved in the disputes raging between England and France in the Old World. The French entered North America relatively late, although they moved more rapidly than the English into the wilderness, following main waterways like the St. Lawrence, the Great Lakes, the Wisconsin, Illinois, Wabash and the Mississippi in pursuit of fishing and fur-trapping. But France severely limited immigration to America. For example, only Catholics were permitted to settle in Canada, whereas England encouraged men and women of every faith and background to establish farming communities and permanent settlements in the New World. Thus, in 1754 the British colonies consisted of 1,500,000 people, while France had only 100,000 people in America, many of whom were scattered thinly throughout several thousand miles of territory.

France had secured strategic positions by establishing forts and fur-trading posts that stretched from Quebec in the Northeast through what is now Detroit and St. Louis and down to New Orleans. The French aimed to retain and develop this vast hinterland, confining the British to the narrow coastal belt east of the Appalachians. In 1752, the French attacked the small British trading post of Pickawillany in the Ohio country, killing its defenders and seizing a large store of goods. Encouraged by their victory, they increased their efforts to secure the fur-trading country that was within their grasp.

In November 1753, Governor Robert Dinwiddie of Virginia dispatched a messenger to carry a letter of warning to the French commandant at Fort Le Boeuf, which is now the town of Waterford in Erie County, Pennsylvania. The French had settled in territory claimed by the English, and Governor Dinwiddie believed his colony's western land claims and his own interests in the Ohio Valley were threatened. The Ohio Company, which had plans to sell land in this territory, was also disturbed by the French occupation. Dinwiddie's messenger was a

21-year-old planter, surveyor and officer in the Virginia militia, Major George Washington.

The French refused to leave, and Washington hurried back to Virginia with Captain Sainte-Pierre's letter rejecting Governor Dinwiddie's ultimatum. Washington reported that military action would be necessary to force the French to relinquish their claim. His journal of his trip to Fort Le Boeuf was published and circulated throughout the colonies, generating support for the defense of the Ohio Valley from an invasion by the French.

In May 1754, French Ensign Coulon de Jumonville and his small detachment were attacked and killed outside of Fort Duquesne by Washington and 40 of his troops. Thus began the final military conflict between France and England in North America, the French and Indian War. The struggle over ownership of the Ohio country, part of the Seven Years' War in Europe, would ultimately decide which empire controlled North America.

Between 1754 and 1758 the French retained complete control over the Ohio River country. The French armies consistently defeated the English in battle. In July 1755, General Edward Braddock of Virginia and more than 1,000 troops were badly beaten near Fort Duquesne.

The centralized government of France was better equipped for fighting a war in North America than was the loose association of English colonial governments. However, the British population in America outnumbered the French by 15 to one, and Britain had a superior navy to quickly reinforce and resupply her troops.

After suffering a series of defeats, the British attacked the French in 1759 on two fronts: one, against the Canadian coastal fortress at Louisbourg, and a second, up the Hudson River Valley past Lakes George and Champlain into St. Lawrence River country. General John Forbes led more than 6,000 troops in an attack on Fort Duquesne, which the French burned rather than surrender. Forbes informed the colonial government that his troops had overtaken Fort Duquesne, and it was renamed "Pittsborough" after the British war minister, William Pitt.

In September 1759, Quebec also fell to the British. Within a year the American phase of the Seven Years' War was over, and the fate of North America was decided. With the signing of the Treaty of Paris on February 10, 1763, France surrendered all of Canada to the British, and everything east of the Mississippi except New Orleans. With a stroke of the pen America was cleared for uninterrupted westward expansion.

Settlement Crosses the Mountains

After the French departed from North America as a result of the Treaty of Paris, the English colonists found the vacant territories ripe

Colonel George Washington (of the Virginia Militia). By Charles Peale, 1772. Courtesy of the New York Public Library.

for land speculation and settlement. During the 18th century land fever was rampant in America, and although the French and Indian War temporarily slowed speculation activities, it did not extinguish the keen interest in opening up the Ohio country. Speculation in wilderness land was a sure way to become rich in the years before and after the American Revolution, as land investment companies were founded by English and colonial investors. The Ohio Company, formed in 1748, was a leading land speculation venture. The Crown granted the Ohio Company 200,000 acres of land along the Upper Ohio River, provided that 100 families were settled there within seven years. The investors hoped to profit from the sale of land, while the British saw it as an opportunity to deter the French.

Founding Fathers such as Benjamin Franklin, Patrick Henry and George Washington realized great wealth through land speculation. In June 1763, the Mississippi Company was founded by a group of prominent men from Maryland and Virginia, including George Washington. They were granted by the Crown 2,500,000 acres in the Mississippi Valley territory.

Indians in the Old Northwest resented the encroachment by white settlers, and in May 1763, Pontiac, an Ottawa chief, led the Six Nations in a campaign to evict white squatters. Known as "Pontiac's Rebellion," the attack effectively rolled back the frontier to the crest of the Alleghenies.

In England the British Board of Trade discussed to what extent colonial settlers should be allowed to occupy the region and make land purchases directly from the Indians, and who should govern the territory. In October 1763, the British issued a proclamation that attempted to resolve the Indians' complaints about intruding settlers. Colonial governors were prohibited from issuing any more land grants, and individuals were forbidden from purchasing land directly from the Indian tribes. The British controlled land speculation through administrators who entered into purchase agreements with the Indian tribes and then passed on to individual owners the land they acquired.

Colonial land speculators devised many ingenious ways to circumvent the proclamation. For example, companies and individuals used land warrants as a means to penetrate the forbidden Indian country. A land warrant did not convey title. It was simply a document that permitted the bearer to locate a specified number of acres, survey them and register the claim in the land office. During the French and Indian War land warrants were issued to soldiers in return for their military service. Virginia alone issued warrants for nearly three million acres beyond the mountains. Shrewd speculators purchased these land rights from the holders for a low price and then requested the Crown to fulfill its obligation to sell the land.

A more direct way to circumvent the proclamation was simply to ignore it. Thousands of settlers crossed the Alleghenies in Pennsylvania and started farms along the rivers that meet near Fort Pitt (now Pittsburgh) to form the Ohio. They were ordinary farmers seeking out new homes in a country once familiar only to fur traders and explorers.

The early pioneers blazed trails that were once used by Indians for hunting game. In 1758, the Forbes Road was opened between Philadelphia and Fort Pitt. During the French and Indian War only a few crude wagons traveled over the road. With the passage of time and thousands of families the road became a well-marked thoroughfare for adventurous Americans.

By 1770 about 5,000 settlers had crossed the Appalachian Mountains, calling themselves the "men of the western waters." During the next few years around 30,000 people settled in the Ohio River country, known as the "gateway to the West."

Before any of these settlers' land titles could become legal, the proclamation line had to be extended farther west. In October 1768, the Indian superintendent for the Southern Department, John Stuart, negotiated the Treaty of Hard Labor with the Cherokees, which won for the settlers some of the North Carolina back country and a great part of what is now West Virginia.

As settlers, hunters and land speculators moved into the Kentucky Valley, the Shawnee became increasingly concerned at what was happening to the land they had once called their own. The resulting conflict between the two opposing civilizations became known as Lord Dunmore's War.

In April 1774, Governor Lord Dunmore of Virginia used a minor Shawnee attack on a surveying party as an excuse for a call to frontiersmen to defend themselves. To the pioneers this order was equivalent to a declaration of war against the Indians. In July and August 1774, 400 Virginia militia crossed the Ohio and raided two Shawnee villages. The Shawnees soon retaliated by waging a surprise attack on 1,100 Virginia militiamen at Point Pleasant. It was a bloody and desperate frontier battle, and after suffering hundreds of casualties, the Indians retreated across the Ohio.

The Shawnees immediately requested a peace conference, fearing further attacks on their villages. Dunmore forced the Shawnee chiefs to sign the Treaty of Camp Charlotte, in which they consented to the occupation of Kentucky and agreed to cease hunting in the territory. Kentucky was now free of hostilities and open for settlement.

THE WILDERNESS ROAD

Land speculators envisioned great opportunities in the fertile plains of Kentucky, Tennessee and the Cumberland. Judge Richard Henderson of North Carolina, founder of the Transylvania Company, negotiated a treaty with the Cherokees for title to half of what is now the state of Kentucky. The Cherokees received £10,000 sterling in trade goods, mostly clothing, ornaments and firearms, in exchange for 20,000,000 acres of their land between the Kentucky and Cumberland rivers. Although the Transylvania Company was not authorized to buy land from the Indians and sell it to white settlers, Judge Henderson refused to allow regulations imposed by the proclamation to interfere in his dream of developing the West. In March 1775, Henderson hired Daniel Boone, the famed frontiersman and "Long Hunter," to mark off a trail from the eastern settlements through the mountains and down the Kentucky River to the Ohio.

"Long Hunters," named for their lengthy journeys into the wilderness, were as skilled as their Indian foes in reading the messages of a fallen branch or the cries of a distant animal. Out of the wilderness they took game, vegetables, salt and hides to make their coonskin caps and leather hunting jackets. They traded their furs for things the wilderness could not provide: hatchets, hunting knives and long rifles.

Daniel Boone and 30 axmen set out on March 10, 1775, to clear a trail that passed through the Cumberland Gap and ended on the Kentucky River, where the settlement of Boonesborough was established. The trail, which became well known as the Wilderness Road, was the only practical route through the mountains, and it was used by thousands of early westbound settlers.

Soon after the Wilderness Road was cleared many settlers began to move into the Kentucky region, and families came to purchase land from the Transylvania Company. They went not only to Boonesborough, but also to nearby places such as Harrodsburg, Boiling Springs and St. Asaph's.

Henderson and his associates intended to establish an independent local government. On May 23, 1775, 18 delegates from Harrodsburg, Boiling Springs, St. Asaph and Boonesborough drew up a plan to provide for the conservation of game, for religious liberty and for the creation of a militia and judicial system. However, the Transylvania territory faced opposition by the governors of North and South Carolina, who did not recognize Henderson's title to the territory. Governor Lord Dunmore of Virginia called the Cherokee treaty illegal, and considered it a violation of the king's proclamation of 1763. Henderson's last hope for securing title to the Kentucky territory was with the recently assembled Continental Congress in Virginia.

Henderson petitioned the Congress to admit the Transylvania territory as the 14th colony. John Adams argued against the proposal, fearing that recognition of the illegal colony would further damage the already strained relations between the other colonies and the Crown.

Within a few months after Henderson's request, Boonesborough suffered severe food shortages and experienced several Indian attacks. Resentment also began to grow among the settlers concerning the rise in land prices and the high price of goods sold at Henderson's company store. In June 1776, 24-year-old surveyor George Rogers Clark was chosen by the disgruntled settlers to journey through the Cumberland Gap to Williamsburg with an appeal to the assembly that Kentucky be made a county of Virginia. During the closing days of June the Virginia assembly had nullified the proclamation of 1763, and declared that it owned the western lands. Now Virginia agreed to incorporate Kentucky as one of its counties.

Although Henderson failed to establish his proprietary colony, his efforts did help publicize the rich lands located beyond the mountains, and contributed to rallying support among the early pioneers for an independent West that was free from British control. Two years later Virginia compensated Henderson for his investment in the Kentucky territory by granting the Transylvania Company 200,000 acres of land between the Green River and the Ohio.

Fort at Boonesborough, 1775. Courtesy of the New York Public Library.

THE WEST IN THE AMERICAN REVOLUTION

At first the early western settlers had little interest in the American Revolution. They were unsympathetic to the rebels' call of "taxation without representation" when their own delegates were denied admission into the colonial legislatures. However, their indifference soon turned to support for the eastern revolutionaries when the British began encouraging the Indians to attack their settlements.

During the War for Independence both the British and Americans tried to make the Indians their allies. The British had a clear advantage over the Americans in their greater supply of manufactured trade goods. Also, the Indians were more likely to view the encroaching American settlers as their natural enemies. Accordingly, the Indian commissioners appointed by the Continental Congress decided to try to secure a pledge of neutrality from the Indian nations.

The commissioners were successful only with the northern Shawnees and Delawares, because these tribes remembered Lord Dunmore's War and feared the Virginia frontiersmen, known as the "Long-Knives."

The Cherokees proclaimed their allegiance to George III, but were badly defeated in other attacks on southern settlements. Joint militia forces from South and North Carolina devastated several Indian villages and broke the once all-powerful tribe. The Cherokees surrendered to the Americans in 1777 their remaining territory in South Carolina in the Treaty of Dewitt's Corner.

In Kentucky pioneers were confronted with Delaware, Shawnee, Ottawa and Miami tribes who saw the war with Britian as an opportunity to evict the American intruders from their hunting grounds. Raids by Shawnee and Delaware warriors began in the summer of 1776. Settlers from small towns either fled Kentucky or moved to more secure settlements. By the beginning of 1777 the entire population of Kentucky was residing in the three largest settlements: Boonesborough, Harrodsburg and St. Asaph.

The settlements were transformed into primitive forts, known as stations. Log cabins were connected by high wooden walls that prevented the Indians from launching surprise attacks. Because the daily threat of Indian ambushes prevented the harvesting of badly needed crops, the settlers were forced to survive mostly on meat and water.

Inhabitants of western New York and the Wyoming Valley of Pennsylvania were also plagued by attacks from British-paid Indians, the Iroquois. By the end of June 1778, no frontier settlement was safe from Indian attack. The defensive policy in the West was clearly not succeeding. George Rogers Clark decided that the only way to end the Indian attacks was by striking against the British forts of the Ohio, and he persuaded Virginia Governor Patrick Henry to sponsor an expedition against the Illinois villages. Clark was commissioned by the Virginia assembly as a lieutenant colonel, with the authority to raise a force of militiamen.

On June 26, 1778, Clark set out from Fort Massac, 10 miles below the Falls of Ohio, with 175 experienced Indian fighters. His troops quietly slipped through the country, rather than travel conspicuously along the river route. Clark launched a surprise attack against the British at Kaskaskia, the British were forced to surrender, and within a month the Americans controlled the Illinois country.

Clark capitalized on his victory by summoning the neighboring Indian tribes to a conference at Cahokia. He had studied how the French and Spaniards successfully dealt with the Indians, and he adapted their methods when conferring with the tribes. Clark appeared confident when addressing the chiefs and warriors from the Chippewa, Ottawa, Potawatomi, Sauk, Fox, Miami and other tribes, some of whom had traveled to the council from as far as 500 miles away. Clark explained in terms the Indians could understand the reasons for the American Revolution. He captivated the Indians with his fiery speeches on freedom from British rule, and persuaded most of the tribes to pledge their support to the Americans. The tribes were so im-

Colonel George Rogers Clark's march against Vincennes, across the Wabash River, through wilderness and flood, 1778. Painting by Ezra Winter. Courtesy of the National Archives.

pressed with Clark that years after the American Revolution many Indians insisted on speaking only with him about treaties, rather than with United States commissioners.

While at Kaskaskia Clark learned that British Captain Henry Hamilton (at Detroit) was planning to recapture the Illinois territory by first establishing a base at Fort Vincennes with his army of 500 soldiers and Indians, and then in the spring launching an assault on the American troops. Clark realized that his small force had little chance of defending Kaskaskia, and he decided to try a preemptive surprise attack on Vincennes.

For 180 miles Clark and his poorly supplied men marched along trails that were deeply flooded. At times the troops had to wade through swamps and creeks, with water up to their shoulders. Clark's stamina was remarkable even for an experienced frontiersman, and his stories and jokes boosted the troops' morale.

Despite the terrible hardships, Clark's men arrived three weeks later at Vincennes. Captain Hamilton was not expecting such a bold maneuver, and when the Americans raided Vincennes in the afternoon, the British officer was napping. A tough battle ensued, with the experienced wilderness fighters picking off the English gunners through the fort's gun ports. It soon became evident to Hamilton that Clark's troops were unbeatable. The British commander surrendered to the Americans.

After the capture of Vincennes, Clark planned to immediately march on Detroit. He requested 500 replacements for the exhausted veterans of Kaskaskia and Vincennes, but only 150 recruits arrived from Virginia. The attack was postponed, and Clark spent the next year trying to raise troops and supplies for the raid. However, the Congress could not spare the men or the money to realize Clark's plan, and he never did launch an assault on Detroit. He turned his attention to defending forts and frontier settlements from attacks by British-sponsored Indians.

Despite Clark's victories in the Northwest during 1778 and 1779, most of that territory remained in British control throughout the war. Clark's successful campaigns did have an impact on American troops fighting on other fronts, however. Troops in the East and in the South were inspired by his brilliant victories, and they went on to defeat the British despite their smaller armies and limited supplies.

Even during the war, settlers continued to move westward on the Wilderness Road, despite the constant threat of Indian ambushes. Many pioneers were attracted by the cheap land—100 acres for 10 shillings. In the spring of 1780 more than 20,000 settlers had poured into the Kentucky region. They believed the war was over in the West, but for the next two years the frontier experienced a series of attacks and counterattacks. At the war's end in 1783 England had a stronger claim to the Old Northwest than in 1780.

What the Americans lost on the battlefield in the Northwest they gained at the peace table in Paris. The American representatives, John Adams, Benjamin Franklin and John Jay, were instructed to negotiate a treaty that met with France's approval. France had been America's ally during the war. However, now that their longtime enemy Britain was defeated, France and her ally Spain opposed American westward expansion. The Comte de Vergennes, the French foreign minister, remarked, "We have no interest whatever to see America play the part of a power." France and Spain had formulated a scheme whereby the Spanish would occupy the Floridas and Britain would keep the country north of the Ohio. Faced with this scheme, the American commissioners decided to negotiate a treaty with Britian independently. The British favored such an arrangement because they preferred American, rather than Spanish, expansion in America.

The Treaty of Paris gave the entire region of the Great Lakes to the United States. The northwestern boundary was to run from Lake Superior to Lake of the Woods and then west to the Mississippi. By abandoning the French and taking advantage of England's desire for a quick peace, the American commissioners secured for their country an immense western territory that might have gone to Spain.

The Western Problem

With the final treaty signed and ratified on September 3, 1783, the American government was now faced with the same problems that confronted England after the Seven Years' War: How could the Indians be displaced from the trans-Appalachian frontier, and the incoming settlers governed? The issue for the new republic was complicated by conflicting state claims to the western territory, as well as by the interests of the land companies.

Massachusetts, Connecticut, Georgia and North Carolina maintained that their original sea-to-sea Crown charters provided each with a territory running to the Pacific. South Carolina disputed Georgia's western boundaries and contended that part of the territories belonged to her. Virginia based her claim on a 1609 charter that granted her control of Kentucky and all lands north and west of the Ohio River. New York claimed the same region as Virginia.

The states without western land claims proposed that all unsold western land be turned over to the federal government. As early as 1776, the six landless states had advocated the cession of the western territories to the United States. At first the states with western claims adamantly refused to cede their territories to Congress, but it soon became evident that holding the lands created several problems. Conflicting state claims made it difficult to determine the amount of land each state would receive. The western territory was occupied mostly by hostile Indians, and it would be a long and arduous task to gain control of the region. The territory required the construction of many public improvements, such as roads, which would have to be financed with eastern money. In the end, the states with western claims reluctantly concluded that ceding the territories to the federal government was the only practical alternative.

Land companies based in the states holding western territories argued vehemently against the cessions, since they hoped the states would award them land grants in the West. After the land speculators presented their position before Congress, popular opinion moved strongly against them. The land speculators were seen as a small group of self-serving individuals who were preventing Congress from acquiring a vast territory that could help reduce the national debt and satisfy the promises made to the Revolutionary War heroes.

As a consequence of the land cessions, Congress now controlled a vast public domain and faced the problem of a growing population of settlers, including Revolutionary War veterans who anticipated receiving land grants in return for their military service. The settlers ignored legal ownership of the territory and began to occupy and cultivate whatever land they considered worthwhile. These "squatters" expected to receive free land from the federal government and protection from the Indians.

Congressional delegates feared that if swift action to govern the western lands was not implemented the settlers might create an independent state or seek the aid of Spain. There were long and bitter congressional debates on how to disperse the public lands. After considering numerous proposals, Congress decided on a plan that became known as the Ordinance of 1785. The ordinance pertained to land north of the Ohio and was enacted primarily to generate revenue from the public lands. Townships six miles square were to be surveyed and then divided into 36 lots of 640 acres. The land was to be auctioned in the eastern states, with a minimum price of $1 an acre plus survey costs. By barring purchases of less than 640 acres the ordinance prevented pioneer farmers from purchasing the land directly from the government, since frontiersmen did not need large tracts and could not afford them. Speculators were now free to purchase large tracts and then sell them in smaller parcels to settlers on credit.

Despite the Ordinance of 1785, thousands of squatters continued to settle on the federal domain in the Ohio country. The United States government tried to drive them back by constructing a fort at the mouth of the Muskingum, Fort Harmar, but this effort did not turn back the flow of emigrants during the summer of 1785. "All mankind," declared one squatter "have an undoubted right to pass into every vacant country and there form their constitution."

While settlers were illegally migrating to the Northwestern Territory, Indian commissioners were negotiating with the Shawnees for land cessions. The Ohio tribes, along with the Shawnees, refused to cede their lands to Congress. In the spring of 1786 bands of Indians raided settlements, while the Iroquois threatened war if their lands were occupied. As Indian attacks became more frequent, Congress assigned more troops to the garrisons in the Old Northwest. A war would ultimately decide who controlled the territory.

Meanwhile, land sales at the eastern auctions were disappointing to a government that desperately needed revenue for reducing the national debt. Buyers were few, and prices rarely rose above the minimum. While Congress continued to debate how the western lands could be sold, two Revolutionary War generals, Rufus Putnam and Benjamin Tupper, formed the Ohio Company for the purpose of buying up depreciated Continental certificates and using them to purchase a huge block of land in the Ohio country. Individuals were able to receive subscriptions with $1,000 in depreciated Continental currency, which was then worth only a few cents on the dollar. It was hoped that Congress would accept the paper money for western lands.

Congress agreed to grant the Ohio Company 6,500,000 acres of Ohio land at one dollar an acre in Continental currency. The actual price came to about 8¢ an acre for good Ohio land. The grant to the Ohio Company encouraged a group of New Englanders to immigrate to the Ohio Country, where they established the town of Marietta, modeled after a traditional New England village, including the usual Congregational Church.

While these land grants were being made to the Ohio Company and to other companies and individuals, Congress finally decided how the territory would be governed. The Northwest Ordinance of 1787 provided for the orderly development of a self-governing territory, and for the eventual creation of three to five states. The principles behind the ordinance were used as a pattern throughout the entire process of westward expansion, from the Appalachians to the Pacific.

The Northwest Ordinance called for three stages of government. First, Congress immediately appointed a governor, a secretary and three judges to make laws, subject to congressional veto. When the population reached 5,000, the people would elect a legislature consisting of two chambers. Finally, when the population reached 60,000 the territory could petition for statehood. In addition, there was also a provision for a bill of rights similar to that of the United States Constitution, and a prohibition of slavery, except for those slaves already in the territory. Five states eventually emerged from the Northwest Territory: Illinois, Indiana, Michigan, Ohio and Wisconsin.

The opening of the territory resulted in more intrusions on Indian lands and increased Indian hostilities against the settlers. Immigrant expeditions in 1790 and 1791 were often poorly planned and accompanied by inexperienced troops. President Washington, determined to subdue the Indians, appointed General Anthony Wayne commander of the Northwest Territory. After battling the Indians for two years, Wayne decisively defeated the warriors of a dozen tribes in less than two hours at the battle of Fallen Timbers in 1794. Although the Indians lost only 50 braves, their spirit to continue fighting was broken when the British commander at nearby Fort Miamis refused to risk war with the United States by supporting the Indians.

With the Treaty of Greenville in 1795 the Northwest tribes agreed to cede two-thirds of what is now Ohio and part of Indiana to the United States, and granted permission for 16 forts to be constructed in the remaining Indian territory. The power of the Northwest Indians was crushed, and a new territory was cleared for expansion. The next task for the United States was driving the English from the posts in the Great Lakes region that they had retained under the Treaty of Paris of 1783.

John Jay. Courtesy of the New York Public Library.

In June 1794, President Washington sent John Jay to London with full authority to negotiate a treaty. England agreed to surrender the Northwest posts within two years, but in return the United States agreed to permit Canadian traders to operate south of the boundary and promised not to tax the furs they carried back to Montreal. The final treaty signed on November 19, 1794, was so unpopular in the United States that Jay was burned in effigy by mobs. In the Senate, the treaty was ratified by a narrow margin.

Jay's Treaty and the Treaty of Greenville opened the trans-Appalachian frontier for increased settlement. Peace in the Northwest Territory encouraged a great number of pioneers to move westward. Early settlers had emigrated mostly from the South through the Cumberland Gap; now, many began to come from the central and northern states.

CHRONICLE OF EVENTS

1753:

October 31: Governor Dinwiddie of Virginia commissions George Washington to deliver a message to the French commandant at Fort Le Boeuf, demanding the French withdraw from the upper Ohio.

December 21: Washington arrives at Fort Le Boeuf in the Ohio territory and informs the commandant, Legardeur de Saint-Pierre, that Virginia demands immediate French withdrawal; the French refuse to leave.

1754:

January 16: Washington returns to Williamsburg and reports to Governor Dinwiddie the intentions of the French to remain in the Ohio territory. Dinwiddie orders the construction of a fort at the confluence of the Allegheny and Monongahela rivers.

The French establish their own Fort Duquesne (now Pittsburgh).

April 1: Five-hundred French troops led by Captain Sieur de Contrecoeur set off from Quebec for an invasion of the Ohio country.

April 2: Washington and 75 volunteers march from Alexandria to assist Captain Trent at the forks of the Ohio River.

April 17: The French invade the Ohio territory and capture the strategic forks of the Ohio.

May 28: French Ensign Coulon de Jumonville and his detachment are killed by Washington and his recruits outside Fort Duquesne. The French and Indian War begins.

July 3: Washington, under siege by French troops from Fort Duquesne, is forced to surrender Fort Necessity, giving control of the Ohio Valley to the French.

1755:

February 20: General Edward Braddock arrives in Virginia to become commander-in-chief of the British forces against the French. He plans campaigns against French-held forts of Beausejour, Crown Point, Niagara and Duquesne.

April 14: Braddock sets out from Virginia for Fort Duquesne. George Washington is in charge of 450 troops that accompany Braddock.

July 9: Braddock is defeated at the Battle of the Wilderness, eight miles from Fort Duquesne; he dies and 1,000 of his troops are killed or wounded. The Indians of the Northwest desert the English, side with the French and attack British settlements.

December: George Washington returns to Virginia and persuades the colonies to build more forts between the Potomac River and the James and Roanoke rivers, hoping to counter the French strength from Fort Duquesne.

1756:

August: General Montcalm destroys the English forts of Oswego and George. Britain yields the Mohawk Valley to the French.

1758:

July 26: A joint force of British and colonial soldiers attacks and seizes the French fort of Louisbourg, Nova Scotia, near the mouth of the St. Lawrence.

August 27: English troops seize Fort Frontenac near present-day Kingston, Ontario.

November 25: The French blow up Fort Duquesne to prevent it from being used by the British.

Forbes Road is opened from Philadelphia to the forks of the Ohio; it opens the West for military and civilian travelers.

1759:

June: British General James Wolfe leads 9,000 troops up the St. Lawrence in preparation for an attack on Quebec.

July 25: British troops seize Fort Niagara.

July 26: French troops are forced to destroy their own outposts to prevent their capture at Fort Ticonderoga and Fort Saint-Frederick.

September 12: English and French troops battle

over Quebec; both Generals Montcalm and Wolfe are killed, but the English are victorious.

1760:

September 8: English forces under General Jeffrey Amherst compel the governor of Quebec to surrender the entire province of Quebec (New France) to the English.
November 20: Detroit falls to the British.

1761:

September 9: Pontiac's Rebellion begins. Ottawa Indians protest the English refusal to supply them with arms. Pontiac, chief of the Ottawas, leads a revolt against the British.

1762:

November 3: France signs a secret treaty with Spain, promising to give Spain all the French territory west of the Mississippi as well as the Isle of Orleans in Louisiana. This is the first step in ending the Seven Years' War, which the French are eager to do.

1763:

February 10: The Treaty of Paris ends both the colonial and European phases of the Seven Years' War. France cedes North American territories to England.
August 2: Pontiac's forces defeated at the battle of Bushy Run, near present-day Pittsburgh.
September 9: The Mississippi Company, led by George Washington, receives a grant of 2.5 million acres from the English Crown for settlement by Virginia soldiers who had served in the French and Indian War.
October 7: George III signs the Proclamation of 1763, limiting English settlements west of the Appalachians and ordering settlers already there to return.
November: Pontiac's forces abandon their raid on Detroit.

1764:

November 17: Pontiac's forces surrender at the Muskingum River in the Ohio Territory.

1768:

August 14: The Treaty of Hard Labor moves the frontier farther west, past the Ohio, with the Cherokees ceding their lands.
November 3: The Indiana Company purchases 1,800,000 acres from the Iroquois, southeast of the Ohio River.
November 5: In the Treaty of Fort Stanwix, the League of Iroquois in the Mohawk Valley agrees to accept £10,460 for southwestern New York, western Pennsylvania and parts of West Virginia, as well as their claim to portions of Kentucky and Tennessee.

1769:

First settlements on the Watauga and Monongahela.
April: Throngs of would-be settlers storm the land office in Pittsburgh seeking to purchase land in the newly opened western territories.
May 1: Daniel Boone sets off from his home on the Yadkin River in North Carolina to see the lands of Kentucky.
June 7: Boone arrives at the Cumberland Gap.
December 27: The Ohio Company receives a grant from the British Crown of 20 million acres, under the Fort Stanwix Treaty.

1770:

The population of the British colonies is estimated at 2,205,000.
October 18: The Treaty of Lochabar with the Cherokees moves the Virginia border west, adding another 9,000 square miles to the colony's territory.

1771:

April: Daniel Boone returns from his trip along the Cumberland Gap.

1773:

September: Daniel Boone leads a party of families along the Cumberland Gap to settle in Kentucky, but they turn back after the Indians capture and kill Boone's oldest son, James.

1774:

August 27: The Transylvania Company is founded by Judge Richard Henderson of North Carolina. For £10,000 Henderson purchases from the Cherokees 20,000 acres of their land between the Kentucky and Cumberland rivers. Henderson hires Daniel Boone to clear a trail, later known as the Wilderness Road, from Virginia to Kentucky.

August: Lord Dunmore's War breaks out between the Shawnees and Virginia colonists.

October 10: The Shawnees are defeated at Point Pleasant by Dunmore's soldiers.

1775:

March 16: Daniel Boone sets out with 30 axmen to mark off the Wilderness Road from the Cumberland Gap to Kentucky. In the next 25 years over 200,000 pioneers will pass along this trail.

March 17: In the Treaty of Sycamore Shoals, the Cherokees sell for £10,000 worth of trading goods their Kentucky land to the Transylvania Company.

April 1: Daniel Boone founds Boonesborough in Kentucky.

April 18: The American Revolution begins with the first shots fired at Lexington and the scuffle at Concord.

1776:

June: Judge Henderson petitions the Continental Congress to admit Transylvania as a 14th state. Congress refuses the request.

1777:

August 6: Colonial soldiers are ambushed by British-backed Mohawk Indians in upstate New York.

1778:

September: Shawnee Indians attack and lay siege to Boonesborough, Kentucky, but the town does not fall.

June: George Rogers Clark captures Kaskaskia. Persuades several Indian tribes to support the Americans.

1779:

February 25: George Rogers Clark captures Vincennes and forces Captain Henry Hamilton to surrender his fort.

1782:

October 6: In Paris, the United States and Great Britain reach agreement on Mississippi and Canada boundaries, independent of France and Spain.

1783:

September 3: Britain and the United States sign the Treaty of Paris, formally ending the Revolutionary War. Under the terms of the treaty, the United States receives all territory as far west as the Mississippi River.

1785:

May 8: Congress passes the Land Ordinance of 1785, which provides that the northwestern territories be surveyed and divided into six-mile-square townships, each further divided into 36 lots of 640 acres. The land is to be auctioned at $1 per acre.

1786:

March 1: The Ohio Company is formed in Boston to purchase land and settle New England homesteaders in 1.5 million acres of the Upper Ohio River.

1787:

July 13: Congress passes the Northwest Ordinance to establish a government north of the Ohio. Eventually 31 states are admitted under the principles of the Northwest Ordinance.

1788:

This year is known as the year of "Great Immigration" to the West.

1789:

April 30: George Washington is president.
November 21: Georgia sells 25,400,000 acres to land companies for $207,580. Settlers found Walnut Hills (today's Vicksburg, Mississippi).

1790:

March 1: Congress passes the Census Act, calling for a routine census of the United States. The 1790 census shows a total population of 3,929,625.
October 18: The Ohio tribe defeats an expedition of Americans near Fort Wayne, Indiana, beginning five years of hostilities in the Northwest Territory.

1791:

March 30: Construction begins on the Knoxville Road, linking the Wilderness Road with Knoxville, south of the Ohio River. The road opens up more frontier areas to settlement.
September 10: Indian hostilities in the Ohio territory require the construction of forts at Hamilton, St. Clair, Jefferson, Greenville and Recovery.

1792:

June 1: Kentucky becomes a state.
September: Cherokee war council plans united action.

1793:

March 1: Congress directs commissioners to seek peace with the Indians.
July 31: First conference with delegates from Indian congress.

1794:

March 24: Washington issues a proclamation denouncing George Rogers Clark's expedition to seize the Louisiana Territory.

General Anthony Wayne. Courtesy of the New York Public Library.

August 8: General "Mad" Anthony Wayne builds Fort Defiance.
August 20: Wayne defeats the Cherokees at the battle of Fallen Timbers.
October 22: Fort Wayne completed and used to secure the territory of northwest Ohio.
November 19: Jay's Treaty results in the withdrawal of British forces from their military forts in the Old Northwest Territory, in return for repayment of debts owed to British subjects before the Revolution.

1795:

August 3: In the Treaty of Greenville, the Indians relinquish two-thirds of present-day Ohio and part of Indiana to the United States, and grant permission for 16 forts to be built in the remaining Indian territory.

EYEWITNESS TESTIMONY

Whereas I have receiv'd Information of a Body of French Forces being assembled in an hostile Manner on the River Ohio, intending by force of Arms to erect certain Forts on the said River, within this Territory & contrary to the Peace & Dignity of our Sovereign the King of Great Britain.

These are therefore to require & direct You the said George Washington Esqr. forthwith to repair to the Logstown on the said River Ohio; & having there inform'd YourSelf where the said French Forces have posted themselves, thereupon to proceed to such Place: & being there arriv'd to present Your Credentials, together with my Letter to the chief commanding Officer, &, in the Name of His Britanic Majesty, to demand an Answer from him thereto.

Robert Dinwiddie, governor of Virginia, to George Washington, commissioning Washington to deliver a letter of warning to the French commandant in the Ohio country, letter of October 30, 1753, in The Papers of George Washington *(1983).*

I was commissioned and appointed by the Honorable Robert Dinwiddie, Esq., Governor, etc. of Virginia, to visit and deliver a letter to the Commandant of the French forces on the Ohio, and set out [from Williamsburg] on the intended journey the same day. The next, I arrived at Fredericksburg and engaged Mr. Jacob Vanbraam to be my French interpreter; and proceeded with him to Alexandria, where we provided necessaries. From thence we went to Winchester and got baggage, horses, etc., and from thence we pursued the new road to Wills Creek, where we arrived the 14th of November. Here I engaged Mr. Gist to pilot us out, and also hired four others as servitors . . . and in company with those persons left the inhabitants the day following.

George Washington, October 31, 1753, in The Journal of Major George Washington *(1959).*

The lands upon the Ohio in the western parts of the colony of Virginia are so notoriously known to be the property of the Crown of Great Britain that it is a matter of equal concern and surprise to me to hear that a body of French forces are erecting a fortress and making settlements upon that river in H.M.'s Dominions . . .

If these facts are true and you shall think fit to justify your procceedings, I must desire you to acquaint me by whose authority and instructions you have lately marched from Canada with an armed force and invaded the King of Great Britain's territories . . .

Robert Dinwiddie, governor of Virginia, to the French commandant at Fort Le Boeuf, letter of October 1753, in The Official Records of Robert Dinwiddie *(1883–84).*

We found the French colors hoisted at a house from which they had driven Mr. John Frazier, an English subject. I immediately repaired to it, to know where the Commander resided. There were three officers, one of whom, Capt. Joncaire, informed me that he had the command of the Ohio, but that there was a general officer at the near fort [Le Boeuf] where he advised me to apply for an answer. He invited us to sup with them and treated us with the greatest complaisance.

The wine, as they dosed themselves pretty plentifully with it, soon banished the restraint which at first appeared in their conversation and gave a license to their tongues to reveal their sentiments more freely. They told me that it was their absolute design to take possession of the Ohio, and by God they would do it. For that, altho' they were sensible the English could raise two men for their one, yet they knew their motions were too slow and dilatory to prevent any undertaking of theirs. They pretend to have an undoubted right to the river from a discovery made by one La Salle 60 years ago. . .

George Washington, November 30, 1753, in The Journal of Major George Washington.

As I have the honor of commanding here in chief, Mr. Washington delivered me the letter which you wrote to the commandant of the French forces.

I should have been glad that you had given him orders, or that he had been inclined to proceed to Canada, to see our General; to whom it better belongs than to me to set forth the evidence and reality of the rights of the King my Master, upon the lands situated along the River Ohio, and to contest the pretensions of the King of Great Britain thereto . . .

As to the summons you sent me to retire, I do not think myself obliged to obey it. Whatever may be your instructions, I am here by virtue of the orders of my General; and I entreat you, Sir, not to doubt one moment but that I am determined to conform myself to them with all the exactness and resolution which can be expected from the best of officers.

Legardeur de Saint-Pierre, commandant of the French troops at Fort Le Boeuf, to Robert Dinwiddie, governor of Virginia, letter of December 14, 1754, in The Official Records of Robert Dinwiddie.

I arrived at Turtle Creek about eight miles from the Forks of Mohongialo, where I was informed by John Frazier, an Indian Trader, that Mr. Washington, who was sent by the Governor of Virginia to the French Camp, was returned. Mr. Washington told Mr. Frazier that he had been very well used by the French General; that after he delivered his Message the General told him his Orders were to take all the English he found on the Ohio, which Orders he was determined to obey, and further told him that the English had no business to trade on the Ohio, for that all the Lands of Ohio belonged to his Master the King of France, all to Alegainay Mountain. Mr. Washington told Mr. Frazier the Fort where he was is very strong, and that they had Abundance of Provisions, but they would not let him see their Magazine; there are about one hundred Soldiers and fifty Workmen at that Fort, and as many more at the Upper Fort, and about fifty Men at Weningo with Jean Coeur; the Rest of their Army went home last Fall, but is to return as soon as possible this Spring . . .

George Croghan, trader on the upper Ohio, journal entry of January 12, 1754, in Thwaites' Early Western Travels *(1904–07).*

Nothing can surprise me more than to see you attempt a settlement upon the lands of the King, my master, which obliges me now, sir, to send you this gentleman, Chevalier Le Mercier, Captain of the Artillery of Canada, to know of you, sir, by virtue of what authority you are come to fortify yourself within the dominions of the King, my master. This action seems so contrary to the last treaty of peace, at Aix la Chapelle, between His Most Christian Majesty and the King of Great Britain, that I do not know to whom to impute such an usurpation, as it is incontestable that the land situated along the Beautiful River belongs to His Most Christian Majesty.

Let it be as it will, sir, if you come into this place, charged with orders, I summon you in the name of the King, my master, by virtue of orders which I have got from my General, to retreat peaceably with your troops from off the lands of the King, and not

to return, or else I will find myself obliged to fulfill my duty, and compel you to it. I hope, sir, you will not deter an instant, and that you will not force me to the last extremity. In that case, sir, you may be persuaded that I will give orders that there shall be no damage done by my detachment.

Sieur de Claude Contrecoeur, French commander, to Edward War, British ensign at Fort Prince George, letter of April 16, 1754, in O'Meara's Guns at the Forks.

When the men had fired away all their ammunition and the General and most of the officers were wounded, they by one common consent left the field, running off with the greatest precipitation. About fifty Indians pursued us to the river, and killed several men in the passage. The officers used all possible endeavours to stop the men, and to prevail upon them to rally; but a great number of them threw away their arms and ammunition, and even their cloaths, to escape the faster.

About a quarter of a mile of the other side of the river, we prevailed upon near one hundred of them to take post upon a very advantageous spot, about two hundred yards from the road . . . We intended to have kept possession of that ground, 'till we could have reinforced. The General and some wounded officers remained there about an hour, till most of the men run off. From that place, the General sent Mr Washington to Colonel Dunbar with orders to send waggons for the wounded, some provisions, and hospital stores . . .

Robert Orme, British lieutenant and aide-de-camp to Major General Edward Braddock, on Braddock's retreat at the battle of the Wilderness, journal entry of July 9, 1755, in Sargent's The History of an Expedition Against Fort Du Quesne *(1855).*

Sir John went forward this morning, and sent me back word . . . that as far as he had gone he found the road good, and every other thing answering our expectations. I cannot therefore entertain the least doubt that we shall now all go on hand in hand and that the same zeal for the service that has hitherto been so distinguishing a part of your character will carry you by Reas Town over the Allegheny Mountains and to Fort Duquesne.

Henry Bouquet, British colonel, to George Washington, anticipating a British victory at Fort Duquesne, in letter of April 1758, The Papers of Henry Bouquet *(1951).*

General Edward Braddock's retreat at the Battle of the Wilderness, 1755. Courtesy of the New York Public Library.

I have the pleasure of acquainting you with signall success of His Majesties Arms over all His Enemies on the Ohio, by having obliged them to burn, and abandon their Fort Duquesne, which they effectuated upon the 24th Inst; and of which I took possession with my light troops the same Evening, and with my little Army the next day—The Enemy having made their escape down the River, part in Boats, and part by land to their Forts and Settlements upon the Mississippi, being abandoned, or at least not seconded by their friends the Indians, whom we had previously engaged to act a neutrall part, after thoroughly convincing them in severall skirmishes, that all their attempts upon our advanced posts, in order to cut off our Communication, were vain, and to no purpose, so they now seem all willing, and well disposed to Embrace His Majesties most Gracious protection.

Give me leave therefore to congratulate you upon this important Event, of having expelled the French from Fort Duquesne, and this prodigious tract of fine rich Country, and of having in a Manner reconciled the various tribes and Nations of Indians inhabiting it, to His Majesties Government.

General John Forbes, to Generals James Abercomby and Jeffrey Amherst, on the capture of Fort Duquesne, letter of November 26, 1758, in Writings of General John Forbes *(1971).*

What a scene! An army in the night dragging itself up a precipice by stumps of trees to assault a town and attack an enemy strongly intrenched and double in numbers! The King is overwhelmed with addresses on our victories; he will have enough to paper his palace.

Horace Walpole, Fourth Earl of Oxford, to British Ambassador Man at Florence, on the British capture of Quebec, letter of 1759, in Parkman's Montcalm and Wolfe *(1884).*

Who can tell what great and glorious things God is about to bring forward in the world, and in this world of America in particular? Oh, may the time come when these deserts, which for ages unknown have been regions of darkness and habitations of cruelty, shall be illuminated with the light of the glorious Gospel, and when this part of the world, which till the later ages was utterly unknown, shall be the glory and joy of the whole earth!

Nathaniel Appleton, citizen of Cambridge, Massachusetts, hailing the end of the French and Indian War, 1760, in Parkman's Montcalm and Wolfe.

God has given us to sing this day the downfall of New France, the North American Babylon, New England's rival.

Eli Forbes, pastor of Brookfield, Massachusetts, 1760, in Parkman's Montcalm and Wolfe.

I have often heard the British officers call the Indians the undisciplined savages, which is a capital mistake—as they have all the essentials of discipline. They are under good command, and punctual in obeying orders: they can act in concert, and when their officers lay a plan and give orders, they will cheerfully unite in putting all their directions into immediate execution; and by each man observing the motion or movement of his right hand companion, they can communicate the motion from right to left, and march abreast in concert, and in scattered order, though the line may be more than a mile long, and continue, if occasion requires, for a considerable distance, without disorder or confusion. They can perform various necessary manœuvers, either slowly, or as fast as they can run: they can form a circle, or semi-circle: the circle they make use of, in order to surround their enemy, and the semi-circle if the enemy has a river on one side of them. They can also form a large hollow square, face out and take trees: this they do, if their enemies are about surrounding them, to prevent from being shot from either side of the tree. When they go into battle they are not loaded or encumbered with many clothes, as they commonly fight naked, save only breech-clout, leggins and mockesons.

James Smith, British captain captured by Indians at the age of 18, in 1755, and escaped four years later, in An Account of the Remarkable Occurrences in the Life and Travels of Colonel James Smith, During His Captivity with the Indians *(1799).*

I mean to destroy the English and leave not one upon our lands.

Pontiac, Ottawa chieftain, May 7, 1763, in Parkman's The Conspiracy of Pontiac *(1851).*

At Break of day this Morning three Men came in from Col. Chaphams who was settled at the Oswegly Old Town about 25 Miles from here, on the Youghyogane River, with an account that Col. Chapham, with one of his Men, two Women and a Child were murdered by Wolfe and some other Delaware Indians, about two o'Clock the day before, the 27th Wolfe with some others robed one Mr. Colman on the Road between this and Ligonier of upwards of £50—The women that were killed at Col. Claphams, were treated in such a brutal manner that Decency forbids the Mentioning.

This Evening we had two Soldiers killed and scalped at the Sawmill.

William Trent, trader and Fort Pitt defender, on Pontiac's rebellion, journal entry of May 29, 1763, in Journal at Fort Pitt *(1914).*

I have the pleasure to inform you that on our march to the relief of this Fort we have been attacked by a considerable body of Indians composed of the Delawares, Shawanes Wyandots and Mingoes, and that after two obstinate engagements on the 5th and 6th Instant we have obtained a compleat victory over the Barbarians by the uncommon resolution of our brave highlanders; before the enemy came to meet us they had closely beset and attacked this Fort and for five days kept an incessant fire upon it.

Captain Basset who has distinguished himself extremely and has been of great service to me, carries my dispatches to the General. I beg leave to refer you to him for the particulars of that bloody affair in which the most warlike of the savage tribes have lost their boasted claim of being invincible . . .

Henry Bouquet, British army colonel, to the governor of England's Northwest Territories, describing the defense of Fort Pitt, letter of August 11, 1763, in The Papers of Henry Bouquet.

At day-break we were attacked by a party of Indians, consisting of eighty warriors of the Kiccapoos and Musquattimes [Mascoutens or Muscatins], who killed two of my men and three Indians, wounded myself and all the rest of my party, except two white men and one Indian; then made myself and all the white men prisoners, plundering us of everything we had. A deputy of the Shawanees who was shot through the thigh, having concealed himself in the woods for a few minutes after he was wounded—not knowing but they were Southern Indians, who are always at war with the northward Indians—after discovering what nation they were, came up to them and made a very bold speech, telling them that the whole northward Indians would join in taking revenge for the insult and murder of their people. This alarmed those savages very much, who began to excuse themselves, saying their Fathers, the French, had spirited them up, telling them that the English were coming with a body of Southern Indians to take their countrie from them . . .

George Croghan, assistant to Sir William Johnson in the Indian Service, recalling his trip into the Ohio country for the purpose of securing the old French posts on the Wabash for the British, journal entry of January 1765, in Thwaites' Early Western Travels.

It was the first of May, in the year 1769, that I resigned my domestic happiness for a time and left my family and peaceable habitation on the Yadkin River in North Carolina to wander through the wilderness of America in quest of the country of Kentucke, in company with John Finley, John Stewart, Joseph Holden, James Monay, and William Cool. We proceeded successfully, and after a long and fatiguing journey through a mountainous wilderness, in a westward direction, on the seventh day of June following we found ourselves on Red River, where John Finley had formerly been trading with the Indians, and, from the top of an eminence, saw with pleasure the beautiful level of Kentucke.

We found everywhere abundance of wild beasts of all sorts through this vast forest. The buffaloes were more frequent than I have seen cattle in the settlements, browsing on the leaves of the cane, or cropping the herbage on those extensive plains, fearless, because ignorant, of the violence of man. Sometimes we saw hundreds in a drove, and the numbers about the salt springs were amazing.

Daniel Boone, 1769, in Filson's The Discovery, Settlement, and Present State of Kentucke *(1784).*

Arrived at this place about sun set. The first object of our attention was a number of poor drunken Indians, staggering & yelling through the Village. It

Colonel Henry Bouquet negotiating with the Delawares and Shawnees on the Muskingum River, 1764. From a drawing by Benjamin West. Courtesy of the New York Public Library.

is the headquarters of Indian traders, & the resort of Indians of different & distant tribes, who come to exchange their peltry & furs for rum, blankets & ammunition etc.

Reverend David McClure, on visiting site of present-day Pittsburgh, diary entry of August 19, 1772, in McClure's Diary *(1899).*

I have learnt from experience that the established authority of any Government in America, and the policy of Government at home are both insufficient to restrain the Americans; and that they do and will remove as their avidity and restlessness incite them. They acquire no attachment to Place; but wandering about seems engrafted in their nature; they do not conceive that Government has any right to forbid their taking possession of a vast tract of country either uninhabited or which serves only as a shelter to a few scattered tribes of Indians. Nor can they be easily brought to entertain any belief of the permanent obligation of Treaties made with those People whom they consider as but little removed from the brute creation.

Lord Dunmore, governor of Virginia, to the
Earl of Dartmouth, secretary of state for the
British colonies, letter of December 24, 1774, in
Thwaites' Documentary History of Lord
Dunmore's War (1905).

It is indiscribable, how enraged the relations of the murdered became, on seeing such abominable acts committed without cause, and even by some white men who had always pretended to be their friends. The cries of the relations of the sufferers soon reached the ears of the respective nations to whom they belonged, and who quickly resolved to take revenge on the long knives (so they called the people of Virginia); for (said they,) "they are a barbarous people." Some however, considering the difficulty of meeting the perpetrators, proposed killing every white man then in their country, until they should believe themselves amply revenged for the valuable lives lost by the long knife men (Virginians). Nothing could equal the rage of the Senecas, in particular; and it was impossible to foresee where the matter would end. Parties after parties came on—the missionaries had to keep within their houses—the enraged Indians insisted that every able man should do his utmost to take revenge. They kept on the look out for traders, to kill them, but these had already generally fled the country, while some were taken under protection by friendly Shawanese Indians, who afterwards conducted them safely to Pittsburg.

John Heckewelder, missionary, surveyor and Indian interpreter, recalling the anger of the Senecas after white settlers killed an Indian family, journal entry of 1774, in History, Manners, and Customs of the Indian Nations (1818).

In the mean time the ravage of the Indians, wherever they could carry it, was dreadfull:—one Shawanese returned to his Town with the Scalps of forty men Women and Children whom he had killed. On the other hand a Party went out, with my permission, and destroyed one of the Shawanese Towns, and meeting a Small Party of Indians, they killed Six or Seven of them, but this produced no Change in the designs of these People.

The real concern, principally, which the Continuation of these Miseries gave me, and, partly, the Accounts Sent by the Officers of the Militia, of the Mutinous and ungovernable Spirit of their men, whom they could by no means bring to any order or discipline or even to Submit to command, determined me to go up into that part of the Country, and to exert my own immediate endeavours on this important occasion.

Lord Dunmore, governor of Virginia, to the
Earl of Dartmouth, secretary of State for the
British colonies, letter of December 24, 1774, in
Thwaites' Documentary History of Lord
Dunmore's War.

I well remember that, when a little boy, the family were sometimes waked up in the dead of night, by an express with a report that the Indians were at hand. The express came softly to the door, or back window, and by a gentle tapping waked the family. This was easily done, as an habitual fear made us ever watchful and sensitive to the slightest alarm. The whole family were instantly in motion. My father seized his gun and other implements of war. My stepmother waked up and dressed the children as well as she could . . . Besides the little children, we caught up what articles of clothing and provision we could get hold of in the dark, for we durst not light a candle or even stir the fire. All this was done with the utmost dispatch and the silence of death. The greatest care was taken not to awaken the youngest child. To the rest it was enough to say Indian and not a whimper was heard afterwards.

Joseph Doddridge, trans-Appalachian settler,
1770s, in Notes on the Settlement and Indian Wars of the Western Parts of Virginia and Pennsylvania from 1763 to 1783 (1876).

They [the Shawnees] presently made known their intentions, and I admitted them immediately to a Conference, wherein all our differences were Settled. The terms of our reconciliation were, briefly, that the Indians should deliver up all prisoners without reserve; that they should restore all horses and other valuable effects which they had carried off; that they Should not hunt on our Side the Ohio, nor molest any Boats passing thereupon; That they Should promise to agree to such regulations, for their trade with our People, as Should be hereafter dictated by the Kings Instructions, and that they Should deliver into our hands certain Hostages, to be kept by us untill we were convinced of their Sincere intention to adhere to all these Articles. The Indians, finding, contrary to their expectation, no punishment likely to follow, agreed to everything with the greatest alacrity, and gave the most Solemn assurances of their quiet and peaceable deportment for the future:

and in return I have given them every promise of protection and good treatment on our Side.

Lord Dunmore, to the Earl of Dartmouth, letter of December 24, 1774, in Thwaites' Documentary History of Lord Dunmore's War.

Whole nations have melted away like balls of snow before the sun. The whites have passed the mountains and settled upon Cherokee lands, and now wish to have their usurpation sanctioned by the confirmation of a treaty. New cessions will be required, and the small remnant of my people will be compelled to seek a new retreat in some far distant wilderness. There they will be permitted to stay only a short while, until they again behold the advancing banners of the same greedy host. When the whites are unable to point out any farther retreat for the miserable Cherokees, they will proclaim the extinction of the whole race. Should we not therefore run all risks, and incur all consequences, rather than submit to further laceration of our country? Such treaties may be all right for men too old to hunt or fight. As for me, I have my young warriors about me. We will have our lands.

Dragging-Canoe, Cherokee son of Chief Little Carpenter, speech to Cherokee council, objecting to selling the tribe's hunting land to Richard Henderson, March 1775, in Kincaid's The Wilderness Road (1947).

I was ordered to take the command of three garrisons during the campaign which Governor Dunmore carried on against the Shawanese Indians; after the conclusion of which the militia was discharged from each garrison and I, being relieved from my post, was solicited by a number of North Carolina gentlemen, that were about purchasing the lands lying on the S. side of Kentucke River from the Cherokee Indians, to attend their treaty at Wataga in March, 1775, to negotiate with them, and mention the boundaries of the purchase. This I accepted, and at the request of the same gentlemen, undertook to mark out a road in the best passage from the settlement through the wilderness to Kentucke, with such assistance as I thought necessary to employ for such an important undertaking.

Daniel Boone, 1775, in Filson's The Discovery, Settlement, and Present State of Kentucke.

thursday 20th—this morning is clear and cool. We start early and git Down to caintuck to Boons foart

Daniel Boone. Courtesy of the New York Public Library.

about 12 o'clock where we stop they come out to meet us and welcome us in with a voley of guns.

fryday 21st—warm this Day they begin laying off lots in the town and preparing for people to go to work to make corn.

Satterday 22nd—they finish laying out lots this Eavening I went a-fishing and caught 3 cats they meet in the night to draw for chose of lots but prefer it till morning.

Sunday 23rd—this morning the peopel meets and draws for chois of lots this is a very warm day.

monday 24th—We all view our lots and some Dont like them about 12 oclock the combses come to town and Next morning they make them a bark canew and set off down the river to meet their Companey.

tuesday 25th—in the eavening we git us a plaise at the mouth of the creek and begin clearing.

Wednesday 26th—We Begin Building us a house and a plaise of Defense to Keep the indians off this day we begin to live without bread.

William Calk, frontiersman, who traveled from Prince William City, Virginia, to Boone's fort on the Kentucky River, journal entries of 1775, in Speed's The Wilderness Road (1971).

Land being thus plenty in *America*, and so cheap as that a labouring Man that understands Husbandry, can in a short Time save Money enough to purchase a Piece of new Land sufficient for a Plantation, whereon he may subsist a Family; such are not afraid to marry; for if they even look far enough forward to consider how their Children when grown up are to be provided for, they see that more Land is to be had at Rates equally easy, all Circumstances considered.

Hence Marriages in *America* are more general, and more generally early, than in *Europe*. And if it is reckoned there, that there is but one Marriage per Annum among 100 Persons, perhaps we may here reckon two; and if in *Europe* they have but 4 Births to a Marriage (many of their Marriages being late) we may here reckon 8, of which if one half grow up, and our Marriages are made, reckoning one with another at 20 Years of Age our People must at least be doubled every 20 Years.

But not withstanding this Increase, so vast is the Territory of *North-America*, that it will require many Ages to settle it fully . . .

Benjamin Franklin, remarking on the abundance of land in the West, 1775, in Observations Concerning the Increase of Mankind, Peopling of Countries *(1775).*

After my compliments to you, I shall acquaint you of our misfortune. On March the 25th a party of Indians fired on my Company about half an hour before day, and killed Mr. Tevetty and his negro, and wounded Mr. Walker very deeply, but I hope he will recover.

On March 28th, as we were hunting for provisions, we found Samuel Tate's son, who gave us an account that the Indians fired on their camp on the 27 day. My brother and I went down and found two men killed and scalped, Thomas McDowell and Jeremiah McPheeters. I have sent a man down to all the lower companies in order to gather them all to the mouth of the Otter Creek. My advice to you, Sir, is to come or send as soon as possible, your company is desired greatly, for the people are very uneasy, but are willing to stay and venture their lives with you; and now is the time to frustrate the intentions of the Indians, and keep the country, whilst we are in it. If we give way to them now, it will ever be the case. This day we start from the battleground, for the mouth of Otter Creek, where we shall immediately erect a fort,

which will be done before you can come or send—then we can send ten men to meet you if you send for them.

Daniel Boone, to Colonel Richard Henderson, letter of April 1, 1775, in McEllroy's Kentucky in the Nation's History *(1909).*

24th. Forty or fifty Indians attacked Boonesborough, killed and scalped Daniel Goodman, wounded Captain Boone, Captain Todd, Mr. Hite and Mr. Stoner . . . 29th. Indians attacked the fort and killed Ensign McConnell.

May . . . 23rd. A large party of Indians attacked Boonesborough fort . . . 26. A party went out to hunt Indians; one wounded Squire Boone . . . 30th. Indians attacked Logan's Fort; killed and scalped William Hudson, wounded Burr Harrison and John Kennedy.

June 5 . . . Daniel Lyons . . . we suppose was killed going into Logan's Fort. John Peters and Elisha Bathey we expect were killed . . . 13th. Burr Harrison died of his woundes . . . 22nd . . . Barney Stagner, Sen., killed and beheaded half mile from the fort. A few guns fired at Boone's . . .

George Rogers Clark, journal entries of 1777, in George Rogers Clark Papers *(1912).*

As some Indian tribes to the westward of the Mississippi have lately, without provocation, massacred many of the Inhabitants of the Frontiers of this Commonwealth in the most cruel and barbarous manner, and it is intended to revenge the Injury and punish the Aggressors by carrying the war into their own country, we congratulate you upon your appointment to conduct so important an enterprise in which we most heartily wish you success, and we have no doubt but some further reward in lands in the country will be given to volunteers who shall engage in this service, in addition to the usual pay, if they are so fortunate as to succeed. We think it just and reasonable that each volunteer entering as a common soldier in this expedition should be allowed three hundred acres of land and the officers in the usual proportion, out of the lands which may be conquered in the country not in the possession of the said Indians, so as not to interfere with the claims of any friendly Indians or of any people willing to become subjects of this Commonwealth, and for this we think you may safely confide in the justice and Generosity of the Va. Assembly.

George Wythe, George Mason and Thomas Jefferson, to George Rogers Clark, letter of January 3, 1778, authorizing Clark to offer land as an inducement for enlisting troops, in Mc-Ellroy's Kentucky in the Nation's History.

Children!—Ottawas, Chippewas, Hurons, Pottawatomies, Shawnees, Delawares, &c.—Let us, before all things, return thanks to the Great Spirit above, who has permitted us to meet together this day . . . With these strings of wampum I open your eyes, that you may see clear and your ears may listen to my words; since I speak by order of the Great King, who is the Father of us all, whether white or brown skins. For myself, I shall never forget the manner in which you have acted since I have resided among you, nor the good will with which you took up your Father's axe, striking as one man his enemies and yours, the Rebels . . . You may remember, when you received a large belt of alliance here last year, the number of nations who took hold of it. You know the consequences have been good, as you have succeeded in almost all your enterprises, having taken a number of prisoners and a far greater number of scalps. You have forced them from the frontiers to the coast.

Henry Hamilton, British commander and lieutenant governor of the Northwest Territory, to Indian war council at Detroit, speech of June 14, 1778, in Bodley's George Rogers Clark *(1926).*

They said we must buy everything from them, and since we had become saucy they would make us give them two bucks for a blanket that we used to get for one. They said we must do as they pleased, and they killed some of us to make the rest afraid . . .

Thus the war began, and the English were driven from one place to another, until they became weak and hired you red men to fight for them, and help them. The Great Spirit became angry at this, and caused your Old Father, the French king, and other great nations to join the Big Knives and fight with them against all their enemies, so that the English have become like deer in the woods. From this you may see that it is the Great Spirit that caused your waters to be troubled, because you fought for the people he was angry with, and if your women and children should cry you must blame yourselves for it, and not the Big Knives.

You can now judge who is in the right. I have already told you who I am. Here is a bloody belt and a white one. Take whichever you please. Behave like men . . .

George Rogers Clark, to Delaware Indians, speech of August 1778 seeking permission for his troops to cross their land to fight the British at Fort Pitt, in George Rogers Clark Papers.

I then ordered out parties to attack the Fort—and firing began very smartly on both sides one of my men thro a bravery known but to Americans walking Carelessly up the main street was slightly woundid over the left eye but no ways dangerous—About 12 OClock the firing from the Fort suspended and I perceived a Flag coming out I ordered my people to stop firing till further orders—I soon perceived it was Capt Helm who after salutations informed me that the purport of his commission was, that Lt Govr. Hamilton was willing to surrender up the Fort and Garrison provided Colo Clarke would grant him Honourable terms

George Rogers Clark, account of the capture of Vincennes, February 27, 1779, in George Rogers Clark Papers.

The Inhabitants of Illinois must not expect settled peace and safety while their and our Enemies have footing at Detroit and can interrupt or stop the Trade of the Mississippi. If the English have not the strength or courage to come to war against us themselves, their practice has been and will be to hire the Savages to commit murder and depredations. Illinois must expect to pay in these a large price for her Freedom, unless the English can be expelled from Detroit. The means of effecting this will not perhaps be found in your or Col. Clarkes power. But the French inhabiting the neighbourhood of that place, it is presumed, may be brought to see it done with indifference or perhaps join in the enterprise with pleasure. This is but conjecture. When you are on the spot you and Col. Clarke may discover its fallacy or reality

Patrick Henry, governor of Virginia, to Colonel John Todd, associate of George Rogers Clark, letter of 1781, in James' The Life of George Rogers Clark *(1928).*

Yesterday Dr. Franklin told me that it would entirely depend upon the approaching treaty, whether the attachments of America were to be renewed & increased, or were to be extirpated; that if it was meant (for instance) to keep America in *danger* (as by retaining garrisoned places, making treaties with the Indians, & the like) persons would be found in America very well disposed to excite an aversion to England, & an union with France; & that as they would certainly succeed, the consequence would be wars, & hatred, in various ways; that for his part, he was for reconciliation, which he thought practicable, even under the circumstances of England as she stands; but that nothing lasting could be done, if America were to be kept *in danger.*

Benjamin Vaughn, American representative at the Paris peace negotiation, to the Earl of Shelburne, British prime minister, on English military posts remaining in the Old Northwest, letter of August 6, 1782, in Stourzh's Benjamin Franklin and American Policy *(1954).*

The Marquis de la Fayette is clever, but he is a Frenchman. Our Allies dont play fair, he told me. They were endeavoring to deprive Us of the Fishery, the Western Lands, and the Navigation of the Mississippi. They would even bargain with the English to deprive us of them. They want to play the Western Lands, Mississippi and whole Gulph of Mexico into the Hands of Spain.

Oswald [British agent for the Earl of Shelburne] talks of Pultney, and a Plott to divide America between France and England. France to have N. England. They tell a Story about Vergennes and his agreeing that the English might propose such a division, but reserving a Right to deny it all. These Whispers ought not to be credited by Us.

John Adams, delegate at the Paris peace negotiation, November 8, 1782, in Diary and Autobiography *(1961).*

On the 10th of August I carried this map to the Count de Vergennes, and left it with him. Dr. Franklin joined with me in pointing out the extravagance of this line; and I must do him the justice to say that in all his letters to me, and in all his conversations with me respecting our western extent, he has invariably declared it to be his opinion that we should insist upon the Mississippi as our western boundary, and that we ought not, by any means, to part with our right to the free navigation of it.

The Count de Vergennes was very cautious and reserved; but M. Rayneval, his principal secretary, who was present, thought we claimed more than we had a right to.

Having thus clearly discovered the views of Spain, and that they were utterly inadmissible, I had little hope of our ever agreeing, especially as the Mississippi was, and ought to be, our *ultimatum.*

John Jay, to Robert Livingston, on the Paris peace treaty negotiations, letter of November 17, 1782, in The Correspondence and Public Papers of John Jay *(1891).*

We were of Opinion that the Country in Contest was of great Value, both on Account of its natural Fertility, and of its Position, it being in our Opinion the Interest of America to extend as far down towards the Mouth of the Mississippi as we possibly could. We also thought it advisable to impress Britain with a strong Sense of the Importance of the Navigation of that River, to their future Commerce on the interior Waters from the Mouth of the River St. Lawrence to that of the Mississippi, and thereby render that Court averse to any Stipulations with Spain to relinquish it. These two objects militated against each other; because to inhance the Value of the Navigation was also to inhance the Value of the Countries contiguous to it, and thereby disincline Britain to the Dereliction of them. We thought therefore that the surest Way to reconcile and obtain both Objects would be a Composition beneficial to both Parties. We therefore proposed that Britain should withdraw her Pretensions to all the Country above the Yassous and that we would cede all below it to her in Case she should have the Floridas at the End of the War, and at all Events that she should have a Right to navigate the River throughout its whole extent. This proposition was accepted and we agreed to insert the contingent Part of it in a separate Article for the express purpose of keeping it secret for the Present.

John Adams, Benjamin Franklin and John Jay, to Robert Livingston, letter of July 18, 1783, in Morris' The Winning of the Peace *(1980).*

Not a soul was then settled on the Ohio between Wheeling and Louisville, a space of five hundred or six hundred miles, and not one hour, day or night, in safety; though it was now winter, not a soul in all Beargrass settlement was in safety but by being in a fort. I then meditated traveling about eighty miles to Craig's Station, on Gilbert's Creek, in Lincoln County. We set out in a few days; nearly all I owned was then at stake. I had three horses, two of them were packed, the other my wife rode, with as much lumber beside as the beast could bear. I had four black people, one man, and three smaller ones. The pack horses were led, one by myself, the other by my man. The trace, what there was being so narrow and bad, we had no chance but to wade through all the mud, rivers, and creeks we came to. Salt River, with a number of its large branches, we had to deal with often; those waters being flush, we often must wade to our middle . . . Those struggles often made us forget the dangers we had from Indians . . . After six days painful travel of this kind, we arrived at Craig's Station a little before Christmas, and about three months after our start from Virginia.

Samuel Taylor, Kentucky emigrant from Virginia, traveling along the Ohio River in 1783, in Speed's The Wilderness Road *(1971).*

. . . that having been excluded from the United States and the King of Great Britain, you are become a free and independent nation, and may make what terms you please. It is not so. You are a subdued people; you have been overcome in a war which you entered into with us, not only without provacation, but in violation of most sacred obligations. The great spirit who is at the same time judge and avenger of perfidy, has given us victory over all our enemies. We are at peace with all but you, you now stand out alone against our whole force.

When we offer you peace on moderate terms, we do it in magnanimity and mercy. If you do not accept it now, you are not to expect a repetition of such offers. Consider well, therefore, your situation and ours. Do not suffer yourselves to be again deceived so as to raise our arm against you. You feel the sad effects of having refused this counsel before—beware how you do it again.

Richard Butler, Arthur Lee and Oliver Wolcot, United States Indian commissioners, speech to Ohio Iroquois, October 1783, in Caruso's The Great Lakes Frontier *(1961).*

I am told that a certain Dispute has arose between the States of Georgia and South Carolina by the latter claiming a Right to back lands as far West as to the Mississippi now if South Carolina has any back lands the Bend of Tenesee must be a Part of it. This dispute between the two States will in my opinion be very favorable to our Designs of obtaining the Georgia Title or the South Carolina Title and either will answer our Purpose equally well for we shall surely settle the Country before the Dispute can be determined and in order to procure a Title from one or both of those States I will certainly attend both their next Assemblies and I have not the least doubt but I shall succeed.

William Blount, Tennessee Company land speculator, to Joseph Martin, North Carolina commissioner, letter of October 26, 1783, in Keith's The John Gray Blount Papers *(1952).*

Here are the finest and most excellent sites for farms, cities, and towns. Here may the industrious and broken-hearted farmer, tired with the slavery of the unfortunate situation in which he was born, lay down his burthen and find rest on these peaceful and plenteous plains; here may Iberia, Britain and Scotia, pour out their superabundant sons and daughters, who with cheerful hearts, and industrious hands, will wipe away the tear of tyrannic toil, and join the children of America in the easy labors of comfort and plenty, and bless the providence of that power who hath directed them to such a land.

Richard Butler, traveler, describing the fertile lands of Kentucky, journal entry of 1784, in James' The Life of George Rogers Clark.

I do certify that all mankind agreeable to every constitution formed in America, have an undoubted right to pass into every vacant country, and there to form their constitution, and that from the confederation of the whole United States, Congress is not empowered to forbid them, neither is Congress empowered from that confederation to make any sale of the uninhabited lands to pay the public debts, which is to be a tax levied and lifted (collected) by authority of the Legislature of each State.

John Amberson, Ohio country settler, posted notice, March 12, 1785, in Butler's Ohio in the Time of the Confederation *(1918).*

In establishing the township and sectional corners, a post is first planted at the point of intersection; then on the tree nearest the post, and standing within the section intended to be designated is numbered with the marking iron the range, township, and number of the section.

The Ohio Gazetter, *report of 1785, in Havighurst's* Wilderness for Sale *(1956).*

At Yellow creek, I dispossessed two families and destroyed their building. The 2d inst., being stormy, nothing was done. The 3d, we disposed eight families. The 4th we arrived at Mingo Bottom, or Old

Town. I read my instructions to the prisoner, [Joseph] Ross, who declared they never came from Congress, for he had late accounts from that honorable body, who, he was convinced, gave no such instructions to the [Congressional] Commissioners [for Indian Affairs]. Neither did he care from whom they came, for he was determined to hold possession, and if I destroyed his house he would build six more within a week. He also cast many reflections on the honorable the Congress, the Commissioners, and the commanding officer. I conceived him to be a dangerous man, and sent him under guard to Wheeling. Finding that most of the settlers at this place were tenants under the prisoner, I have them a few days, at which time they promised to move to the east side of the Ohio river, and to demolish their buildings.

Ensign John Armstrong, to Colonel Josiah Harmar, on evicting settlers in the Ohio country, report of April 12, 1785, in Butler's Ohio in the Time of the Confederation.

The *first* settler in the woods is generally a man who has outlived his credit or fortune in the cultivated parts of the State. His time for migrating is in the month of April. His first object is to build a small cabbin of rough logs for himself and family. The floor of this cabbin is of earth, the roof is of split logs— the light is received through the door, and, in some instances, thro' a small window made of greased paper. A coarser building adjoining this cabbin affords a shelter to a cow, and pair of poor horses. The labor of erecting these buildings is succeeded by killing the trees on a few acres of ground near his cabbin; this is done by cutting a circle round the trees, two or three feet from the ground. The ground around these trees is then ploughed and Indian-corn planted in it. The season for planting this grain is about the 20th of May—It grows generally on new ground with but little cultivation, and yields in the month of October following, from 40 to 50 bushels per acre. After the first of September it affords a good deal of nourishment to his family, in its green or unripe state, in the form of what is called *roasting ears*. His family is fed during the summer by a small quantity of grain which he carries with him, and by fish and game. His cows and horses feed upon wild grass, or the succulent twigs of the woods. For the first year he endures a great deal of distress from hunger—cold—and a variety of accidental causes, but he seldom complains or sinks under them.

Dr. Benjamin Rush, western Pennsylvania settler, to a friend in England, letter of 1786, in Harpster's Crossroads *(1938).*

Shall all this country now be cultivated entirely for the use of the Spaniards? Shall we be their bondsmen as the children of Israel were to the Egyptians? Shall one part of the United States be slaves, while the other is free? In case we are not countenanced and succured by the United States (if we need it) our allegiance will be thrown off, and some other power applied to.

Anonymous Kentucky pioneer, to friend in New England, letter of 1786 expressing outrage over John Jay's proposed treaty with the Spanish to suspend U.S. navigation of the Mississippi for 25 years, in James' The Life of George Rogers Clark.

Today you demand hostages till your prisoners are returned! You next say you will divide the lands! I now tell you it is not the custom of the Shawnees to give hostages. Our words are to be believed. When we say a thing we stand to it; we are Shawnees! As to the lands, God gave us this country! We do not understand measuring out the lands. It is all ours! You say you have goods for our women and children. You may keep your goods and give them to other nations. We will have none of them.

Kehenepelity, Shawnee war chief, to Richard Butler, Indian commissioner, January 28, 1786, in Caruso's The Great Lakes Frontier *(1961).*

I had suffered exceedingly in yᵉ war, and after it was over, by paper money and yᵉ high price of articles of living. My salary small and family large, for several years I thought yᵉ people had not done me justice, and I meditated leaving them. Purchasing lands in a new country appeared to be yᵉ only thing I could do to secure a living to myself, and family in that unsettled state of public affairs.

Manasseh Cutler, Revolutionary War veteran, journal entry of 1787, in Life, Journals and Correspondence of Rev. Manasseh Cutler *(1888).*

Proceeded to Laurel Creek and Ascended the hill. I think this and many more of the scenes we have passed through, we have seen Nature display'd in her greatest undress, at other times we have seen her dress'd Beautiful, beyond expression. The road excessive bad, some of the Land fine, The Timber Excellent, and grows to an Amazing height, the

Generality of it from 50 to 60 feet high. The day by reason of the Badness of the roads, could not reach a stage, the hill being 20 miles across and our horses a good deal tired. We in Company with another waggon were obliged to Encamp in the woods, after a Suitable place, at a Convenient distance from a run of water was found, a level piece of ground was pitched upon for our encampment. Our men went to give refreshment to the Horses, we Females having had a good fire made up, set about preparing Supper, which consisted of an Excellent dish of Coffee, having milk with us, those who chose had a dish of cold ham and pickled beets with the addition of Bread, Butter, Biscuit and Cheese, made up our repast. After supper, Sister, the Children, and myself took up our lodging in the waggon, the men with their Blankets laid down at the fire side.

Mary Dewees, western Pennsylvania pioneer, journal entry of October 13, 1787, in Journal from Philadelphia to Kentucky *(1904).*

The subscriber having succeeded with Congress in obtaining that most excellent tract of land on the northwest bank of the Ohio, between the great and little Miami rivers, begs leave to state some particulars to those gentlemen who may not meet with a small pamphlet already published on the subject.

In the first place it ought to be observed, that no dispute respecting titles in the first instance, can possibly arise, these will be clear and certain, as the whole purchase will be surveyed into sections of one mile square, and every line well marked, and the sections numbered, and every number which may be sold shall be recorded to the first person applying to the subscriber therefor. The land is allowed (all circumstances considered) to be the best tract in the federal country: It lies in north latitude thirty-eight degrees, and the same with Virginia. Horses, cattle and hogs can live well in the woods, where there is abundance of food through the winters, which are very moderate: Every kind of grain and vegetable raised in the middle states grows here, with the addition of cotton and indigo, which may be raised in sufficient quantities for family use.

John Cleves Symmes, land speculator, describing land for sale in the Ohio country, advertisement of January 8, 1788, in Brunswick Gazette.

The subduing a new country, notwithstanding its natural advantages, is alone an arduous task; a task,

however, that patience and perseverance will at last surmount, and these virtues, so necessary in every situation, but peculiarly to yours, you must resolve to exercise. Neither is reducing a country from a state of nature to a state of civilization irksome as it may appear from a slight or superficial view; even very sensible pleasures attend it; the gradual progress of improvement fills the mind with delectable ideas; vast forest converted into arable fields, and cities rising from places where were largely the habitations of wild beasts, give a pleasure something like the attendant of creation. If we can form an idea of it, the imagination is ravished, and a task communicated of even the "joy of God to see a happy world."

Arthur St. Clair, first governor of the Northwest Territory, to the Ohio country settlers, address of July 28, 1788, in Hildreth's Pioneer History of the Ohio Valley *(1848).*

The settlers here appear highly satisfied with the measures we have taken, and very many will go out to those lands. As they must be settled in the spring or early next summer, it will be necessary for as many as wish to receive the donations to be out as soon as possible. We have had an addition of about one hundred within two weeks, and more are expected. We are constantly putting up buildings, but arrivals are faster than we can provide convenient covering. Between forty and fifty houses are so far done as to receive families, and ten more are in building, about one-half of which I expect will be able to receive families next week.

Samuel Holden Parsons, Marietta, Ohio, settler, to Reverend Manasseh Cutler, letter of December 11, 1788, in Life and Letters of Samuel Holden Parsons *(1905).*

The whole number of indian warriors south of the Ohio, and east of the Mississippi may be estimated at 14,000—Those to the northward of the Ohio and to the southward of the Lakes at about 5000—In addition to these the old men, women and children may be estimated at three for one Warrior, the whole amounting to 76,000 souls.

It is highly probable that by a conciliatory system, the expence of managing the said indians and attaching them to the United States for the next ensuing period of fifty years may on average cost 15,000 dollars annually.

A system of coercion and oppression, pursued from time to time for the same period as the convenience of the United States might dictate, would probably amount to a much greater sum of money— But the blood and injustice which would stain the character of the nation, would be beyond all pecuniary calculation.

Secretary of War Henry Knox, to President
George Washington, letter of June 15, 1789, in
The Papers of George Washington.

. . . we were making preparations to solemnize the 13th anniversary of the Independence of the United States. I shall now, having nothing else to write, give you the particulars of our proceedings on that day.

In the afternoon we assembled at the northwest block house, where a short oration was pronounced, after which the militia paraded, discharged fourteen cannons, fired their muskets fourteen times, performed various evolutions, etc and were dispersed. The officers of the Government, together with a few other gentlemen, then repaired to Fort Harmar where we partook of an excellent dinner, and with good wine and under the discharge of cannons, we drank the following toasts:

1. The United States.
2. The President of the United States.
3. The Senate and House of Representatives.
4. The Secretary of War.
5. His most Christian Majesty [the King of France].
6. Perpetual union between France, Spain and America.
7. In memory of those heroes who fell in America in defense of the liberty of their country.
8. The Marquis de LaFayette.
9. The friendly powers of Europe.
10. The day.
11. Governor St. Clair and the Western Territory.
12. Agriculture, commerce and sciences.
13. Dr. Franklin.
14. The citizens of Marietta.

Enoch Parsons, Marietta, Ohio, settler, to his
mother, letter of July 21, 1789, in Parsons'
Life and Letters of Samuel Holden Parsons.

. . . [the United States has] no desire to destroy the red people, although they have the power; but, should you decline this invitation, and pursue your unprovoked hostilities, their strength will be exerted against you; your warriors will be slaughtered, your towns and villages ransacked and destroyed your

wives and children carried into captivity, and you may be assured that those who escaped the fury of our mighty chiefs, shall find no resting place on this side of the great lakes.

General Charles Scott, to the Miami tribe of the
Ohio country, urging them to relinquish their
land claims and sign a peace treaty, message of
May 1791, in U.S. Congress' American State
Papers, Indian Affairs *(1832–61).*

For some time past the western frontiers have been alarmed by depredations committed by some hostile tribes of Indians; but such measures are now in train as will, I presume, either bring them to sue for peace before a stroke is struck at them, or make them feel the effects of an enmity too sensibly to provoke it again unnecessarily, unless, as is much suspected, they are countenanced, abetted, and supported in their hostile views by the B——h. Tho' I must confess I cannot see much prospect of living in tranquillity with them so long as a spirit of land jobbing prevails, and our frontier Settlers entertain the opinion that there is not the same crime (or indeed no crime at all) in killing an Indian as in killing a white man.

President George Washington, to David Hum-
phreys, secretary of foreign affairs, letter of July
20, 1791, in The Writings of George Washington.

With the first 1500 alone I can take the whole of Louisiana for France. If France will be hearty and secret in this business—my success borders on certainty.

George Rogers Clark, to Citizen Edmond
Charles Genet, French emissary, on recruiting
troops to take Louisiana, letter of February 2,
1793, in George Rogers Clark Papers.

Brothers: Money, to us, is of no value, and to most of us unknown: and as no consideration whatever can induce us to sell the lands on which we get sustenance for our women and children, we hope we may be allowed to point out a mode by which your settlers may be easily removed, and peace thereby obtained.

Brothers: We know that these settlers are poor, or they would never have ventured to live in a country which has been in continual trouble ever since they crossed the Ohio. Divide, therefore, this large sum of money, which you have offered to us, among these people: give to each, also, a proportion of what you say you would give to us, annually, over and above this very large sum of money: and, we are persuaded, they would most readily accept of it, in lieu of the lands you sold them. If you add, also, the great sums you must expend in raising and paying armies, with a view to force us to yield you our country, you will certainly have more than sufficient for the purposes of repaying these settlers for all their labor and their improvements.

Brothers: You have talked to us about concessions. It appears strange that you should expect any from us, who have only been defending our just rights against your invasions. We want peace. Restore to us our country, and we shall be enemies no longer.

Wyandot Indians, to United States commissioners, message of August 16, 1793, in U.S. Congress' American State Papers, Indian Affairs.

It's with infinite pleasure that I now announce to you the brilliant success of the Federal army under my Command in a General action with the combined force of the Hostile Indians & a considerable number of the Volunteers & Militia of Detroit on the 20th Instant, on the banks of the Miamis in the vicinity of the British post & Garrison at the foot of the rapids . . .

General Anthony Wayne, to Secretary of War Henry Knox, on the victory over the Ohio tribes at the battle of Fallen Timbers, letter of August 28, 1794, in Anthony Wayne, A Name in Arms (1959).

Perhaps it is not very much to be regretted that all our differences are merged in this treaty, without having been decided; disagreeable imputations are thereby avoided, and the door of conciliation is fairly and widely opened by the *essential* justice done, and the conveniences granted to each other by the parties.

The term limited for the evacuation of the posts could not be restricted to a more early day; that point has been pressed. The reasons which caused an inflexible adherence to that term, I am persuaded, were these, viz.: That the traders have spread through the Indian nations goods to a great amount; that the return for those goods cannot be drawn into Canada at an earlier period; that the impression which the surrender of all the posts to American garrisons will make on the minds of the Indians cannot be foreseen. On a former occasion it was intimated to them (not very delicately) that they had been forsaken, and given up to the United States; that the protection promised them on our part, however sincere, and however, in other respects, competent, cannot entirely prevent those embarrassments which, without our fault, may be occasioned by war . . .

John Jay, to Secretary of State Edmund Randolph, on Jay's Treaty mandating the withdrawal of British forces from their military forts in the Old Northwest Territory, letter of November 19, 1794, in The Correspondence and Public Papers of John Jay (1893).

2. The Trans-Mississippi Frontier: 1795–1810

THE WEST IN AMERICAN DIPLOMACY

As the 18th century came to a close, Spain controlled the Mississippi Gulf region, East Florida, West Florida and Louisiana, including the present state of that name as well as a vast domain extending from the Mississippi to the Rockies. The main western commercial route was along the Mississippi River, which was vital to westerners shipping their raw materials to foreign markets. Growth and economic progress in the West depended heavily on the Ohio-Mississippi River connection.

By the early 1790s a considerable number of settlers from Kentucky and Tennessee had moved into the Gulf region. Spain controlled navigation along the Mississippi, and at times the river was officially closed to all but Spanish traffic. However, corruption among Spanish officials was commonplace, and Americans gained access to the river, usually by paying a bribe.

Many southwesterners were disturbed that the United States expressed no interest in alleviating their problems with the Spanish government. Some even considered declaring their independence from the Union and possibly forming an alliance with Spain.

In 1793, "Citizen" Edmond Charles Genet arrived in the United States as an emissary of France's Revolutionary Convention. Genet planned to capture Florida and Louisiana with the support of discontented Americans, including George Rogers Clark, who resented the small compensation for his Revolutionary War service. Clark advertised for recruits in Kentucky, offering a bounty of a dollar a day plus 1,000 acres of captured land for each year served.

The Genet plot soon collapsed in 1794 when President Washington prohibited enlistments. Congress passed a law imposing fines and imprisonment on Americans who assembled a private army. However, the incident did impress on the federal government the seriousness of the problems plaguing the southwesterners, and President Washington became concerned about the threatened independence movement.

Jay's Treaty with England opened the door to negotiations with Spain, which was no longer allied with the British. With the Treaty of San Lorenzo, Spain accepted the boundary north of the 31st parallel, agreed to withdraw her troops from north of that line, and, most important, to permit the free navigation of the Mississippi.

During the summer of 1795, an estimated 26,000 people traveled over the Old Walton Road, the main passageway to the Cumberland settlements of north-central Tennessee. Tens of thousands more immigrated into the Ohio Valley by floating along the Ohio River on unwieldly flatboats. Many of these settlers occupied Indian territories before the federal government had negotiated treaties with the tribes. Congress attempted to protect the Indians from the white settlers by passing a series of laws. Individuals were prohibited from purchasing land from the Indians or selling them liquor inside the Indian territories. Squatters who occupied unceded territories were subject to eviction. However, these measures failed to regulate the growing number of white settlers. Prosecutors were unable to win convictions against traders and squatters when they were tried before indignant frontier juries.

While Americans were settling the trans-Appalachian region, France was negotiating with Spain for the return of the Louisiana Territory. The Spanish were eager to sell Louisiana, seeing the vast wilderness, inhabited by only about 50,000 people, as a burden on their treasury. For years it had cost her more than it had returned and expenses were likely to soar as American settlers moved into the region from Kentucky, Ohio and Tennessee. In 1800, France signed the secret Treaty of Ildefonso whereby Spain returned Louisiana in exchange for territorial acquisitions in Italy. The official transfer was not actually made until 1803, when the United States began negotiating the Louisiana Purchase with France.

Soon after the secret treaty, however, rumors circulated in America about an impending transfer of Louisiana to France, to the displeasure of the Westerners, who preferred the relatively weak Spain as a neighbor. Whereas Spain could be pressured into keeping the Mississippi open, powerful France would be impossible to control. President Jefferson, viewing France's occupation of Louisiana as a threat to the nation's westward expansion, sent James Monroe, a popular figure in the West, to Paris to negotiate for the purchase not of all Louisiana but only of New Orleans and the Floridas. Jefferson believed the United States could control the mouth of the Mississippi by owning these territories.

While Monroe was en route to Paris, Robert R. Livingston, the American ambassador in France, received a surprise offer to purchase all of Louisiana from Napoleon. The First Consul was facing the prospect of another war with England, and needed the funds to be obtained from selling Louisiana. After Monroe arrived in Paris, a three-week bargaining session took place. For the small price of $15 million the United States acquired 828,000 square miles of territory, which doubled the size of the nation. On November 30, 1803, Louisiana was transferred formally from Spain to France, and then, on December 20, from France to the United States.

With the Louisiana Purchase, the Mississippi Valley was no longer subject to the transportation problems that had threatened the economic progress of the West. Southwesterners who once talked of rebellion and secession now embraced the Union.

EXPLORING THE WEST

Jefferson had been considering a transcontinental expedition as early as 1793, when as vice president of the American Philosophical Society he proposed that the French naturalist André Michaux "explore the country along the Missouri, and thence westward to the Pacific." However, plans for the journey collapsed when Michaux became involved in the Genet conspiracy. In 1802, Jefferson again began making plans for an exploration of the territory west of the Mississippi—before Napoleon even offered Louisiana to the United States.

What stirred Jefferson into action was the recent publication of British explorer Alexander Mackenzie's *Voyages*, an account of his 1793 trek across Canada from Montreal to the Pacific. Mackenzie proposed that Britain develop a passage through North America by way of the Columbia and Missouri rivers in order to tap the lucrative fur trade in the Pacific Northwest and to establish a commercial trade route to Asia. Jefferson, now considering America and England as rivals for the domination of the Pacific Northwest, was determined to secure the Columbia River and its surrounding territory for the United States. Jefferson also wanted to know if there was an undiscovered water route through the North American continent to the Pacific Coast and the Orient—the long-sought-after "Northwest Passage."

On January 18, 1803, Jefferson delivered a secret request to Congress for an appropriation of $2,500 to finance an American exploration beyond the Mississippi. Jefferson emphasized the commercial and scientific benefits of such an exploration, and omitted his concerns about British control of the Pacific Northwest. Some of the lawmakers probably read his intentions; in any event, Jefferson received the $2,500 he requested.

With the revelation in July 1803 of the Louisiana Purchase, the expedition became public and was no longer subject to the sanction of foreign powers. The scope of the expedition was expanded to asserting America's sovereignty over the immense region that had suddenly become United States territory. The explorers about to plunge into the unknown country would have to overcome the elements of a harsh frontier and hostile Indians likely to consider the white men as intruders.

Although Jefferson had no wilderness experience, he realized that the mission could be entrusted only to experienced frontiersmen. He appointed Meriwether Lewis, his 28-year-old secretary, as the commander of the expedition. Lewis was an accomplished hunter, who had experienced Indian raids while growing up on the Georgia border, and had served seven years in the army on the western frontier. Jefferson left all subsequent recruiting to Lewis' discretion.

Lewis invited his 32-year-old friend, William Clark, with whom he had served under General Anthony Wayne, to join him as the company's co-commander. Clark was the youngest brother of George Rogers Clark, the controversial Revolutionary War hero in the West. Clark's self-taught knowledge of natural science, his skills as a frontiersman and soldier and his familiarity with Indian ways made him an ideal candidate for this job. The two young leaders then recruited a group of men, mostly with military backgrounds, who were experienced hunters and boatmen familiar with the wilderness and the Indians, and who had the ability to endure great bodily fatigue.

The Lewis and Clark Expedition, consisting of 45 soldiers, trappers and voyageurs, started up the Missouri from St. Louis on May 14, 1804. They traveled in two narrow canoes, called pirogues, and on a keelboat, 55 feet long and propelled by 22 oars. The first stage of the expedition, lasting 166 days, was to the Mandan Indian villages in present-day North Dakota. This was not unexplored territory, as many traders had traveled up the Missouri past the mouth of the Platte. In 1796, a Spanish representative, the Welshman John Evans, had also reached the Mandan towns, and Lewis and Clark often consulted Evans' map of the Missouri during their upriver journey. The explorers were also familiar with some points on the upper Missouri through maps used by surveyors of the Hudson's Bay and the North West Fur Companies. But they knew nothing of the territory between the Mandan villages and the Cascade Mountains.

After traveling up the Missouri for about 1,600 miles, the Lewis and Clark Expedition reached the Mandan villages near present-day Bismarck in November 1804. Spending the winter here in preparation for the next leg of the trip west, the party constructed a temporary settlement, named Fort Mandan.

Over the next five months, Lewis and Clark interviewed Indians and traders, seeking information on the land that was beyond the headwaters of the Missouri. They soon learned that the river would become unnavigable a few hundred miles past the Yellowstone, and the party would require horses to continue its journey. Fortunately, a Shoshone Indian captive, Sacajawea, the wife of a French Canadian trapper, offered her services as a guide.

In April 1805, about one-third of the expedition returned to St. Louis in the keelboat, as planned, taking with them scientific data and samples of the flora and fauna of the upper Missouri. The rest of the party, under Lewis and Clark, then left Fort Mandan and headed past the mouth of the Yellowstone River into the wilderness of present-day eastern Montana. After 1,200 miles of upriver travel, they encountered a fork in the river. Lewis explored the Marias, the north fork, while Clark continued on the south fork. Clark soon reached the Great Falls of the Missouri, and was rejoined by Lewis, who had discovered that the Marias led only another 70 miles north before it became unnavigable.

The Great Falls of the Missouri, in western Montana, also proved to be the limit of navigation on the Missouri, and the expedition had to carry its supplies and canoes over an 18-mile portage to the Three Forks of the Missouri. Sacajawea led the men along the westernmost branch and then into another tributary, the Beaverhead, which soon became impassible for the canoes. Expedition members resorted to another portage as they crossed the initial ranges of the Rocky Mountains.

On August 15, 1805, the Lewis and Clark Expedition crossed the Continental Divide via the Lemhi Pass, at an elevation of over 7,300 feet, in present-day Montana. For the expedition to continue the explorers needed horses as transport to replace their canoes. All depended on locating and establishing friendly relations with the mountain Indians, the Shoshone. After traveling for months without sighting one Indian, they finally encountered a Shoshone tribe. By an incredible coincidence the band's chief turned out to be Sacajawea's brother. The explorers were able to buy horses and prevent the failure of their expedition.

In late September they emerged from the treacherous Lolo Pass into the Clearwater River, where a friendly band of Nez Perce gave them food and shelter. After resting for one week, the expedition resumed its journey toward the Pacific. Using canoes supplied by the Indians, the men and Sacajawea traveled down the Clearwater to its tributary, the Salmon, which led finally to the western-flowing Snake River.

As hoped, the Snake's swift current soon led them into the Columbia River. They traveled through the Cascade Mountains along the Columbia, and finally, on November 7, 1805, Lewis entered in his journal: "Great joy in camp we are in view of the Ocian, this great Pacific Octean which we been so long anxious to See."

A few miles inland, on the Columbia estuary, the Lewis and Clark Expedition established its winter headquarters, Fort Clatsop, near the site of what is now Astoria, Oregon. Jefferson had instructed Lewis and Clark to seek a seaward route home from the Oregon coast by ob-taining passage on a trading vessel, either by way of Cape Horn or the Cape of Good Hope. But they had arrived on the coast too late in the season to meet up with any ships, and so were forced to spend a rainy, cold winter and prepare for an overland journey eastward in the spring.

After wintering on the Oregon coast for four months, the expedition began its return trip to St. Louis in early March. As the explorers ap-proached the Continental Divide on their homeward journey, Lewis and Clark separated to search for more feasible overland passes. Clark headed southeastward toward Yellowstone, while Lewis traveled northeastward toward the Great Falls. In early August the parties reu-nited below the mouth of the Yellowstone, confirming that there ex-isted no practical route connecting the Missouri and the Colum-bia.

On September 23, 1806, the Lewis and Clark Expedition returned to St. Louis after its monumental journey. The survivors had passed over thousands of miles of largely unknown country, revealed much about the newly acquired Louisiana Territory, improved America's claim to the Pacific Northwest and established friendly relations with a dozen Indian tribes. Moreover, Lewis and Clark had established once and for all that there was no all-water route through the western part of North America to the Pacific.

As the nation cheered the success of the Lewis and Clark Expedi-tion, Jefferson was turning his attention to the conflict between Ameri-can and British territorial claims. In order to assert American sover-eignty, Jefferson ordered Lieutenant Zebulon Pike to lead an expedition up the Mississippi into the Great Lakes to remind English traders that they were operating on American territory. English posts were illegally flying the British flag, and the traders were not paying duties on their goods.

Twenty-six-year-old Zebulon Pike, accompanied by 20 soldiers, set sail on a 70-foot keelboat from an Army post near St. Louis on August 9, 1805. Pike's company journeyed through the maze of islands on the Mississippi, and on an island at the junction of the Mississippi and Minnesota rivers, near present-day Minneapolis, Pike purchased a mil-itary reservation of 100,000 acres from the Sioux Indians. Near present-day Little Falls, Minnesota, 1,500 miles from St. Louis, half of his com-pany set up winter quarters, while Pike pressed forward on sleds through the snow-covered countryside. Pike returned to St. Louis in the spring after having met little resistance from the British traders to America's claim of sovereignty on the upper Mississippi.

In the southwest, Spain was disputing the new territorial boundaries resulting from the Louisiana Purchase. The United States argued that its claim extended to the Rio Grande, whereas Spain maintained that the Red River, which passes through the western part of present-day

Louisiana and then along the southern border of Oklahoma, was the correct boundary.

In July 1806, General James Wilkenson, the governor of the Territory of Upper Louisiana, ordered Lt. Pike to explore the headwaters of the Arkansas and Red rivers and to descend the Red to Natchitoches, near the Spanish border. Although Wilkenson's description of the expedition resembled more an espionage mission than a geographical exploration, the young officer obeyed his orders without question. The American general, it was later discovered, received $12,000 from Spain in 1804 for keeping the Spanish authorities informed of Jefferson's intentions in the Southwest.

Wilkenson was associated with former Vice President Aaron Burr, who had helped him obtain his governor's post. When Burr's political career tumbled after he killed Alexander Hamilton in a duel, Burr traveled west in 1805 and conferred with Wilkenson. It is speculated that Burr and Wilkenson were planning to organize a private army to seize New Orleans and separate Louisiana from the United States. Provoking war between the United States and Spain was part of their supposed scheme.

Pike was unaware that he was a participant in an unsavory plan. In late October 1806, his party of 15 men moved up the Arkansas and were soon scouting for the Rockies. Pike sighted a great peak rising in the northwest, and in mid-November set out with three men to explore the mountain, which later became known as Pikes Peak. After traveling for three days and reaching only the mountain's foothills, Pike returned to camp.

In the spring of 1807, Pike's expedition crossed the Sangre de Cristos Mountains and emerged on the upper Rio Grande, where a temporary stockade was built on undisputed territory that Spain had owned for the past two centuries. A Spanish patrol out of Santa Fe discovered the stockade, and Pike along with his company were escorted back to the present-day capital city of New Mexico for questioning. In June 1807, Pike and his men were marched across northern Mexico to Natchitoches, where they arrived on American soil. Pike's papers and maps were confiscated, but he was able to reconstruct enough material to publish an account that brought him wide acclaim.

When Pike was first starting out from St. Louis, Wilkenson, believing that some members of the press and many government officials were already aware of the plot, wrote to Jefferson revealing Burr's intentions. He then negotiated a truce with the Spanish by establishing a neutral area between Natchitoches and the Sabine. Jefferson notified Congress that Burr was involved in a conspiracy to create a private empire in the Southwest. Burr was charged with treason and later tried before the Supreme Court.

Although Wilkenson, who was not charged, testified against his former benefactor, Burr was acquitted. According to Chief Justice John

Marshall's opinion, the case presented only an intention to commit an act of war, whereas treason was punishable only if the act was actually carried out. Despite his victory in court, Burr's reputation was irreparably tarnished. Wilkenson was court-martialed in 1811 for his alleged acceptance of fees from the Spanish but ultimately acquitted. Beyond the guilt or innocence of Burr and Wilkenson, the collapse of the Burr conspiracy proved that separatism was no longer popular in the West.

Lewis and Clark's prodigious reports describing the abundance of game, the immense mountain ranges and the friendly Indians in the Pacific Northwest ignited the curiosity of frontiersmen in St. Louis, the center of the western fur trade. Previously, journeys to such distant regions had been undertaken only with government support; but with the returning explorers' accounts of the number of beaver around the Columbia River's headwaters, private investors saw the opportunity to profit from financing transcontinental expeditions. Hundreds of trapper-traders were eager to travel thousands of miles across the country if they were provided with the initial capital for boats and equipment.

THE FUR TRADE

Manuel Lisa was one of the early organizers of a commercial expedition to the Far West. He was a Spaniard of South American descent, born in New Orleans. Lisa's destination was the Yellowstone River in present-day eastern Montana. His partner was an experienced frontiersman, George Drouiland, who had traveled through the mountains with Lewis and Clark. The expedition was sponsored by William Morrison, proprietor of a leading Mississippi Valley trading company.

Lisa led 42 trappers 2,000 miles up the Missouri, then up the Yellowstone River to the mouth of the Big Horn, where his men built a blockhouse, named Fort Manuel. They spent the winter hunting, trapping and exploring the Northern Rockies frontier. These private explorers plotted the courses of rivers, discovered passes through the mountains and paved the way for settlers by establishing trade with the Indians.

Lisa's party returned to St. Louis in the summer of 1808 with plenty of furs and strong advice for future expeditions. Because only large companies could finance these time-consuming journeys, and because small parties would be subject to attack by hostile Indians, the city's leading traders pooled their resources to form the Missouri Fur Company. Among the partners were Manuel Lisa, William Clark and Major Andrew Henry.

The company's first expedition, consisting of all the partners and 172 other men, set out for Fort Manuel in the spring of 1809. The frontiersmen traveled up the Missouri on nine large barges, carrying enough trading goods to supply five or six posts. Part of the expedition remained at Fort Mandan in present-day North Dakota, obtaining beaver pelts from the Plains Indians, while the other traders moved on to Fort Manuel, where they spent the winter of 1810 profitably trading with the Crow tribe.

Some of the partners at Fort Manuel believed better furs could be procured from the nearby Blackfeet. Although the traders knew the tribe was hostile to whites because two of its warriors had been killed by Meriwether Lewis on his return trip, they believed a large expedition could offer sufficient protection. While trappers were cautiously searching in the forest for beaver pelts, they were attacked by a powerful Blackfoot war party. Five men were killed, and a large store of goods was destroyed. Later, three more trappers were killed, including George Drouillard, who had traveled with Lewis and Clark.

Adding to the difficulties with the Blackfeet was the cold winter, which made game scarce. In the spring of 1811, the trappers returned to St. Louis with only 40 packs of beaver. With resources almost depleted, the Missouri Fur Company withdrew from the Northern Rockies, abandoning Fort Manuel in 1811 and Fort Mandan a year later.

The Missouri Fur Company's failure to establish an American fur trade in the Far West did not dissuade others from trying to reap the rich rewards to be had in the Rocky Mountains. In 1808, the American Fur Company was organized by John Jacob Astor, a German immigrant who had founded one of the leading fur trading firms in the country. He planned an operation on a grand scale that could compete with the two powerful English fur trading concerns, the Hudson's Bay Company and the North West Company. His plan included creating a chain of posts across the Far West from the Great Lakes to the Pacific, with his headquarters at the mouth of the Columbia, whence furs could be shipped to the Orient.

The overland route ensured that British ships in the Pacific Northwest could not prevent American fur traders from transporting their goods. Although the project was essentially a commercial venture, it also served to strengthen America's presence west of the mountains first explored by Lewis and Clark. President Jefferson, a strong proponent of American westward expansion, endorsed Astor's plan, as did many members of Congress.

Astor formed a subsidiary company, the Pacific Fur Company, to command a post on the Columbia River. In 1810, two expeditions set out for the Pacific. One set sail on September 8 from New York City, aboard Astor's first ship, the *Tonquin*. They sailed around Cape Horn and arrived in March of 1811 at the mouth of the Columbia, where they built a blockhouse and founded Astoria, America's first permanent settlement in the Pacific Northwest. The second party, known as the "Overland Astorians," left St. Louis in March 1811. After a rigor-

*John Jacob Astor. Courtesy of the
New York Public Library.*

ous journey across the Plains, they arrived at Astoria in February 1812.

The outpost prospered, and by the summer Astoria's warehouses had accumulated stacks of pelts. A returning expedition set out for St. Louis on June 29, 1812, crossing the Rockies through the South Pass and descending the Platte River. This route later became famous as the Oregon Trail.

The Astorians were unaware of the start of the War of 1812. When a British warship approached to capture their post, Astor's partners realizing they were unable to resist, sold the entire enterprise to the North West Company for only $58,000.

The War of 1812 suspended American activity in the Pacific Northwest for a generation. Astoria was a failure, losing $400,000 and costing 61 lives. However, Astor's venture did acquaint more American frontiersmen with a region that had been previously unknown.

CHRONICLE OF EVENTS

1795:

August 3: In the Treaty of Greenville, the Indians relinquish two-thirds of Ohio and part of Indiana to the United States, and grant permission for 16 forts to be built in the remaining Indian Territory.

August 25: Governor St. Clair proclaims the end of the Indian war.

October 27: In the Treaty of San Lorenzo, Spain relinquishes claims north of the 31st parallel, and permits the free navigation of the Mississippi River.

1796:

Thousands of new settlers travel by foot or on wagons along the Old Walton Road into north-central Tennessee.

March 1: Jay's Treaty ratified by the U.S. Senate.

May 18: Congress mandates the survey of all lands in the Northwestern Territory in preparation for the auctioning of land tracts of 640 acres for $2 an acre.

June 1: Tennessee admitted as a state.

July 11: The British withdraw from their frontier forts, and Americans occupy Fort Miami and Detroit.

October 29: Captain Ebenezer Dorr commands the *Otter*, the first American ship to sail along the California coast and into Monterey Bay.

December: Mississippi River opened to American ships.

1798:

April 7: Congress creates the Mississippi Territory from the lands ceded by Spain; the territory first includes parts of Alabama and Mississippi, and later includes Tennessee and West Florida.

1799:

December 14: George Washington dies at the age of 67 at Mount Vernon.

General Arthur St. Clair. Courtesy of the New York Public Library.

1800:

The Northwest Territory is divided into the Ohio and Indiana territories. William Henry Harrison is appointed governor of the Indiana Territory.

Total United States population is estimated at 5,308,483, including 869,849 slaves. Population of Kentucky is 220,000

May 1: In the secret Treaty of San Ildefonso between Spain and France, the Louisiana Territory is returned to France, the original Old World owner.

May 10: The Harrison Land Law is passed, providing for the sale of half-sections of public domain land in 320-acre sections at $2 per acre, to be paid in installments over four years. Enables individual settlers to buy land from the United States government

October 1: Spain publicly agrees to transfer Louisiana to France.

1801:

March 4: Thomas Jefferson is inaugurated as the third president of the United States.

December 5: Robert R. Livingston, American ambassador to France, meets French Foreign Minister Talleyrand for the first time. Talleyrand denies that a secret treaty has provided for France to take Louisiana.

1802:

February: Albert Gallatin, secretary of the treasury, proposes that funds from the sale of public lands be used to finance the construction of roads from the Atlantic Ocean to the Ohio River. (Road-building begins the following year).

1802

April 30: Congress passes the first Enabling Act, authorizing any territory organized under the Northwest Ordinance to hold a convention, draft a constitution and prepare for entry into the Union.

October 28: Robert Livingston writes to Jefferson that Joseph Bonaparte, brother of France's first consul, has casually inquired whether the United States would be interested in purchasing East and West Florida, and the southern parts of Alabama and Mississippi.

1803:

January 12: Congress authorizes Jefferson to initiate negotiations with France and Spain for the purchase of New Orleans and the provinces of East and West Florida.

January 18: In a secret message to Congress, Jefferson requests an appropriation of $2,500 to send an exploratory expedition to the West. Congress grants the request, making possible the Lewis and Clark Expedition.

March 1: Ohio is admitted as the 17th state. Ohio's population is estimated at 70,000. Slavery is forbidden by the state's constitution, the first instance of this in United States history.

March 3: Congress approves the sale of all un-committed public lands in the Mississippi Territory.

April 11: French diplomat Talleyrand asks Livingston what price the United States would be willing to pay for the entire Louisiana Territory.

April 15: Livingston and James Monroe begin negotiations with France for the Louisiana Purchase.

May 2: The Louisiana Purchase is signed. The United States acquires 828,000 square miles of land between the Mississippi River and the Rocky Mountains for approximately $25 million, doubling the size of the nation.

July: Jefferson suggests removing the Indians to the west of the Mississippi River. The bill passes the Senate, but fails in the House.

August 31: Meriwether Lewis and William Clark begin their expedition with a trip down the Ohio River.

November 30: Spain formally cedes Louisiana to France.

December 20: The French turn over New Orleans and lower Louisiana to the United States.

1804:

March 9: Upper Louisiana is transferred from Spanish to French control, and then formally ceded to the United States.

March 26: The Land Act sets cash payment for western public lands at $1.64 per acre for a minimum of 160 acres, reduced from the previous price of $2.00.

May 14: Lewis and Clark lead an expedition of twenty-nine men (16 others will accompany them to the Mandan villages in present-day North Dakota) out of St. Louis on a keelboat and two pirogue boats.

August 13: Governor William Henry Harrison purchases the land between the Wabash and Ohio rivers from the Delaware Indians.

October 1: William C. Claiborne is appointed first governor of the Louisiana Territory.

October 27: The Lewis and Clark Expedition reaches the Mandan Indian towns on the Missouri River. The explorers have traveled 1,600 miles in 23 weeks.

1805:

January 11: The Indiana Territory is divided, its northern section becoming the Michigan Territory.

April 7: Part of the Lewis and Clark Expedition begins its return trip to St. Louis, with specimens from the wilderness that has been explored.

April 26: The Lewis and Clark company reaches the mouth of the Yellowstone River.

May 26: Lewis and Clark sight the Rocky Mountains.

August 9: Lieutenant Zebulon M. Pike sets out from St. Louis to find the sources of the Mississippi River.

August 15: Lewis and Clark cross the Continental Divide.

September 23: Zebulon Pike, representing the United States Army, pays $2,000 to the Minnesota Sioux for a nine-square-mile tract at the mouth of the Minnesota River. Pike sets up Fort Snelling, the first United States government presence in this region.

November 2: The Lewis and Clark Expedition reaches the Cascade Mountains.

December 7: The Lewis and Clark company builds Fort Clatsop in present-day Oregon. They spend the winter recording data and organizing maps of the region.

1806:

February 19: President Jefferson issues a report on the Lewis and Clark Expedition entitled "Message from the President of the United States Communicating Discoveries Made in Exploring the Missouri, Red River and Washita by Captains Lewis and Clark, Doctor Sibley and Mr. Dunbar."

March 29: Congress approves the construction of the Cumberland Road from Cumberland, Maryland, to Zanesburg, Virginia, on the Ohio River.

April 30: Zebulon Pike returns to St. Louis after exploring the upper Mississippi and reaching Cass Lake in present-day Minnesota, but has not discovered source of the Mississippi River.

June 15: Lewis and Clark begin climbing the Rocky Mountains from the western side.

July 15: General James Wilkenson, secretly on Spain's payroll, orders Pike to explore the Southwest.

September 23: The Lewis and Clark Expedition returns to St. Louis, over 36 months after its departure.

October 21: Wilkenson informs President Jefferson of Burr's intention to seize New Orleans and separate Louisiana from the Union.

November 16: Zebulon Pike sights what will be called "Pikes Peak," in Colorado.

1807:

January 22: Jefferson officially informs Congress of Aaron Burr's alleged conspiracy to start a private territory in the Southwest.

February 19: Aaron Burr is arrested in Alabama.

April 19: Manuel Lisa sets out from St. Louis for the Yellowstone River.

August 17: Inventor Robert Fulton takes his steamboat *Clermont* up the Hudson River from New York City to Albany in 32 hours.

September 1: Burr and his associates are acquitted of treason by the Supreme Court.

November 21: Manuel Lisa builds Fort Manuel on the Yellowstone River, at the mouth of the Big Horn.

1808:

April: John Jacob Astor founds the American Fur Company.

July 12: The *Missouri Gazette*, published in St. Louis, becomes the first newspaper west of the Mississippi River.

August: Manuel Lisa returns to St. Louis from Yellowstone.

November 10: The Osage Indians cede all of their lands in present-day Missouri and Arkansas.

1809:

March 1: The Illinois Territory is created from part of the Indiana Territory.

March 9: The Missouri Fur Company is organized; among the 10 partners are Manuel Lisa and William Clark.

June: The Missouri Fur Company sets out for the Mandan villages and Fort Manuel.

1810:

Total United States population is estimated at 7,239,000, up 36.4% since 1800.

March: The Missouri Fur Company builds a fort at the Three Forks in present-day Montana.

April 12: A Blackfoot war party attacks Missouri Fur Company trappers, killing five men.

June 23: John Jacob Astor founds the Pacific Fur Company to take advantage of the rich resources in the Pacific Northwest.

July: A party from the Missouri Fur Company returns to St. Louis with a small number of pelts.

September 8: Astor's ship, the *Tonquin,* sails from New York for the Pacific, as part of the American Fur Company's plan to establish a fur trade in the Pacific Northwest.

EYEWITNESS TESTIMONY

The termination of the long, expensive and distressing war in which we have been engaged with certain Indians North west of the Ohio, is placed in the option of the United States, by a treaty, which the Commander of our Army has concluded, provisionally, with the hostile tribes in that Region.

In the adjustment of the terms, the satisfaction of the Indians was deemed an object worthy no less of the policy, than of the liberality of the United States, as the necessary basis of durable tranquility. This object, it is believed, has been fully attained.

President George Washington, Seventh Annual
Address to Congress, December 8, 1795, in
The Writings of George Washington *(1939).*

If the Anglo-Americans possess these rich countries they would become masters of the Gulf of Mexico. They would have everything in their hands to create a formidable marine power which, in their service, would make all the commerce of America and of our colonies dependent upon them. It is not necessary, then, to demonstrate that the Anglo-Americans would become strong at our expense and would seize upon the richest provinces. On the other hand, it is desirable for us to rival them in negotiating for Louisiana . . . country we should have, in abundance, timber for building, pasturage for animals, rice, indigo, cotton, peltries, and a thousand other valuable products which would be at the ports of our colonies. We would then be more powerful in the New World than in Europe; we would attach the Americans to our political existence; they would be forced to observe strictly the treaties of France.

Anonymous French diplomat, 1796, in James'
The Life of George Rogers Clark *(1928).*

The great cause of so many quarrels with the Indians has been, that the latter have always looked upon the attack of individuals as expressive of the disposition of the whole nation; and not unfrequently have private quarrels been the cause of shedding much blood. And it is worthy of remark, that the most violent prejudices exist on both sides, between the Indians and those white people who live on the frontiers of the United States: so much so, that I have

The Treaty of Greenville, 1795. By a member of General Anthony Wayne's staff. Courtesy of the New York Public Library.

heard them talk with the same unconcern of killing an Indian, as of killing a deer or a turkey . . .

Francis Baily, English traveler, journal entry of March 31, 1797, in Journal of a Tour in Unsettled Parts of North America *(1856).*

When I walk through the streets I see every person in his shop employed about something. One makes shoes, another hats, a third sells cloth, and everyone lives by his labor. I say to myself, which of all these things can you do? Not one. I can make a bow or an arrow, catch fish, kill game, and go to war, but none of these is of any use here . . . I should be a piece of furniture, useless to my nation, useless to the whites, and useless to myself.

Little Turtle, Miami chief, on the occasion of his visit to Philadelphia, 1797, in Young's Little Turtle *(1917).*

. . . the Spaniards have lately formed a settlement, called St. Louis, and have taken a great deal of pains to encourage Americans to settle there; induced by the temptations they held out, a great many emigrated thither, and still continue to do so, to the great retardation of the settlements in the western parts of the United States. However, there is one thing which is likely to make amends for this temporary evil, and that is, that such Americans as do emigrate thither will take with them all their local habits and dispositions, and that unconquerable spirit of independence which characterises them.

Francis Baily, English traveler, journal entry of June 1797, in Journal of a Tour in Unsettled Parts of North America.

. . . it appears their Commissioners treated the business so mysteriously as to make these people believe we had sold their lands; first having defrauded us by having all that country included in the confirmation of Mr. Livingston's deed to Mr. Oliver Phelps, to which the Senecas signed their names, only supposing that they sold part of their own country, and to which I signed as a witness. This was made use of to convince the Caughnawagas they had no right to the country they inhabit; and I learn that it was not till after much argument that your Government owned that they never paid any money to me or the Five Nations on account of these lands, and that they never looked on any Indians to have a right to them, either Caughnawagas or Five Nations.

Joseph Brant, Mohawk chieftain, to Thomas Morris, letter of April 4, 1799, in Stone's The Life of Joseph Brant *(1838).*

They are furnishing their hunters and Indians with arms; they hold conversations and impress mischievous thoughts on their hearers, in accord with their restless and ambitious character, and with the bonds which bind them to their countrymen of the west [part of the United States]. They have a custom of patting their children on the shoulder when the latter are very robust and saying to them "You wil go to Mexico."

[The bishop reports] that the same thing is taking place on the upper Mississippi, in the Illinois district [*distrito de Jlinesses*] and its vicinity, where there has been a remarkable introduction of those adventurers who are penetrating into the interior toward New Mexico.

Joseph Antonio Caballero, Spanish minister, to colleague Antonio Coruel, letter of November 13, 1799, in Robertson's Louisiana Under the Rule of Spain, France, and the United States *(1969).*

There is on the globe one single spot, the possessor of which is our natural and habitual enemy. It is New Orleans, through which the produce of three-eighths of our territory must pass to market, and from its fertility it will erelong yield more than half of our whole produce, and contain more than half of our inhabitants. France, placing herself in that door, assumes to us the attitude of defiance.

Thomas Jefferson, to Robert Livingston, letter of April 8, 1802, in Letters and Addresses *(1907).*

The inhabitants of Kentucky eagerly recommend to strangers the country they inhabit as the best part of the United States, as that where the soil is most fertile, the climate most salubrious, and where all the inhabitants were brought through the love of liberty and independence!

André F. Michaux, French scientist, 1802, in Travels to the West of the Allegheny Mountains *(1805).*

You will be surprised when I inform you that we still remain in the dark respecting the future fate of our neighbouring province of Louisianna—we cannot learn that any official intelligence on the subject has ever been communicated to the Govr. of the province by the Court of Madrid—that it has once been ceded is not doubted, but various are the reports which have been of late circulated pro and con. The future proximity of a govt. forming a member of Our/soi disant [self-styled]/Sister republic, presents not the most pleasing ideas to the reflecting part of our Citizens: it is impossible to predict what embarrassments may be placed upon the navigation & commerce of this river by the aspiring ruler of the french nation; but we must be willfully blind not to see that the position of the U. S. in this quarter must be . . . unfavorably altered by the expected change the contrast is . . . [ind]eed very great—The Spaniards stand some what in awe of us, and . . . I suspect, very much dread the power of france—

William Dunbar, scientist and Mississippian, to Robert Bird, commercial trader, letter of July 25, 1802, in The Life, Letters and Papers of William Dunbar *(1930).*

From what has been said of Louisiana and the adjacent states, it is clear that the Republic, as sovereign of the two shores of the Mississippi at its mouth, holds in its hands the key to its navigation. That navigation, moreover, is of the highest importance to the western states of the federal government; for the mountains which separate several of their provinces from Philadelphia, make the expense of transportation by the interior so excessive, that, without the resource of the river, all commercial connection between the two parts of the United States would become impossible.

Duc Denis Decrés, Spanish minister, from secret instructions for the captain-general of Louisiana, November 26, 1802, in Robertson's Louisiana Under the Rule of Spain, France, and the United States.

An intelligent officer with ten or twelve chosen men, fit for the enterprize and willing to undertake it, taken from our posts, where they may be spared without inconvenience, might explore the whole line, even to the Western ocean, have conferences with the natives on the subject of commercial intercourse, get admission among them for our traders as others are admitted, agree on convenient deposits for an interchange of articles, and return with the information acquired in the course of two summers.

President Thomas Jefferson, secret request to Congress for appropriations to explore the Louisiana Territory, December 1802, in The Papers of Thomas Jefferson *(1950).*

The general sentiment upon the Affair and upon the Navigation of the Mississippi which is justly regarded as the basis of the prosperity of the Western States, is such as to convince a very superficial observer, that an act of the greatest vigour, such for instance as taking possession of the Island of New Orleans, would be the most popular step the President could take; if it were conducted with tolerable Capacity or seconded by judicious measures for securing hereafter the perfect freedom of that port. If a pacific system be that which Mr. Jefferson is determined to adopt at all events, the greatest danger he has to apprehend will be, either from the inhabitants of the Western States, who, if the negociation should go into great length and the right of depôt be interdicted, will most probably take upon themselves to vindicate their claims by some act of violence: or from the Arrival of the French, with whom a negociation will be conducted on less easy terms than with the Spaniards . . .

Edward Thornton, English ambassador to the United States, to Lord Hawkesberry, letter of January 3, 1803, in Robertson's Louisiana Under the Rule of Spain, France, and the United States.

When they [the Indians] withdraw themselves to the culture of a small piece of land, they will perceive how useless to them are their extensive forests, and will be willing to pare them off from time to time in exchange for necessaries for their farms & families. To promote this disposition to exchange lands which they have to spare and they want, we shall push our trading houses, and be glad to see the good and influential individuals among them run into debt, because we observe that when these debts get beyond what the individuals can pay, they become willing to lop them off by a cession of lands.

President Thomas Jefferson, to William Henry Harrison, governor of the Indiana Territory, letter of February 27, 1803, in The Papers of Thomas Jefferson.

The desire to spare the continent of North America from the war that threatened it, of settling various

Thomas Jefferson. Courtesy of the New York Public Library.

points of litigation between the Republic and the United States, and to remove all new causes for misunderstanding that their competition and neighborhood would have given rise to between them; the position of the French colonies, their need of men, agriculture, and aid; and finally, the force of circumstances, foresight for the future, and the intention of compensating by an advantageous arrangement for the inevitable loss of a country which war was about to place at the mercy of another nation: all these reasons have decided the government to cause all the rights that it had acquired from Spain to the sovereignty and to the possession of Louisiana to pass to the United States.

Charles Talleyrand, French foreign minister, to Duc Denis Decrés, French official in Louisiana, letter of May 23, 1803, in Robertson's Louisiana Under the Rule of Spain, France, and the United States.

The acquisition of Louisiana is important for the United States, so far as it assures them the mouth of the Mississippi, but the acquisition of the vast territories, which the above-mentioned province is sup-

posed to contain, is truly an evil, insomuch as it gives an extent of territory already before burdensome to the United States. It is true that until now we have seen its population increase in an incalculable ratio; but, notwithstanding the territory which they possess is now so extensive that even supposing the continuation of the same ratio—which is not believable—two centuries at least would be necessary to populate the country as heavily as are some of the most deserted provinces of Spain.

Marqués de Casa Irujo, Spanish minister in the United States, to Pedro Guerra Ceballos, Spanish official, letter of September 12, 1803, in Robertson's Louisiana Under the Rule of Spain, France, and the United States.

This accession of territory for ever assures the territory of the United States. I have just given England a maritime rival who sooner or later will humble its pride.

Napoleon Bonaparte, France's first consul, 1803, in Robertson's Louisiana Under Spain, France, and the United States.

We have lived long, but this is the noblest work of our whole lives. The treaty which we have just signed has not been obtained by art or dictated by force; equally advantageous to the two contracting parties, it will change vast solitudes into flourishing districts. From this day the United States take their place among the powers of the first rank; the English lose all exclusive influence in the affairs of America.

Robert R. Livingston, American ambassador in Paris, 1803, in Robertson's Louisiana Under Spain, France, and the United States.

The acquisition of New Orleans would of itself have been a great thing, as it would have ensured to our western brethern the means of exporting their produce: but that of Louisiana is unappreciable, because, giving us the sole dominion of the Mississippi, it excludes those bickerings with foreign powers, which we know of a certainty would have put us at war with France immediately; and it secures to us the course of a peaceable nation.

President Thomas Jefferson, to James Dickenson, statesman, letter of August 9, 1803, in The Writings of Thomas Jefferson *(1891).*

The object of your mission is to explore the Missouri River, & such principal stream of it, as, by it's course and communication with the waters of the

William Clark, by Charles Willson Peale. Courtesy of the New York Public Library.

Pacific ocean, whether the Columbia, Oregan, Colorado or any other river may offer the most direct & practicable water communication across the continent for the purposes of commerce.

President Thomas Jefferson, June 20, 1803, instructions to Meriwether Lewis, in The Papers of Thomas Jefferson.

I determined to go as far as St. Charles a french Village 7 Leags. up the Missourie, and wait at that place untill Capt. Lewis could finish the business in which he was obliged to attend to at St. Louis and join me by Land from that place 24 miles.

I Set out at 4 oClock P.M, in the presence of many of the neighbouring inhabitents, and proceeded on under a jentle brease up the Missouri to the upper Point of the 1st Island

William Clark, journal entry of May 14, 1804, in DeVoto's The Journals of Lewis and Clark *(1953).*

In the after part of the day I also walked out and ascended the river hills which I found sufficiently

fortiegueing. on arriving to the summit [of] one of the highest points in the neighborhood I thought myself well repaid for my labour; as from this point I beheld the Rocky Mountains for the first time.

Meriwether Lewis, journal entry of May 26, 1805, in DeVoto's The Journals of Lewis and Clark.

Our vessels consisted of six small canoes, and two large perogues. This little fleet altho' not quite so rispectable as those of Columbus or Capt. Cook, were still viewed by us with as much pleasure as those deservedly famed adventurers ever beheld theirs; and I dare say with quite as much anxiety for their safety and preservation. we were now about to penetrate a country at least two thousand miles in width, on which the foot of civilized man had never trodden; the good or evil it had in store for us was for experiment yet to determine, and these little vessells contained every article by which we were to expect to subsist or defend ourselves. . . . enterta[in]ing as I do, the most confident hope of succeeding in a voyage which had formed a da[r]ing project of mine for the last ten years, I could but esteem this moment of my departure as among the most happy of my life.

Meriwether Lewis, after wintering in what is now central South Dakota, journal entry of April 7, 1805, in DeVoto's The Journals of Lewis and Clark.

. . . the grandest sight I ever beheld, the hight of the fall is the same of the other but the irregular and somewhat projecting rocks below receives the water in it's passage down and brakes it into a perfect white foam which assumes a thousand forms in a moment sometimes flying up in jets of sparkling foam to the hight of fifteen or twenty feet and are scarcely formed before large roling bodies of the same beaten and foaming water is thrown over and conceals them.

Meriwether Lewis, at the Great Falls of the Missouri, journal entry of June 13, 1805, in DeVoto's The Journals of Lewis and Clark.

We were desirous to oblige the United States, but we had never before Sold Land, and we did not know the value of it, we trusted our beloved white men traders and interpreters to Speak for us, and we have given away a great Country to Governor Harrison for a little thing, we do not say we were cheated, but we made a bad bargain and the Chiefs who made it are all dead, deposed, yet the bargain Stands, for we never back what we had given.

Sauk and Fox tribal delegation, July 27, 1805, speech to Illinois government officials, in Jackson's Thomas Jefferson and the Stony Mountains *(1981).*

You will be pleased to take the course of the River and calculate distances by time, noting rivers, creeks, Highlands, Prairies, Islands, rapids, shoals, mines, Quarries, Timber, water[,] Soil, Indian Villages and Settlements, in a Diary to comprehend reflections on the wind and weather.

It is interesting to government to be informed of the Population and residence of the several Indian Nations, of the Quantity and Species of Skins and Furs they barter per annum, and their relative price to goods; of the Tracts of Country on which they generally make their hunts, and the People with whom they trade.

General James Wilkenson, to Lieutenant Zebulon M. Pike, instructions to explore the upper Mississippi, letter of July 30, 1805, in The Journals of Zebulon Montgomery Pike *(1966).*

A fine morning. We proceeded on about two miles, and discovered a number of the natives, of the Snake nation, coming along the bank on the South side. Captain Lewis had been as far as the waters of the Columbia river and met them there. We continued on about two miles further to a place where the river forks, and there halted and encamped, after much fatigue and difficulty. The water is so shallow that we had to drag the canoes, one at a time, almost all the way. The distance across from this place to the waters of the Columbia river is about 40 miles, and the road or way said to be good. There were about 20 of the natives came over with Captain Lewis, and had the same number of horses. Here we unloaded the canoes, and had a talk with the Indians; and agreed with them that they should lend us some of their horses to carry our baggage to the Columbia river.

Patrick Gass, officer with the Lewis and Clark Expedition, on meeting Shoshone Indians near the south fork of the Missouri River, journal entry of August 17, 1805, in Gass' A Journal of the Voyages and Travels of a Corps of Discovery Under the Command of Capt. Lewis and Capt. Clarke *(1807).*

Meriwether Lewis. Courtesy of the Library of Congress.

we made them [the Indians] sensible of their dependance on the will of our government for every species of merchandize as well for their defence & comfort; and apprized them of the strength of our government and it's friendly dispositions towards them.

Meriwether Lewis, finally sighting Indians (Shoshones) after traveling 1,200 miles along the Missouri River, journal entry of August 17, 1805, in DeVoto's The Journals of Lewis and Clark.

As the Indians who were on their way down the Missouri had a number of spare ho[r]ses with them

I thought it probable that I could obtain some of them and therefore desired the Cheif to speak to them and inform me whether they would trade. they gave no positive answer but requested to see the goods which I was willing to give in exchange. I now produced some battle axes which I had made at Fort Mandan with which they were much pleased. knives also seemed in great demand among them. I soon purchased three horses and a mule. for each horse I gave an ax a knife handkercheif and a little paint

Meriwether Lewis, on buying horses from the Shoshones for the expedition's trek over the Bitterroot mountains, journal entry of August 24, 1805, in DeVoto's The Journals of Lewis and Clark.

our guide could not inform us where this river discharged itself into the columbia river, he informed us that it continues it's course along the mountains to the N. as far as he knew it and that not very distant from where we then were it formed a junction with a stream nearly as large as itself which took it's rise in the mountains near the Missouri to the East of us and passed through an extensive valley generally open prarie which forms an excellent pass to the Missouri. the point of the Missouri where this Indian pass intersects it, is about 30 miles above the *gates of the rocky Mountain,* or the place where the valley of the Missouri first widens into an extensive plain after entering the rockey Mountains.

Meriwether Lewis, discovering that the Snake River leads into the Columbia, journal entry of September 9, 1805, in DeVoto's The Journals of Lewis and Clark.

I addressed them in a Speech which though long, and touching on many points, yet the principal ones were the Granting of the Land at this place, Falls of Saint Anthony & St. Croix; and the making peace with the Chippeway's. I was replied to by *Le Fils de Penichon, Le Petit Corbeau,* and *L'Orignal levé.* They gave me the Land required; about 100000 Acres (equal to 200000 Dollars) and promised me a safe passport for myself and any Chiefs I might bring down; but spoke doubtfully relative to the peace. I gave them presents to the amount of about 200 dollars, and as soon as the Council was over, I suffered the Traders to present them with some liquor, which, with what I myself gave, was equal to 60 gallons. In one half hour they were all Embarked for their respective Villages.

Zebulon Pike, on purchasing 100,000 acres from the Sioux at present-day Minneapolis-St. Paul, journal entry of September 23, 1805, in The Journals of Zebulon Montgomery Pike *(1966).*

Great joy in camp we are in view of the Ocian, this great Pacific Octean which we been so long anxious to See. And the roreing or noise made by the waves brakeing on the rockey Shores (as I suppose) may be heard disti[n]ctly.

William Clark, journal entry of November 7, 1805, in DeVoto's The Journals of Lewis and Clark.

The north west company, were about to push their trade down the Mississippi, until they would have met the traders of Michilimackinacj, but I gave them to understand, that it could not be admitted.

Zebulon Pike, 1806, "Observations on the North West Company," in The Journals of Zebulon Montgomery Pike.

The persons who usually visit the entrance of this river for the purpose of traffic or hunting I believe are either English or Americans; the Indians inform us that they speak the same language with ourselves, and give us proofs of their varacity by repeating many words of English, as musquit, powder, shot, [k]nife, file, damned rascal, sun of a bitch &c. whether these traders are from Nootka sound, from some other late establishment on this coast, or immediately from the U'States or Great Brittain, I am at a loss to determine, nor can the Indians inform us.

Meriwether Lewis, at the mouth of the Columbia River in the Pacific Northwest, journal entry of January 9, 1806, in DeVoto's The Journals of Lewis and Clark.

It was reasonably expected that while the limits between the territories of the United States and Spain were unsettled neither party would have innovated on the existing state of their respective positions. Some time since, however, we learnt that the Spanish authorities were advancing into the disputed country to occupy new posts and make new settlements. Unwilling to take any measures which might preclude a peaceable accommodation of differences, the officers of the United States were ordered to confine themselves within the country on this side of the Sabine River which, by delivery of its principal post, Natchitoches, was understood to have been itself delivered up by Spain, and at the same time to permit no adverse post to be taken nor armed men to remain within it. In consequence of these orders the commanding officer at Natchitoches, learning that a party of Spanish troops had crossed the Sabine River and were posting themselves on this side the Adais, sent a detachment of his force to require them to withdraw to the other side of the Sabine, which they accordingly did.

*President Thomas Jefferson, special message to
Congress, March 19, 1806,* The Writings of
Thomas Jefferson.

Collected our horses early with the intention of makeing an early Start. Some hard Showers of rain detained us we took our final departu[r]e from the quawmash fields and proceeded with much dificuelty owing to the Situation of the road which was very sliprey, and it was with great dificulty that the loaded horses Could assend the hills and Mountains   the[y] frequently sliped down both assending and decending those steep hills. the rain seased and sun shown out. after detaining about 2 hours we proceeded on passing over some ruged hills or Spurs of the rocky Mountain . . .

*William Clark, on the expedition's return trip,
journal entry of June 15, 1806, in DeVoto's*
The Journals of Lewis and Clark.

. . . you may find yourself approximate to the settlements of New Mexico, and therefore it will be necessary you should move with great circumspection, to keep clear of any Hunting or reconnoitring parties from that province, & to prevent alarm or offence because the affairs of Spain, & the United States appear to be on the point of amicable adjustment, and more over it is the desire of the President, to cultivate the Friendship & Harmonious Intercourse, of all the Nations of the Earth, & particularly our near neighbours the Spaniards. In the course of your tour, you are to remark particularly upon the Geographical structure; the Natural History; and population; of the country through which you may pass, taking particular care to collect & preserve, specimens of every thing curious in the mineral or botanical Worlds . . .

*James Wilkenson, to Zebulon Pike, instructions
to explore the Southwest, letter of June 24,
1806, in* The Journals of Zebulon Montgomery Pike.

Set out decended to the Mississippi and down that river to St. Louis at which place we arived about 12 oClock. we Suffered the party to fire off their pieces as a Salute to the Town. we were met by all the village and received a harty welcom from it's inhabitants

*William Clark, returning to St. Louis 36½
months after departure, journal entry of September 23, 1806, in DeVoto's* The Journals of
Lewis and Clark.

The portion of the continent watered by the Missouri and it's branches from the Cheyenne upward is richer in beaver and otter than any country on earth particularly that proportion of its subsidiary streams lying within the Rocky Mountains.

*Meriwether Lewis, to President Jefferson, letter
of September 23, 1806, in Jackson's* Letters of
the Lewis and Clark Expedition, with Related Documents *(1962).*

A body of the associates is to descend the Allegany River, & the first general Rendezvous will be held near the rapids of the Ohio, on or before the 20th. of next month, from which this Corps is to proceed in light boats . . . [to] the City of New Orleans under the expectation of being joined in the Route, by a Body of auxiliaries from the State of Tennessee & other Quarters. It is unknown under what auspices this Enterprize had been projected, from whence the means of its support are derived, or what may be the intentions of its Leaders, in relation to the Territory of Orleans; But it is believed, that the maritime cooperation, will depend on a British Squadron from the West Indies, under the ostensible command of American Masters.

James Wilkenson, to President Thomas Jefferson, on Aaron Burr's plot to seize New Orleans, letter of October 20, 1806, in Abernethy's
The Burr Conspiracy *(1954).*

At two o'clock in the afternoon I thought I could distinguish a mountain to our right, which appeared like a small blue cloud; viewed it with the spy glass, and was still more confirmed in my conjecture, yet only communicated it to doctor Robinson, who was in front with me, but in half an hour, they appeared in full view before us. When our small party arrived on the hill they with one accord gave three *cheers* to the *Mexican mountains.* Their appearance can easily be imagined by those who have crossed the Alleghany; but their sides were whiter as if covered with snow, or a white stone. Those were a *spur* of the grand western chain of mountains, which divide the waters of the Pacific from those of the Atlantic oceans, and it divided the waters which empty into the bay of the Holy Spirit, from those of the Mississippi; as the Alleghany does, those which discharge themselves into the latter river and the Atlantic. They appear to present a natural boundary between the province of Louisiana and New Mexico and would be a defined and natural boundary.

Zebulon Pike, sighting what later became known as Pikes Peak, journal entry of November 15, 1806, in The Journals of Zebulon Montgomery Pike.

Reports have for some time circulated from one end of the United States to the other, that Aaron Burr—with others, in the western states are preparing gun boats, provisions, money, men, &c to make war upon the Spaniards in South America—that his intention is to establish a new empire in the western world & That he contemplates forming his Empire from South America & the western States of North America.

Senator William Plummer, journal entry of November 28, 1806, in Abernethy's The Burr Conspiracy.

The plan of Col. Burr is finally and completely developed. We have received a private communication from the Governor informing us that Mr. Burr's plan is to collect about 1300 men, to rendezvous at the mouth of red river and to proceed from there to Orleans, to attack the city, to seize upon the bank and treasury, and upon the artillery and to form an independent government under the protection of Spain. This plan has been communicated to Mr. Harrison by Mr. Blennerhassett, and Mr. Harrison has proceeded to Washington, with the information.

Lewis Cass, Ohio legislator, to his wife, letter of December 5, 1806, in Abernethy's The Burr Conspiracy.

Some time in the latter part of September, I received intimations that designs were in agitation in the western country, unlawful and unfriendly to the peace of the union; and that the prime mover in these was Aaron Burr, heretofore distinquished by the favor of his country.

President Thomas Jefferson, special message to Congress, January 22, 1807, in The Writings of Thomas Jefferson *(1891).*

After breakfast the commanding officer addressed me as follows: "Sir, the governor of New Mexico, being informed you had missed your route, ordered me to offer you, in his name, mules, horses, money, or whatever you may stand in need of to conduct you to the head of Red river; as from Santa Fe to where it is sometimes navigable, is eight days journey and we have guides and the routes of the traders to conduct us." "What, said I, (interrupting him) is not this the Red river," "No sir! the Rio del Norte." I immediately ordered my flag to be taken down and rolled up, feeling how sensibly I had committed myself, in entering their territory, and was conscious that they must have positive orders to take me in.

Lt. Zebulon Pike, upon being informed by a Spanish officer that his company is trespassing on Spanish territory, journal entry of February 26, 1807, in The Journals of Zebulon Montgomery Pike.

According to appearances, Spain has saved the United States from the separation of the Union which menaced them. This would have taken place if Wilk-

Zebulon Montgomery Pike, by Charles Willson Peale. Courtesy of the Library of Congress.

inson had entered cordially into the views of Burr—which was to be expected, because Wilkinson detests this government, and the separation of the Western States has been his favorite plan. The evil has come from the foolish and pertinacious perseverance with which Burr has persisted in carrying out a wild project against Mexico. Wilkinson is entirely devoted to us. He enjoys a considerable pension from the King.

Marques de Casa Yrujo, Spanish minister in the United States, to Pedro de Cevallos, Spain's foreign minister, letter of February 28, 1807, in Adams' History of the United States *(1889–91).*

The present indictment charges the prisoner [Aaron Burr] with levying war against the United States, and alleges an overt act of levying war. That overt act must be proved, according to the mandates of the Constitution and of the Act of Congress, by two witnesses. It is not proved by a single witness.

Supreme Court Justice John Marshall, August 31, 1807, in Cabell's The Trial of Aaron Burr *(1900).*

The inhabitants of the Ohio country in general have very little of that unmeaning politeness, which we so much praise and admire in the Atlantic States. They are as yet the mere children of nature and neither their virtues nor their vices are calculated to please refined tastes. They are brave, generous, and humane, and in proportion to their population are able to produce the most effective military force of any in our country. This preeminence may chiefly be attributed to their exposed situation on an Indian frontier

Christian Schultz, traveler, journal entry of 1807, in Travels on an Inland Voyage *(1810).*

I am the Father of the English, of the French, of the Spanish, and of the Indians. I created the first man, who was the common father of all these people, as well as yourselves; and it is through him, whom I have now awakened from his long sleep, that I now address you. But the Americans I did not make. They are not my children, but the children of the Evil Spirit. They grew from the scum of the great water, when it was troubled by the Evil Spirit, and the froth was driven into the woods, by a strong east wind. They are numerous, but I hate them. They are unjust. They have taken away your lands, which were not made for them.

The Prophet, Shawnee medicine man and brother of Tecumseh, to Mississippi Valley and Great Lakes tribes, speech of June 1808, in Banta's The Ohio.

I repeat that we will never do an unjust act towards you—On the contrary we wish you to live in peace, to increase in numbers, to learn to labor as we do and furnish food for your ever increasing numbers, when the game shall have left you. We wish to see you possessed of property and protecting it by regular laws. In time you will be as we are: you will become one people with us; your blood will mix with ours: and will spread with ours over this great island

President Thomas Jefferson, to a delegation of Old Northwest Indians, speech of January 1809, in Horsman's Expansion and American Indian Policy *(1967).*

It has every prospect of becoming a source of incalculable advantage not only to the individuals engaged but to the community at large. Their extensive preparations, and the extensive force with which they intend to ascend the Missouri, may bid defiance to any hostile force they may meet with. The streams which they descend from the Rocky Mountains afford the finest of hunting, and here, we learn, they intend to build their fort.

The Louisiana Gazette hails the Missouri Fur Company, article of March 8, 1809.

Amongst intelligent Americans, the question of—whether it can or cannot be peopled by civilized man? has often been agitated. Accustomed, as they are, to a profusion of timber, for buildings, fuel, and fences, they are not aware of the small quantity of that article that may be dispensed with, in a country abounding in another substance for fuel; nor can they conceive, that fences, and even buildings, may be constructed with the application of a very small portion of timber. Under these impressions, the belief in America is, that the prairie cannot be inhabited by the whites; even Mr. Brackenridge says it cannot be cultivated. My own opinion is, that it can be cultivated; and that, in process of time, it will not only be peopled and cultivated, but that it will be one of the most beautiful countries in the world.

John Bradbury, naturalist and author who accompanied the overland Astorian expedition of 1811, in Travels in the Interior of America *(1818).*

Brothers: You ought to realize what you are doing with the Indians. It is a very bad thing, and we do not like it. Since I have lived at Tippecanoe, we have tried to do away with all tribal distinctions, and take away power from the town chiefs who have done us mischief by signing away our land; it is they who sold it to the Americans; and it is our wish that our affairs shall be managed by the warriors.

Brothers: This land was sold, and the good received for it went only to a few . . . In the future we are prepared to punish those chiefs who may come forward to propose selling the land. If you continue to purchase it from them, it will cause war among the different tribes; and in the end I do not know what will be the consequences for the white people.

Tecumseh, Shawnee chief, to William Henry Harrison, governor of the Indiana territory, and the Supreme Court judges of the territory, on rights to the land along the Wabash, speech of August 12, 1810, in Oskison's Tecumseh and His Times *(1938).*

Are then those extinguishments of native title, which are at once so beneficial to the Indian, the Territory and the United States, to be suspended upon the account of the intrigues of a few individuals? Is one of the fairest portions of the globe to remain in a state of nature, the haunt of a few wretched savages, when it seems destined, by the Creator, to give support to a large population, and to be the seat of civilization, of science, and true religion?

William Henry Harrison, to the Indiana legislature, speech of November 12, 1810, in Tucker's Tecumseh: Vision of Glory *(1973).*

Sell [our] country! Why not sell the air, the clouds and the great sea, as well as the earth?

Tecumseh, to William Henry Harrison, refusing to cede Indian lands in the Ohio country to the United States, speech of August 13, 1810, in Tucker's Tecumseh.

I saw no living thing in the course of my evening ramble, except a few buzzing insects. But there is a pleasure in giving wing to fancy, which anticipates the cheerful day when this virgin soil will give birth to millions of my countrymen. Too happy, if my after fame might but survive on the plains of the Missouri. If the vast expanse of ocean is considered as a sublime spectacle, this is even more so; for the eye has still greater scope, and, instead of its monotony, now

reposes upon the velvet green, or feeds on the endless variety of hill and dale. Instead of being closed up in a moving prison, deprived of the use of our limbs, here we may wander at our will. The mind naturally expands, or contracts, to suit the sphere in which it exists—in the immeasurable immensity of the scene, the intellectual faculties are endued with an energy, a vigor, a spring, not to be described.

Henry Marie Brackenridge, Astorian expedition member, 1811, in Journal of a Voyage Up the River Missouri *(1854).*

From this station I sent messages to the different tribes around, who soon assembled, bringing with them their furs. Here we stayed for ten days. The number of Indians collected on the occasion could not have been less than 2,000. Not expecting to see so many, I had taken but a small quantity of goods with me; nevertheless, we loaded all our horses. So anxious were they to trade, and so fond of tobacco, that one morning before breakfast I obtained 110 beavers for leaf tobacco, at the rate of five leaves per skin; and at last, when I had but one yard of white cotton remaining, one of the chiefs gave me twenty prime beaver skins for it.

Alexander Ross, Astorian expedition clerk, 1811, in The Adventures of the First Settlers on the Oregon or Columbia River *(1849).*

. . . the Indians of the Missouri are superlatively honest towards strangers. I never heard of a single instance of a white man being robbed, or having any thing stolen from him in an Indian village. It is true, that when they find white men trapping for beaver on the grounds which they claim, they often take from them the furs they have collected, and beat them severely with their *wiping sticks*; but so far is this from being surprising, that it is a wonder they do not kill them, or take away their rifles.

John Bradbury, naturalist, on the civility of the Aricara Indians, journal entry of July 4, 1811, in Travels in the Interior of America.

From the site of the establishment the eye could wander over a varied and interesting scene. The extensive sound, with its rocky shores, lay in front; the breakers on the bar, rolling in wild confusion, closed the view on the west; on the east, the country as far as the Sound had a wild and varied aspect; while towards the south, the impervious and magnificent forest darkened the landscape as far as the eye could reach. The place thus selected for the emporium of the West might challenge the whole continent to produce a spot of equal extent presenting more difficulties to the settler: studded with gigantic trees of almost incredible size, many of them measuring fifty feet in girth, and so close together, and intermingled with huge rocks, as to make it a work of no ordinary labor to level and clear the ground. With this task before us every man, from the highest to the lowest, was armed with an axe in one hand and a gun in the other: the former for attacking the woods, the latter for defense against the savage hordes which were constantly prowling about.

Alexander Ross, on the founding of Astoria in the Pacific Northwest, 1811, in The Adventures of The First Settlers on the Oregon or Columbia River.

. . . we paid a visit to the hostile camp; and those savages, who had never seen white men, regarded us with curiosity and astonishment, lifting the legs of our trousers and opening our shirts, to see if the skin of our bodies resembled that of our faces and hands. We remained some time with them, to make proposals of peace; and having ascertained that this warlike demonstration originated in a trifling offence on the part of the *Kreluits*, we found them well disposed to arrange matters in an amicable fashion. After having given them, therefore, some looking-glasses, beads, knives, tobacco, and other trifles, we quitted them and pursued our way.

Gabriel Franchere, American Fur Company trader, on meeting the Pacific Northwest Indians, 1812, in A Narrative of a Voyage to the Northwest Coast of America *(1854).*

By information received from these gentlemen, it appears that a journey across the continent of North America might be performed with a waggon, there being no obstruction in the whole route that any person would dare to call a mountain, in addition to its being much the most direct and short one to go from this place to the mouth of the Columbia river.

Any future party, who may undertake this journey, and are tolerably acquainted with the different places where it would be necessary to lay up a small stock of provisions, would not be impeded, as in all probability, they would not meet with an Indian to interrupt their progress, although on the other route, more north, there are almost insurmountable barriers.

The Missouri Gazette, *on the American Fur Company's overland expedition, article of 1812, in Thwaites'* Early Western Travels.

In the present critical conjuncture there is no time to be lost. Let us then by a timely measure save what we can, lest a British ship of war enter the river and seize all. We have been long enough the dupes of a vacillating policy, a policy which showed itself ·at Montreal on our first outset, in refusing to engage at once a sufficient number of able hands.

Donald MacKenzie, fur trader, on the sale of Astoria to the North West Company, 1812, in Ross' The Adventures of the First Settlers on the Oregon or Columbia River.

On the twelfth of December the death warrant of short-lived Astoria was signed. On that day Captain Black went through the customary ceremony of taking possession, not only of Astoria but of the whole country. What the vague term of "whole country" in the present case meant, I know not. Does it mean the Columbia? Does it mean all the country lying west of the Rocky Mountains? Or does it merely mean the coast of the Pacific? That part of the ceremony which referred to the "whole country" might have been dispensed with, for the country had already been taken possession of in the name of His Britannic Majesty, and that many years ago, by Drake, by Cooke, by Vancouver, and lastly by Black. The name of Astoria was now changed to that of Fort George . . .

Alexander Ross, 1812, in The Adventures of the First Settlers on the Oregon or Columbia River.

3. The West in the War of 1812 and Economic Depression: 1811–1820

FRONTIER CONFLICT

By 1810 the Ohio Valley was plagued by an economic depression and threatened by growing Indian unrest. In the fertile fields of the Midwest, newcomers from the East raised such an abundance of cotton, grain and rice that they were unable to sell all of their harvest. Farmers who journeyed south to sell their crops found the prices in New Orleans as low as in Cincinnati. In addition, Britain's blockade of Napoleon's European ports prevented farmers from exporting their goods overseas. As a result, many Westerners blamed Britain, rather than overproduction, for their problems.

Early-19th-century agricultural practices were unsophisticated and wasteful. Farmers often cleared a few acres, exhausting the soil, then sold their land and moved on to a new location, creating a constant demand for new farmland. Although the Louisiana Purchase had doubled the size of the country, emigrants considered the land too far away and too barren for cultivation. Westerners looked hungrily toward the Great Lakes region occupied by the British, who exerted a considerable influence over the Indians in the Old Northwest. A conquered Canada could also be used to force the British to allow American ships to enter blockaded European ports.

In the South, more Americans were settling in West Florida, owned by Spain. Many were attracted by Spain's generous land policy, and by 1809, 90% of the inhabitants of the Pearl River region were loyal to the United States. In September 1810, a group of Americans seized the Spanish fort at Baton Rouge, claiming that the Louisiana Purchase extended east to the Perdido River, the western border of present-day Florida. They declared Western Florida independent of Spain and petitioned the United States for annexation. President James Madison promptly granted their request.

Since the turn of the century nearly 110 million acres of prime hunting land had been acquired from the Indians through bribery, threats and treaties with tribal factions. Governor William Henry Harrison of the Indiana Territory had an overwhelming desire to secure Indian land cessions. In September 1809, Harrison held a council with various tribes at Fort Wayne, offering trade goods to the Delaware and Potawatomi chiefs, who wished to increase their annuities by selling some of their territories. The result was the Treaty of Fort Wayne, in which 3,000,000 acres of Indian land were transferred to the United States in return for $7,000 in cash and an annuity of $1,750.

In response to these actions, two Shawnee brothers—a one-eyed mystic known as the Prophet, and Tecumseh, an eloquent spokesman for his people—tried to unite the disorganized tribes into a confederacy. Where Tippecanoe Creek runs into the Wabash River in Indiana, the two brothers founded Prophetstown, the capital of their proposed Indian nation. Delegates came from hundreds of miles away to hear the Prophet's fiery speeches about rejecting American goods, especially whiskey, and returning to the traditional ways of their ancestors. Tecumseh traveled from tribe to tribe, and also crossed the Detroit River to Fort Malden, Canada, where he met with Matthew Elliot, the British superintendent of Indian affairs. Tecumseh proposed an independent Indian nation situated between the Ohio River, the upper lakes and the upper Mississippi. The border state would enable British Canadians to control the Great Lakes waterway to the St. Lawrence and to dominate the Ontario Peninsula. Since the plan involved British interference in United States Indian affairs, they did not officially support Tecumseh. However, Tecumseh and his followers concluded that if a conflict arose between the Indians and the Americans, Britain certainly would come to their aid.

When William Henry Harrison learned of Tecumseh's absence from Prophetstown, he decided to move 1,000 soldiers against the Indian village at the mouth of Tippecanoe Creek. The Prophet soon heard of the impending assault, and in the predawn hours of November 7, 1811, his braves launched a surprise attack on the American camp. But Harrison's experienced fighters quickly repelled the Indians. The following day a scout informed Harrison that Prophetstown was deserted. Harrison advanced on the Indian village, destroyed it, then returned to the capital of Vincennes.

There were no clear victors at the battle of Tippecanoe. Although Harrison's men defended their ground, they suffered as many casualties as the Indians. Nor did Indian hostilities cease in the West; when Tecumseh returned, he directed his followers to attack American outposts. By the spring of 1812 settlers were fleeing their frontier posts, and even the heavily populated regions of Ohio feared Indian attack.

William Henry Harrison. Courtesy of the New York Public Library.

Tippecanoe had ignited Indian resistance in the Northwest, leading to a major war with the whites.

THE WEST IN THE WAR OF 1812

Westerners were convinced that the British were behind the Indian uprisings. Governor Harrison espoused the popular opinion, "The whole of the Indians on this frontier have been completely armed and equipped from the British King's stores at Malden." Sentiment in the West was overwhelming for war with Britain in order to seize Canada and end Britain's alliance with the Indians. Farmers in the West believed war with Britain would also alleviate the economic depression by opening European ports to American merchant ships.

The congressional elections of 1810 swept into office a young group known as the "War Hawks," proponents of war with Britain. The West was represented by the eloquent Henry Clay of Kentucky; and John C. Calhoun led the Southerners, who hoped to seize all of Florida from Spain, Britain's ally. Eastern seaboard states protested the call to war, while Westerners pressured President Madison into supporting their cause. On June 1, 1812, Madison delivered a war message to Congress. Three weeks later, on June 18, Congress declared a state of war between the United States and England, marking the start of the War of 1812.

The War of 1812 was a Westerner's war. British harassment of American commerce and impressment of American seamen were the principal causes of the conflict, but the Northeast, which was most affected by these actions, wanted no part of the war. It was those in the Northwest who demanded the conquest of Canada; those in the Southwest and South who called for the seizure of Florida from Spain. But the war, which was to have been won easily and swiftly, resulted in a series of disasters from which the United States was fortunate enough to emerge without a loss of territory.

The young nation was unprepared for a major conflict with one of the world's paramount military powers. The United States had only a half-dozen warships, and its army consisted of 6,700 poorly trained men, led by two generals of questionable competence, Henry Dearborn and Thomas Pinckney. A call for volunteers resulted in few enlistments, forcing the regular army to rely on the state militias for troops. Despite these adversities, the West was confident that Canada, defended by only 4,500 British troops, could be conquered within a year.

By July Americans found themselves on the defensive in the Michigan Territory. The British army, aided by 280 Ottawas and Chippewas, launched a surprise attack on Fort Mackinac, located between Lakes Huron and Michigan. Without a shot being fired, American troops were forced to surrender.

Tecumseh caused further trouble for American troops by blocking a supply train at the River Basin, 35 miles south of Detroit. British commanders Henry Proctor and Isaac Brock advanced on Detroit with 300 regulars and 400 militia. General William Hull, governor of the Michigan Territory, was forced to retreat across the Detroit River into Detroit, and on August 16 surrendered his army of nearly 1,400 men.

British triumphs encouraged Indians throughout the West. Tecumseh announced to his followers that a British victory would push American settlement back behind the line established by the Treaty of Greenville. After three months of fighting, the West no longer looked to invading Canada, but to defending its own frontiers.

In the Missouri region, every tribe between the Great Lakes and the Rocky Mountains was under British influence. Remote outposts were regularly attacked by war parties. There were rumors that an invading Indian force, possibly amounting to thousands of warriors, was about to descend the Mississippi and Missouri. The campaign never materialized, however, and the frontier was subject only to hit-and-run raids throughout the war. Nevertheless, the threat of Indian uprisings curtailed westward movement in the Missouri region for the next 10 years. American fur-trappers fled the mountains, and many of these men, who had once ventured to the shores of the Pacific, now considered the Plains their barrier.

In September 1813, an American victory was finally achieved when 27-year-old Captain Oliver Hazard Perry overtook a British fleet in Lake Erie and broke the supply line to Detroit. With this single event the outcome of the war in the West was reversed, as the British and Tecumseh were confronted with American sea power in the interior of the continent. General William Henry Harrison, now U.S. commander in the West, immediately took advantage of the victory by moving on the remaining British and Indians at the Thames River in Ontario. At the battle of the Thames on October 5, 1813, the British were decisively defeated, and Tecumseh was slain. Indian power in the Ohio and Wabash country was crushed. Tecumseh's followers dispersed and the Indians were convinced they could not rely upon their British allies.

In the Southwest, Americans were less successful. The Creeks, allies of the British, were forcing frontiersmen into the protection of hastily built blockhouses. On August 30, 1813, Fort Mims was raided, and nearly 500 men, women and children were slaughtered. The people of the Southern states demanded retaliation against the Creek nation.

General Andrew Jackson, who would later serve two terms as president, commanded 5,000 Tennessee militiamen in raids on two Creek villages, destroying one and subduing another. On March 27, 1814,

Captain Oliver H. Perry's victory on Lake Erie, September 10, 1813. Courtesy of the Library of Congress.

Jackson led 3,000 troops in an attack that lasted several hours at the battle of Horseshoe Bend. American troops outnumbered the Creeks, and over 800 warriors were killed on the battlefield. Jackson ordered the surviving Creeks to sign a peace treaty, which included their surrender of sites for military roads and posts, cessation of all trade with the Spaniards and cession of two-thirds of their land, or 22 million acres. On August 9, 1814, the Treaty of Fort Jackson was signed, and Indian power in the Southwest was broken.

A few weeks later, the United States faced a major setback in the East. On August 24, after landing in Maryland, British troops defeated American forces and burned the Capitol and the White House. But by mid-September, Maryland militia had succeeded at stopping the British advance.

In September 1814, American warships on Lake Champlain turned back a British fleet approaching New York. Four months later, Andrew Jackson successfully repelled 10,000 more British soldiers at New Orleans, losing only 80 Americans while killing or wounding 2,000 British troops in 20 minutes. Although the battle of New Orleans was a triumphant victory for the Americans, it did not determine the outcome of the war. Two weeks before Jackson's victory, a peace treaty had been signed at Ghent, in the Netherlands.

By the Treaty of Ghent, territorial boundaries remained as they were before the war. With the close of the European war, however, Britain no longer interfered in American ocean trade. The United States did not attain its original war aims, but the resulting peace was a welcome benefit for the West. The upper lakes region seized by the British was returned, and fur-trading disputes in northern Minnesota were ended. Hostile Indians could no longer rely on the British for support. The West was opened for further expansion, moving the frontier to the Mississippi.

ACROSS THE APPALACHIANS TO THE MISSISSIPPI

The end of the fighting brought thousands of emigrants across the Alleghenies. In the five years following the war a half-million emigrants had crossed the Ohio in the North, and a quarter of a million moved toward the Mississippi in the South. Among the issues left unresolved was how to deal with the eastern tribes. For years the Indians had been subject to random attack by encroaching settlers. Congress and the president were now determined to regulate the settlement of the new lands, for the sake of both the Indians and the settlers.

In 1816 and 1817, the federal government assumed responsibility for the frontier by establishing Forts Crawford, Edwards and Armstrong on the Mississippi, Howard at Green Bay and Smith on the Arkansas. At each outpost regular army troops were assigned to keep peace between Indians and whites, oversee settlement of lands and expel unauthorized settlers. As the forts restored order to the frontier, the federal government expanded its control over more and more tribes. United States Indian commissioners obtained land cessions from the tribes by pressuring them to sign treaties that relinquished their land claims in return for annuities and gifts. Indians were relocated to reservations or to the barren wilderness beyond the Mississippi.

The orderly opening of new land to settlement encouraged throngs of pioneers to move westward. Southeastern farmers from the Carolinas, Georgia and eastern Tennessee were attracted to the rich soil of the Lake Plains country, Illinois, Indiana and Michigan. Others came from the back country of Virginia and Maryland, traveling along the National Road, a broad, paved highway of crushed stone, built across the mountains by the federal government. Migrating farm families carried few household belongings in their small wagons as they drove their flocks of cows and pigs before them. One traveler on the National Road in 1817 wrote, "We are seldom out of sight, as we travel on this grand track, towards the Ohio, of family groups before and behind us."

In the Southeast, Andrew Jackson's successful campaigns against the Creeks opened up great tracts of virgin land ideal for cotton plantations. This migration differed considerably from that to the Old Northwest; instead of coming from all parts of the United States, these pioneers came from only one section: the seaboard states of the South Atlantic. By the end of the War of 1812 the southern roads to the lower Mississippi Valley region were crowded with migrating planters who traveled by wagon, while their gangs of slaves, sometimes shackled, traveled on foot.

Slaves cleared the land and planted the first crop of cotton. As more plantations sprang up, there was an increasing demand for slave labor. Slaves in the West were often overworked, poorly fed and subject to illness. Especially dangerous were the swampy cotton plantations of Mississippi and the sugar plantations of Louisiana, where scores of slaves died from the poor conditions.

The planter's slave labor enabled him to expand his cultivated lands more rapidly than could the small farmers around him, and his large-scale operation resulted in a larger return on his investment. Profits were used to buy out his smaller competitors and purchase more slaves to farm the land.

While the federal government was administering the settlement of new lands and relocating the Indians, it was also negotiating with

General Andrew Jackson, portrait made shortly after the battle of New Orleans, 1815, when he was 48. Courtesy of the New York Public Library.

Great Britain and Spain over the previously undetermined northern and southern boundaries of the Louisiana Purchase. In 1818, the United States and Britain agreed on the 49th parallel as a boundary, from Lake of the Woods to the Rocky Mountains. However, they were unable to reach an agreement on the ownership of the Oregon country, and it was decided that citizens of both the United States and Britain would have equal rights of settlement and trade in the Pacific Northwest for 10 years.

Spain was plagued with domestic problems at home, and revolutions in Latin America were unraveling her empire. In 1819, Spain signed the Adams-Onis Treaty, whereby she ceded Florida in return for America relinquishing all claims to Texas, which then interested only a few Americans. The Spanish-American boundary as defined by the treaty was a line running along the eastern and northeastern borders of present-day Texas, then north to the Arkansas River and west to the Pacific. Spain reaffirmed its possession of all of the present states of Texas, New Mexico, Utah, Arizona, Nevada and California, along with portions of Oklahoma, Kansas, Colorado and Wyoming. By agreeing to these terms with Spain, the United States accepted the Rocky Mountains as the virtual western limit to the nation's territory and renounced any future plans for southwestward expansion.

THE GREAT AMERICAN DESERT

Some interest continued in the Pacific Northwest, stimulated mostly by the explorations of Lewis and Clark and by the activities of the early American fur-traders. On June 6, 1819, Major Stephen H. Long set out from Pittsburgh to find the source of the Red River. Long ascended the Platte River in 1820, explored the eastern slopes of the Rockies along the South Platte, climbed Pikes Peak, then returned by way of the Arkansas River. He did not find the headwaters of the Red River, and his reports on the inhabitability of the central and southern Plains gave rise to the myth of the "Great American Desert."

Long reported, "In regard to this extensive section of country between the Missouri River and the Rocky Mountains, we do not hesitate in giving the opinion that it is almost wholly unfit for cultivation." His description of the region as a useless wasteland discouraged any attempt at settling the area for two generations. The "Great American Desert" label persisted up until the 1850s.

THE PUBLIC LANDS

The outpouring of settlers moving westward after the War of 1812 was matched by a renewed enthusiasm for land speculation. The federal government tried to satisfy the pioneers' hunger for good land by selling public domain lands largely on credit, and in 1818 and 1819, three-and-a-half-million newly surveyed acres were sold to optimistic farmers. The United States Treasury recorded $44 million in sales, but only half that amount was received. Thousands of farmers bought all the land on which they could make the down payment but soon were unable to meet the succeeding installments. However, Congress was reluctant to evict thousands of angry farmers. In addition, the entire West opposed the farmers' dispossession, realizing that at some point they might experience the same fate.

Congress received a flood of petitions from the West for assistance. A series of relief bills were passed that postponed farmers' payments and allowed settlers to return excess acreage to the government for credits toward the balance of their holdings. In spite of these relief measures, $21 million was still overdue by 1820.

Financial conditions in the West were further worsened by the banks in the region, which were often badly managed by their amateur owners. The banks printed their own currency, which was often backed by little or no specie. Because the notes were poorly printed and easily copied, counterfeiting became so prevalent throughout the West that notes were accepted only in the community where they were issued.

In response to this deteriorating situation, the second Bank of the United States was created in 1816. The federal bank resumed the practice of specie payments for currency and oversaw the activities of smaller banks throughout the country. The Bank of the United States immediately caused some of the unsound western institutions to fold, and the West soon found its money supply diminished and its credit contracted. When the Panic of 1819 occurred, the West attributed the country's economic downturn to the federal bank's control over state institutions. In fact, the collapse was caused chiefly by the bad banking practices and fraudulent currency operations prevalent throughout the West in the preceding years.

In Congress, Easterners and Westerners argued over the price and distribution of western lands. The East, fearing labor shortages caused by western migration, wanted land prices kept high, while the West wanted the prices decreased to benefit the settlers and encourage further settlement.

Out of these debates eventually emerged the Land Act of 1820. Under the law, the credit system was abolished by mutual agreement. The smallest lot was reduced to 80 acres, and the cost per acre was reduced to $1.25. Although the minimum purchase requirements were reduced, far more speculators than individual farmers were able to buy land.

Several new states entered the Union during the years of renewed westward movement. North of the Ohio emerged the states of Illinois, Indiana and Michigan; and in the South, Alabama, Louisiana and Mississippi. The last two territories to achieve statehood during the years known as the "Great Migration" were Maine and Missouri, admitted in 1820 and 1821, respectively.

When Missouri applied for statehood, there were 11 free states and 11 slave states. Equality in the Senate was of great importance to the South because its influence in the House was declining. After a heated debate Congress passed the "Missouri Compromise," in which Maine was admitted as a free state and Missouri as a slave state, with the provision that no later states formed from the Louisiana Purchase and north of the principal southern boundary of Missouri (36° 30' N) would allow slavery.

Between 1810 and 1820 thousands of settlers moved beyond the Mississippi in the North and in the South. States such as Kentucky, Ohio and Tennessee now considered themselves old and well-settled regions and began to resemble northeastern states rather than frontier territories. The western frontier was advancing past the Mississippi and toward the Pacific.

CHRONICLE OF EVENTS

1811:

July: Tecumseh, the Shawnee Indian chief, travels among the tribes from Ohio to as far west as Iowa, trying to organize a confederacy that would resist encroaching settlers.

July 31: Settlers of Vincennes in the Indiana Territory urge Governor William Henry Harrison to attack the Indian settlement on the Tippecanoe Creek.

August: Wilson Price Hunt, John Jacob Astor's principal partner in the Pacific Fur Company, discovers an overland route to the Pacific via the Snake and Columbia rivers.

September 26: General Harrison leads a company of 1,000 soldiers out of Vincennes to attack the Indian settlement known as Prophetstown, 150 miles north on the Tippecanoe Creek.

The steamboat *New Orleans* is launched on the Ohio River, becoming the first steamboat to sail on western waters.

October: William Henry Harrison marches toward Tippecanoe.

October 6: Harrison sets out for Tecumseh's settlement on the Tippecanoe, planning to meet with the Shawnee chief about a possible compromise.

November 7: Shawnees launch a surprise attack on Harrison's camp.

The confrontation between Tecumseh and William Henry Harrison at Vincennes in August 1810 reflected the tensions between Indians and settlers in the Wabash Valley. Courtesy of the New York Public Library.

November 8: Harrison wages a counterattack on Prophetstown; most of the Indians have fled, the village is destroyed, and one-quarter of Tecumseh's men are killed or wounded.

December 16: Believed to be the strongest earthquake in American history occurs, centering at New Madrid, Missouri. Tremors are felt over 300,000 square miles, and for several hours the Mississippi River actually flows backward.

1812:

April 30: Louisiana is admitted to the Union.

June 1: President James Madison requests both houses of Congress to declare war on Great Britain.

June 4: Madison proclaims a state of war between the United States and Great Britain.

June 18: Congress declares a state of war between the United States and Great Britain.

June 28: British at Fort Malden, on the Canadian shore of the Detroit River, hear of declaration of war.

July 12: General William Hull, commander of American troops in the western territories, leads a company of 2,200 soldiers across the Detroit River to occupy Sandwich, Canada.

July 17: The American post on Michilimackinac Island, between Lakes Huron and Michigan, surrenders to the British without any resistance.

August 15: Fort Dearborn, present-day Chicago, surrenders to the British.

August 16: General Hull surrenders Fort Detroit and 1,400 soldiers without a fight. The entire Old Northwest is subject to raids by the British and Tecumseh's braves.

September 17: President Madison and Secretary of War Eustis appoint William Henry Harrison commander of the army in the Northwest.

1813:

January 22: Americans are defeated at Frenchtown, present-day Monroe, Michigan, with great losses.

February 1: Harrison advances to Maumee and builds Fort Megis in present-day Ohio.

May 9: Harrison successfully defends Fort Megis against Tecumseh and the British.

July 18: A British fleet prepares to attack Lake Erie.

August 4: Captain Oliver H. Perry leaves Lake Erie.

August 30: In the Fort Mims massacre in lower Alabama hundreds of settlers are killed by Creeks allied with the British.

September 10: Perry defeats the British fleet in the battle of Lake Erie.

October 4: General Andrew Jackson assembles a force of 5,000 militiamen to raid Creek villages.

October 5: Harrison defeats the British and their Indian allies at Moravian Town on the Thames River in Ontario, Canada. Tecumseh dies in the battle, the Indian confederacy is broken and the British threat in the Northwest is eliminated.

October 23: Americans sell Astoria to the North West Company after learning that a British warship is approaching the settlement.

1814:

March 27: In the battle of Horseshoe Bend, Jackson commands 3,000 troops against Creek warriors; over 800 Indians are killed.

August 9: In the Treaty of Fort Jackson, the Creeks cede two-thirds of their territory.

August: Peace negotiations between the United States and Britain begin in Ghent, the Netherlands.

December 24: The Peace Treaty of Ghent is signed, ending the War of 1812.

1815:

January 8: The battle of New Orleans is fought; the British have 2,000 casualties, while Jackson loses only seven killed and six wounded.

1816:

December 11: Indiana is admitted as the 19th state of the Union.

1817:

March 4: James Monroe becomes the fifth U.S. president.

July 4: Digging begins at Rome, New York, on the Erie Canal, connecting New York City and Albany with the West.

December 10: Mississippi is admitted as the 20th state of the Union.

1818:

The Cumberland Road reaches Wheeling, Virginia (now West Virginia), on the Ohio River.

October 20: The United States and Britain sign the Convention of 1818, setting the boundary between the United States and British North America at the 49th parallel. The Oregon country is open to people of both nations for 10 years.

December 3: Illinois is admitted to the Union as the 21st state. Slavery is prohibited.

1819:

The "Panic of 1819" stems from wild land speculation in the West and unregulated currency. Congress enacts bills for debtors' relief in the western states.

February 16: The House of Representatives passes the Missouri Bill, prohibiting further slavery in Missouri and freeing children born to slaves at the age of 25 after Missouri becomes a state. The bill is defeated by the Senate on February 27.

February 22: The Treaty of Amity, Settlement and Limits with Spain sets the previously unresolved boundaries of the Louisiana Purchase. United States acquires Florida and relinquishes claims to Texas.

June 6: Major Stephen H. Long leaves Pittsburgh to find the source of the Red River.

1820:

Total U.S. population is 9,638,453. Population west of the Appalachian Mountains is 2,236,000. Ohio's population has grown from 45,365 in 1810 to 581,434.

February 17: The Senate passes the Missouri Compromise, which admits Missouri into the Union as a slave state and Maine as a free state. Slavery is prohibited north of latitude 36° 30'. There are now 12 free and 12 slave states.

April 24: The Land Act of 1820 abolishes credit provisions and reduces the minimum purchase to 80 acres at a per-acre price of $1.25.

September 2: A stagecoach line now runs from Louisville, Kentucky to Vincennes and then on to St. Louis.

December 26: In San Antonio, Moses Austin asks Spanish Governor Antonio Martínez for permission to settle 300 American families in Texas. On January 17, 1821, Austin is granted a charter to settle 300 families in Texas.

EYEWITNESS TESTIMONY

No man in the nation desires peace more than I. But I prefer the troubled ocean of war, demanded by the honor and independence of the country, with all its calamities, and desolations, to the tranquil, putrescent pool of ignominious peace. If we can accommodate our differences with one of the belligerents only, I should prefer that one to be Great-Britain. But if with neither, and we are forced into a selection of our enemy, then am I for war with Britain; because I believe her prior in aggression, and her injuries and insults to us were atrocious in character. I shall not attempt to exhibit an account between the belligerents of mercantile spoliations, inflicted and menaced. On that point we have just cause of war with both. Britain stands preeminent, in her outrage on us, by her violation of the sacred personal rights of American freedom, in the arbitrary and lawless impressment of our seamen—the attack on the Chesapeake.

Henry Clay, Kentucky congressman, in Congress, speech of February 22, 1810, in The Papers of Henry Clay *(1959).*

I am not, sir, in favor of cherishing the passion of conquest. But I must be permitted to conclude by declaring my hope to see, ere long, the *new* United States (if you will allow me the expression) embracing not only the old thirteen States, but the entire country East of the Mississippi, including East Florida and some of the territories to the north of us also.

Henry Clay, to Congress, speech of December 28, 1810, in The Papers of Henry Clay.

Taking into view the tenor of these several communications, the posture of things with which they are connected, the intimate relation of the country adjoining the United States eastward of the river Perdido to their security and tranquillity, and the peculiar interest they otherwise have in its destiny, I recommend to the consideration of Congress the seasonableness of a declaration that the United States could not see without serious inquietude any part of a neighboring territory in which they have in different respects so deep and so just a concern pass from the hands of Spain into those of any other foreign power.

President James Madison, to Congress, on annexing West Florida, special message of January 3, 1811, in The Writings of James Madison *(1908).*

If the intentions of the British Government are pacific, the Indian department of Upper Canada have not been made acquainted with them: for they have very lately said everything to the Indians, who visited them, to excite them against us.

William Henry Harrison, to Secretary of War William Eustis, letter of February 1811, in Pratt's Expansionists of 1812.

I am decidedly of opinion, that upon every principle of policy our interest should lead us to use all our endeavours to prevent a rupture between the Indians and the subjects of the United States. Upon these considerations, I think it would be expedient to instruct the officers of the Indian department to use all their influence to dissuade the Indians from their projected plan of hostility, giving them clearly to understand that they must not expect any assistance from us.

Sir James Craig, governor-in-chief of Canada, to Brigadier General Isaac Brock, letter of February 4, 1811, in Tupper's The Life and Correspondence of Major-General Sir Isaac Brock *(1847).*

From the present state of our foreign relations, particularly with England, I am induced to believe, there is little prospect of a continuance of peace. In event of war with England, this part of the United States, will be particularly situated. The British land forces at Amherstburg and St. Joseph's, are about equal to those of the United States, at this place and Michilimackinack. The population of Upper Canada is more than twenty to one as compared to this territory. That province contains about one hundred thousand inhabitants, while our population does not amount to five thousand. A wilderness of near two hundred miles separates this settlement from any of the states. Besides, the Indiana Territory and states of Ohio and Kentucky are thinly inhabited, have extensive frontiers, and their forces will be necessary for their own defence.

William Hull, governor of Michigan Territory, to Secretary of War William Eustis, letter of June 15, 1811, in Klinck's Tecumseh: Fact and Fiction in Early Records *(1961).*

I ascertained that the quiet possesion of East Florida could not be obtained by an amicable negotiation with the power that exists there . . . that the inhabitants of the province are ripe for revolt.

General George Matthews, to Secretary of State James Monroe, letter of August 3, 1811, in Adams' History of the United States *(1889–91).*

My letter of yesterday will inform you of the arrival and departure of Tecumseh from this place, and of the route which he has taken. There can be no doubt his object is to excite the southern Indians to war against us. His mother was of the Creek nation, and he builds much upon that circumstance towards forwarding his views. I do not think there is any danger of further hostility until he returns: and his absence affords a most favorable opportunity for breaking up his confederacy, and I have some expectations of being able to accomplish it without a recourse to actual hostility.

William Henry Harrison, to the War Department, report of August 6, 1811, in Drake's The Life of Tecumseh *(1969).*

From the friendly course pursued by Mr. Jefferson, towards our red neighbors, and which has been followed by Mr. Madison, we had supposed the Indians would never more treat us otherwise than as brethren. But we have been mistaken—British intrigue and British gold, it seems, has greater influence with them of late than American justice and

General William Henry Harrison attacking Shawnee Indians at the battle of Tippicanoe, 1811. Courtesy of the Library of Congress.

benevolence . . . We have in our possession information which proves beyond doubt, the late disturbances to be owing to the too successful intrigues of British emissaries with the Indians.

The Kentucky Gazette, *article of August 27,*
1811.

The course to be pursued with The Prophet . . . must depend, in a great measure . . . on his conduct . . . You will approach and order him to disperse, which he may be permitted to do on condition of satisfactory assurances . . . If he neglects or refuses . . . he will be attacked and compelled to it by the force under your command . . . His adherents should be informed that in case they shall hereafter form any combination of a hostile nature . . . they will be driven beyond the great waters.

Secretary of War William Eustis, to William
Henry Harrison, on advancing toward the In-
dian village of Prophetstown, instructions of
September 18, 1811, in Adams' History of the
United States.

Let the white race perish! They seize your land, they corrupt your women, they trample on the grass of your dead. Back whence they came, upon a trail of blood, they must be driven. Back, back, aye, into the great waters whose accursed waves brought them to our shores. Burn their houses, destroy their stock! The red man owns the country and the palefaces must never enjoy it. War now, war forever! War upon the living, war upon the dead. Dig their bones from the grave. Our country must give no rest to a white man's bones.

Tecumseh, to the Creeks' annual tribal council,
speech of October 1811, in Tucker's Tecumseh:
Vision of Glory *(1973).*

I cannot but notice the villainy practiced in the Indian country by British agents and traders . . . They labor by every unprincipled means to instigate the Savage against the American . . . Never until a prohibition of the entrance of all foreigners, and especially British subjects, into the Indian Country takes place, will we enjoy a lasting peace with the credulous, deluded, and cannibal savages.

Isaac Van Voorhis, Chicago surgeon, on the
British in the Old Northwest, October 1811, in
Lavender's The Fist in the Wilderness
(1964).

Gentlemen say, that this government is unfit for any war, but a war of invasion. What, is it not equivalent to invasion, if the mouths of our harbors and outlets are blocked up, and we denied egress from our waters?

Henry Clay, to Congress, on Britain's embargo
of American ships, speech of December 31,
1811, in Colton's The Life and Times of
Henry Clay *(1846).*

Under pretended blockades, without the presence of an adequate force and sometimes without the practicability of applying one, our commerce has been plundered in every sea, the great staples of our country have been cut off from their legitimate markets, and a destructive blow aimed at our agricultural and maritime interests

President James Madison, to Congress, declara-
tion of war against Britain, special message of
January 1, 1812, in The Writings of James
Madison *(1908).*

The Americans we must fight, not the English. The Americans are our eternal foes, the hungry devourers of the country of our fathers.

Tecumseh, to the Upper Creeks, at a midnight
conference on fighting the Americans and mak-
ing an alliance with the English, speech of
1812, in Tucker's Tecumseh: Vision of
Glory.

In reviewing the conduct of Great Britain toward the United States our attention is necessarily drawn to the warfare just renewed by the savages on one of our extensive frontiers—a warfare which is known to spare neither age nor sex and to be distinguished by features peculiarly shocking to humanity. It is difficult to account for the activity and combinations which have for some time been developing themselves among tribes in constant intercourse with British traders and garrisons without connecting their hostility with that influence and without recollecting the authenticated examples of such interpositions heretofore furnished by the officers and agents of that Government.

President James Madison, to Congress, on Brit-
ish-sponsored Indian raids in the Old North-
west, special message of January 1, 1812, in
The Writings of James Madison.

The Americans burned the Prophets Village and all the Corn of the Shawnees, but the Kikapoos saved theirs by having had it previously buried. Twenty five Indians only are killed; the Kikapoo does not know the number of Americans killed, but he says their loss must have been considerable, not less than one hundred.

Colonel Matthew Elliot, British army, to General Isaac Brock, commander of British forces in upper Canada, on the battle of Tippecanoe, letter of January 12, 1812, in Klinck's Tecumseh: Fact and Fiction in Early Records.

A part of your army now recruiting may be as well supported and disciplined at Detroit as at any other place. A force adequate to the defence of that vulnerable point would prevent a war with the savages, and probably induce the enemy to abandon the province of Upper Canada without opposition. The naval force on the Lakes would in that event fall into our possession, and we should obtain the command of the waters without the expense of building such a force.

General William Hull, to Secretary of War William Eustis, letter of March 6, 1812, in Adams' History of the United States.

For what are we going to fight? To satisfy the revenge or ambition of a corrupt and infatuated ministry? to place another and another diadem on the head of an apostate republican general? to settle the balance of power among an assassin tribe of Kings and emperors? "or to preserve to the prince of Blood, and the grand dignitaries of the empire" their overgrown wealth and exclusive privileges? No. Such splendid achievements as these can form no part of the objects of an american war. But we are going to fight for the reestablishment of our national charector, misunderstood and vilified at home and abroad; for the protection of our maritime citizens, impressed on baord British ships of war and compelled to fight the battles of our enemies against ourselves; to vindicate our right to free trade, and open a market for the productions of our soil, now perishing on our hands because the mistress of the ocean has forbid us to carry them to any foreign nation; in fine, to seek some indemnity for past injuries, some security against future aggressions by the conquest of all the British dominions upon the continent of north america.

General Andrew Jackson, orders to his troops, March 7, 1812, in The Correspondence of Andrew Jackson *(1926).*

. . . the Intelligencer may talk of negociation and honorable accommodation' with England; but when we view the effects of her policy in the West—when we hear of the tragic scenes that are now acting on our frontiers, after the slaughter of Tippecanoe, it is really surprising to hear that there is any doubt about the 'active preperations for warlike operations.'

The National Intelligencer, *editorial of April 21, 1812.*

But the period has now arrived, when the United States must support their character and station among the Nations of the Earth, or submit to the most shameful degradation. Forbearance has ceased to be a virtue. War on the one side, and peace on the other, is a situation as ruinous as it is disgraceful. The mad ambition, the lust of power, and commercial avarice of Great Britain, arrogating to herself the complete dominion of the Ocean, and exercising over it an unbounded and lawless tyranny, have left to Neutral Nations—an alternative only, between the base surrender of their rights, and a manly vindication of them.

John C. Calhoun, congressman from South Carolina, report to Congress, June 3, 1812, in The Papers of John C. Calhoun *(1959).*

My friends, I am well pleased at what you have done: that you have accepted the hatchet of your British father, and are willing to assist him in fighting against the Americans. As for these men, my friend Walk-in-the-Water and the others, I shall bring them and their people to this side of the river, where I can have them under my own eye, for they are in my way at Brownstown.

British General Matthew Elliot, to Wyandot chiefs Morrow and Spitlog, speech of 1812, in Tucker's Tecumseh, Vision of Glory.

You burn with anxiety to learn on what theatre your arms will find employment. Then turn you eyes to the South! Behold in the province of West Florida, a territory whose rivers and harbors are indispensable to the prosperity of the western, and still more so, to the eastern division of our state.

General Andrew Jackson, proclamation to his division of the Tennessee militia, 1812, in Bassett's The Life of Andrew Jackson *(1911).*

Can it be expected that those savage butcheries will have an end until we take possession of Malden and other British forts on the Lakes? And must the settlements in our territories be entirely destroyed, and the blood of the women and children drench the soil before this can be done?

The Kentucky Gazette, editorial of May 26, 1812.

The capitulation of Detroit has produced no despair; it has, on the contrary, awakened new energies and aroused the whole people of this State. Kentucky has at this moment from eight to ten thousand men in the field; it is not practicable to ascertain the precise number. Except our quota of the hundred thousand militia the residue is chiefly of a miscellaneous character, who have turned out without pay or supplies of any kind, carrying with them their own arms and their own subsistence. Parties are daily passing to the theatre of action; last night seventy lay on my farm; and they go on, from a solitary individual, to companies of ten, fifty, one hundred, etc. The only fear I have is that the savages will, as their custom is, elude them, and upon their return fall upon our frontiers.

Henry Clay, to Secretary of State James Monroe, letter of August 25, 1812, in Adams' History of the United States.

We shall drive the British from our Continent—they will no longer have an opportunity of intriguing with our Indian neighbors, and setting on the ruthless savages to tomahawk our women and children. That nation will lose her Canadian trade, and, by having no resting place in this country, her means of annoying us will be diminished.

Felix Grundy, Tennessee congressman, 1812, in Pratt's Expansionists of 1812.

Britain has commenced war in the Western Country, equally so as France would have done, was she to burn New York. The citizens of the Eastern States, and members in Congress, may abandon 7,000 seamen—they may term it, a trifling impropriety on the part of England, but the old Revolutionary Heroes here are not to be deceived by the misrepresentation of any man whatever. The Government must not abandon the Western Country to the British.

The Reporter, article of May 30, 1812.

In the name of my Country and by the authority of my Government I promise you protection for your *persons, property* and *rights.* Remain at your homes.

Pursue your peaceful and customary avocations. Raise not your hands against your brethren, many of your fathers fought for the freedom & *Independence* we now enjoy. Being children therefore of the same family with us, and heirs to the same Heritage, the arrival of an army of Friends must be hailed by you with a cordial welcome. You will be emancipated from Tyranny and oppression and restored to the dignified station of freemen. Had I any doubt of eventual success I might ask your assistance, but I do not. I come prepared for every contingency. I have a force which will look down all opposition and that force is but the vanguard of a much greater. If, contrary to your own interest & the just expectation of my country, you should take part in the approaching contest, you will be considered and treated as enemies, and the horrors and calamities of war will Stalk before you.

Brigadier General William Hull, U.S. Army, to Canadian citizens, after crossing the Detroit River and occupying the village of Sandwich, proclamation of July 12, 1812, in Brannan's Official Letters of the Military and Naval Officers of the United States during the War with Great Britain in the Years 1812, 13, 14 & 15 (1823).

Two species of warfare have been used by the United States in their contests with the tribes upon the north-western frontier, viz: rapid and desultory expeditions by mounted men, having for their object, the surprise and destruction of particular villages; or the more tardy, but effectual, operations of an army composed principally of infantry, penetrating the country of the enemy, and securing the possession by a chain of posts.

William Henry Harrison, to Secretary of War William Eustis, letter of August 10, 1812, in Klinck's Tecumseh: Fact and Fiction in Early Records.

He who attracted most my attention was Shawnee chief, Tecumseh, brother of the Prophet, who for the last two years has carried on contrary to our remonstrances an active warfare against the United States. A more sagacious or more gallant warrior does not, I believe exist. He was the admiration of every one who converses with him.

British General Isaac Brock, dispatch of August 29, 1812, in Adams' History of the United States.

The Americans have not yet defeated us by land; neither are we sure that they have done so by water; we therefore, wish to remain here, and fight our enemy, if they should make an appearance. If they defeat us, we will then retreat with our father.

At the battle of the Rapids last war, the Americans certainly defeated us; and when we retreated to our father's fort at that place the gates were shut against us. We were afraid that it would now be the case, but instead of that we now see our British father preparing to march out of his garrison.

Father! You have got the arms and ammunition which our great father sent for his red children. If you have an idea of going away, give them to us, and you may go and welcome.

As for us, our lives are in the hands of the Great Spirit. We are determined to defend our lands, and if it be his will we wish to leave our bones upon them.

Tecumseh, to British Colonel Henry Proctor, replying to Proctor's request for the Indians to retreat with British troops into Canada, September 13, 1813, in Edmonds' Tecumseh and the Quest for Indian Leadership *(1984).*

There was something so majestic, so dignified, and yet so mild, in his countenance as he lay stretched on the ground, where a few minutes before he rallied his men to the fight, that while gazing on him with admiration and pity, I forgot he was a savage. He had such a countenance as I shall never forget. He had received a wound in the arm, and had it bound up, before he received the mortal wound.

U.S. Major Thomas Rowland, recounting the death of Tecumseh at the battle of the Thames, October 9, 1813, in Tucker's Tecumseh: Vision of Glory.

They will not quietly suffer the common highway of nations, intended by a kind Providence for the common intercourse and benefit of all, to be converted into a domain of her crown. No; the ocean cannot become property. Like light and air, it is insusceptible of the idea of property.

John C. Calhoun, to Congress, on continued financial support for war against Britain, speech of February 25,1814, in The Papers of John C. Calhoun.

We have laid the foundation of a lasting peace to those frontiers which had been so long and so often infested by the savages. We have conquered. We

The death of Tecumseh, at the battle of the Thames, 1813. Courtesy of the Library of Congress.

have added a country to ours, which, by connecting the settlements of Georgia with those of Mississippi Territory, and both of them with our own, will become a secure barrier against foreign invasion, or the operation of foreign influence over our red neighbors in the South and we have furnished the means not only of defraying the expenses of the war against the Creeks, but of that which is carrying on against their ally Great Britain. How ardently, therefore, is it to be wished that government may take the earliest opportunity, and devise the most effectual means, of populating this section of the Union.

General Andrew Jackson, to the citizens of Fayetteville, speech of May 16, 1814, in Parton's Life of Andrew Jackson.

We have just received despatches from Ghent, which I shall lay before Congress to-day. The British sine qua non excluded us from fishing within the sovereignty attached to her shores, and from using these in curing fish; required a cession of as much of Maine as would remove the obstruction to a *direct* communication between Quebec and Halifax; confirmed to her the Passamaquoddy Islands as always hers of right; included in the pacification of Indian allies, with a boundary for them (such as that of the Treaty of Greenville) against the United States mutually guarantied, and the Indians restrained from selling their lands to either party, but free to sell them to a *third* party; prohibited the United States from having an armed force on the lakes or forts on their shores; the British prohibited as to neither; and substituted for the present North Western limit of the U. States a line running direct from the West end of Lake Superior to the Mississippi, with a right of G. Britain to the navigation of this river.

President James Madison, to Thomas Jefferson, letter of October 10, 1814, in Letters and Other Writings of James Madison *(1884).*

We must fall upon them & murder them all or we must still pursue the course which has hitherto been followed so successfully, viz, that of obtaining their Confidence & Attachment by treating them with Justice and Humanity and convincing them that their only resource against want and misery is in the annuities they receive from us.

William Henry Harrison, to Secretary of War Alexander Dallas, on expelling the Indians, letter of June 26, 1815, in Cleaves' Old Tippecanoe *(1969).*

One of the principal topics of conversation in all places was the public lands—the price and the quality—the choice of location, tracts, quarter sections, entries, &c., &c.

Gorham A. Worth, 1817–21, in Recollections of Cincinnati *(1916).*

Old America seems to be breaking up and moving westward. We are seldom out of sight, as we travel on this grand track towards the Ohio, of family groups, behind and before us, some with a view to a particular spot; close to a brother perhaps, or a friend, who has gone before, and reported well of the country. Many, like ourselves, when they arrive in the wilderness, will find no lodge prepared for them.

A small wagon (so light that you might almost carry it, yet strong enough to bear a good load of bedding, utensils, and provisions, and a swarm of young citizens,—and to sustain marvellous shocks in its passage over these rocky heights), with two small horses; sometimes a cow or two, comprises their all; excepting a little store of hard-earned cash for the

land office of the district; where they may obtain a title for as many acres as they possess half-dollars, being one-fourth of the purchase money.

Morris Birkbeck, English immigrant and author, traveling along the Cumberland Road, 1817, in Notes on A Journey in America from the Coast of Virginia to the Territory of Illinois *(1818).*

The conditions of the sale will be as follows . . . ¼ of purchase money to be paid in hand . . . ¼ in six months, notes with interest to be given for the last two payments . . . If the purchaser builds a house or a stable of wood, brick, or stone within two years from the time purchase is made, sixteen feet by twenty and one story high, or larger, on each lot purchased . . . he will be given a FULL WARRANTEE DEED, with a provision that the actual owner or occupant shall pay one dollar a year forever to be appropriated for the support of a school; but if the house or stable is not built, at the end of two years then the lot shall be forfeited, together with all the improvements and payments made.

Broadside advertisement on land for sale in the Ohio country, February 1, 1817, in Havighurst's Wilderness for Sale *(1956).*

The projected canal to connect the waters of Lake Erie with those of the Hudson will no doubt greatly accelerate the population and prosperity of this country, an event and undertaking no doubt exceedingly gigantic, but which will inevitably produce as majestic a change in our country as the object appears difficult to accomplish.

John Williams, Detroit merchant, to a friend, Samuel Abbott, letter of May 1817, in Dain's Every House A Frontier *(1956).*

The land is rich natural meadow, bounded by timbered land, within reach of two navigable rivers, and may be rendered immediately productive at a small expence. The successful cultivation of several prairies has awakened the attention of the public, and the value of this description of land is now known; so that the smaller portions, which are surrounded by timber, will probably be settled so rapidly as to absorb, in a few months, all that is to be obtained at the government rate, of two dollars per acre.

Morris Birkbeck, English immigrant and author, on land in southern Illinois, July 26, 1817, in Notes on A Journey in America.

Some came in wagons and light carriages, overland; some on horseback; some in arks; some in skiffs; and some by steamboat, by New Orleans. One Welshman landed at Charleston, S. C. "How did you get there?" I asked. "Oh," he innocently replied, "I just bought me a horse, sir, and inquired the way."

George Flower, an Illinois settler from England, 1817, in History of the English Settlement in Edwards County, Illinois *(1882).*

The Illinois Territory, I have no doubt, furnishes greater inducements to emigration, than any other Territory belonging to the United States, to such men as are not holders of Slaves. I have no hesitation in saying, that one hand there can make as much annually, as any three in any other part with which I am acquainted. If is far the most fertile soil in the U. States; and quantity of prairie gives it advantages over and above what it would enjoy, from fertility alone. In the general, the farmer has nothing to do, but fence in his fields: plough his ground and plant his crop. He may then expect, from an acre, from 50 to 100 bushels [of] corn; and from 10 to 50 of wheat; the quality of both which articles is superior to that of any I ever saw.

Anonymous immigrant to Illinois Territory, to Illinois Intelligencer, *letter of September 18, 1817.*

A great number of farmers have more land inclosed in one fence than they can well manage: Ask one of these the reason, he replies, "I want help." An assistant enables him to cultivate a portion of his land that would otherwise become overrun with weeds. The emigrant cannot expect full wages at the commencement, but if he be attentive, he may in one year become so expert as to be entitled to what is usually paid to husbandman, from twelve to fifteen dollars per month, and board.

John Bradbury, English naturalist and traveler, 1817, in Travels in the Interior of America *(1818).*

This acquisition will connect our settlements in this state with those in the territory of Michigan and will enable us to present an iron frontier in the event of any difficulties with the British or Indians in this quarter.

Lewis Cass, governor of Michigan Territory, to President James Monroe, on obtaining a land cession from the Indians, letter of September 30, 1817, in Dain's Every House A Frontier.

Here, whatever their origin, whether English, Scottish, Irish, German, or French—all are Americans: and of all the imputations on the American character, jealousy of strangers is surely the most absurd and groundless.

Morris Birkbeck, 1818, in Notes on a Journey in America.

. . . this is the country for a man to enjoy himself . . . Ohio, Indiana, and the Missouri Territory; where you may see prairies 60 miles long and ten broad, not a stick nor a stone in them, at two dollars an acre, that will produce from seventy to one hundred bushels of Indian corn per acre: too rich for wheat or any other kind of grain. I measured Indian corn in Ohio State, last September more than fifteen feet high, and some of the ears had from four to seven hundred grains. I believe I saw more peaches and apples rotting on the ground than would sink the British fleet. I was at many plantations in Ohio where they no more knew the number of their hogs than myself . . .

Samuel Crabtree, an English settler in the Ohio country, to his brother, letter of April 1818, in Knight's Important Extracts from Original and Recent Letters *(1818).*

Our future population will be principally from the northern states, and avowed enemies to slavery. The wealthy southern planter, will not part with the plantation Gods, which he worships, starves and whips, for the blessings of the western woods, while we are a territory, and doubtful as to the future toleration of slavery. To those that are uninterested, I need not say a word as to the horrors of slavery, and to those who are, they would be words thrown away.

Daniel Pope Cook, Illinois Territory representative, editorial in the Illinois Intelligencer, *April 15, 1818.*

The Public sales taking place so near the end of the year and the great quantity of land sold, more than could have been calculated in the time allow'd by Law, occationed a hundred mistakes in our books, which has taken nearly all winter to correct.

Nathaniel Ewing, Illinois land office receiver, 1818, in Rohrbough's Land-Office Business *(1968).*

The west is fit for only poor men, who are the only proper pioneers of the wilderness.
William Faux, English traveler and author, in Memorable Days in America, 1818–1820 *(1823).*

The city of New-Orleans is a place of immense business. In the course of fifty years it will probably be, in a mercantile point of view, second to none in the world. At this place inland and maritime commerce combine their energies. An immense tract of the most productive country in the world, is continually sending its produce, through a thousand channels, to this great mart. Already five or six hundred vessels, some of which are very large, may occasionally be seen lying at the Levee; and upon this embankment are vast piles of produce of every description. Foreign vessels frequently arrive here with from 500,000 to 1,000,000 dollars in specie, for the purpose of purchasing cargoes of sugar, cotton, and tobacco.
Estwick Evans, 1818, in A Pedestrious Tour of Four Thousand Miles Through the Western States and Territories *(1819).*

The Executive Government have ordered (and, as I conceive, very properly) Amelia Island to be taken possession of; this order ought to be carried into execution at all hazards, and, simultaneously, the whole of East Florida seized and held as an indemnity for the outrages of Spain upon the property of our Citizens; This done, it puts all opposition down, secures to our Citizens a compleat indemnity, and saves us from a war with Great Britain, or some of the Continental Powers combined with Spain; this can be done without implicating the Government: let it be signified to me through any channel, (say Mr. J. Rhea) that the possession of the Floridas would be desirable to the United States, and in sixty days it will be accomplished.
General Andrew Jackson, to President James Monroe, letter of January 6, 1818, in The Correspondence of Andrew Jackson.

Our company consisted of my father and mother and eight children, with six negroes; Joseph Bryan, my brother-in-law, and his wife and two negroes; my wife and me and two small sons and two negroes. We had good horses and wagons and guns and big dogs. We set out on the 10th of March, 1818. I felt as if I was on a big camp hunt.

The journey, the way we traveled, was about 500 miles, all wilderness; full of deer and turkeys, and the streams were full of fish. We were six weeks on the road; and altogether it was, as I thought and felt, the most delightful time I had ever spent in my life. My brother Garland and I "flanked it" as the wagons rolled along and killed deer, turkeys, wild pigeons; and at nights, with pine torches, we fished and killed a great many with my bow and arrows, whenever we camped on my water course. Little creeks were full of fish at that season.

At length we reached Tuscaloosa, Ala. It was at that time a small log cabin village; but people from Tennessee were arriving daily, and in the course of that year it grew to be a considerable town.
Gideon Lincecum, southwestern pioneer, March 1818, in Autobiography *(1904).*

To this territory the purchase is very important, because it connects us with more than a half million of people who inhabit the state of Ohio, and from this day we cease to be an insulated point, insecure and almost inaccessible. We are a constituent part of the American Union.
Detroit Gazette, *on Indian land cessions in the states of Ohio and Indiana, March 13, 1818.*

In the settlement of a country, there are many things to be done, which require the united strength of many; this money cannot purchase: but that kind and generous feeling, which men (not rendered callous by wealth or poverty) have for each other, comes to their relief. The neighbors, (even unsolicited) appoint a day, when as a frolic, they shall (for instance,) build the new settler a house.—On the morning appointed, they assemble; and divide themselves into parties: one party cut down the trees; another lops them and cuts them into proper lengths; a third, (with horses or oxen) drag them to the intended spot; another party make shingles for the roof; and at night all the materials are on the spot: and the night of the next day, the family sleep in their new habitation.—No payment is expected, nor would be received: it is considered a duty; and lays him under obligation, to assist the next settler. But this cooperation of labour is not confined to new settlers; it occurs frequently, in the course of a year, amongst the old settlers with whom it is a bond of amity and social intercourse; and in no part of the world, is good neighbourship, in greater perfection, than in America.

John Knight, English Ohio Valley settler, 1818 guidebook describing house-raising on the frontier, in The Emigrants Best Instructor *(1818).*

Nothing so strongly indicates the superiority of the western country as the vast emigration to it from the eastern and southern states . . . I was informed by an inhabitant of Cayuga, in April, 1816, that more than fifteen thousand wagons had passed over the bridge at that place within the last eighteen months, containing emigrants to the western country.

Morris Birkbeck, 1818, in Notes on A Journey in America.

MECHANICS of every description are much wanted at Edwardsville: more particularly the following, *a Taylor, Shoemaker, Waggon Maker, Hatter, Saddler, Tanner and Currier.* From *four* to *six* Carpenters and *Joiners,* and from *four* to *six ax-men,* and from *six* to *eight farming labourers,* will find immediate employment and good wages

Advertisement in the Illinois Intelligencer *of March 18, 1818.*

New ones are continually rising or endeavoring to rise, with or without capital, as the case may be. Others, which have for a time maintained an extensive credit, are failing and, from inability or disinclination, refuse to redeem their bills. Notes are often found in circulation on banks, which have a "name" indeed, but no "local habitation." A great part of the community are unable to detect these frauds, and the loss which is sustained by them must be immense.

Detroit Gazette, *April 17, 1818.*

But were slavery admitted, many emigrants, who now pass through our territory, on their way to Boon's lick, and other parts of the Missouri territory, followed by a long concourse of slaves, might settle in Illinois. Perhaps they might; and this is the most plausible argument which has been adduced in favor of the admission of slavery. Yet for my own part, I would rather see our rich meadows and fertile woodlands inhabited alone by the wild beasts and birds of the air, than that they should ever echo the sound of the slave driver's scourge, or resound with the cries of the oppressed African. I would rather that

our citizens should live fearlessly and contentedly in their peaceful and modest cabins, than that, surrounded by a host of slaves, and inhabiting splendid palaces and gilded domes, they should live in constant apprehensions of an attack from those who are, and who ought to be, their mortal enemies.

Anonymous editorial in the Illinois Intelligencer, *July 1, 1818.*

There is considerable business being done here, as it is on the road from the southern States to St. Louis, and the Missouri, and the land office is here. The number of waggons, horses, and passengers crossing, and wading across the Ohio, was so great, that a great part of the morning was spent in waiting for my turn; at length I grew impatient, and taking the opportunity of a skiff, turned my back on Illinois, and landed in the state of Kentucky.

William Tell Harris, English traveler and author, September 1818, Remarks Made During a Tour Through the United States of America *(1821).*

The country we have passed is rather mountainous; affording very little bottom land, and that little not well managed. There are four or five villages, of some little consequence, scattered along the banks of the Allegany, which afford the mind a temporary relief from the gloominess imparted by the rude and barren scenery, which almost continually presents itself. These towns, however, afford but a scanty and dear supply, for the numerous wants of the passing emigrants. I saw, on my route, the 20 *cents per acre* land in Pennsylvania, so much talked of among our neighbours; but as I do not like it myself, I cannot recommend it to others. This place fully equals, and perhaps exceeds, the description generally given of it. The approach to it on the river is delightful: you are surrounded by rugged hills and finely cultivated vallies, decorated with neat cottages and elegant mansions. An immense column of dusky smoke, which is seen ascending, spreading in vast wreaths among the clouds, marks the site of Pittsburgh.

John Stillman Wright, western New York farmer, December 3, 1818, in Letters from the West; or A Caution to Emigrants *(1819).*

Probably from thirty to fifty wagons daily cross the Mississippi at the different ferries, and bring in an average of four to five hundred souls a day. The emigrants are principally from Kentucky, Tennessee,

Virginia and the states further south. They bring great numbers of slaves, knowing that Congress has no power to impose the agitated restriction, and that the people of Missouri will never adopt it.
St. Louis Enquirer, *1819, in Stevens' Centennial History of Missouri (1921).*

From some cause, it happens that in the western and southern states, a tract of country gets a name, as being more desirable than any other. The imaginations of the multitudes that converse upon the subject, get kindled, and the plains of Mamre in old time, or the hills of the land of promise, were not more fertile in milk and honey, than are fashionable points of immigration. During the first, second, and third years of my residence here, the whole current of immigration set towards this country, Boone's Lick . . . Boon's Lick was the common . . . point of union for the people. Ask one of them whither he was moving, and the answer was, "To Boon's Lick to be sure."
Timothy Flint, minister and author, in Recollections of the Last Ten Years in the Valley of the Mississippi *(1826).*

The same price for eatables, that we gave two years ago, when we saw five dollars put into our pockets oftener than we now see one dollar placed there.
Detroit Gazette, *on nationwide depression, January 22, 1819.*

Bear in mind, fellow-citizens, that the question now before us is not whether slavery shall be permitted or prohibited in the future State of Missouri, but whether we will meanly abandon our rights and suffer any earthly power to dictate the terms of our Constitution.
The Missouri Gazette, *on the congressional provision restricting slavery in Missouri, editorial of April 7, 1819.*

It is a question in which Congress have no right to interfere, and to which we as the people will never submit. The restriction attempted to be imposed upon us by the *seventy-eight members* of the *House of Representatives* who voted for it, were those exclusively from the *eastern states.* They view with a jealous eye the march of power westward, and are well aware the preponderance will soon be against them; therefore they have combined against us; but let them pause before they proceed further, or the grave they

are preparing for us, may be their own sepulchre.
The Missouri Intelligencer, *editorial of May 9, 1819.*

Counterfeiting goes on prosperously, and presents itself in so many forms that it is difficult to guard against it. We can hardly take up a newspaper without seeing some fresh evidence of the prostration of morals caused by the paper system.
Niles' Weekly Register, *May 15, 1819.*

I regret as much as any person can do the existence of slavery in the United States; I think it wrong in itself, nor on principle would I be understood as advocating it; but I trust I shall always be the advocate of the people's right to decide on this question, as on all others, for themselves, leaving to their own wisdom and forecast the adoption of such a Constitution, and the enaction of such laws as they shall consider best comforts with their prosperity and happiness. I consider it, not only unfriendly to the slaves themselves to confine them to the south, but wholly incompetent for Congress to interfere upon the subject, being a piece of domestic policy which the state of Missouri has a clear right to decide for herself, as every other state in the Union has done.
John Scott, Missouri territorial delegate, circular of July 16, 1819, in Shoemaker's Missouri's Struggle for Statehood.

The events which have occurred in both the Floridas show the incompetency of Spain to maintain her authority; and the progress of the revolutions in South America will require all her forces there. There is much reason to presume that this act will furnish a strong inducement to Spain to cede the territory, provided we do not wound too deeply her pride by holding it. If we hold the posts, her government cannot treat with honor, which, by withdrawing the troops, we afford her an opportunity to do.
President James Monroe, to Andrew Jackson, on withdrawing from captured Spanish posts at Pensacola, letter of July 19, 1819, in The Writings of James Monroe *(1902).*

They are building a steamboat at Wheeling, which is to go, they say 1800 miles up the Missouri River.
Thomas Hulme, English traveler, journal entry of July 28, 1819, in Cobbett's A Year's Residence in the United States of America *(1818).*

President James Monroe. Courtesy of the New York Public Library.

It is believed that on an average, there is not a copper coin in the possession of more than one individual out of three hundred in this territory who are in the practice of receiving and paying money.
Detroit Gazette, *September 17, 1819.*

It [Florida] was surrounded by the Territories of the United States on every side except on that of the ocean. Spain had lost her authority over it, and falling into the hands of adventurers connected with the savages, it was made the means of unceasing annoyance and injury to our Union in many of its most essential interests. By this cession, then, Spain ceded a territory in reality of no value to her and obtained concessions of the highest importance by the settlement of long standing differences with the United States affecting their respective claims and limits, and likewise relieved herself from the obligation of a treaty relating to it which she had failed to fulfill, and also from the responsibility incident to the most flagrant and pernicious abuses of her rights where she could not support her authority.
President James Monroe, third annual message to Congress, December 7, 1819, in The Writings of James Monroe.

The settlers never dreamed that cotton would be reduced from 25 to 10 cents per pound, or that the common currency of the country would become so depreciated that $100 would only pay $85 debt at the land office.
Alabama Republican, *October 20, 1820.*

4. Early Traders and Explorers: 1821–1830

The "Permanent" Indian Frontier

With an increasing number of emigrants settling between the Appalachians and the Mississippi, the federal government began initiating treaties with the eastern tribes for land cessions and the Indians' relocation to barren land west of the Mississippi. After all, Lewis and Clark had described most of the area as a desert; Zebulon Pike compared the southwest to the sandy deserts of Africa; and Stephen H. Long reported that it was "wholly unfit for cultivation."

After the War of 1812, federal commissioners summoned tribe after tribe to councils where they forced the chiefs to cede their territories in return for annuities and presents, and compelled them to sign land cession treaties with the United States. No longer supported by their British allies, the Indians were unable to resist America's demands for their ancestral lands. Between 1817 and 1821 dozens of tribes in Ohio surrendered their territories and agreed either to live in the confines of a reservation or to move to the wilderness beyond the Mississippi. By the end of 1821 nearly all of Illinois, Indiana and Michigan was controlled by the federal government and was open for settlement.

Farmers from the East were attracted to the fertile soil of the Lake Plains country. They referred to the plentiful northern lands as "God's country." Other pioneers came from Kentucky and Tennessee, where they had been held back by a generation of Indian warfare. Thousands of small farmers from the Carolinas, Georgia and eastern Tennessee were driven to the Old Northwest because their lands had been absorbed by large plantation owners.

They came in droves. Pioneers traveled westward along the National Road to Wheeling, where they then floated down the Ohio River on keelboats. Others from the South reached the western waterways by following the old Wilderness Road from Kentucky to Louisville and Cincinnati. Along the Ohio River settlers journeyed to Lafayette and Vincennes in Indiana, to Alton and St. Louis in Missouri, or to the rich farming lands surrounding these towns.

Major Stephen H. Long. Courtesy of the New York Public Library.

The rush of settlers to the southern Lake Plains region convinced the federal government that more Indian territories must be opened to the pioneers. By 1825, a definite Indian removal policy was established. For the next four years tribes were forced to cede either their ancestral lands or their newly acquired reservations in Illinois, Indiana and Ohio and to relocate to the inhospitable territory beyond the Mississippi.

A definite boundary between the United States and Indian country had emerged. It ran from the mouth of Green Bay (northern Lake Michigan) west to the Mississippi, leaving the upper Wisconsin region to the Indians. After following the Mississippi, it swung south through Iowa to the northern border of Missouri; then it bent west at the Missouri River and dropped south again along the western boundaries of Missouri and Arkansas. North of the Platte was to be the home of the tribes already residing there, and the land south of the Platte to the Red River border of Texas was assigned to the relocated eastern tribes. The territory was granted to the Indians for "as long as the grass grows and the rivers run."

THE FUR TRAPPERS

During the early 1820s there was a renewed interest in fur trapping in the central Rocky Mountain region. William H. Ashley of Missouri was one of the early pioneers of the fur trade in the Rockies. In 1822, he advertised in the *Missouri Gazette* for a group of "enterprising young men" to undertake a fur-trading expedition to the upper Missouri. Ashley planned to ascend to the Three Forks of the Missouri with an expedition that would spend three years trapping along all the streams in that region. After experiencing Indian hostilities that prevented the party from successfully trapping near the Three Forks, Ashley sent a small detachment across present-day South Dakota. The group, led by Jedediah Smith and Thomas Fitzpatrick, crossed the Continental Divide and found excellent beaver grounds on the upper Green River.

The following spring Fitzpatrick returned to St. Louis by way of the South Pass and the Platte River, and informed Ashley of the rich country found and of the passable land route to the region. In the fall of 1824, Ashley organized a trapping party and led it to the Green River. He divided his men into "brigades," sending them in various directions to trap beaver, and arranged a location where they all would meet in early July 1825, thus originating the fur trade's customary rendezvous in the mountains.

These early frontiersmen were responsible for exploring the country around the sources of the Platte, Green, Yellowstone and Snake rivers. They were the first to travel from the Great Salt Lake southwesterly to southern California and the first to cross the Sierras and the deserts of Utah and Nevada between California and the Great Salt Lake. As far as is known, these private explorers were also the first to travel by land up the Pacific Coast from San Francisco to the Columbia River in present-day Oregon and Washington. Their thorough exploration of the central Rocky Mountain region pushed the frontier forward to the Far West.

The Santa Fe Trade

In 1821, a successful Mexican revolution ended Spain's colonial rule over New Mexico and opened the way for American trade with Santa Fe. William Becknell, a Missouri Indian trader who has been called the "Father of the Santa Fe Trail," was one of the first Americans to recognize the potential profits to be derived from commerce under the new Mexican government. Becknell and 20 plainsmen originally set out from Franklin, Missouri, for the Southern Rockies, where they intended to trade with the Comanches for furs. While working their way up through the tortuous Raton Pass they met a company of Mexican rangers, who told Becknell that Mexico was independent and would welcome American goods. The company immediately headed for Santa Fe, where they turned their small quantity of goods into great sacks of silver dollars. Becknell's favorable reports aroused considerable interest in this new commercial market across the Mexican border.

Becknell launched a second expedition from Santa Fe in June 1822, with 21 men and three loaded wagons. Realizing the difficulty of crossing the steep Raton Pass with his wagons, Becknell pioneered a new and shorter route across the Cimarron Desert. Thus the Santa Fe Trail was marked out and opened for future expeditions. Besides opening a new commercial route, Becknell was the first to use wagons for long-distance trading.

The early expeditions encouraged so many others that by 1824 the Santa Fe trade was well established. In that year, 80 men, with 25 wagons, 150 packhorses and $30,000 worth of goods, journeyed to Santa Fe and returned to Franklin, Missouri, with silver and furs worth $190,000. As the number of traders grew, there was an increasing demand for the government to lay out a road and provide military escorts to protect the Santa Fe traders from Indian attacks. Senator Thomas Hart Benton of Missouri took up the cause of his constituents by introducing a bill that provided for the building of a road to the Mexican border through Indian country and for the establishment of a garrison at the crossing of the Arkansas. Congress responded by appropriating $30,000 for surveying the road and obtaining Indian concessions.

The Santa Fe trade consisted primarily of compact but valuable commodities, because of the long trip across the Plains. Goods usually included cottons, hardware, looking glasses, shawls, silks and velvets, and were carried on wagons, each drawn by eight to 12 mules or oxen and holding 3,000 to 7,000 pounds of merchandise. The goods were exchanged for bullion and beaver skins.

The Santa Fe trade prospered despite many obstacles. Traders had to cross arid plains and one real desert. Caravans were subject to Indian attack, particularly by Comanches, who were attracted by the merchants' ammunition and horses. (However, descriptions of Indian attacks were grossly exaggerated. Usually, Indians never attacked a well-organized caravan, and only eight travelers on the trail were killed by Indians in its first 10 years of use.) Because the import tax at Santa Fe was exorbitant, sometimes as high as 60% of the value of the imports, bribing customs officials was an ordinary part of conducting business. Despite these various difficulties the trade prospered; an average trip realized a gross profit of from 10% to 40%.

The trade with Santa Fe expanded the federal government's presence in the Southwest. Fort Leavenworth was established in 1827 for the principal purpose of preventing Indians from interfering with the Santa Fe trade. Military escorts were provided at government expense to protect the traders as far as the United States boundary.

The Santa Fe trade was never overwhelmingly important to the American economy. Nevertheless, it played a major role in advancing the frontier. The Santa Fe traders helped to some extent to dispel the myth of the "Great American Desert." The permanent Indian frontier was beginning to unravel, and American attention was turning toward the Mexican territory of the Southwest.

THE ROOTS OF TEXAS

The organized colonization of Texas was conceived by Moses Austin, who once had a prosperous mining business in Missouri but in 1818 suffered financial ruin. Undiscouraged by his losses, Austin turned his attention toward establishing a colony of settlers in Texas. In the fall of 1820 he crossed the barren wilderness of eastern Texas on horseback and arrived in San Antonio after a journey of more than 800 miles. At first, Austin was not welcomed by Texas Governor Antonio Martinez, who was under orders to keep all foreigners out of Texas, particularly Americans. Austin was about to comply with this order when he met an old friend from Louisiana, the Dutch adventurer Baron de Bastrop. Through Bastrop's influence Austin was granted another interview with the governor. In their second meeting, Austin persuaded Martinez to allow him to settle 300 American families on Spanish soil—by demonstrating that, as a one-time citizen of Louisiana, he was a former subject of the Spanish monarch.

On his return trip from Texas, Moses Austin was overcome by exposure and died in June 1821; his last request was that his 27-year-old son, Stephen Fuller Austin, should follow through on establishing the proposed colony. At age 20 Stephen Austin had become a member of the territorial legislature of Missouri, a position he held for six years, and, while his father was in Texas, was serving as a circuit court judge in Arkansas Territory. Father and son planned to meet in Nacogdoches, Texas, during the summer. As young Austin was about to enter Texas with a party of a dozen men he received word of his father's death. After returning to Natchitoches in Louisiana to confirm the report, Austin continued on to Nacogdoches and to San Antonio. On August 12, 1821, as Austin rode into San Antonio, the town was celebrating the news of Mexico's independence from Spain.

Austin informed Governor Martinez of his father's death and asked that he be allowed to carry out his contract. Martinez acquiesced, with generous terms: He might settle any land he needed, anywhere in Texas, without payment of any kind to the government.

In response to a request by the governor, Austin drew a sketch of his settlement plans. According to this document each head of a fam-

Stephen Austin. Courtesy of the Texas Historical Commission.

ily was to receive 640 acres for himself, 320 for his wife, 160 for each child, and 80 for each slave. Martinez approved the plan, and Austin proceeded to the Colorado River and selected a site for his 300 families, along the lower course of the Brazos and Colorado rivers.

Austin then turned his energy toward colonizing the land. He returned to Louisiana in the late fall and advertised his settlement at 12½ cents an acre, in order to underwrite expenses and compensate Austin for his services. By December 1821, Austin had led the first party of settlers to the banks of the lower Brazos, and here was established the town of San Felipe de Austin, the earliest Anglo-American settlement in Texas.

As authorization for his plan of colonization Austin had a letter from the governor of Texas, and he assumed no further approval was required. To Austin's great surprise, he learned in March 1822 that he needed confirmation from the Congress of Mexico. Austin immediately set out on the 1,200-mile journey to Mexico City.

Confusion prevailed in Mexico during this turbulent period. For 12 months Austin waited for an answer from the Mexican Congress. In April 1823, one year after his arrival in the capital, his petition was reviewed. Soon afterward his colony was granted authorization.

The Mexican Colonization Law provided that Austin's 300 families were entitled to one *labor* (177 acres) for farming, with an additional 74 *labors* for stock-raising. The entire amount equaled a *sitio*, or square league. The land was to be assigned and laid out by the governor of

Texas. Austin was to found a town located near the settlements, and all settlers were required to be of the Roman Catholic faith and of good character.

The Mexican Congress wanted to outlaw slavery. Austin was against the institution on principle, but felt immigrants would not settle in his colony unless they were permitted the economic incentive to which they had been accustomed for decades. He negotiated a compromise under which slaves could be imported but not sold after their arrival, and their children were to be freed at the age of 14.

When Austin returned to his settlement in August 1823, he found that many of the original settlers had returned to their homes in the states. Not discouraged, he once again turned his energies to promoting his colony. Settlers began arriving once more, and were now allowed to choose their land from any area they wished. By September 1824, land titles had been issued to 272 families. A census of the colony in 1825 showed a total of 1,800 persons, 443 of whom were slaves.

Settlers came from all parts of the United States, but most were from Kentucky and Tennessee, and a few came from as far away as Ireland and Germany. Some came by water, embarking at ports along the Atlantic, while others journeyed overland, crossing the Sabine, generally at Gaines's Ferry, or coming through southwestern Arkansas.

The empresario movement brought settlers into other Texas colonies as well. And the Mexican government did not attempt to close the eastern frontier from unauthorized settlers. Below the old San Antonio Road, including Austin's colony and the area east of the Sabine, the region's population expanded rapidly. By 1827 the estimated population of Texas, exclusive of Indians, was 10,000.

As Mexican officials watched the increase of Anglo-Americans in Texas, they became more concerned about the future of the Mexican territory. Austin was well aware of Mexico's anxieties about the incoming settlers, and during the early years of the immigration movement he used his influence to prevent misunderstandings between the Americans and the Mexican authorities. But as more and more Americans crossed the border, it became impossible to keep the peace.

The "Fredonian Rebellion" of 1826–27 greatly stimulated Mexican fears about an American occupation of Texas. In April 1825, Haden Edwards received permission to establish a colony of 800 families in eastern Texas. His grant was obtained not from the national government, as was Austin's, but from the states of Coahuila and Texas. Mexican families had already settled some of these lands, and Haden's contract stipulated that early settlers who could establish valid claims to their lands were to be recognized and granted privileges equal to the new settlers. Soon after his arrival, Edwards began transferring the claims of previous settlers, and charging them a small fee per acre. The early settlers gained the attention of the governor, and Edwards' grant was canceled.

Edwards and his brother Benjamin launched a revolt after obtaining a promise of aid from a band of Cherokees who had settled nearby. On December 16, 1826, Benjamin Edwards rode into Nacogdoches with 15 men and declared an independent republic under the name of Fredonia. He took possession of an old fort and proclaimed a government. Edwards was confident that Austin and his colony would support his rebellion. He was mistaken. Austin's colony not only opposed their revolt, but also joined the Mexican troops that drove the rebels across the Sabine and crushed the Fredonian uprising.

Although most Anglo-Americans in Texas opposed the Fredonian Rebellion, the Mexicans remained skeptical of American colonization and interpreted the incident as an indication of America's desire to absorb Texas. Mexican fears over the security of Texas went back to the boundary settlement of the Adams-Onis Treaty in 1819, when Thomas Hart Benton and other prominent U.S. politicians expressed their disapproval of America's relinquishing any claims to Texas. Mexico's fears were confirmed in 1829, when, Andrew Jackson, soon after becoming president, offered $5 million for Texas. The Mexican government was outraged and demanded that Jackson recall his representative.

To forestall more uprisings similar to the Fredonian Rebellion, the Mexican government passed a new colonization law on April 6, 1830; it forbade the entrance of foreigners along her northern border unless they were provided with passports from Mexican agents. The act also forbade citizens from adjacent foreign countries to settle as colonists in the frontier states and territories of Mexico. Settlement by Mexicans in Texas was encouraged, but no attempt was made to interfere with the colonies already established, such as Austin's.

Debate Over the Pacific Northwest

When John Jacob Astor was forced to sell his Pacific Fur Company to the North West Company in 1813, the door was opened for Britain to increase its presence in the Pacific Northwest. In 1825, the Hudson's Bay Company established Fort Vancouver on the north bank of the Columbia River. Out of necessity, the outpost became self-supporting. Herds of cattle were imported from California, pigs from Hawaii and sheep from Canada. A sawmill and gristmill were built, and during the summer idle fur trappers cleared the fields for wheat, corn and oats. By 1828 the British traders not only supported themselves, but also produced a surplus of crops that were exported to Alaska and California. The English dominated the Oregon country to such an extent that a few visionary Americans were concerned that the United

States would lose the opportunity to establish settlements in the Pacific Northwest.

Dr. John Floyd, a Virginia congressman and a friend of William Clark, the explorer, first alerted the nation to the impending loss of Oregon on December 19, 1820, when he proposed in Congress that a select committee be appointed to "inquire into the situation of the settlements upon the Pacific Ocean and the expediency of occupying the Columbia River." The motion was passed and Dr. Floyd became chairman of the committee, whose report had the same impact on settling the Pacific Northwest as Richard Hakluyt's famous *Discourse on Western Planting* had on settling the English colonies in America. Floyd's report described in glowing detail the agricultural and geographical attributes of the Oregon country. As a result, the public was awakened to its potential for settlement. In 1822, Floyd introduced a bill that urged the annexation of the Oregon country, stressing the importance of the fur trade and the potential for establishing commerce between the Mississippi and the Columbia. But at that time Floyd's proposal appeared absurd to most members of Congress, and many considered Oregon to be as remote as Africa.

Although wagon trains were crossing the desert plains in the newly opened trade with Santa Fe, congressmen were convinced that a successful settlement at the mouth of the Columbia was impossible. Even after a major competitor in the Pacific Northwest, the Russians, acknowledged in 1824 that the 54°40' line was the southern limit of her territory, there remained little support for occupying the Oregon country. Floyd countered that in 1775 Kentucky was considered "too far away even to be a part of the Union." New York congressmen replied that Oregon's climate was "bleak and inhospitable" for the successful cultivation of cereal crops. Congress also feared that passage of the bill would result in creating either an independent colony or an independent state, neither of which would benefit the United States. The debate came to an end in January 1823, when after prolonged discussion Floyd's bill was defeated in the House. The idea of an American settlement on the Pacific was too visionary for the average congressman to comprehend.

Despite Floyd's failure to win the support of Congress, he did have a significant effect on settling the Oregon country. He was the first to describe the possibilities of the region from the immigrant's point of view. It was the pioneer farmer who was to be drawn to the attractive Willamette Valley, and who ultimately established an American claim to the Pacific Northwest.

American interest in Oregon was kept alive by the activities of private citizens. A substantial amount of information existed regarding the Pacific Northwest, including accounts and journals by fur traders and explorers. A Charlestown, Massachusetts, schoolteacher, Hall Jackson Kelley, replaced John Floyd as the nation's leading Oregon promoter. In 1828, Kelley organized the American Society for Encouraging a Settlement of the Oregon Territory. He planned on founding a New England–type town in Oregon, which he hoped would evolve into a new state.

Kelley wrote letters to Congress asking for support, but received only a pledge that protection would be given to any settlement he might establish in the Oregon country. He issued a general circular calling for immigrants to travel overland to the mouth of the Columbia. Only a few applicants enlisted for the first expedition, which was to leave in June 1832, but among these was a Cambridge, Massachusetts, ice dealer, Nathanial J. Wyeth, who was destined to play a major role in settling Oregon and opening the Far West. Wyeth would lead an expedition across the continent over a historic route later christened the Oregon Trail.

CHRONICLE OF EVENTS

1821:

The Hudson's Bay Company takes over its rival, the North West Company, securing a monopoly on the fur trade in the Pacific Northwest.

January 21: Moses Austin is granted a charter from the Spanish governor of Texas for settling 300 American families there.

February 22: The U.S. Senate approves the Adams-Onis Treaty.

March 2: Congress passes the Relief Act, which enables previous purchasers of government land in the West to pay off their debts at the reduced price set by the Land Act of 1820, with more time to meet installment payments.

June 10: Moses Austin dies in Missouri, while preparing to lead his group of families into Texas. His son, Stephen F. Austin, will continue his plans for settlement.

August 10: Missouri is admitted as the 24th state, the 12th that permits slavery.

August 12: Stephen F. Austin arrives at Bexar, Texas, to take possession of the land granted to his father, Moses Austin, by the Spanish governor.

September 1: William Becknell leads a trading party from Independence, Missouri, toward Santa Fe.

November 16: William Becknell arrives at Santa Fe, having mapped an overland route that will become known as the "Santa Fe Trail."

1822:

John Jacob Astor forms a branch of the American Fur Company in St. Louis. For the next 10 years, Astor's company will dominate fur-trading west of the Mississippi.

William Henry Ashley and Andrew Henry form the Rocky Mountain Fur Company in St. Louis.

March 20: William Henry Ashley publishes an advertisement in the *Missouri Republican* calling for 100 young men to ascend the Missouri River to its source and develop the fur trade in the region.

May 22: William Becknell sets out from Franklin, Missouri, on his second trip to Santa Fe, leading 21 men and three wagons. The expedition blazes the Cimarron Cutoff, a shorter but more dangerous route than the "Mountain Route" of the Santa Fe Trail.

September 3: The Fox and Sauk tribes sign a treaty that permits them to live on the lands they had previously ceded in the Wisconsin Territory and Illinois.

October 27: A 280-mile section of the Erie Canal is opened, connecting Rochester and Albany, New York.

1823:

Stephen F. Austin begins to settle San Felipe de Austin on the Brazos River as the colonial seat of government. Mexico gives new land grants to American settlers.

Arikara Indians attack a trading party led by General William Ashley, lieutenant governor of the Missouri Territory. The federal government retaliates by sending an army group led by Colonel Henry Leavenworth to punish the Indians.

April 14: The new Mexican government approves Stephen F. Austin's settlement of Texas.

1824:

Fur trader James Bridger discovers the Great Salt Lake, which he believes is an ocean because of its salt water.

The federal government creates Forts Gibson and Towson in present-day Oklahoma to prepare for relocation of the Cherokee, Chickasaw, Choctaw, Creek and Seminole tribes.

The first annual rendezvous for the fur trappers of the Rocky Mountains is held at Green River, Wyoming.

Dr. John McLaughlin of the Hudson's Bay Company establishes Fort Vancouver.

February: Jedediah Strong Smith, a guide for

James Bridger. Courtesy of the Kansas State Historical Society.

the Rocky Mountain Fur Company, leads an expedition through the South Pass of the Rocky Mountains.

February 10: Both houses of Congress pass the General Survey Bill, which gives the president the authority to initiate surveys and estimates of roads and canals required for commercial, postal and military purposes.

April 17: Russia signs a treaty with the United States acknowledging 54°40′ N as the southern limit of her territory in the Pacific Northwest.

October 4: The Mexican Congress adopts a constitution making Mexico a republic.

1825:

The Republic of Mexico declares that California is her territory, and sends Jose Maria de Enchenadia to form a territorial government there.

The U.S. government makes Kansas an independent territory.

Congress approves a boundary that defines an official Indian territory—the region known as the "Great American Desert," in present-day Oklahoma and Kansas.

February 12: The Creek Indian Treaty is signed; the Creeks agree to cede all of their lands in Georgia to the federal government.

March 3: Congress approves a federal survey to mark the Santa Fe trail between the Missouri River and New Mexico.

March 24: Mexico opens the state of Texas-Coahuila to American colonization.

July 4: Construction resumes on the Cumberland Road, to extend it from Wheeling, Virginia, through Ohio. From Wheeling, it will be named the National Road.

August 10: The Osage tribe agrees to give up more of its lands by signing a treaty with federal commissioners at Grove, Kansas.

October 26: The Erie Canal opens for traffic. It is 363 miles long.

December 6: President John Quincy Adams delivers his first annual presidential address to Congress. He recommends road and canal construction, and exploration of the interior and the Pacific Northwest.

1826

July 18: William Henry Ashley sells his interest in the Rocky Mountain Fur Company to Jedediah Smith, David Jackson and William Sublette at the Cache Valley summer rendezvous.

August 16: Jedediah Smith leaves Cache Valley on the South West Expedition with 17 men.

October 3: Jedediah Smith and company reach the Colorado River.

November 10: Jedediah Smith leads an expedition across the Mohave Desert.

November 27: Smith and his company arrive in San Diego, the first Americans to take this route into California.

December 16: Benjamin Edwards arrives in Nacogdoches, Texas, declaring himself the ruler of the Republic of Fredonia. Stephen F. Austin recruits a small army and helps Mexican authorities suppress the Fredonian Revolt.

1827

May: Fort Leavenworth is built on the Santa Fe trade route to protect commercial traffic on this prospering overland route.

July 26: The Cherokees in the state of Georgia declare themselves a sovereign nation. Georgia responds by annexing the Cherokee territories.

August 6: United States and Great Britain agree to a joint occupation of the Oregon country, renewing the Convention of 1818.

August 18: Jedediah Smith expedition is attacked by Mohave Indians while crossing the Colorado River; 10 men are killed.

August 28: Jedediah Smith and surviving members enter the San Bernardino Valley.

November: Jedediah Smith and company reach San Francisco.

1828

July 9: Jedediah Smith and his men reach the Umpqua River in Oregon.

July 14: Smith's party is attacked by Umpqua Indians; only Smith and three of his men escape.

August 10: Smith expedition reaches Fort Vancouver.

1829

March 4: In his first inaugural address, President Andrew Jackson calls for a fair and liberal policy toward the Indians.

July 26: In the Michigan Territory, the Chippewa, Ottawa and Potawatami Indians cede their lands to the federal government.

August 25: President Andrew Jackson offers to purchase the Texas region from Mexico and is refused.

1830:

Total U.S. population is 12,866,000; one-fourth lives west of the Appalachian Mountains.

The town of Chicago is laid out at Fort Dearborn.

January: Antonio Armijo, the Mexican governor of New Mexico, leads an expedition across the Mohave River and the Cajun Pass, opening what will become known as the "Old Spanish Trail."

April: In Fayette, New York, Joseph Smith and 30 followers found the Mormon Church.

April 6: The Mexican government forbids further American colonization of Texas and prohibits the importation of slaves into the region.

April 10: William L. Sublette leads 10 wagons, each drawn by five mules, and two one-mule Dearborn carriages out of St. Louis. They are the first wagons to travel on the Oregon Trail.

May 28: President Andrew Jackson signs the Indian Removal Act, relocating eastern Indians to the lands west of the Mississippi River.

May 29: The Pre-emption Act is enacted, allowing settlers, who have farmed land within the previous year, to buy it at a minimum of $1.25 per acre.

July 15: The Fox, Sauk and Sioux tribes sign a treaty that gives the United States most of present-day Iowa, Minnesota and Missouri.

Eyewitness Testimony

If you can obtain a permit for me to land with my property at the place I have requested to say Mouth of the *Colorado* and permission is given to Establish a Town and Settle 300 families One year would make a Change in the State and condition of Saint Antonio beyond any thing, you can now believe I have a full confidence that a Town at the Mouth of Colorado in three years would become of the utmost Consequence and an interest in this Town would give some thousand of Dollars to the friends of this establishment without any violation of Confidence or injury to Government. people of the first class would immediately Resort to this Establishment with property that would secure their fidelity to the King and Constitution of Spain.

Moses Austin, to Baron de Bastrop, Dutch national living in Bexar, Mexico, letter of January 26, 1821, in The Austin Papers *(1924).*

The next day, after crossing a mountain country, we arrived at SANTA FE and were received with apparent pleasure and joy. It is situated in a valley of the mountains, on a branch of the Rio del Norte or North river, and some twenty miles from it. It is the seat of government of the province; is about two miles long and one mile wide, and compactly settled. The day after my arrival, I accepted an invitation to visit the Governor, whom I found to be well informed and gentlemanly in manners; his demeanor was courteous and friendly. He asked many questions concerning my country, its people, their manner of living, etc.; expressed a desire that the Americans would keep up an intercourse with that country, and said that if any of them wished to emigrate, it would give him pleasure to afford them every facility

William Becknell, Missouri trader, journal entry of November 14, 1821, in Hulbert's Southwest on the Turquoise Trail *(1933).*

Wolves and panthers were destructive to our stock. I have carried a gun on more than one occasion to assist the killing of wolves that were after our stock. I was chased by a panther nearly a mile, taking refuge in an old cabin. When just having closed the door, it sprang upon the roof and I had to remain there all night.

Elizabeth Clemmons Smith, who emigrated at the age of 11 with her parents from North Carolina to Pike County, Illinois, 1821, in Sprague's Women and the West *(1940).*

We are part of a Considerable Company of Farmers who wish to remove to your Grant, being generally poor, and not at all acquainted with the geography of either this Country or that we must rely on you for all the necessary information as well as assistance to effect our Journey thither. If you will be so obliging as to write us word how this can be effected and how much of a settlement is already formed, whither provisions Can be had near your Grant, it will be too late to attempt to remove this session but if our information suits we intend to be ready early in the fall we would wish to be informed whither there are many Indians in that quarter and whither Friendly or hostile—

Andrew Mitchell and William H. McCurdy, Pensacola farmers, to Stephen F. Austin, on immigrating to Texas, letter of January 31, 1822, in The Austin Papers.

TO Enterprising Young Men: The subscriber wishes to engage ONE HUNDRED MEN, to ascend the river Missouri to its source, there to be employed for one, two or three years. For particulars enquire of Major Andrew Henry, near the Lead Mines, in the County of Washington, (who will ascend with, and command the party) or to the subscriber at St. Louis. William H. Ashley.

Missouri Gazette, advertisement of February 13, 1822.

We Went up the [River] twelve miles pasing at Seven miles a large pond of Watter of about 40 acers on the West Side of the River—the Bottom of Which is about one mile Wide the mountains High on Each Side—the tops of Which are a great Hight above vegatation at about ten miles We Crost a fork   Puting In on the West Sid about one third as large as the River it appeers to Head to the West—Heare the River makes a turn to the north as fare as We Cold See up it—We Camped With vanbebers party the Head killed one Elk—our Cors West 12 miles—Heare the mountains Put Close to the River Which [is] very Croked

Jacob Fowler, frontiersman and trader, at the South Fork of the Rio Grande, journal entry of March 2, 1822, in The Journal of Jacob Fowler *(1970).*

We started with an escort of fifty men, following the Wind River down to the Yellow Stone, where we built our boats to descend the river. On the sixth day after leaving camp, while we were packing our effects for an early start, the alarm of "Indians!" was given, and, on looking out, we saw an immense body of them, well mounted, charging directly down upon our camp. Every man seized his rifle, and prepared for the living tornado. The general gave orders for no man to fire until he did. By this time the Indians were within half pistol shot. Greenwood (one of our party) pronounced them Crows, and called out several times not to shoot. We kept our eyes upon our general; he pulled trigger, but his gun missed fire, and our camp was immediately filled with their warriors. Most fortunate was it for us that the general's gun did miss fire, for they numbered over a thousand warriors, and not a man of us would have escaped to see the Yellow Stone.

Jim Beckwourth, mountain man, recalls William Ashley's fur-trading expedition in the Rockies, 1822, in The Life and Adventures of James P. Beckwourth *(1926).*

In regard to my grant and settlement, I have only been here a few days and I have not had time for the full examination of my papers by Congress. I found the government here fully informed, (through the Governor of Texas), of all that had been done in relation to the grant; the steps I had taken, and the progress of the settlement—so far all seems satisfactory, and I can, I think, safely assure you, that Congress will in a few days sanction all that has been done, as well as the measures necessary to the future prosperity of the settlement.

We have just heard of the acknowledgement of the independence of this government by the United States—an event exciting the most lively sensations here—and fraught I hope, with solid and lasting benefits to both nations.

Stephen F. Austin, to Joseph H. Hawkins, New Orleans attorney and Texas sponsor, letter of May 1, 1822, in The Austin Papers.

Those formerly engaged in the trade have increased their capital and extended their enterprise, many new firms have engaged in it and others are preparing to do so. It is computed that a thousand men chiefly from this place [St. Louis] are now employed on the waters of the Missouri and half that number on the upper Mississippi.

Missouri Intelligencer, *article of September 17, 1822.*

Brother we have repeatedly complained to your Government of the injuries done to our Nation by our white Brethren of the frontier States, in direct violation of the good faith solemnly pledged by your Government to our Nation in our Treaties. There appear[s] to be a great relaxation in enforcing those obligations. Intruders of considerable numbers have been tolerated to remain on our lands to secure their crops from year to year, and in place of removing off when their crops were secured, it has been only a stimulant for others to move on our lands.

Cherokee delegation, to Secretary of War John C. Calhoun, message of October 24, 1822, in The Papers of John C. Calhoun *(1959).*

For a few days past our wharves and taverns have been literally thronged with people emigrating to this new country [Michigan], nearly all of whom appears to belong to the most valuable class of settlers—practical farmers, of moderate capital and good habits.

Detroit Gazette, *March 21, 1823.*

As to your objection to remove to Green Bay, it is entirely at your option to go or stay; the Government will never take any steps to compel you to do either; you are at perfect liberty to follow your inclination in this respect. But it is believed that your interest would be promoted by a removal to that country. The distance which it would place between you and the white settlements would prevent the collisions which now frequently happen between you; the various tribes composing the Six Nations, which are now scattered over several distinct and distant reservations could there be united in one body on one tract of country owned in common by all, where game is plenty and where your settlements would

John C. Calhoun. Courtesy of the New York Public Library.

be, for many years to come, unmolested by the too near approach of those of the white people.

*John C. Calhoun, to Red Jacket, Major Berry
and Corn Planter, chiefs of the Seneca nation,
on relocating their tribe, speech of March 1823,
in The Papers of John C. Calhoun.*

Sir, to these remarks we beg leave to observe and to remind you that the Cherokee are not foreigners but original inhabitants of America, and that they now inhabit and stand on the soil of their own territory and that the limits of this territory are defined by the treaties which they have made with the government of the United States, and that the states by which they are now surrounded have been created out of land which was once theirs, and that they cannot recognize the sovereignty of any state within the limits of their territory.

*Cherokee delegation, to Secretary of War John
C. Calhoun, on ceding their lands in Georgia
and relocating to Arkansas, message of February 11, 1824, in The Papers of John C. Calhoun.*

I am persuaded (perhaps this ought to be taken with some grains of allowance,) that Oregon is destined to be the great place of North America. It is more distant from any probable war than any point on the globe; it more completely looks over the whole commerce of the world than any other. In war it is more easily defended: it has an easy access to the vast valley of the Mississippi: it has the only large river in the world, in a climate combining soil, timber, health, and internal resources. Wherefore, he who can go, and grow with the country, will, and must, in three or four years, possess wealth and influence, and greater security, than can be obtained any where else, from the broils of turbulent Europe!

*John Floyd, Virginia congressman, letter of
March 17, 1824, in Hulbert's The Oregon
Crusade (1935).*

My impression is equally strong that it would promote essentially the security and happiness of the tribes within our limits if they could be prevailed on to retire west and north of our States and Territories on lands to be procured for them by the United States, in exchange for those on which they now reside. Surrounded as they are, and pressed as they will be, on every side by the white population, it will be difficult if not impossible for them, with their kind of government, to sustain order among them. Their interior will be exposed to frequent disturbances, to remedy which the interposition of the United States will be indispensable, and thus their government will gradually lose its authority until it is annihilated.

*President James Monroe, to Congress, special
message of March 30, 1824, in The Writings
of James Monroe (1902).*

We spent that day with Cordaro [Indian chief] and the Spaniards, and held a council or "talk" with them. Cordaro made a speech dissuading me from going to Santa Fe on account of the treatment which the Americans had always received from the Government there. "They will imprison you," said he to me, "as they have imprisoned all Americans that ever went to Santa Fe. You will meet the fate of all your countrymen before you." The Spanish officers, who were all present at this harangue, smiled and said there was no danger of any ill-treatment to us, now that they had an independent government.

*Thomas James, trader, recalling his 1824 expe-
dition to Santa Fe, in Three Years Among
the Indians and Mexicans (1966).*

Arrived at Santa Fe about dusk. This is quite a populous place, but is built entirely of mud houses; some parts of the city are tolerably regularly built, others very irregularly. The inhabitants appear to be friendly, and some of them are very wealthy; but by far the greater part are the most miserable, wretched, poor creatures that I have ever seen; yet they appear to be quite happy and contented in their miserable priest-ridden situation.

Meredith Miles Marmaduke, member of the Augustus Storrs expedition over the Santa Fe Trail, journal entry of July 28, 1824, in Journal of M.M. Marmaduke of a Trip from Franklin, Missouri, to Santa Fe, New Mexico *(1911).*

Although tracts of fertile land, considerably extensive, are occasionally to be met with, yet the scarcity of wood and water, almost uniformly prevalent, will prove an insuperable obstacle in the way of settling the country. This objection rests not only against the immediate section under consideration, but applies with equal propriety, to a much larger portion of the country. Agreeably to the best intelligence that can be had concerning the country both northward and southward of the section, and especially to the inferences deducible from the account given by Lewis and Clark of the country situated between the Missouri and the Rocky Mountains, above the River Platte, the vast region commencing near the sources of the Sabine, Trinity, Brassos, and Colorado, and extending northwardly to the 49th degree of north latitude, by which the United States territory is limited in that direction, is, throughout, of a similar character. The whole of this region seems peculiarly adapted as a range for buffaloes, wild goats, and other wild game, incalculable multitudes of which find ample pasturage and subsistence upon it.

Senator Mahlon Dickerson (New Jersey), to the U.S. Senate, speech of 1824 opposing the Oregon Bill, in Hulbert's Where Rolls Oregon.

Considering, then, our now circumscribed limits, the attachments we have to our native soil, and the assurances which we have, that our homes will never be forced from us, so long as the Government of the United States shall exist, we must *positively decline* the proposal of a removal beyond the Mississippi, or the sale of any more of our territory.

Creek Council at Broken Arrow, to United States commissioners, response of December 1824, in Green's The Politics of Indian Removal *(1982).*

To remove them from it [their present territory] by force, even with a view to their own security and happiness, would be revolting to humanity and utterly unjustifiable. Between the limits of our present States and Territories and the Rocky Mountains and Mexico there is a vast territory to which they might be invited with inducements which might be successful. It is thought if that territory should be divided into districts by previous agreement with the tribes now residing there and civil governments be established in each, with schools for every branch of instruction in literature and the arts of civilized life, that all tribes now within our limits might gradually be drawn there . . .

President James Monroe, final annual message to Congress, on Indian removals, December 7, 1824, in The Writings of James Monroe.

In looking to the interests which the United States have on the Pacific ocean, and on the western coast of this continent, the propriety of establishing a military post at the mouth of the Columbia river, or at some other point in that quarter, within our acknowledged limits, is submitted to the consideration of Congress. Our commerce and fisheries on that sea, and along the coast, have much increased, and are increasing. It is thought that a military post, to which our ships of war might resort, would afford protection to every interest, and have a tendency to conciliate the tribes to the northwest, with whom our trade is extensive. It is thought, also, that, by the establishment of such a post, the intercourse between our Western States and Territories and the Pacific, and our trade with the tribes residing in the interior, on each side of the Rocky Mountain, would be essentially promoted.

President James Monroe, final annual message to Congress, December 7, 1824, in The Writings of James Monroe.

The only very rugged part of the route is in crossing the Big Horn mountain, which is about 30 miles wide. I had the Big Horn river explored from Wind River mountain to my place of embarkation. There is little or no difficulty in the navigation of that river from its mouth to Wind River mountain. It may be ascended that far at a tolerable stage of water with a boat drawing three feet water. The Yellowstone river is a beautiful river to navigate.

William Ashley, report of 1825, in Dale's The Ashley-Smith Explorations and the Discovery of a Central Route to the Pacific.

Our most valuable inhabitants here own negroes. I am therefore anxious to know what the laws are upon that subject. Can they be introduced as the labouring servants of emigrants? and, when are they free? They are an important species of property here and our planters are not willing to remove without they can first be assured of their being secured to them by the laws of your Govt.

Charles Douglas, Alabama farmer, to Stephen F. Austin, inquiring about settling in Texas, letter of February 15, 1825, in The Austin Papers.

Westward, we can speak without reserve, and the ridge of the Rocky Mountains may be named without offence, as presenting a convenient, natural and everlasting boundary. Along the back of this ridge, the Western limit of the republic should be drawn, and the statute of the fabled god, Terminus, should be raised upon its highest peak, never to be thrown down. In planting the seed of a new power on the coast of the Pacific ocean, it should be well understood that when strong enough to take care of itself, the new Government should separate from the mother Empire as the child separates from the parent at the age of manhood.

Senator Thomas Hart Benton (Missouri), to U.S. Senate, speech of March 1, 1825, in Merk's Albert Gallatin and the Oregon Problem *(1950).*

You desire to be separate from the whites; & to have a Country of your own which shall not in future be encroached upon. This is exactly the wish of your Great Father. He sees how much inconvenience you suffer from your close connection with the whites. He knows that to remedy it you must have a country to yourselves & be protected in it by the United States. I advise you therefore, the more certainly to secure this great end, to give land on your Eastern Boundary & take an equal quantity on the Western. The farther back your eastern line is removed, the better for you, as it will secure to you the more certainly one great object, which is separation from the whites.

Secretary of War John C. Calhoun, to Cherokee delegation, on ceding their Arkansas territory to the United States, letter of March 2, 1825, in The Papers of John C. Calhoun.

Their present prospect for civilization is very promising; and little doubt can be entertained but, in a short time, these people will be well prepared to be admitted as citizens of the state of Ohio; and to remove them just at this time . . . would be, in my judgment, a most cruel act.

Reverend James B. Finley, to Lewis Cass, governor of Michigan Territory, on the Wyandots at Upper Sandusky, Ohio, letter of 1825, in Life Among the Indians *(1857).*

It is among the anomalies of history, that a country deemed so inaccessible from swamps in 1818, as to be unfit to be given in bounty lands to the soldiers of the late army, should, within six years thereafter, be found to possess qualities of so different a nature, as to attract crowds of emigrants from the fertile banks of the Genesee, and to divert, in a measure, the current of migration from the Wabash and the Illinois. Time, better means of comparison, and the spirit of exploration, which characterizes the present era, without showing the advantages of other parts of the western country to be less than has been claimed for them, have, at the same time, shown the advantages of Michigan Territory to be in many respects equal:—while its vicinity to the parent settlements, and the ease and cheapness of access, together with the quality of the land and the permanent benefits anticipated from the completion of the Erie Canal, give it, in the minds of many, a superiority.

Henry Rowe Schoolcraft, geologist and ethnologist, 1825, in Travels in the Central Portions of the Mississippi Valley *(1825).*

The country which you now possess, and that which we now remain on, was by the Great Spirit originally given to his red children. Our brothers, the white men, visited us when we were like the trees of the forest. Our forefathers smoked the pipe of peace and friendship with the forefathers of the white man, and when the white man said, we wish to live with the red man and inhabit the same country, we received their presents, and said, welcome; we will give you land for yourselves and for your children. We took the white man by the hand, and held fast to it. We became neighbors, and the children of the white man grew up, and the children of the red man grew up in the same country, and we were brothers. The white men became numerous as the trees of the forest, and the red men became like the buffalo. *Friends and Brothers:* You are like the mighty storm; we are like the tender and bending tree; we must bow before you; you have torn us up by the roots, but still you are our brothers and friends. You have promised to replant us in a better soil, and to watch over us and nurse us.

William McIntosh (aka Tustunnuge Hutkee), Creek chieftain, to the Georgia legislature, April 12, 1825, in Griffith's McIntosh and Weatherford, Creek Indian Leaders *(1988).*

Distance is conquered by science, and in the neighborhood of the Lakes, is no longer a thing to be regarded. Detroit is virtually nearer to New York, than Cumberland, in Maryland, is to Baltimore.

Niles' Weekly Register (Detroit), on the utility of the Erie Canal, November 19, 1825.

The route proposed, after leaving St. Louis and passing generally on the north side of the Missouri river, strikes the river Platte a short distance above its junction with the Missouri; then pursues the waters of the Platte to their sources, and in continuation, crosses the head waters of what Gen. Ashley believes to be, the Rio Colorado of the West, and strikes for the first time, a ridge, or single connecting chain of mountains running from north to south [the Bear River Divide]. This, however, presents no difficulty, as a wide gap is found, apparently prepared for the purpose of a passage. After passing this gap, the route proposed, falls directly on a river, called by Gen. Ashley, the Buenaventura, and runs with that river to the Pacific Ocean.

St. Louis Enquirer, describing William Ashley's overland route to the Pacific, newspaper article of March 11, 1826.

The absent parties began to arrive, one after the other, at the rendezvous. Shortly after, General Ashley and Mr. Sublet came in, Accompanied with three hundred pack mules, well laden with goods and all things necessary for the mountaineers and the Indian trade. It may well be supposed that the arrival of such a vast amount of luxuries from the East did not pass off without a general celebration. Mirth, songs, dancing, shouting, trading, running, jumping, singing, racing, target-shooting, yarns, frolic, with all sorts of extravagances that white men or Indians could invent were freely indulged in.

James Beckwourth, fur trapper with William Ashley's expedition, describing the rendezvous at Willow Valley (in present-day Utah), 1826, in The Life and Adventures of James P. Beckwourth.

James P. Beckwourth. Courtesy of the New York Public Library.

His return march to St. Louis occupied about seventy days, each mule and horse carrying nearly two hundred pounds of beaver fur—the animals keeping their strength and flesh on the grass which they found, and without losing any time on this long journey. The men also found an abundance of food; they say there was no day in which they could not have subsisted a thousand men, and often ten thousand. Buffaloe furnished the principal food—water of the best quality was met with every day. The whole route lay through a level and open country, better for carriages than any turnpike road in the United States. Wagons and carriages could go with ease as far as General Ashley went, crossing the Rocky Mountains at the sources of the north fork of the Platte, and descending the valley of the Buenaventura towards the Pacific Ocean.

Charles Keemle, editor of the Missouri Herald, *November 8, 1826, in Morgan's* Jedediah Smith and the Opening of the West.

We had taken very little rest for four nights, and being exceedingly drowsy, we had scarcely laid ourselves down, before we were sound asleep. The Indians had still followed us, too far off to be seen by day, but had probably surveyed our camp each night. At about 11 o'clock this night, they poured upon us a shower of arrows, by which they killed two men, and wounded two more; and what was most provoking, fled so rapidly that we could not even give them a round. One of the slain was in bed with me. My own hunting shirt had two arrows in it, and my blanket was pinned fast to the ground by arrows. There were sixteen arrows discharged into my bed. We extinguished our fires, and it may easily be imagined, slept no more that night.

James Ohio Pattie, fur trapper, on being followed by Mojave Indians after trapping along the Colorado River, 1826, in The Personal Narrative of James O. Pattie of Kentucky *(1833).*

. . . you also think that this colony will unite in such mad schemes—I have a better opportunity of knowing the force of the Gov^t than you have, and I assure you that were it necessary they could march five thousand troops to that district in two months and you would find that every man in this colony able to bear arms would freely and cheerfully join them—Some of those people have been so far deluded as to believe that the Gov^t of the United States would aid them, such an idea is too absurd for any reasonable man to think of so far from aiding them that Gov^t would if called on send troops to aid this Gov^t in establishing peace and good order on the frontier of the two nations and to expel from there all persons who might be disturbing it.

Stephen F. Austin, to Burril J. Thompson, Fredonian rebel leader, on his disapproval of the uprising and his own colony's support for the Mexican troops, letter of December 24, 1826, in The Austin Papers.

We have now the means of making *this empire shake to its very centre.* We ask you not to risk your lives and properties with us in this enterprize, unless your own feelings and your own judgments sanction such a cause. The rights and properties of every American and Spaniard will be held sacred, unless he raises arms against us. We will not dictate to you what course you should pursue.—Should you think proper to leave the struggle to us alone, We are nevertheless willing to fight for your rights and security in common with our own. Should we secure the Independence of this country, of which we have not an earthly doubt, you will of course share its blessings with us. We have undertaken this glorious cause with a determination to be freemen or to perish under the flag of liberty. We at least are determined to live or to die like Americans and like the sons of freemen.

General Committee for Independence (American settlers in Nacogdoches, Texas), proclamation of December 25, 1826, in The Austin Papers.

. . . put the question to your own bosoms and ask what would you as citizens of the U.S. of the north living in that nation think or say should a few foreigners settled without legal authority on the frontier immagine that the local subordinate officers who had charge of them had done them an injustice and should for that cause without first seeking the legal remidy condemn abuse and villify the whole american people and rise in open rebellion against the Govt. calling in the aid of savage allies and desperadoes to wage a war of desolation and massacre against the defenceless inhabitants of the frontier? What would you think of such foreigners? what would you do, if called on by your Govt. to march against them? as patriots, as friends to the cause of liberty and virtue and justice you would say reclaim them convince them of their delusions by reason and persuasion and should these fail put them down by force of arms and expel them [from] the country—you are now placed presisely in the situation above indicated—you are now Mexicans and you owe the same duties to the Government of your adoption, that you once owed to that of your nativity and reason justice and patriotism will at once point out to you what those duties are, and I feel no hesitation in pledging myself for you that you will faithfully perform them.

Stephen F. Austin, to Texas colonists, on the independence movement in Nacogdoches, address of January 5, 1827, in The Austin Papers.

. . . this River I have nam'd Sastise River . . . also a mount equal in height to Mount Hood on Vancouver [Mt. Jefferson] I have nam'd Mount Sistse ["Sastise"] its bearings by our Compass from our present encampment East South East . . . I have given these names from the Tribes of Indians who are well known by all the neighboring Tribes . . . by giving English names it often tends to lead strangers astray.

Peter Skene Odgen, fur trader and explorer, on sighting and naming Mount Shasta in northern California, journal entry of February 15, 1827, in Peter Skene Ogden's Snake Country Journal, 1826–1827 *(1961).*

Is it possible, said the companions of my sufferings, that we are so near the end of our troubles. For myself I durst scarcely believe that it was really the Big Salt Lake that I saw. It was indeed a most cheering view, for although we were some distance from the depo, yet we knew we would soon be in a country where we would find game and water, which were to us objects of the greatest importance and those which would contribute more than any others to our comfort and happiness.

Those who may chance to read this at a distance from the scene may perhaps be surprised that the sight of this lake surrounded by a wilderness of more than 2000 Miles diameter excited in me those feelings known to the traveller, who, after long and perilous journeying, comes again in view of his home. But so it was with me for I had travelled so much in the vicinity of the Salt Lake that it had become my home in the wilderness.

Jedediah Smith, journal entry of June 26, 1827, in The Travels of Jedediah Smith *(1934).*

On the south border of this lake is a number of hot and boiling springs, some of water and others of most beautiful fine clay, resembling a mush pot, and throwing particles to the immense height of from twenty to thirty feet.—The clay is of a white, and of a pink color, and the water appears fathomless, as it appears to be entirely hollow underneath. There is also a number of places where pure sulphur is sent forth in abundance.

William Ashley, describing area that is present-day Yellowstone Park, in Philadelphia Gazette *of July 8, 1827.*

I then steered my course N.W. keeping from 150 miles to 200 miles from the sea coast. A very high range [Sierra Nevada] of mountains lay on the East. After travelling three hundred miles in that direction through a country somewhat fertile, in which there was a great many Indians, mostly naked and destitute of arms, with the exception of a few Bows and Arrows and what is very singular amongst Indians,

they cut their hair to the length of three inches; they proved to be friendly; their manner of living is on fish, roots, acorns and grass.

Jedediah Smith, to General William Clark, superintendent of Indian affairs, letter of July 17, 1827, in Hulbert's Where Rolls Oregon.

The western people have a claim from the laws of God and nature to the exclusive possession of the entire valley of the Mississippi. This magnificent valley was, and it ought to be, theirs, in all its extent and circumference—to the head spring of every stream that drains it, to the summit ridge of the mountains which enclose it. It was, and ought to be, theirs, in all its borders and dimensions, with all its woods and groves, with all its fountains, springs and floods. No foreign flag should wave over any part of it. Not an inch of its soil should be trod, not a drop of its waters should be drunk, by any foreign power. The American people alone should have it; and as execrations, loud and deep, pursue the negotiator who dismembered it [Adams]—who despoiled this imperial valley of two of its noblest rivers and 200,000 square miles of its finest territory—so will benedictions, fervent and lasting, thicken over the head, and crown the honors, of the American President who shall restore it to its natural possessors and to its pristine integrity.

"La Salle" (Senator Thomas Hart Benton of Missouri), 1827 editorial in St. Louis Beacon, *in Barker's* Mexico and Texas *(1928).*

This lake is bounded on the south [north] and west by low Cedar Mountains, which separate it from the plains of the Great Salt Lake. On the south and east also, it is bounded by great plains. The Indians informed us that the country lying southwest, was impassible for the horses owing to the earth being full of holes. As well as we could understand from their description, it is an ancient volcanic region. This river is inhabited by a numerous tribe of miserable Indians. Their clothing consists of a breechcloth of goat or deer skin, and a robe of rabbit skins, cut in strips, sewed together after the manner of rag carpets, with the bark of milk week twisted into twine for the chain. These wretched creatures go out barefoot in the coldest days of winter.

Daniel Potts, fur trapper with the Ashley-Smith expedition, July 28, 1827, in Morgan's Jedediah Smith and the Opening of the West.

I must request you to draw the attention of the Secretary of War to the moving or emigrating Indians, who are continually coming on to this side of the Mississippi. Those that have come on, and not permanently settled, (many of them,) are scattered, for the purpose of procuring subsistence; and frequent complaints are made against them by the white people, and considerable expense incurred in reconciling the difficulties. No means is under my control to prevent further difficulties, until funds are placed in my hands for the purpose.

It will not only be necessary to place funds in my hands to move the Indians out of the settlements, but to assist them in commencing their new settlements.

William Clark, superintendent of Indian affairs, to Colonel Thomas L. McKenney, letter of December 10, 1827, in Cochran's The New American State Papers: Indian Affairs *(1972).*

. . . the incoming stream of new settlers is increasing; the first news of them comes by discovering them on land already under cultivation, where they have been located for months; the old inhabitants set up a claim to the property, basing their titles of doubtful priority, and for which there are no records, on a law of the Spanish government; and thus arises a lawsuit in which the *alcalde* has a chance to come out with some money . . . The whole population here is a mixture of strange and incoherent parts without parallel in our federation.

Mexican General Manuel Mier Teran, describing American colonists in Texas, 1828, in Barker's Mexico and Texas.

. . . the plan of collocating the Indians on suitable lands West of the Mississippi, contains the elements of their preservation; and will tend, if faithfully carried into effect, to produce the happiest benefits upon the Indian race. I have not been able to perceive in any other policy, principles which combine our own obligations to the Indians, in all that is humane and just, with effects so favorable to them, as is contained in this plan.

Secretary of War James Barbour, to Congressman William McLean, letter of April 29, 1828, in Prucha's American Indian Policy in the Formative Years *(1962).*

The town of Franklin, as also our own village, presents to the eye of the beholder, a busy, bustling and commercial scene, in buying, selling and packing goods, practicing mules, etc., etc., all preparatory to the starting of the great spring caravan to Santa Fe. A great number of our fellow citizens are getting ready to start, and will be off in the course of a week on a trading expedition. We have not the means of knowing how many persons will start in the first company, but think it probable the number will exceed 150, principally from this and the adjoining counties.

The Intelligencer (Franklin, Missouri), May 2, 1828.

As independent powers, we negotiated with them [the Indians] by treaties; as proprietors, we purchased of them all the lands which we could prevail upon them to sell; as brethren of the human race, rude and ignorant, we endeavored to bring them to the knowledge of religion and of letters. The ultimate design was to incorporate in our own institutions that portion of them which could be converted to the state of civilization. In the practice of European States, before our Revolution, they had been considered *as*

John Quincy Adams. Courtesy of the New York Public Library.

children to be governed; as tenants at discretion, to be dispossessed as occasion might require; as hunters to be indemnified by trifling concessions for removal from the grounds from which their game was extirpated. In changing the system it would seem as if a full contemplation of the consequences of the change had not been taken. We have been far more successful in the acquisition of their lands than in imparting to them the principles or inspiring them with the spirit of civilization.

President John Quincy Adams, final message to
Congress, December 2, 1828, in Richardson's
Messages and Papers of the Presidents
(1896).

Its salubrity of climate, its fertility of soil, its peculiar facilities and local advantages for commerce with the trading world, its commodious harbors for the safety and convenience of the navigating interests, its grand river Oregon, diversifying and watering by its thousand streams a wide-spread and beautiful country, its probable abundant productions, and more probable growth in population, have already excited the envy of some, and the admiration of all civilized nations, and will be found to contribute greatly to the resources of the wealth and power of the republic. It is also believed, that a permanent settlement of that country would render our Indian trade safer and more profitable; would give a specific value to millions of property now valueless to Government, and would conduct the streams of commerce, on that part of the globe, through their proper channels, into the reservoir of our national finance.

Hall Jackson Kelley, to Congress, memorial of
1828, in Hulbert's The Call of the Columbia
(1934).

To-day we passed two large rafts lashed together, by which simple conveyance several families from New England were transporting themselves and their property to the land of promise in the western woods. Each raft was eighty or ninety feet long, with a small house erected on it; and on each was a stack of hay, round which several horses and cows were feeding, while the paraphernalia of a farm-yard, the ploughs, waggons, pigs, children, and poultry, carelessly distributed, gave to the whole more the appearance of a permanent residence, than of a caravan of adventurers seeking a home.

James Hall, English traveler, on immigrants
using rafts on the Ohio River, 1828, in Letters
From the West *(1828).*

I have full confidence you will effect the purchase of Texas, so important for the perpetuation of that harmony and peace between us and the Republic of Mexico so desirable to them and to us to be maintained forever and if not obtained, is sure to bring us into conflict, owing to their jealousy and the dissatisfaction of those Americans now settling in Texas under the authority of Mexico—who will declare themselves independent of Mexico the moment they acquire sufficient numbers. This our government will be charged with fomenting, altho' all our Constitutional powers will be exercised to prevent. You will keep this steadily in view, and their own safety if it is considered will induce them to yield *now* in the present reduced state of their finances.

President Andrew Jackson, to Colonel Anthony
Butler, private letter of October 19, 1829, in
Rives' The United States and Mexico *(1913).*

The road begins in Maryland and it terminates at Wheeling. It passes through the states of Maryland, Pennsylvania, and Virginia. All the direct benefit of the expenditure of the public money on that road, has accrued to those three states. Not one cent in any Western State. And yet we have had to beg, entreat, supplicate you, session after session, to grant the necessary appropriations to complete the road. I have myself toiled until my powers have been exhausted and prostrated to prevail on you to make the grant. We were actuated to make these exertions for the sake of the collateral benefit only to the West; that we might have a way by which we should be able to continue and maintain an affectionate intercourse with our friends and brethren—that we might have a way to reach the Capitol of our country, and to bring our councils, humble as they may be, to consult and mingle with yours in the advancement of the national prosperity.

Henry Clay, to Congress, speech of January 14,
1829, in The Papers of Henry Clay *(1959).*

The great body of the chiefs of the Cherokees are most *positively opposed* to the war; and I have pointed out to them the ruinous consequences, which must result to them; and the Creeks also, and the probable evils to the United States; The war will, or may have a tendency to draw upon the frontiers of both nations those numerous hoards of Indians, who have never yet, dared to invade *them!* It will surely have great influence upon those of the Cherokees, and Creeks yet remaining on the East side of the Mississippi, and in all probability, deter them from removing to a country, which they, will understand is involved in a war; and where they must meet the hazards and dangers in the causes of which they had no participancy.

General Sam Houston, to Colonel Matthew Arbuckle, letter of July 8, 1829, in The Writings of Sam Houston *(1938–43).*

The Rocky mountains are deemed by many to be impassable, and to present the barrier which will arrest the westward march of the American population. The man must know but little of the American people who supposes they can be stopped by any thing in the shape of mountains, deserts, seas, or rivers; and he can know nothing at all of the mountains in question, to suppose that they are impassable. I have been familiar with these mountains for three years, and have crossed them often, and at various points between the latitude 42 and 54; that is to say, between the head waters of the Rio Colorado of the gulf of California, and the Athabasca of the Polar sea. I have, therefore, the means to know something about them, and a right to oppose my knowledge to the suppositions of strangers. I say, then, that nothing is more easily passed than these mountains. Wagons and carriages may cross them in a state of nature without difficulty, and with little delay in the day's journey.

Joshua Pilcher, president of the Missouri Fur Company, to Secretary of War John H. Eaton, 1829, in Hulbert's Where Rolls Oregon.

Indeed, to seek a place on the coast where the Indians have not suffered in consequence of their intercourse with foreigners, will be, I am persuaded, a fruitless attempt. The Russian-Fur, the North-West, and the Hudson-Bay, companies and traders from the United States have occupied every post of importance from Norfolk Sound to the Columbia river.

Jonathan Smith Green, missionary, report of an exploring tour of the northwest coast of North America, 1829, in Hulbert's Where Rolls Oregon.

To operate against the Indians who have heretofore committed outrages upon our Santa Fe traders, one hundred men would be all sufficient; but it is reasonable to suppose that the success of the offenders on this route will induce others to join them. Let us consider the force of the Indians in that quarter who

are now recognised as our enemies; those who have taken a menacing attitude, and those who are, or pretend to be, friendly, but who may be brought to action against us. In this way it may be better seen whether protection is necessary, and what that protection ought to be.

William Ashley, to A. Macomb, commander-in-chief of the Army, on military protection for fur traders, report of March 1829, in Hulbert's Where Rolls Oregon.

The condition and ulterior destiny of the Indian tribes within the limits of some of our States have become objects of much interest and importance. It has long been the policy of Government to introduce among them the arts of civilization, in the hope of gradually reclaiming them from a wandering life. This policy has, however, been coupled with another wholly incompatible with its success. Professing a desire to civilize and settle them, we have at the same time lost no opportunity to purchase their lands and thrust them farther into the wilderness. By this means they have not only been kept in a wandering state, but been led to look upon us as unjust and indifferent to their fate. Thus, though lavish in its expenditures upon the subject, Government has constantly defeated its own policy, and the Indians in general, receding farther and farther to the west, have retained their savage habits. A portion, however, of the Southern tribes, having mingled much with the whites and made some progress in the arts of civilized life, have lately attempted to erect an independent government within the limits of Georgia and Alabama.

President Andrew Jackson, to Congress, first annual message of December 8, 1829, in Richardson's Messages and Papers of the Presidents.

It is that I may be able to help those who stand in need that I face every danger—it is for this, that I Traverse the Mountains covered with Eternal Snow—it is for this that I pass over the Sandy Plains, in heat of summer, thirsting for water, and am well pleased if I can find a Shade, instead of water where I may cool my overheated Body—it is for this that I go for days without eating, & am pretty well satisfied if I can gather a few roots . . .

Jedediah Smith, to his brother, letter of December 24, 1829, in Hafen's The Old Spanish Trail *(1954).*

Their machinations in the country they wish to acquire are then brought to light by the visits of explorers, some of whom settle on the soil, alleging that their presence does not affect the question of the right of sovereignty or possession of the land. These pioneers originate, little by little, movements which complicate the political state of the country in dispute, and then follow discontents and dissatisfaction, calculated to fatigue the patience of the legitimate owner, and diminish the usefulness of the administration and the exercise of authority. When things have come to this pass, which is precisely the present state of things in Texas, diplomatic intrigue (*el manejo diplomático*) begins.

Lúcas Ignacio Alaman, Mexican secretary of foreign relations, to Mexico's Congress, on preserving the Texas territory, report of February 8, 1830, in Rives' The United States and Mexico.

The doctrine, that Indians are an erratic people, who have only run over lands of extensive bounds in pursuit of the chase, [and] are not therefore justly entitled to the same, is inapplicable to our people, who have settled habitations in villages and towns . . . We beg permission to be left, where your treaties have left us, in the enjoyment of rights as a separate people, and to be treated as unoffending, peaceable inhabitants of our own, and not a borrowed country.

Creek Nation, to Congress, petition of February 9, 1830, in Green's The Politics of Indian Removal.

The imprudence and thoughtlessness of some on the Sabine frontiers and the excessive noise that has been made in the U.S. papers about the purchase of Texas, seems to have had a much greater weight in Mexico than a matter so essentially unimportant ought to have had. It appears to have caused an impression that the North Americans are all turbulent and that the Gov^t of the north wish to take Texas by force right or wrong. All these impressions are erronious and have been created by the reports of some evil minded persons for the purpose of trying to extort from this Govt. unjust and arbitrary measures against the colonist, so as to foment discontent in Texas. Those persons have also been trying to sow the seeds of suspicion and jealousy against the Govt. of the U.S. with the hope no doubt that a war might be brought about between the two nations, in which event Texas would be lost to Mexico in one campain.

Stephen F. Austin, to Thomas F. Leaming, Philadelphia lawyer, on the Mexican Colonization Law of April 6, 1830, letter of June 14, 1830, in The Austin Papers.

The United States owe the Creeks money. They have paid them none in three years. The money has been appropriated by Congress. It is withheld by the Agents. The Indians are destitute of almost every comfort for the want of what is due to them. If it is longer withheld from them, it can only be so, upon the grounds, that the poor Indian, who is unable to compel the United States to a compliance with solemn treaties, must linger out a miserable degraded existence, while those who have power to extend to him the measure of justice, will be left in *full* possession of *all* the *complacency* arising from the solemn *assurance*, that they are either the *stupid* or *guilty* authors of his degradation and misery.

"Tah-Lohn-Tus-ky" (Sam Houston), article of July 7, 1830, Arkansas Gazette.

The usual progress of the wagons was from fifteen to twenty five miles per day. The country being almost all open, level, and prairie, the chief obstructions were ravines and creeks, the banks of which required cutting down, and for this purpose a few pioneers were generally kept ahead of the caravan. This is the first time that wagons ever went to the Rocky mountains; and the ease and safety with which it was done prove the facility of communicating over land with the Pacific ocean.

Jedediah Smith, David E. Jackson and William L. Sublette, to Secretary of War John H. Eaton, report of October 29, 1830, in Hulbert's Where Rolls Oregon.

English traders, at the present time possess the country. The will of the Hudson Bay Company, is the supreme law of the land. The natives are subservient to it, and American traders dare not resist it. Hence, the inland trade is fast on the wane, and has become disastrous, if not in most cases, ruinous. While it is so constantly exposed to the rapacity of treacherous Indians, and to the avarice of the English, it must remain utterly valueless. It might, however, be reclaimed, and forever protected by a colony occupying the shores of the Columbia. And what better means could the American Republic desire, for the protection of the lives and property of her citizens, in that territory, and on the Western Ocean.

Hall Jackson Kelly, describing Oregon, 1830, in
Hulbert's The Call of the Columbia.

Asks he how thrives the country back?
Let him just ride to Pontiac;
Or take the stage to Washtenaw,
The finest land he ever saw,
Except St. Joseph's, which, 'tis said,

Is where the Paradise was laid.
St. Joseph's now is a disease,
Which emigration seems to seize,
And carries off, at sundry times,
Whole families—to distant climes,
Where fertile counties proudly claim
Old Hickory's and Van Buren's name.

Henry Whiting, military officer and poet, on
travelers bound for the Michigan country, poem
of 1830, in Buley's The Old Northwest:
Pioneer Period (1950).

5. Across the Plains: 1831–1840

THE DISPOSSESSED

When the Cherokees in Georgia were faced with removal by the federal government in 1827, they declared themselves a sovereign nation and adopted a constitution modeled after that of the United States. Georgians vehemently rejected the claim and annexed the Cherokee counties.

The Cherokees appealed to the federal government for protection. Under President Andrew Jackson, who showed little sympathy for the Indians, Congress passed a Removal Bill in May 1830, which authorized the president to relocate any eastern tribe, by force if necessary, to lands beyond the Mississippi. In desperation the Cherokees asked the Supreme Court to issue an injunction against Indian removal. In the case of *The Cherokee Nation v. Georgia*, the Court ruled in 1831 that the Indians did not constitute a foreign nation and therefore had no right to bring the suit before the Court.

Payment of annuities to the Cherokees was halted, debts owed to them were canceled, Cherokee lands were seized and their homes appropriated. Agents descended upon the Cherokees, provoking disputes between families and attempting to break tribal unity. Christian missionaries appealed to the Supreme Court on the Cherokees' behalf. Chief Justice John Marshall ruled in the case of *Worcester v. Georgia* that the Cherokees possessed the status of a "dependent nation" under the protection of the federal government, and that Georgia had no right to harass them. Georgia refused to comply with the decision, and Jackson considered the order too absurd to enforce.

In the North, squatters were settling on lands occupied by the Sauk and Fox tribes in Illinois. By a treaty of 1804 with William Henry Harrison the tribes had ceded to the United States their entire territory east of the Mississippi River, comprising northwestern Illinois, southwestern Wisconsin and part of eastern Missouri. However, they had been permitted to remain on the lands until the territory was needed for settlement. That time had arrived in 1829, when a rush of farmers descended upon the principal Sauk Indian village, which is now a part of Rock Island, Illinois, and forced the peaceful natives from their fields.

Keokuk, the leading Sauk chieftain, urged his people to follow him across the Mississippi to safer grounds, but one minor chief refused. Black Hawk, a proud 60-year-old warrior who despised the Americans, proclaimed that he and his followers would continue occupying the lands of their ancestors. The remaining Sauk lived undisturbed until the spring of 1831, when Illinois officials decided that they threatened the frontier. A force of 1,500 troops assembled, ordered Black Hawk and his followers to leave and then marched against the villages.

Black Hawk retreated with his followers to the west side of the Mississippi. After spending a miserable winter in the Iowa country, missing the planting season, and suffering from starvation, Black Hawk recrossed the Mississippi in the spring of 1832 with a large band of warriors, women and children. Although he insisted that his intent was peaceful, a wave of panic swept over the Illinois frontier. General Henry Atkinson commanded a heavy force of volunteers and regulars in pursuit of Black Hawk. The chief tried to surrender, but when one of his representatives was fired upon, he decided to fight the Americans. A brief skirmish ensued, and Black Hawk defeated the inexperienced soldiers. It was only a temporary victory, however, and resulted in bringing more soldiers into the field against Black Hawk and his followers.

The conflict lasted until early August, when the band was almost annihilated at the mouth of the Bad Axe River in Wisconsin as it attempted to recross the Mississippi to Iowa. By the end of the battle only 150 of the thousand Indians who had set out for the Rock River Valley three months before remained alive, and they were taken prisoners, including Black Hawk himself. The Bad Axe Massacre, as it is called, was one of the bloodiest tragedies in the history of American-Indian affairs.

As the price for peace the Sauk and Fox Indians had to cede to the United States a 50-mile wide tract of land in Iowa, running along the west bank of the Mississippi from Missouri's northern boundary to the vicinity of Prairie du Chien. The Black Hawk War achieved the desired effect of intimidating other Northwestern tribes into surrendering their lands. Tribe after tribe ceded their territories, and by 1837 nearly all of the Old Northwest had been transferred to the United States. In those five years 190,879,937 acres were secured from the Indians at a cost of $70,059,505 in gifts and annuities.

EXPANDING FRONTIERS

Even while the Black Hawk War raged, emigrants from New England and the Middle Atlantic states were settling in northern Indiana, northern and central Illinois, and southern Michigan. Improved transportation systems for reaching the West greatly influenced the course of the new migration. Some pioneers from the Middle states continued to use the old routes—the National Road, the Forbes Road or the Catskill Turnpike—to reach the Ohio, then made their way down the river and northward to central Indiana or Illinois. More were taking advantage of the newly completed all-water route from the Hudson River to Lake Erie. Almost overnight the Erie Canal became the most important route to the West.

When in the early 1830s eastern newspapers and guidebooks advertised the rich soil and dense forests to be found in the Michigan Territory, a rush of farmers poured into the region. Newcomers first arrived at Detroit, then moved on to settle in southern Michigan. Others immigrated to Illinois, first stopping at Chicago, and then fanning out over northern Illinois, settling in such choice spots as the Rock and Illinois river valleys. By the end of the 1830s northern Illinois was so populated that the overflow of settlers spilled into Wisconsin.

The demand for land was accelerating under the pressures of a new cycle of prosperity and increasing emigration from Ireland, Germany and England. Between 1830 and 1840 more than half a million European immigrants entered the United States. Government land sales grew from a little under four million acres during 1833 to more than 20 million during 1836. All public land, good or bad, was sold for $1.25 an acre. Settlers raced into the wilderness, searching for choice plots,

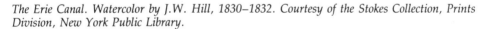

The Erie Canal. Watercolor by J.W. Hill, 1830–1832. Courtesy of the Stokes Collection, Prints Division, New York Public Library.

while hundreds of thousands of less desirable acres remained untouched.

In the Southwest a new frontier was emerging. Its pioneers were the small farmers of Missouri, Kentucky, Mississippi, Arkansas and Louisiana. When a disastrous economic depression swept over the nation in 1837, many of these family farmers were forced to sell out to the "planter aristocracy" of the South. Many Southern states had backed unsound banks and invested carelessly in internal improvement schemes. The states were now left with staggering debts, which would burden farmers with higher taxes for many years.

While the pioneers of the upper Mississippi Valley could move to the virgin soil of Iowa or Minnesota, southerners were limited to only a few unsettled and poorly soiled regions. Ahead was the barrier of the Permanent Indian Frontier, and beyond that the "Great American Desert." They turned their sights on the far western country described by traders and explorers. The lower Mississippi Valley frontiersmen left their homes to establish new settlements in Texas, Oregon and California.

TEXAS INDEPENDENCE

Although the Mexican Colonization Law of April 6, 1830, was designed to prevent further settlement by the United States, Americans continued to enter Texas, many of them settling in Austin's colony. Based on a loose interpretation of the law, the Mexican government permitted Austin's colony to continue. The law of 1830 did result in limiting the number of "respectable" immigrants from entering Texas, but it did not prevent undesirable squatters from crossing the border.

With the successful Mexican revolution of Antonio Lopez de Santa Anna, Texans hoped their grievances could be settled. At a colonial convention at San Felipe on October 1, 1832, the delegates agreed to dispatch Stephen F. Austin to Mexico City to petition for a reversal of the severe tax laws and restrictions against American immigration, and to present a new state constitution that would permit Texas to govern itself independently from Coahuila.

The Mexican authorities regarded independence from Coahuila as a step toward secession from the Republic of Mexico. However, Austin was successful in having the Mexican Congress repeal the portion of the Law of April 6, 1830, excluding American settlement in Texas. On his return trip Austin was arrested at Saltillo, because a letter he had written to Texans advising them to form a state government without Mexican approval had fallen into the hands of government officials.

Austin was hauled back to Mexico City, where he spent months in prison without ever being charged, and was then released on September 1, 1835.

Overwhelmed by persistent uprisings, Santa Anna abolished the constitution of 1824, which had established a federal system of government in Mexico, and replaced it with a powerful centralized national authority. He increased the military garrisons throughout the country and suspended all civil government in Texas-Coahuila. The Mexican leader ordered the army to crush any rebellious states, and to advance northward toward Texas to enforce customs collections at Anahuac and Brazoria.

At Anahuac, William B. Travis, a young lawyer, gathered a few dozen settlers and on June 30, 1835, forced the new customs garrison out of town. General Martin Perfecto de Cos, determined to make an example of Travis, marched his army toward San Antonio. About 70 miles east of San Antonio, the citizens of Gonzales were able to turn back Cos by firing on his troops with a six-pounder brass cannon loaded with iron balls and pieces of chain. The Texans were now under the false impression that they could overcome the entire Mexican army.

In November 1835, a convention was assembled at San Felipe, where the Texans formed a provisional government in the American tradition and created a plan for organizing a regular army. Persuaded by Austin, the delegates voted down a resolution that Texas secede from Mexico. However, Austin was rejected as the provisional governor and elected instead to a commission to solicit aid from the United States.

In February 1836, travelers along the El Camino Real were reporting that Santa Anna was advancing with an army of 4,000 men toward San Antonio. One-hundred-and-fifty men under William Travis defended the town from behind the adobe walls of the Alamo Mission. Among them was Davy Crockett, the frontiersman and backwoods congressman from Tennessee. The Texans were confident that hundreds of volunteers from the United States were on their way.

On February 23, 1836, Santa Anna surrounded the Alamo and ordered the garrison to surrender or be destroyed. Santa Anna began a bombardment with light artillery. The shooting killed no one, but caused Travis to send out his famous appeal: "To the People of Texas & all Americans in the world . . . If this call is neglected, I am determined to sustain myself as long as possible & die like a soldier who never forgets what is due to his own honor & that of his country— VICTORY OR DEATH!"

Before dawn on Sunday, March 6, Santa Anna launched his attack. A brutal battle ensued. Santa Anna's orders were to take no prisoners. Before the Texans were overpowered by the Mexican army, they had killed 1,544 troops. "Remember the Alamo" became a rallying cry throughout Texas.

On March 1, 1836, at a little town known as Washington-on-the-Brazos, 59 delegates assembled and agreed on a Declaration of Independence, then appointed Sam Houston as commander-in-chief of the army. A constitution for the Republic of Texas was adopted, borrowing heavily from the constitution of the United States. Slavery was legalized, and each Texan was granted one *labor* (177 acres) for farming, with an additional 74 labors for stock-raising, the whole constituting a *sitio* or square league.

While retreating from Santa Anna's troops, Houston shaped his own troops into efficient, fighting soldiers. On April 21, 1836, Houston was prepared to meet the enemy on the banks of the San Jacinto River in eastern Texas. His well-trained army of 783 men took the Mexican troops by total surprise; the battle of San Jacinto was over in 18 minutes. Houston inflicted a decisive blow, killing 630 of the Mexicans and capturing 730 more, including Santa Anna himself.

The remaining Mexican troops, between 4,000 and 5,000, chose to retreat across the Rio Grande rather than counterattack. Most Texans wanted to hang Santa Anna, but Houston and Texas President David Burnett protected him. Treaties were signed with Santa Anna, calling for the end of hostilities. He was released by Houston under the promise that he would help convince the Mexican government to grant full independence to Texas. Upon his return to Mexico City, Santa Anna was ousted from the government and went into a brief retirement. Although Mexico insisted that Texas was not independent, unsettled conditions farther south prevented the former government from attempting to exert its authority for several years.

Texans wanted and expected annexation by the United States. However, the United States was reluctant to risk war with Mexico. Bitter debates raged in Congress, where for three weeks John Quincy Adams argued that the southern slave states had instigated the revolution for "the avowed purpose of adding five or six more slaveholding States to this Union." Deciding that annexation would have to await a different political atmosphere, Texas withdrew its request for admission to the Union.

Under the leadership of Sam Houston, who was overwhelmingly elected as president of Texas in September 1836, Texans set out to show the world that they could survive on their own. Immigration multiplied as settlers were attracted by a generous land grant program that gave away two square miles (1,280 acres) to each new family. The Panic of 1837 caused tens of thousands of Americans to lose their farms in the South and their factory jobs in the North, and scores of settlers and adventurers poured into Texas.

THE OREGON COUNTRY

While some pioneers advanced into the Southwest to secure Texas from Mexico, others moved toward the Pacific Northwest to seize the Oregon country from England's fur traders. By 1831 Hall Jackson Kelly's Oregon Emigration Society had a considerable number of members, including Nathaniel J. Wyeth, a Cambridge icemaker, who planned to establish a supply base for fur trappers on the Columbia River. While Kelly was interested in creating a New England–type town, Wyeth's motivations were purely commercial.

When Kelly's group would not move beyond the discussion stage, Wyeth decided to form his own expedition. By December 1831, 31 men had enlisted for his overland journey. After spending 10 days during March 1832 on an island in Boston harbor preparing themselves for the frontier trek, Wyeth's party went by ship to Baltimore, then proceeded by way of Pittsburgh and Cincinnati to St. Louis. At Independence, Missouri, Wyeth's expedition was attached to the annual caravan of the Rocky Mountain Fur Company, under the experienced leadership of William L. Sublette.

At Pierre's Hole in present-day Wyoming, half of Wyeth's party deserted, broken by the severe hardships of the trail. Wyeth continued on with 11 men toward Fort Walla Walla, the Hudson's Bay Company post, and then pushed on to Fort Vancouver, where he arrived in late October 1832. Upon arriving, Wyeth learned that his ship and cargo from Boston had been lost at sea. Most of his men decided to quit, taking jobs with the Hudson's Bay Company. Unable to pursue his trading plans, Wyeth returned to Boston in February 1833.

Wyeth's expedition publicized the Columbia country but did not result in any permanent settlements. Missionaries, not traders, were mostly responsible for founding the first American settlements in the Oregon country. Missionary activity in Oregon can actually be traced to a chance journey undertaken by four Oregon-country Indians, three Nez Perces and one Flathead, who in October 1831 accompanied a group of fur trappers on their return trip from the Rocky Mountains to St. Louis. The Indians came east to satisfy their curiosity about the white man's way of life. Reports circulated that they had made the arduous journey to ask that ministers visit their tribes and give them religious instruction.

William Walker, an educated Wyandot Indian from the East, heard about the visiting Indians during his visit to St. Louis. He sent off an enthusiastic letter to a friend, who passed it on to the *Methodist Christian Advocate and Journal,* where it was published on March 1, 1833.

Almost overnight every religious person in the United States became concerned with the plight of the Indians who had traveled 2,000 miles to request the word of God. One single letter did more to stimulate interest in the Oregon country than all the efforts of Wyeth and Kelly, and the pleas to Congress by politicians and explorers.

Reverend Jason Lee and his nephew Daniel Lee volunteered to establish a Methodist mission in the Pacific Northwest. When Lee learned about Wyeth's return from his first expedition, he rushed off to Cambridge to obtain all the possible information regarding the Northwest. Wyeth was planning a second expedition, and, although he was a nonbeliever, he invited the Lees to accompany him on the journey.

The missionaries arrived at Fort Vancouver on September 15, 1834, where they received a hearty welcome from Dr. John McLoughlin of the Hudson's Bay Company. With the assistance of Dr. McLoughlin, Lee's party established a settlement in the Willamette Valley, near present-day Salem. Living nearby were about 20 families, most of them employees of the Hudson's Bay Company with Indian wives, who had started farms on the fertile lands. The first agricultural community in the Oregon country was destined to become the nucleus for future American settlements in the Pacific Northwest.

Within one year the Lees' mission consisted of a house, a barn, a school for Indian children and 30 acres of plowed land. In early 1836, Samuel Parker, a 57-year-old Presbyterian minister, visited the Lees' mission. He too had become interested in missionary activity in the Northwest after reading William Walker's letter in the *Christian Advocate.* Parker and his companion, Dr. Marcus Whitman, had traveled with the American fur company caravan from St. Louis. At the Green River rendezvous it was decided that there was great potential for missionary work in the Northwest, and Whitman returned east to enlist more missionaries and to bring his future bride, Narcissa Prentiss.

By March 1836, Marcus Whitman and a new recruit, Henry Spalding, and their wives were making their way toward the Oregon country. The first white women to cross the American continent, they created much excitement among the Indians and fur trappers at the Green River rendezvous. The Whitmans, helped by the Hudson's Bay Company, built a mission east of the Cascade Mountains at Waiilatpu on the Walla Walla River, while the Spaldings moved to the center of the Nez Perce country, at Lapwai.

During the winter of 1837 more American missionaries reached the Columbia, including five more women. Two were soon married to Jason Lee and Cyrus Shepard, a member of Lee's original expedition party. The Willamette Valley now included 51 American settlers. They had established successful farms and were looking toward the future. In March 1838, a group of them petitioned Congress for United States jurisdiction over the region.

Congress was once again taking notice of the Oregon country. Senator Lewis F. Linn of Missouri introduced a bill in 1838 that provided for the military occupation of the Columbia and the creation of a territorial government for Oregon. Attached to the bill was a report covering the history of American claims to the region and also an account of the Spalding-Whitman expedition over the mountains to the Oregon country.

Oregon fever was beginning to take shape among Mississippi Valley farmers, who were impressed with the great number of cattle being exported by the Willamette Cattle Company. Easterners were learning about the Pacific Northwest through the accounts of official explorers, such as the report of Lieutenant Charles Wilkes on the Willamette Valley and the Methodist Mission. American settlement in California was also beginning to stir the imagination of many Easterners, with the publication of travel books by those who had visited the region.

In 1840, after spending four months visiting every port up and down the coast, Richard H. Dana wrote *Two Years Before the Mast*, in which he cited the remarkable attractions of the land: "In the hands of an enterprising people, what a country this might be!" Within a few years endless lines of covered wagons would be moving across the Oregon Trail.

CHRONICLE OF EVENTS

1831:

In *Cherokee Nation v. Georgia*, the Supreme Court rules that the Cherokee Indians are a domestic, dependent nation, not a foreign nation.

The mechanical reaper, which will revolutionize prairie farming, is invented by Cyrus McCormick.

May 15: Departing from Independence, Missouri, 200 men and 100 wagons, transporting goods worth $200,000, make the journey to Santa Fe. Josiah Gregg, author of *Commerce of the Prairies* (1844), the classic account of the early history of the Santa Fe Trail, accompanies this caravan.

May 27: Jedediah Strong Smith is killed by Comanche Indians along the Santa Fe Trail.

June 27: Chief Black Hawk agrees to move west of the Mississippi River.

August: Joseph Smith chooses Independence, Missouri, as the Holy City of Zion for the Mormon Church.

October: Nez Perce and Flathead tribesmen arrive at St. Louis from Oregon to learn more about the religion of the white man. This will lead to increased missionary activity in the Far West.

1832:

Hall Jackson Kelley journeys to Oregon.

Nathanial J. Wyeth recruits men for an expedition to the Pacific Northwest. He reaches Oregon, but returns East after finding his ship and supplies were lost at sea.

February 6: The Emigrant, published in Ann Arbor, Michigan, suggests the construction of a transcontinental railroad.

April: Chief Black Hawk leads 400 braves and their families back to Illinois. When his emissary is killed, Black Hawk attacks a large force of white troops. The Black Hawk War begins.

July 13: Henry R. Schoolcraft finds the source of the Mississippi River at Lake Itasca in Minnesota.

August 2: The last battle of the Black Hawk War occurs on the Bad Axe River in Wisconsin. After many of the Black Hawk's people are massacred, including women and children, he escapes and hides among the Winnebago Indians. The Black Hawk War is ended.

August 27: Black Hawk is turned over to U.S. troops by the Winnebago Indians. He is imprisoned for about a year, then released to live with his remaining people in Iowa.

October 15: Congress authorizes the War Department to enlist mounted troops, known as dragoons, for use on the Western Plains to protect wagon trains on the Santa Fe Trail.

December 2: Sam Houston, former governor of Tennessee, crosses the Red River and enters Texas for the first time.

1833:

Chicago is incorporated as a village.

Bent's fort is built near present-day La Junta, Colorado; it is used as a trading post for beaver skins, replacing the annual fur trappers' rendezvous.

The Black Hawk Purchase, a 50-mile-wide strip of land running along the west bank of the Mississippi from Missouri's northern boundary to the vicinity of Prairie du Chien, opens the Iowa country for settlement.

March 1: The Methodist Christian Advocate and Journal publishes a story by William Walker, an educated Wyandot Indian, describing Oregon-country Indians who desire to learn more about the white man's religion. Missionaries are inspired to travel to Oregon.

March 4: Andrew Jackson is inaugurated for his second presidential term.

April 1: A convention of Texas settlers votes to separate from Mexico.

1834:

Fort William established, the first permanent trading post in Wyoming.

The area known as the Black Hawk Purchase is attached to the Territory of Michigan.

Joseph Reddeford Walker leads an expedition from Salt Lake down the Humboldt River, crossing the Sierra Nevada Mountains to the California coast. They are the first white men to see and describe the Yosemite Valley, and they discover an easy route around the southern end of the Sierra Mountains—the Walker Pass.

January 3: Stephen F. Austin is arrested and imprisoned by Mexican officials, for eight months, after presenting resolves to Mexican President Antonio Lopez de Santa Anna. The resolves request separate statehood for Texas, apart from Coahuila.

April: Nathaniel J. Wyeth leaves for the Far West from Independence, Missouri, with the Rocky Mountain Fur Company.

June 30: An Act of Congress establishes a Department of Indian Affairs.

September: Wyeth reaches the Pacific Coast, builds Fort William on an island at the mouth of the Willamette River in Oregon.

The Reverend Jason Lee, a Methodist missionary, arrives at Fort Vancouver. He creates the first American farming settlement in Oregon near present-day Salem.

1835:

Samuel Parker and Dr. Marcus Whitman travel to Oregon for missionary work.

June 30: Texans led by William B. Travis seize the Mexican garrison at Anahuac.

September: Stephen F. Austin returns to Texas after being released from a Mexican prison. Austin now favors war between Texas and Mexico as the only recourse for American settlers in Texas.

October: A convention of Texans rejects Mexican rule, calls for self-government and declares the right of secession from the Republic of Mexico.

December 9: The Texan army led by Colonel Benjamin Milan captures San Antonio.

December 15: Santa Anna announces a constitution for all Mexican territories.

1836:

Construction begins on the Illinois and Michigan Canal, which will connect Chicago with the Illinois River and increase commerce on the Mississippi River system.

The Wisconsin Territory is formed from part of the Michigan Territory that lies west of the present state of Michigan.

February 23: The siege of the Alamo is carried out by a Mexican army of 4,000 troops, led by Mexican President Santa Anna. The defenders refuse to surrender and are killed when the fort falls on March 6.

March 2: Texas settlers declare their independence from Mexico. David G. Burnett is chosen as the provisional president and Sam Houston as the army commander.

March 27: Three-hundred-and-thirty defenders of Goliad, a Texan outpost, are captured and shot to death by order of Santa Anna.

April 21: Sam Houston defeats the Mexican army and captures Santa Anna at the battle of San Jacinto.

July 1: A congressional resolution calls for recognition of Texas, but President Jackson, fearing war with Mexico, declines.

July 15: Arkansas is admitted to the Union as the 25th state, and the 13th that permits slavery.

September: Settlers of the Republic of Texas request it to be annexed as part of the United States.

September 12: Marcus Whitman and Henry F. Spaulding and their wives reach Vancouver. Narcissa Prentiss Whitman and Eliza Spaulding are the first white women to cross the North American continent.

October 22: Sam Houston is sworn in as the president of Texas.

November 7: California declares independence from Mexico, but there is no military reaction from Mexico.

Sam Houston. Courtesy of the Library of Congress.

1837:

The Sioux and Chippewa Indians surrender their claim to the St. Croix valley of Minnesota, resulting in a land boom and settlers emigrating from England.

Chicago is incorporated as a city, with 3,000 inhabitants.

The first plow with steel moldboard is invented by John Deere, revolutionizing Prairie farming.

January 26: Michigan is admitted as the 26th state, the 13th free state.

March 3: Andrew Jackson recognizes the independent Republic of Texas, the last act of his presidency.

1838:

January 12: Joseph Smith flees Kirtland, Ohio, to escape arrest after the collapse of the Mormon bank. He and his associate, Sydney Rigdon, relocate in the far west of the Missouri frontier.

July 4: The Iowa Territory is created by separating the western regions of the Wisconsin Territory, with the Mississippi River as the border. The new territory includes all of present-day Iowa, most of Minnesota, and two-thirds of North and South Dakota.

1839:

The Trail of Tears: Cherokee, Choctaw, Chickasaw, Creek and Seminole Indians are forced to march from their lands in the south to the Indian country in present-day Oklahoma. Several thousand die on the journey.

Thomas J. Farnham leads an expedition of 13 men from Peoria, Illinois, to the Willamette Valley in Oregon, with a train of pack horses.

August: John Augustus Sutter, a Swiss immigrant trader, arrives in the upper Sacramento Valley, the first white pioneer in that region.

September 23: Texan independence is recognized by France, the first European nation to do so.

1840:

Forty-thousand Indians from the Five Civilized Tribes are resettled in Indian Territory in present-day Oklahoma by this year.

EYEWITNESS TESTIMONY

It was ascertained that a great war chief [General E.P. Gaines], with a large number of soldiers, was on his way to Rock River. The war chief arrived, and convened a council at the agency. He said: "I hope you will consult your own interest and leave the country you are occupying, and go to the other side of the Mississippi."

I replied: "That we had never sold our country. We never received any annuities from our American father! And we are determined to hold on to our village!"

The war chief said: "I came here, neither to beg nor hire you to leave your village. My business is to remove you, peaceably if I can, but forcibly if I must! I will now give you two days to remove in—and if you do not cross the Mississippi within that time, I will adopt measures to force you away!"

Black Hawk, recalling army orders for him and his followers to leave their lands in Illinois, 1831, in Autobiography of Ma-ka-tai-me-she-kia-kiak, or, Black Hawk *(1882).*

I have witnessed all the Treaties of my Nation with your Government since the Old British War. I have even been the friend of the white man [and] I have never seen the necessity of complaining until now. [But] your white sons and daughters are moving into my country in a band, and are spoiling my lands and taking possession of the Red peoples improvements that they have made with their own labour. Contrary to the consent of the Nation. Your soldiers have refused to prevent it. This makes me sorry and have caused me to give you the talk Believing at the same time that you will not give a deaf ear to it . . . These are the kind of characters that settle among us. They steal our property they swear to lies they make false accounts against us they sue us in your State courts for what we know nothing of the Laws that we are immeaneable to are in words that we have no possible means to understanding.

Tuskeneah, Creek chieftain, to President Andrew Jackson, May 21, 1831, in Green's The Politics of Indian Removal *(1982).*

Though the Indians are acknowledged to have an unquestionable, and heretofore unquestioned, right to the lands they occupy, until that right shall be extinguished by a voluntary cession to our govern-

ment; yet it may well be doubted, whether those tribes which reside within the acknowledged boundaries of the United States can, with strict accuracy, be denominated foreign nations. They may, more correctly, perhaps, be denominated domestic dependent nations. They occupy a territory to which we assert a title independent of their will, which must take effect in point of possession, when their right of possession ceases. Meanwhile, they are in a state of pupilage; their relation to the United States resembles that of a ward to his guardian. They look to our government for protection; rely upon its kindness and its power; appeal to it for relief to their wants; and address the President as their great father . . .

Supreme Court, decision in Cherokee Nation v. Georgia, *1831, in Schmeckebier's* The Office of Indian Affairs *(1927).*

You asked, "Who I am"—I am a Sauk; my fathers were great men, & I wish to remain where the bones of my fathers are laid. I desire to be buried with my fathers. Why then should I leave their fields?

Black Hawk, to General Edmund P. Gaines and Governor John Reynolds of Illinois, speech of June 1831, in Whitney's The Black Hawk War *(1970).*

The familiar note of preparation, "Catch up! catch up!" was now sounded from the captain's camp, and re-echoed from every division and scattered group along the valley. On such occasions, a scene of confusion ensues, which must be seen to be appreciated. The woods and dales resound with the gleeful yells of the light-hearted wagoners, who, weary of inaction, and filled with joy at the prospect of getting under way, become clamorous in the extreme. Scarcely does the jockey on the race-course ply his whip more promptly at that magic word 'Go,' than do these emulous wagoners fly to harnessing their mules at the spirit-stirring sound of 'Catch up.' Each teamster vies with his fellow who shall be soonest ready; and it is a matter of boastful pride to be the first to cry out—"All's set!"

Josiah Gregg, Santa Fe trader, on setting out for Santa Fe from Council Grove, Missouri, May 27, 1831, in Commerce of the Prairies *(1966).*

. . . he [Chief Keokuk] wished that the General would not apply force to the Black Hawk band, until he [Keokuk] could get all his friends & relations across the Mississippi. But as they had planted corn at Rock River, it was now too late in the season to prepare new fields to plant more they would suffer from want of food.

General Edmund P. Gaines, memorandum of talks with Sauk chieftain Keokuk, June 1831, in Whitney's The Black Hawk War.

The principles which have uniformly governed me since I began colonizing in this country in 1821 are so different from those which appear to have influenced others who have attempted colonization in Texas that neither this colony, nor myself ought to be confounded with the others—My object, the sole and only desire of my ambition since I first saw Texas, was to redeem it from the wilderness—to settle it with an intelligent honorable and interprising people. To make a fortune, a great pecuniary speculation for myself, was and always has been and now is, a secondary consideration with me, When I left my native Govt. and became a citizen of this I consider[d] that all and every kind of political obligation ceased as to the first, and became fully as binding as to the second, as if this had been my native country.

Stephen F. Austin, to Thomas E. Leaning, a Philadelphia relative, letter of July 23, 1831, in The Austin Papers (1924).

It is not uncommon for ladies to mount their mustangs and hunt with their husbands, and with them to camp out for days on their excursions to the sea shore for fish and oysters. All visiting is done on horseback, and they will go fifty miles to a ball with their silk dresses, made perhaps in Philadelphia or New Orleans, in their saddlebags.

Mary Austin Holley, Texas settler, 1830s, in Texas: Observations, Historical, Geographical and Descriptive (1836).

Each man and each youth, over 14 years of age, will receive 200 acres of land. Each unmarried female, over 14 years, will likewise receive 200 acres. Every individual above that age, will be required to pay $50, for which sum he will be carried to Oregon, and receive a right to 200 acres of land. Children will pay a less sum, and receive no land. Emigrants will furnish their own bedding and small stores. Other freight will be taken in vessels round Cape Horn, at $2 a barrel. Farmers and mechanics will carry their tools, and such materials as they may immediately

want. As small a quantity of baggage as possible must be carried by the overland expedition.

Circular, to "All Concerned in the Oregon Expedition," 1831, in Hulbert's The Call of the Columbia (1934).

The Blackfeet Indians have this year, for the first time, made their appearance in great force on the trace.

To insure the safety of the caravans, it is the custom of the traders, on reaching the rendezvous on the western boundary of Missouri, to elect a caravan bachi [captain], and other officers, who are invested with such authority as may be voluntarily conceded from day to day, or such as they may have the address to enforce. This is greater or less, as the dangers increase or diminish. When on the march, as night approached, the wagons are thrown into a square, and made to resemble, with much aid of the imagination, a camp fortified by Roman legions. Guards are always set, and these watch or sleep, as their interest or love of repose may predominate.

Alphonso Wetmore, courier on the Santa Fe Trail, to Secretary of War Lewis Cass, letter of October 11, 1831, in Hulbert's Southwest on the Turquoise Trail (1933).

The place where it is now contemplated to establish a colony, is at the junction of the Multnomah river with the Columbia. The point of land on which it is proposed to build the city, has the Columbia river on the north, and the Multnomah on the west and south. It is represented as a pleasant, healthy and fertile situation. It is 85 miles from the mouth of the Columbia river.

Hall Jackson Kelley, in "A General Circular to All . . . who wish to Emigrate to the Oregon Territory," 1831, in Hulbert's The Call of the Columbia (1934).

We arrived at a town or settlement called *Independence.* This is the last white settlement on our route to the Oregon, and this circumstance gave a different cast to our peregrination, and operated not a little on our hopes, and our fears, and our imaginations. Some of our company began to ask each other some serious question; such as, Where are we going? and what are we going for? and sundry other questions, which would have been wiser had we asked them before we left Cambridge, and ruminated well on the answers. But *Westward ho!* was our watchword, and checked all doubts, and silenced all expressions of fear.

John B. Wyeth, brother of Nathaniel J. Wyeth, April 1832, in Oregon; or a Short History from the Atlantic Ocean to the Region of the Pacific *(1833).*

I am sorry to learn that you have taken your Band across the Mississippi and carried them up on Rock river contrary to the treaty you made last year with General Gaines & Governor Reynolds. Your great father will be angry with you for doing so. I advise you to come back and recross the Mississippi without delay. It is not too late to do what is right—and what is right do at once. If you do not come back and go on the other side of the great river I shall write to your great father & tell him of your bad conduct. You will be sorry if you do not come back.

Some foolish people have told you that the British will assist you—do not believe it—you will find when it is too late that it is not true.

General Henry Atkinson, to Chief Black Hawk, message of April 24, 1832, in Whitney's The Black Hawk War.

. . . the Sacs are on Rock River about 30 miles above Ogee's ferry, in a state of Starvation and are anxious to recross the Mississippi but dare not descend Rock River for fear of being intercepted by the Militia & indiscriminately slaughtered without affording them an opportunity of explaining the cause of their recent movements. They aver most positively to the Potowatimies that they have no design of committing any wrong whatever towards the people of their great Father.

Thomas Owen, U.S. Indian agent, to John Reynolds, governor of Illinois, on the desperate situation of Black Hawk and his followers, report of May 12, 1832, in Whitney's The Black Hawk War.

We accordingly met, Captain Wyeth in the chair, or on the stump, I forget which. Instead of every man speaking his own mind, or asking such questions as related to matters that lay heaviest on his mind, the Captain commenced the business by ordering the roll to be called; and as the names were called, the clerk asked the person if he would go on. The first name was Nathaniel J. Wyeth, whom we had dubbed *Captain*, who answered—"I shall go on."— The next was William Nud, who, before he answered, wished to know what the Captain's plan

and intentions were, whether to try to commence a small colony, or to trap and trade for beaver? To which Captain Wyeth replied, that *that* was none of our business. Then Mr. Nud said, "I shall not go on;" and as the names of the rest were called, there appeared *seven* persons out of the *twenty-one*, who were determined to return home. Of the number so determined was, besides myself, Dr. Jacob Wyeth, the captain's brother, whose strength had never been equal to such a journey.

John B. Wyeth, in present-day Idaho, July 1832, in Oregon; or A Short History from the Atlantic Ocean to the Region of the Pacific.

On the 8th of July we reached Pierre's Hole, at the head of Lewis River, a rendezvous for trappers and Indians. We remained at this place until the 17th, at which time my party had been reduced by desertion and dismissal to 11 men. We then started for the Columbia, arriving at Cape Disappointment on November 8, 1832, one man having died on the route. There I learned that the vessel on which I relied for supplies had been wrecked at the Society Islands. This intelligence discouraged the party so much that all but two requested their discharge. Of the eight who left me, five returned to the United States by sea, one died near the mouth of the Columbia in 1834 and two remained as settlers.

Captain Nathaniel J. Wyeth, to J.G. Palfrey, letter of December 13, 1847, in The Correspondence and Journals of Captain Nathaniel J. Wyeth, 1831–6. *(1899).*

Came in sight of the Black hills and crossed Larrimee fork of the Platte in getting over one of my rafts broke the tow line the raft went down stream lodged on a snag and upset wetting most of the goods on it and loosing two Horse loads as it lodged in the middle of the river and the stream [being] very rappid the goods were with difficulty passed ashore here an alarm was occasioned by the appearance of 4 men on the bluf[f]s behind us and an attack was expected every moment which would have been bad as our party was much scattered in crossing They However proved to be a part of a party of 19 men in the employ of Gant & Blackwell. They last winter lost all but 3 of their animals and in going to Sante Fee got enclosed by snow in the mountains and nearly starved to Death, and at first they were hard to tell from Indians or devils   they are now in good health having felt well for some time   all of them joined Mr. Fitzpatricks party and proceeded on foot with us to the mountains.

Nathaniel J. Wyeth, journal entry of June 13, 1832, in The Correspondence and Journals of Captain Nathaniel J. Wyeth, 1831–6.

Started about 9 and after about 6 miles passed the grand falls of the Columbia just above which a small river puts into the Columbia about the size of the small rivers above the Wallah [Waiiah] for instance   these falls now the water is low are about 25 feet   when the water is high these falls are covered   the water not having a sufficient vent below   the water here rises about 40 feet   just before arriving at the falls are considerable rapids   the falls are easily passed in boats at high water   we hired the Indians about 50 for a quid of tobacco each to carry our boat about 1 mile round the falls   the goods we carried ourselves   shortly after passing the falls we passed what are called the dalles (small) or where the river is dam[m]ed up between banks steep and high of not more than 100 feet apart through which the whole waters of the mighty Columbia are forced with much noise and uproar . . .

Nathaniel J. Wyeth, journal entry of October 23, 1832, in The Correspondence and Journals of Captain Nathaniel J. Wyeth, 1831–6.

Started at 10 ock and arrived at the fort of Vancouver at 12, 4 miles   Here I was received with the utmost kindness and Hospitality by Doct. McLauchland [McLoughlin] the acting Gov. of the place   Mr McDonald Mr Allen and Mr Mckay gentlemen resident here   Our people were supplied with food and shelter from the rain which is constant   they raise at this fort 6000 bush. of wheat 3 of Barley 1500 potatoes 3000 peas a large quantity of punkins   they have coming on apple trees, peach Do. and grapes. Sheep, Hogs, Horses, Cows, 600 goats, grist 2, saw mill 2. 24 lb guns powder magazine of stone   the fort is of wood and square   they are building a Sch. of 70 Tons   there are about 8 settlers on the Multnomah   they are the old engages of the Co. who have done trapping.

Nathaniel J. Wyeth, journal entry of October 29, 1832, in The Correspondence and Journals of Captain Nathaniel J. Wyeth, 1831–6.

A party of whites, being in advance of the army, came upon our people, who were attempting to cross the Mississippi. They tried to give themselves up—the whites paid no attention to their entreaties—but commenced *slaughtering* them! In a little while the whole army arrived. Our braves, but few in number, finding that the enemy paid no regard to age or sex, and seeing that they were murdering helpless women and little children, determined to *fight until they were killed.* As many women as could, commenced swimming the Mississippi, with their children on their backs. A number of them were drowned, and some shot, before they could reach the opposite shore.

Black Hawk, recalling the final battle of the Black Hawk War at Bad Axe River in present-day Wisconsin, August 2, 1832, in the Autobiography of Ma-ka-tai-me-she-kia-kiak, or, Black Hawk.

He is now a prisoner to the white man, but he can stand the torture. He is not afraid of death. He is no coward—Black Hawk is an Indian. He has done nothing of which an Indian need be ashamed. He has fought the battles of his country against the white man, who came year after year to cheat his people and take away their lands. You know the cause of our making war. It is know to all white men. They ought to be ashamed of it. The white men despise the Indians and drive them from their homes. But the Indians are not deceitful. Indians do not steal. Black Hawk is satisfied. He will go to the world of spirits contented. He has done his duty. His Father will meet and reward him. The white men do not scalp the heads, but they do worse—they poison the heart. It is not pure with them. His countrymen will not be scalped, but they will in a few years become like the white man, so that you cannot hurt them; and there must be, as in the white settlements, as many officers as men, to take care of them and keep them in order. Farewell to my nation! Farewell to Black Hawk!

Black Hawk, to General Joseph M. Street, speech of surrender, August 1832, in A.R. Fulton's The Red Men of Iowa *(1882).*

The peculiarities . . . of character, which may be said to distinguish the population of the West, are all created by the peculiar circumstances in which the people have been placed in that new world. They are,

1. A *spirit of adventurous enterprise:* a willingness to go through any hardship or danger to accomplish an object. It was the spirit of enterprise which led to the

settlement of that country. The western people think nothing of making a long journey, of encountering fatigue, and of enduring every species of hardship. The great highways of the west—its long rivers—are familiar to very many of them, who have been led by trade to visit remote parts of the valley.

2. *Independence of thought and action.*—They have felt the influence of this principle from their childhood. Men who can endure any thing: that have lived almost without restraint, free as the mountain air, or as the deer and the buffalo of their forests—and who know that they are Americans all—will act out this principle during the whole of life. I do not mean that they have such an amount of it as to render them *really* regardless alike of the opinions and the feelings of everyone else. But I have seen many who have the virtue of independence greatly perverted or degenerated . . .

3. *An apparent roughness,* which some would deem *rudeness of manners.*

Reverend Robert Baird, 1832, in View of the Valley of the Mississippi: or the Emigrant's and Traveller's Guide to the West *(1832).*

The occupancy of this valuable region by a few thousand of the hardy and enterprising sons of American freedom, would secure to our government one of the most valuable tracts of land in the world, and prevent its augmenting the power and physical resources of an enemy. It might save that and this country from the disastrous consequences of a foreign and corrupt population, and benefit the nation and mankind, by a race of people, bold, free, intelligent, and virtuous. Unless this country is soon occupied by some of our own people, there is every reason to believe that some other nation will avail itself of the advantages which it offers.

Hall Jackson Kelly, to members of Congress, on the settlement of the Oregon country, letter of September 21, 1832, in Hulbert's The Call of the Columbia.

That a party of young, brave, hardy men may cross the continent to the mouth of the Columbia, we know; but that a large body of the inhabitants of New-England, wholly unacquainted with Indian life, and encumbered with baggage and their families, can do so, we hold impossible. We think we have proved that it is so. Our facts cannot be disputed, and the inference is as clear as a geometrical dem-

onstration. We do not know that the prime mover of the folly we have exposed is actuated by any evil motive; we do not believe it. We look upon him as an unfortunate man, who, deluded himself, is deluding others, and conceive it our duty to warn those who are about to follow him on the road to ruin. To conclude, we advise those who have been so unfortunate as to embark in this enterprise to erase their names from the list as soon as possible.

William Joseph Snelling, criticizing Hall Jackson Kelly in New-England Magazine, *February 1832.*

To effect the settlement, a communication by land would be indispensable; a chain of military posts must be extended from St. Louis to Columbia river; a strong fortification must be erected at some convenient place on the river; and a respectable naval force must be maintained there for the security of the settlement. It would become a source of great and increasing expense, incomparably greater than the amount of revenue derived from our trade in that ocean, and probably greater than the profits of the trade to the country. It is not reasonable to suppose all this can be effected without alarming the fears and exciting the jealousy of the Indian nations on both sides of the Rocky Mountains, and without encountering the risk of an Indian war, and endangering the quiet and safety of our frontier settlements, as well as the settlement at Columbia river.

Congressman Silas Woods, to Congress, speech of 1832, in Hulbert's Where Rolls Oregon.

I am in possession of some information, that will doubtless be interesting to you; and may be calculated to forward your views if you should entertain any; touching the acquisition of Texas, by the Government of the United States. That such a measure is desirable by nineteen twentieths of the population of the Province, I can not doubt. They are now without laws to govern or protect them. Mexico is involved in civil war. The Federal Constitution has never been in operation. The Government is essentially despotic and must be so, for years to come. The rulers have not honesty, and the people have not *intelligence.* The people of Texas are determined to form a State Government, and separate from Coahuila, and unless Mexico is soon restored to order, and the Constitution revived and re-enacted, the

Province of Texas will remain separate from the confederacy of Mexico.

General Sam Houston, to President Andrew Jackson, reporting on his visit to Texas, letter of February 13, 1833, in The Writings of Sam Houston *(1938-43).*

We are told that the President looks with great anxiety and solicitation to our situation; that he knows our position is an embarrassing one, and that a change is called for by every consideration of present convenience and future security; and that the Government is desirous of entering into a satisfactory arrangement, by which all our difficulties will be terminated, and the prosperity of our people fixed upon a permanent basis. Yet we are assured that you are well convinced that these objects *can only be attained by a cession of our possessory rights* in Georgia, and by *our removal* to the country west of the Mississippi; that you can see no cause of apprehension, as we do, that such removal will be injurious, either in its immediate or remote consequences.

John Ross, Cherokee chief, to Secretary of War Lewis Cass, letter of February 14, 1833, in U.S. Senate's *Document 512, Correspondence on Removal of Indians West of the Mississippi River, 1831–1833 (1833).*

It appeared that some white man had penetrated into their country, and happened to be a spectator at one of their religious ceremonies, which they scrupulously perform at stated periods. He informed them that their mode of worshipping the supreme Being was radically wrong, and instead of being acceptable and pleasing, it was displeasing to him; he also informed them that the white people *away* toward the rising of the sun had been put in possession of the true mode of worshipping the great Spirit. They had a book containing directions how to conduct themselves in order to enjoy his favor and hold converse with him; and with this guide, no one need go astray, but every one that would follow the directions laid down there, could enjoy, in this life, his favor, and after death would be received into the country where the great Spirit resides, and live for ever with him.

William Walker, Indian trader, to G.P. Disosway, Indian agent, reporting the arrival of Indians from the Oregon country in St. Louis, letter of March 1833, in Hulbert's The Oregon Crusade *(1935).*

The subject of canals and railroads awakens at this moment the keenest interest in Michigan; and, after the route of the projected grand communication between Lakes Erie and Michigan, through the peninsula, shall be determined upon by the general government, I have no doubt but that large and advantageous outlays of private capital upon similar works will be made at other points. Of the plans talked of as best worthy the attention of government, that of a grand railroad from Chicago to Detroit, with a lateral one perhaps to Monroe, seems to be considered as the least chimerical; though there are not a few who advocate a canal immediately across the peninsula, in a direct line from the mouth of the Maumee to Lake Michigan . . .

Charles Fenno Hoffman, newspaper correspondent, December 3, 1833, in Hoffman's A Winter in the West *(1966).*

I have been accused of having magnificent schemes for Texas, and I confess that I have had them . . . It is depopulated; I wish to people it. The population that is there is backward; I wish it to be advanced and improved by the introduction of industrious farmers, liberal republicans. I want the savage Indians subdued, the frontier protected, the lands cultivated, roads and canals opened, river navigation developed and the rivers covered with boats and barges carrying the produce of the interior to the coast for export in exchange for foreign products.

Stephen F. Austin, to Rafael Llanos, Nuevo Leon senator and friend, on his arrest by the Mexican government, letter of January 14, 1834, in The Austin Papers.

We have made arrangements to cross the mountains with Capt. W[yeth], whose company will consist of about fifty. He expects to leave Liberty (which is about one hundred miles above St. Louis) in April. From St. Louis to the Flat Head country is about one thousand five hundred miles; thence to the Pacific nine hundred miles. This journey is to be performed on horseback, at the rate say of twenty miles per day. And when this journey, from the shores of the Atlantic to the shores of the Pacific, is accomplished, the most laborious part of our work is yet before us. It will still remain for us to transport our outfit nine hundred miles up the river to the place of destination.

Our dependence for subsistence is almost exclusively upon the rifle, as it is impossible to carry provisions for such a journey on horseback. You will hear from me again soon. "Brethren, pray for us."

Jason Lee, missionary, in The Christian Advocate, *February 21, 1834.*

Mr. Wm. Sublette is building a trading fort at Laramies Fork, on the Platte, about thirty days' march from Independence, Mo. Here I think is a very favorable location for a missionary establishment.— Mr. Sublette mentioned it to me, of his own accord, as a favorable place. The Sous Indians, which are a powerful and numerous tribe, range along near this place, and will in future, no doubt, often frequent his place, as well as many other tribes. A party will pass up from the settlements yearly, connected with the fort, and many others on their way to the Rocky Mountains. I hope you will investigate this subject; and perhaps your board may see fit to establish a mission there immediately.

Jason Lee, missionary, to The Christian Advocate *(September 26, 1834), letter of July 1, 1834, in Hulbert's* The Oregon Crusade.

Much of this vast waste of territory belongs to the Republic of the United States. What a theme to contemplate its settlement and civilization. Will the jurisdiction of the federal government ever succeed in civilizing the thousands of savages now roaming over these plains and her hardy freeborn population here plant their homes, build their towns and cities, and say here shall the arts and sciences of civilization take root and flourish? Yes, here, even in this remote part of the great West before many years will these hills and valleys be greeted with the enlivening sound, of the workman's hammer, and the merry whistle of the ploughboy. But this is left undone by the government, and will only be seen when too late to apply the remedy. The Spaniards are making inroads on the south—the Russians are encroaching with impunity along the seashore to the north, and further northeast the British are pushing their stations into the very heart of our territory, which even at this day, more resemble military forts to resist invasion than trading stations. Our government should be vigilant. She should assert her claim by taking pos-

session of the whole territory as soon as possible— for we have good reason to suppose that the territory *west* of the mountain will some day be equally as important to a nation as that on the east.

Zenas Leonard, clerk on Joseph Reddeford's expedition across the Rocky Mountains, looking north from San Francisco Bay, 1834, in Narrative, Adventures of Zenas Leonard: Fur Trader and Trapper *(1904).*

This evening we are encamped on the banks of the aforesaid fork. Tis here that Mr S. [Sublette] designes erecting a smaller fort. In a day or two he will recommence his march to the rocky mountains with such of his men as he does not leave for the erection of the fort. The Black Hills are around us. They are spurs of the R.M. [Rocky Mountains].

William Marshall Anderson, on establishing the first permanent trading post in present-day Wyoming, journal entry of May 30, 1834, in The Rocky Mountain Journals of William Marshall Anderson *(1967).*

This is the Best country I ever saw for a Poor man or a rich one, an Industrious man or a Lazy one.—I see no kind of business but looks Promising, and I believe the country is perfectly Healthy. I do not Know nor see what can make it otherwise. The Place I mention above has but one disadvantage. It is 28 miles to Chicago, and 40 miles to Ottawa. The Proposed Canal will run from Chicago to Ottawa, the head water of the Illinois, and the place lays about 8 or 9 miles from the rout of the Canal. It has the advantage of Grist Mills & Saw Mills, with half a mile also a Store and tavern, and a thick Settled neighborhood.

Morris Sleight, Illinois settler from Hyde Park, New York, to Hannah Sleight, his wife, letter of July 9, 1834, in Angle's Prairie State, Impressions of Illinois *(1968).*

Our journey, to-day, has been particularly laborious. We were engaged for several hours, constantly in ascending and descending enormous rocky hills, with scarcely the sign of a valley between them; and some of them so steep, that our horses were frequently in great danger of falling, by making a misstep on the loose, rolling stones. I thought the Black

Hills, on the Platte, rugged and difficult of passage, but they sink into insignificance when compared with these.

John Townsend, Philadelphia physician and naturalist, August 7, 1834, in present-day Custer County, Idaho, between the Sawtooth and Lost River ranges, in A Narrative of a Journey Across the Rocky Mountains to the Columbia River *(1839).*

We are so completely overrun by emigrants or movers with carriages, wagons, cattle horses, dogs and sheep that we are compelled to speak. Our streets are a moving mass of living men, women, children and everything joyously wending their way to their new habitations.

The Cincinnati Mirror, *September 6, 1834.*

We have passed for months through a country swarming with Indians who thirsted for our blood, and whose greatest pride and glory consisted in securing the scalp of a white man. Enemies, sworn, determined enemies to all, both white and red, who intrude upon his hunting grounds, the Blackfoot roams the prairie like a wolf seeking his prey, and springing upon it when unprepared, and at the moment when it supposes itself most secure. To those who have always enjoyed the comforts and security of civilized life, it may seem strange that persons who know themselves to be constantly exposed to such dangers—who never lie down at night without the weapons of death firmly grasped in their hands, and who are in hourly expectation of hearing the terrific war whoop of the savage, should yet sleep soundly and refreshingly, and feel themselves at ease; such however is the fact.

John Townsend, after passing the Cascades on the Columbia River, September 15, 1834, in A Narrative of a Journey Across the Rocky Mountains, to the Columbia River.

The Cherokees are nearly all prisoners. They have been dragged from their houses, and encamped at the forts and military posts, all over the nation. In Georgia, especially, multitudes were allowed no time to take anything with them, except the clothes they had on. Well-furnished houses were left a prey to plunderers, who, like hungry wolves, follow in the train of the captors. These wretches rifle the houses, and strip the helpless, unoffending owners of all they have on earth. Females, who have been habit-

uated to comforts and comparative affluence, are driven on foot before the bayonets of brutal men.

Evan Jones, missionary, June 16, 1835, on the "Trail of Tears," in Schmeckebier's The Office of Indian Affairs.

Our people yet abhor the idea of leaving all that is dear to them—the graves of their relatives; but circumstances have changed their opinions; they have become convinced of their true situation; that they cannot live in the same field with the white man. Our people have done that which we did not believe they would have done at the time we made the treaty; they have sold their reservations—it is done and cannot now be helped; the white man has taken possession, and has every advantage over us; it is impossible for the red and white man to live together.

Opothleyoholo, Creek chieftain, 1835, in Green's The Politics of Indian Removal.

The American Fur Company have between two and three hundred men constantly in and about the mountains, engaged in trading, hunting and trapping. These all assemble at rendezvous upon the arrival of the caravan, bring in their furs, and take new supplies for the coming year, of clothing, ammunition, and goods for trade with the Indians. But few of these men ever return to their country and friends. Most of them are constantly in debt to the company, and are unwilling to return without a fortune; and year after year passes away, while they are hoping in vain for better success.

Reverend Samual Parker, describing the activities of the mountain men at Green River, in present-day Wyoming, 1835, in Journal of an Exploring Tour Beyond the Rocky Mountains *(1842).*

I hope to see Texas forever free from Mexican domination of any kind. It is yet too soon to say this publicly, but that is the point we shall end at—and it is the one I am aiming at. But we must arrive at it by steps and not all at one jump.

Stephen F. Austin, to David B. Burnett, chairman of the Committee for Texas independence, letter of October 5, 1835, in The Austin Papers.

Fellow-Citizens and Compatriots: I am besieged by a thousand or more of the Mexicans under Santa Anna. I have sustained a continued bombardment for twenty-four hours, and have not lost a man. The

The fall of the Alamo. Woodcut from Davy Crockett's Almanack, 1837. *Courtesy of the Library of Congress.*

enemy have demanded a surrender at discretion; otherwise the garrison is to be put to the sword, if the place is taken. I have answered the summons with cannon shot, and our flag still waves proudly from the walls. I shall never surrender nor retreat! Then I call on you, in the name of liberty, of patriotism, and of everything dear to American character, to come to our aid with all dispatch. The enemy are receiving re-inforcements daily, and will no doubt increase to three or four thousand in four or five days. Though this call may be neglected, I am determined to sustain myself as long as possible, and die like a soldier who never forgets what is due to his own honor or that of his country. Victory or death!

Lieutenant Colonel William B. Travis, Texas militia, on defending the Alamo, dispatch of February 24, 1836, in Brown's History of Texas *(1892).*

Your country demands your aid. The enemy is pressing upon us. families, the wives and children of your neighbours, are driven from their firesides, and compelled to take shelter in woods and forests, while the enemy gathers confidence and audacity from every disaster we encounter. Under these painful circumstances, equally reproachful to our national character, and dangerous to our national existence, too many citizens are lingering in idleness and lethargy at home or ingloriously flying before an enemy, whom we have heretofore affected to dispise. Is it possible that the free citizens of Texas, the descendants of the heroes of 76 can take panic at the approach of the paltry minions of a despot, who threatens to desolate our beautiful country? Let us rather "rush to the rescue" Let every man able to poise a rifle or wield a sabre *fly to the army*, and soon, very soon your families will be safe. Our country cleansed from the pollution of every hostile fort, and the "bond of promise" will smile benignantly over the land. Fellow citizens! The Blood of the martyrs of freedom, the heroes of the "Alamo" call aloud for vengeance.

President David G. Burnet, Republic of Texas, to the citizens of Texas, March 29, 1836, in Brinkley's Official Correspondence of the Texas Revolution *(1936).*

This morning we are in preparation to meet Santa Anna. It is the only chance of saving Texas. From time to time I have looked for reinforcements in vain. The Convention's adjourning to Harrisburg struck terror through the country. Texas could have started at least four thousand men. We will be only about seven hundred to march, besides the camp guard.

But we go to conquest. It is wisdom growing out of necessity to meet and fight the enemy now. Every consideration enforces it. The troops are in fine spirits, and now is the time for action. We will use our best efforts to fight the enemy to such advantage as will insure victory, though the odds are greatly against us. I leave the result in the hands of an all-wise God, and I rely confidently upon His providence. My country will do justice to those who serve her. The right for which we fight will be secured, and Texas shall be free.

Sam Houston, to Colonel Rusk, letter of April 19, 1836, in Crane's Life and Select Literary Remains of Sam Houston of Texas *(1972).*

A young man by the name of Robbins dropped his gun in the confusion of the battle, and happening to run directly with a Mexican soldier, who had also lost his musket, the Mexican seized Robbins, and both being stout men, rolled to the ground. But Robbins drew out his bowie-knife and ended the contest by cutting the Mexican's throat. On starting out from our camp to enter upon the attack, I saw an old man, by the name of Curtis, carrying two guns. I asked him what reason he had for carrying more than one gun. He answered, 'Damn the Mexicans; they killed my son and son-in-law in the Alamo, and I intend to kill two of them for it or be killed myself.' I saw the old man again during the fight, and he told me that he had killed his two men, and if he could find Santa Anna himself he would cut out a razor-strop from his back . . .

General Rusk, report of the battle of San Jacinto, April 1836, in Crane's Life and Select Literary Remains of Sam Houston of Texas.

He [Santa Anna] asked me if Gen. Houston commanded in person at the battle; how many we killed, and how many prisoners we had taken, and when they would be shot? I told him I did not think they would be shot; that I had never known Americans to kill prisoners of war.

Colonel Joel W. Robison, Texas militia, recalling the capture of Santa Anna, April 21, 1836, in Carne's Life and Select Literary Remains of Sam Houston of Texas.

Art. 1st.　He will not take up arms, nor cause them to be taken up, against the people of Texas, during the present war for Independence.

Art. 2nd.　He will give his orders that in the shortest time the Mexican troops may leave the territory of Texas.

Art 3rd.　He will so prepare things in the cabinet of Mexico, that the mission that may be sent thither by the government of Texas may be well received, and that by means of negotiations all differences may be settled and the independence that has been declared by the convention may be acknowledged.

Secret treaty of May 14, 1836, between the Republic of Texas and General Antonio Lopez de Santa Anna of Mexico, in Brown's History of Texas.

My Friends: I have been a witness of your courage on the field of battle, and know you to be generous. Rely with confidence on my sincerity, and you shall never have cause to regret the kindness shown me. In returning to my native land, I beg you to receive the sincere thanks of your grateful friend Farewell.

General Antonio Lopez de Santa Anna, to Texan soldiers, farewell address of June 1, 1836, in Crane's Life and Select Literary Remains of Sam Houston of Texas.

A spot of earth almost unknown to the geography of the age, destitute of all available resources, few in numbers, we remonstrated against oppression, and, when invaded by a numerous host, we dared to proclaim our independence and to strike for freedom on the breast of the oppressor. As yet our course is onward. We are only in the outset of the campaign of liberty.

President Sam Houston, Republic of Texas, to the Texas Congress, after taking oath of office, address of October 22, 1836, in Crane's Life and Select Literary Remains of Sam Houston of Texas.

Here and there, and frequently too, we encountered a solitary broken-down waggon, full of some new settler's goods. It was a pitiful sight to see one of these vehicles deep in the mire; the axletree broken; the wheel lying idly by its side; the man gone miles away, to look for assistance; the woman seated among their wandering household goods with a baby at her breast, a picture of forlorn, dejected patience; the team of oxen crouching down mournfully in the mud, and breathing forth such clouds of vapour from their mouths and nostrils, that all the damp mist and fog around seemed to have come direct from them.

Charles Dickens, English author, 1830s, in
American Notes for General Circulation
(1842).

Already, in fact, the white race is advancing through the forests which surround it, and in a few years the Europeans will have cut the trees which reflect in the limpid waters of the lake, and will have forced the animals which populate its banks to retreat toward new wilds.

*Alexis de Tocqueville, on advancing settlement
in the Michigan Territory, 1830s, in Buley's*
The Old Northwest: Pioneer Period.

I never saw insulation, (not desolation,) to compare with the situation of a settler on a wide prairie. A single house in the middle of Salisbury Plain would be desolate. A single house on a prairie has clumps of trees near it, rich fields about it; and flowers, strawberries, and running water at hand. But when I saw a settler's child tripping out of home-bounds, I had a feeling that it would never get back again. It looked like putting out into Lake Michigan in a canoe.

*Harriet Martineau, English author, describing
the Illinois prairies, 1836, in* Society in America *(1837).*

Theirs is a life of strangely blended success and reverses. To-day in abject poverty; to-morrow rolling in wealth; the day after, as poor as ever; according to the success or failure of their speculations; but still, as a nation, their prosperity is gradually, but most certainly increasing. As a soldier, the motto of a western man is "to conquer or die;" but conquering with him, means to make money; to build up a fortune from nothing, to buy lots at Chicago, Cleveland, or at St. Louis, and to sell them the next year at the rate of a thousand *per cent.*

*Michael Chevalier, observing advancing settlers
in the Old Northwest, 1830s, in* Letters on
America *(1835).*

We are really a moving village—nearly four hundred animals with ours, mostly mules and seventy men. The Fur Com. has seven wagons and one cart, drawn by six mules each, heavily loaded; the cart drawn by two mules carries a lame man, one of the proprieters

of the Com. We have two waggons in our com[pany.] Mr. & Mrs. S. and Husband and myself ride in one, Mr. Gray and the baggage in the other. Our Indian boys drive the cows and Dulin the horses. Young Miles leads our forward horses, four in each team. Now E. if you wish to see the camp in motion, look away ahead and see first the pilot and the Captain Fitzpatrick, just before him—next the pack animals, all mules loaded with great packs—soon after you will see the waggons and in the rear our company. We all cover quite a space. The pack mules always string along one after the other just like Indians.

*Narcissa Prentiss Whitman, missionary, to sis-
ter Harriet and brother Edward Prentiss, at the
Platte River, letter of June 3, 1836, in Drury's*
First White Women Over the Rockies
(1963).

Crossed a ridge of land today; called the divide, which separates the waters that flow into the Atlantic from those that flow into the Pacific, and camped for the night on the head waters of the Colorado. A number of Nez Perces, who have been waiting our arrival at the Rendezvous several days, on hearing we were near came out to meet us, and have camped with us to night. They appear to be gratified to see us actually on our way to their country.

*Eliza Hart Spalding, missionary, diary entry of
July 4, 1836, in Drury's* First White Women
Over the Rockies.

Husband has had a tedious time with the wagon to-day. It got stuck in the creek this morning when crossing, and he was obliged to wade considerably in getting it out. After that, in going between the mountains, on the side of one, so steep that it was difficult for horses to pass, the wagon was upset twice; did not wonder at this at all; it was a greater wonder that it was not turning somersaults continually. It is not very grateful to my feelings to see him wearing out with such excessive fatigue, as I am obliged to. He is not as fleshy as he was last winter. All the most difficult part of the way he has walked, in laborious attempts to take the wagon. Ma knows what my feelings are.

*Narcissa Prentiss Whitman, at the junction of
Smith's Fork and the Bear, on the present-day
Idaho-Wyoming boundry, journal entry of July
18, 1836, in Drury's* First White Women
Over the Rockies.

We are now in Vancouver. The New York of the Pacific Ocean.

Narcissa Prentiss Whitman, diary entry of September 12, 1836, in Drury's First White Women Over the Rockies.

Reached this place yesterday after a pleasant journey of 6 days from the time we left Fort Walla Walla (being detained 2 days by head winds)—met with the warmest expressions of friendship, & find ourselves in the midst of civilization, where the luxuries of life seem to abound. Saw many wretched natives along the river, who appeared destitute of the means of living comfortable in this life, & ignorant of the rich provision made for that which is to come. May they soon be blest with the light of the Gospel of our Lord Jesus Christ & with the means for securing a more comfortable subsistance for this life.

Eliza Hart Spalding, arriving at Fort Vancouver, diary entry of September 14, 1836, in Drury's First White Women Over the Rockies.

Our country found itself invaded not by an established nation that came to vindicate its rights, whether true or imaginery; nor by Mexicans who, in a paroxysm of political passion, came to defend or combat the public administration of the country. The invaders were all men who, moved by the desire of conquest, with rights less apparent and plausible than those of Cortés and Pizarro, wished to take possession of that vast territory extending from Béxar to the Sabine belonging to Mexico. What can we call them? How should they be treated? All the existing laws, whose strict observance the government had just recommended, marked them as pirates and outlaws. The nations of the world would never have forgiven Mexico had it accorded them rights, privileges, and considerations which the common law of peoples accords only to constituted nations.

General Antonio Lopez de Santa Anna, to ''His Fellow Citizens,'' 1837, in Cortes' The Mexican Side of the Texas Revolution *(1976).*

The possession of land is the aim of all action, generally speaking, and the cure for all social ills, among men in the United States. If a man is disappointed by politics or love, he goes and buys land. If he disgraces himself, he betakes himself to a lot in the West.

Harriet Martineau, English author, 1837, in Society in America *(1837).*

Now the river is alive with flats, rafts, and steamboats. Indeed, a mighty change has occurred! The Valley of the Ohio teems with inhabitants.—Four new states with an enterprising population of, from two to three million, already exist in this Terratory.—and another, grown past boyhood within a few days, threatens to demand admittance into our Union, of next Congress. These almost increditable things are wonders indeed.—This is a land of wonders.

Rufus B. Sage, newspaper compositor and author, to Jerusha Sage, his mother, from Marietta, Ohio, letter of April 16, 1837, in His Letters and Papers *(1956).*

The traveller who passes through this most productive valley, meets continually with much calculated to excite his admiration. For miles, his course frequently meanders along the borders of some gently rolling prairie, whose surface, as far as the eye can reach, seems gemmed with flowers of all varieties, the brilliancy of whose coloring baffles all description. Again, his path, more open than before, will lead him through these beautiful *parterres* of nature, and long the banks of many a sweet stream, that winds round and round in almost innumerable convolutions, as if flowing with reluctance to pour out its treasures on the waters of the Wabash. Again, leaving this enchanting region, he journeys amid the deep solitudes of a western forest, whose silence is broken only at intervals by the bounding footstep of the deer, or the sharp crack of the rifle.

Henry L. Ellsworth, Indiana settler, describing the Wabash Valley, 1837, in Mitchell's Illinois in 1837 *(1837).*

I do believe slavery to be a sin before the sight of God and that is the reason and the only insurmountable reason why we should not annex Texas to the Union.

Congressman John Quincy Adams, to Congress, speech of January 16, 1838, in Hecht's John Quincy Adams: A Personal History of an Independent Man *(1972).*

For the horseback journey, they ought to have good strong colored clothes, a gentleman should have home-made blue cloth for his clothes, a strong stout box coat, thick boots and shoes, a cap and a broad brimmed felt hat. A lady should have a good green merino or pongee dress, and a loose calico dress to wear when she does not need her cloak. Her underclothes as well as the gentlemens should all be colored. They ought to have three changes to wear on the journey and at least four to wear in the States, and after they get here. They should have a Florence bonnet or a variegated straw. They should have a small dark bedquilt, a pr. of sheets, 4 prs of pillow cases and two pillows. Calico cases are best for the journey. A lady should have a pair of gentlemen's calf shoes, and be well-supplied with stockings and shoes.

Myra Fairbanks Eells, missionary at Waiilutpu mission in the Oregon country, to her sister, advice for western travelers, letter of October 4, 1838, in Drury's First White Women Over the Rockies.

They felt that they were bidding farewell to the hills, valleys and streams of their infancy; the more exciting hunting grounds of their advanced youth; as well as the stern and bloody battle fields, where they had contended in riper manhood, on which they had received wounds, and where many of their friends and loved relatives had fallen, covered with gore and with glory. All these they were leaving behind them to be desecrated by the plowshare of the white man. As they cast mournful glances back toward these loved scenes that were rapidly fading in the distance, tears fell from the cheek of the downcast warrior, old men trembled, matrons wept, the swarthy maiden's cheek turned pale, and sighs and half-suppressed sobs escaped from the motley groups as they passed along, some on foot, some on horseback, and others in wagons—sad as a funeral procession.

Sanford C. Cox, settler, recalling the removal of the Potawatomi Indians, 1838, in Recollections of the Early Settlement of the Wabash Valley *(1860).*

The Santa Fé caravans have generally avoided every manner of trade with the wild Indians, for fear of being treacherously dealt with during the familiar intercourse which necessarily ensues. This I am convinced is an erroneous impression; for I have always found, that savages are much less hostile to those with whom they trade, than to any other people. They are emphatically fond of traffic, and, being anxious to encourage the whites to come among them, instead of committing depredations upon those with whom they trade, they are generally ready to defend them against every enemy.

Josiah Gregg, 1839, in Commerce of the Prairies *(1844).*

All kinds of people from all nations of the world live together here like brothers and sisters; and in spite of the fact that there are no garrisons of soldiers, police, and the like, you never hear anything about theft, begging, or any noticeable ill will between neighbors. To me everybody is good, kind, and accommodating. Nobody here can take anything away from you by force; but he can do this by cunning, power of money, and forestallment. This I hope to prevent on our claims by the help of Congress and so, in time, to succeed in uniting the Norwegians who are still here.

Hans Barlien, Norwegian immigrant, to Reverend Jens Rynning, on settling in Missouri, letter of April 23, 1839, in Blegen's Land of Their Choice: The Immigrants Write Home *(1955).*

Taking into consideration the soil, the timber, the water, and the climate, Iowa territory may be considered the best part of the Mississippi valley. The Indians so consider it, as appears from the name which they gave it. For it is said that the Sioux [Sac] and Fox Indians, on beholding the exceeding beauties of this region, held up their hands, and exclaimed in an ectasy of delight and amazement, "I-O-W-A," which in the Fox language means, "this is the land."

The Buffalo Journal, March 1839, in Goodwin's The Trans-Mississippi West *(1922).*

The rapidity with which the frontier settlements are now made, the great facilities afforded to emigrants, of carrying with them all the necessaries and most of the conveniencies of life, their entire security from danger and the density and proximity of their settlements, at once, conclusively prove that the character of the people of Iowa has nothing peculiar in it but what has been derived from other and older sections of the civilized world. Almost every State in the Union and many foreign countries are contributing to its population. The States of Ohio, Pennsylvania and New York, are perhaps among the first in affording the greatest number of emigrants; while, at the same time, the Northern States, together with Virginia, Kentucky, Tennessee, &c. are also doing their part in furnishing Iowa with industrious and enterprising citizens.

Isaac Galland, Iowa Territory settler, 1840, in Iowa Emigrant *(1840).*

We passed several towns to day, as Liverpool, Havanna, Beardstown—the former a small settlement, but which its inhabitants intend to make larger, as they have already a railroad in contemplation across the Mississippi. Beardstown is a place of some importance. It is a county town, and its commerce greater than any upon the river. Mechanics of all descriptions are to be found here, as bakers, shoe makers, tailors, blacksmiths, cabinet makers, silversmiths, carpenters, joiners, coopers, painters &c, &c. There are also here steam flour mills, saw mills, breweries, distilleries, &c. A canal is projected here, to connect the Illinois with the Wabash, (which divides the state of Illinois from Indiana,) by means of the Sangamon and Vermilion forks. While passing these towns one is surprised at their rapid growth, for when Schoolcraft rowed his canoe up this river twenty years since, it was a wilderness only inhabited by Indians.

Eliza R. Steele, author, traveling along the Illinois River, 1840, in Angle's Prairie State.

The poor man at the east, with a large family, laboring, for example, upon the ungenerous soil of New England, finding that there is a country westward, where labor is dear and broad acres yielding an abundance of the necessaries of life are cheap, is induced to migrate with his household goods and all his effects, to this "land of promise," where provision may be made for his children. Houses must be built for the population. They require, as they advance, all the appliances which belong to a civilized form of society; and, to supply this demand, the mechanics in the various trades follow in his track, who are succeeded by the merchants, and he in his turn is followed by the members of the different professions, who find that the avenues to wealth and distinction at the east are more crowded than in the broad and growing region of a new country.

Anonymous settler, July 1840, in The Merchants' Magazine and Commercial Review.

Nearly every man lived on a piece of land of his own, and this was usually in eighty or one hundred and sixty acre tracts. Their stock was small, and mostly their families were large. Almost every man

was the son of a farmer in an older settlement who had come in to this to have a farm of his own, out of what his father could spare; or some man who had been a farm laborer or renter in an older place, had bought land and was opening out a home. Among such a people there were no rich, and none very poor. Most of them lived very plainly. They usually had enough to eat, though they were liable to run short a while before harvest. All that would bring money was sold to provide for taxes and such payments as only money would make; and those who had payments to make on their land were pretty sure to sell themselves bare, and were often hard put to it to maintain themselves in provisions.

William Cooper Howells, recalling pioneer life in the old Northwest, 1830s, in Recollections of Life in Ohio *(1895).*

During my tarry here, several American citizens unconnected with the mission, called on me to talk of their fatherland, and inquire as to the probability that its laws would be extended over them. The constantly repeated inquiries were, "Why are we left without protection in this part of our country's domain? Why are foreigners permitted to domineer American citizens, drive their traders from the country, and make us dependent on them for the clothes we wear, as we are their own apprenticed slaves." I could return no answer to these questions, exculpatory of this national delinquency; and therefore advised them to embody their grievances in a petition, and I forward it to Congress. They had a meeting for that purpose, and afterward put into my hand, as the result of it, a petition signed by 67 "citizens of the United States, and persons desirous of becoming such," the substance of which was a description of the country—their unprotected situation—and, in conclusion, a prayer that the Federal Government would extend over them the protection and institutions of the Republic.

Thomas J. Farnham, visiting the Willamette settlement in the Oregon country, 1840, in Travels in the Great Western Prairies, The Anahuac and Rocky Mountains, and in the Oregon Territory *(1841).*

6. Manifest Destiny: 1841–1847

The Overland Route

Before 1841, most American settlers arrived in California by sea; in the 1840s most followed the overland route. Settlers attracted to California by handbills and promoters after 1841 differed considerably from those who had arrived earlier. The overland travelers came mainly from the Mississippi Valley. They were attracted to the interior valleys rather than the coastal areas, and were interested in agriculture rather than commerce.

Prospective emigrants learned about California through books and reports written by explorers and visitors. California settlers promoted the territory by corresponding regularly with their friends in the East, and some of the letters were clearly written for publication in local newspapers. One early and permanent resident, Thomas O. Larkin, who arrived in California in 1832 and in 1843 became the United States consul, became a regular correspondent for major newspapers in Boston and New York. Larkin's letters were so remarkably practical that they became sort of a settlers' guide, with recommendations on the equipment necessary for overland travel, descriptions of California agriculture, and advice on what to do upon "arriving on the banks of the Sacramento."

The first organized migration to California originated in Platte County, on the far western frontier of Missouri. Enthusiasm had developed there because of reports of a returned California trapper, Antoine Robidoux, who described California as "a perfect paradise, a perpetual spring." The people of Platte County formed the Western Emigration Society, which disseminated information about California throughout the Mississippi Valley. In late 1840, 500 members of the society signed a pledge to meet at Sapling Grove in eastern Kansas in May 1841, and prepared for an expedition across the continent.

Several merchants and landowners of Platte County were so concerned about the number of prospective emigrants that they launched a campaign disparaging California. It proved so effective that when the designated day came in May 1841, only 69 people appeared at Sapling Grove, and of those only one had signed on the previous fall. This was John Bidwell, a 21-year-old adventurer who would command the company and later become known as the "Prince of California Pioneers."

The first overland group consisted of 54 men, five women and 10 children. They had 14 sturdy wagons and a sizable herd of horses, mules and oxen. Not one of the entire group knew which way to travel, except westward. Fortunately, during the early stages of their trip, they fell in with Thomas Fitzpatrick, the well-known trapper, who was guiding Father De Smet on his expedition to establish a mission for the Flathead Indians in Montana's Bitterroot Valley.

The party followed the route taken by fur trappers to the Platte River, Fort Laramie, Independence Rock and the Sweetwater River to the Rockies, through the South Pass, and the Green River Valley to Soda Springs near present-day Pocatello, Idaho. Fitzpatrick was unfamiliar with the Mexican province, and preferred to take the known route to the Columbia rather than the unknown trail to California. The parties separated where the north-flowing Bear River drops south toward the Great Salt Lake. Fitzpatrick and De Smet followed the trail toward Oregon with 32 emigrants, while John Bidwell led the others, including one woman and her baby, on toward their original destination, the California valleys.

When the emigrants reached the desert that Jedediah Smith and Joseph Walker had once crossed, they plunged into the unknown, abandoning their wagons in favor of pack animals to gain time. On September 23, 1841, they arrived at the Humboldt River, which they followed to the Sink. A month later they came to the Walker River, where some members proposed a return to Fort Hall before the winter snows began, but the question was put to a vote and the majority favored pressing on. Near the end of October, with their supply of beef exhausted and surrounded by impassable mountains, the emigrants despaired of ever reaching California. But they soon discovered a westward-flowing river, the Stanislaus, which they followed to the Sonora Pass. When the weary emigrants arrived in the San Joaquin Valley, some thought California must still be 500 miles away. However, with the aid of an Indian guide they arrived at the ranch of Dr. John Marsh, near Mount Diablo, on November 4, 1841. After a journey of six months, the first overland migration to California was achieved.

During 1842 and 1843 relatively few emigrants followed the first migration to California. In 1843, bills in Congress promised to grant every adult male settler in the Pacific Northwest 640 acres, another 160 to his wife and 160 to each child. The sovereignty of the Oregon country was in dispute with Great Britain, at the time and, although the bills did not pass, many emigrants were convinced that one soon would. In the spring of 1843, 1,000 emigrants headed for Oregon over a trail that only one year before had carried fewer than 100 pioneers.

As early as 1844, there were calls for building a transcontinental railroad that would transport goods from eastern factories and farms to western ports and thence to the Orient. Senator Stephen A. Douglas of Illinois advocated that the Indians be removed from the Platte Valley, territorial governments be established in Nebraska and Oregon, and a transcontinental railroad be surveyed immediately, so that the United States could "drive Great Britain and her ships and commerce from China."

The Road to Manifest Destiny

James K. Polk, the Democratic candidate for the presidency in 1844, campaigned on a platform that called for occupying Oregon ("54°40′ or fight!"), extending the United States border to the southern tip of Alaska, and for the "reannexation of Texas." Outgoing Whig president John Tyler stole some of Polk's thunder by introducing a joint resolution to annex Texas in his annual message to Congress in December 1844. Despite strong opposition by abolitionists, the resolution was adopted by both the House and the Senate. No more than four additional states could be created from the territory, and slavery was restricted to south of the Missouri Compromise line of 30°30′. Soon after Tyler signed the resolution on March 1, 1845, Mexico broke off all diplomatic relations with the Polk administration.

American pioneers settling in the Mexican provinces of Texas and California would inevitably lead to hostilities between Mexico and the United States. For generations these territories had been seen by the Mexicans as barriers against aggressive frontiersmen from the United States. During the 1840s Americans were filled with the spirit of "manifest destiny," a term coined in a newspaper editorial in 1845. Americans believed their democratic institutions so perfect that no boundaries could contain them. Every president from Jackson to Polk had wanted to acquire the northern Mexican provinces; Polk was determined to secure them, but he viewed war as a last resort. He and his predecessors had tried intrigue, bribery and purchase, but Mexico would not willingly relinquish her territories.

On June 11, 1845, as tension with Mexico mounted, Polk ordered General Zachary Taylor to position his troops near the mouth of the Nueces River, ready to defend Texas in case Mexico attacked. Simultaneously, a reconnaissance group from the Bureau of Engineers, commanded by John Charles Fremont, moved up the Arkansas River to Bent's Fort. The company consisted of 48 cartographers, scientists, soldiers and trappers, including scout, trapper and Indian agent Kit Carson.

President James K. Polk. Courtesy of the New York Public Library.

In 1842 and 1843 Fremont had explored the Oregon Trail for the War Department's Corps of Topographical Engineers. In his detailed reports Fremont described his miraculous climb of Fremont Peak in the Wyoming Rockies; braving the Great Salt Lake in a raft; battling snowdrifts; and fighting off Indians in the Mohave Desert. Fremont's accounts excited the nation, and were also used by westbound emigrants as a source of information about distances, campgrounds, fords and mountain passes.

In 1845, the Corps of Engineers had instructed Fremont to examine the Southern Rockies and return with his information before Congress adjourned. He may also have been under secret orders to survey the situation in California in case trouble erupted between Mexico and the United States.

THE MORMONS AND THE GREAT SALT LAKE

In spring 1845, the Mormons were contemplating a migration to "Upper California," the great expanse of land between present-day Utah and the Pacific. The Mormon religion, also known as the Church of Jesus Christ of Latter-Day Saints, was founded in 1830 by Joseph Smith, a young farmhand from upstate New York. The Mormons were driven from their home at Kirkland, Ohio, to Jackson County in western Missouri, near Independence. In the early 1830s, Mormon converts had flocked to the little Ohio town, where they cleared fields, built homes and established a prosperous religious community. But the Panic of 1837 had destroyed their dreams. Joseph Smith had launched a flimsy banking enterprise that had collapsed along with most of the other banks of the nation, leaving the Mormons heavily in debt and surrounded by angry creditors. When most of the Saints turned against him, Smith responded by ordering them out of the Church, and he then fled along with a few followers to join a small Mormon community recently established in Missouri.

However, they were abolitionists in a slaveholding region, prosperous landowners and unorthodox believers. In 1838, Governor Lillburn Boggs sent 6,000 troops into the area and forced the Mormons out of Missouri. They fled to the east bank of the Mississippi River in Illinois and established a community named Nauvoo. Smith created the name of Nauvoo based upon the Hebrew word "NAWA," interpreted to mean "beautiful place."

Smith proclaimed that no Illinois laws, including ones forbidding polygamy, would be recognized in the settlement without his consent. Non-Mormons resented the newcomers; when angry mobs formed throughout the countryside, Smith, his brother Hyrum, and two others surrendered to the authorities, hoping to be protected from the impending violence. Although they were promised state protection in a jail in the nearby town of Carthage, a mob broke into the building at five in the afternoon of June 27, 1844, and fatally shot the two brothers.

The Mormon Church was on the verge of collapsing when 43-year-old Brigham Young succeeded Joseph. In mid-April 1847, a well-organized pioneer caravan led by Young and consisting of 146 young men and women riding in 73 wagons set out for Fort Laramie. Young chose not to follow the Oregon Trail along the south bank of the Platte, but instead blazed a new route north of the stream that was better suited to wagon travel. The party reached Fort Laramie in early June, then pushed on to Fort Bridger, where experienced mountain man James Bridger tried to discourage the group from passing into the desert that lay ahead.

Young ignored Bridger's warnings and crossed the steep Uinta Range, traversed a sun-baked desert and entered the eastern spurs of the Wasatch Mountains. On July 24, 1847, the party arrived at the mountain-fringed valley of the Great Salt Lake that was to be their future home. According to Mormon legend, upon arrival, Young said, "This is the place." Within a decade, some 22,000 Saints were residing

Brigham Young. Courtesy of the
Library of Congress.

in the vicinity of the Great Salt Lake or in towns along the "Mormon Corridor," a result of the largest organized migration in the history of the American West.

THE DONNER PARTY

As Brigham Young set out from Iowa in search of a new homeland for the Mormons, George and Jacob Donner were organizing an overland migration in Illinois. The tragedy that befell the Donner party in 1846 would mark the year as a notable one in the history of overland migrations. The group left Independence, Missouri, in the spring with almost 100 members. As other parties joined them along the way, their numbers increased to 200. All went well as far as Fort Bridger. There the party divided, the larger group followed the usual route by Fort Hall, but the remaining 89 took what seemed to be a more expeditious route to California, described in the *Emigrants' Guide* (1845), by Lansford W. Hastings, as the Hastings Cutoff.

The larger company arrived in California with little suffering. But the smaller one was not as fortunate. They reached the south side of the Great Salt Lake at the cost of a month's time, and autumn was upon them when they started across the desert. In the late fall they arrived at the foot of the Sierra-Nevada Mountains, disorganized and torn by internal disputes. They became snowbound near the shores of Alder Creek, later named Donner Lake, where they suffered severely from cold and famine.

Dissension divided the Donner Party: One group tried to proceed through the passes in December, but experienced terrible losses. The remaining members resorted to eating the flesh of those who had died in order to survive. It was not until mid-February of 1847 before the first of several rescue expeditions from the Sacramento Valley were able to rescue the surviving members. Of the original 89 persons who set out from Fort Bridger, only half survived.

THE MEXICAN WAR

As emigrants crossed the continent in search of new homes in California, relations between Mexico and the United States were steadily deteriorating. The breaking point came when Texas was formally admitted as the 28th state of the Union on December 29, 1845. Texas entered the Union with a series of longstanding border disputes with Mexico. Most controversial was the southern boundary. As a republic, Texas had claimed the Rio Grande as its southern border, a claim Mexico denied because the province of Texas-Coahuila had never extended south of the Nueces. Although the only support for the Texans' claim was a dubious agreement obtained under duress from General Santa Anna, President Polk felt obligated to support their claim. Tensions increased between the two nations when Polk declared that the Nueces-Grande strip belonged to the United States.

Despite the rising tension, Polk still hoped to settle the dispute peacefully. He sent envoy John Slidell to Mexico City with the authority not only to purchase California but also to settle the Texas boundary by assuming all claims against Mexico in return for the Rio Grande line. When the Mexican officials refused to meet with him, Slidell sent Polk the message: "Be assure that nothing is to be done with these people until they shall have been chastised."

The president received the message on January 12, 1846, and now foresaw war with Mexico as inevitable. There remained only the problem of provoking Mexico into firing the first shot. On January 13, 1846, Polk ordered General Zachary Taylor to position his troops in the disputed area between the Nueces and the Rio Grande. For three months Taylor's troops waited on the border, hoping to incite the Mexicans into an attack. On May 9, 1846, when Polk was about to draft a message to Congress recommending war, based upon Mexico's refusal to honor its financial obligations or peacefully settle the boundary dispute, he received a dispatch from the Rio Grande. Mexican troops under the command of General Mariano Arista had crossed the Rio Grande from Matamoros on April 25, ambushed an American patrol and killed or wounded 16 men. This was the opportunity Polk was waiting for. He quickly drafted a new message, and on May 11, 1846, requested a declaration of war from Congress.

Polk told Congress, "Mexico has passed the boundary of the United States, has invaded our territory and shed American blood upon the American soil." Two days later Congress declared that "by the Act of the Republic of Mexico a state of war exists." The president was authorized to recruit an army of 50,000 troops, and Congress appropriated $10,000,000 for military operations.

The American people were divided on the issue of war with Mexico. Many in the northeastern states were opposed because they viewed the conflict as a ploy by southern states to expand their agricultural interests and to secure more slaveholding territories. The Northeast provided only 7,930 volunteers, while the expansionist West enlisted almost 40,000 and the South 21,000. The Northeast, the nation's most prosperous region, also refused to financially support the war.

Whether Americans supported it or not, they were at war with Mexico. Polk and his military advisors had two principal war aims. The first was to acquire the northern Mexican provinces. On the day war was declared, Polk told his cabinet, "In making peace with our adversary, we shall acquire California, New Mexico, and other further territory, as an indemnity for this war, if we can." The second objective was to end the dispute quickly.

The war would be waged on two fronts. One army would march westward through Santa Fe into southern California, and a second army would move south toward Mexico City. Polk believed the joint campaign would result in a speedy conclusion, as a prolonged war would diminish his popularity and possibly contribute to the success of the Whig Party in the next election.

The Army of the West, which was assigned the mission of conquering New Mexico and California, was commanded by Colonel Stephen W. Kearny. Kearny's troops were an eclectic group: 300 regular dragoons, 1,000 Missouri frontiersmen, 500 Mormon youths recruited from Brigham Young's camp at Council Bluffs and an assortment of other recruits—a total of 2,700 men. On June 30, 1846, they set out from Fort Leavenworth for a journey of 800 miles across the plains and deserts to Santa Fe. For days they went without adequate water and food, but the resilient plainsmen were accustomed to these hardships.

By August 13, Kearny's troops were within sight of Santa Fe. News reached the Americans that 3,000 Mexican troops were waiting for them along the rim of a narrow canyon through which they must pass. Kearny relied on diplomacy, rather than engaging the Mexicans in battle. James Magoffin, a wealthy Santa Fe trader who was a member of Kearny's company, was sent to persuade the New Mexican officials that it was not worth risking a catastrophe by opposing the Americans. The governor of New Mexico, Manuel Armijo, agreed to flee with his troops southward and permit the American troops to march into Santa Fe unmolested.

Kearny issued a proclamation to the city's residents declaring America's intention to annex New Mexico, promised a democratic government and designated a governor to administer the province. Most New Mexicans supported the liberal declarations, and American troops marching through New Mexico found the citizens generally loyal to the United States.

In California, Commodore John D. Sloat sailed into Monterey on July 7 and occupied the port without much resistance. A few days later San Francisco was seized and northern California was formally annexed to the United States. Captain John C. Fremont led his "California company of mounted riflemen" toward San Diego for the conquest of southern California. Commodore Robert F. Stockton, who had replaced Sloat, sailed toward Los Angeles. Mexican General Jose Castro fled for the border before the advancing Americans. On August 13, 1846, Fremont and Stockton entered Los Angeles, where the commodore officially annexed all of California to the United States and assigned Fremont as its military governor.

Within six months after the declaration of war, the United States had acquired California and New Mexico. The remaining task was to inflict such a decisive defeat upon Mexico that the possession of these territories would be permanent. The campaign fell to General Zachary Taylor, whose troops were positioned on the Rio Grande and were prepared to begin a conclusive march on Mexico City. On August 19, 1846, Taylor launched an invasion of Monterey as the first step. The town of Matamoros fell without any serious resistance, and after three days of desperate fighting, Monterey also surrendered to the American forces.

The American troops, totaling 4,800, advanced to Buena Vista and awaited the arrival of 15,000 Mexican troops led by General Santa Anna. Santa Anna struck on February 22, 1847, when he mistakenly thought Taylor was retreating. After a raging two-day battle, Santa Anna was unable to repel the invaders and ordered a retreat.

The battle of Buena Vista paved the way for an invasion of Mexico City. However, General Taylor was denied the honor of marching into the capital. President Polk, becoming concerned about the growing popularity of "Old Rough and Ready," a Whig, decided to seize the city not from the north, but by an amphibious operation led from the Gulf Coast by relatively unknown General Winfield Scott.

Sailing from New Orleans, Scott's troops landed south of Vera Cruz on March 9, 1847. Cannon were moved ashore, and after an 18-day siege, Vera Cruz surrendered. The road that lay ahead to Mexico City was a tortuous route that crossed through a few miles of mountain passes where Santa Anna and his defenders were prepared to fight the Americans at every step.

All the way to Mexico City American troops were harassed by small parties of Mexican soldiers. By May 15, 1847, Scott had reached the city of Puebla. Aware of the impossibility of keeping supply lines open with bands of guerillas roaming the region, Scott decided to move boldly forward with 10,000 men, subsisting off the countryside. Near the end of August 1847, the Americans finally arrived at the gates of Mexico City.

The long-sought goal was far from achieved. The Mexican capital was a fortified city, and the two gates to the city were guarded by throngs of Mexican troops. The Americans burrowed under the city's stone walls and fought the defenders at close range. After three days, on September 17, 1847, Santa Anna ran up a white flag, and the Mexican War was over. The terms of surrender were all that remained to be decided.

Santa Anna abdicated his presidency, and Mexico tottered on the verge of anarchy. Fearing that more fighting would be required if a peace treaty was not concluded at once, Scott directed Nicholas P. Trist, the chief clerk of the State Department, to meet with the representatives of the Mexican provisional government at the city of Guadalupe Hidalgo. Under the treaty, signed on February 2, 1848, Mexico accepted the Rio Grande boundary for Texas and ceded all of New Mexico and California. In return Mexico received $15 million and the United States assumed $3.5 million in American claims brought against the Mexican government. In March, the Senate ratified the treaty, but without the Wilmot Proviso, leaving open the question of slavery.

The slavery question had been linked to the war as early as August 1846 when the Polk administration had sought to put through Congress a $2 million appropriation bill for war expenses. Congressman David Wilmot, a dissident Pennsylvania Democrat, tried to amend the bill: "Provided, That, as an express and fundamental condition to the acquisition of any territory from the Republic of Mexico by the United States . . . neither slavery nor involuntary servitude shall ever exist in any part of said territory." The Proviso divided both parties down sectional lines; southern Whigs and Democrats denounced it as an invasion of states' rights, while northerners of both parties praised the antislavery amendment.

Following the ratification of the treaty, some outspoken politicians argued that the manifest destiny of the United States was to annex all of Mexico. One New York senator envisioned an American Union "embracing the whole of the North American continent." The territorial gains between 1845 and 1848 were enough to satisfy all but the most zealous advocates of manifest destiny. By the Treaty of Guadalupe Hidalgo, the United States acquired an immense western territory stretching from Texas to the Pacific and north to Oregon. The United

States gained 1.2 million square miles, virtually doubling its territory. The human cost for the United States was 13,283 killed and 4,152 wounded.

THE ISSUE OF SLAVERY

The added territories gained from the war with Mexico ignited the simmering controversy over the question of slavery between North and South. Should Congress ban slavery there? Was slavery an issue to be decided by the states themselves or by the federal government? Following the Mexican War there were bitter debates in Congress, in state legislatures and on streetcorners, until a temporary solution was reached with the Compromise Resolutions of 1850.

Senator Henry Clay of Kentucky offered eight compromise resolutions in an attempt to organize the territories while still dealing with the tortuous issue of slavery. The resolutions included admitting California as a free state and allowing territorial governments for New Mexico and Utah without reference to slavery. By the Compromise's terms, the boundaries of Texas would be adjusted and the United States would assume Texas' public debt. The last resolutions involved slavery: that the fugitve slave law would be strengthened, but no slavery would be allowed in Washington, D.C.

Southerners realized the arid lands of the West were not suited to cotton growing and a slave economy. But if the South extended its political control over the region, perhaps it could break the North's hold on national leadership. Southerners argued that the North had no right to dictate the government of the West when it was mostly Southern blood that had won the region. Northern abolitionists demanded that Congress ban slavery from the western territories, under the provision in the Constitution that authorized it to "make all needful rules and regulations respecting the territory or other property belonging to the United States."

Moderates on both sides of the Mason–Dixon Line proposed various solutions. Some favored having Congress extend the Missouri Compromise line of 36°30′N to the Pacific, while others felt the Supreme Court should decide the question. The western border states advocated "squatter sovereignty," under which settlers in each territory would decide whether they wanted slavery.

Soon the question of slavery in the Southwest would take on a new urgency. In 1848, James Marshall, a workman at John Sutter's mill in the lower Sacramento Valley, discovered flakes of a dull yellow metal that turned out to be gold. Despite Sutter's efforts to keep the find a secret, within a year tens of thousands of gold hunters from all over the nation and the world were heading for California. Some sailed by ship around South America while others took the overland trails. The California Gold Rush was on. By the end of 1849, 100,000 people were living in California. Congress would finally have to decide the question of slavery in the West and establish a form of government for the new territories.

CHRONICLE OF EVENTS

1841:

March 4: William Henry Harrison, who campaigned as a "man of the frontier," is inaugurated as the ninth president. He becomes sick, and one month later dies; Vice President John Tyler is sworn in as his successor.

April 6: Joseph Smith moves to Nauvoo, Illinois, and makes this town the center of his Church of Jesus Christ of Latter-Day Saints.

September: Father Pierre Jean de Smet establishes Mary's Mission in the Bitterroot Valley of Montana.

September 4: Congress passes the Distribution-Preemption Act, encouraging settlement of frontier territory.

November: The first large wagon train of settlers reaches Sacramento, California, via the Oregon Trail.

December 16: Senator Lewis Linn of Missouri seeks protection for settlers traveling along the Oregon Trail; his bill calls for constructing forts along the route.

1842:

May 16: 130 people in 18 wagons depart Independence, Missouri, to join Whitman's mission in Walla Walla, Oregon.

May: Colonel John C. Fremont of the U.S. Army Topographical Corps surveys the Wind River chain of the Rocky Mountains in southern Wyoming.

August 9: In the Webster-Ashburton Treaty between Britain and the United States, Britain cedes the area south of a line drawn from Lake Superior to Lake of the Woods.

September 11: Mexican soldiers capture San Antonio in the Republic of Texas.

October 3: American missionary Marcus Whitman leaves Oregon for Washington, D.C., to generate public interest in the Oregon country.

1843:

James Bridger opens Fort Bridger on the Black Fork of the Green River in southwest Wyoming; it becomes an important stop on the Oregon Trail.

May 8: Secretary of State Daniel Webster resigns over a dispute over the annexation of the Republic of Texas.

May 22: One-thousand pioneers leave Elm Grove, Missouri, bound for Oregon.

May 29: John C. Fremont and guide Kit Carson explore the Snake and Columbia river valleys and the San Joaquin Valley in California.

June 15: A truce is declared between Mexico and the Republic of Texas.

July: A convention in Cincinnati calls for adoption of a resolution to make 54°40'N the international boundary for the Oregon Territory, pushing the north line to include the present-day state of Washington.

July 24: President Tyler appoints Abel Upshur to succeed Daniel Webster as secretary of state. Upshur favors annexing Texas.

August 23: Santa Anna warns the United States that annexation of the Republic of Texas would be tantamount to declaring war against Mexico.

October 16: Texas President Sam Houston, concerned about losing Great Britain's support, refuses annexation negotiations with U.S. officials.

1844:

February: Secretary of State Abel Upshur sends the Texas government a message arguing the advantages of Texas joining the United States.

March: Fremont arrives at Sutter's Fort in Sacramento via the Sierra Nevada.

March 6: John C. Calhoun replaces Abel Upshur, who was killed in an explosion on the warship *Princeton*.

April 12: The Republic of Texas signs a treaty with the United States ceding public lands in the republic to the U.S.

May 27–29: James K. Polk campaigns for president under the slogan "54°40' or Fight!" asserting U.S. rights to the land that will become Washington state.

John C. Fremont (seated) and his guide, Kit Carson. Courtesy of the New York Public Library.

June 8: The Senate rejects admitting Texas as a state after antislavery forces convince the majority that the act would incite a confrontation between North and South.

June 27: Joseph Smith, leader of the Mormons, and his brother Hyrum are killed by an angry mob after being jailed in Carthage, Illinois.

August 7: Fremont returns to St. Louis, Missouri, with maps and journals of his expeditions; when published, they will guide a generation of westward-bound settlers.

August 8: Brigham Young succeeds Smith as leader of the Mormon Church.

December 3: President John Tyler, in his annual message to Congress, suggests that Congress annex Texas by a joint resolution instead of by adopting a treaty.

December 4: James Polk is elected president, defeating Henry Clay. Polk favors acquiring Texas, California and Oregon as U.S. territories.

December 12: Anson Jones succeeds Sam Houston as president of the Republic of Texas.

1845:

January 25: By a margin of 120 to 98, the House of Representatives votes to annex the Republic of Texas in a joint resolution.

February 3: The House passes a bill to establish a government for Oregon with a northern border of 54°40′N. The Senate refuses to consider the bill because it prohibits slavery in the region.

February 27: The Senate passes the Joint Resolution on the annexation of the Republic of Texas by a vote of 27 to 25.

March: The Report of the Exploring Expedition to the Rocky Mountains in the Year 1842 and to Oregon and North California in the Years 1843–44 is published by John C. Fremont.

March 1: Lame-duck President John Tyler signs the Joint Resolution annexing the Republic of Texas, the first use of this procedure to acquire a territory.

March 4: James Polk is inaugurated as president, declaring that the United States has "clear and unquestionable" title to Oregon and that the annexation of Texas is a matter between only Texas and the United States.

March 6: The Mexican minister to the United States, General Juan Almonte, in Washington, D.C., protests President Polk's reference to Texas and demands his passport to leave the United States.

March 28: The Mexican government, in protest of the Texas annexation treaty, severs diplomatic relations with the United States.

May 28: President Polk sends U.S. Army troops to the southwest border of Texas to protect the republic against a Mexican invasion.

June 11: General Zachary Taylor is ordered to position his troops near the Rio Grande River, the disputed border of the Republic of Texas and Mexico.

June 15: President Tyler officially guarantees protection by U.S. troops if the republic of Texas agrees to the terms of the annexation treaty.

June 23: In a special session, the Congress of the Republic of Texas votes for annexation by the United States.

September 16: President Polk offers to pay as much as $40 million to Mexico for the territories of Mexico and California.

October 13: Annexation and a new state constitution are approved by a majority of Texan-American voters.

December 2: President James Polk, in his first annual message to Congress, calls for an end to the joint occupation of Oregon.

December 27: The phrase "manifest destiny" is coined in a *New York Morning News* editorial.

December 29: Texas is admitted to the Union as the 28th state.

1846:

January 4: Mexico's President Paredes declares that he will defend all territories he regards as Mexican.

January 27: Captain John C. Fremont reaches Monterey, in Mexican California; it is suspected that he is under secret orders to survey the territory for acquisition.

February 10: Twelve-thousand Mormons led by Brigham Young begin their exodus from Illinois, traveling to Council Bluffs on the Missouri River, where they wait to learn of their final destination.

April 12: Mexican General Ampudia orders U.S. Generals Taylor and Worth to retreat from Mexican territory and to recross the Nueces River; Taylor refuses and asks for a U.S. Navy blockade of the mouth of the Rio Grande.

April 24: About 1,600 Mexican soldiers surround a scouting party of 63 Americans at the north bank of the Rio Grande. Eleven Americans are killed, five are wounded and the remainder are captured.

April 26: General Taylor sends a message to Polk that hostilities have begun.

May 11: President Polk asks Congress for a declaration of war against Mexico.

May 13: Congress authorizes $10 million and the recruitment of 50,000 soldiers when it votes to declare war on Mexico.

June 15: The Senate approves a new treaty with Great Britain abolishing joint occupation of the Oregon territory by the two countries and setting the U.S.–British boundary at the 49th parallel.

August 17: Commodore Robert Stockton announces that California has been annexed by the United States and establishes himself as governor.

August 19: General Taylor begins his advance to the Mexican city of Monterey with a force of 4,800 men.

September 14: Santa Anna becomes commander-in-chief of the Mexican army.

September 22: Americans are driven from Los Angeles, Santa Barbara and San Diego by Mexican troops led by Jose Maria Flores.

September 25: General Taylor captures the Mexican city of Monterey. He agrees to an eight-week truce with Mexico.

November: The Donner Party is snowbound on Alder Creek, later known as Donner Lake, in the Sierra Nevada. Of the original 89 who had set out from Independence, Missouri, in July, only 45 survive.

November 2: President James Polk orders Taylor to rescind the truce with Mexico.

November 16: General Taylor captures Saltillo, the capital of Coahuila.

December 28: Iowa is admitted to the Union as the 29th state; slavery is prohibited.

1847:

January 10: General Kearny and Commander Stockton retake Los Angeles, which ends the fighting between Mexicans and Americans in California.

January 13: The Treaty of Cahuenga giving generous terms to the defeated Mexicans, is signed in the San Fernando Valley with Captain Fremont representing the United States and Andres Pico, Mexico.

February 22: Santa Anna, with 15,000 troops, demands an unconditional surrender from General Taylor and his 4,800 troops. Taylor refuses and the battle of Buena Vista ensues, with American victory. The war in northern Mexico is over.

April 16: Brigham Young leads a small group of followers from Council Bluffs to their new Zion—the Great Salt Lake Basin.

September 13: General Scott captures Mexico City, raising the American flag over "the halls of Montezuma."

November 22: The Mexican government signals that it is interested in peace talks.

EYEWITNESS TESTIMOMY

Our ignorance of the route was complete. We knew that California lay west, and that was the extent of our knowledge. Some of the maps consulted, supposed of course to be correct, showed a lake in the vicinity of where Salt Lake now is; it was represented as a long lake, three or four hundred miles in extent, narrow and with two outlets, both running into the Pacific Ocean, either apparently larger than the Mississippi River.

John Bidwell, California pioneer, recalling the first overland emigrant wagon train bound for California in 1841, in Echoes of the Past *(1928).*

The situation of Upper California will cause its separation from Mexico before many years. The country between it and Mexico can never be any thing but a barren waste, which precludes all intercourse except that by sea, always more or less interrupted by the course of the winds, and the unhealthfulness of the lower or seaport towns of Mexico. It is very probable that this country will become united with Oregon, with which it will perhaps form a state that is destined to control the destinies of the Pacific. This future state is admirably situated to become a powerful maritime nation, with two of the finest ports in the world,—that within the straits of Juan de Fuca, and San Francisco. These two regions have, in fact, within themselves every thing to make them increase, and keep up an intercourse with the whole of Polynesia, as well as the countries of South America on the one side, and China, the Philippines, New Holland, and New Zealand, on the other. Among the latter, before many years, may be included Japan. Such various climates will furnish the materials for a beneficial interchange of products, and an intercourse that must, in time, become immense . . .

Lieutenant Charles Wilkes, commander of the U.S. South Sea Surveying and Exploring expedition, 1841, in Narrative of the United States Exploring Expedition During the Years 1838, 1839, 1840, 1841, 1842 *(1845).*

This morning I started from my residence, near Napoleon, Ripley county, Indiana, for the Oregon Territory, on the Columbia River, west of the Rocky Mountains; though many of my friends tried to dissuade me from going, telling me of the many dangers and difficulties I should have to go through, exposed to hostile Indians and the wild beasts, and also on account of my advanced age, being at this time in my 64th year. But my mind leads me strongly to go; I want to preach to the people there, and also to the Indians, as well as to see the country.

Joseph Williams, Methodist missionary, journal entry of April 26, 1841, in Hafen's To the Rockies and Oregon, 1839–1842 *(1955).*

I gave you a hint as to the possibility of acquiring Texas by treaty—I verily believe it could be done—Could the north be reconciled to it would anything throw so bright a lustre around us? It seems to me that the great interests of the north would be incalculably advanced by such an acquisition—How deeply interested is the shipping interest? Slavery—I know that is the objection—and it would be well founded if it did not already exist among us—but my belief is that a rigid enforcement of the laws against the slave trade, would make in time as many free States, south, as the acquisition of Texas would add of slave States—and then the *future* (distant it might be) would present wonderful results.

President John Tyler, to Secretary of State Daniel Webster, letter of October 11, 1841, in Smith's The Annexation of Texas *(1971).*

After a journey of four months and a half on horseback through the desert, and in spite of our actual want of bread, wine, sugar, fruit, and all such things as are called the conveniences of life, we find our strength and courage increased, and are better prepared than ever to work at the conversion of the souls that Providence entrusts to our care.

Pierre-Jean De Smet, Jesuit missionary, on selecting the Bitter Root Valley in present-day Montana as the place for the first mission in the Far West, October 18, 1841, in Life, Letters and Travels of Father De Smet Among the North American Indians *(1905).*

There were some Sioux warriors at Fort Laramie when we arrived, and they joined with the trappers and traders to persuade Frémont not to proceed, saying that in all probability he would meet the hostile Sioux and that his party would be destroyed.

Frémont replied that he had been sent by his government to perform a certain duty, that no matter what obstacles lay before him he would continue his march and accomplish his mission or die in the attempt; and if his party were slain, his government would eventually punish its destroyers. We continued our march to the South Pass, where Frémont accomplished all of his objectives, and returned to Fort Laramie sometime in September. During the expedition I had performed the duties of guide and hunter. At Laramie, I quit the employ of Frémont, who returned to the States by the same route over which he had come out.

Kit Carson, 1842, in Kit Carson's Autobiography *(1935).*

From the impression on my mind at this time, and subsequently on our return, I should compare the elevation which we surmounted immediately at the Pass, to the ascent of the Capitol hill from the avenue, at Washington. It is difficult for me to fix positively the breadth of this pass. From the broken ground where it commences, at the foot of the Wind river chain, the view to the southeast is over a champaign country, broken, at the distance of nineteen miles, by the Table rock; which, with the other isolated hills in its vicinity, seems to stand on a comparative plain. This I judged to be its termination, the ridge recovering its rugged character with the Table rock. It will be seen that it in no manner resembles the places to which the term is commonly applied—nothing of the gorge-like character and winding ascents of the Allegheny passes in America: nothing of the Great St. Bernard and Simplon passes in Europe.

John C. Fremont, August 8, 1842, describing his ascent of the South Pass on the Oregon Trail, in Report of the Exploring Expedition to the Rocky Mountains in the Year 1842 and to Oregon and North California in the Years 1843–44 *(1845).*

American trappers have frequently stalked into the Californian towns with their long rifles, ready for all sorts of mischief, practically setting the government at defiance, and putting the inhabitants in bodily fear; and, in 1836, the American residents, as also some of the American skippers on the coast, supported the revolution, in the hope of its merely transferring California from Mexico to the United States.

Sir George Simpson, English visitor to California, 1842, in Narrative of a Journey Round the World *(1847).*

For a time, until we reached the Platte River, one day was much like another. We set forth every morning and camped every night, detailing men to stand guard. Captain Fitzpatrick and the missionary party would generally take the lead and we would follow. Fitzpatrick knew all about the Indian tribes, and when there was any danger we kept in a more compact body, to protect one another. At other times we would be scattered along, sometimes for half a mile or more. We were generally together, because there was often work to be done to avoid delay. We had to make the road, frequently digging down steep banks, filling gulches, removing stones, etc. In such cases everybody would take a spade or do something to help make the road passable. When we camped at night we usually drew the wagons and carts together in a hollow square and picketed our animals inside in the corral. The wagons were common ones and of no special pattern, and some of them were covered. The tongue of one would be fastened to the back of another. To lessen the danger from Indians, we usually had no fires at night and did our cooking in the daytime.

John Bidwell, first leader of overland settlers to California, 1842, in A Journey to California with Observations About the Country, Climate and the Route to the Country *(1842).*

Ye rugged mounts, ye vales, ye streams and trees,
    To you a hunter bids his last farewell,
I'm bound for shores of distant, western seas,
    To view far-famed Multnomah's fertile vale;
I'll leave these regions, once-famed hunting
    grounds,
    Which I, perhaps, again shall see no more,
And follow down, led by the setting sun
    Or distant sound of proud Columbia's roar.

Osborne Russell, fur trapper, "The Hunter's Farewell," diary entry of June 22, 1842, in Hurbert's Where Rolls Oregon *(1933).*

Shall we be such fools as to be governed by their [Illinois] laws which are unconstitutional? No. We will make a law for gold and silver; then their law ceases, and we can collect our debts. Powers not delegated to the states, or reserved from the states, are constitutional. The constitution acknowledges that the people have all power not reserved to itself. I am a lawyer. I am a big lawyer, and comprehend heaven, earth and hell, to bring forth knowledge that shall cover up all lawyers, doctors and other big bodies.

Joseph Smith, to Nauvoo City Council, speech of February 23, 1843, in Linn's The Story of the Mormons *(1923).*

The Oregon fever is raging in almost every part of the Union. Companies are forming in the east, and in several parts of Ohio, which added to those of Illinois, Iowa, and Missouri, will make a pretty formidable army, the largest portion will probably join companies at Fort Independence, Missouri, and proceed together across the mountains. It would be reasonable to suppose that there will be at least five thousand Americans west of the Rocky Mountains next autumn.

The Niles National Register, article of May 6, 1843.

If it is in contemplation to keep open the communications with Oregon Territory, a show of military force in this country is absolutely necessary; and a combination of advantages renders the neighborhood of Fort Laramie the most suitable place, on the line of the Platte, for the establishment of a military post. It is connected with the mouth of the Platte and the Upper Missouri by excellent roads, which are in frequent use, and would not in any way interfere with the range of the buffalo, on which neighboring Indians mainly depend for support. It would render any posts on the Lower Platte unnecessary; the ordinary communication between it and the Missouri being sufficient to control the intermediate Indians. It would operate effectually to prevent any such coalitions as are now formed among the Gros Ventres, Sioux, Cheyennes, and other Indians, and would keep the Oregon road through the valley of the Sweet Water and the South Pass of the mountains constantly open.

John C. Fremont, July 22, 1843, in A Report of an Exploration of the Country Lying Between the Missouri River and the Rocky Mountains on the Line and Great Platte Rivers *(1843).*

The winter of 1842–43 had been used to make out the maps and write the report. I was secretary and amanuensis, and had full knowledge of the large scope and national importance of these journeys—a knowledge as yet strictly confined to the few carrying our aim. Even to the Secretary of war, and Mr. Fremont's immediate commander, the Colonel of the Topographical Engineers, they were only geographical surveys to determine lines of travel.

Jessie Benton Fremont, on John C. Fremont's first expedition to the Rocky Mountains in 1843, in The Origins of the Fremont Expedition *(1891).*

There are sixty wagons. They have been divided into fifteen divisions or platoons of four wagons each, and each platoon is entitled to lead in its turn. The leading platoon of today will be the rear one of tomorrow, and will bring up the rear unless some teamster, through indolence or negligence, has lost his place in the line, and is condemned to that uncomfortable post. It is within ten minutes of seven; the corral but now a strong barricade is everywhere broken, the teams being attached to the wagons. The women and children have taken their places in them. The pilot (a borderer who has passed his life on the verge of civilization, and has been chosen to the post of leader from his knowledge of the savage and his experience in travel through roadless wastes) stands ready in the midst of his pioneers and aids to mount and lead the way.

Jesse Applegate, commander of an overland wagon train, 1843, in A Day with the Cow Column *(1868).*

To admit Texas as a non-slave holding State, or to permit her to remain an independent and sovereign non-slave holding state, will be fatal to the Union, and ruinous to the whole country. I have no doubt that a proposition to admit her into the Union would be received, at first, with a burst of repugnance at the North; but the more the subject is reflected on, the more clearly will they see that the measure is absolutely necessary. To the South, it is a question of *safety;* to the North, it is one of interest. *We* should introduce rivals of our most productive industry [cotton growing], and should be, so far, losers; they [the North] would profit by that very rivalry. I have never known the North to refuse to do what their interest required, and I think it will not be difficult to convince them that their interest requires the admission of Texas into the Union as a slaveholding State.

Secretary of State Abel Upshur, to John C. Calhoun, letter of August 14, 1843, in Merk's Slavery and the Annexation of Texas *(1972).*

I have established a small fort, with a blacksmith shop and a supply of iron in the road of the emigrants on Black Fork of Green River, which promises fairly. In coming out here they are generally well supplied with money, but by the time they get here they are in need of all kinds of supplies, horses, provisions, smith-work, etc. They bring ready cash from the states, and should I receive the goods ordered, will have considerable business in that way with them, and establish trade with the Indians in the neighborhood, who have a good number of beaver among them.

James Bridger, to Pierre Choteau, Jr., fur trader and financier, letter (written for Bridger) of December 10, 1843, in Alter's James Bridger, A Historical Narrative *(1925).*

FORT LARAMIE and FORT JOHN are about one mile apart and west of the river. You now begin to cross the Black Hills, and will find some pretty rough roads, the ridges are high, and country barren. There is no difficulty in finding good camping places however; some travellers take the road that follows the river, and avoid the Black Hills,—it is said to be better travelling when the fords are good; the road crosses the river three times. At a distance of seven miles from the Fort, you find a steep hill to descend; it is a long hill, and requires great care. Four miles and a half further, you find a steep hill to ascend and descend; the road is rough, rocky and crooked— half way over, there is a sudden turn in the road that is dangerous, if great care is not used. You leave the river at the fort, and do not touch it again for 80 miles.

Joseph E. Ware, guidebook author, 1844, in The Emigrant's Guide to California *(1972).*

I instructed the Twelve Apostles to send out a delegation, and investigate the locations of California and Oregon, and hunt out a good location where we can remove to after the Temple is completed, and where we can build a city in a day, and have a government of our own, get up into the mountains, where the devil cannot dig us out, and live in a healthy climate where we can live as old as we have mind to.

Joseph Smith, diary entry of February 20, 1844, in Linn's The Story of the Mormons.

. . . by day our teams ware moving to the river which we had been expecting [to] fall but which began to rise again   we let down by cords over a steep rock bluff through mud knee deep an[d] in the rain pouring in torrents   me[n] women and children dripping in mud and water over Shoe mouth deep and I Thought I never saw more determined resolution even amongst men than most of the female part of our company exhibited   The leaving of home of near andear friend the war whoop and Scalping Knif

The long dreary Journey the privations of a life in a Tent with all the horrors of flood and field and even the element seemed to combine to make us uncomfortable   But still there was a determined resolution sufficient to overcome all obsicles   with the utmost exertion we crssed over 20 waggons by about 10 o'clock when the waters became too deep to cross and in about an hour it rose so as to swim a horse

James Clyman, fur trader, on leading an Oregon-bound emigrant train, journal entry of May 24, 1844, in Journal of a Mountain Man *(1984).*

Resolved, that the time, in our opinion, has arrived when the adherents of [Joseph] Smith, as a body, should be driven from the surrounding settlements into Nauvoo; that the Prophet and his miscreant adherents should then be demanded at their hands, and, if not surrendered, a war of extermination should be waged, to the entire destruction, if necessary for our protection, of his adherents.

Town of Warsaw, Hancock County, Illinois, resolution of 1844, in Linn's The Story of the Mormons.

After twenty-five years, the American population has begun to extend itself to the Oregon. Some hundreds went a few years ago; a thousand went last year; two thousand are now setting out from the frontiers of Missouri; tens of thousands are meditating the adventure. I say to them all, Go on! The Government will follow you, and will give you protection and land!

Senator Thomas Hart Benton (Missouri), address of June 3, 1844, to the U.S. Senate, in Abridgement of the Debates of Congress, from 1789 to 1856 *(1857–1861).*

This accession to our territory has been a bloodless achievement. No arm of force has been raised to produce the results. The sword has had no part in the victory. We have not sought to extend our territorial possessions by conquest, or our republican institutions over a reluctant people. It was the deliberate homage of each people to the great principle of our federative union. If we consider the extent of territory involved in the annexation, its prospective influence on America, the means by which it has been accomplished, springing purely from the choice of the people themselves to share the blessings of

Thomas Hart Benton. Courtesy of the New York Public Library.

our union, the history of the world may be challenged to furnish a parallel.

President John Tyler, to Congress, annual message of December 3, 1844, in Richardson's Messages and Papers of the Presidents *(1896).*

All persons, designing to travel by this route, should, invariably, equip themselves with a good gun; at least, five pounds of powder, and twenty pounds of lead; in addition to which, it might be advisable, also, for each to provide himself with a holster of good pistols, which would, always, be found of very great service, yet they are not indispensable. If pistols are taken, an additional supply of ammunition should, also, be taken; for, it almost necessarily follows, that the more firearms you have, the more ammunition you will require, whether assailed by the Indians, or assailing the buffalo. If you come in contact with the latter, you will find the pistols of the greatest importance; for you may gollop your horse, side by side, with them, and having pistols, you may shoot them down at your pleasure; but should you come in mortal conflict with the former, the rifle will be found

to be much more effective, and terrific; the very presence of which, always, affords ample security. Being provided with arms and ammunition, as above suggested, the emigrant may consider himself, as far as his equipment is concerned, prepared, for any warlike emergency, especially, if nature has, also, equipped him with the requisite energy and courage.

Lansford W. Hastings, advice for overland travelers, 1845, in The Emigrants' Guide to Oregon and California *(1845).*

Our title to the country of the Oregon is "clear and unquestionable," and already are our people preparing to perfect that title by occupying it with their wives and children. But eighty years ago our population was confined on the west by the ridge of the Alleghanies. Within that period—within the lifetime, I might say, of some of my hearers—our people, increasing to many millions, have filled the eastern valley of the Mississippi, adventurously ascended the Missouri to its headsprings, and are already engaged in establishing the blessings of self-government in valleys of which the rivers flow to the Pacific. The world beholds the peaceful triumphs of the industry of our emigrants. To us belongs the duty of protecting them adequately wherever they may be upon our soil.

President James Polk, inaugural address, March 4, 1845, in Richardson's Messages and Papers of the Presidents.

The Republic of Texas has made known her desire to come into our Union, to form a part of our Confederacy and enjoy with us the blessings of liberty secured and guaranteed by our Constitution. Texas was once part of our country—was unwisely ceded away to a foreign power—is now independent, and possesses an undoubted right to dispose of a part or the whole of her territory and to merge her sovereignty as a separate and independent state in ours.

President James Polk, inaugural address, March 4, 1845, in Richardson's Messages and Papers of the Presidents.

It is utterly useless to think of arranging our difficulties with Mexico in an amicable way for the present or for some time to come. All parties here are clamorous for war, and no one is found bold enough to advocate an amicable adjustment of the difficulties between the two countries. Even those who believe war a ruinous and most disastrous measure for Mexico are compelled to join the public clamour in order to maintain their positions. As an instance illustrative of the feeling that prevails here towards the U.S., a resolution was introduced into [the Mexican] Congress a few days since, declaring any man who advocated peace with the U.S. a traitor to his country, and that he should be dealt with accordingly.

Wilson Shannon, U.S. minister to Mexico, to Secretary of State James Buchanan, letter of April 6, 1845, in Manning's Diplomatic Correspondence of the United States: Inter-American Affairs, 1834–1860 *(1923–1939).*

In the name of Israel's God, and by virtue of multiplied ties of country and kindred, we ask your friendly interposition in our favor. Will it be too much for us to ask you to convene a special session of Congress and furnish us an asylum where we can enjoy our rights of conscience and religion unmolested? or will you in a special message to that body, when convened, recommend a remonstrance against such unhallowed acts of oppression and expatriation as this people have continued to receive from the States of Missouri and Illinois? or will you favor us by your personal influence and by your official rank? or will you express your views concerning what is called the "Great Western Measure" of colonizing the Latter-day Saints in Oregon, the northwestern Territory, or some location remote from the States, where the hand of oppression shall not crush every noble principle and extinguish every patriotic feeling?

Committee of the Church of Jesus Christ of Latter-Day Saints, to President James Polk, letter of April 24, 1845, in Golder's The March of the Mormon Battalion *(1928).*

I propose that we proceed to the purchase (of lands) on Grand River, Iowa, and fence in a field of two miles square, build about 20 log cabins, plow some land and put in spring crops and thus spend our time until the weather settles; select men and families to take care of our improvements and the rest proceed westward . . . Then those who follow can tarry on Grand River or go on to the Missouri bottoms and other places where there will be plenty of feed for their cattle, and tarry through the winter, and come on another season as soon as they can make their way through.

Brigham Young, 1845, in Larson's Prelude to the Kingdom: Mormon Desert Conquest *(1947).*

On looking out at the passing train, we see among the foremost a very comfortable covered wagon, one of the sheets drawn aside, and an extremely nice-looking lady seated inside, very quietly sewing; the bottom of the wagon is carpeted, there are two or three chairs, and at one end there is a bureau, surmounted by a mirror; various articles of ornament and convenience hanging around the sides—a perfect prairie boudoir. Blessed by Woman! Shedding light and happiness wherever she goes; with her the wild prairie will be a paradise! Blessed be He who gave us this connecting link between Heaven and man, to win us from our wilder ways!

The Expositor *(Independence, Missouri), on a wagon train bound for Oregon via the overland route at Independence, newspaper account of May 3, 1845.*

The point of your ultimate destination is the western frontier of Texas, where you will select and occupy, on or near the Rio Grande del Norte, such a site as will consist with the health of the troops, and will be best adapted to repel invasion, and to protect what in the event of annexation will be our western border. You will limit yourself to the defence of the territory of Texas, unless Mexico should declare war against the United States.

Secretary of War George Bancroft, to General Zachary Taylor, dispatch of June 14, 1845, in McAfee and Robinson's Origins of the Mexican War: A Documentary Source Book *(1982).*

Orders came last evening by express from Washington City directing General Taylor to move without any delay to some point on the coast near the Sabine or elsewhere, and as soon as he shall hear of the acceptance by the Texas convention of the annexation resolutions of our Congress he is immediately to proceed with his whole command to the extreme western border of Texas and take up a position on the banks of or near the Rio Grande, and he is to expel any armed force of Mexicans who may cross that river.

General Ethan Allen Hitchcock, diary entry of June 30, 1845, in Hitchcock's Fifty Years in Camp and Field *(1909).*

What a people we are! What a country is this of ours! How wide in extent—how rich in productions—how various in beauty! I have asked in my travels, for the West, in the streets of the Queen of the West—a fairy City, which but as yesterday was a wilderness. They smiled at my inquiry, and told me it was among the "Hoosiers" of Indiana, the "Suckers" of Illinois, or the "Badgers" of Wisconsin. Then I passed along, crossing great rivers and broad Prairies, and again I asked for the West. They said it was in Iowa. I arrived at the Capitol. They complained that *they* were "too far down East." "But go," they said, "if you wish to see the West, days and days, and hundreds and hundreds of miles up the Missouri—farther than from us to New England, and beyond the Rocky Mountains, and among the Snake Indians of Oregon, and you may find it." It was the work of months to find the West, and I turned about in despair—and here I am, in this Empire City of Wisconsin—which but as yesterday was a wilderness.

Josiah Bushnell Grinnell, Upper Mississippi Valley settler from New England, 1845, in Home of the Badgers *(1845).*

. . . our manifest destiny [is] to overspread and to possess the whole of the continent which Providence has given us for the development of the great experiment of liberty and federated self-government entrusted to us.

John Louis O'Sullivan, editor of The New York Morning News, *December 27, 1845.*

We do not believe it possible that our country *can* be prospered in such a war as this. It may be victorious, it may acquire immense accessions of territory; but these victories, these acquisitions, will prove fearful calamities, by sapping the morals of our people, by inflating them with pride and corrupting them with the lust of conquest and of gold, and leading them to look to the commerce of the Indies and the dominion of the seas for those substantial blessings which follow only in the wake of peaceful, contented Labour. So sure as the universe has a Ruler will every acre of territory we acquire by this war prove to our nation a curse and the source of infinite calamities.

Horace Greeley, editor of The New York Tribune, *opposing the Mexican-American War, editorial of 1845, in Ingersoll's* The Life of Horace Greeley *(1890).*

Wagons should be selected with the greatest care; those should be taken which are made out of the best material, well put together, and properly proportioned. The irons on the wheels should be as tight as possible, without breaking or straining the wood; and the whole wagon should only be heavy enough to bear the required load. It is necessary to have the tires tight on the wheels, on account of the hot dust and sand through which they have to go, and which is very liable to loosen them from the wood.

Overton Johnson and William H. Winter, 1846, in Route Across the Rocky Mountains with a Description of Oregon and California *(1846).*

Arriving after an immense journey upon the unpeopled shores of the Pacific at the season of the closing in of winter, exhausted and destitute, neither despondency nor hesitation palsied for a moment the undertaken work; but with energies overpowering all obstacles, the opening spring beheld farms, houses, mills, and towns, growing apace, as with the pith and sinews of many years. Suffice it to say, that this hardy band, accompanied by 122 wagons, in the short space of five months penetrated to the Pacific, opening and traveling along a road of 1,000 miles of plains and 1,000 of vast mountains on whose summits the eternal snows are perpetually visible, without other guide than an indomitable perseverance, or other protection than their invincible rifles, and the wives and progeny clustered around them.

William Gilpin, politician and newspaper editor, on emigrants settling in the Oregon country, 1846, in Settlement of Oregon—Emigrants of 1843 *(1846).*

Let each company provide themselves with all the teams, wagons, provisions, clothing and other necessities for the journey that they can. When the companies are organized let them go to with their might to prepare for those who are to tarry.

When the companies with their captains and presidents decide how many can go next spring, then choose out a sufficient number of able bodied and expert men to take teams, seeds, farming utensils, to go as pioneers to prepare for putting in spring crops.

Let each company bear an equal proportion, according to the dividend of their property, in taking the poor and widows and fatherless and the families of those who have gone into the army, that the cries of the widows and the fatherless come not up into the ears of the Lord against this people.

Let each company prepare houses, and fields for raising grain, for those who are to remain behind this season. . . .

Let every man use all his influence and property to remove this people to the place where the Lord shall locate a Stake of Zion.

Brigham Young, on his plan for relocating 50,000 Mormons to the Far West, January 14, 1846, in Larson's Prelude to the Kingdom: Mormon Desert Conquest.

Our pioneers are instructed to proceed West until they find a good place to make a crop, in some good valley in the neighborhood of the Rocky Mountains, where they will infringe upon no one and be not likely to be infringed upon. Here we will make a resting place, until we can determine a place for a permanent location.

Mormon Circular of High Council, January 1846, in Stanley's A Biography of Parley P. Pratt: The Archer of Paradise *(1937).*

As we journeyed onward, mothers gave birth to offspring under almost every variety of circumstances imaginable, except those to which they had been accustomed: some in tents, others in wagons—in rain storm and in snow storm. I heard of one birth which occurred under the rude shelter of a hut, the sides of which were formed of blankets fastened to poles stuck in the ground, with a bark roof through which the rain was dripping.

Kind sisters stood holding dishes to catch the water as it fell, thus protecting the newcomer and its mother from a shower-bath as the little innocent first entered on the stage of human life; and through great faith in the ruler of events, no harm resulted to either.

Eliza R. Snow, plural wife of Brigham Young, diary entry of 1846, in Mullen's The Latter-Day Saints: The Mormons Yesterday and Today *(1966).*

We'll find the place which God for us prepared,
Far away in the West,
Where none shall come to hurt or make afraid;
There the Saints will be blessed.
We'll make the air with music ring.
Should praises to our God and King;
Above the rest these words we'll tell—
All is well! All is well!

And should we die before our journey's through,
Happy day! All is well!

We then are free from toil and sorrow, too;
With the just we shall dwell!
But if our lives are spared again
To see the Saints their rest obtain,
O how we'll make this chorus swell—
All is well! All is well!

"Come, Come Ye Saints," favorite Mormon hymn, in Mullen's The Latter-Day Saints: The Mormons Yesterday and Today.

SOLDIERS! You have been enlisted in time of peace to serve in that army for a specific term, but your obligation never implied that you were bound to violate the laws of God, and the most sacred rights of friends! The United States government, contrary to the wishes of a majority of all honest and honorable Americans, has ordered you to take *forcible* possession of the territory of a *friendly* neighbor, who has never given her consent to such occupation.

General Mariano Arista (Mexico), to soldiers of the United States Army, on their way to Matamoros in Northern Mexico, message of April 20, 1846, in McAfee and Robinson's Origins of the Mexican War: A Documentary Source Book.

I solemnly announce that I do not decree war against the government of the United States of America, because it belongs to the august Congress of the nation, and not to the Executive, to decide definitely what reparation must be exacted for such injuries. But the defence of Mexican territory which the troops of the United States are invading is an urgent necessity, and my responsibility before the nation would be immense if I did not order the repulse of forces which are acting as enemies; and I have so ordered. From this day defensive war begins, and every point of our territory which may be invaded or attacked shall be defended by force.

President Mariano Paredes, proclamation of April 23, 1846, in Rives' The United States and Mexico: 1821–1848 *(1913).*

The war has commenced on the part of Mexico. On the night of the 25th instant, Capt. Thornton, of the dragoons, with a squadron consisting of his own and Capt. Hardee's company, were ordered to reconnoiter the Mexican army, which Gen. Taylor had been informed were crossing the Rio Grande twenty-seven miles above here. The squad was ambuscaded and fired on, and a number [unknown] killed, and all besides taken by the Mexicans. They sent in two wounded, with a note to Gen. Taylor. Capt. Hardee is a prisoner, but no news of Capt. Thornton and Lieuts. Mason and Kane. You will believe me when I tell you the war is commenced in Mexico, and that Gen. Taylor is about to be surrounded and cut off from his supplies at Pont Isabel where there is not more than four hundred men of all descriptions. You will believe me when I tell you that this army will have the d—dest hardest fighting that ever any army had in this world, and, unless reinforcements are largely and speedily sent to its assistance, it must be cut off, as the enemy are in great force, and I fear have been very much underrated.

Colonel Robert Fitzpatrick, report of April 27, 1846, in the Niles' National Register *(May 16, 1845).*

The cabinet held a regular meeting today; all the members present. I brought up the Mexican question, and the question of what was the duty of the administration in the present state of our relations with that country. The subject was very fully discussed. All agreed that if the Mexican forces at Matamoros committed any act of hostility on Gen. Taylor's forces, I should immediately send a message to Congress recommending an immediate declaration of war. I stated to the cabinet that up to this time, as they knew, we had heard of no open act of aggression by the Mexican army, but that the danger was imminent that such acts would be committed. I said that in my opinion we had ample cause of war, and that it was impossible that we could stand in *status quo,* or that I could remain silent much longer; that I thought it was my duty to send a message to Congress very soon and recommend definitive measures. I told them that I thought I ought to make such a message by Tuesday next, that the country was excited and impatient on the subject, and if I failed to do so I would not be doing my duty.

President James Polk, diary entry of May 9, 1846, in Diary of James Polk During His Presidency *(1910).*

After a severe affair of yesterday, principally with artillery, with six thousand of the best Mexican troops we succeeded after a continued contest of five hours in driving the enemy from his position & occupying the same laying on our arms; at day light he was still in sight, apparently disposed to renew the contest, but on our making the arrangements for doing so he retired on the Matamoros road & took a strong position at this place, & awaited the attack which we commenced at about four o'clock P. M. & after a severe contest of two hours a close quarters we succeeded in gaining a complete victory, dispersing them in every direction taking their artillery, baggage or means of transportation, a number of standards &c, with a great loss of killed, wounded & prisoners, one of the first is a Genl of artillery, & among the latter is Genl Lavega one of the most accomplished officers of their army; the war I have no doubt is completely brought to a close on this side the Rio Grande; the enemy who escaped having recrossed said river—So brilliant an achievement could not be expected without heavy loss on our side, we have many killed & wounded . . .

General Zachary Taylor, to Robert C. Wood, U.S. Army physician, on the battle of Palo Alto, letter of May 9, 1846, in Letters of Zachary Taylor: From the Battlefields of the Mexican War *(1970).*

The cup of forbearance had been exhausted even before the recent information from the frontier of the Del Norte. But now, after reiterated menaces, Mexico has passed the boundary of the United States, has invaded our territory and shed American blood upon the American soil. She has proclaimed that hostilities have commenced, and that the two nations are now at war.

As war exists, and, notwithstanding all our efforts to avoid it, exists by the act of Mexico herself, we are called upon by every consideration of duty and patriotism to vindicate with decision the honor, the rights, and the interests of our country.

President James Polk, to Congress, message of May 11, 1846, in Richardson's Messages and Papers of the Presidents.

It is known that a large body of Mormon emigrants are en route to California for the purpose of settling in that country. You are desired to use all proper means to have a good understanding with them to the end that the United States may have their cooperation in taking possession of and holding that country. It has been suggested here that many of these Mormons would willingly enter into the service of the United States, and aid us in our expedition against California. You are hereby authorized to muster into service such as can be induced to volunteer not, however, to a number exceeding one third of your entire force.

Secretary of War William L. Marcy, to Colonel Stephen W. Kearny, letter of June 3, 1846, in Golder's The March of the Mormon Battalion.

Feb. 26, Hungry times in camp, plenty of hides but the folks will not eat them, we eat them with tolerable good appetite, thanks be to the Almighty God. Mrs. Murphy said here yesterday that she thought she would commence on Milton and eat him, I do not think she has done so yet, it is so distressing, the Donners told the California folks four days ago that they would commence on the dead people if they did not succeed that day or next in finding their cattle, then ten or twelve feet under the snow, and did not know the spot or near it, they have done it ere this.

March 1, Ten men arrived this morning from Bear Valley with provisions, we are to start in two or three days and cache our goods here, they say the snow will remain until June.

Patrick Breen, member of the Donner Party expedition, journal entries of 1846, in Diary of Patrick Breen *(1910).*

The scene of "catching up," as the yoking and attaching of the oxen to the wagons is called in emigrant phraseology, is one of great bustle and confusion. The crack of the ox-goad, the "whoa-haws" in a loud voice, the leaping and running about of the oxen to avoid the yoke, and the bellowing of the loose stock, altogether create a most Babel-like and exciting confusion. The wagons commenced moving at nine o'clock, and at ten the camp was entirely deserted. In consequence of there being no order of march to-day, the train of wagons was strung out two or three miles in length.

Edwin Bryant, overland traveler and author, departing for California from Independence, Missouri, May 1846, in What I Saw in California *(1985).*

A plan of the campaign against Mexico and the manner of prosecuting the war was fully considered. I brought distinctly to the consideration of the cabinet the question of ordering an expedition of mounted men to California. I stated that if the war should be protracted for any considerable time, it would in my judgment be very important that the United States should hold military possession of California at the time peace was made, and I declared my purpose to be to acquire for the U.S. California, New Mexico, and perhaps some others of the northern provinces in Mexico whenever a peace was made. In Mr. Slidell's secret instructions last autumn these objects were included. Now that we were at war, the prospect of acquiring them was much better, and to secure that object military possession should with as little delay as possible be taken of all these provinces. In these views the cabinet concurred.

President James Polk, diary entry of May 30, 1846, in Diary of James Polk During His Presidency.

On a rainy day, near sunset, we reached the landing of this place, which is situated some miles from the river, on the extreme frontier of Missouri. The scene was characteristic, for here were represented at one view the most remarkable features of this wild and enterprising region. On the muddy shore stood some thirty or forty dark slavish looking Spaniards, gazing stupidly out from beneath their broad hats. They were attached to one of the Santa Fé companies, whose wagons were crowded together in the banks above. In the midst of these, crouching over a smoldering fire, was a group of Indians, belonging to a remote Mexican tribe. One or two French hunters from the mountains, with their long hair and buckskin dresses, were looking at the boat; and seated on a log close at hand were three men, with rifles lying across their knees. The foremost of these, a tall, strong figure, with a clear blue eye and an open, intelligent face, might very well represent that race of restless and intrepid pioneers whose axes and rifles have opened a path from the Alleghenies to the western prairies. He was on his way to Oregon, probably a more congenial field to him than any that now remained on this side the great plains.

Francis Parkman, author and historian, 1846, in The Oregon Trail *(1849).*

If I live through all this—and I think from all appearances now I shall come off the winner—I shall be fit for one of the *Oregon pioneers*. We are here without a stick of wood to get anything to eat, all that was provided at the last camp having been used last night & this morning—some of the men though have gone off, perhaps several miles to find some. I believe there is not a tree in sight of camp. And this should no longer be called the lost spring for it is "runing high" now, and taking all before it.

Susan Shelby Magoffin, Santa Fe Trail traveler, diary entry of June 23, 1846, in Down the Santa Fe Trail and Into Mexico *(1962).*

I must remark here, by the way, that the sight of an emigrant wagon in these wildernesses and deserts, produces the same emotions of pleasure as are felt by the way-worn and benighted traveller, within the boundaries of civilization, when approaching some hospitable cottage or mansion on the roadside. More intense, perhaps, because the white-tent-cloth of the wagon is a certain sign of welcome hospitality, in such form as can be afforded by the ever liberal proprietor, who without stint, even though he might have but a single meal, would cheerfully divide it among his stranger visiters. Civilization cannot always boast of such dispensers of hospitality; but among the emigrants to the Pacific, it is nearly universal.

Edwin Bryant, along the wagon trail to California, August 18, 1846, in What I Saw in California.

The American desert, is, perhaps, not less sterile, sandy, parched and destitute of water and every green herb and living thing than the African Sahara. In the course of a long day's march we could scarcely find a pool of water to quench the thirst, a patch of grass to prevent our animals perishing, or an oasis to relieve the weary mind. Dreary, sultry, desolate, boundless solitude reigned as far as the eye could reach, and seemed to bound the distant horizon. We suffered much with the heat, and thirst, and the driven sand—which filled our eyes, and nostrils, and mouths, almost to suffocation. Many of our animals perished on the desert. A Mexican hare, or an antelope, skimming over the ground with the utmost velocity, was the only living creature seen upon the plain. The Roman army under Metellus, on its march through the desert of Africa, never encountered more serious opposition from the elements than did our army in its passage over this American Sahara.

Anonymous soldier, with Colonel Doniphan's Army of the West, recalls the march toward Santa Fe, in August 1846, in George's Heroes and Incidents of the Mexican War, Containing Doniphan's Expedition *(1971).*

We understand that we shall probably meet the Mexicans to-morrow at another pass. Last night we took two Mexican prisoners, who were men of some note, one of them being a relative of Governor Amigo. He remarked to Gen. Kearney that although the position of the Mexicans was so strong at the pass, he could tell him how to defeat them—just fire five or six cannon, no matter which way, and he would ensure them all to run. To this Gen. Kearney replied that if that was the case, they must be a very cowardly people. But the Mexican said, far from it, they are very courageous; but they do not want to fight; they had rather be under your government than under our own. Before we reached the pass, however, on the 18th, they had fled, without waiting for the firing of our cannon. They retreated about 15 miles, and encamped in the mountains around us. It is a novel sight to see 200 camp fires lighted up among the rocks and hills and trees, with the men moving from fire to fire like so many spirits.

Jacob S. Robinson, a soldier with Colonel Doniphan's Army of the West, on approaching Santa Fe, August 17, 1846, in A Journal of The Santa Fe Expedition Under Colonel Doniphan *(1932).*

New Mexicans, we have come amongst you to take possession of New Mexico, which we do in the name of the government of the United States. We have come with peaceable intentions and kind feeling toward you all. We come as friends, to better your condition and make you part of the Republic of the United States. We do not mean to murder you or rob you of your property. Your families shall be free from molestation: your women secure from violence. My soldiers will take nothing from you but what they pay you for. In taking possession of New Mexico we do not mean to take away your religion from you.

Colonel Stephen W. Kearny, to the citizens of Santa Fe, address of August 19, 1846, in George's Heroes and Incidents of the Mexican War.

The people of this section [of] the country in our first appearance were the most abject contemptible looking objects I ever saw. They had been frightened allmost to death by the stories the priests and rich (for they are the two classes that rule the country) had told them of the *barbarian*[s] that were marching against them, but now after we have mingled a few days with them, they begin to look a little more cheerful and assume somewhat the appearance of *men*. They supposed our force was much larger than it is and say that if they had known we were so weak they would have fought us.

Andrew T. McClure, soldier, 1st Regiment of Missouri Mounted Volunteers, to Rio Vigita, his wife, letter of August 20, 1846, on seizing Santa Fe, in Smith and Judah's Chronicles of the Gringos: The U.S. Army in the Mexican War, 1846–1848 *(1968).*

After travelling about ten miles we struck a wagon-trail, which evidently had been made several years. From the indentations of the wheels, where the earth was soft, five or six wagons had passed here. The appearance of this trail in this desolate region was at first inexplicable; but I soon recollected that some five or six years ago an emigrating expedition to California was fitted out by Colonel Bartlettson, Mr. J. Chiles, and others, of Missouri, who, under the guidance of Captain Walker, attempted to enter California by passing round the southern terminus of the Sierra Nevada; and that they were finally compelled to abandon their wagons and every thing they had, and did not reach their destination until they had suffered incredible hardships and privations. This, it appeared to me, was evidently their trail; and old as it was, and scarcely perceivable, it was nevertheless some gratification to us that civilized human beings had passed here before, and left their mark upon the barren earth behind them.

Edwin Bryant, near the Salt Lake flats, August 1846, in What I Saw in California.

Some time we passed the grave of one who had sickened and died on the way. The earth was usually torn up, and covered thickly with wolf-tracks. Some had escaped this violation. One morning, a piece of plank, standing upright on the summit of a grassy hill, attracted our notice, and riding up to it, we found the following words very roughly traced upon it, apparently with a red-hot piece of iron:—

MARY ELLIS.
Died May 7th, 1845.
aged two months.

Such tokens were of common occurrence.

Francis Parkman, traveling along the Oregon Trail, 1846, in The Oregon Trail.

On the 13th of August, having been joined by Major Frémont with about eighty riflemen, and Mr. Larkin, late American consul, we entered this famous "City of the Angels," the capital of the Californias, and took unmolested possession of the government house.

Thus, in less than a month after I assumed the command of the United States force in California, we have chased the Mexican army more than three hundred miles along the coast; pursued them thirty miles in the interior of their own country; routed and dispersed them, and secured the Territory to the United States; ended the war; restored peace and harmony among the people; and put a Civil government into successful operation.

Commodore Robert F. Stockton, to Secretary of the Navy George Bancroft, letter of August 28, 1846, in Smith and Judah's Chronicles of the Gringos.

From the columns of this small sheet [*The Californian*] we gleamed some farther items of general intelligence from the United States, all of great interest to us. The leading paragraph, under the editorial head, was, in substance, a call upon the people of California to set about the organization of a territorial government, with a view to immediate annexation to the United States. This seemed and sounded very odd. We had been traveling in as straight a line as we could, crossing rivers, mountains, and deserts, nearly four months beyond the bounds of civilization, and for the greater distance beyond the boundries of territory claimed by our government; but here, on the remotest confines of the world as it were, where we expected to visit and explore a foreign country, we found ourselves under American authority, and about to be "annexed" to the American Union.

Edwin Bryant, August 30, 1846, in What I Saw in California.

We were late in breaking up our camp on the following morning, and scarcely had we ridden a mile when we saw, far in advance of us, drawn against the horizon, a line of objects stretching at regular intervals along the level edge of the prairie. An intervening swell soon hid them from sight, until, ascending it a quarter of an hour after, we saw close before us the emigrant caravan, with its heavy white wagons creeping on in slow procession, and a large drove of cattle following behind. Half a dozen yellow-visaged Missourians, mounted on horseback, were cursing and shouting among them, their lank angular proportions enveloped in brown homespun, evi-

Expulsion of the Mormons from Nauvoo, Illinois, 1846. Courtesy of the Library of Congress.

dently cut and adjusted by the hands of a domestic female tailor. As we approached, they called to us: "How are ye, boys? Are ye for Oregon or California?" *Francis Parkman, 1846, in* The Oregon Trail.

This scene of confusion, fright and distress was continued throughout the forenoon. In every part of the city scenes of destitution, misery and woe met the eye. Families were hurrying away from their homes, without a shelter,—without means of conveyance,—without tents, money, or a day's provision, with as much of their household stuff as they could carry in their hands. Sick men and women were carried upon their beds—weary mothers, with helpless babes dying in the arms, hurried away—all fleeing, they scarcely knew or cared whither, so it was from their enemies, whom they feared more than the waves of the Mississippi, or the heat, and hunger and lingering life and dreaded death of the prairies on which they were about to be cast. The ferry boats were crowded, and the river bank was lined with anxious fugitives, sadly awaiting their turn to pass over and take up their solitary march to the wilderness.

M. Brayman, legal counsel to Governor Ford of Illinois, report of October 20, 1846, on the expulsion of the Mormons from Nauvoo, Illinois, in September 1846, in Linn's The Story of the Mormons.

I told him I did not desire to extend slavery, that I would be satisfied to acquire by Treaty from Mexico the Provinces of New Mexico & the Californias, and that in these Provinces slavery could probably never exist, and the great probability was that the question would never arise in the future organization of territorial or State Governments in these territories. I told him that slavery was purely a domestic question, and to restrict the appropriation which had been asked for, so as to require the President to insert it in a Treaty with a Foreign Power, was not only inappropriate and out of place, but that if such a

Treaty were made it must be opposed by every Senator from a slave-holding State, and as one third of the Senators could reject a Treaty it could not be ratified, though it might be satisfactory in all other respects.

President James Polk, on discussing a proposed anti-slavery amendment with David Wilmot, diary entry of December 23, 1846, in Diary of James Polk During His Presidency.

You are surrounded by twenty thousand men, and cannot, in any human probability, avoid suffering a rout, and being cut to pieces with your troops; but as you deserve consideration and particular esteem, I wish to save you from a catastrophe, and for that purpose give you notice, in order that you may surrender at discretion, under the assurance that you will be treated with the consideration belonging to the Mexican character; to which end you will be granted an hour's time to make up your mind, to commence from the moment when my flag of truce arrives in your camp. With this view, I assure you of my particular consideration.

Santa Anna, to General Zachary Taylor, before the battle of Buena Vista, message of February 22, 1847, in Weems' To Conquer A Peace: The War Between the United States and Mexico *(1974).*

Sir:

In reply to your note of this date, summoning my forces at discretion, I beg leave to say I decline according to your request.

General Zachary Taylor, to Santa Anna, message of February 22, 1847, in Rives' The United States and Mexico.

About 11.30 the discharge of a few rockets by *our* rocketeers caused a stampede amongst the Mexicans—they fired escopettes and muskets from all parts of their walls. Our mortars reopened about 1.30 with the greatest vigor—sometimes there were six

The battle of Palo Alto, May 8, 1846. Courtesy of the Library of Congress.

shells in the air at the same time. A violent Norther commenced about 1 o'clock making the trenches very disagreeable. About three quarters of an hour, or an hour after we reopened we heard a bugle sound in town. At first we thought it a bravado—then reveillé, then a parley—so we stopped firing to await the result. Nothing more was heard, so in about half an hour we reopened with great warmth. At length another chi-wang-a-wang was heard which turned out to be a parley. During the day the terms of surrender of the town of Vera Cruz and castle of San Juan de Ulua were agreed upon, and on 29th of March, 1847 the garrison marched out with drums beating, colors flying and laid down their arms on the plain between the lagoon and the city . . .

Lieutenant George B. McClellan, on the battle of Vera Cruz, diary entry of March 25, 1847, in The Mexican War Diary of General George B. McClellan *(1917).*

Our positions will be ticklish, if Santa Anna should compel Taylor and Wool even to fall back. All Durango, Zacatecas and Chihuahua will be down upon my little army. We are out of the reach of help, and it would be as unsafe to go backward as forward.— High spirits and a bold front, is perhaps the best and the safest policy. My men are rough, ragged, and ready, having one more of the R's than Gen. Taylor himself. We have been in service nine months, and my men, after marching two thousand miles, over mountains and deserts, have not received one dollar of their pay, yet they stand it without murmuring. Half rations, hard marches, and no clothes! but they are still game to the last, and curse and praise their country by turns, but fight for her all the time.

Colonel Alexander Doniphan, to Major Ryland, after occupying Chihuahua, letter of March 1847, in George's Heroes and Incidents of the Mexican War, Containing Doniphan's Expedition.

But the third day the enemy alternately scattered their shot, and now every spot was a place of danger. This was the actual condition of the desolate families, suffering so much anguish, without advice, hope, sleep or food, solely engaged in preserving their lives, yet more aggravated by the reflection of the uncertain fate of their sons and brothers, remaining on the fortifications, who in return sympathized with this condition of their parents, known to be subjected to the explosion of every bomb upon their own

habitation. Most of the families whose houses had been destroyed, had lost every thing, all the property remaining to them was the clothes on their backs because what the flames did not consume, was buried under the ruins. Hundreds of persons, as well as fathers of numerous families of children, heretofore relying upon certain incomes, to-day find themselves without a bed to lie upon, without covering or clothing to shelter them, and without any victuals.

Niles' National Register, *on the battle of Vera Cruz, May 8, 1847.*

. . . we come to Brigers Fort & we lost another ox   we sold some of our provisions & baut a yoak of Cows & oxen and thay pursuaded us to take Hastings cutof over the salt plain   thay said it saved 3 Hundred miles.   we went that road & we had to go through a long drive of 40 miles With out water   Hastings said it was 40 but i think 80 miles   We traveld a day and night & a nother day and at noon pa went on to see if he coud find Water.   he had not bin gone long till some of the oxen give out and we had to leve the wagons and take the oxen on to water.

Virginia Reed, Donner party survivor, to Mary C. Keyes, her cousin, letter of May 16, 1847, in Stewart's Ordeal By Hunger: The Story of the Donner Party *(1936).*

The most direct route, for the California emigrants, would be to leave the Oregon route, about two hundred miles east from Fort Hall; thence bearing west southwest, to the Salt Lake; and thence continuing down to the bay of St. Francisco.

Lansford Hastings, 1845, in The Emigrants' Guidebook to Oregon and California.

Neither have I the least idea of "joining" you, or in any way assisting the unjust war waging against Mexico. I have no wish to participate in such "glorious" butcheries of women and children as were displayed in the capture of Monterey, &c. Neither have I any desire to place myself under the dictation of a petty military tyrant, to every caprice of whose will I must yield implicit obedience. No sir-ee! As long as I can work, beg, or go to the poor house, I won't go to Mexico, to be lodged on the damp ground, half starved, half roasted, bitten by mosquetoes and centipedes, stung by scorpions and tarantulas— marched, drilled, and flogged, and then stuck up to

Members of the Donner Party. Courtesy of the California Department of Parks and Recreation.

be shot at, for eight dollars a month and putrid rations. Well, I won't.

Anonymous young man of Massachusetts, letter of June 16, 1847, to the Cambridge Chronicle.

On this spot . . . the pioneers arrived on Thursday 23rd of July last, at five P.M.; the next morning removed to the spot where the city will be built; at noon consecrated and dedicated the place to the Lord; the same afternoon four plows were tearing up the ground; next day the brethren had planted five acres of potatoes and irrigated all the land at night . . . During the short space between 23rd of July and 28th August we ploughed and planted about eighty-four acres with corn, potatoes, beans, buckwheat, turnips and a variety of garden sause. We irrigated all the land.

Thomas Buloch, secretary to Brigham Young, to his brother in England, on settling the Great Salt Lake Valley, letter of July 1847, in Neff's History of Utah *(1940).*

For my own part I am happily disappointed in the appearance of the valley of the Salt Lake, but if the land be as rich as it has the appearance of being, I have no fear but the Saints can live here and do well while we will do right. When I commune with my own heart and ask myself whether I would choose to dwell here in this wild looking country amongst the Saints surrounded by friends, though poor, enjoying the privileges and blessings of the everlasting priesthood, with God for our King and Father; or dwell amongst the gentiles with all their wealth and good things of the earth, to be eternally mobbed, harassed, hunted, our best men murdered and every good man's life continually in danger, the soft whisper echoes loud and reverberates back in tones of stern determination; give me the quiet wilderness and my family to associate with, surrounded by the Saints and adieu to the gentile world till God says return and avenge you of your enemies.

William Clayton, member of the Mormon expedition to the Great Salt Lake Basin, journal entry of July 22, 1847, in William Clayton's Journal *(1921).*

[General Scott] took off his hat, and waving it around his head—his white locks giving him the appearance of some inspired old patriarch—shouted forth in the voice of a Stentor: 'Now, my lads, give them a Cerro Gordo shout!' A simultaneous hurrah arose on the morning air, from twenty-five hundred brazen throats, that shook the walls of the palace and must have given a death-blow to the hopes of any Mexican patriots who were looking on. The cry was joined in and prolonged by the by-standers of the other corps, and before its echoes had died away, the division, with its bands playing and banners flying, was in motion. It was, indeed, a thrilling spectacle to behold this vanguard of the American army moving to the conquest of Mexico.

Lieutenant Raphael Semmes (U.S. Navy), recalling General Winfield Scott's occupation of the city of Puebla, August 7, 1847, in Service Afloat and Ashore During the Mexican War *(1851).*

General Mora was presented to General Scott. All gave way at once for the interview between the two generals and Mr. Trist, the American commissioner. The Mexican handed a parcel to General Scott, who handed it over to Mr. Trist, who broke the seal and read the enclosure. The parties have now been in conference over half an hour under the shade of a

General Zachary Taylor (second from left) at his headquarters near Monterrey, 1847. Painting by William Carl Brown, Jr. Courtesy of the West Point Museum, U.S. Military Academy.

tree. We outsiders suppose communications have been opened between the Mexican Government and ours, and we hope it may be the beginning of a peace.

General Ethan Allen Hitchcock, at Coyoacan, diary entry of August 21, 1847, in Fifty Years in Camp and Field: Diary of E.A.H., U.S.A. *(1909).*

At about daylight on the 14th when on the point of opening the fire of our batteries upon the citadel, a white flag appeared in that direction, coming to announce that the Mexican army had abandoned it as well as the city during the night, leaving an officer in charge of the citadel to surrender it to us. As I was the only staff officer present who could speak the Spanish language, I was sent with Lieutenant Lovell, one of General Quitman's aides, to see if the information was correct; the bearer of the flag being kept as a hostage until our return. Upon entering the citadel, the officer left in charge of it, offering to turn over everything, *provided we would furnish him with our receipts!* I looked at him in utter amazement and finally told him that in such cases, we "gave our receipts with the points of our swords! That if he did not give up the property under his charge willingly, we would *take it.*" He then made a bow and gave that eternal answer, *"Para servir a Vmds., Señores."* [At your service, Sirs]. Lovell then made the signal we had agreed upon, and our troops marched in, taking possession of the citadel, the property, the documents and the officer!

Lieutenant Pierre Gustave Beauregard recalls the capture of Mexico City, September 14, 1847, in With Beauregard in Mexico, The Mexican War Reminiscences of P.G.T. Beauregard *(1956).*

Although the Mexicans kept up a resistance for a time, it was soon overcome; but while it lasted the American soldiers showed more ferocity than had been exhibited by them during the whole course of the war. The remembrance of the murder of their wounded comrades on the field of Molino del Rey was still fresh, and, where resistance was made, quarter was rarely given. General Pérez was killed fighting; Colonel Caño, engineer of the castle, and a host of inferior officers and soldiers fell in the tumult; and although the struggle lasted but a few minutes, it was not until the soldiers were satiated with revenge, and the first fury consequent upon the successful assault had passed away, that the bloodshed was put a stop to.

Roswell S. Ripley, aide to General J. Pillow, on the battle of Chapultepec, September 13, 1847, in The War With Mexico *(1849).*

. . . this small force has beaten . . . the whole Mexican army, of (at the beginning) thirty-odd thousand men—posted, always in chosen positions, behind entrenchments, or more formidable defences of nature and art; killed or wounded, of that number, more than 7,000 officers and men; taken 3,730 prisoners, one-seventh officers, including 13 generals, of whom 3 had been presidents of this republic; captured more than 20 colors and standards, 75 pieces of ordnance, besides 57 wall-pieces, 20,000 small arms, an immense quantity of shots, shells, powder, &c., &c.

General Winfield Scott, on the capture of Mexico City, report of September 1847, in Rives' The United States and Mexico.

At 7 o'clock this morning Gen. Scott, with his staff, rode in and took quarters in the national palace, on the top of which the regimental flag of the gallant rifles and the stars and stripes were already flying, and an immense crowd of blanketed leperos, the scum of the capital, were congregated in the plaza as the commander-in-chief entered it. They pressed our soldiers, and eyed them as though they were beings of another world. So much were they in the way, and with such eagerness did they press around, that Gen. Scott was compelled to order our Dragoons to clear the plaza. They were told, however, not to injure or harm a man in the mob—they were all our friends.

George W. Kendall, newspaper correspondent of the New Orleans Picayune, *on General Scott's final military action in Mexico City, September 14, 1847.*

Seeing further resistance useless, our soldiers ceased firing, and on the 16th of September (sad day!) the

General Scott's entrance into the Grand Plaza at Mexico City, September 14, 1847. Courtesy of the Library of Congress.

enemy was in possession of the Mexican capital. Though we inflicted havoc and death upon the Yankees, we suffered greatly ourselves. Many were killed by the blowing up of the houses, many by the bombardment, but more by the confusion which prevailed in the city, and altogether we cannot count our killed, wounded and missing since the actions commenced yesterday at less than 4,000, among whom are many women and children. The enemy confesses a loss of over 1,000, it is no doubt much greater. What a calamity! But Mexico will yet have vengeance. God will avenge us for our sufferings.

Anonymous Mexican merchant, on the American occupation of Mexico City, September 16, 1847, in Smith and Judah's Chronicles of the Gringos.

It seems certain that Mexico must ultimately submit to such terms of peace as the United States shall dictate. An heterogeneous population of seven millions, with very limited resources and no credit; distracted by internal dissensions, and by the ambition of its chiefs, a prey by turns to anarchy and to military usurpers; occupying among the nations of the civilized world, either physically or mentally, whether in political education, social state, or any other respect, but an inferior position; cannot contend successfully with an energetic, intelligent, enlightened and united nation of twenty millions, possessed of unlimited resources and credit, and enjoying all the benefits of a regular, strong, and free government. All this was anticipated; but the extraordinary successes of the Americans have exceeded the most sanguine expectations. All the advanced posts of the enemy, New Mexico, California, the line of the lower Rio Norte, and all the sea ports, which it was deemed necessary to occupy, have been subdued.

Albert Gallatin, financier and public official, 1847, on the defeat of Mexico and the acquisition of new territories for the United States in Peace with Mexico (1847).

It rains and snows. We start this morning around the falls with our wagons . . . I carry my babe, and lead, or rather carry, another through snow, mud and water, almost to my knees. It is the worst road . . . I went ahead with my children and I was afraid to look behind me for fear of seeing the wagons turn over into the mud . . . My children gave out with cold and fatigue and could not travel, and the boys had to unhitch the oxen and bring them and carry the children on to camp. I was so cold and numb. I could not tell by feeling that I had any feet at all . . . I have not told you half we suffered. I am not adequate to the task.

Elizabeth Smith Geer, Oregon Territory pioneer from Indiana, on passing over the Oregon Trail, diary entry of November 1847, in Schlissel's Women's Diaries of the Westward Journey.

The cession to the United States by Mexico of the Provinces of New Mexico and the Californias, as proposed by the commissioner of the United States, it was believed would be more in accordance with the convenience and interests of both nations than any other cession of territory which it was probable Mexico could be induced to make.

It is manifest to all who have observed the actual condition of the Mexican Government for some years past and at present that if these Provinces should be retained by her she could not long continue to hold and govern them. Mexico is too feeble a power to govern these Provinces, lying as they do at a distance of more than 1,000 miles from her capital, and if attempted to be retained by her they would constitute but for a short time even nominally a part of her dominions. This would be especially the case with Upper California.

. . . The Provinces of New Mexico and the Californias are contiguous to the territories of the United States, and if brought under the government of our laws their resources—mineral, agricultural, manufacturing, and commercial—would soon be developed.

President James Polk, third annual message to Congress, December 7, 1847, in Richardson's Messages and Papers of the Presidents.

7. The Gold Rush and the Debate Over Slavery in the West: 1848–1859

THE CALIFORNIA GOLD RUSH

A Swiss immigrant to the United States, John Augustus Sutter, was destined to play a prominent role in the California Gold Rush. Sutter arrived in California in 1839, and within a year had charmed the Mexican authorities into granting him 49,000 acres on the south bank of the American River near the Sacramento River. Here he established a self-contained estate, complete with a fort, gristmill, grainfields, herds, orchards and a small army of workers. As a Mexican citizen and minor official, Sutter was a generous and hospitable patron, especially to American emigrants and other visitors.

Until 1848, Sutter's empire remained undisturbed, but after one of his hands discovered gold while building a sawmill on his land, Sutter's estate was no longer considered private property. Within a year hordes of prospectors from throughout the nation and around the world began descending on Sutter's mill. The discovery of gold had triggered the great Gold Rush of 1849.

In the wake of the Mexican War, Mexico had ceded California to the United States. Despite Sutter's support for statehood, the new authorities did not recognize his land title. Four years after gold was discovered, Sutter was bankrupt. For the next several years he continued to petition state and national authorities for compensation and for title to his property, but was unsuccessful in his efforts.

The East learned of the discovery at Sutter's mill in September 1848, when reports, accompanied by a little box of dust and nuggets, arrived from Thomas O. Larkin, the American consul at Monterey. Within a month 61 crowded ships were sailing around South America destined for the "diggings" in California. Fortune seekers who could not afford the exorbitant cost of the sea passage spent the winter preparing for the overland journey. By the middle of May 1849, 5,000 wagons were trudging westward along the California Trail, stretching from present day Utah to Sacramento.

Many of these untrained emigrants knew nothing of overland travel, only the little information they had gleaned from guidebook writers and newspaper reporters. Thousands lost their lives to the cholera that lurked in muddy watering holes, while others fell victim to starvation or Indian attack. By the fall of 1849 skeletons of dead horses and cattle littered the sides of the heavily used trails for hundreds of miles. Unmarked human graves were also quite common.

The most severe portion of the journey lay near the end of the ordeal, where the Forty-Niners would have to overcome the steep and barren slopes of the Sierra Nevadas. Fatigued emigrants often abandoned their wagons and ate their starving pack animals, hoping to build up their stamina for the climb. Others sought a route around the southern tip of the mountains and wandered unexpectedly into the Death Valley region. Those who survived these obstacles were more than prepared for the long days of work ahead at the diggings.

At the mining camps, appropriately named Poker Flat, Whiskey Bark, Hell's Delight, Skunk Gulch, Dry Diggings, among others, rooms rented for $1,000 a month and eggs cost $10 a dozen. The assembled characters included Missouri farmers, Navy sailors, Georgia planters, English storekeepers, Mexican peasants, Chinese and Indians, along with a number of desperados and gamblers. All were drawn to California by the magnet of gold. By the end of 1849, 100,000 people were living in California, most of whom were respectable citizens desiring a better way of keeping order than the vigilante committees created to preserve the peace.

THE GREAT COMPROMISE

The lack of law and order in California forced Congress into finally deciding whether slavery would be permitted in the newly acquired territories. It was clear that some form of government had to be established in the western territory. President Zachary Taylor urged Californians to prepare a constitution and apply for admission as a state directly, thus avoiding the issue of congressional authority over the territories. On August 1, 1849, Californians elected 48 delegates to a state constitutional convention that met in Monterey the following September. By October 1850 the delegation had drafted an acceptable constitution that included a controversial clause, the prohibition of slavery. The document was overwhelmingly ratified by the voters in November. A governor and legislature was chosen, and California was on its way to becoming a state. It was now up to Congress to approve its admission.

In his first annual message to Congress, President Taylor had strongly urged the legislative body to admit California and organize New Mexico and Utah as territories without any reference to slavery. However, Southerners were alarmed at the prospect of a free California disturbing the Senate balance between free and slave states. John C. Calhoun, the elder statesman from South Carolina, championed the South's cause, declaring, "We have borne the wrongs and insults of the North long enough." William H. Seward of New York spoke for the Northern Abolitionists, retorting, "You cannot roll back the tide of social progress." Never before had the nation faced such bitter debate.

Henry Clay of Kentucky, a venerable Whig, and Stephen A. Douglas of Illinois, a young Democrat, hammered out a proposal that was destined to preserve the Union for another decade, the Compromise of 1850. Under the compromise, California entered the Union as a free state, and the remaining two sections were divided into the territories of New Mexico and Utah. Settlers would decide for themselves whether they should become free or slave states. The slave trade in the District of Columbia was abolished, and the Fugitive Slave Act was strengthened. The Fugitive Slave Act was a concession to the Southern states. The Act made it easier for slaveowners to recapture ex-slaves or simply pick up blacks they claimed had run away.

The resolutions by Clay and Douglas triggered one of the outstanding debates in the Senate's history. On February 5, 1850, Henry Clay began a brilliant speech that spanned two days. Asking the North to accept the compromise, he said, "You have nature on your side—fact upon your side—and this truth staring you in the face that there is no slavery in those territories." Clay reminded Southerners of the benefits derived from the Union, and argued that peaceful secession was impossible. He was supported by Douglas and other moderates who realized that compromise was the only solution to avoiding a costly war.

To the extremists any discussion of a compromise was repugnant. Calhoun insisted that the South would accept only a constitutional amendment that protected its institution of slavery, while Seward vehemently argued that slavery was an immoral, backward, dying institution.

A moderate Northerner, Daniel Webster of Massachusetts, was able to stir congressional sentiment toward compromise with his magnificent "Seventh of March" speech. In the last great oration of his life, Webster pleaded "not as a Massachusetts man, nor as a Northern man, but as an American" for unity. Webster's support of the Compromise outraged radical antislavery advocates in New England, but his statesmanlike act was largely responsible for the Compromise's ultimate passage.

When President Taylor died on July 9, 1850, the Compromise gained another champion, Millard Filmore. The new president pressured congressmen into accepting the resolutions, and during the early weeks of September the bills were finally passed, forming the Compromise of 1850. Clay and Webster were able temporarily to extinguish the fire that had been lit by manifest destiny.

Throughout the 1850s the controversy over slavery brought the nation closer and closer to civil war. The Compromise of 1850 could only delay the inevitable separation of North and South. With every advance of settlement the sensitive question of slavery in the territories was reopened.

"BLEEDING KANSAS"

Northerners considered the slavery controversy in the West settled. The Missouri Compromise specified that all lands east of the Rockies and north latitude 36°30'N should become free territories, all south of the line, slave. The Compromise of 1850 covered the territories acquired from Mexico. However, these measures were far from acceptable to Southerners, who saw slavery as a dynamic institution that must expand to survive. Southern Democrats seized the opportunity to acquire more slave-holding territory when the Kansas-Nebraska bill was presented to Congress in January 1854.

Stephen A. Douglas of Illinois, the act's sponsor, proposed that the unorganized region of the Great Plains be divided into the two territories of Kansas and Nebraska. Both would be open to slavery during the territorial period, but ultimately the people would decide by popular vote whether they wanted the institution. Douglas understood that slavery could not legally exist north of the 36°30'N line as long as the Missouri Compromise remained law. The Kansas-Nebraska Act virtually repealed the ordinance by declaring that the true intent of Congress was "not to legislate slavery into any Territory or State, nor to exclude it therefrom, but to leave the people thereof perfectly free to" decide the issue.

The bill, backed by President Franklin Pierce, was passed on May 25, 1854. Immediately squatters began crossing the border, seeking new farms for settlement with their families. Most came from north of the Ohio River, and very few owned slaves. It is likely that if outside forces had not interfered, Kansas would have established antislavery communities without much strife. But Northern abolitionists were furious at what they considered the South's attempt to win over Kansas, and they decided to eradicate the institution by sending enough Free-Soilers into the territory to outvote the slaveholders.

The abolitionists quickly formed emigration societies to send Free-Soilers to the disputed Kansas territory. The New England Emigration

Stephen A. Douglas. Courtesy of the New York Public Library.

Society, led by Eli Thayer of Massachusetts, was one of the most prominent. By the summer of 1854 Thayer was boasting that his society would have 1,000 settlers in Kansas by the end of August and 20,000 by the first of the year. These claims turned out to be grossly exaggerated. Only 4,209 pioneers moved to Kansas from New England, the abolitionist center, during those critical years, and of those only 1,240 were sponsored by the Emigration Aid Society. However, rumors spread throughout the territory that 20,000 Free-Soilers supported by $5 million were on their way.

In fall 1854, an election was set to choose a legislature. Missourians were in a majority at that time, but they were unwilling to leave the election to chance. On the day of the election 5,000 "Border Ruffians," all heavily armed, descended on Kansas, took control of the voting booths and cast four times as many ballots as there were registered voters in the territory. Although the territorial governor, Andrew H. Reeder, was a proslavery Democrat, he protested against the fraudulent election. At the town of Shawnee Mission a proslavery legislature convened and passed laws limiting offices to proslavery advocates and providing for the imprisonment of anyone who declared the institution illegal in the territory; they also enacted measures for punishing anyone speaking or writing against slaveholding. Governor Reeder continued to object to the new government and was soon dismissed.

Free-staters responded by holding their own election to choose delegates for a constitutional convention that would seek admission for Kansas as a free state. In October 1855, the delegates met at Topeka and drafted a constitution that prohibited slavery. Two months later the constitution was overwhelmingly ratified and a Northern government was organized. Kansas now had two separate governments, each with its own legislature, governor and delegate to Congress. The proslave advocates were situated around Leavenworth and Atchison in the Missouri Valley, and the Free-staters resided in Topeka and Lawrence on the Kansas River. The Southerners were supported by the Missouri "Border Ruffians," who were eager to wipe out the abolitionist crusaders. Civil conflict was inevitable.

The hostilities began in spring 1856 when a proslave sheriff visiting Lawrence was shot in the back by an unknown gunman. Although the Free-staters denied any responsibility, a Southern grand jury indicted half the leading citizens of Lawrence for treason. The federal marshal appointed to deliver the warrants marched into the town on May 21, 1856, accompanied by a posse of 800 "Border Ruffians." The mob ransacked the town, destroying the printing press of the local newspaper, tearing down a hotel and burning the homes of several presumed abolitionists.

Overnight Kansas became a testing ground for the forces of freedom and slavery. Southerners proclaimed the "Border Ruffians" as proud soldiers fighting for their sacred cause, while the Northerners glorified the Free-staters as the crusaders of freedom. In New Haven, Connecticut, the Reverend Henry Ward Beecher, in addressing a group of Kansas-bound settlers, urged them to enter the territory armed with the dreaded Sharp's rifle, one of the first successful breechloaders. From then on Easterners entering the disputed territory carried with them rifles that were christened "Beecher's Bibles." All-out civil war in Kansas was approaching.

Soon after the Lawrence raid fighting once again erupted. The turmoil was ignited by John Brown, a religious fanatic whose Old Testament God demanded the spilling of blood for blood. Upset with the pillage of Lawrence, he believed he was divinely appointed to avenge the wrongs inflicted by the Southerners. On the night of May 24, 1856, Brown, with his four sons and a few followers, snuck up quietly on the neighboring hamlet of Pottawatomie Creek and hacked five Southerners to death. The "Pottawatomie Massacre" inflamed the war in "Bleeding Kansas." For the next three months "Border Ruffians" and Northern fanatics roamed the territory, burning, pillaging and murdering. An estimated $2 million worth of property and 200 lives were lost.

"Bleeding Kansas" divided the nation, as many Southerners came to believe that all Northerners were fanatics who were determined to annihilate the slaveholder, and many Northerners accepted the behavior of the "Border Ruffians" as typical of all Southerners. The days of compromise were past. Free-staters were now eager to force their will on the minority South. "Bleeding Kansas" and the controversy over slavery played a major role in the presidential election of 1856.

As the election approached, Northerners abandoned the Whig Party and flocked to the new Republican Party, which incorporated the antislavery forces of the Know-Nothings and the Free-Soilers, and which did not advocate compromise with the minority South. The Republicans chose as their candidate explorer John C. Fremont. Their platform demanded the immediate admission of Kansas as a free state. It also called for the construction of a transcontinental railroad to the Pacific. While the Democrats also endorsed the Pacific railroad, their platform endorsed the Kansas-Nebraska Act and asserted that popular sovereignty, i.e., "non-interference by Congress with Slavery in States and Territories," was the appropriate solution to the problem of slavery in the new territories.

In a close election, the Democratic proslavery candidate, James Buchanan, defeated the "Pathfinder of the West." Fremont came closer than any previous presidential candidate to uniting the North and West against the South. He carried every free state except Indiana, Illinois, Pennsylvania, New Jersey and California.

In March 1857, the Supreme Court issued a momentous decision in the case of *Dred Scott v. Sanford* that further exacerbated the conflict between North and South. Dred Scott, a slave, sued for his freedom on the basis that his master, an Army surgeon, had taken him into Illinois and then to the Wisconsin Territory, where slavery had been barred by Congress in the Missouri Compromise of 1820. Chief Justice Taney and a majority of the Court ruled that the Missouri Compromise was unconstitutional because it violated the property rights protected by the Fifth Amendment, since it denied slave owners the right to take their property wherever they chose. Effectively opening the West to slavery, the decision enraged the North and drove the nation closer to civil war.

THE MORMON CONFLICT

Meanwhile, with more Americans moving westward, Brigham Young's dream of an independent desert nation was coming to a close. Mormon independence was threatened in 1850 when the federal government created the Utah Territory, which included all of present-day Utah, most of Nevada, the western third of Colorado and part of Wyoming.

Mormon fears of federal interference were eased when President Millard Filmore appointed Brigham Young governor and four Saints to other administrative posts. For the next five years the Mormon state continued to function smoothly, with property disputes settled by church courts, justice administered according to ecclesiastical law and government affairs conducted without regard to the statutes of the United States. Then in 1855 three anti-Mormon judges were appointed to the territory, two were disgruntled former Saints, and the third an avowed enemy of the Mormon Church. They returned to Washington in 1857 and characterized Brigham Young as a tyrannical dictator who commanded his followers to eliminate all opposition and defy the federal authorities.

These accusations aroused a barrage of complaints against the Saints. The surveyor general of the United States charged that the Mormons refused to permit him to operate in the territory. Indian agents complained that "lawless" young men from Utah were settling on Indian lands. Overland immigrants involved in land or livestock disputes with the Mormons complained to Congress. The reports fueled the nation's growing antipathy for the Mormon practice of polygamy. By the mid-1850s, several books had condemned plural marriage as immoral, newspapers railed against it and ministers called from the pulpit for the elimination of the sinful practice. In this heated atmosphere every charge against the Mormons was magnified.

In May 1857, President James Buchanan ordered 2,500 troops to Utah with instructions to enforce federal authority over the Saints. Unaware of the expedition's purpose, the Mormons were convinced that their foes in Washington were determined to assassinate their leaders and annihilate their church. They believed themselves once again under persecution.

Into this atmosphere of tension came the Fancher Company of 140 emigrants from Arkansas bound for California. A few in the group were "Missouri Wild Cats" who taunted the Mormons they met, boasting that they had been among the mob in 1838 that had killed 17 Mormons at Haun's Mill, and spreading the rumor that the United States Army was on its way to decimate the Mormon settlement.

On September 7, 1857, the Fancher party was attacked by Indians at Mountain Meadows in southern Utah, with seven men killed and the rest of the party under siege. One of the emigrants managed to escape and tried to summon aid from the Mormons, but he was slain by a fanatical Saint who resented the earlier insults of the Missourians. A group of Mormons, fearing that their entire community would be punished for the murder, decided to kill every member of the train. A message was sent to the besieged train that the Indians had been pacified and it was safe for them to leave. As the emigrants emerged they were ruthlessly shot down by the Mormons. Within minutes 120 persons lay dead, while only 17 children were spared. The tragedy became known as the Mountain Meadows Massacre.

Federal officials were convinced that if federal troops ever clashed with the Mormons, there would be further bloodshed. The only solution was a peaceful settlement to the Mormon War. Colonel Thomas

Kane, an old friend of the Saints, met with Brigham Young and convinced the Mormons that the United States had no intention of interfering with their religion and that federal troops should be permitted to enter the territory. A compromise was struck where President Buchanan pardoned the Mormons for their "rebellion" and Young yielded his governorship to a gentile—but as head of the church continued in effect to rule the Utah Territory.

CONNECTING THE CENTERS

During the early 1850s pressure was mounting by Westerners, especially California miners, for a direct overland route that would assure the regular movement of the mails. In 1857, Congress passed the Post Office Appropriation Act, which authorized the postmaster general to solicit bids for a semiweekly or weekly mail service from "such point on the Mississippi River as the contractors may select, to San Francisco." According to the bill, the company selected must guarantee delivery within 25 days in return for an annual subsidy of $600,000.

A firm headed by two experienced expressmen, John Butterfield and William G. Fargo, was chosen to establish a route from St. Louis or Memphis through Fort Smith, El Paso and Fort Yuma to San Francisco. After a year of preparation the Butterfield Overland Mail started its first stagecoaches across the continent. Distributed across the wilderness route were 1,800 horses and mules, at 165 wooden and adobe stations.

Western travel was revolutionized by the Butterfield Overland Mail stages, known as Concord Coaches after the Abbott-Downing Company of Concord, New Hampshire, which built them. Better designed for journeys across the Plains and deserts than earlier stages, their heavy wheels prevented the coaches from sinking in soft sand, and their iron-reinforced bodies absorbed some of the worst shocks. Service was launched with much fanfare on September 15, 1858, from a station at Tipton, Missouri, and simultaneously from one in San Francisco. For three weeks they raced across the prairies, one traveling east and the other west, as frontiersmen gathered from miles around to witness the latest breakthrough in communications.

On the morning of October 10, 1858, a dust-covered stage rode into San Francisco, 24 days out of Missouri, while the eastbound coach had arrived in St. Louis a few days earlier. Both coaches maintained an astonishing average of nearly 120 miles a day. For the next three years the Butterfield Overland Mail prospered as its coaches whizzed across the continent, two each week in each direction, through rain and snow and desert heat, with only brief stops for station breaks. However, by 1860, Westerners were demanding an even faster mail service.

Preparations were underway for a fantastic scheme that would carry the mails by relays of horsemen from Missouri to California in 10 days—the Pony Express.

As early as 1845 a transcontinental railroad had been proposed to Congress. Asa Whitney, a New York businessman and China trader, suggested that the government grant a 60-mile-wide strip between Lake Superior and the Oregon country to any firm willing to finance construction. After Congress shelved his visionary plan, Whitney continued for the next decade to promote the idea of a railroad to the Pacific. By 1853, Congress realized the need for a government-funded, transcontinental railroad.

Sectional antagonism contributed to the debate over which route was best for a transcontinental railroad. Southerners insisted the government support a line along the Butterfield Overland Mail route, while Northerners promoted a railway through the South Pass in present-day Wyoming. Congress decided the problem could best be settled by the topography, and in spring 1853, the legislature commissioned the Army to survey all feasible routes between the Mississippi Valley and the Pacific.

Two years later, 10 thick volumes were presented to Congress, showing that four routes were practical: one between Lake Superior and Portland, another through the South Pass to San Francisco, a third along the Red River to Southern California, and a fourth across southern Texas and the Gila Valley. The route would remain undecided until 1862, after the Confederate states had seceded, when Northerners agreed on the Central Route, between Sacramento and Omaha on the Missouri River.

"Pikes Peak or Bust"

By the late 1850s, the days of the individual prospector were coming to an end. Gold continued to be mined in California, but eastern financiers provided the capital while machines did the work. Many thousands of prospectors failed to find enough gold to pay for their grubstakes, but many continued to hunt the grounds of the West, from the Pacific to the Rockies and from the mountains of British Columbia to the desert valley near the Gila River. Occasionally a rich pocket was struck and miners throughout the West raced to the new "diggings." One of the wildest rushes in the nation's history took place during 1859 in the Pikes Peak region of Colorado, near the Rocky Mountains.

A small strike had been made in the spring of 1858 by a member of William Green Russell's mining expedition along the headwaters of the South Platte. News of the discovery made its way to the Mississippi

Valley, and soon Missouri newspapers were publishing exaggerated accounts of the strike. There were reports of prospectors whose daily take with only a shovel and washing pan was $20. By the spring of 1859, it was "Pikes Peak or Bust" for thousands of farmers and laborers ruined in the financial panic of 1857.

Eager prospectors poured over Pikes Peak guidebooks, which described land that was yellow with gold. Throughout the eastern Rockies they panned every stream, chipped away at every promising rock outcropping and found nothing. In the expression of the times, they had been "humbugged." By midsummer the 50,000 miners who had reached Colorado had returned East.

While the 59ers were returning from Pikes Peak a few prospectors were digging for gold in the mountains surrounding the Carson River Valley in Nevada. In June 1859, two of them, Peter O'Riley and Patrick McLaughlin, uncovered the richest lode in United States history. Henry Comstock, a drifter and reputedly one of the laziest men working at the mine, talked himself into receiving a share of the claim. In fact, Comstock bragged so widely about "his" discovery that soon others began referring to it as the "Comstock Lode."

After the heavy bluish quartz was assayed in Nevada City, California, as pure silver and gold, worth $3,876 a ton, news spread overnight about the incredible riches to be found in the Washoe District. Thousands of prospectors poured into Virginia City, but only a few could mine, for the gold was locked in quartz veins that could be retrieved only with expensive machinery. Less than a dozen of the 3,000 mines claimed proved profitable, but their payoffs were incredible. At Davidson Mountain, $15 million worth of precious metal was mined during the next four years.

The wealth transformed Virginia City into a thriving metropolis, with five newspapers and a stock exchange. Prospectors who failed to strike it rich at the Comstock Lode sought out other mines in western Nevada, while others put aside their wash pans and established the first permanent settlements in the Rocky Mountain country. The Far West was becoming more tame, with emigrants founding townships and the overland expresses bringing news and mail from the East. Meanwhile, as the West was expanding, back East the nation began its descent into civil war.

CHRONICLE OF EVENTS

1848:

January 24: Gold is discovered at Sutter's Creek, a branch of the American River in the lower Sacramento Valley.

February 2: The United States and Mexico sign the treaty of Guadalupe Hidalgo, ending the Mexican-American War. The United States acquires the territories of New Mexico, California and the Rio Grande border of Texas, an addition of 1,193,061 square miles. U.S. agrees to pay $15 million for land and assumes payment of $3.25 million in claims Americans have brought against Mexico.

May 29: Wisconsin admitted to the Union as a free state.

August 14: The Territory of Oregon is formally organized when President Polk signs the Oregon Bill.

November 7: Mexican War hero Zachary Taylor is elected president.

1849:

February 12: San Franciscans gather to set up a temporary government for their region.

March 10: The Mormons vote to form the state of Deseret, with boundaries set and provision for elections.

July 2: The legislature of the state of Deseret adopts a resolution petitioning Congress for admission into the Union.

December 4: President Taylor, in his first annual message to Congress, urges admission of California to the Union.

1850:

Fargo, North Dakota, is established as a post for the Wells Fargo Express Company.

January 29: Senator Henry Clay offers the Compromise of 1850, admitting California as a free state and creating territorial governments for New Mexico and Utah without reference to slavery.

chartered with a grant of 2.7 million acres of land from Cairo to Galena.

March 12: California requests statehood.

July 1: The first overland mail service west of the Missouri River is established, with monthly deliveries between Independence, Missouri, and Salt Lake City, Utah.

July 31: A territorial government is established for the Mormon state of Deseret, now renamed the Utah Territory.

July 25: Gold is discovered in the Rogue River in Oregon.

August 13: The Senate approves the admission of California as the 31st state, with slavery prohibited.

September 26: Brigham Young is officially appointed governor of the Utah Territory by President Fillmore.

1851:

July 23: The Treaty of Traverse des Sioux is signed, in which the Sioux relinquish their lands in Iowa and Minnesota.

1852:

November 2: Franklin Pierce, a Democrat and a supporter of the Compromise of 1850, defeats Winfield Scott in the presidential election.

1853:

March 2: Congress organizes the Washington Territory out of the Oregon Territory, using the 46th parallel as the southern boundary.

March 3: Congress appropriates $150,000 to pay for a survey by the War Department of various routes for a transcontinental railroad.

April 8: Exploration begins for a railroad route between the 47th and 49th parallels.

October 25: Captain John W. Gunnison and a company of eight surveyors are attacked and killed by Indians in the Utah Territory, where they were surveying sites for the transcontinental railroad. U.S. officials believe that Mormons were involved.

December 30: Gadsden Purchase. Cession of

Sutter's Fort, 1848. Courtesy of the New York Public Library.

29,640 square miles of desert, near the southern boundary of New Mexico and Arizona, is secured from Mexico for a purchase of $10 million.

1854:
January 23: Stephen A. Douglas challenges the Missouri Compromise by introducing a bill organizing the country west of the Missouri River into the territories of Kansas and Nebraska; territorial governments would decide whether to be slave or free.
April 26: Abolitionists in Boston form the Massachusetts Emigrant Aid Society to settle Kansas with anti-slave pioneers.
May 22–30: The Kansas-Nebraska Act is passed by Congress. The act establishes two territories, with the settlers to decide the issue of slavery in each.
July: The federal government opens a land office in the new Kansas Territory to distribute property. Proslavery forces are taking claims without regard for the law.

1855:
The U.S. Army subdues the Utes and Jicarilla Apache tribes, removing the threat of attack along the western portion of the Santa Fe Trail.
January 28: A railroad is completed across the Isthmus of Panama, opening an alternate route across North America.
September: Antislavery colonists in Kansas organize the Free State Party.
September 5: Antislavery colonists meet at Big Springs, Kansas, to reject the proslavery legislature. They ask admission to the Union as a free state.
December 15: The Kansas Territory by popular election adopts the Topeka Constitution proposed by the Free-staters. The constitution prohibits entry of slaves into the territory.

1856:

February 11: President Franklin Pierce issues a proclamation warning both the Free-staters and the "Border Ruffians" in Kansas to cease their disruptive activities.

March 17: Stephen A. Douglas introduces a bill calling for a constitutional convention in Kansas, denouncing the antislavery Topeka government in Kansas.

May 21: Civil war erupts in the Kansas Territory.

May 24: Abolitionist John Brown leads the Pottawatomie Massacre, murdering five proslavery colonists living near Dutch Henry's Crossing at Pottawatomie Creek, Kansas.

June 9: The first of 10 handcart brigades leaves Iowa City for Salt Lake City. Two companies totaling 497 persons, all converted to the Mormon faith, carry their belongings in two-wheeled handcarts for miles along the Mormon Trail. They reach Salt Lake City on September 26.

November 4: Democratic candidate James Buchanan defeats Republican John Fremont in the presidential election. The nation is split along proslavery and antislavery lines; Buchanan has won in 14 slave states.

1857:

The last length of track is laid connecting New York City to St. Louis, Missouri.

March 6: In the Dred Scott decision, the Supreme Court declares that the Missouri Compromise of 1820 and all laws banning the importation of slaves in the territories are unconstitutional.

August 28: Fort Abercrombie is established on the banks of the Red River of the North in present-day North Dakota, to protect settlers in the Red River Valley from Sioux attacks.

September 15: With the Utah Territory under martial law, Brigham Young forbids any U.S. armed forces to enter Utah.

September 16: The Butterfield Overland Mail Company is awarded a federal contract to provide mail and passenger service from St. Louis and Memphis to Arkansas, then to Texas, Los Angeles and San Francisco.

December 8: President James Buchanan, in his annual message to Congress, requests money for soldiers and supplies to end the revolution in the Utah Territory.

1858:

Yankton Sioux cede southeastern Dakota to the United States.

May 11: Minnesota is admitted to the Union as a nonslave state. It is the 32nd state of the Union.

September 16: The Butterfield Overland Mail Company starts its first run from St. Louis to San Francisco. Twenty-three days, 23 hours and 3,000 miles later, the destination is reached.

1859:

February 14: Oregon is admitted as the 33rd state, the 18th nonslave state.

March: The '59ers rush to the gold fields of Colorado, near the Rocky Mountains.

June 10: The richest gold and silver mine in U.S. history is discovered, the Comstock Lode in present-day Nevada.

October 4: An anti-slave constitution is ratified in the Kansas Territory.

EYEWITNESS TESTIMONY

The "California Star" Express (60 days to Independence, Mo., by way of Salt Lake,) will leave this place [San Francisco] on the 1st of April, and New Helvetia on the 15th. Postage on letter 50 cents.
The California Star, Announcement of January 15, 1848.

I reached my hand down and picked it up; it made my heart thump, for I was certain that it was gold. The piece was about half the size and of the shape of a pea. Then I saw another piece in the water. After taking it out I sat down and began to think right hard. I thought it was gold, and yet it did not seem to be of the right color: all the gold coin I had seen was of a reddish tinge; this looked more like brass. I recalled to mind all the metals I had ever seen or heard of, but I could find none that resembled this. Suddenly the idea flashed across my mind that it might be iron pyrites. I trembled to think of it! The question could soon be determined. Putting one of the pieces on a hard river stone, I took another and commenced hammering it. It was soft, and it didn't break; it therefore must be gold, but largely mixed with some other metal, very likely silver; for pure gold, I thought would certainly have a brighter color.
James Marshall recalls his initial discovery of gold on January 24, 1848, on the American River in California at Sutter's mill, in The Century Magazine *(Feb. 1891).*

After the water was out we went in and searched for gold. This was done every morning. Small pieces of gold could be seen remaining on the bottom of the clean washed bed rock. I went into the race and picked up several pieces; several of the laborers gave me some which they had picked up, and from Marshall I received a part. I have had a heavy ring made of this gold, with my family's coat of arms engraved on the outside, and on the inside is engraved, "The first gold discovered in January, 1848."
John Augustus Sutter, recalling the first gold discovery at his California mill, in Patterson's Twelve Years in the Mines of California *(1862).*

GOLD MINE FOUND.—In the newly made raceway of the Saw Mill recently erected by Captain Sutter, on the American Fork, gold has been found in considerable quantities. One person brought thirty dollars worth to New Helvetia, gathered there in a short time. California, no doubt, is rich in mineral wealth; great chances here for scientific capitalists. Gold has been found in almost every part of the country.
San Francisco Californian, report of March 15, 1848.

Mines are discovered in many places; but quicksilver is to enrich California beyond all other mines. There is one now in operation belonging to Barron, Forbes & C., an English house in Mexico. The workmen at this mine have only the common try-pots, a few picks and crowbars, and for a few days past have bottled off $300 per day . . . Almost the same expense and labor employed in Pennsylvania, in obtaining a ton of iron, will obtain a ton of quicksilver in California. Neither you nor your readers are expected to believe the most incredible story; yet, such is the fact.
"Paisano" (Thomas O. Larkin), in the New York Herald, *March 30, 1848.*

When peace shall have been made, I do not think Mexico will again be anxious to enter into war with us. I have no doubt that in twenty years all the country lying between the Rio Grande and the Sierra Madre will be annexed to the U.S. and this will be accomplished without a war, if our country shall not interfere. All the northern States are even now almost ripe for a revolution, and if the Mexican government does not grant them many more privileges than it has heretofore, they will in a few years declare themselves independent and ask to be admitted into our Union. Mexico with a population of which three fifths are ignorant, superstitious Indians, can never form a solid government. The only means by which she can ever attain a respectable place among nations is to introduce colonies of foreigners and to give to each a certain quantity of her useless land.
Lieutenant Edmund Bradford, to John Tazewell, letter of May 19, 1848, in Smith and Judah's Chronicles of the Gringos *(1968).*

The whole country, from San Francisco to Los Angeles and from the sea shore to the base of the Sierra Nevada, resounds with the sordid cry of "*gold!* GOLD!! GOLD!!!" while the field is left half planted, the house half built, and everything neglected but the manufacturer of shovels and pickaxes, and the means of transportation to the spot where one man obtained $128 worth of the *real stuff* in one day's

Gold mining in California. Courtesy of the New York Public Library.

washing, and the average for all concerned is $20 per diem.
San Francisco Californian, *report of May 29, 1848.*

I have to report the State Department one of the most astonishing excitements and state of affairs now existing in this country, that, perhaps, has ever been brought to the notice of the government. On the American fork of the Sacramento and Feather river, another branch of the same, and the adjoining lands, there has been, within the present year, discovered a placer, a vast tract of land containing gold, in small particles. This gold, thus far, has been taken on the bank of the river, from the surface to eighteen inches in depth, and is supposed deeper, and to extend over the country. On account of the inconvenience of washing, the people have, to this time, only gathered the metal on the banks, which is done simply with a shovel, filling a shallow dish, bowl, basket, or tin pan with a quantity of black sand, similar to the class used on paper, and washing out the sand by movement of the vessel.

Thomas O. Larkin, American consul in California, to Secretary of State James Buchanan, letter of June 1, 1848, in The Larkin Papers *(1951).*

There are now about four thousand white persons, besides a number of Indians engaged at the mines, and from the fact, that no capital is required, they are working in companies on equal shares or alone with their basket. In one part of the mine called the "dry diggins," no other implements are necessary than an ordinary sheath knife, to pick the gold from the rocks. In other parts, where the gold is washed out, the machinery is very simple, being an ordinary trough made of plank, round on the bottom, about two feet long and two feet wide at the top, with a riddle or seive at one end to catch the larger gravel, and three or four small bars across the bottom, about half an inch high to keep the gold from going out with the dirt and water at the lower end. This machine is set upon rockers, which gives a half rotary motion to the water and dirt inside. But far the largest number use nothing but a large tin pan or an Indian basket, into which they place the dirt and shake it until the gold gets to the bottom and the dirt is carried over the side in the shape of muddy water. It is necessary in some cases, to have a crowbar, pick and shovel, but a great deal is taken up with large horns, shapen spoon fashion at the large end.

San Francisco Californian, on gold mining at Sutter's mill, report of August 16, 1848.

If we were to go to San Francisco and dig up chunks of gold, or find it here in the valley it would ruin us. Many wanted to unite Babylon and Zion; it's the love of money that hurts them. If we find gold and silver we are in bondage directly. To talk of going away from this valley we are in for anything is like vinegar to my eyes. They that love the world have not their affections placed upon the Lord.

Brigham Young, to the Mormon Battalion, October 1, 1848, in Golder's The March of the Mormon Battalion, *(1928).*

The discovery of these vast deposits of gold has entirely changed the character of Upper California. Its people, before engaged in cultivating their small patches of ground, and guarding their herds of cattle and horses, have all gone to the mines, or on their way thither. Labourers of every trade have left their workbenches, and tradesmen their shops. Sailors desert their ships as fast as they arrive on the coast, and several vessels have gone to sea with hardly enough hands to spread a sail. Two or three are now at anchor in San Francisco, with no crew on board. Many desertions, too, have taken place from the garrisons within the influence of these mines; twenty-six soldiers have deserted from the post of Sonoma, twenty-four from that of San Francisco, and twenty-four from Monterey.

Major Edwin Mason, report of 1848, in Fremont's Geographical Memoir Upon Upper California *(1849).*

New Mexico and Upper California have been ceded by Mexico to the United States, and now constitute a part of our country. Embracing nearly ten degrees of latitude, lying adjacent to the Oregon Territory, and extending from the Pacific Ocean to the Rio Grande. . . . it would be difficult to estimate the value of these possessions to the United States. They constitute of themselves a country large enough for a great empire, and their acquisition is second only in importance to that of Louisiana in 1803. Rich in mineral and agricultural resources, with a climate of great salubrity, they embrace the most important ports on the whole Pacific coast of the continent of North America. The possession of the ports of San Diego and Monterey and the Bay of San Francisco will enable of the United States to command the already valuable and rapidly increasing commerce of the Pacific.

President James Polk, to Congress, message July 6, 1848, in Richardson's Messages and Papers of the Presidents *(1896).*

The digging and washing for gold continues to increase on the Sacramento placer, so far as regards the number of persons engaged in the business, and the size and quantity of the metal daily obtained. I have had in my hands several pieces of gold, about twenty-three carats fine, weighing from one to two pounds, and have it from good authority that pieces have been found weighing sixteen pounds. Indeed, I have heard of one specimen that weighed twenty-five pounds. There are many men at the placer, who in June last had not one hundred dollars, now in possession of from five to twenty thousand dollars, which they made by digging gold and trading with the Indians.

Thomas O. Larkin, American consul in California, to Secretary of State James Buchanan, letter of November 16, 1848, in Fremont's Geographical Memoir Upon Upper California.

Oh, Sally, dearest Sally!
Oh, Sally fer your sake.
I'll go to Californy.
An' try to raise a stake.

"Joe Bowers From Pike," a song popular during the Gold Rush period, in Kirsch and Murphy's West of the West.

Under the Constitution every State has the right of establishing from time to time altering its municipal laws and domestic institutions independently of every other State and of the General Government, subject only to the prohibitions and guaranties expressly set forth in the Constitution of the United States. The subjects thus left exclusively to the respective States were not designed or expected to become topics of national agitation. Still, as under the Constitution Congress has power to make all needful rules and regulations respecting the Territories of the United States, every new acquisition of territory has led to discussions on the question whether the system of involuntary servitude which prevails

in many of the States should or should not be prohibited in that territory. The periods of excitement
from this cause which have heretofore occurred have
been safely passed, but during the interval, or whatever length, which may elapse before the admission
of the Territories ceded by Mexico as States it appears
probable that similar excitement will prevail to an
undue extent.

President Zachary Taylor, to the Senate, mes-
sage of January 23, 1849, in Richardson's Messages and Papers of the Presidents.

At first every appearance was hostile. They were
importunate in demanding various things, acted with
the air of victors, some of the younger ones pressed
close to the wagon, and looked in, with boisterous
exclamations and impertinent gestures. But I was
enabled to keep a firm unblenching front, taking care
that my little Mary did not stir from my side. She
was too young to realize any danger, and thought
the whole rather amusing. My husband met them
from the first with a calm, business-like air, as if he
thought they wanted to hold a consultation with him;
and when they became overbearing, he still kept on
making speeches to them, though we could not perceive that they understood what he said. Their behavior changed several times quite strangely. They
would draw nearer together and consult with puzzled looks, some of them still guarding the team.
Then they would scowl and seem to differ among
themselves. Thus they kept us for perhaps an hour,
when, all at once, my husband raised the big ox-
whip, shouted to the cattle, and rushed them forward
so suddenly that those nearest Indians instinctively
stepped aside, then pompously exclaiming "I'm going
to move on" he called the old man to follow, and we
were once more in motion. But would they let us
keep on? I looked through a small gap in the wagon.
They were evidently puzzled by such unusual behavior, and as evidently divided in their counsels.

Sarah Royce, wagon train traveler, encounter-
ing an Indian party along the trail from the
Great Salt Lake to the Sierra, 1849, in A Frontier Lady, Recollections of the Gold Rush
and Early California *(1932).*

This overland journey is one of the most unfortunate undertakings to which man may allow himself
to be lured, because he cannot possibly have any
conception before starting of this kind of travelling.
To be sure, there is a beaten path which you see

clearly before you, but there are no stopping-places
with even the slightest signs of civilization. Everyone
is going and no one is coming back. You leave your
camp in the hope of finding water, and a grazing
place for the cattle a few miles further on; but sometimes it happens that you are forced to halt in a place
where neither grass nor water can be found. This
means intense suffering for the cattle and often an
irretrievable loss.

Herman B. Scharmann, gold prospector, de-
parting from Independence, Missouri for Cali-
fornia, May 20, 1849, in Overland Journey
to California *(1918).*

It may be interesting to give here a few instances
of the enormous and unnatural value put upon property at the time of my arrival. The Parker House
rented for $110,000 yearly, at least $60,000 of which
was paid by gamblers, who held nearly all the second
story. Adjoining it on the right was a canvas-tent
fifteen by twenty-five feet, called "Eldorado," and
occupied likewise by gamblers, which brought $40,000.
On the opposite corner of the plaza, a building called
the "Miner's Bank," used by Wright & Co., brokers,
about half the size of a fire-engine house in New
York, was held at a rent of $75,000. A mercantile
house paid $40,000 rent for a one-story building of
twenty feet front; the United States Hotel, $36,000;
the Post-Office, $7,000, and so on to the end of the
chapter. A friend of mine, who wished to find a place
for a law-office, was shown a cellar in the earth,
about twelve feet square and six deep, which he
could have at $250 a month. One of the common
soldiers at the battle of San Pasquale was reputed to
be among the millionaires of the place, with an income of $50,000 *monthly.* A citizen of San Francisco
died insolvent to the amount of $41,000 the previous
Autumn. His administrators were delayed in settling
his affairs, and his real estate advanced so rapidly in
value meantime, that after his debts were paid his
heirs had a yearly income of $40,000.

Bayard Taylor, New York Tribune *correspon-*
dent, on the high cost of living in San Francisco
during the gold rush, July 1849, in Eldorado,
or Adventures in the Path of Empire
(1850).

We went into San Francisco shortly before the rainy
season—about three months after I had first seen it.
Already it was changed out of recognition by the
crowds of people added, and the buildings which
had grown up. Houses were rapidly going up for

winter; night and day and Sunday, the sounds of hammers never ceased. Ready-made houses were to be had, and some very pretty little ones from China. One of these was bought and put up for me on a lot we had in what was then called Happy Valley, next to where is now the Palace Hotel.

Jessie Benton Fremont, on the growth of San Francisco during the gold rush, 1849, in A Year of American Travel *(1877).*

Oh, the Good time has come at last,
    We need no more complain, Sir.
The rich can live in luxury
    And the poor can do the same, Sir.
For the Good time has come at last,
    And as we all are told, Sir.
We shall be rich at once now.
    With California Gold, Sir.

"Oh, the Good Time Is Come at Last," ballad, 1849, in Hulbert's Forty-Niners: The Chronicle of the California Trail *(1949).*

At length a ridge of gold scales, mixed with a little sand, remains in the pan, from the quantity of which some estimate may be formed of the richness of the place. If there are five to eight grains, it is considered that "it will pay." If less gold is found, the miner digs deeper or opens a new hole, till he finds a place affording a good *prospect*. When this is done, he sets his cradle by the side of the stream, in some convenient place, and proceeds to wash all the dirt. This is aptly named *prospecting*, and is the hardest part of a miner's business. Thus have we been employed the whole of this day, digging one hole after another—washing out many test-pans—hoping, at every new attempt, to find that which would reward our toil, and we have made *ten cents* each.

Daniel B. Woods, gold prospector at Salmon Falls, on the South Fork of the American River, July 4, 1849, in Sixteen Months at the Gold Diggings *(1973).*

Well here we are in the gold mines of California, & mining has been tried "& found wanting!" We left Sac. City October 18, with our provisions &c in Chapins wagons en route for the Consumne River distant some 28 or 30 miles & arrived here the 21. We are about S.E. from the city, in a rolling country & on a small rapid stream tumbling over a rocky bed. The appearance of the country through which we passed was somewhat better than that down the Sac. River, as we saw it, but yet I have not been in any

part of the "beautiful valley" of which we used to hear. On locating here we immediately went to work making "washers." Doc & John being somewhat "under the weather" I did nearly all the work on the mine alone. I cut down a pine tree, cut it off the proper length peeled & cut down one side & with axe & adz hollowed it out till I reduced it to about ½ inch in thickness by nearly two days of hard labor & blistering of hands &c, & another day put in the "ripples" dash screen &c & took it down to the rocky bar where we are to commence our fortunes! & since have worked away like a trooper, rain or shine, with but indifferent success.

Elisha Douglass Perkins, California gold miner, diary entry of November 1, 1849, in Gold Rush Diary *(1967).*

Go West, young man, and grow up with the country.

Horace Greeley, 1850, in Hints Toward Reform *(1857).*

What do you, who reside in the free States, want? . . . You want that there shall be no slavery introduced into the territories acquired from Mexico. Well, have you not got it in California already, if admitted as a State? Have you not got it also in New Mexico, in all human probability? What more do you want? You have got what is worth a thousand Wilmot provisos. You have got nature itself on your side. You have the fact itself on your side. You have the truth staring you in the face, that no slavery is existing there. Well, if you are men, if you can rise from the mud and slough of party struggles, and elevate yourselves to the height of patriots, what will you do? You will look at the fact as it exists.

Henry Clay, to the Senate, on the resolutions for the Compromise of 1850, speech of February 5, 1850, in The Works of Henry Clay *(1857).*

Every smoke that rises in the Great West marks a new customer to the courting room.

Horace Greeley, on the Compromise of 1850, editorial of 1850 in The New York Tribune, *in Lavender's* The Great West *(1985).*

If the Union is to be dissolved for any existing cause, it will be because slavery is interdicted or not allowed to be introduced into the ceded territories; or because slavery is threatened to be abolished in the District of Columbia; or because fugitive slaves

Henry Clay. Portrait by John Neagle. Courtesy of the New York Public Library.

are not restored, as in my opinion they ought to be, to their masters. These, I believe, would be the causes, if there be any causes which can lead to the dreadful event to which I have referred. Let us suppose the Union dissolved; what remedy does it, in a severed state, furnish for the grievances complained of in its united condition? Will you be able at the South to push slavery into the ceded territory? How are you to do it, supposing the North, or all the States north of the Potomac, in possession of the navy and army of the United States? Can you expect, I say, under these circumstances, that if there is a dissolution of the Union you can carry slavery into California and New Mexico? Sir, you can not dream of such an occurrence.

Henry Clay, to the Senate, on the resolutions for the Compromise of 1850, speech of February 6, 1850, in The Works of Henry Clay.

. . . all the evils of incongruous conjunctions are exemplified in this conjunction of the territorial government bills with the California State admission bill. They are subjects not only foreign to each other, but involving different questions, and resting upon principles of different natures. One involves the slavery and anti-slavery questions; the other is free from them. One involves constitutional questions: the other does not. One is a question of right, resting upon the constitution of the United States and the treaty with Mexico: the other is a question of expediency, resting in the discretion of Congress. One is the case of a State, asking for an equality of rights with the other States: the other is a question of territories, asking protection from States. One is a sovereignty— the other a property. So that, at all points, and under every aspect, the subjects differ; and it is well known that there are senators here who can unite in a vote for the admission of California, who cannot unite in any vote for the territorial governments; and that, because these governments involve the slavery questions, from all which the California bill is free. That is the rock on which men and parties split here.

Thomas Hart Benton, to the Senate, speech of February 1850, in Thirty Years' View *(1856).*

Two Territories, Oregon and Minnesota, are already in progress, and strenuous efforts are making to bring in three additional States from the territory recently conquered from Mexico; which, if successful, will add three other States in a short time to the northern section, making five States; and increasing the present number of its States from fifteen to twenty, and of its Senators from thirty to forty. On the contrary, there is not a single territory in progress in the southern section, and no certainty that any additional State will be added to it during the decade. The prospect then, is, that the two sections in the Senate, should the efforts now made to exclude the South from the newly-acquired territories succeed, will stand, before the end of the decade, twenty northern States to twelve southern, (considering Delaware as neutral,) and forty northern Senators to twenty-four southern. This great increase of Senators, added to the great increase of members of the House of Representatives and the electoral college on the part of the North, which must take place under the next decade, will effectually and irretrievably destroy the equilibrium which existed when the Government commenced.

John C. Calhoun, to the Senate, opposing the Compromise Resolutions, speech of March 4, 1850, in Rives' The Congressional Globe *(1850).*

There is a power in this nation greater than either the North or the South—a growing, increasing, swelling power, that will be able to speak the law to the nation . . . That power is the country known as the great West—the Valley of the Mississippi, one and indivisible from the gulf to the great lakes, and stretching, on the one side and the other, to the extreme sources of the Ohio and Missouri—from the Alleghenies to the Rocky mountains. There, sir, is the hope of this nation—the resting-place of the power that is not only to control, but to save, the Union? . . . This is the mission of the great Mississippi valley, the heart and soul of the nation and the continent.

Stephen A. Douglas, to the Senate, speech of March 13, 1850, during the debates over organizing the territories gained from the Mexican War, in Rives' The Congressional Globe.

But what I mean to say is, that it is as impossible that African slavery, as we see it among us, should find its way, or be introduced, into California and New Mexico, as any other natural impossibility. California and New Mexico are Asiatic in their formation and scenery. They are composed of vast ridges of mountains, of great height, with broken ridges and deep valleys. The sides of these mountains are entirely barren; their tops capped by perennial snow. There may be in California, now made free by its constitution, and no doubt there are, some tracts of valuable land. But it is not so in New Mexico. Pray, what is the evidence which every gentleman must have obtained on this subject, from information sought by himself or communicated by others? I have inquired and read all I could find, in order to acquire information on this important subject. What is there in New Mexico that could, by any possibility, induce any body to go there with slaves? There are some narrow strips of tillable land on the borders of the rivers; but the rivers themselves dry up before midsummer is gone. All that the people can do in that region is to raise some little articles, some little wheat for their *tortillas*, and that by irrigation. And who expects to see a hundred black men cultivating tobacco, corn, cotton, rice, or any thing else, on lands in New Mexico, made fertile only by irrigation?

Daniel Webster, to the Senate, speech entitled "The Constitution of the Union," March 7, 1850, in The Works of Daniel Webster (1872).

The road is closely lined with emigrants. We can count one hundred waggons ahead and behind us. Many teams passed us today. All pushing on, I fear,

too rapidly. Teams will fag and finally give out. Our teams are doing finely, all things considered. Look as well, if not better, than when we started. We will not drive too hard at first; favor our animals all we can. We had one bad accident occur today. One of our teams ran around; broke the [wagon] tongue. All stopped, and in twenty minutes, we had it so well repaired that the team drove on and I think the tongue will stand for some days. Our sick men are better. We passed a fresh made grave today. The head board states his age to be 21 years, emigrating from Randolph County, Missouri, name Robert Malone. He was consigned to the dust from which he came this morning. Came to his death by accidentally shooting himself through the head. Many such accidents occur on the plains.

Willis Read, overland traveler and gold miner, passing the dividing ridge between the Kansas and Mississippi Rivers, diary entry of May 14, 1850, in A Pioneer of 1850 (1927).

The tents do not protect one from such winds— We were out of the range of Buffalo to day, no game of any kind beyond the land of flowers too almost except the Cactus which is just beginning to bloom and is very beautiful—We met a party of "Arapahoes" to day   they approached us rather timidly at first were quite sociable afterwards & had a long talk which they carried on by signs. Mr Macarty understood them—When we were ready to start the Drum was beaten unexpectedly—& Indians and horses took to their heels pretty much frightened until they found it was only the signal for our departure

Anna Maria De Morris, overland traveler, on traveling along the Santa Fe Trail, near the Banks of the Arkansas, diary entry of June 15, 1850, in Holmes' Covered Wagon Women.

In Memory of Samuel Oliver
of Waukesha, Wisconsin,
who was killed by an arrow shot
from a party of Indians, July 5th, 1850
while standing guard at night

Anonymous emigrant traveling to California on a wagon train, diary entry of July 1850, in Stewart's The California Trail (1962).

Still detained here on acct of rain. It rained incessantly all last night & this morning. It looks very gloomy. When it stops for a few moments the mountains seem to smoke. There are campt near us the 10 Californians. They have been there one year, made a fortune & glad to get back home. They say some 200 miles this side of there they found men without food eating their horses & mewls. One young man rather than eat his horse plunged in the river & drowned himself. There are also with the Californians men from Fort Larimee in search of deserters this season. Still rains & as cold as winter.

Lucena Parsons, overland traveler, journal entry of August 19, 1850, in Holmes' Covered Wagon Women *(1983).*

There are but few women; among these thousands of men, we have not seen more than ten or twelve.

Margaret Frink, wife of a California gold prospector, journal entry of August 20, 1850, in Holmes' Covered Wagon Women.

Talked of an arrangement to leave the train and push on to Sutters Fort on foot. A little farther on we found some abandoned wagons. On one is written "20 miles to Salmon Trout River." Road becomes very deep and sandy. As we advance we find dead oxen, remains of wagons, carts, harness and baggage strewn along the trail in profusion. Panic had evidently overtaken the emigrants ahead of us. In their distress, panic, loss of cattle, hunger, thirst and fatigue, they seem to have cast everything away to save life. We begin to fear our guide book has deceived us, and that we have made a fatal mistake in the road. Farther on we met a courier from Turner, who was in advance, directing Moses [the wagon master] to leave everything but the carriages, the passengers, and their necessary bedding and provisions for a few days and push on with all the stock to the run to save them from total destruction.

Bernard J. Reid, gold miner traveling to Sutter's fort, diary entry of September 10, 1850, in Overland to California with the Pioneer Line *(1983).*

. . . this morning is vary clear and bright this day we have traveled seventeen miles to day noon we had the best grass I ever saw it looked like a perfect wheete field we then went on a litle ways and come to the river their we found a man that had bin killed buy the Indians and his heart taken out he was buried yesterday and their lay a dead Indian it apears he was alone and the Indians came upon him and he shot one an then they shot him he was found with four arrows shot in his breast and the Indian found shot under the arm

Sarah Davis, overland traveler, journal entry of September 19, 1850, in Holmes' Covered Wagon Women.

Have been at work all the past week, and still am $8 in debt for boarding. I dug 50¢ worth on Monday, $1.00 Tuesday, Wednesday $1.70. Thursday $2.00, Friday $2.00 and Saturday $6.00. Bought a spade on Tuesday for $4.00. Paid $10 last night in gold dust in account of my week's board. Am not discouraged yet, but find it very hard work for a little filthy lucre. Am anxious to get enough to take me to San Francisco to get letters from home and answer them. Hope to go in one week more.

Bernard J. Reid, gold miner, diary entry of September 30, 1850, in Overland to California with the Pioneer Line.

Grand Father and Father: I am glad to see so many Indians and whites meeting in peace. It makes my heart glad, and I shall be more happy at home. I am glad you have taken pity on us, and come to see us. The buffalo used to be plenty in our country, but it is getting scarce. We got enough to come here and keep us a while, but our meat will not last long. As the sun looks down upon us—(so) the Great Spirit sees me I am willing, Grand Father, to do as you tell me to do. I know you will tell me right, and that it will be good for me and my people. We regard this as a great *medicine day*, when our pipe and water shall be one, and we all shall be at peace. Our young men, Grand Father, whom you want to go with you to the States, are ready, and they shall go. I shall look to their return when the grass begins to grow again. If all the nations here were willing to do what you tell them, and do what they say as we are, then we could sleep in peace; we would not have to watch our horses or our lodges in the night.

Old Bark, Cheyenne chief, to treaty council at Fort Laramie, speech of September 1851, in Hoig's The Peace Chiefs of the Cheyennes *(1980).*

Express lines have furthered the interests of our commercial classes, and become of indispensable service to the mining population; penetrating the most remote recesses of the mineral region, and intersecting the country, threading the rivers and streams to their head waters, and following the highways, the byway and the wilderness track, wherever the adventurer has pushed his explorations, and established among human wants that of facile communication with his neighbor and the busy world.

Newspaper (Alta, California) editorial of October 20, 1851, in Winther's Express and Stagecoach Days in California.

We were eighteen days encamped together, during which time the Indians conducted themselves in a manner that excited the admiration and surprise of every one. The different tribes, although hereditary enemies, interchanged daily visits, both in their national and individual capacities; smoked and feasted together; exchanged presents, adopted each others children according to their own customs, and done all that was held sacred, or solemn in the eyes of these Indians, to prove the sincerity of their peaceful and friendly intentions—both amongst themselves, and with the citizens of the United States, lawfully residing among them, or passing through the country.

David Dawson Mitchell, Indian Affairs superintendent, to Luke Lea, Indian Affairs agent, on the Fort Laramie peace treaty council, report of November 11, 1851, in Hoopes' Indian Affairs and Their Administration *(1932).*

San Francisco, ho! We passed through the "Golden Gate," at about 11 last night and came up to the wharf at near 12. I turned in early but with noise and excitement could not sleep. Soon after 1 I went on deck for a short time and saw El Dorado. Contrary to the idea I had formed, that the city and country back were one flat plain for miles, there are high hills all around the city and it extends partly up their side. Seeing an immense number of ships at anchor and at the wharves, and seeing houses near the water & white-hull boats rowing around the ship, and mistaking, for a moment in the dim light, the tops of the hills for the outlines of long, massive blocks of brick stores, I began to think we had made some mistake and had somehow got round Cape Horn and arrived safely at New York.

Captain Edward Davis Townsend, after sailing around Cape Horn, diary entry of January 2, 1852, in The California Diary of General E.D. Townsend *(1970).*

This company having completed its organisation as above is now ready to undertake the general forwarding agency and commission business; the purchase and sale of gold dust, bullion, and specie, also packages, parcels and freight of all description in and between the City of New York and the City of San Francisco, and the principal cities and towns in California, connecting at New York with the lines of the American Express Company, the Harnden Express, Pullen, Virgil & Co. European Express.

They have established offices and faithful agents in all the principal cities and towns throughout the eastern, middle and western states, energetic and faithful messengers furnished with iron chests for the security of treasure and other valuable packages accompany each express upon all their lines as well as in California and in the Atlantic States.

Wells, Fargo & Company, announcement of May 20, 1852, in The New York Times.

In the spring of 1852 I established myself in Beckwourth Valley, and finally found myself transformed into a hotel-keeper and chief of a trading-post. My house is considered the emigrant's landing-place, as it is the first ranch he arrives at in the golden state, and is the only house between this point and Salt Lake. Here is a valley two hundred and forty miles in circumference, containing some of the choicest land in the world. Its yield of hay is incalculable; the red and white clovers spring up spontaneously, and the grass that covers its smooth surface is of the most nutritious nature. When the weary, toil-worn emigrant reaches this valley, he feels himself secure; he can lay himself down and taste refreshing repose, undisturbed by the fear of Indians.

Jim Beckwourth, on his settlement in the Sierra Nevada, 1850s, in The Life and Adventures of James P. Beckwourth *(1926).*

. . . sometimes I am taking care of Babies and nursing at the rate of Fifty Dollars a week but I would not advise any Lady to come out here and suffer the toil and fatigue that I have suffered for the sake of a little gold neither do I advise any one to come. Clarks Simmon wife says if she was safe in the States she would not care if she had not one cent. She came in here last night and said, "Oh dear I am so homesick that I must die," and then again my other associate came in with tears in her eyes and said that she had cried all day. she said if she had as good a home as I had got she would not stay twenty five minutes in California. I told her that she could not pick up her duds in that time. she said she would not stop for duds nor anything else but my own heart was two sad to cheer them much.

Mary B. Ballou, wife of a California gold pro-
spector, to Selden Ballou, her son, letter of Oc-
tober 30, 1852, in A Woman's View of the
Gold Rush *(1962).*

Every effort has been made to protect our frontier
and that of the adjoining Mexican States from the
incursions of the Indian tribes. Of about 11,000 men
of which the Army is composed, nearly 8,000 are
employed in the defense of the newly acquired territory (including Texas) and of emigrants proceeding
thereto. I am gratified to say that these efforts have
been unusually successful. With the exception of
some partial outbreaks in California and Oregon and
occasional depredations on a portion of the Rio
Grande, owing, it is believed, to the disturbed state
of that border region, the inroads of the Indians have
been effectually restrained.

President Millard Fillmore, third annual mes-
sage to Congress, December 6, 1852, in Rich-
ardson's Messages and Papers of the Presidents.

The apprehension of dangers from extended territory, multiplied States, accumulated wealth, and
augmented population has proved to be unfounded.
The stars upon your banner have become nearly
threefold their original number; your densely populated possessions skirt the shores of the two great
oceans; and yet this vast increase of people and
territory has not only shown itself compatible with
the harmonious action of the States and Federal Government in their respective constitutional spheres,
but has afforded an additional guaranty of the strength
and integrity of both.

President Franklin Pierce, first inaugural ad-
dress, March 4, 1853, in Richardson's Messages and Papers of the Presidents.

The time has come when the long disputed question of a railroad to the Pacific ocean is assuming a
practical form, and is about to receive its solution in
the authoritative examination of the country, and the
selection of the route. An appropriation has been
made by Congress for the examinations, and the
selection of the route is referred to the next Congress.
This is well, and will give the CENTRAL route a fair
chance, although the MEMPHIS, or SOUTHERN route
has gained an immense advantage over it in the
numerous surveys which have been made, and the
long concentration of the public opinion upon it.

Thomas Hart Benton, to the people of Missouri,
letter of March 4, 1853, in Heap's Central
Route to the Pacific *(1957).*

I will now give you briefly my opinion of the
railroad to connect the valley of the Mississippi river
with the Pacific coast. I am in favor of the construction of such a road by the General Government for
that purpose. I will vote to appropriate land and
money. I believe it absolutely necessary for the land
and money. I believe it absolutely necessary for the
preservation of the integrity of this Union . . . As to
where it shall commence or where it shall end, that
is a matter to be determined when the surveys and
operations now in progress shall be completed, and
the route it must take between the termini is entirely
dependent upon these surveys. We may bluster about
a northern, a southern and a central route; but it all
amounts to nothing; nothing but the actual surveys
can determine it.

Senator David R. Atchison (Missouri), speech
of June 1853, in Ray's The Repeal of the
Missouri Compromise *(1909).*

The heat increased as we advanced into the desert,
and most of the party had divested themselves of
the greater part of their clothing. The guns, which
we carried across the pummels of our saddles, were
hot to the touch; and, to add to our annoyance and
suffering, the wind, ladened with an impalpable sand,
blew fiercely from the southward, feeling as if issuing
from the mouth of a furnace, and obliterating in
many places all traces of the road. The mules, already
jaded by travelling across the sandy plain, went
slowly along, their heads drooping to the ground.

Gwinn Harris Heap, journalist, on crossing the
California desert with a railroad survey expedi-
tion, journal entry of August 6, 1853, in Central Route to the Pacific.

If Nebraska be made a free Territory then will
Missouri be surrounded on three sides by free territory, where there will always be men and means to
assist in the escape of our slave . . . With the emissaries of abolitionists around us, and the facilities of
escape so enlarged, this species of property would
become insecure, if not valueless, in Missouri. The
Free-Soilers and Abolitionists look to this result, and
calculate upon the facilities which will be offered by
the incorporation of this Territory with a provision
against slavery, as a means of abolishing slavery in
Missouri.

St. Louis Republican, *editorial of 1853, in*
Nevins' Ordeal of the Union *(1947).*

In view of the fact that at no distant day the whole country over which those Indians now roam must be peopled by another and more enterprising race, and also of the consideration that the channels of commerce between the east and the west will eventually, in part at least, pass through their country, it was regarded as incumbent to provide, as far as practicable, for any action the government might see proper to take upon that subject. Already the idea of a great central route to the Pacific by railway has become deeply impressed upon the public mind; and while many courses are contemplated, two of them at least are designated as passing through this section of country.
Thomas Fitzpatrick, Bureau of Indian Affairs
agent for the Upper Platte and Arkansas, to
Alfred Cummings, Bureau of Indian Affairs
commissioner, on the Fort Atkinson treaty with
the Apaches, Comanches and Kiowas, report of
November 19, 1853, in Hoopes' Indian Affairs
and Their Administration.

How are we to develop, cherish and protect our immense interests and possessions on the Pacific, with a vast wilderness fifteen hundred miles in breadth, filled with hostile savages, and cutting off all direct communication. The Indian barrier must be removed. The tide of emigration and civilization must be permitted to roll onward until it rushes through the passes of the mountains, and spreads over the plains, and mingles with the waters of the Pacific. Continuous lines of settlement with civil, political and religious institutions all under the protection of law, are imperiously demanded by the highest national considerations. These are essential, but they are not sufficient. No man can keep up with the spirit of this age who travels on anything slower than the locomotive, and fails to receive intelligence by lightning. We must therefore have Rail Roads and Telegraphs from the Atlantic to the Pacific, through our own territory. Not one line only, but many lines, for the valley of the Mississippi will require as many Rail Roads to the Pacific as to the Atlantic, and will not venture to limit the number. The removal of the Indian barrier and the extension of the laws of the United States in the form of Territorial governments are the first steps toward the accomplishment of each and all of those objects.

Stephen A. Douglas, to Nebraska convention,
favoring the Nebraska bill, letter of December
17, 1853, in Johannsen's Stephen A. Douglas
(1973).

The legal effect of this is neither to legislate slavery into these territories nor out of them, but to leave the people do as they please. If they wish slavery, they have a right to it. If they do not want it, they will not have it, and you should not force it upon them.
Stephen A. Douglas, to the Senate, favoring the
Kansas-Nebraska bill, speech of January 30,
1854, in Rhodes' History of the United
States From the Compromise of 1850
(1893).

The sun has set for the last time upon the guaranteed and certain liberties of all the unsettled and unorganized portions of the American continent that lie within the jurisdiction of the United States. Tomorrow's sun will rise in dim eclipse over them. How long that obscuration shall last is known only to the Power that directs and controls all human events. For myself, I know only this: that no human power can prevent its coming on, and that its passing off will be hastened and secured by others than those now here, and perhaps only by those belonging to future generations.
William H. Seward, to the Senate, lamenting
the passage of the Kansas-Nebraska Act, speech
of May 25, 1854, in Thayer's A History of
the Kansas Crusade *(1971).*

A Territory which one short year ago was unanimously considered by all, North and South, as sacredly secured by irrepealable law to FREEDOM FOREVER, has been fully betrayed by traitor hearts and traitor voices, and surrendered to slavery.
The New York Tribune, *condemning the passage of the Kansas-Nebraska Act, editorial of*
June 1854, in Robinson's The Kansas Conflict
(1972).

Citizens of the West, of the South, and Illinois! stake out your claims, and woe be to the abolitionist or Mormon who shall intrude upon it, or come within reach of your long and true rifles, or within point-blank shot of your revolvers. Keep a sharp lookout lest some dark night you shall see the flames curing from your house or the midnight philanthropist hurrying off your faithful servant.

The Argus (Platte, Missouri), editorial of
1854, in Robinson's The Kansas Conflict.

The *Worcester Spy* announces that the first band of emigrants for Kansas under the charge of the Emigrant Aid Company will start from Boston on the 17th inst. We wish them the utmost success their hearts can desire in getting there, for the hardy pioneers of Kansas will doubtless have tar and feathers prepared in abundance for their reception. Kansas is open for settlement both to the North and the South. Slavery has been kept out of Territories by Congressional enactments, but has never failed to carry the day and firmly establish itself upon new Territories when allowed to enter.

Lynchburg Republican (Virginia), endorsing
slavery in Kansas and the intimidation of antislavery settlers, editorial of July 1, 1854.

If the design of the Mormon rulers in selecting the Great Basin as the seat of their power was to isolate their people from the rest of the world, they certainly made a happy choice. The Mormon capital is unapproachable from any civilized point except by a tedious journey of from eight hundred to one thousand miles. In a severe winter it is entirely inaccessible.

Benjamin G. Ferris, secretary of Utah Territory, 1854, in Utah and the Mormons
(1854).

Why is Kansas a failure as a free State? I will tell you. You sent out there some thousand or two thousand men—for what? To make a living; to cultivate a hundred and sixty acres; to build houses; to send for their wives and children; to raise wheat; to make money; to build saw-mills; to plant towns. You meant to take possession of the country, as the Yankee race always takes possession of a country, by industry, by civilization, by roads, by houses, by mills, by churches; but it will take a long time—*it takes two centuries to do it.*

Wendell Phillips, proslavery advocate, speech of
September 1855, in Thayer's A History of the
Kansas Crusade.

As citizens of Kansas Territory, we desire to call your attention to the fact that a large force of armed men from a foreign State have assembled in the vicinity of Lawrence, and are now committing depredations upon our citizens, stopping wagons, opening and appropriating their loads, arresting, detaining, and threatening travellers upon the public road, and that they claim to do this by your authority. We desire to know if they do appear by your authority, and if you will secure the peace and quiet of the community by ordering their instant removal, or compel us to resort to some other means and to higher authority.

Citizens Council of Lawrence, Kansas, to Wilson Shannon, Governor of Kansas Territory,
letter of December 1855, in Robinson's The
Kansas Conflict.

More speedy measures must be devised for strengthening Zion . . . The system of ox-trains is too slow and expensive, and must give way to the telegraph line of handcarts and wheelbarrows. It would be much more economical both in time, labor, and expense, if, instead of spending several weeks to obtain and accustom to the yoke, a lot of wild ungovernable cattle, impairing the health of many of the brethren by excessive labor and fatigue, and bringing disease and death into the camps by long delays on the miasmatic banks of the Missouri River, on the arrival of a company of Saints on the frontier they could have the necessary handcarts ready and load them, and be 200 or 300 miles on their journey, with the same time and labor that would otherwise be expended in getting started.

Franklin D. Richards, president of the European Mormon Mission, newspaper editorial in
the Millennial Star, December 22, 1855.

Some seemed to have no more definite notion of the position of Kansas, than of the distance of the fixed stars. They thought of it as indefinitely remote—somewhere 'out west' towards the Pacific Ocean. One individual placed it two thousand miles from Council Bluffs; another brought it within two thousand miles of Cincinnati, while an Irish friend inquired if it was indeed a newly discovered continent.

C.B. Boyton and T.B. Mason, emigrant guidebook authors, 1855, in Dondore's The Prairie
and the Making of Middle America (1926).

Some of the flags which floated beside that of the Union had for mottoes, 'Superiority of the white race,' 'Kansas the outpost,' 'South Carolina'; while one had the national stripes, with a tiger in place of the Union; another had alternate stripes of black and white. While the cannon were being placed for the destruction of the Eldridge House, David R. Atchison, late Vice-President of the United States, was

conspicuous among the mob. When the final doom of the hotel and printing offices was pronounced, it was said by the officials to be by order of the Government, as the Grand Jury of Douglas County had ordered them abated as nuisances. The only charge against the Eldridge House was its ownership by the Emigrant Aid Company.
Citizens of Lawrence, Kansas Territory, to I.B. Donelson, U.S. Marshal, Kansas Territory, letter of May 21, 1856, in Robinson's The Kansas Conflict.

Though the prisoners were spared, I regret to say the town was not, for Atchison's men got completely out of hand, battered down the ''Free State Hotel,'' and sacked most of the houses. It was a terrible scene of orgy, and I was very glad when, about midnight, we of Miller's company were ordered off to Lecompton to report the day's doings to Governor Shannon. There we were kept several days, scouring the country for Free Soilers, and impressing arms, horses, and corn.
R.H. Williams, ''Border Ruffian,'' recalling the attack on Lawrence, Kansas, May 21, 1856, in With the Border Ruffians *(1982).*

All here is excitement and confusion. We have just heard of the murder on Saturday night of Allen Wilkinson, Doyle and his two brothers, and William Sherman; all living in Franklin County, near Potawatomie Creek. The body of another man has been found at the ford of Potawatomie. These murders, it is supposed, were committed by the abolitionists of Osawatomie and Potawatomie creeks, on their return from Lawrence.

How long shall these things continue? How long shall our citizens, unarmed and defenseless, be exposed to this worse than savage cruelty? Wilkinson, it is said, was taken from his bed, leaving a sick wife and children, and butchered in their sight. The two young Doyles were unarmed, and shot down on the prairie like dogs.
William A. Heiskell, settler, to Wilson Shannon, Governor of Kansas Territory, letter of May 26, 1856, in Robinson's The Kansas Conflict.

Nothing is clearer in the history of our institutions than the design of the nation, in asserting its own independence and freedom, to avoid giving countenance to the extension of slavery. The influence of the small but compact and powerful class of men interested in slavery, who command one section of the country and wield a vast political control as a consequence in the other, is now directed to turn back the impulse of the Revolution and reverse its principles. The extension of slavery across the continent is the object of the power which now rules the government; and from this spirit have sprung those kindred wrongs of Kansas so truly portrayed in one of your resolutions, which prove that the elements of the most arbitrary governments have not been vanquished by the just theory of our own.
John C. Fremont, accepting the Republican nomination for president, speech of July 8, 1856, in Nevins' Fremont: Pathmaker of the West *(1939).*

Free Soil, Free Speech, Free Men, Fremont!
Republican Party, slogan of 1856, in McPherson's Battle Cry of Freedom *(1988).*

Started at 5 o'clock without any breakfast and had to pull the carts through 6 miles of heavy sand. Some places the wheels were up to the boxes and I was so weak from thirst and hunger and being exhausted with the pain of the boils that I was obliged to lie down several times, and many others had to do the same. Some fell down. I was very much grieved today, so much so that I thought my heart would burst—sick—and poor Kate—at the same time—crawling on her hands and knees, and the children crying with hunger and fatigue. I was obliged to take the children and put them on the hand cart and urge them along the road in order to make them keep up. About 12 o'clock a thunder storm came on, and the rain fell in torrents. In our tent we were standing up to our knees in water and every stitch we had was the same as if we were dragged through the river. Rain continued until 8 o'clock the following morning.
Twiss Berminghan, member of the Second Mormon Handcart Company to the Great Salt Lake Valley, on passing through Nebraska, journal entry of August 3, 1856, in Hafen's Handcarts to Zion *(1960).*

One of the greatest, if not the greatest, obstacle to overcome in the production of peace and harmony in the territory, is the unsettled condition of the claims to the public lands. These lands are very considerably covered by settlers, many of whom have expended much labor and money in the improvement of their claims, to which, as yet, they have no legal title. These improved claims have excited the cupidity of lawless men; many of whom, under pretense of being actuated by either anti-slavery or pro-slavery proclivities, drive off the settlers and take possession of their property. The persons thus driven off, having no legal title to their claims, have no redress at the hands of the law, and in many instances have patiently and quietly submitted to their wrongs, and left the country: while others, and still a greater portion, have retreated to the towns, combined together, and prepared themselves to defend and maintain what they justly conceive to be their rights, by meeting violence with violence.

John W. Geary, governor of the Kansas Territory, to Secretary of State William L. Marcy, letter of September 22, 1856, in Welch's Border Warfare in Southeast Kansas *(1977).*

Upon these considerations it is the opinion of the Court that the Act of Congress [the Missouri Compromise Act] which prohibits a citizen from holding property of this kind in the Territory of the United States north of the line mentioned is not warranted by the Constitution, and it is therefore void; and that neither Dred Scott himself, nor any of his family, were made free by being carried into this territory, even if they had been carried there by the owner with the intention of becoming a permanent resident.

Chief Justice of the Supreme Court Roger B. Taney, on Dred Scott v. Sanford, March 6, 1857, in Miller's The Petitioners: The Story of the Negro and the United States Supreme Court *(1966).*

A slave is not mere chattel. He bears the impress of his Maker and is amenable to the laws of God and man and he is destined to an endless existence.

Associate Justice of the Supreme Court John McLean, dissenting opinion on the Court's Dred Scott decision, March 6, 1857, in Miller's The Petitioners: The Story of the Negro and the United States Supreme Court.

There are certain points which are settled and beyond the reach of the fanatics of the Nation. The [Dred Scott] decision is a closing and clinching confirmation of the settlement of the issue Whoever now seeks to revive sectionalism arrays himself against the Union.

The Pennsylvanian, editorial of March 10, 1857.

The idea that any decision of the Supreme Court can reestablish slavery in the Free States is a bug-bear—an absurdity. The only result, therefore, that we can arrive at is that, however repugnant, the Dred Scott decision may be to the feelings of a portion of the Northern States, it can have no practical effects injurious to our tranquility or to our institutions. The subject of slavery will be left to be decided, as it ultimately must be, by the laws which govern labor and production. It is, indeed most devoutly to be desired that this great question should be left to be determined exclusively by those laws, free from interference of the hotheads of the press and of the pulpit. If we would but permit Nature to have her own way for only a few short years.

Harper's Weekly, editorial of March 28, 1857.

Dred Scott—This doughty gentlemen of color has become the hero of the day, if not of the age. He was thrown Anthony Burns, Bully Bowlegs, Uncle Tom and Fred Douglass into temporary, if not everlasting oblivion, annihilated the Missouri Compromise and almost healed the wounds of bleeding Kansas.

Washington Union, newspaper editorial of April 23, 1857.

The community and, in part, the civil government of Utah Territory are in a state of substantial rebellion against the laws and authority of the United States. A new civil governor is about to be designated, and to be charged with the establishment and maintenance of law and order. Your able and energetic aid, with that of the troops to be placed under your command, is relied to insure the success of his mission.

Lieutenant Colonel George W. Lay, aide-de-camp to General Winfield Scott, to General William S. Harney, commander of Fort Leavenworth, instructions of June 29, 1857, in Hafen's The Utah Expedition *(1958).*

I have the honor to report that, on the 29th ultimo, while pursuing the Cheyennes down Solomon's Fork of the Kansas, we suddenly came upon a large body of them, drawn up in battle array, with their left resting upon the stream and their right covered by a bluff. Their number has been variously estimated from two hundred and fifty to five hundred; I think there were about three hundred. The cavalry were about three miles in advance of the infantry, and the six companies were marching in three columns. I immediately brought them into line, and, without halting, detached the two flank companies at a gallop to turn their flanks, (a movement they were evidently preparing to make against our right,) and we continued to march steadily upon them. The Indians were all mounted and well armed, many of them had rifles and revolvers, and they stood, with remarkable boldness, until we charged and were nearly upon them, when they broke in all directions, and we pursued them seven miles. Their horses were fresh and very fleet, and it was impossible to overtake many of them. There were but nine men killed in the purusit, but there must have been a great number wounded.

Colonel Edwin V. Sumner, to Secretary of War John B. Floyd, report of August 9, 1857, in Hafen's Relations with the Indians of the Plains, 1857–1861 *(1959).*

We do not want to fight the United States, but if they drive us to it, we shall do the best we can; and I will tell you, as the Lord lives, we shall come off conquerors, for we trust in Him. The United States are sending their armies here to simply hold us still until a mob can come and butcher us as has been done before. We are supporters of the constitution of the United States, and we love that constitution and respect the laws of the United States; but it is by the corrupt administration of those laws that we are made to suffer.

Brigham Young, to Captain Van Villet, conversation of September 1857, in Tullidge's Life of Brigham Young *(1876).*

The 5th Inf. and Reno's battery came in about 2 P.M. They report that two supply trains that were on the Green River were attacked and burned by the Mormons. This is open war. We have, fortunately, 6 months provisions with us. The ball is opened, and attacks on our trains is their system of warfare. The excitement is tremendous. Mountaineers are leaving the Territory and everything is being burned by the Mormons to prevent our advancing. Today Col. Alexander held a council of war to decide upon what to do.

Captain Jesse Gove, 10th Infantry Battalion, to Maria Gove, his wife, letter of September 30, 1857, in The Utah Expedition, 1857–1858; Letters of Captain Jesse A. Gove *(1928).*

It is my duty to inform you that I shall use the force under my control, and all honorable means in my power, to obey literally and strictly the orders under which I am acting. If you, or any acting under your orders, oppose me, I will use force, and I warn you that the blood that is shed in this contest will be upon your head.

Captain Edmund B. Alexander, to Brigham Young, letter of October 12, 1857, in Hafen's The Utah Expedition.

I write in the midst of revolution—Our town is filled with armed men—For several weeks our town has been threatened with conflagration & pillage— This morning we were awakened with the cry that the enemy were upon us, and such was the fact—A large body of armed men came into our town, just at day-break, and declared their intention to lay the town in ashes, unless certain individuals who, from their political opinions, had become obnoxious to them, should be delivered into their custody—

Epaphroditus Ranson, United States land office receiver, to James W. Denver, governor of the Kansas Territory, on tensions between abolitionists and proslavery advocates, letter of February 11, 1858, in Welch's Border Warfare in Southeast Kansas.

Settlers are flying with their families to this palys (place), leaving their property behind—Scores are leaving Osage valley, daily, and fleeing to save their lives having received notices, of which, the following is a literal copy, taken from one in my possession, which was taken from a settlers door, and brought to me by Captain Anderson.

"Leave this claim in 24 hours."

Joseph Williams, Kansas Territory judge, to Governor James W. Denver, letter of March 5, 1858, in Welch's Border Warfare in Southeast Kansas.

You have settled upon territory which lies, geographically, in the heart of the Union. The land you live upon was purchased by the United States and paid for out of their Treasury; the proprietary right and title to it is in them, and not in you. Utah is bounded on every side by States and Territories whose people are true to the Union. It is absurd to believe that they will or can permit you to erect in their very midst a government of your own, not only independent of the authority which they all acknowledge, but hostile to them and their interests.

President James Buchanan, to citizens of the Utah Territory, proclamation of April 6, 1858, in Richardson's Messages and Papers of the Presidents.

We are some days travel from the nearest Mormon settlements near Salt Lake, but we hope to find good grass and water. We had been told for some days back, that Brigham Young had issued a decree that the brethren should not on any consideration let the gentiles have any kind of provision under penalty of excommunication. Their winter had been very severe and their crops promised very poorly, and as there was a prospect of a large emigration to Salt Lake, it stood them in hand to be as economical as possible, so our prospects were quite dubious.

Mary Rockwood Powers, journal entry of 1858, in A Woman's Overland Journey to California *(1985).*

We have the honor to report that we reached this city on the 7th instant. We lost no time in placing ourselves in communication with the chief men of the Mormon people. After the fullest and freest conference with them we are pleased to state that we have settled the unfortunate difficulties existing between the government of the United States and the people of Utah. We are informed by the people and chief men of the Territory that they will cheerfully yield obedience to the Constitution and laws of the United States. They consent that the civil officers of the Territory shall enter upon the discharge of their respective duties. They will make no resistance to the army of the United States in its march to the valley of Salt Lake or elsewhere. We have their assurance that no resistance will be made to the officers, civil or military, of the United States in the exercise of their various functions in the Territory of Utah.

Ben McCulloch, peace commissioner to Utah, to Secretary of War John B. Floyd, report of June 12, 1858, in Hafen's The Utah Expedition.

"A house divided against itself cannot stand." I believe this government cannot endure permanently half slave and half free. I do not expect the Union to be dissolved; I do not expect the house to fall; but I do expect it will cease to be divided. It will become all one thing, or all the other. Either the opponents of slavery will arrest the further spread of it, and place it where the public mind shall rest in the belief that it is in the course of ultimate extinction, or its advocates will push it forward till it shall become alike lawful in all the States, old as well as new, North as well as South.

Abraham Lincoln, to the Republican state convention at Springfield, Illinois, on the Dred Scott decision and the Kansas-Nebraska Act, speech of June 16, 1858, in Abraham Lincoln, Complete Works *(1886–1906).*

We travel night and day and only stop long enough to change teams and eat. The stations are not all yet finished, and there are some very long drives—varying from thirty-five to seventy-five miles—without any opportunity of procuring fresh teams. Many obstacles have been overcome, and I am sanguine of the ultimate success of the enterprise, however much I may now doubt its efficiency as an expeditious mail or available passenger route.

Waterman L. Ormsby, special correspondent for the New York Herald, *on traveling with the Overland Mail Company's stage line, September 28, 1858, in* The Butterfield Overland Mail *(1942).*

The overland mail arrived to-day at St. Louis from San Francisco in twenty-three days and four hours. The state brought through six passengers.

John Butterfield, to President James Buchanan, telegram of October 9, 1858, in Root and Connelley's The Overland Stage to California *(1950).*

I cordially congratulate you upon the result. It is a glorious triumph for civilization and the union. Settlements will soon follow the course of the road, and the east and the west will be bound together by a chain of living Americans which can never be broken.

President James Buchanan, to John Butterfield, praising the initial transcontinental run of the Butterfield Overland Mail Express, telegram of October 9, 1858, in Root and Connelley's The Overland Stage to California.

Where Gold Hill now stands, I had noticed indications of a ledge and had got a little color. I spoke to "Old Virginia" about it, and he remembered the locality, for he said he had often seen the place when hunting deer and antelope. He also said that he had seen any quantity of quartz there. So he joined our party and Comstock also followed along. When we got to the ground, I took a pan and filled it with dirt, with my foot, for I had no shovel or spade. The others did the same thing, though I believe that some of them had shovels. I noticed some willows growing on the hillside and I started for them with my pan.

The Overland Mail starts from the eastern side. Wood engraving from Leslie's Illustrated Newspaper, *October 23, 1858. Courtesy of the Library of Congress.*

The place looked like an Indian spring, which it proved to be.

I began washing my pan. When I had finished, I found that I had in it about fifteen cents. None of the others had less than eight cents, and none more than fifteen. It was very fine gold; just as fine as flour. Old Virginia decided that it was a good place to locate and work.

John Bishop, prospector at the Comstock Lode near Virginia City, Nevada, recalling the first discovery of gold, January 28, 1859, in Quille's The Big Bonanza (1947).

Kansas, without any protection for freedom, has become a free state, or at least she is this day prepared to be a free State, and will never be anything less. In defiance of numerous obstacles in the way of obtaining her freedom, she has bravely secured it. In the immediate vicinity of the Platte Purchase, the most intensely pro-slavery portion of Missouri, there, almost in the bosom of slave States, there, far re-moved from the States of the North, which furnish emigrants to the West, and with all the force of the General Government against freedom, and for slav-ery in the Territory, the free-State heroes have triumphed; and not only that, but they have put forth many times the power which was requisite to accomplish the grand result.

Congressman Eli Thayer (Massachusetts) to the Congress speech of February 24, 1859, in A History of The Kansas Crusade.

Those two little words, "Pike's Peak," are every-where. The latest from Pike's Peak is eagerly de-voured, no matter what it is. The quickest, safest route to Pike's Peak is what thousands want to know. Pike's Peak is in everybody's mouth and thoughts, and Pike's Peak figures in a million dreams. Every clothing store is a depot for outfits for Pike's Peak. There are Pike's Peak hats, and Pike's Peak guns, Pike's Peak boots, Pike's Peak shovels, and Pike's

John Butterfield

John Butterfield. Courtesy of the New York Public Library.

Ben Holladay. Courtesy of the New York Public Library.

Peak goodness-knows-what-all, designed expressly for the use of emigrants and miners, and earnestly recommended to those contemplating a journey to the gold regions of Pike's Peak. We presume there are, or will be, Pike's Peak pills, manufactured with exclusive reference to the diseases of Cherry valley, and sold in conjunction with Pike's Peak guide books; or Pike's Peak schnapps to give tone to the stomachs of overtasked gold diggers; or Pike's Peak goggles to keep the gold dust out of the eyes of the fortune hunters; or Pike's Peak steelyards (drawing fifty pounds) with which to weight the massive chunks of gold quarried out of Mother Earth's prolific bowels . . .

Missouri Republican, report of March 10, 1859.

Many persons who have had much experience in prairie traveling prefer leaving the Missouri River in March or April, and feeding grain to their animals until the new grass appears. The roads become muddy and heavy after the spring rains set in, and by starting out early the worst part of the road will be passed over before the ground becomes wet and soft. This plan, however, should never be attempted unless the animals are well supplied with grain, and kept in good condition. They will eat the old grass in the spring, but it does not, in this climate, as in Utah and New Mexico, afford them sufficient sustenance.

Captain Randolph B. Marcy, soldier and guidebook author, in The Prairie Traveler: A handbook for Overland Expeditions *(1859).*

We'll cross the bold Missouri, and we'll steer for
 the west,
And we'll take the road we think is the shortest
 and the best;
We'll travel, o'er the plains, where the wind is
 blowing bleak,
And the sandy wastes shall echo with—Hurrah for
 Pike's Peak.

We'll sit around the campfire when all our work is
 done,
And sing our songs, and crack our jokes, and have
 our share of fun;
And when we're tired of jokes and songs, our blankets we will seek,
To dream of friends, and home, and gold. Hurrah
 for Pike's Peak.

Of course the companies who returned before any
of the discoveries of importance were made, being
themselves discouraged and disheartened, would endeavor to discourage any of their friends from emigrating. They saw no mining operations that would
pay here, and hence they would be likely to disbe-
lieve any reports in contradiction to their experience.
A certain pride of opinion would lead them to adhere
to their first assertions. On the contrary, certain
mountain traders, who themselves made no discoveries, but who are interested in inducing emigration
hither for their own private ends, have, as I understand, circulated extravagant reports of the immense
richness of the mines. For instance: some of these
traders have asserted that they had taken out forty
thousand dollars worth of gold dust, when in fact
they had only taken a few panfulls of gravel from
one of our mines, and carried it to the States as
specimens.

*Luke Tierney, guidebook author and gold pros-
pector, advice to prospectors traveling to the
Pikes Peak region, 1859, in Hafen's* Pike's
Peak Gold Rush Guidebooks of 1859
(1941).

People are beginning to make the astounding discovery that "Pike's Peak is a humbug." The fact has
been known for a long time, but not till now has it
been made evident to the emigrant, bent with feverish haste, to the imagined land of gold. Two or three
months ago thousands passed through this state to
the "Cherry creek mines," lured thither by the cruelty and atrociously false stories concocted by persons in the border towns, who had outfitting goods
to dispose of, and by speculators in the new region,
who had town lots to sell. The poor emigrants solemnly believed every word of these fabricated stories.

St. Louis Evening News, *report of May 19,
1859.*

Coarse gold has been found, but not in sufficient
quantities to justify working. I saw, last evening,
some very good specimens of gold taken out 25 miles
from here, and will start for that place the day after
tomorrow. We will very likely stop there and work
until October, when I go home, for I would not spend
another winter here for any amount of money. Those

sentimentalists, who sigh for a "lodge in some vast
wilderness," can find several by coming to this place.

*Rufus Cable, gold prospector at Pikes Peak, to
the* Western Weekly Argus, *letter of June 9,
1859.*

We have this day personally visited nearly all the
mines or claims already opened in this valley, (that
of a little stream running into Clear creek at this
point;) have witnessed the operation of digging,
transporting, and washing the vein-stone, (a partially
decomposed, or rotten quartz, running in regular
veins from south-west to north-east, between shat-
tered walls of an impure granite,) have seen the gold
plainly visible in the riffles of nearly every sluice,
and in nearly every pan of the rotton quartz washed
in our presence; have seen gold (but rarely) visible
to the naked eye, in pieces of the quartz not yet fully
decomposed, and have obtained from the few who
have already sluices in operation accounts of their
several products, as follows:

Zeigler, Spain & Co., (from South Bend, Ind.,)
have run a sluice, with some interruptions, for the
last three weeks; they are four in company, with one
hired man. They have taken out a little over three
thousand pennyweights of gold, estimated by them
as worth at least $3,000; their first day's work pro-
duced $21; their highest was $495.

*Horace Greeley, Henry Villard and Albert Rich-
ardson, journalists, in the* Rocky Mountain
News, *article of June 11, 1859.*

The mines at Virginia Town and Gold Hill are
exceeding the most sanguine expectations of their
owners. At Virginia Town, particularly the claims on
the main leads promise to excel in richness the far-
famed Allison lead in California in its palmiest days.

Claims are changing hands at almost fabulous prices.
No fictitious sales either, but bona-fide business operation. The main lead, on which is the celebrated
Comstock and other claims, appears to be composed
of ores producing both silver and gold, and the more
it is prospected the richer is proving.

Territorial Enterprise *(Virginia City, Nevada), article of October 1, 1859.*

The first circumstance that strikes a stranger tra-
versing this wild country is the vagrant instincts and
habits of the great majority of its denizens—perhaps
I should say, of the American people generally, as
exhibited here. Among any ten whom you succes-

sively meet, there will be natives of New England, New York, Pennsylvania, Virginia or Georgia, Ohio or Indiana, Kentucky or Missouri, France, Germany, and perhaps Ireland. But, worse than this; you cannot enter a circle of a dozen persons of whom at least three will not have spent some years in California, two or three have made claims and built cabins in Kansas or Nebraska, and at least one spent a year or so in Texas. Boston, New York, Philadelphia, New Orleans, St. Louis, Cincinnati, have all contributed their quota toward peopling the new gold region.

The next man you meet driving an ox-team, and white as a miller with dust, is probably an ex-banker or doctor, a broken merchant or manufacturer from the old states, who has scraped together the candle-ends charitably or contemptuously allowed him by his creditors on settlement, and risked them on a last desperate cast of the dice by coming hither.

Horace Greeley, on visiting the gold mining town of Denver, in An Overland Journey from New York to San Francisco, in the Summer of 1859 *(1860).*

8. Overland Transportation and Civil War in the West: 1860–1869

THE OVERLAND EXPRESS

By 1858, Congress was debating the relative merits of the two overland mail routes—the Butterfield, via El Paso, and the "Central" via Salt Lake City. Although the proposed southern route was longer, it was favored by the Post Office Department for its frequent service and year-round travel. The central route, which passed through higher mountain ranges, was considerably shorter and was the favorite route of travel for emigrants.

Northern congressmen derisively labeled the southern road as the roundabout "oxbow route," while Southerners justified its great distance by pointing to the Southwest's plentiful grasslands and healthy climate. The southern route also had support from the postmaster general, Aaron B. Brown of Tennessee, an ardent Southerner, who threw out all the bids from the northern companies, and selected the offer of a firm headed by two seasoned expressmen, John Butterfield and William G. Fargo. They proposed to use a road from St. Louis or Memphis through Fort Smith, El Paso and Fort Yuma to San Francisco.

A year of preparation was involved before the Butterfield Overland Mail started its first stagecoaches across the continent. First, a "road" was marked out over 2,812 miles between Tipton, Missouri, and San Francisco. "Stations" were constructed at intervals, where horses and mules could be sheltered, and food provided for passengers. The menu was for strong stomachs: bacon, beans, bread and what passed in the West for coffee. At each outpost was placed an "agent" and every 200 miles of road was entrusted to a "district agent."

The coaches introduced by the Butterfield Overland Mail Company revolutionized travel. Known as Concord Coaches for their manufacturer—the Abbott-Downing Company of Concord, New Hampshire—

they were far better suited for journeys across plains and deserts than any earlier vehicles. The wheels were heavy, with broad iron ties that would not sink in soft sand. Some of the worst shocks of overland travel were absorbed by the iron-reinforced wooden body, which was swung on leather thoroughbraces. The driver and conductor, and sometimes a passenger or two, rode high up on a boxlike structure, while to the rear was a triangular "boot," which contained the mail sacks and any luggage. Usually four horses or a half-dozen mules pulled the red- or green-painted stagecoaches.

On September 16, 1858, the Butterfield Overland Mail Company began its first run from St. Louis to San Francisco. By October 10, the overland stage had reached its destination, crossing 3,000 miles in just 23 days and 23 hours. For the next three years Butterfield Overland Mail coaches raced over trails between East and West, two each week in each direction, through rain and snow and desert heat. By 1859, the company's prosperity encouraged the postmaster general to subsidize two alternate routes, the Kansas and Stockton Express between Kansas City and Stockton, California, and the San Antonio Express connecting Texas with San Diego.

The freighting firm of Russell, Majors and Waddell was carrying the mail over the central route on a semimonthly schedule. William H. Russell, one of the firm's partners, proposed to Congress that fast and reliable service could be maintained during the winter months if subsidies were provided for adequate stock and stations. Russell's scheme was the famed Pony Express, where relays of horsemen would carry the mail between Missouri and California in 10 days.

Russell discussed his plan with Senator William Gwin of California, who suggested that a demonstration was needed before Congress would award the mail contract to Russell's firm. Preparations were soon underway. One-hundred-ninety way stations were situated at 10-mile intervals between Saint Joseph, Missouri, and San Francisco; 500 horses were selected for speed and stamina, and the best riders were hired. By April 3, 1860, arrangements were complete for demonstrating Russell's grand experiment in rapid overland transportation.

On that day large crowds assembled in Saint Joseph and San Francisco to cheer the two Pony Express riders. Each rode his horse at full gallop for 10 miles, then came barrelling into a station where another horse was saddled and waiting. Each rider rode about 75 miles at this fast pace then turned over his mail pouches to another and rested for the return trip. Eighty riders were constantly in the saddle, 40 of them heading east, 40 west, traveling over rolling prairies and tortuous mountain passes, and never stopping for snow or sleet or even Indian attack.

The Pony Express fairly maintained its 10-day schedule during the summer and fall months, and throughout the winter was able to deliver the mails in about 14 days. But the venture was more romantic than profitable. The short-lived Pony Express carried the mails between California and Saint Joseph, Missouri, only until October 1861, when the first transcontinental telegraph made it obsolete. Deeply in debt, after he and his partners had poured $500,000 into the venture while also losing money on the company's stagecoach line, Russell stooped to embezzling government securities with the help of a friend who worked as a clerk in the Interior Department. His scheme was soon exposed, but through the work of his clever lawyers he escaped imprisonment for any long period of time. Russell still hoped in 1861 to receive another mail contract from Congress, but the bond scandal was too unsavory for Congress to overlook.

Although Russell, Majors and Waddell went bankrupt, the Pony Express proved the feasibility of the central route for year-round travel. The southern Butterfield route was abandoned in favor of the central route across the Great Plains, and the Pony Express was replaced by Ben Holladay's Overland Stage Line, which could carry the mails, freight and also passengers across the continent.

THE BLUE AND THE GRAY IN THE WEST

By 1861, the sectional controversy between North and South was about to erupt into full-scale civil war. Except for Texas, the states and territories of the trans-Mississippi West were little concerned with slavery and the cotton economy. Nevertheless, almost every western state or territory had been forced to align itself with either the North or the South.

Governor Sam Houston strongly pled with Texas politicians to refrain from secession, but he was forced out of office, and at a state convention in February 1861 Texans voted to secede from the Union. Almost immediately Texas militiamen captured and occupied federal forts within the state's borders. Ben McCulloch, Indian fighter and Texas Ranger, led 300 troops into San Antonio's Main Plaza, where he accepted the surrender of General D.E. Twiggs, the 2,700 troops under his command and all of United States property in Texas.

With the victory in Texas, the Confederacy planned to win over the wavering border state of Missouri, seize New Mexico and occupy the gold fields of California, Colorado and Nevada. None of these plans were ever realized. The outcome of the war was decided on battlefields farther east—at Gettysburg and Vicksburg, at Chattanooga and Antietam. Yet the fighting in the West did influence to some extent the outcome of these campaigns.

In most western regions the Civil War had an affect on the Indians, who, except for the Five Civilized Tribes in the Indian Territory, had

Construction of telegraph lines across the Plains. Painting by George M. Ottinger, Harper's Weekly, *November 2, 1867. Courtesy of the New York Public Library.*

no interest in the issues dividing North and South. Albert Pike, representing the Confederacy, met with the Tribes and reminded them that the United States had appropriated their lands in the East. Hoping to gain the Indians' beef herds and to enlist warriors in the Confederate Army, Pike promised that the Confederacy, when victorious, would create an independent Indian nation. The Creeks, Choctaws, Chickasaws and Seminoles were impressed with Pike's proposal and agreed to sign treaties with the Confederacy.

Through the blazing heat of July 1861 Colonel John R. Baylor of Texas marched a force of volunteers from San Antonio to the Rio Grande, and without much of a fight captured Fort Bliss, near El Paso. Forty miles upriver, federal troops and their families began evacuating Fort Fillmore. Baylor proceeded northward and in late July 1861 was able to capture the fort without firing a shot. Baylor decreed that all territory in Arizona and New Mexico south of the 34th parallel belonged to the Confederate States of America.

On August 10, 1861, at a small stream called Wilson's Creek in southwestern Missouri, Confederate General Sterling Price led an army of 13,000 troops against 5,000 Union soldiers under the command of General Nathaniel Lyon. Price's troops triumphed, and Lyon was killed in action. The Confederate force roared through central Missouri, and by September 20 had captured 2,800 federal troops.

Price was pushed back as John C. Fremont, commander of the Western Department of the Union Army, organized a force of 30,000 troops to repel the invading Confederates. Fremont, however, was replaced by Samuel Curtis, a West Point graduate, after issuing an order freeing all slaves and confiscating rebel property in the region. The unauthorized order damaged President Lincoln's plan to keep Missouri and

Bivouac of Confederate troops at Las Moras, Texas, with stolen U.S. wagons, etc., July 1861. Sketched by a member of the corps. Courtesy of the Library of Congress.

other border states in the Union. Confederate forces in Missouri were eventually routed at Pea Ridge, Arkansas, in March 1862.

The Confederate assault along the Rio Grande resumed in February 1862 when Colonel Henry Hopkins Sibley arrived in New Mexico with replacement troops for Colonel Baylor's army. The federal defense of New Mexico was under the command of Colonel Edward R.S. Canby, whose 19th United States Infantry was stationed at Santa Fe. By coincidence, Canby was the brother-in-law of Confederate Colonel Sibley.

With 1,750 men Sibley overpowered Canby's 4,000 Union defenders at Fort Craig. Sibley was able to push back the federal troops, but could not take the fort. He continued marching north toward Albuquerque, which he captured without much opposition, and by March 23 occupied Santa Fe. Sibley was so impressed with his easy victories that he planned to continue toward Fort Union and eventually seize the Pikes Peak gold region.

As Sibley's overconfident troops approached Fort Union on March 26, 1862, they expected another easy victory. But they were surprised by the "Pikes Peakers," a hearty army of irregulars from the Denver City gold mines. Two days later the battle of La Glorietta Pass took place, later to become known as the "Gettysburg of the West." It represented the last serious Confederate threat to Union control of the Southwest.

The battle was a draw until evening, when, unknown to the Confederates, several hundred troops from the First Colorado Volunteers, under the command of Major John M. Chivington, made their way through the almost impassable mountains to the south of the battle-field. Chivington's men caught the Confederate supply column, consisting of 73 wagons and 600 mules and horses, by total surprise and destroyed it. The Confederate force retreated to Texas. The high point of Confederate victories in the West had came to an end.

STRUGGLE ON THE PLAINS

By the start of the Civil War, the Indians of the northern Plains were growing increasingly disturbed at the caravans of emigrants, rumbling overland stages, railroad surveying crews and military expeditions passing through their region. The Indians were most annoyed by the thousands of prospectors who ignored their land claims and drove them from their homes. A few young Indian chiefs realized that they were caught between the advance of the mining frontier, from the West, and the agricultural frontier, from the East. More Indians were coming to believe that if their race was to avoid annihilation it must make a stand against white aggression.

Although the Civil War provided an excellent opportunity for the Indians to roll back the white man's advancing frontier, there were only a few attacks on white settlers during these years. One such uprising, by the Sioux of Minnesota during 1862, stemmed more from a misunderstanding between Indians and whites than from an attempt to expel the settlers.

On August 18, 1862, after six whites were murdered by a small band of Indians near New Ulm, Minnesota, survivors panicked and spread rumors of widespread Indian uprisings. Most of the Minnesota Sioux were astonished by the murders. Fearing the revenge of the whites, the Sioux concluded that they must either fight or flee westward. Part of the Indians prepared for war under the command of Little Crow, while others moved westward.

Little Crow and his 1,300 warriors began an offensive against the outlying settlements of the Minnesota River Valley. Men, women and children were killed, barns and houses were burned, and the frontier was thrown into a state of panic. The Minnesota state government requested federal troops to quell the uprising. By September 1862, volunteer troops under the command of Colonel Henry Hastings Sibley had defeated the Indians.

Sibley's troops captured 1,700 warriors, held a grand court-martial and condemned over 300 of them to death. Through the intervention of President Lincoln all but 39 of the death sentences were commuted. The punishment against the Sioux was swift, and in the following year a punitive military expedition was waged against the rest of Little

Crow's band. In 1863, Congress confiscated all Sioux lands in Minnesota, and in the next year the dispossessed Indians were relocated to Dakota.

While the Sioux in the North were battling whites, the Apaches and the Navajos in the Southwest were being subjected to the removal policy of Union General James Carleton. His motives were mixed. On the one hand, harassed settlers appealed to him for relief against the menacing Indians. He was also convinced that Arizona and New Mexico were full of precious minerals that would result in a rush comparable to California's as soon as the Indians were removed. He ordered all Apache and Navajo males "to be slain whenever and wherever they can be found, and women and children were to be taken prisoner." Indians who did not resist were to be confined to a reservation at Bosque Redondo, along the Pecos River in central New Mexico.

In January 1864, Colonel Kit Carson led 375 troops in a brief battle against a large group of Navajos in present-day Arizona. After defeating the Navajos, Carson convinced 2,400 men, women and children to surrender and begin the march to Bosque Redondo. The 300-mile trek became known as the "Long Walk."

Fighting began in the Colorado country in February 1861 after federal agents called the chiefs from the Arapaho and Cheyenne tribes to a council at Fort Lyon. The commissioners forced the chiefs to abandon all their claims to the territory guaranteed them at the 1851 Fort Laramie council in return for a small reservation between the Arkansas River and Sand Creek in eastern Colorado. Many Arapaho and Cheyenne warriors refused to abandon their territories. They disassociated themselves from the chiefs responsible for the new treaty and took to the warpath. During the next three years, mining camps, overland stages, mail stations and emigrant trains were subject to frequent attack. The federal government could offer little protection, for troops were needed in the East to fight the Confederates.

In August 1864, Governor John Evans of Colorado issued a proclamation calling on all citizens to pursue the Indians and "to kill and destroy" them. He also put into service two volunteer regiments of the state cavalry. By the end of August the warring tribes were ready to negotiate a peace settlement. At a council at Fort Lyon, the Cheyenne Chief Black Kettle expressed his desire for peace, but the federal commander informed him that he did not have the authority to end the war. In late September, Black Kettle and other Cheyenne and Arapaho chiefs held a conference with Governor John Evans, who refused to accept their overtures for peace and declared that the war would continue. Writing from Fort Leavenworth, Major General Samuel R. Curtis echoed Evans' sentiment, "I want no peace till the Indians suffer more."

The chiefs, still yearning for peace, turned again to Fort Lyon, hoping the newly appointed commander would accept their surrender. At first, Major Scott J. Anthony promised the Indians protection, but then, fearing he had exceeded his authority, ordered them to leave the fort. Believing the war was over, Black Kettle led his 700 followers to a camp on Sand Creek. Unknown to the Indians, Colonel John M. Chivington of the Colorado militia was leading a regiment of 1,000 territorial volunteers for an attack upon them. On November 29, 1864, at Sand Creek, one of the bloodiest events in the history of Indian warfare took place.

The Indians were taken by complete surprise. In the early morning hours the camp was surrounded by the Colorado troops. The Indians' first reaction was to run, but most were unable to escape the terrible slaughter. In vain Black Kettle raised first an American flag, then a white flag. Chivington's troops shot down men, women and children, and committed other atrocities. Within a few hours 450 Indians lay dead, with only Black Kettle and a few younger warriors managing to escape.

As word of the Chivington Massacre spread across the Plains, Cheyenne and Arapaho warriors were inspired to renew their attacks. During the winter of 1864–65, raiding parties pillaged ranches, destroyed telegraph wires, attacked overland mail stations and engaged in bitter battles with Colorado and federal troops. Fearing another massacre, the Cheyennes and Arapahos agreed to surrender unconditionally and relinquish their Sand Creek reservation in return for lands elsewhere.

While peace was descending upon the Southwest, a new conflict with the Sioux was breaking out in the North. Many Sioux were disturbed by the advance of the mining frontier into the Montana Territory, and they were provoked into action by news that the United States planned to build the "Powder River Road" or "Bozeman Trail," which would destroy one of their favorite hunting grounds in the foothills of the Big Horn Mountains.

Chief Red Cloud warned that any attempt to build the road would be resisted. Federal troops were deployed in the Big Horn country, and they began building forts along the proposed highway. During the summer of 1866 troops were under almost constant attack. Skirmishes reached a climax on December 21, 1866, when Captain William J. Fetterman marched 82 troops out of Fort Phil Kearny on Powder River to aid a beseiged train of woodcutters. Fetterman and every one of his troops were killed in an ambush attack.

The Fetterman Massacre and subsequent Sioux raids made soldiers along the Powder River virtual prisoners within the walls of their forts throughout the spring of 1867. As a result of the Sioux War and a report on the Chivington Massacre, Congress began to reexamine its Indian policy and established a Peace Commission to persuade the various tribes to abandon their nomadic ways in return for protected lives on remote reservations.

In October 1867, peace commissioners held a council at Medicine

Red Cloud. Courtesy of the New York Public Library.

Lodge Creek in Kansas with representatives of the Kiowa and Comanche tribes. The Indians agreed to accept a three-million-acre reservation between the Red and Washita rivers in western Indian Territory. One week later the Cheyenne and Arapaho accepted a barren area between the Cimarron and Arkansas rivers.

Next, the peace commissioners turned their attention to ending the Sioux War. They realized the Sioux would never stop fighting as long as the government insisted on building the Powder River Road. At a council held at Fort Laramie the commissioners agreed to abandon the Powder River Road along with the three forts that guarded the highway. The Sioux agreed to cease fighting and to move to a permanent reservation in the Dakota Territory.

Not all southern Plains chiefs, especially the younger warriors, accepted the Fort Laramie and Medicine Lodge treaties. To some Indians the terms provided exactly what they did not want—fixed homes and farms. The frontiers of Texas, Colorado, Kansas and New Mexico continued to experience sporadic attacks by raiding bands from various tribes. The Plains Indians were also becoming aware of another invasion of their lands—railroad builders laying track westward for the first transcontinental railroad.

THE IRON ROAD

Congress had passed a law on July 1, 1862, launching construction of the nation's first transcontinental railroad. The line would follow the Central route between Sacramento and Omaha, on the Missouri River in Nebraska Territory. Two companies would build the road. The Central Pacific was assigned the task of laying the line from the west, while the Union Pacific would construct the road from the east. The lines would be joined in the Far West. The first track was set down in 1863, and work inched forward during the next few years.

At the end of 1865 only 40 miles of track stretched west from Omaha, as workers and material were difficult to obtain from a war-torn nation. After the war, throngs of laborers headed west to work on the railroads. In 1867, the Chicago and Western Railroad reached Council Bluffs, Iowa. Yet plentiful labor did not solve the Union Pacific's construction problems. All materials had to be shipped to the barren Plains from the East—ties from the forests of Minnesota, stone from the quarries of Wisconsin and rails from the steel mills of Pennsylvania. Hundreds of wagons were constantly in motion, hauling supplies to the crews. Work along the road was also frequently halted by Indian attack.

The men who built the Union Pacific lived in tent cities that moved west with the road. These overnight towns, spread out across the plains at 60- or 70-mile intervals, attracted an assortment of characters, from saloon keepers and prostitutes to gamblers and outlaws.

By spring 1868 the Central Pacific was moving across the deserts of Nevada, while the Union Pacific was battling through the South Pass. Foremen pushed their crews forward, laying between five miles and 10 miles of track a day. The competition between the Central Pacific and the Union Pacific was so great that they seemed destined never to meet. Congress had set no junction point and in the last days the two lines were moving so fast that their graders went past each other. Washington finally ruled that the two roads must join at Promontory, Utah, a short distance from Ogden, Utah.

On May 10, 1869, at Promontory Point, the Central and Union Pacific lines were brought together in a special ceremony. Officials from both companies and honored guests assembled to watch the final spikes as they were driven into the railroad ties: one of silver from Nevada, one of gold, silver and iron from Arizona, and two gold ones from California. As the two companies' engines came nose to nose, the telegraph flashed the news to the country, beginning a series of celebrations from east to west.

THE LONG DRIVE

Following the Civil War a few enterprising Texas cattlemen had seen the expanding northern-route railroads as an opportunity to turn their millions of cattle into substantial profits. In their own state good steers could be purchased for $3 or $4 a head from ranchers. In the upper Mississippi Valley buyers were willing to pay up to $40 a head for marketable steers. If a cattleman could transport a few thousand long-horns to northern markets he could realize a huge profit. Texans were aware that the steers could be driven overland without much difficulty through the open Plains. Consequently, in 1866 the ''Long Trail'' drives across Plains and Prairie began.

The first big drives were not very successful. Drivers unfamiliar with the trail would sometimes lose a quarter of the few thousand animals that began the trip. Herds passing through Indian Territory were frequently stampeded by Indians, who then demanded rewards for returning the steers. Missouri farmers, fearing that their cows might become infected with the dreaded Texas Fever, also went out to repel the herds. Only a few steers managed to reach market, but the $35-a-head price convinced Texan cattlemen that the Long Drive could be successful if a less hazardous route to market were established.

Joseph G. McCoy, an Illinois stockman, saw the tremendous opportunities and persuaded the railroads to grant him special rates for shipping cattle from the Plains to Chicago. He next chose a small Plains town on the Kansas Pacific tracks where the Long Drive would end—Abilene, Kansas.

During the spring of 1867, McCoy built stockyards, pens, loading chutes, barns, a livery stable and even a hotel to house the cowhands. The following year cattlemen were driving thousands of longhorn over the trail northward; they called it the Chisholm Trial, in honor of Jesse Chisholm, a half-breed Scotch-Cherokee Indian trader, who in the preceding years had moved goods and furs along the route. Between 1867 and 1871 approximately 40,000 freight cars carried a million and a half steer to the new meat-processing plants in Kansas City and Chicago.

As more railroad lines cut across the Plains, new cattle towns, such as Wichita, Ellsworth and Dodge City became terminal points for the Long Drives. They were sleepy hamlets most of the time, but when the mounted cowboys arrived, they were transformed into hurly-burly towns. Like the mining camps, the ''cow towns'' were places of easy money, rugged individuals, barroom brawls and gunfights. The legends and myths surrounding the ''Wild West'' were about to take shape.

CHRONICLE OF EVENTS

1860:

April 3–13: The first relay of the Pony Express carries 49 letters from St. Joseph, Missouri, to Sacramento, California, in 10 days.

November 6: Abraham Lincoln is elected president.

1861:

January 29: Kansas is granted statehood. The antislavery constitution of Kansas is accepted by the Republican-dominated Congress.

February 18: Cheyenne and Arapaho tribes agree to abandon their claims to most of Colorado. They agree to relocate to a small reservation in the eastern part of the state.

February 23: Texas secedes from the Union.

February 28: Congress creates the Territory of Colorado.

March 2: Congress creates the Territory of Nevada.

April 12: Confederate forces fire on Fort Sumter in South Carolina; the Civil War begins.

April 30: Federal troops evacuate Indian Territory forts, leaving the Five Civilized Nations under Confederate control.

May–October: The Confederacy negotiates treaties with five Indian nations residing in the Indian Territory (present-day Oklahoma).

July 25: Union troops from Fort Fillmore in New Mexico battle with Confederates. Union troops abandon the fort.

August 1: Captain John Boyer, who defeated Union troops at Fort Fillmore, decrees that all territory in Arizona and New Mexico south of the 34th parallel belongs to the Confederacy.

August 10: The battle of Wilson's Creek, in southwestern Missouri; a 5,000-man Union army is defeated by a much larger Confederate force.

August 30: General John C. Fremont declares martial law throughout Missouri, confiscating property, including slaves of those who oppose the Union.

October 24: The first telegraph message is sent between San Francisco and Washington, D.C.; the transcontinental line makes the Pony Express obsolete and it ceases service.

1862:

Feburary 21: Union control of the entire Southwest is threatened by the Confederacy's capture of Albuquerque and Santa Fe.

March 8: The battle of Pea Ridge, Arkansas, the most significant Civil War battle in the trans-Mississippi West, results in the deaths of two Confederate generals, McCulloch and McIntosh.

March 28: The battle of La Glorietta Pass, 20 miles southeast of Santa Fe; the First Colorado Volunteer Regiment forces Confederate troops back down the Rio Grande River into Texas. The battle is later called the "Gettysburg of the West."

May 20: Lincoln signs the Homestead Act, offering to any citizen who is head of a family and over 21 years of age, 160 acres of public land after residing on it for five years. The Act opens up millions of acres on the Great Plains.

July 1: Congress passes the Pacific Railroad Act, authorizing the Union Pacific and the Central Pacific companies to build the first transcontinental railroad over a central route between Sacramento and Omaha on the Missouri River.

August 17–September 26: Peace with Indians in Minnesota is broken when Santee Sioux, led by Chief Little Crow, begin a six-week attack against white settlers.

November 5: After a series of trials in Minnesota, 303 Santee Sioux are sentenced to death and 16 to lengthy prison terms for crimes against whites in the state.

December 6: President Lincoln commutes the death sentences of all but 39 of the convicted Santee Sioux in Minnesota.

1863:

January 1: The first claim under the Homestead Act is filed by Daniel Freeman, at a location a few miles west of Beatrice, Nevada.

January: The Bear River Campaign, near Salt Lake City; 700 California volunteers launch an attack against Shoshoni and Bannock Indians who have been attacking mining camps and Mormon settlements. Indian power in northern Utah and southern Idaho is destroyed.

February 24: Congress creates the Territory of Arizona from the western section of New Mexico Territory.

March: Almost 500 Mescalero Apache Indians surrender to New Mexico volunteers led by Colonel Kit Carson. They are relocated to an Indian reservation on the Pecos River.

March 3: Congress creates the Territory of Idaho.

July 4: Union forces under General Ulysses S. Grant capture the Confederate stronghold of Vicksburg on the Mississippi River.

July 8: Port Hudson, Mississippi, the only remaining Confederate fort on the Mississippi River, falls to Union forces.

August 21: Lawrence, Kansas is attacked by approximately 450 irregular Confederate raiders; 150 civilians are killed, 30 wounded and most of the town is burned.

September 10: Federal troops occupy Little Rock, Arkansas, after Confederates evacuate the state capital.

1864:

January–March: Navajo Indians in northeast Arizona Territory surrender to volunteer troops under Colonel Kit Carson, and begin a 300-mile trek, known as the "Long March," to their assigned reservation.

April 11: A pro-Union state government is established in Little Rock, Arkansas.

May 26: Congress creates the Territory of Montana from Idaho Territory.

June 30: Yosemite Valley Park, in California, is authorized as the nation's first state park.

September 28: Seven chiefs from the Cheyenne and Arapaho tribes, led by Black Kettle and White Antelope, meet with Colorado military forces and Governor Evans, near Denver, Colorado. The Indians are accused of hostile attacks, but the Indians deny the acts or blame them on the Sioux.

October 23: The battle of Westport, Missouri; the Confederates are forced to retreat southward along the Missouri-Kansas border.

October 31: Nevada is admitted to the Union.

November 29: Colorado volunteers, commanded by Colonel Chivington, attack a Southern Cheyenne and Arapaho village at Sand Creek in Colorado. Atrocities are committed by the undisciplined troops, mostly against women and children.

1865:

January: Cheyenne, Arapaho and Sioux warriors launch a series of revenge attacks along the valley of the South Platte River in Colorado.

April 9: Confederate General Robert E. Lee surrenders to General Ulysses S. Grant at Appomattox Court House, Virginia, ending the Civil War.

April 15: President Abraham Lincoln dies after being shot by John Wilkes Booth the previous evening. Andrew Johnson of Tennessee is sworn in as president.

May 20: Confederate General E. Kirby Smith, commander of Confederate troops west of the Mississippi River, surrenders at Palmitto Hill on the Rio Grande in Texas.

July 10: The Union Pacific Company lays its first rail out of Omaha, Nebraska.

October 14: In the Little Arkansas Treaties, Southern Plains tribes cede to the United States their claims to the territory north of the Arkansas River and agree to relocate to territories south of the stream.

December 25: The Union stockyards open in

Chicago, making Chicago the hub for transcontinental commerce.

1866:

June: At Fort Laramie a delegation of Brule and Oglala Sioux, led by Red Cloud, meet with American officials. Americans wish to expand a route that runs across some prime buffalo range of the Sioux. Negotiations are ended when Colonel Henry B. Carrington arrives with 700 soldiers; Red Cloud considers their presence a threat to use force.

July 16: The First Sioux War begins in the Powder River country. Sioux warriors and allies from northern tribes wage war along the Bozeman Road. Red Cloud has gathered a force of 3,000 Indian warriors.

December 21: The Fetterman Massacre; Captain William J. Fetterman and 80 soldiers are ambushed and killed near Fort Phil Kearney, the worst defeat the U.S. Army has suffered to date in Indian warfare.

1867:

March: The Kansas Pacific Railroad reaches Abilene, Kansas. The town is established as a terminus for Texas cattle to be shipped by rail to the East.

March 30: The Alaska Purchase; Russia transfers Alaska to the United States for $7,200,000.

April: General Winfield Scott Hancock leads a large force of cavalry and infantry across western Kansas. At Pawnee Fork, his troops capture and burn a Cheyenne village. In retaliation the Indians stop almost all travel across western Kansas.

August 2: The Wagon Box Fight; woodcutters near Fort Phil Kearney flee to a line of wagon boxes when they are attacked by about 800 Sioux warriors, under Red Cloud. Equipped with repeating rifles, they inflict 200 Indian casualties for every five whites.

September 5: The first shipment of 20 cattle cars leaves Abilene, Kansas, on the Kansas Pacific Railroad, bound for the East.

October: William F. Cody is hired to kill 12 buffalo per day along the path of the Kansas Pacific Railroad as it progresses westward to supply meat to workers building the railroad. After killing more than 4,000 buffalo during the next eight months, he becomes known as "Buffalo Bill."

October 21: At Medicine Lodge Creek in southwestern Kansas 7,000 Indians gather, as the leaders of the southern tribes hold a council with federal peace commissioners. Treaties are signed, and the Kiowas and Comanches are assigned a 3,000,000-acre reservation between the Red and Washita Rivers in western Indian Territory.

December 4: The Grangers, an agricultural interest party, is founded by Oliver Hudson Kelley in Washington, D.C.

1868:

April 29: Sioux and Northern Cheyenne tribal leaders hold a treaty council with U.S. peace commissioners at Fort Laramie. The Indians agree to accept designated reservations in Dakota Territory west of the Missouri River, but are promised use of their hunting grounds east of the Big Horn Mountains in southern Montana Territory.

July 25: The Territory of Wyoming is created.

July 28: The Fourteenth Amendment to the U.S. Constitution is ratified. It grants full citizenship to blacks and all other persons either born in the United States or naturalized, with the exception of the Native Americans, who are denied citizenship.

November 27: Lieutenant Colonel George Custer leads the Seventh Cavalry in an attack on a large Cheyenne camp on the upper Washita River in western Indian Territory. Chief Black Kettle is among the 103 Indians killed.

1869:

March 4: Ulysses S. Grant is inaugurated as the 18th president of the United States.

May 10: The first transcontinental railroad is

completed at Promontory Point in Utah Territory, as the Central Pacific's Jupiter and the Union Pacific's No. 119 touch after gold and silver spikes are driven.

July 11: The battle of Summit Springs, in northeast Colorado Territory; eight companies of the U.S. Cavalry attack the camps of Tall Bull and his Cheyenne "Dog Soliders." Tall Bull and 52 Indians are killed, ending the Indian threat in Kansas and the surrounding country.

December 10: The legislature of the Territory of Wyoming grants the right to vote and hold office to women over 21 years of age, the first state or territory in the nation to do so.

EYEWITNESS TESTIMONY

Men and brethren! let us resolve to have a railroad to the Pacific—to have it soon. It will add more to the strength and wealth of our country than would the acquisition of a dozen Cubas. It will prove a bond of union not easily broken, and a new spring to our national industry, prosperity, and wealth. It will call new manufacturers into existence, and increase the demand for the products of those already existing. It will open new vistas to national and to individual aspiration, and crush out filibusterism by giving a new and wholesome direction to the public mind. My long, fatiguing journey was undertaken in the hope that I might do something toward the early construction of the Pacific Railroad; and I trust that it has not been made wholly in vain.

Horace Greeley, editorial in the New York Tribune, *1860, in Ingersoll's* The Life of Horace Greeley *(1890).*

The first courier of the Pony Express will leave the Missouri River on Tuesday, April 3, at 5 o'clock p.m. and will run regularly weekly thereafter, carrying a letter mail only.

William H. Russell, president of the Central Overland California and Pikes Peak Express Company, announcement in the Missouri Republican, *March 26, 1860.*

The mail must go. Hurled by flesh and blood across 2,000 miles of desolate space—Fort Kearney, Laramie, South Pass, Fort Bridger, Salt Lake City. Neither storms, fatigue, darkness, mountains or Indians, burning sands or snow must stop the precious bags. The mail must go.

M. Jeff Thompson, mayor of St. Joseph, Missouri, starting point for the Pony Express, speech of April 3, 1860, in Monaghan's The Overland Trail *(1947).*

I _____, do hereby swear, before the Great and Living God, that during my engagement, and while I am in the employ of Russell, Majors and Waddell, I will under no circumstances, use profane language; that I will drink no intoxicating liquors; that I will not quarrel or fight with any other employee of the firm, and that in every respect, I will conduct myself honestly, be faithful to my duties, and so direct all my acts as to win the confidence of my employers. So help me God.

Pony Express rider oath, 1860, in Bradley's The Story of the Pony Express *(1920).*

In stretching my own route I found myself getting further and further west. Finally I was riding well into the foothills of the Rockies. Still further west my route was pushed. Soon I rode from Red Buttes to Sweetwater, a distance of seventy-six miles. Road-agents and Indians infested the country. I never was quite sure when I started out when I should reach my destination, or whether I should never reach it at all.

William F. Cody ("Buffalo Bill"), on his days as a Pony Express rider in 1860, in The Life of Honorable William F. Cody known as Buffalo Bill *(1879).*

The Promised Land is gained and we are in Denver tonight. We entered the city of the plains at 10 o'clock A.M. We soon found Dora. They are camping on the banks of Cherry Creek, a dry, sandy channel. There are no houses to be had, and hundreds of families are living in wagons, tents, and shelters made of carpets and bedding. I like the looks of the place. Everybody seems glad to welcome the coming pilgrims, as we are called, anybody from "back in the States." It is estimated there are five thousand people in and around Denver. It seems so near the mountains that I thought I could easily walk over there, but Dora says they are 12 miles away. The atmosphere is so dry and clear it brings distant objects nearer.

Mollie Dorsey Sanford, emigrant from Nebraska Territory, journal entry of June 26, 1860, in Mollie: The Journal of Mollie Dorsey Sanford *(1959).*

It has not fallen to my lot to visit any Indians who seemed more disposed to yield to the wishes of the government than the Cheyennes and Arrapahoes. Notwithstanding they are fully aware of the rich mines discovered in their country, they are disposed to yield up their claims without any reluctance. They certainly deserve the fostering hand of the government, and should be liberally encouraged in their contemplated new sphere of life.

Albert B. Greenwood, Indian Affairs agent, report of October 25, 1860, in Hafen's Relations with the Indians of the Plains, 1857–1861 *(1959).*

I think there can be no doubt that many of the Southern States will secede from the Union. The State

Emigrants crossing the Plains, 1869. Courtesy of the Library of Congress.

of Texas will be among the number, and, from all appearances at present, it will be at an early day; certainly before the 4th of March next. What is to be done with public property in charge of the army? The arsenal at this place has some ordinance and other munitions of war. I do not expect an order for the present for the disposition of them, but I would be pleased to receive your views and suggestions. My course, as respects myself, will be to remain at my post and protect this frontier as long as I can, and then when turned adrift make my way home, if I have one.

General David E. Twiggs (USA), to General Winfield Scott, Commander in Chief of the U.S. Army, letter of December 13, 1860, in Johnson and Buel's Battles and Leaders of the Civil War *(1887).*

We had had a consuming desire, from the beginning, to see a pony-rider, but somehow or other all that passed us and all that met us managed to streak by in the night, and so we heard only a whiz and a hail, and the swift phantom of the desert was gone before we could get our heads out of the windows. But now we were expecting one along every moment, and would see him in broad daylight. Presently the driver exclaims:

"HERE HE COMES!"

Every neck is stretched further, and every eye strained wider. Away across the endless dead level of the prairie a black speck appears against the sky, and it is plain that it moves. Well, I should think so! In a second or two it becomes a horse and rider, rising and falling, rising and falling—sweeping toward us nearer and nearer—growing more and more distinct, more and more sharply defined—nearer and still nearer, and the flutter of the hoofs comes faintly to the ear—another instant a whoop and a hurrah from our upper deck, a wave of the rider's hand, but no reply, and man and horse burst past our excited faces, and go winging away like a belated fragment of a storm!

Mark Twain, on the Pony Express, 1861, in Roughing It *(1872).*

We gathered buffalo-chips to boil our coffee and cook our buffalo and antelope steak, smoked for a while around the smouldering fire until the animals were through grazing, and then started on our lonely way again. Sometimes the coach would travel for a hundred miles through buffalo herds, never for a moment getting out of sight of them. Often we saw fifty thousand to a hundred thousand on a single journey out or in. The Indians used to call them their cattle, and claimed to own them.

W.H. Ryus, overland stage driver, 1861, in
Inman's The Old Santa Fe Trail *(1897).*

Late in January was held the election for delegates to a State convention which should consider the question of secession. San Antonio was crowded. Women vied with each other in distributing the little yellow ballots, on which were printed in large type, "For Secession," or "Against Secession." Many an ignorant Mexican received instructions that the ballot "with the longest words" was the right one. The *carteros* from New Mexico, who were in town with their wagon-trains, were bought by the secessionists, and some were known to have voted three times. It was well known that the Federal civil officers were loyal; the French and German citizens were emphatically so; and yet against the will of the people, "by superior political diplomacy," secession triumphed in San Antonio by a small majority.

Mrs. Caroline Baldwin Darrow, citizen of San
Antonio, Texas, January 1861, in Johnson and
Buel's Battles and Leaders of the Civil War.

In regard to the homestead law, I have to say that in so far as the government lands can be disposed of, I am in favor of cutting up the wild lands into parcels, so that every poor man may have a home.

President Abraham Lincoln, address of February
12, 1861, in Abraham Lincoln, Complete
Works *(1920).*

I have considered it a physical problem, worthy of the highest efforts of a great people, to overcome that difficulty which, in all history, has shown that men could not be aggregated together under one Government if they were divided by impassable mountains. I have thought it an achievement worthy of our age and of our people, to couple with bonds of iron the people of the Pacific with the valley of the Mississippi, and show that even the snow-capped mountains intervening could not divide them.

Senator Jefferson Davis (Mississippi) to the
Senate, on the Pacific railroad bill, speech of
January 5, 1861, in Jefferson Davis: Constitutionalist, His Letters, Papers and
Speeches *(1923).*

Whereas, By virtue of an Act of the Legislature of the State of Texas, an election was ordered to be held on the 23d of February, A.D. 1861, at which the people of Texas were called upon to vote in favor of or against "Secession" from the government of the United States, and,

Whereas, said election was held, and returns thereof, received on the 2d day of March, have been opened and counted as required by law, and it appearing that a majority of those votes, as well as a majority of those received since that period, are in favor of "Secession."

Governor Sam Houston (Texas), proclamation
of March 4, 1861, in Roberts' Confederate
Military History *(1962).*

One section of our country believes slavery is right, and ought to be extended, while the other believes it is wrong, and ought not to be extended. This is the only substantial dispute. The fugitive-slave clause of the Constitution, and the law for the suppression of the foreign slave-trade, are each as well enforced, perhaps, as any law can ever be in a community where the moral sense of the people imperfectly supports the law itself. The great body of the people abide by the dry legal obligation in both cases, and a few break over in each. This, I think, cannot be perfectly cured; and it would be worse in both cases after the separation of the sections than before.

President Abraham Lincoln, first inaugural ad-
dress, March 4, 1861, in Abraham Lincoln,
Complete Works *(1886–1906).*

In view of your recent service in New Mexico and knowledge of that country and the people, the President has intrusted you with the important duty of driving the Federal troops from that department, at the same time securing all the arms, supplies, and materials of war. You are authorized to take into the Confederate States service all disaffected officers and soldiers on the original commissions of the former and enlistments of the latter.

General Samuel Cooper, adjutant and inspector
general of the Confederate Army, to General
Henry H. Sibley (CSA), dispatch of July 8,
1861, in the United States War Department's
The War of Rebellion *(1880–1901).*

I have the honor to report that I had an engagement with the U.S. forces, numbering over 500 cavalry and infantry with four pieces of artillery, at Mesilla, on the evening of the 25th of July, in which the enemy were repulsed with a loss of 3 killed and 7 wounded.

On the 27th I captured at San Augustine Springs the entire command of the enemy under Major Lynde, consisting of eight companies of infantry, three of Mounted Rifles, with four pieces of artillery, together with all their transportation, arms, ammunition, commissary and quartermaster's stores; all of which, with Fort Fillmore, are now in my possession.

Lieutenant Colonel John R. Baylor (CSA), report of August 3, 1861, in the United States War Department's The War of Rebellion.

Lyon repeated his order for the regiment to come forward. The regiment moved promptly by the flank, and as it approached Lyon he directed the two companies of Iowa troops to go forward with it, himself leading the column, swinging his hat. A murderous fire was opened from the thick brush, the 2d Kansas deployed rapidly to the front and with the two companies of the 1st Iowa swept over the hill, dislodging the enemy and driving them back into the next ravine; but while he was at the head of the column, and pretty nearly in the first fire, a ball penetrated Lyon's left breast, inflicting a mortal wound. He slowly dismounted, and as he fell into the arms of his faithful orderly, Lehmann, he exclaimed, ''Lehmann, I am killed,'' and almost immediately expired.

Brevet Brigadier General William M. Wherry, Sixth U.S. Infantry, recalls the battle of Wilson's Creek, Missouri, August 10, 1861, in Johnson and Buel's Battles and Leaders of the Civil War.

This proved to be the decisive engagement, and as volley after volley was poured against our lines, and our gallant boys were cut down like grass, those who survived seemed to be nerved to greater effort and a determination to win or die. At about this time (11:30 A.M.) the first line of battle before us gave way. Our boys charged the second line with a yell, and were soon in possession of the field, the enemy slowly withdrawing toward Springfield. This hour decided the contest and won for us the day. It was in our front here, as was afterward made known, that the brave commander of the Federal forces, General Lyon, was killed, gallantly leading his men to what he and

they supposed was victory, but which proved (it may be because they were deprived of his enthusiastic leadership) disastrous defeat.

Brigadier General N.B. Pearce (CSA), recalls the battle of Wilson's Creek, Missouri, August 10, 1861, in Johnson and Buel's Battles and Leaders of the Civil War.

The battle was fought ten miles from Springfield. The enemy were nine or ten thousand strong; our force was about the same. The battle lasted six and a half hours. The enemy were repulsed and driven from the field, with the loss of six pieces of artillery, several hundred stands of small-arms, eight hundred killed, one thousand wounded, and three hundred prisoners. Gen. Lyon was killed, and many of their prominent officers. Our loss was two hundred and sixty-five killed, eight hundred wounded, and thirty missing. We have possession of Springfield, and the enemy are in full retreat toward Rolla.

Brigadier General Ben McCulloch (CSA), to L.P. Walker, on the battle of Wilson's Creek, dispatch of August 12, 1861, in Moore's The Rebellion Record *(1977).*

The cry, ''They (Lyon's troops) are firing against us!'' spread like wild fire through our ranks; the artillerymen, ordered to fire, and directed by myself, could hardly be brought forward to serve their pieces; the infantry would not level their arms until it was too late. The enemy arrived within ten paces of the muzzles of our cannon, killed the horses, turned the flanks of the infantry, and forced them to fly. The troops were throwing themselves into the bushes and bye-roads, retreating as well as they could, followed and attacked incessantly by large bodies of Arkansas and Texas cavalry. In this retreat we lost five cannon, of which three were spiked, and the colors of the Third, the color-bearer having been wounded, and his substitute killed.

Colonel Franz Sigel (USA), on the battle of Wilson's Creek, Missouri, report of August 18, 1861, in Moore's The Rebellion Record.

In order, therefore, to suppress disorders, maintain the public peace, and give security to the persons and property of loyal citizens, I do hereby extend and declare established martial law throughout the State of Missouri. The lines of the army occupation in this State are for the present declared to extend from Leavenworth, by way of posts of Jefferson City, Rolla, and Ironton, to Cape Girardeau on the Mississippi River. All persons who shall be taken with arms in their hands within these lines shall be tried by court-martial, and if found guilty, will be shot. Real and personal property of those who shall take up arms against the United States, or who shall be directly proven to have taken an active part with their enemies in the field, is declared confiscated to public use, and their slaves, if any they have, are hereby declared free men.

Major General John C. Fremont (USA), proclamation of August 30, 1861, in Moore's The Rebellion Record.

Two points in your proclamation of August 30th give me some anxiety. First, should you shoot a man, according to the proclamation, the Confederates would very certainly shoot our best man in their hands in retaliation; and so, man for man, indefinitely. It is therefore my order that you allow no man to be shot, under the proclamation, without first having my approbation or consent.

Secondly, I think there is great danger that the closing paragraph, in relation to the confiscation of property, and the liberating slaves of traiterous owners, will alarm our Southern Union friends, and turn them against us—perhaps ruin our rather fair prospect for Kentucky.

President Abraham Lincoln, to Major General John C. Fremont (USA), letter of September 12, 1861, in Abraham Lincoln, Complete Works.

The Pacific to the Atlantic sends greetings; and may both oceans be dry before a foot of all the land that lies between them shall belong to any other than one united country.

San Francisco, to New York City, first Pacific telegraph message of October 22, 1861, in Root and Connelley's The Overland Stage to California *(1950).*

An army under my command enters New Mexico, to take possession of it in the name and for the benefit of the Confederate States. By geographical position, by similarity of institutions, by commercial interests, and by future destinies New Mexico pertains to the Confederacy.

Upon the peaceful people of New Mexico the Confederate States wage no war. To them we come as friends, to re-establish a governmental connection agreeable and advantageous both to them and to us; to liberate them from the yoke of a military depotism

erected by usurpers upon the ruins of the former free institutions of the United States; to relieve them from the iniquitous taxes and exactions imposed upon them by that usurpation; to insure and to revere their religion, and to restore their civil and political liberties.

General Henry H. Sibley (CSA), to the people of New Mexico, proclamation of January 17, 1862, in the United States War Department's The War of Rebellion.

I have the honor to report to you, for the information of the President, that I encountered the enemy at this point (6 miles above Fort Craig) in force at 11 o'clock yesterday morning, and after one of the most severely contested actions, lasting until 5 p.m., the enemy was driven from the field with a loss, as estimated, of 4 captains of the Regular Army and some 300 killed and wounded, and capture of his entire battery, the disabling of one 24-pounder, and the abandonment of another in the river. We have but few prisoners; among them is Capt. William H. Rossell, of the Tenth Infantry.

General Henry H. Sibley (CSA), to General Samuel Cooper at Richmond, Virginia, on the battle of Valverde, near Santa Fe, report of February 22, 1862, in the United States War Department's The War of Rebellion.

The news has come by messenger that the Rebels are marching on to Fort Union on the borders of New Mexico. The cry comes to our Regiment at Denver to come to the rescue. Our two companies are ordered to meet the regiment at Hulls Ranch on the Arkansas. Already preparations are being made to make forced marches. Poor boys! it is a long rough journey. No doubt the rebel forces outnumber ours two to one. Gen. Canby is in the field, and to his rescue are they going. Some of our brave boys are marching on to certain death. It may be my husband. God knows! The women of the company have to be sent to Denver until it is all over.

Mollie Dorsey Sanford, journal entry of March 1, 1862, in Mollie: The Journal of Mollie Dorsey Sanford.

The command was given to charge, and the troops started upon double-quick. Captain Wynkoop, with 30 of his men, were deployed to the mountain side to silence their guns by picking off their gunners, which they did effactually, Captain Lewis capturing and spiking the gun after having five shots discharged at him. The remainder of the command surrounded the wagons and buildings, killing 3 and wounding several of the enemy. The wagons were all heavily loaded with ammunition, clothing, subsistence, and forage, all of which were burned upon the spot or rendered entirely useless. During the engagement one of the wagons containing ammunition exploded, severely wounding Private Ritter, of Company A, First Colorado Volunteers; the only person injured. We retook 5 privates, who had been taken in the forenoon in the battle between Slough's and Scurry's forces, from whom we gleaned our first intelligence of the general engagement, and upon reaching the summit of the mountain we were met by Lieutenant Cobb, bringing an order from Colonel Slough for our advance to support the main column, which we hastened to obey. We also took 17 prisoners, and captured about thirty horses and mules, which were in a corral in the vicinity of the wagons.

Major John M. Chivington (USA), First Regiment Colorado Volunteers, on the battle of La Glorietta Pass, New Mexico, report of March 28, 1862, in the United States War Department's The War of Rebellion.

The battle continued over five hours. The fighting was all done in thick covers of cedars, and having met the enemy where he was not expected the action was defensive from its beginning to its end. Major Chivington's command continued on toward Johnson's, where some 200 of the enemy were posted, and fell upon the enemy's train of 60 wagons, capturing and destroying it and capturing and destroying one 6-pounder gun, and taking 2 officers and about 15 men prisoners. The loss of this train was a most serious disaster to the enemy, destroying his baggage and ammunition, and depriving him of provisions, of which he was short. Much praise is due to the officers and men of Major Chivington's command.

About 5 o'clock p.m. a flag of truce came from the enemy, and measures were taken by both forces to gather up the dead and take care of the wounded. Our loss is not great.

Colonel John P. Slough (USA), First Regiment Colorado Volunteers, on the battle of La Glorietta Pass, New Mexico, report of March 30, 1862, in the United States War Department's The War of Rebellion.

We have been surrounded with every description of embarrassment, general and individual. Whole trains had been abandoned, and scantily provided, as they had originally been, with blankets and clothing, the men had, without a murmur, given up the little left them. More than all this, on the representation of their officers that forage could not be procured with one accord the regiment agreed to be dismounted.

General Henry H. Sibley (CSA), to General Samuel Cooper at Richmond, Virginia, on the battle of La Glorietta Pass, New Mexico, report of March 31, 1862, in the United States War Department's The War of Rebellion.

Our brave soldiers, heedless of the storm, pressed on, determined, if possible, to take their battery. A heavy body of infantry, twice our number, interposed to save their guns. Here the conflict was terrible. Our men and officers, alike inspired with the unalterable determination to overcome every obstacle to the attainment of their object, dashed among them. The right and centre had united on the left. The intrepid Ragnet, and the cool, calm courageous Pyron, had pushed forward among the rocks, until the muzzle of the opposing forces' guns passed each other. Inch by inch was the ground disputed, until the artillery of the enemy had time to escape with a number of their wagons. The infantry also broke ranks and fled from the field. So precipitate was their flight, that they cut loose their teams and set fire to two of their wagons. The pursuit was kept up until forced to halt from the extreme exhaustion of the men, who had been engaged for six hours in the hardest contested fight it had ever been my lot to witness. The enemy is now known to have numbered fourteen hundred men, Pike's Peak miners and regulars, the flower of the United States army.

Lieutenant Colonel William R. Scurry (CSA), to Major A.M. Jackson, on the battle of La Glorietta Pass, letter of March 31, 1862, in Commager's The Blue and the Gray (1950).

On the 26th we got word that the enemy were coming down the canyon in the shape of two hundred Mexicans and about two hundred regulars. Out we marched with two cannon expecting an easy victory, but what a mistake. Instead of Mexicans and Regulars, they were regular demons, and iron and lead had no effect upon, in the shape of Pike's Peakers.

George M. Brown (CSA), to his wife, on the battle of La Glorietta Pass, New Mexico, letter of April 20, 1862, in Hollister's Boldly They Rode: A History of the First Colorado Regiment of Volunteers (1949).

The Confederate force, in rapid retreat, had taken the route by the Renesco through a mountainous and difficult country exceedingly destitute of water. They will probably reach the Rio Grande in the neighborhood of Santa Barbara, where Colonel Steele would probably meet them with supplies. Scouts and prisoners report this force as greatly demoralized, and that they have abandoned everything that could impede their flight. The sick and wounded have been left by the wayside, without care and often without food.

Colonel Edward R.S. Canby (USA), to the adjutant general of the U.S. Army, after the battle of La Glorietta Pass, New Mexico, report of May 4, 1862, in the United States War Department's The War of Rebellion.

I am, sir, for opening these lands for the landless of every nation under heaven. I care not whether he comes to us from the populous cities of our older States, or from the enlightened though oppressed nations of Europe.

Senator Samuel Pomeroy (Kansas), on the Homestead Act, speech of May 5, 1862, in the Smokey Hill and Republican Union *(Junction City, Kansas), May 29, 1862.*

I have the honor to inform you that I have advanced thus far from California with a force of regulars and volunteers sufficient in numbers to occupy this [New Mexico] Territory.

I have assumed to represent the U.S. Authority, and for the time being have placed the Territory under martial law.

Colonel James H. Carleton (USA), First California Volunteers, to Colonel Edward R.S. Canby, dispatch of June 15, 1862, in the United States War Department's The War of Rebellion.

A general war with nearly all tribes of Indians east of the Missouri river is close at hand. I am expecting daily an interruption on my line, and nothing but prompt decisive action on the part of the government will prevent it.

Ben Holladay, to Postmaster General Montgomery Blair, requesting more soldiers to protect his overland stagecoach line, telegram of August 26, 1862, in Frederick's Ben Holladay: The Stagecoach King *(1940).*

So far as I am concerned, if they are hungry let them eat grass!

Andrew Myrick, Lower Agency trader, on the Minnesota Sioux not receiving their annuity payments, August 1862, in Folwell's History of Minnesota *(1921–30).*

It began to be whispered about that now would be a good time to go to war with the whites and get back the lands. It was believed that the men who had enlisted last had all left the state, and that before help could be sent the Indians could clean out the country, and that the Winnebagoes, and even the Chippewas, would assist the Sioux. It was also thought that a war with the whites would cause the Sioux to forget the troubles among themselves and enable many of them to pay off some old scores. Though I took part in the war, I was against it. I knew there was no good cause for it, and I had been to Washington and knew the power of the whites and that they would finally conquer us. We might succeed for a time, but we would be overpowered and defeated at last. I said all this and many more things to my people, but many of my own bands were against me, and some of the other chiefs put words in their mouths to say to me. When the outbreak came Little Crow told some of my band that if I refused to lead them to shoot me as a traitor who would not stand up for his nation, and then select another leader in my place.

Jerome Big Eagle, Mdewakanton Sioux chief, on the Minnesota Sioux uprising of 1862, in Anderson and Woolworth's Through Dakota Eyes *(1988).*

Capt Marsh left this post [Fort Ridgley] at 10 1/2 this morning to prevent Indian depredations at the Lower Agency. Some of the men have returned—from them I learn that Capt Marsh is killed and only thirteen of his company remaining. The Indians are killing the settlers and plundering the country. Send reinforcements without delay.

Lieutenant Thomas P. Gere (USA), to Alexander Ramsey, governor of Minnesota, on the Sioux uprising, dispatch of August 18, 1862, in Carley's The Sioux Uprising of 1862 *(1976).*

All that I then knew was the fact that I was seized by an Indian and very roughly dragged from the wagon, and that the wagon was drawn over my body and ankles. I was not dead. I suppose the Indians then left me for a time, how long I do not know, as I was for a time almost, if not quite, insen-

sible. When I was shot the sun was shining, but when I came to myself it was dark. My baby, as my children afterward told me, was, when they found it, lying about five yards from me, crying. One of my step-children, a girl of thirteen years of age, took the baby and ran off. The Indians took two with them.
Justina Kreiger recalls the Minnesota Sioux uprising of August 1862, in Bryant and Murch's History of the Great Massacre By the Sioux Indians in Minnesota *(1864).*

The Indian who took me prisoner gave me to his niece, *Wenona.* The whites called her Maggie. Her husband's name was *Wakinyan Waste,* or Good Thunder. I was forced to call them father and mother. We remained at the village of Little Crow about a week, or perhaps a little more, and then moved toward Yellow Medicine, and camped about fifteen miles above Crow's village. The next morning they heard the soldiers were coming, and they awoke me and took off the squaw dress they had compelled me to wear, and put my own on me again.
Mary Schwandt recalls her August 1862 captivity by the Sioux during the Minnesota Sioux uprising, in Bryant and Murch's History of the Great Massacre By the Sioux Indians in Minnesota.

Many times have I reluctantly retired for the night on the cold damp ground with my child on my arm, unable to sleep, thinking of my friends and home. If by chance my eyes were closed in sleep, I would sometimes dream of seeing Indians perpetrating some act of cruelty on innocent white captives. Occasionally I would dream of having made my escape from my captors, and was safe among my relatives and friends in a civilized country. But on awakening from my slumber, Oh the anguish of mind, the heart-crushing pangs of grief, to again realize that I was still a prisoner among the Indians!
Mrs. N.D. White recalls her captivity during the Minnesota Sioux uprising of 1862, in Sprague's Women and the West *(1940).*

Say to them: 'Go to the Bosque Redondo, or we will pursue and destroy you. We will not make peace with you on any other terms. You have deceived us too often and robbed and murdered our people too long—to trust you again at large in your own country. This war shall be pursued against you if it takes years, now that we have begun, until you cease to exist or move. There can be no other talk on the subject.'
General James H. Carleton (USA), to Colonel Kit Carson, on fighting the Mescalero tribe in New Mexico territory, October 12, 1862, in Sabin's Kit Carson Days *(1935).*

The commanding officer at this place has called to speak to you upon a very serious subject this afternoon. Your Great Father at Washington, after carefully reading what the witnesses have testified in your several trials, has come to the conclusion that you have each been guilty of wantonly and wickedly murdering his white children; and, for this reason, he has directed that you each be hanged by the neck until you are dead, on next Friday, and that order will be carried into effect on that day at ten o'clock in the morning.
Colonel Stephen Miller (USA), to 39 Minnesota Sioux prisoners, December 21, 1862, in Bryant and Murch's History of the Great Massacre By the Sioux Indians in Minnesota.

The skies smiled yesterday upon a ceremony of vast significance to Sacramento, California and the Union. With rites appropriate to the occasion and in presence of dignitaries of the State, representatives of every portion of the commonwealth, and a great gathering of citizens, ground was formally broken at noon for the commencement of the Central Pacific Railroad—the California link of the continental chain that is to unite American communities now divided by thousands of miles of trackless wilderness.
Sacramento Union, *January 8, 1863.*

I thought at first that the noise came from a company of colored recruits who were camped just west of our house; thought that they had got to quarrelling among themselves. I got up and went to the window to see what was the matter, and as I drew aside the curtain the sight that met my eyes was one of terror—one that I never shall forget. The bushwhackers were just passing by my house. There were 350 of them, all mounted and heavily armed; they were grim and dirty from their night's ride over the dusty roads and were a reckless and bloodthirsty set of men. It was a sight we had somewhat anticipated, felt that it might come, and one that we had dreaded ever since the commencement of the war. I turned to my wife and said: "The bushwhackers are here."

They first made for the main street, passing up as

far as the Eldridge House to see if they were going to meet with any opposition, and when they found none they scattered out all over town, killing, stealing and burning.

Gurdon Grovenor, citizen of Lawrence, Kansas, recalls the attack by Confederate irregulars led by Captain William C. Quantrill on August 21, 1863, in Connelley's Quantrill and the Border Wars *(1910).*

Disaster has again fallen on our State. Lawrence is in ashes. Millions of property have been destroyed, and, worse yet, nearly 200 lives of our best citizens have been sacrificed. No fiends in human shape could have acted with more savage barbarity than did Quantrill and his band in their last successful raid. I must hold Missouri responsible for this fearful, fiendish raid. No body of men large as that commanded by Quantrill could have been gathered together without the people residing in Western Missouri knowing everything about it. Such people cannot be considered loyal, and should not be treated as loyal citizens; for while they conceal the movements of desperadoes like Quantrill and his followers, they are, in the worst sense of the word, their aiders and abettors, and should be held equally guilty.

Governor Thomas Carney (Kansas), to Major General John M. Schofield (USA), letter of August 24, 1863, in Breihan's Quantrill and His Civil War Guerrillas *(1959).*

To gather them together little by little onto a Reservation away from the haunts and hills and hiding places of their country, and there be kind to them: there teach their children how to read and write: teach them the art of peace; teach them the truths of Christianity. Soon they will acquire new habits, new ideas, new modes of life: the old Indians will die off and carry with them all latent longings for murdering and robbing: the young ones will take their places without these longings: and thus, little by little, they will become a happy and a contented people, and Navajoe Wars will be remembered only as something that belongs entirely to the Past.

General James H. Carleton (USA), to General Lorenzo Thomas, letter of September 6, 1863, in Trafzer's The Kit Carson Campaign *(1982).*

The Cheyennes will have to be soundly whipped before they will be quiet. If any of them are caught in your vicinity kill them, as that is the only way.

Colonel John M. Chivington (USA), dispatch of May 31, 1864, in the United States War Department's The War of Rebellion.

In regard to these Indian difficulties, I think if great caution is not exercised on our part that there will be a bloody war. It should be our policy to try and conciliate them, guard our mails and trains well to prevent theft, and stop these scouting parties that are roaming over the country who do not know one tribe from another who will kill anything in the shape of an Indian. It will require but few murders on the part of our troops to unite all these warlike tribes of the plains, who have been at peace for years and intermarried amongst one another.

Major T.I. McKenny (USA), on the Indian situation in Colorado Territory, report of June 15, 1864, in the United States War Department's The War of Rebellion.

The Indians are getting very mischievous and troublesome, they have killed several emigrants and stolen a great deal of emigrant stock. two men traveling alone were pounced upon one night by eight indians, who shot both of them killing one instantly and only wounding the other who crawled in to the brush and hid. their horses took fright and ran off the indians after them. The indians soon returned and sacked the wagons taking away blankets, clothing, three gallons of whiskey, and several hundred dollars in gold and greenbacks but they couldnt find the other man, if some person could have followed them he could have taken every thing from them in two hours, for they would have been drunk enough to know nothing in that time.

Corporal Harvey Johnson (USA), Company G, Eleventh Ohio Cavalry, to his family, on Indian hostilities near Deer Creek Station, Dakota Territory, letter of June 16, 1864, in Tending the Talking Wire: A Buck Soldier's View of Indian Country *(1979).*

Any man who kills a hostile Indian is a patriot; but there are Indians who are friendly and to kill one of these will involve us in greater difficulty. It is important therefore to fight only the hostile, and no one has been or will be restrained from this.

Governor John Evans (Colorado Territory), proclamation of August 10, 1864, in Hafen's The Overland Mail *(1926).*

I want you to give all the chiefs of the soldiers here to understand that we are for peace, and that we

Black Kettle and Chiefs holding a council with U.S. military officers at Camp Weld, September 28, 1864. At center, holding the peace pipe is Black Kettle and kneeling (left) is Major Edward W. Wynkoop. Courtesy of the Colorado Historical Society.

have made peace, that we may not be mistaken by them for enemies. I have not come with a little wolf's bark, but have come to talk plain with you. We must live near the buffalo or starve. When we came here we came free, without any apprehension, to see you, and when I go home and tell my people that I have taken your hand and the hands of all the chiefs here in Denver, they will feel well, and so will all the different tribes of Indians on the plains, after we have eaten and drunk with them.

Black Kettle, Cheyenne chief, to Colonel John M. Chivington, Major Edward W. Wyncoop and other U.S. Army officers, council at Camp Weld, Colorado Territory, speech of September 28, 1864, in Hoig's The Sand Creek Massacre *(1961).*

When I looked toward the chief's lodge, I saw that Black Kettle had a large American flag up on a long lodgepole as a signal to the troop that the camp was friendly. Part of the people were rushing about the camp in great fear. All the time Black Kettle kept calling out not to be frightened; that the camp was under protection and there was no danger. Then suddenly the troops opened fire on this mass of men, women, and children, and all began to scatter and run. At the beginning of the attack Black Kettle, with his wife and White Antelope, took their position before Black Kettle's lodge and remained there after all others had left the camp. At last Black Kettle, seeing that it was useless to stay longer, started to run.

George Bent, half-Cheyenne, recalls the Sand Creek Massacre in southeastern Colorado, November 29, 1864, in Grinnell's The Fighting Cheyennes *(1966).*

In the last ten days my command has marched three hundred miles—one hundred of which the snow was two feet deep. After a march of forty miles last night I at daylight this morning attacked a Cheyenne village of one hundred and thirty lodges, from nine hundred to a thousand warriors strong. We killed chiefs Black Kettle, White Antelope and Little

Robe, and between four and five hundred other Indians; captured between four and five hundred ponies and mules. Our loss is nine killed and thirty-eight wounded. All did nobly. I think I will catch some more of them about eighty miles on the Smoky Hill.

Colonel John Chivington (USA), to Major General S.R. Curtis, report of November 29, 1864, in Grinnell's The Fighting Cheyennes.

The affair at Fort Lyon, Colorado, in which Colonel Chivington destroyed a large Indian village, and all its inhabitants, is to be made the subject of congressional investigation. Letters received from high officials in Colorado say that the Indians were killed after surrendering, and that a large proportion of them were women and children.

Rocky Mountain News *(Denver), December 20, 1864.*

Wanted, 5000 laborors for constant and permanent work, also experienced foreman. Apply to J.H. Strobridge, Superintendant on the work, near Auburn.

Sacramento Union, *advertisement of January 7, 1865, for workers on the construction of the transcontinental railroad.*

All manner of depredations were inflicted on their persons; they were scalped, their brains knocked out; the men used their knives, ripped open women, clubbed little children, knocked them in the head with their guns, beat their brains out, mutilated their bodies in every sense of the word.

It would be hard for me to tell who did these things: I saw some of the first Colorado regiment committing some very bad acts there on the persons of the Indians, and I likewise saw some of the one-hundred-day men in the same kind of business.

John S. Smith, Indian interpreter, before a congressional inquiry into the Sand Creek Massacre, testimony of January 15, 1865, in Hoig's The Sand Creek Massacre.

I went over the ground soon after the battle. I should judge there were between 400 and 500 Indians killed. I counted 350 lying up and down the creek. I think about half killed were women and children. Nearly all, men, women, and children, were scalped.

Asbury Bird, First Colorado Cavalry, before a congressional inquiry into the Sand Creek Massacre, affidavit of January 1865, in Hoig's The Sand Creek Massacre.

As to Colonel Chivington, your committee can hardly find fitting terms to describe his conduct. Wearing the uniform of the United States, which should be the emblem of justice and humanity; holding the important position of commander of a military district, and therefore having the honor of the government to that extent in his keeping, he deliberately planned and executed a foul and dastardly massacre which would have disgraced the veriest savage among those who were the victims of his cruelty.

Committee on the Conduct of War, U.S. House of Representatives, report on the massacre of Cheyenne Indians, 1865, in Hoig's The Sand Creek Massacre *(1961).*

You of course understand that we settle the Indian troubles this season, and at such time as you consider it proper and for the interest of the government you can make an informal treaty for cessation of hostilities, appointing some place for meeting the Indian chiefs for having a full understanding with them, and myself or such persons as the government sees fit go there. You must be the judge when it is proper to do this, and the Indians must be given to fully understand that when all hostilities cease, any act of robbery, murder, etc., by their people will precipitate our whole force on them. It is my opinion before this is done they should be made to feel the full power of the government and severely punished for past acts.

Major General Grenville M. Dodge, to General Patrick E. Connor, on the Powder River campaign in the Northern Plains, instructions of June 10, 1865, in Hafen's Powder River Campaigns and Sawyers Expedition of 1865 *(1961).*

Seizing upon every advantageous position, the enemy's fire was returned deliberately and with effect. The fighting continued three hours. The last volley of the war, sunset of the 13th of May, 1865, between White's Ranch and the Boca Chica, Tex. Our entire loss in killed, wounded, and captured was 4 officers and 111 men.

Colonel Theodore H. Barrett, 62nd U.S. Colored Infantry, to Adjutant-General Lorenzo Thomas, report of August 10, 1865, on the final battle of the Civil War, at Palmitto Hill on the banks of the Rio Grande in Texas, in the United States War Department's The War of Rebellion.

Statesmen and warriers, traders and the rest
May boast of their profession and think it is the
    best.
Their taste I'll never envy, I'll have you understand
Long as I can be a driver on the jolly overland.

It's thus you're safely carried throughout the
    mighty West,
Where chances to make fortunes are ever famed the
    best.
And thus the precious pouches of mail are brought
    to hand
Through the ready hearts that center in the jolly
    overland.

"Driver's Song" (1865), by Nat Stein, express
agent at Virginia City, Montana Territory,
sung by Ben Holladay Stage Coach Line driv-
ers, in Frederick's Ben Holladay: The Stagecoach King.

Upon this little section of road four thousand laborers were at work—one-tenth Irish, the rest Chinese.
They were a great army laying siege to Nature in her
strongest citadel. The rugged mountains looked like
stupendous ant-hills. They swarmed with Celestials,
shoveling, wheeling, carting, drilling and blasting
rocks and earth, while their dull, moony eyes stared
out from under immense basket-hats, like umbrellas.
At several dining-camps we saw hundreds sitting on
the ground, eating soft boiled rice with chop-sticks
as fast as terrestrials could with soup-ladles. Irish
laborers received thirty dollars per month (gold) and
board; Chinese, thirty-one dollars, boarding themselves.

Albert D. Richardson, journalist, on the con-
struction crew building the transcontinental
railroad, near Sacramento, California, 1865, in
Beyond the Mississippi *(1867).*

When I arrived at Boise, Indian affairs in that
country could not well have been worse. That whole
country, including Northern California and Nevada,
Eastern Oregon and Idaho, up to Montana, you
might say was in a state of siege. Hostile Indians
were all over that country, dealing death and destruction everywhere they wished. People were afraid to
go outside of their own doors without protection.
There was scarcely a day that reports of Indian
depredations were not coming in.

General George Crook, November 1866, in
General George Crook: His Autobiography
(1946).

There are so many parties in and out of business
on the Plains who desire an Indian War as a means
of speculation, that they are ever busy circulating
stories to the effect that warriors of such and such
tribe have put on their war paint, and declared hostility to death against the whites.

Anonymous newspaper correspondent, Alta,
California, October 11, 1866.

Presently the escort fell in line and we moved
toward the stockade, but just before entering a halt
was made, and I looked eagerly for the occasion of
the delay. It almost took my breath away, for a
strange feeling of apprehension came over me. We
had halted to give passage to a wagon, escorted by
a guard from the wood train, coming from the opposite direction. In that wagon was the scalped and
naked body of one of their comrades, scarcely cold,
who had been murdered so near the fort that the
signals by the picket, given almost simultaneously,
were now fully understood. My whole being seemed
to be absorbed in the one desire,—an agonized but
un-uttered cry, "Let me get within the gate!"

Frances C. Carrington, wife of Colonel Henry
B. Carrington, recalls approaching Fort Phil
Kearny, in Wyoming Territory, in 1866, in My
Army Life *(1971).*

Do send me reinforcements forthwith. Expedition
now with my force is impossible. I risk everything
but the post and its store. I venture as much as
anyone can, but I have had a fight today unexampled
in Indian warfare. My loss is ninety-four [81] killed.
I have recovered forty-nine bodies and thirty-two
more are to be brought in in the morning that have
been found. Among the killed are Brevet Lieutenant-
Colonel Fetterman, Captain F.H. Brown, and Lieutenant Grummond.

Colonel Henry B. Carrington, to commander at
Fort Laramie, dispatch of December 21, 1866,
in Brininstool and Hebard's The Bozeman
Trail *(1922).*

At the time of my arrival it had become apparent
to any sensible observer that the Indians of that
country would fight to the death for home and native
land, with spirit akin to that of the American soldier
of our early history, and who could say that their
spirit was not comendable and to be respected.

Francis Carrington, on the Indians in Wyoming
Territory, 1866, in My Army Life.

As bearers of the United States mail they felt themselves king of the road and were seldom loth to show it. "Clear the road! Git out of the way thar with your bull teams!" was a frequent salutation.

General James F. Rusling, on the attitude of overland stage coach drivers, 1866, in Across America *(1875).*

In my first drive across the 96 mile desert, I lost 300 head of cattle. We were three days and nights in crossing and during that time we had no sleep or rest, as we had to keep the cattle moving constantly, in order to get them to water before they died of thirst. I rode the same horse for three days and nights, and what sleep I got was on his back. When the cattle reached the water they had no sense at all. They stampeded into the stream, swam right across it, and then doubled back before they stopped to drink. During this trip the steers got as gentle as dogs."

Charlie Goodnight, Texas trail driver, recalls his first trail drive across Texas to Fort Sumner, New Mexico, 1866, in Pioneer Days in the Southwest from 1850 to 1879 *(1909).*

Abilene was selected because the country was entirely unsettled, well watered, excellent grass and nearly the entire area of country was adopted to holding [Texas] cattle. And it was the point east at which a good depot for cattle business could have been made.

Joseph G. McCoy, Illinois stockman, 1867, in Historic Sketches of the Cattle Trade of the West and Southwest *(1940).*

I have a great many chiefs with me that have commanded more men than ever you saw, and they have fought more great battles than you have fought fights. A great many Indians think they are better armed than they were formerly, but they must recollect that we are also. My chiefs cannot derive any distinction from fighting with your small numbers. They are not anxious for wars against Indians, but are ready for a just war, and know how to fight, and lead their men. Let the guilty then beware. I say this to you to show you the importance of keeping treaties made with us, and of letting the white man travel unmolested.

General Winfield Scott Hancock, to Cheyenne "Dog Soldiers," during council at Fort Larnard, Kansas, speech of April 13, 1867, in Stanley's My Early Travels and Adventures in America and Asia *(1895).*

I want the Great Father at Washington and all the soldiers and troops to go slowly. I don't want the prairies and country to be bloody, but just hold on for a while. I don't want war at all. I want peace. As for the Kiowas talking war, I don't know anything about it. Nor do I know anything about the Comanches, Cheyennes, and Sioux talking about war. The Cheyennes, Kiowas, and Comanches are poor. They are all of the same colour. They are all red men. This country here is old, and it all belongs to them. You are cutting off the timber, and now the country is of no account at all. I don't mean anything bad by what I say. I have nothing bad hidden in my breast at all; everything is all right. I had heard that there were many troops coming out to this country to whip the Cheyennes, and that is the reason we were afraid and went away. The Cheyennes, Arapahoes, and Kiowas heard that there were troops coming out to this country; so did also the Comanches and Apaches; but did not know whether the soldiers were coming for peace or for war.

Satanta, Kiowa chief, to Colonels Edward W. Wynkoop and Jesse H. Leavenworth, during a council at Fort Hayes, Kansas, speech of May 3, 1867, in Stanley's My Early Travels and Adventures in America and Asia.

The white men are coming out here so fast that nothing can stop them—coming from the east and coming from the west, like a prairie on fire in a high wind. The reason of it is because the whites are a great people, and they are spreading out and we cannot help it. Those on one sea in the west want to communicate with another sea in the east, and that is the reason they are building these waggon roads, and railroads and telegraphs. The Great Father had a council with these tribes, and asked their permission to run roads through here, and you and the others gave your permission. That treaty was made at the mouth of the Little Arkansas; and last fall it was signed again, and it is too late to reconsider it now. I don't know where the railroad is going to run. It may run on the Smoky Hill, and they may find a better road on this line. At any rate, if the road comes here I cannot help it, and you have already given your assent to it.

General Winfield Scott Hancock, to Santanta, during a council at Fort Hayes, Kansas, speech of May 3, 1867, in Stanley's My Early Travels and Adventures in America and Asia.

The Texas cattle trade—guarding the herd. Courtesy of the Library of Congress.

And here are the drovers, the identical chaps I first saw at Fair Oaks, and last saw at Gettysburg. Every man of them unquestionably was in the Rebel Army. Some of them have not yet worn out all of their distinctive gray clothing—keen-looking men, full of reserved force, shaggy with their hair, undoubtedly terrible in a fight, yet peaceably great at cattle-driving, and not demonstrative in their style of wearing six-shooters.

Anonymous correspondent, New York Daily Tribune, *November 6, 1867.*

This was joyous news to the drover, for the fear of trouble and violence hung like an incubus over his waking thoughts alike with his sleeping moments. It was almost too good to be believed; could it be possible that someone was about to afford a Texan drover any other reception than outrage and robbery? They were very suspicious that some trap was set, to be sprung on them; they were not ready to credit the proposition that the day of fair dealing had dawned for Texan drovers, and the era of mobs,

brutal murder, and arbitrary proscription ended forever.

Yet they turned their herds toward the point designated, and slowly and cautiously moved on northward, their minds constantly agitated with hope and fear alternately.

Joseph G. McCoy, on the opening of the stockyards in Abilene, Kansas, 1867, in Historic Sketches of the Cattle Trade of the West and Southwest.

> O say, little dogies, when you goin' to lay down
>   And quit this forever shifting around?
> My limbs are weary, my seat is sore;
> Oh, lay down doggies, like you've laid before—
>   Lay down, little dogies, lay down
>   Hi-oo, hi-oo, oo-oo

Popular cowboy song of the 1860s, in Lomax's Cowboy Songs (1922).

In a pursuit of Indians, much time is necessarily lost in following the trail. Unlike in civilized warfare, if the solecism may be allowed, there are no roads to follow, no inhabitants no question by the wayside, no "intelligent contraband" to give "reliable information" as to the whereabouts and intentions of the enemy. On the contrary there are no data to govern a pursuing party except to follow the trail as the hound follows his game, and here again the white man is compelled to acknowledge the superiority of the Indian. Trailing is peculiarly and undeniably an Indian accomplishment. This is proven by the fact that all expeditions against hostile Indians, are provided with a sufficient number of friendly Indians from half-civilized tribes who are employed exclusively as trailers. I have met many frontiersmen who claimed to possess this faculty in an equal degree with the Indian; but I have had opportunities of comparing the relative merits of the two in this respect, and am forced to give my decision in favor of the red man.

Lieutenant Colonel George Armstrong Custer,
to Turf, Field and Farm, *letter of November*
11, 1867, in Dippie's Nomad: George A.
Custer in Turf, Field and Farm *(1980).*

Fully seventy-five thousand cattle arrived at Abilene during the summer of 1868, and at the opening of the market in the spring fine prices were realized and snug fortunes were made by such drovers as were able to effect a sale of their herds. It was the custom to locate herds as near the village as good water and plenty of grass could be found. As soon as the herd is located upon its summer grounds a part of the help is discharged, as it requires less labor to hold than to travel. The camp was usually located near some living water or spring where sufficient wood for camp purposes could be easily obtained. After selecting the spot for the camp, the wagon would be drawn up. Then a hole dug in the ground in which to build a fire of limbs of trees or drift wood gathered to the spot, and a permanent camp instituted by unloading the contents of the wagon upon the ground.

Joseph G. McCoy, Illinois stockman, 1868, in
Historic Sketches of the Cattle Trade of the
West and Southwest.

I was about to turn in my saddle and direct the signal for attack to be given—still anxious as to where the other detachments were—when a single rifle shot rang sharp and clear on the far side of the village from where we were. Quickly turning to the band leader I directed him to give us "Garry Owen." At once the rollicking notes of that familiar marching and fighting air sounded forth through the valley, and in a moment were re-echoed back from the opposite sides by the loud and continued cheers of the men of the other detachments, who, true to their orders, were there and in readiness to pounce upon the [Cheyenne] Indians the moment the attack began. In this manner the battle of the Washita commenced. The bugles sounded the charge, and the entire command dashed rapidly into the village. The Indians were caught napping; but realizing at once the dangers of their situation, they quickly overcame their first surprise and in an instant seized their rifles, bows, and arrows, and sprang behind the nearest trees, while some leaped into the stream, nearly waist deep, and using the bank as a rifle-pit began a vigorous and determined defense. Mingled with the exultant cheers of my men could be heard the defiant war-whoop of the warriors, who from the first fought with a desperation and courage which no race of men could surpass.

Lieutenant Colonel George Armstrong Custer,
on the battle of Waschita River, in present-day
Oklahoma, November 27, 1868, in My Life on
the Plains *(1874).*

On they came. A light car, drawn by a single horse, gallops up to the front with its load of rails. Two men seize the end of a rail and start forward, the rest of the gang taking hold by twos until it is clear of the car. They come forward at a run. At the word of command the rail is dropped in its place, right side up, with care, while the same process goes on at the other side of the car. Less than thirty seconds to a rail for each gang, and so four rails go down to the minute! Quick work, you say, but the fellows on the U. P. are tremendously in earnest. The moment the car is empty it is tipped over on the side of the track to let the next loaded car pass it, and then it is tipped back again; and it is a sight to see it go flying back for another load, propelled by a horse at full gallop at the end of 60 or 80 feet of rope, ridden by a young Jehu, who drives furiously. Close behind the first gang come the gaugers, spikers, and bolters, and a lively time they make of it. It is a grand Anvil Chorus that those sturdy sledges are playing across the plains. It is in triple time, three strokes to a spike. There are ten spikes to a rail, four hundred rails to a mile, eighteen hundred miles to San Francisco. That's the sum, what is the quotient?

William A. Bell, journalist, 1860s, in New
Tracks in North America *(1869).*

All the supplies for this work had to be hauled from the end of the track, and the wagon transportation was enormous. At one time we were using at least 10,000 animals, and most of the time from 8,000 to 10,000 laborers. The bridge gangs always worked from five to twenty miles ahead of the track, and it was seldom that the track waited for a bridge. To supply one mile of track with material and supplies required about forty cars, as on the plains everything—rails, ties, bridging, fastenings, all railway supplies, fuel for locomotives and trains, and supplies for men and animals on the entire work, had to be transported from the Missouri River. Therefore, as we moved westward, every hundred miles added vastly to our transportation. Yet the work was so systematically planned and executed that I do not remember an instance in all the construction of the line of the work being delayed a single week for want of material.

Grenville M. Dodge, chief engineer of the Union Pacific Railroad, 1860s, in How We Built the Union Pacific Railway *(1910).*

Here had sprung up in two weeks, as if by the touch of Aladdin's Lamp, a city of three thousand people; there were regular squares arranged into five wards, a city government of mayor and aldermen, a daily paper, and a volume of ordinances for the public health. It was the end of the freight and passenger, and beginning of the construction, division; twice every day immense trains arrived and departed, and stages left for Utah, Montana, and Idaho; all the goods formerly hauled across the plains came here by rail and were reshipped, and for ten hours daily the streets were thronged with motley crowds of railroad men, Mexicans and Indians, gamblers, "cappers," and saloon-keepers, merchants, miners, and mulewhackers.

J.H. Beadle, correspondent of the Cincinnati Commercial, *on a construction town along the plains during the building of the transcontinental railroad, 1868, in* The Underdeveloped West; or Five Years in the Territories *(1873).*

The Post-Office Department has received a telegram from Promontory Point, stating that the mails have been delivered at that place to the Central Pacific Road, and that the through line has been regularly established. The Butterfield Company were last informed that their contract would cease on the junctions of the roads. The cost by the Butterfield

Announcing the grand opening of the Union Pacific Railroad, May 10, 1869. Courtesy of the Library of Congress.

Joining of track for the first transcontinental railroad, Promontory, Utah Territory, 1869. Courtesy of the National Archives.

Jesse Chisholm, whose name the trail bears. Courtesy of the New York Public Library.

route for transporting the mails was $1,100 a mile, and by the railroad $200 a mile per annum.

The New York Daily Tribune, *May 12, 1869.*

A cold norther, with rain, blew up just before day. Continued to rain until 9 A.M. Norther blew all day. Some of the hands drove the cattle about four miles, while the boss, myself, and four of the hands spent the day hunting for a yoke of our oxen. Found them in another herd and got them back to our camp about sunset. Made camp on Rock Creek near the Kansas line. Twenty thousand head of cattle are being grazed in this vicinity, waiting for buyers.

J.H. Barker, Texas trail driver, diary entry of October 8, 1869, in Gard's The Chisholm Trail *(1954).*

I woke up one morning on the Old Chisholm Trail, Rope in my hand and a cow by the tail.

Feet in the stirrups and seat in the saddle, I hung and rattled with them Longhorns cattle.

Popular cowboy song, 1860s, in Gard's The Chisholm Trail.

9. Opening the Plains: 1870–1879

THE FARMERS' FRONTIER

During the last three decades of the 19th century more land was settled than in all of America's past. Following the Civil War, thousands of farmers surged westward. They swarmed into Kansas and Nebraska, moved on to the grasslands of North and South Dakota, and occupied the rolling foothills of Montana and Wyoming.

The unfamiliar Plains region was opened to farmers not by adventurous trailblazers but by ingenious inventors who applied the techniques of the industrial revolution to the American frontier. On this vast grassland there was no lumber for building homes and barns, nor was there much water for raising crops. In order to succeed in this subhumid region, new farming methods and especially new machinery had to be devised.

During the post–Civil War years the United States was entering upon its machine age. Within one decade inventors developed the barbed wire fences, well-drilling machinery and farm implements that made it possible for ambitious farmers to conquer the Plains country.

With irrigation impossible and wells costly, western farmers turned to a method known as "dry farming." After each rainfall farmers harrowed their fields, allowing every drop of precious liquid to be stored near the plants' roots. Due to the subnormal rainfall the Plains farmer had to till five times as much land as he did back East. Consequently, he needed machines that would substitute for human labor. This demand triggered improvements in farm machinery, such as the invention of the chilled-iron plow in 1868 by James Oliver of Indiana. The plow was equipped with a smooth-surfaced moldboard that could slip quickly through humus prairie soils without much clogging. Other inventors improved upon Oliver's invention by covering wearing surfaces with steel. Plowing speed was further increased with the invention of the sulky plow, which lifted the farmer from the furrow to a seat on the machine. By 1877 thoroughly modern plows were in use throughout the Great Plains.

Other inventions speeded planting. The spring-toothed harrow, developed by a Michigan mechanic in 1869, proved ideal for use on Prairie soils, for its flexible teeth bounced over obstacles and automatically dislodged debris. End-gate seeders enabled the farmer to scatter seed from the end of a wagon. Corn planting was advanced with the check-rower, an implement that spaced corn in equidistant hills and made possible alternate cultivation horizontally and transversely across a field.

Harvesting machinery was essential in a region where the crop might suffer from storms or heat if not gathered at just the moment of maturity. Reapers used in the past were inadequate. They simply cut wheat or oats and placed the stalks on a platform where it was then tied by farmhands into bundles. Usually, a large number of workers had to work furiously to keep up with the machine. Plains farmers needed a laborsaving machine that would both cut and tie bundles of grain. In 1878, the first successful cord binder was perfected. It enabled two men and a team of horses to harvest 20 acres of wheat a day.

The Industrial Revolution freed Plains farmers from the time constraints of the past. They no longer had to limit their planting to the amount they could reap by hand in the 10-day period when grain was prime. Farm machinery gave them the means to engage in extensive agriculture.

HOMESTEADING

When the settlement of the Great Plains began, the Homestead Act of 1862 governed the distribution of land. Under the terms of this law, all heads of families and all males over 21 could claim 160 acres of the public domain, provided that he lived on and cultivated the land for five years. However, very few farmers had the means to move their families to the frontier or to purchase expensive farm equipment.

Corruption was rampant under the Homestead Act. Speculators often acquired public land by establishing fraudulent claims. For example, frontiersmen were sent out to occupy the land with rented cabins on wheels, then went to the nearest land office and made their claim. After six months, the pretending homesteader transferred his plot to the speculator. Land speculators combined these plots with land they had purchased from the railroad companies, then, with increasing population, sold off these plots to emigrants at higher prices.

In response Congress passed a number of amendments aimed at remedying the abuses of the Homestead Act. First, the Timber Culture Act of 1873 allowed any homesteader to apply for an additional 160 acres, which would become his if he planted at least one-fourth of it with trees within four years. Speculators were not attracted to the expense of planting trees and the long wait for ownership. As a result, the Timber Culture Act enabled thousands of legitimate homesteaders to expand their holdings.

The second amendment, the Desert Land Act of 1877, although designed to benefit the pioneer, was lobbied through Congress by the cattle industry. The bill provided that anyone could secure tentative title to 640 acres on the Great Plains or in the Southwest by an initial payment of .25¢ an acre. After three years if a portion of the land was irrigated and he was willing to pay an additional dollar a acre, the tract became his. The act was often subject to fraudulent claims established by cattlemen, who rounded up a few witnesses, who swore they had seen water on the claim (usually a bucket of water dumped on the ground), then secured title by paying $1.25 an acre.

While thousands of acres were fraudulently acquired under the Pre-emption and Homestead Acts, the largest land jobbers in the West were the railroads. The railroads stood to benefit doubly from western settlement. Homesteaders would not only buy their land from the railroads but also initiate traffic that was previously lacking in the sparsely settled region. These lands were secured between 1850 and 1871, when Congress awarded 181 million acres of public land to encourage construction of the transcontinental railroad. When the settling of the Great Plains began, the railroads were the nation's largest landowners.

Speculators and railroad companies eager to attract purchasers circulated throughout the eastern United States and western Europe inflated stories about the rewards of farming on the Great Plains. A Union Pacific land agent claimed that the Platte Valley was "a flowery meadow of great fertility clothed in nutritious grass, and watered by numerous streams." Often personal success stories were promoted, such as the farmer whose $8,000 investment in Kansas lands supposedly yielded $11,000 a year.

Although the Homestead Act failed to provide "free land for the homeless," it did promote the trans-Mississippi country throughout the eastern United States and also in Europe. Three groups were attracted to the Great Plains: first, Mississippi Valley farmers dissatisfied with the overcrowded conditions in their region; second, European immigrants to the United States, such as the Irish who worked on the railroads and the Germans living on the upper Mississippi Valley; third, the sturdy farmers of Denmark, Norway and Sweden.

Boom and Bust on the Plains

Despite the discrepancies between the railroad advertisements and the reality of the frontier, pioneers were encouraged to remain on the Great Plains by the promise of profit from supplying food for a growing native population. Life was hard when houses had to be built where there was no timber, water obtained where there were no springs and heat supplied where there was nothing to burn. Some pioneers failed to overcome these obstacles and fled back East. Those rugged settlers who remained opened up a new frontier for the nation's farmers in the post-Civil War years.

Increasing railroad connections between the East and the West contributed to the settlement of the Great Plains. When the Illinois Central Railroad reached Sioux Falls, the southeastern section of Dakota became desirable to farmers who could now easily transport their harvest to Chicago. Similarly, the most northerly transcontinental line, the Northern Pacific, attracted adventurous pioneers to settle in Bismarck and other surrounding outposts.

In 1873, construction along the Northern Pacific came to an abrupt halt after the company had exhausted its capital. The nation's leading brokerage house, Jay Cooke and Company, was held responsible for the collapse of one of the most heavily promoted transcontinental lines. Cooke had created an unsound financial structure by paying out huge bonuses in return for the sale of the company's bonds and by the distribution of generous blocks of stock to influential politicians. The Northern Pacific had so little actual cash that construction could continue only as long as investors continued to buy stock. When rumors spread about mismanagement in the spring of 1873, Cooke's firm was forced to close its doors. Unchecked railroad speculation, particularly with respect to the Northern Pacific line, was one of the chief underlying causes of the Panic of 1873. Shortly after Cooke's firm folded, many other banks also failed, plunging the nation into a prolonged depression.

Farmers on the Great Plains, already suffering from financial difficulties caused by the Panic of 1873, were hit with another disaster in 1874—the grasshopper invasion. The insects came without warning and devoured everything in sight: cornstalks, crops, leaves and the bark from trees, the lumber on house walls, and even the clothes within the cabins. Dejected farmers packed their wagons and returned East, some carrying signs proclaiming they came "from Kansas, where it rains grasshoppers, fire and destruction." During the late 1870s, emigration was temporarily reduced by the nation's economic downturn and by severe winter storms that were sweeping across the Great Plains.

THE EXODUSTERS

In 1879, a remarkable migration of southern blacks to the sod-house frontier of Kansas took place within the space of a few months. Although freed from plantation slavery 14 years earlier, their economic freedom was limited in the post-Reconstruction South. Most were landless tenant farmers who were attracted to Kansas for the opportunity to establish homestead claims. In the spring of that year, large groups of blacks from Louisiana, Mississippi, Tennessee and Texas fled by the thousands to the one sure Promised Land they knew—the Kansas of John Brown, the quintessential free state. Some migrants called themselves Exodusters, making the analogy to the Israelites' departure from Egypt as described in the Old Testament's *Book of Exodus*.

It is estimated that by the end of 1879, nearly 20,000 southern blacks had traveled on steamboats up the Mississippi, passed through St. Louis and then moved on to Kansas by rail. St. Louis was a pivotal point in the journey undertaken by the Exodusters. It was the place where they left the South. Some even compared the city to the Red Sea.

About one-fourth of the migrants arrived with enough money to immediately take up a homestead, while others worked for wages in eastern Kansas until they accumulated enough money to either rent or buy a farm. Men held odd jobs by the day or month on farms, on the railroads or in the mines, while women worked as washerwomen or domestics. Although relatively poor, the Exodusters thought themselves better off than they had been in the South.

Of the Exoduster settlements, Nicodemus, in Graham County, northwest Kansas, was the most successful and prosperous. They homesteaded land on the Prairie, burrowed into hillsides for shelter and broke the heavy prairie sod for planting with grubbing hoes and managed to plant several acres of corn per family. While some white settlers resented the newcomers, others aided the Exodusters with men and teams of horses.

Despite periodic droughts and crop failures Nicodemus thrived up until the mid-1880s. The collapse of the agricultural boom and a depressed economy forced many Exodusters to give up their homesteads and to seek work in the towns of eastern Kansas or move to Colorado or Missouri. Nicodemus suffered hard times like many other Prairie farm communities, but it remains to this day the most famous black settlement in Kansas. Descendants of the original settlers still own most of the land in the township.

THE BLACK HILLS OF DAKOTA

For years there had been rumors about gold in the Black Hills of present-day South Dakota. In summer 1874, Lieutenant Colonel George Armstrong Custer led a reconnaissance mission to this undisputed

Sioux Indian territory, where it was discovered that there were indeed rich deposits of gold throughout the region. At first, Army officials tried to prevent the rush of miners from invading the Indian territory, but they were unable to hold back the throngs of miners who were determined to strike it rich at the "diggings." In September 1875, federal negotiators offered the Sioux $6 million for their sacred hills. After the offer was refused, the Army decided to allow the prospectors to enter the area at their own risk.

By the winter of 1875, tens of thousands of miners were descending upon the Black Hills. With the advance of the Northern Pacific railroad toward their territory, and now the invasion of land guaranteed them by the federal government, the Sioux prepared for another war. Younger braves left their reservation to join bands of "non-treaty" Indians in the country east of the Big Horn River. In response, all Sioux were ordered to return to their reserve, regardless of treaty gurantees that permitted them to hunt on the northern Plains. Sitting Bull and Crazy Horse, two leaders of the Teton Sioux, refused and began preparations for war along the Little Big Horn. After the Indian Office failed to dissuade the warriors, the Army was ordered to remove them.

The military dispatched three columns of converging troops against the Indians' headquarters in Big Horn country. Brigadier General Alfred Terry's column consisted of 1,200 troops, including most of Lieutenant Colonel George Armstrong Custer's Seventh Cavalry, which was expected to easily overpower the Sioux. In mid-June of 1876, Terry arrived at the junction of the Rosebud and Yellowstone rivers without sighting the Sioux. However, scouts had reported that a large band of Indians had crossed the Rosebud en route to Sitting Bull's headquarters on the Little Big Horn. Custer was ordered to track the Indians to their camp, then surround them so they could not retreat into the Big Horn Mountains.

On June 25, 1876, Custer came upon an encampment of Sioux and Cheyenne in the valley of the Little Big Horn. Without waiting for the other two columns, and fearing that he might miss his chance for glory, he ordered his troops to advance. Instead of surprising a small Indian camp, Custer had carelessly attacked Sitting Bull's headquarters, where thousands of warriors were awaiting his troops. Instantly, Custer and his men were surrounded. In less than a half hour the battle of Little Big Horn—"Custer's Last Stand"—was over, with 225 soldiers, including Custer, dead.

Despite their victory at Little Big Horn, the Sioux and the Northern Cheyenne were driven eastward during the summer, and in 1877 they were forced to move onto a number of confining reservations near the Missouri River. A few scattered bands continued to roam the hills, but they did not pose any major threat. Chief Sitting Bull refused to surrender and fled to Canada, where he remained until 1881. Faced with starvation, he and his followers returned to the United States and surrendered to federal authorities.

Sitting Bull was imprisoned for two years, then lived on a reservation and even toured with Buffalo Bill Cody's Wild West Show for a year. Although he had little to do with the Indian Ghost Dance agitation that took place in 1890 at the Standing Rock reservation in South Dakota, Sitting Bull was accused by Indian agent James McLaughlin of inciting the Sioux to militancy. On December 15, 1890, shortly before the Wounded Knee massacre, Indian police accidentally killed Sitting Bull when they came to arrest him.

Although the Sioux War was the last major Indian war, occasional raids occurred afterward throughout the northern frontier country. For example, in 1877, when the relatively peaceful Nez Perce Indians of Idaho were ordered to relinquish part of their reservation, a young band of warriors under Chief Joseph carried on a running fight against settlers and U.S. Army troops for four months before surrendering.

As railroads pushed steadily across the northern Plains during the 1870s and as improvements in food storage were introduced, the market for western beef increased. The Plains ranchers were soon providing meat for all of the East and much of Europe. With the Sioux driven onto reservations, great herds of cattle were driven north from Colorado or Wyoming to the promising grasslands of Montana. By 1880 the cattle industry was firmly established throughout the Great Plains.

BONANZA FARMING

Gold mining in the Black Hills triggered a second "Dakota Boom" during the late 1870s. The 10,000 prospectors who had flocked to the mines created an unparalleled market for farm produce, and enterprising farmers settled on the Prairies to meet their growing needs. Equally important to opening up the Dakota Territory were officials of the bankrupt Northern Pacific Railroad. Realizing their line could never prosper until the lands surrounding its right of way were settled, they decided to initiate a demonstration of the area's fertility. An expert wheat farmer from Minnesota, Oliver Dalrymple was given 18 sections of Red River Valley land and enough capital for its development. Doing away with traditional farming methods, he hired a large group of workers and bought tons of machinery. The result was extraordinary—a yield of 25 bushels to the acre on a 4,500-acre plot that cost only $9.95 an acre to cultivate. With wheat selling at 90 cents a bushel the profits were over 100%. It was discovered that the Red River Valley was excellent wheat country. Eastern capital soon flowed in as syndicates bought up estates of from 5,000 to 10,000 acres along the Red River. By 1878 "bonanza farms" filled the 300-mile length of the valley.

As farmers, homesteaders and ranchers settled across the northwestern Plains, another stream of pioneers moved into the Southwest, especially into the unpopulated lands of Texas. In the Indian Territory (present-day Oklahoma) were millions of fertile acres assigned to 22 Indian tribes as their reservations. Frontiersmen resented the presence of the 75,000 Indians, who did not farm the region. As the 1870s came to a close a vociferous campaign was underway by eager homesteaders to open the Indian Territory to white settlement.

CHRONICLE OF EVENTS

1870:

February 15: Construction of a second transcontinental railroad, the Northern Pacific, begins in Duluth, Minnesota, on Lake Superior.

1871:

March 3: The Indian Appropriations Act is passed by Congress. The act declares that no Indian tribe or nation will be recognized as a sovereign power by the federal government; tribes shall be subject to all the laws of Congress and the administrative decrees of executive officials.

April 30: With the massacre of 100 Indians at Camp Grant, Arizona, another Apache War begins in New Mexico and Arizona territories. The conflict will continue sporadically until the capture of the Apache leader Geronimo in 1886.

1872:

March 1: An act of Congress creates the nation's first national park, Yellowstone, encompassing 2,142,720 acres in the far northwestern section of Wyoming Territory and in a small section of Montana Territory.

November 28: The Modoc Indians, living away from their assigned Klamath Reservation in southern Oregon, are attacked by U.S. Cavalry troops. The Modocs take refuge in the lava beds south of Tule Lake, in northern California.

1873:

March 3: The Timber Culture Act is passed by Congress. In return for planting 40 acres of trees, one can obtain 160 acres of government land. By this legislation, over 65,000 homesteaders receive 10 million acres of land.

September 18: Jay Cooke and Company, a leading brokerage firm and financial agent for the Northern Pacific Railroad, fails. Soon thereafter, many other banks fail, plunging the country into a severe depression. Construction is abandoned on the Northern Pacific Railroad at Bismarck in Dakota Territory.

November 1: The manufacture of barbed wire begins in Dekalb, Illinois. The invention solves the problem of fencing in cattle on the open prairies, where timber is sparse.

1874:

A grasshopper plague devastates the prairies from Texas to the Canadian border. Western migration is significantly reduced, as thousands of families return East.

June 27: In the battle of Adobe Walls, in the Texas Panhandle, 29 white buffalo hunters hold off 700 Arapaho, Cheyenne, Comanche and Kiowa warriors.

August 12: A military expedition led by Lieutenant Colonel George Custer discovers gold in the Black Hills of western Dakota Territory. In response, miners descend upon the Sioux preserve.

August–December The Red River Wars are ended, and Indian power on the northern Texas plains is broken, when hundreds of Comanches and Kiowas surrender at Fort Sill, Texas.

1875:

October: The U.S. government tries to purchase Indian lands north of the Platte River, but the Indians refuse to sell their only remaining holdings.

November 9: Indian Inspector E.C. Watkins identifies hundreds of Hunkpapa Sioux, under Sitting Bull, and Oglala Sioux, under Crazy Horse, as hostile Indians. He orders their removal to reservations by January 1876.

December: The U.S. government orders all Indians in the Black Hills of Dakota and Wyoming territories to move to reservations or face military action.

1876:

February 1: The Sioux Indians under Sitting Bull refuse to return to their reservations; the Interior Department turns the Indians over to the War Department.

February 10: Brigadier General Alfred H. Terry, commander of the Department of Dakota, receives orders for military action against the Sioux and Cheyenne tribes.

May 17: General Terry, along with Lieutenant Colonel George Custer and 12 companies of the Seventh Cavalry, leaves Fort Abraham Lincoln in Dakota Territory as part of a three-prong attack upon the Sioux and Cheyenne.

June 25: The battle of Little Big Horn, the largest gathering of Indians ever encountered by military troops in North America. Indians numbering 10,000 to 15,000 from various tribes, including Cheyenne, Miniconjoux Sioux, Oglala Sioux, Blackfeet and Hunkpapa Sioux are strung out for at least three miles. The battle lasts only half an hour. Custer and his entire command of 265 are killed.

July 4: News of Custer's defeat reaches the East; there is a public outcry for revenge.

August 1: President Ulysses S. Grant issues a proclamation admitting Colorado to the Union as the nation's 38th state.

November 25: The Cheyenne village of Dull Knife is attacked by U.S. troops as part of an expanded campaign to drive all Indians from the Big Horn and Powder River region.

1877:

March 3: The Desert Land Act is passed by Congress. The act offers to sell any person 640 acres at $1.25 per acre if he irrigates some portion of it. The average settler, however, cannot afford the expense of irrigation. Most of the land is acquired by speculators and ranchers.

September 3: Upon learning he is about to be imprisoned, Crazy Horse, chief of the Oglala Sioux, pulls a knife on a soldier at Fort Robinson in Nebraska. Crazy Horse is killed in the skirmish.

October 5: Chief Joseph of the Nez Perce surrenders his tribe in the Bear Paw Mountains of northern Montana Territory.

1878:

The Great Dakota Boom begins; farmers settle in the territory. Homestead grants total 1,377,000 acres.

1879:

The "Exodus of 1879": About 20,000 blacks from the South seek homesteads in Kansas, but most are forced to turn back in the mid-1880s due to lack of capital.

1879:

March 29: The Wyoming Stock Growers Association is formed, signifying the importance of the cattle industry in the territory.

September 29–October 5: Warfare breaks out between the Ute Indians and U.S. troops in northwestern Colorado Territory. The Utes are forced to surrender and are relocated to Utah; their former reservation of 12,000,000 acres is opened for settlement.

EYEWITNESS TESTIMONY

The stillness is horrible, and the solemn grandeur of the scene surpasses conception. You feel the absence of sound—the oppression of silence. Down, down, you see the river attenuated to a thread. If you could only hear that gurgling river, lashing with puny strength the massive walls that imprison it and hold it in their dismal shadow, if you could but see a living thing in the depth beneath you, if a bird would but fly past you, if the wind would move any object in that awful chasm, to break for a moment the solemn silence which reigns there, it would relieve that tension of the nerves which the scene has excited, and with a grateful heart you would thank God that he had permitted you to gaze unharmed upon this majestic display of his handiwork. But as it is, the spirit of man sympathizes with the deep gloom of the scene, and the brain reels as you gaze into this profound and solemn solitude.

Nathaniel Pitt Langford, explorer and naturalist, describing a canyon in present-day Yellowstone National Park, journal entry of 1870, in The Discovery of Yellowstone Park *(1972).*

"Grand Canyon, Colorado River, Arizona," 1871–1879. Photograph by John K. Hillers, Records of the Geological Survey. *Courtesy of the National Archives.*

The well worn household goods will not generally pay freight. Many families sell their most valuable things and invest the money in land, living simply for a few years in their new homes. Don't come to farm without enough means to buy four cows, a stove and a few household goods, an ax and a few tools, and a few months' supplies, and own with others, if not alone, a team, a plow and a wagon. Families living on the cars should provide a good Lunch Basket to save expense. Be careful of confidence men, don't lend money on any security to strangers.

Circular, advice to westbound emigrants traveling on the transcontinental railroad, 1870, in Quiett's They Built the West *(1965).*

It perhaps ought to be stated here, for the benefit of widows and single women over twenty-one years of age, that they are as much entitled to homesteads as men, and the women of Dakota generally avail themselves of the privilege. We can point you to young women in Dakota who carry on quite a stroke of farming now, who came here penniless a few years ago. One woman has now three hundred and twenty acres of land, paid for from her wages as servant girl, at $4.00 per week. It is the investment of what she has saved from her wages in the last two years. We, of Dakota, believe in Women's Rights, especially the right to take a homestead and manage it to their own liking.

James S. Foster, commissioner of immigration for Dakota Territory, 1870, in Outlines of History of the Territory of Dakota and Emigrant's Guide to the Free Lands of the Northwest *(1870).*

Returning to our claims with the ox team we now proceeded to plow up sod and build a temporary sod house to serve us as shelter in place of a tent. This primitive structure was completed in a few days. In one end of this temporary abode we made a bedstead of poles. A tick filled with hay and a blanket for cover constituted our bed. After breaking up some ten acres of prairie, thus making a good showing to comply with the homestead law, we went on to the next quarter section and did the same there. Altogether during that summer we built four such dugouts and sod houses. As they were meant to be only temporary, we built each of them with an opening for a door and a window, but no actual door or window was installed. A piece of canvas hung up at the opening served for the purpose of a door.

Anonymous Kansas homesteader, 1870, in
Roenigk's Pioneer History of Kansas
(1933).

Kansas was always distinctly erratic, like a child—happy and laughing one minute and hateful and contrary the next.

Anne. E. Bingham, Kansas settler, 1870s, in
Richardson and Rister's The Greater Southwest *(1934).*

If you come, bring your own bedclothes with you. The feathers that are used in featherbeds cost $.75 a pound so that a featherbed will run into some $20. Cotton cloth is cheap, $.12½ a yard (a yard is one and a half *alen*) for a nice calico material; thus clothes are not expensive. Furniture (nice) is expensive and hard to get, but I imagine that the cost of transportation would be too high if you were to bring your own furniture from Norway. Yet I would bring at least a chest of drawers or a chiffonier. It is a good

thing, however, that simple, everyday chairs cost only $1.25 apiece.

Elise Amalie Waerenskjold, Texas immigrant,
to a friend in Norway, letter of May 1, 1870,
in Blegen's Land of Their Choice *(1955).*

Every settler who comes into any of these mountain territories, every mine that is opened, every Indian who goes onto reserves and is fed, every soldier who is brought into the country, creates an additional demand for stock cattle and beef.

Dr. H. Latham, western railroad surgeon, to
the Omaha World Herald, *letter of June 5,*
1870.

This first year that I was on the trail, every river from the Red River to the Arkansas was "big swimming" as the boys termed it. We were fortunate in having no serious accidents, but we lost a number of both cattle and horses by drowning. We had some bad hail- and thunder-storms. Sometimes we went for days at a stretch with scarcely a wink of sleep, because of winds and rain, which made the cattle

Transport of Texas beef on the Kansas-Pacific Railway—a "cattle-shoot" in Abilene, Kansas, 1871. Courtesy of the Library of Congress.

hard to control. In some places on the trail the country would become very boggy after a long rainy spell, and we had to resort to all sorts of schemes to snatch a little sleep when an opportunity presented itself. When three riders could get away at a time they would go a little way from the cattle and dismount, each man holding his horse by the bridle rein. Then they would lie down in the form of a triangle, each man using his neighbor's ankles for a pillow. In this manner the sleeper's heads were up out of the mud and water.

James H. Cook, cowboy, on his first trail drive, 1870s, in Fifty Years on the Old Frontier *(1923).*

We had no unpleasant experiences with the Indians, although they came to camp and tried to trade with the men. We narrowly escaped having trouble with a couple of what we supposed to be rustlers. While alone in camp one afternoon two men came up and were throwing rocks in among the grazing

Charlie Goodnight (below) and Oliver Loving (right), pioneers of the Goodnight-Loving cattle trail. Courtesy of the New York Public Library.

cattle. I called to them to stop and said, "Don't you know you'll stampede those cattle," and they answered, "That's what we're trying to do." Just then some of the men rode up and the rustlers left hurriedly.

Amanda Burks, Texas trail driver, recalling her days on the trail in the 1870s, in Hunter's The Trail Drivers of Texas *(1963).*

Oh, give me a home where the buffaloes roam,
Where the deer and the antelope play,
Where seldom is heard a discouraging word,
And the sky is not cloudy all day.

"Home on the Range" (1870s), popular song on the cattle trails, in Lomax's Cowboy Songs *(1922).*

In the excitement of a stampede a man was not himself, and his horse was not the horse of yesterday. Man and horse were one, and the combination accomplished feats that would be utterly impossible under ordinary circumstances.

Charlie Goodnight, cattle trail driver, 1870s, in Pioneer Days in the Southwest from 1850 to 1879 *(1909).*

Two years ago our beef and cattle were shipped from the East. Today cattle buyers from Chicago and New York are at every station on our railroads, and buying cattle in all our valleys for eastern consumption. It is safe to predict that 15,000 herds of beeves will be shipped from our valleys east the present season.

Anonymous Union Pacific Railroad surgeon, 1870, in Triggs' History of Cheyenne and Northern Wyoming *(1876).*

These herds were held close enough to each other that when one herd stampeded they all went, as the jar and rumble traveled through the ground, telegraphing the move to all the other herds. Sometimes the results were fatal. One night I was with a herd of three-year-old steers that stampeded. We were trying to head them when we heard another stampeding herd (four-year-old steers and up) coming toward us. As the running herds neared each other, the bosses of both bunches yelled for all hands to quit the lead and get out of the way. The two herds met head-on in a deep gulch. About one hundred steers were killed and a lot more crippled, but owing to the bosses calling us out of the way in time, not a single man or horse was hurt.

Ed Lemmon, cowboy and author, on driving a herd of cattle from Texas to Nebraska in 1871, in Boss Cowman *(1969).*

Free Homes for the Millions!

Popular slogan of the 1870s, advertising land in Nebraska, in Olson's History of Nebraska *(1966).*

Land for the Landless! Homes for the Homeless!

Popular slogan in Nebraska, 1870s, in Fite's The Farmers' Frontier: 1865–1900 *(1966).*

The jam was terrible, and the poor woman was obliged to beg for more room from fear of fainting. The applications poured in as fast as they could be taken care of all day, the crowd inside and out never growing smaller, for as fast as one applicant, with papers properly fixed up, would worm his way through the crowd to the door, and be cast out, panting and dripping with perspiration, another would squeeze in, and become a part of the solid surging mass within.

Beatrice Express *(Nebraska), November 18, 1871, on the rush for land by homesteaders.*

After a year or two settlers usually start to crawl out of their sod huts and build comfortable wooden houses. Several of the Danes in Dannebrog reached that stage this spring. They don't need granaries because the grain is threshed by machine immediately after it is harvested. They don't need the straw as the horses are fed hay and grain in the winter. The cattle can stay outside most of the year because the winter is much shorter here in Nebraska than in Denmark. The pastures are excellent in the summer, so cattle raising is the chief source of income for settlers.

P. Andersen, Nebraska immigrant, to Lange- lands Avis *(Denmark), letter of May 17, 1872, in Hale's* Danes in North America *(1984).*

One year ago this was a vast houseless, uninhabited prairie, with no trace of approaching civilization to frighten the timid antelope, or turn the buffalo from this course . . . Today I can see more than thirty dwellings from my door yard aside from these in the village . . .

T.J. Adams, Nebraska homesteader, April 19, 1872, in Dick's The Sod-House Frontier *(1937).*

There—within ten or twelve days of us—with a magnificent climate, and social and educational advantages more rapidly and abundantly provided than has ever before been known in the history of the world, *millions of acres of land, of the richest and most fruitful character, may be had, at prices so low that it seems almost incredible, and like a mockery to call it purchase.*

The price, in fee, does not average the amount of a year's rent on ordinary farms in this country . . . Nay, in many parts, *fine farms may be had for nothing by any families from any part of the world, who choose to come and live on them; and "homesteads" are sacred, so that no misfortune, bringing a man into debt, can result in the pauperizing or "eviction" of his family.*

Reverend Dr. A. King, Nebraska lecturer, on the advantages of homesteading, 1872, in Ol- son's History of Nebraska.

One of the greatest and most constant difficulties with which we had to contend . . . was to keep ourselves supplied with fuel, as we were compelled to go so far off, and hardly knew where to go to get it. In summer we needed it only for cooking, and used to scrape up anything almost that would burn—

cornstalks, sunflowers, and anything in the way of brushwood that we could find on the place. A good many young trees had started up in the ravine since we had been on the land and had kept out the fires, and I was doing all I could to encourage that very thing; so, of course, I would not think of cutting them down to burn. But in the winter it was different; we had to have something to burn that would give warmth. All the timber had been taken from the "Oaks," but there were yet a few trimmings scattered about. So we used to put the hayrack on the wagon and go with that. We would have to hunt around all day—usually three of us—to get a load of any size. And after preparing it, it kept one almost constantly stuffing it into the stove as it burned away so quickly. But these things were not to be counted; for we must have fuel, though of an inferior kind, or freeze; and we could never give up to that without a desperate struggle.

John Turner, Nebraska farmer, 1870s, in Pioneers of the West *(1963).*

The population of Wichita is decidedly heterogeneous. Here may be seen people of every class, shade and character. The sleek and well dressed speculator, with airs suggestive of genteel living and plethoric purses; the independent, money-making, money-spending, somewhat don't-care-a-cuss-ativeness cattle drover; the rollicking, reckless, free-and-easy herder; the substantial citizen; the professional gambler, and the long-haired desperado of the plains, are here brought together of necessity.

Daily Commonwealth (Topeka, Kansas) October 15, 1872.

Thousands upon thousands of hides are being brought in here by hunters. In places whole acres of ground are covered with these hides spread out . . . to dry. It is estimated that there is, south of the Arkansas and west of Wichita, from one to two thousand men shooting buffalo for their hides.

Wichita Eagle (Kansas), November 7, 1872.

Some came to Dodge City out of curiosity; others strictly for business; the stockman came because it was a great cattle market, and here, in the Arkansas river, was the place appointed for the cattle going north to be classed and passed on, for bargains to be

Accompanied by a neighbor's child, a Kansas woman heads homeward with a barrow-load of cow chips. Most pioneer stoves were fueled by these hardened cattle droppings, dubbed the anthracite of the plains. Courtesy of the Kansas State Historical Society.

closed, and new contracts made for next year; the cowboy came because it was his duty as well as his delight, and here he drew his wages and spent them; the hunter came because it was the very heart of the greatest game country on earth; the freighter came because it was one of the greatest overland freight depots in the United States, and he hauled material and supplies for nearly four hundred miles, supplying three military posts, and all the frontier for that far south and west; last but not least, the gambler and the bad man came because of the wealth and excitement, for obscene birds will always gather around a carcass.

Robert M. Wright, Dodge City resident, 1870s,
in Dodge City: The Cowboy Capital *(1913).*

The buffalo is our money. It is our only resource with which to buy what we need and do not receive from the government. The robes we can prepare and trade. We love them just as the white man does his money. Just as it makes a white man feel to have his money carried away, so it makes us feel to see others killing and stealing our buffaloes, which are our cattle given to us by the Great Father above to provide us meat to eat and means to get things to wear.

Bull Bear, Comanche chief, 1872, in Haley's
The Buffalo War *(1976).*

In our intercourse with the Indians it must always be borne in mind that we are the most powerful party . . . We are assuming, and I think with propriety, that our civilization ought to take the place of their barbarous habits. We therefore claim the right to control the soil they occupy, and we assume that it is our duty to coerce them, if necessary, into the adoption and practice of our habits and customs . . . I would not seriously regret the total disappearance of the buffalo from our western prairies, in its effect upon the Indians, regarding it rather as a means of hastening their sense of dependence upon the products of the soil.

Secretary of the Interior Columbus Delano,
1872, in Haley's The Buffalo War.

There I saw my first great cattle herd, two thousand four-year-old steers in a big corral, ready to start up the trail to Kansas. It was a thrilling sight. The corral was made of big oak logs, and each picket was securely lashed with rawhide. It seemed impossible for the cattle to break out of that pen, but that's what happened a night or so after we left. The Indians stampeded the herd. They rode up to the corral shaking blankets and robes. The big steers knocked over the heavy fence like a toy and scattered over the country. Three Mexican herders were killed, along with many cattle. Many other steers were crippled. It took several days to round them up, and some of them were never found.

Frank Collinson, Texas cowboy, 1873, on his
first cattle drive, in Life in the Saddle *(1964).*

In 1873 we had a little country fair down here about where the Norman School now stands, and a man by the name of Rose, that lived in Clinton, exhibited at the fair a strip of wood about an inch square about sixteen feet long, and drove into this wood some sharp brads, leaving the points stick out, for the purpose of hanging it on a smooth wire, which was the principal fencing material at that time. This strip of wood, so armed to hang on the wire was to stop cattle from crawling through. Mr. Glidden, Mr. Haish and myself were at the fair, and all three of us stood looking at this invention of Mr. Rose's, and I think that each of us at that hour conceived the idea that barbs could be placed on wire in some way instead of being driven into the strip of wood.

I.L. Ellwood, inventor of the barbed wire fence,
1873, in Webb's The Great Plains.

All the other Indians having sued for peace, and the Indians occupying this rough country having been so severely chastised, I had some of the prisoners sent out to communicate with the hostiles, holding out the "olive branch," offering them peace on certain conditions, which were that they should all move in on the different reservations and abstain from all depredations from that time forward. They promptly responded to my proposition, and all within reach came in at once.

General George Crook, on the surrender of the
Apaches in the Arizona Territory, April 1873,
in General George Crook: His Autobiography *(1946).*

You see, we're nearly dead from want of food and exposure—the cooper cartridge has done the business for us. I am glad of the opportunity to surrender, but I do it not because I love you, but because I am afraid of you General.

Old Cha-lipun, Apache chief, to General George
Crook, April 1873, in General George Crook:
His Autobiography.

The farmers who have opened the country around Wichita have an almost insurmountable difficulty to encounter, many of them having to borrow money from the soulless money men of Wichita, at three per cent a month on mortgage. The money men who have done this thing excuse themselves by saying other men have done the same. As well might they commit murder and allege as an excuse that there are other murders.

Anonymous Kansas farmer, to the Wichita Eagle, *on the Panic of 1873, letter of May 22, 1873.*

A large number of Indians added to the harlequin appearance of the Denver streets the day I was there. They belonged to the Ute tribe, through which I had to pass, and Governor Hunt introduced me to a fine-looking young chief, very well dressed in beaded hide, and bespoke his courtesy for me if I needed it. The Indian stores and fur stores and fur depôts interested me most. The crowds in the streets, perhaps owing to the snow on the ground, were almost solely masculine. I only saw five women the whole day. There were men in every rig: hunters and trappers in buckskin clothing; men of the Plains with belts and revolvers, in great blue cloaks, relics of the war; teamsters in leathern suits; horsemen in fur coats and caps and buffalo-hide boots with the hair outside, and camping blankets behind their huge Mexican saddles; Broadway dandies in light kid gloves; rich English sporting tourists, clean, comely, and supercilious looking; and hundreds of Indians on their small ponies, the men wearing buckskin suits sewn with beads, and red blankets, with faces painted vermilion and hair hanging lank and straight, and squaws much bundled up, riding astride with furs over their saddles.

Isabella L. Bird, English visitor and author, October 23, 1873, in A Lady's Life in the Rocky Mountains *(1966).*

When I reached Yosemite, all the rocks seemed talkative, and more telling and lovable than ever. They are dear friends, and seemed to have warm blood gushing through their granite flesh; and I love them with a love intensified by long and close companionship. After I had bathed in the bright river, sauntered over the meadows, conversed with the domes, and played with the pines, I still felt blurred and weary, as if tainted in some way with the sky of your streets. I determined, therefore, to run out for a while to say my prayers in the higher mountain temples. "The days are sunful," I said, "and, though now winter, no great danger need be encountered, and no sudden storm will block my return, if I am watchful."

John Muir, naturalist, to a friend, letter of 1873, in Steep Trails *(1918).*

I will say to those holding the bonds of the Northern Pacific Railroad that by changing them into good lands now owned by the road in the valley of the Red River of the North and East of that point is the only means of ever saving themselves from total loss.

Colonel William B. Hazen, commander at Ford Buford, Dakota Territory, to the New York Tribune, *letter of February 27, 1874.*

Nearly one-half the area of our American domain is yet but sparsely settled, and a large proportion of our Northwestern territories, though fertile in soil, suffers from a scarcity of timber and running streams. It is the duty of the government to develop its hidden resources, and encourage its people in new fields of industry and enterprise. Enact such generous laws as will induce immigration, and open new homes and harvest fields all over the broad and uninhabited prairies of the West. Then will our own grain fields supply Europe with bread, and bring money to our shores, in return for the millions in gold which we are taxed yearly to pay as interest on our national debt.

Congressman Moses K. Armstrong (Dakota Territory) to Congress, speech of 1874, in The Early Empire Builders of the Great West *(1901).*

The Indians were about one hundred yards from the house when the hunters turned loose their guns. At the first fire a number of horses and riders went down. We had no time to see anything more, for they were on us in a flash for the next few minutes, which seemed like hours, it was each man for himself.

The house soon filled up with smoke, and as of course every chink was closed but the loopholes, it became stifling in the place, and every man perspired freely. Now and then there was a shout from a hunter as his shot told, and words of encouragement were exchanged.

Seth Hathaway, buffalo hunter, recalls the battle of Adobe Walls in the Texas Panhandle, June 27, 1874, in Baker and Harrison's Adobe Walls *(1986).*

HARPER'S WEEKLY.

JOURNAL OF CIVILIZATION

Vol. XVIII.—No. 937.] NEW YORK, SATURDAY, DECEMBER 12, 1874. [WITH A SUPPLEMENT. PRICE TEN CENTS.

Slaughtered for the hide. Cover of Harper's Weekly, *December 12, 1874. Courtesy of the Library of Congress.*

They began on the green corn and garden crops, and made a clean sweep. In the morning the corn was waving in all its beauty—and it is about the loveliest crop that grows—a splendid green, and so high and dense that a man riding through it on horseback would not be seen; in the evening nothing remained but the bare, upright stalks, which were rapidly blackening under the influence of their bites, and through which one could see all over the field. Flowers, leaves, silk, ears, all had vanished down their rapacious maws. They cleared off all the apples, peaches, and grapes, of which fruits we had a splendid show; but not a single one of either escaped.

Percy C. Ebbutt, Kansas settler from England, on the grasshopper invasion of 1874, in Emigrant Life in Kansas *(1975).*

In a clear, hot July day a haze came over the sun. The haze deepened into a gray cloud. Suddenly the cloud resolved itself into billions of gray grasshoppers sweeping down upon the earth. The vibration of their wings filled the ear with a roaring sound like a rushing storm. As far as the eye could reach in every direction the air was filled with them. Where they alighted they covered the ground like a heavy crawling carpet. Growing crops disappeared in a single day. Trees were stripped of leaves. Potatoes, turnips and onions were pursued into the earth. Clothing and harness were cut into shreds if left exposed. Wheat and oats were mostly in the shock, but the grasshoppers covered the shocks, cut the bands and gnawed the grain.

Addison E. Sheldon, Nebraska farmer, July 26, 1874, in Olson's History of Nebraska.

Subsequent examinations at numerous points confirm and strengthen the fact of the existence of gold in the Black Hills. On some of the water courses almost every panful of earth produced gold in small, yet paying quantities. Our brief halts and rapid marching prevented anything but a very hasty examination of the country in this respect; but in one place, and the only one within my knowledge where so great a depth was reached, a hole was dug 8 feet in depth. The miners report that they found gold among the roots of the grass, and, from that point to the lowest point reached, gold was found in paying quantities. It has not required an expert to find gold in the Black Hills, as men without former experience in mining have discovered it at an expense of but little time or labor.

Lieutenant Colonel George Armstrong Custer, to the assistant adjutant general, Dakota Territory, dispatch of August 15, 1874, in Maguire's Guide to the Black Hills *(1878).*

In the evening, just as we had finished our meal, one of the chiefs called Billy, came in and we had a long talk with him. Said he came up to see how many there were of us, wanted to know how long we were going to stay, when we were going, and what we were doing. They don't recognize the boundary line as laid down on the maps, but claim all the western slope for their reserve, including all of Middle Park & all this portion of country up to the Saguache range, and complained very much indeed of the incroachments of the white men, the miners & the toll roads particularly. Found fault also with the hunters who came in and took away their game.

"Photographing in High Places," in the Teton Range, by William Henry Jackson, kneeling beside his tentlike "darkbox" and preparing his wet plates. Courtesy of the National Archives.

William Henry Jackson, U.S. Geological Survey photographer, on meeting a tribe of Ute Indians in Colorado Territory, diary entry of August 21, 1874, in The Diaries of William Henry Jackson *(1959).*

The captain with a smile turned to us and said, "Boys, they are going to fight us. See how beautifully the old chief forms his line of battle." From a little boy I had longed to be a ranger and fight the Indians. At last I was up against the real thing and with not so much as an umbrella behind which to hide. I was nervous. I was awfully nervous.

We were now within one hundred steps of the redskins. Then came the order to dismount, shoot low, and kill as many horses as possible. The captain said as we came up that every time we got an Indian on foot in that country we were sure to kill him. With the first shot everybody, Indians and rangers, began firing and yelling.

James B. Gillett, Texas Ranger, on an Indian battle along the Texas frontier, August 1875, in Six Years With the Texas Rangers *(1943).*

[The buffalo hunters] have done more in the past two years . . . to settle the vexed Indian question than the entire regular army has done in the past thirty years. They are destroying the Indians' commissary . . . Send them powder and lead, if you will; but, for the sake of lasting peace, let them kill, skin, and sell until the buffaloes are exterminated. Then your prairies can be covered with speckled cattle and the festive cowboy, who follows the hunter as a second forerunner of an advanced civilization.

General Philip H. Sheridan, 1875, in Haley's The Buffalo War.

Your people make big talk, and sometimes make war, if an Indian kills a white man's ox to keep his wife and children from starving; what do you think my people ought to say when they see their [buffalo] killed by your race when you are not hungry?

Little Robe, Cheyenne chief, 1870s, in Haley's The Buffalo War.

Many men have gone to Nebraska without ten dollars clear, and have succeeded well; but in such cases they obtained situations before starting, or there was at the time an active demand for labour of the kind which they could sell, or they were extremely fortunate. In times when railway construction was being pushed with great energy, good labourers found no difficulty in getting employment at rates enabling them to save money at the same time that they were preparing, at little expense, homesteads for themselves. There were also many opportunities for mechanics, and a considerable number for good clerks and men of business capacity. Now neither clerks, mechanics, nor railway labourers are wanted in any considerable numbers. There has been a large influx of poor settlers who have hoped to eke out their living by day labour, while they were acquiring titles to homesteads, and the number of farmers able to hire has not increased in like proportion; and it would be manifestly unwise to trust the chances of such a resource.

Edwin A. Curley, English visitor and author, 1875, in Nebraska; Its Advantages, Resources, and Drawbacks.

Uncle Sam, it appears, has consented at last
To scatter a few of his coppers
In behalf of those who, in the year that is past
Were cursed and cleaned out by the hoppers
Now I, being one of ten thousand in need,

Would willingly better my status;
So, if you can't give me my quota in seed,
Just send me a peck of potatoes.

Anonymous Nebraska farmer, 1875, in Fite's
The Farmers' Frontier: 1865–1900.

In Cheyenne there must have been fifty paroled miners who had been taken out of the Black Hills by the cavalry. We and everybody else probed them for news. Had they struck anything good before the soldiers came? And where would they go if staked to a new outfit? Spring Creek? Rapid Creek? Nigger Gulch? As may be imagined, many lies were told; many an impoverished prospector lived high on his hints and promises. The pockets and shallow gravel bottoms had, no doubt, yielded considerable gold dust. The Warren Bank had an attractive display of nuggets and coarse gold in its window. Several storekeepers set up gold scales on their counters. It all helped to stir up things to fever pitch.

George W. Stokes, gold prospector, 1875, in
Deadwood Gold: A Story of the Black Hills
(1926).

Coloron owns this country. Buffalo are Indian's cattle. White man's cattle eat all grass, buffalo die, no feed. White man must go. Coloron no big fool. No more talk.

Old Coloron, Ute chieftain, to Joseph W.
Bowles, Colorado Territory stockman, message
of 1876, in Peake's The Colorado Range Cattle Industry *(1937).*

Tell Coloron if he don't behave himself I will shoot a hole in him so big that a dog can crawl in. Now all of you, git.

Joseph W. Bowles, to Old Coloron, message of
1876, in Peake's The Colorado Range Cattle
Industry.

A hatless and breathless herder dashed up to the officer on an unsaddled mule. With blanched face and protruding eyeballs he called out that the Indians were running off the herd.

The general came hastily out, just in time to see a cloud of dust rising through a gap in the bluffs, marking the direction taken by the stampeded mules. Instantly he shouted with his clear voice to the bugler to sound the call, "Boots and saddles," and keep it up until he told him to stop. The first notes of the trumpet had hardly sounded before the porches of the company quarters and the parade were alive with

men. Every one, without stopping to question, rushed from the barracks and officers' quarters to the stables. The men threw their saddles on their horses and galloped out to the paradeground. Soldiers who were solely on garrison duty, and to whom no horse was assigned, stole whatever ones they could find, even those of the messengers tied to the hitching-posts. Others vaulted on to mules barebacked. Some were in jackets, others in their flannel shirt-sleeves. Many were hatless, and occasionally a head was tied up with a handkerchief. It was anything but a military-looking crowd, but every one was ready for action, and such spirited-looking creatures it is rarely one's lot to see.

Elizabeth B. Custer, wife of George Armstrong
Custer, at Fort Lincoln in Dakota Territory,
1870s, in Boots and Saddles *(1885).*

I want to know what you are doing on this road. You scare all the buffalo away. I want to hunt in this place. I want you to turn back from here. If you don't, I will fight you again. I want you to leave what you have got here and turn back from here. I am your friend.

Sitting Bull, Sioux chief, note to U.S. Army
troops at Yellowstone, 1876, in Vestal's Sitting
Bull: Champion of the Sioux *(1957).*

The land in which we stand is full of white men; our game is all gone and we have come on great trouble.

Spotted Tail, Oglala Sioux chief, 1876, in
Hyde's Red Cloud's Folk: A History of the
Oglala Sioux *(1937).*

We want no white men here. The Black Hills belong to me. If the whites try to take them, I will fight.

Sitting Bull, 1876, in Brown's Bury My Heart
at Wounded Knee *(1971).*

At 8:30 o'clock, without any warning, we heard a few shots from behind the bluffs to the north. "They are shooting buffalo over there," said the Captain. Very soon we began to know, by the alternate rise and fall of the reports, that the shots were not all fired in one direction. Hardly had we reached this conclusion, when a score or two of our Indian scouts appeared upon the northern crest, and rode down the slopes with incredible speed. "Saddle up, there— saddle up, there, quick!" shouted Colonel Mills, and immediately all the cavalry within sight, without waiting for formal orders, were mounted and ready

Chief Sitting Bull. Courtesy of the Library of Congress.

so on. Custer will go up the Rosebud tomorrow with his whole regiment and thence to the headwaters of the Little Horn, thence down the Little Horn.

I only hope that one of the two columns will find the Indians.

General Alfred Terry, to General Philip Sheridan, letter of June 21, 1876, in Gray's Centennial Campaign: The Sioux War of 1876 *(1976).*

As we cut our way through them, the fighting was hand to hand and it was instant death to him who fell from his saddle, or was wounded. As we dashed through them, my men were so close to the Indians that they could discharge their pistols right into the breasts of the savages, then throw them away and seize their carbines, not having time to replace their revolvers in their holsters. . . . Our horses were on the dead run with, in many instances, two and three men on one animal. We plunged into the Little Big Horn and began the climb of the opposite bluffs. This incline was the steepest that I have ever seen horse or mule ascend. . . . In this narrow place (the ford)

for action. General Crook, who appreciated the situation, had already ordered the companies of the 4th and 9th Infantry, posted at the foot of the northern slopes, to deploy as skirmishers, leaving their mules with the holders. Hardly had this precaution been taken, when the flying Crow and Snake scouts, utterly panic stricken, came into camp shouting at the top of their voices, "Heap Sioux ! heap Sioux !" gesticulating wildly in the direction of the bluffs which they had abandoned in such haste. All looked in that direction, and there, sure enough, were the Sioux in goodly numbers, and in loose, but formidable, array. The singing of the bullets above our heads speedily convinced us that they had called on business.

John F. Finerty, Chicago Times *correspondent, on the battle of Rosebud Creek during the Sioux War, June 17, 1876, in* War-Path and Bivouac *(1980).*

No Indians have been met with as yet, but traces of a large and recent village have been discovered 20 or 30 miles up the Rosebud. Gibbon's column will move this morning on the north side of the Yellowstone for the mouth of the Big Horn, where it will be ferried across by the supply steamer, and whence it will proceed to the mouth of the Little Horn, and

Lieutenant Colonel George Armstrong Custer. Courtesy of the Library of Congress.

there were necessarily much crowding and confusion and many of the men were compelled to cling to the horses' necks and tails for support, to prevent their being trampled to death or falling back into the river. Into the mass of men and horses, the Indians poured a continuous fire and the Little Big Horn was transferred into a seeming river of human blood.

Major Marcus Reno, on the battle of Little Big Horn, June 25, 1876, in Hunt's I Fought With Custer *(1987).*

Then the Sioux rode up the ridge on all sides, riding very fast. The Cheyennes went up the left way. Then the shooting was quick, quick. Pop-pop-pop very fast. Some of the soldiers were down on their knees, some standing. Officers all in front. The smoke was like a great cloud, and everywhere the Sioux went the dust rose like smoke. We circled all around them—swirling like water around a stone. We shoot, we ride fast, we shoot again. Soldiers drop, and horses fall on them. Soldiers in line drop, but one man rides up and down the line—all the time shouting. He rode a sorrel horse, with white legs and white forelegs. I don't know who he was. He was a brave man.

Two Moon, Cheyenne chief, on the battle of Little Big Horn, June 25, 1876, in Hunt's I Fought With Custer.

I charged in. A tall, well-built soldier with yellow hair and mustache saw me coming and tried to bluff me, aiming his rifle at me without shooting. I dodged it. We grabbed each other and wrestled there in the dust and smoke. It was like fighting in a fog. This soldier was very strong and brave. He tried to wrench my rifle from me. I lashed him across the face with my quirt, striking the coup. He let go, then grabbed my gun with both hands until I struck him again.

But the tall soldier fought hard. He was desperate. He hit me with his fists on the jaw and shoulders, then grabbed my long braids with both hands, pulled my face close and tried to bite my nose off. I yelled for help: "Hey, hey, come over and help me!" I thought that soldier would kill me.

White Bull, or Pte-san-hunka, Sioux chief, recalls attacking George Armstrong Custer at the battle of Little Big Horn, June 25, 1876, in Howard's The Warrior Who Killed Custer *(1968).*

When the command got together we followed the Custer trail to the highest point on the bluffs. Many scattered Indians were riding about at some distances, but the country was badly broken into gullies, and there was no sound of firing in any direction. We saw a lot of white objects scattered about which I thought were rocks but which we found afterwards were the naked bodies of Custer's men.

Lieutenant Charles A. Varnum, on the battle of Little Big Horn, June 25, 1876, in Custer's Chief of Scouts *(1982).*

After 3 miles march we came upon the village, or rather what had been the village. Half a dozen lodges with dead Indians were still standing, while any quantity of poles and a heterogeneous lot of equippage were scattered about, showing that they had moved in great haste. A large number of horses, dead, wounded, and sound were in sight. The sound ones were picked up. Half a mile farther we came in sight of Maj. Reno's 7th Cos. who were corralled on a high bluff on the east bank, 3 or four miles above us, & about a mile from where the first attack was made. We moved on up. Lt. Bradley, who was on the east bank, sent in to say that he had seen 42 bodies of soldiers, and soon after that he had found 190 in half a mile further up. We found 40 more and quite a number of dead horses. We soon had a scout from Maj. Reno, and the command went into Camp. [1st] Lt. [Donald] McIntosh & [2d Lt. Benjamin H.] Hodgson [7th Cav.] were found close to the camp & buried. Our Dr's went up to Reno to care for the wounded of whom there were 41. The stench from the dead bodies and dead horses was something terrible. The rest of the day was spent in making litters and bringing the wounded into our camp and burying the dead which latter task was not completed at dark. All the bodies except that of Genl Custer were more or less mutilated.

Captain Henry B. Freeman, diary entry of June 27, 1876, in The Freeman Journal: The Infantry in the Sioux Camp of 1876 *(1977).*

The Indian lands are the best in the state, and justice would demand, as well as every consideration of policy and humanity, that these fertile lands should be thrown open to settlement, and the abode of civilized and industrious men.

Anonymous Indian agent in Kansas, July 13, 1876, in Robbins' Our Landed Heritage *(1962).*

One does not sell the earth upon which people walk.

Crazy Horse, Oglala Sioux chief, 1870s, in
Brown's Bury My Heart at Wounded Knee.

Our next objective point is Crazy Horse. He should be followed up and struck as soon as possible. There should be no stopping for this or that thing. The Indians cannot stand a continuous campaign. I cannot tell whether we can go yet. That depends on our getting the things we want. The best time to strike the Indians is in the winter. They cannot remain together in large bodies at that season. The necessities of subsistence compel them to separate, and then is the time to throw a large force on each band, and crush them all in detail.
General George Crook, journal entry of October
21, 1876, in General George Crook: His
Autobiography.

This war did not spring up here in our land; this war was brought upon by the children of the Great Father who came to take our land from us without price, and who, in our land, do a great many evil things . . . This war has come from robbery—from the stealing of our land.
Spotted Tail, Sioux chief, on the Black Hills
War, 1876, in Brown's Bury My Heart at
Wounded Knee.

I have never seen such a sight as was presented in the captured village, when 2,000 men were scattered through it in orderless confusion, picking up buffalo robes and other articles, and burning the lodges, while at the head of a gulch a hundred yards away a circle of men were held at bay by a handful of Indians in a hole, and off to the south the pickets were engaged.

Occasionally a bullet would come in among us, but no one appeared to mind it much, though we were horrified for a moment when White, a scout, was heard to wail out, 'My God, I've got it,' and seen to fall, shot through the heart. And again a few minutes later, when, a rush having been made at the Indians by the rapidly increasing forces at the gulch, two soldiers were carried back wounded.
Lieutenant Walter S. Schoyler, aide to General
George Crook, to his father, on Crook's Yellow-
stone Expedition against the Sioux and Chey-
enne in Colorado Territory, letter of November
1, 1876, in General George Crook: His Au-
tobiograhy.

Eaten out by grasshoppers.
Going back East to live with wife's folks.
Sign on back of covered wagons leaving Ne-
braska, 1876, in Olson's History of Nebraska.

I had heard of stampedes where they ran over everything in their way, and I thought, "now should I get out into that big field of animals and they should make a run, there would be annihilation." Then I thought, "to go back to camp with word that I was turned back by the main herd would be construed as weakness."

Looking to the southwest and west, I saw a moving sea of that one countless host. I decided that I was just as safe going ahead as turning back. So, taking the landmark in view that I was to go to, I started on, and was soon among them. Of course there were intervals of bare ground; but they were small in comparison to the ground actually covered by the buffaloes. As I drove on, they would veer to my right in front and to my left in rear; the others following on behind them, would hardly seem to vary their course.
John R. Cook, buffalo hunter, 1877, on a buf-
falo hunt on the southwest Plains, in The Border and the Buffalo *(1938).*

We left the Lockhart pasture about the first of April, took the Chisholm Trail and "lit out." My first stampede was on Onion Creek; as usual, this occurred at night, about 12 o'clock. The herd was bedded about one hundred yards from the wagon, two men on guard. In their fright the cattle broke for the wagon, and we asleep at the camp, being aroused by the roar of tramping hoofs, scrambled up on the wagon. One of the older men jumped up and shook a blanket before them and turned them off the other way. The first thing I remember was the boss calling out, "Boys, get down and get your horses." It was then that I discovered that I had quit my pallet and was astride one of the hind wheels. Of course, we hurriedly got our horses, went around the cattle, after about a mile's run, held them, and they quieted down. Old hands at the business will know that we slept no more that night. This trip was marked by excessive rainfall, big rains falling at night, and one hailstorm, adding greatly to the hardship of the cowboy's lot; but we didn't mind it much and, with songs and jokes, kept up our spirits.
G.W. Mills, Texas trail driver, on driving a
herd from Texas to Nebraska, 1877, in Hunter's
The Trail Drivers of Texas.

We took out homesteads directly. We might have 'filed' on the land [established a preemption claim], and that filing would have been good for 30 months, at the end of which time (or before) we could have bought the land or put a homestead on it. As it is, we must live on it five years. The first two years we live "off and on"—that is, we must sleep on it once in a while and make some improvements on it within 6 months, or it will be forfeited. It is to be our home, but we can hire out by the day or month as we like. A man here has three rights—homestead, filing and timber filing. By taking land under the first he must live on it five years, and at the end of five years of actual residence can "prove up" and get a deed.

Howard Ruede, Kansas homesteader, 1877, in Sod House Days *(1937).*

You know very well that the government has set apart a reservation, and that the Indians must go upon it. If an Indian becomes a citizen, like old Timothy of Alpona, he can have land like any other citizen outside, but he has to leave his tribe, and take land precisely as a white man does. The government has set apart the large reservation for you and your children, that you may live in peace, and prosper.

General Oliver O. Howard, Indian commissioner, to Chief Joseph and other Nez Perce leaders, at Lapwai council in Montana Territory, May 3, 1877, in Nez Perce Joseph *(1881).*

I would have given my own life if I could have undone the killing of white men by my people. I blame my young men and I blame the white man . . . My friends among the white men have blamed me for the war. I am not to blame. When my young men began the killing my heart was hurt. Although I did not justify them, I remembered all the insults I had endured, and my blood was on fire. Still I would have taken my people to the buffalo country without fighting, if possible.

I could see no other way to avoid war. We moved over to White Bird Creek, sixteen miles away, and there encamped, intending to collect our stock before leaving; but the soldiers attacked us and the first battle was fought.

Chief Joseph, recalls the beginning of the Nez Perce War, 1877, in Beal's I Will Fight No More Forever *(1966).*

Our post is all in commotion. The two companies of cavalry will leave in a few hours. They don't dare

Chief Joseph. Courtesy of the National Archives.

wait even for more troops, though dispatches have already been sent everywhere to gather up the scattered troops in the Department. My dear old husband will have to follow Colonel Perry's command, as soon as he gets back here. These poor people from Mt. Idaho say, "One thing is certain. An Indian war is upon us." You know these devils always begin on helpless outlying settlements. Poor Mrs. Theller is busy getting up a mess kit for her husband. Major Boyle remains in charge of the post. The talk among the officers is that there will be a great deal of trouble.

Emily Fitzgerald, wife of U.S. Army Captain Jenkins A. Fitzgerald, on the beginning of the Nez Perce War, letter of June 15, 1877, in Brown's The Flight of the Nez Perce *(1967).*

Seated on my horse on the bluff and overlooking this movement as well as the dim light permitted, with every sense on the strain for the first sign of alarm, I was startled by a single shot on the extreme left of the line; and as if answering the shot as a signal, the whole line opened, and the men, rushing forward with a shout, plunged into the stream and climbed up the opposite bank, shooting down the startled Indians as they rushed from their tents pell-mell, men women and children together. Like a flock of startled quail, the first impulse was to seek shelter in the brush behind the abrupt creek bank; but finding themselves rushing directly into the arms of our men, many broke for the bluffs on the opposite side of the valley, some of them dropping into any hole offering protection. Within twenty minutes we had complete possession of the camp and orders were given to commence destroying it.

Colonel John Gibbon, recalls the battle of Big Hole during the Nez Perce War, August 1877, in Brown's The Flight of the Nez Perce.

Tell General Howard I know his heart. What he told me before I have in my heart, I am tired of fighting. Our chiefs are killed. Looking Glass is dead. The old men are all killed. It is the young men who say yes or no. He who led the young men is dead. It is cold and we have no blankets. The little children are freezing to death. My people, some of them, have run away to the hills and have no blankets, no food; no one knows where they are, perhaps freezing to death. I want time to look for my children and see how many of them I can find. Maybe I shall find them among the dead. Hear me, my chiefs, I am tired; my heart is sick and sad. From where the sun now stands, I will fight no more forever.

Chief Joseph, in the Bear Paw Mountains, to the U.S. Army, speech of surrender, October 5, 1877, in McWhorter's Hear Me, My Chiefs *(1952).*

My fathers, you know well how the Americans have treated us, and what they have done for us. They take me for their son, but they have come behind me with their guns. When first our nation learned to shoot with the gun to kill meat for our children and women it was by the English we were taught; but since that time I [we] have been in misery; I tell you the truth: Since I was raised I have done nothing bad. The Americans tried to get our country from us; our country, the Black Hills country, was filled with gold; they knew that the gold was there. I told them not to go into it. I did not wish to leave my golden country; I had not given them the land any more than you would have given it. The Great Almighty and the Queen know that there is no harm in me and that I did nothing wrong.

Sitting Bull, speech to Canadian officials at a council in Canada, October 1877, in Adams' Sitting Bull: An Epic of the Plains *(1973).*

The valley and bench lands of Wyoming, capable of producing crops common to this latitude, have a total area of 20,000 square miles or aggregate nearly 13,000,000 acres. With unlimited natural facilities for irrigation, fencing and building material always convenient and unexcelled fertility of soil, there is no reason why a strictly agricultural population of 50,000 people should not flourish within our borders and supply to the mineral-producing residents and non-producing population the food which otherwise must come from abroad.

Robert E. Strahorn, 1877, in The Hand-book of Wyoming and Guide to the Black Hills and Big Horn Regions.

We have had an opportunity to watch the practical effect of woman suffrage here from the first, and have seen none of the evil results prophesied for it by its opponents. We have never heard of a case of domestic trouble growing out of it; women have not been degraded or demoralized; on the contrary, they have, in a quiet, lady-like manner, exercised their elective franchise, as a rule, in favor of law, order and good government. Their influence has done much to refine the politics of our Territory, and to divest them of their objectionable features. All lovers of law and order, of whatever political faith, acknowledge the benefits of woman's refining influence in our local government.

Anonymous Wyoming settler, 1877, in Strahorn's The Hand-book of Wyoming and Guide to the Black Hills and Big Horn Regions.

The curse of this country is land-grabbing. Few men are satisfied with one claim; they must have a pre-emption, homestead and timber-filing, and between the three they have so much work they don't know which end they stand on. This week we have really done no work, as the weather has been very unfavorable. I would not like to live in Graybill's house, as I think it will settle very much. The sod is very wet and rotten. We can eat corn bread (Johnny-cake is what they call it here) as well as the old settlers. The hens lay now, and we get milk at Jakey's so that we have corn bread about every other day for breakfast. Fried pork, cornbread and molasses, and coffee are good breakfast. Geo. and I think so. Expenses last month amounted to $7.97½, divided thus: Well outfit $2.55; household goods, 75¢; provisions 67½¢; corn $1; rails for hog pen, $2.14; sun-

Homesteaders rest by their covered wagons in Colorado, 1870s. Courtesy of the New York Public Library.

dries 86¢. This month the bill already foots up over $10, but there is wheat sufficient to make flour to last two months.

Howard Ruede, Kansas homesteader, letter of February 15, 1878, in Sod-House Days: Letters From A Kansas Homesteader, 1877–1878.

If the control and management of the Indians were left to the average western man, he would first capture them, i.e., take all their guns, ponies and feathers, then domicile them on the Missouri River at convenient points and keep them well fed. Such a course would stop all Indian wars, cause to cease all raids and other troubles in the Sioux Country and save millions annually to the Government.

But your scheming sentimentalist will have no such commonsense solution of the Indian question. They want to make little angels of the papooses and big angels of the head chiefs. The flighty head of the interior department proposes to turn the war chiefs into husbandmen, to make farmers of savages and require them to become self sustaining in a country where a New England Yankee would starve.

The Press and Dakotian (Dakota Territory), March 29, 1878.

Seven years ago Colorado was without railway communication, and generally styled "out of the world." To-day her energetic citizens point with pride to eight different railroads tracking her broad prairies and plunging even to the hearts and heights of her mountains. The total number of miles of these lines operated is 1,133. Half of these have been constructed while the railway interest has been paralyzed in almost all other sections, and Colorado's showing is due almost wholly to the invincible pluck of her citizens, the wondrous wealth of her mines and the riches in her grasses and farm lands. Seven of these lines, aggregating nearly 1,000 miles, were built while she was yet a territory. The daily mail, telegraph and express radiate from her capital city to every nook and corner.

Robert E. Strahorn, 1878, in To the Rockies and Beyond, or A Summer on the Union Pacific Railway and Branches *(1878).*

All the present and future agriculture of more than four-tenths of the area of the United States is dependent upon irrigation, and practically all values for agriculture industries inhere, not in the land but the water. Monopoly of land need not be feared. The question for legislators to solve is to devise some practical means by which water rights may be distributed among individual farmers and water monopolies prevented.

John Wesley Powell, surveyor and conservationist, on irrigating the Rocky Mountain region, in Report on the Lands of the Arid Region of the United States *(1878).*

The Big Horn country will attract general attention next season. Big Horn City in the northwestern portion of Wyoming, is gaining very rapidly. One year ago there was not a white inhabitant in the Big Horn valley, now a respectable settlement exists, and the rich valleys round about are being ornamented with new cabins.

Cheyenne Sun (Wyoming Territory), January 10, 1879.

We cannot advise any married man to come here [Kansas] with less than $800 or $1000, to make a start on a farm . . . and then it will take plenty of grit, hard work and rigid economy to get through the first year or two . . .

Pamphlet of advice for Kansas immigrants, 1879, in Water's Steel Trails to Santa Fe *(1950).*

If they come here and starve, all well. It is better to starve to death in Kansas than be shot and killed in the South.

The Colored Citizen (Kansas) on blacks immigrating to Kansas, March 29, 1879.

Attention Colored Men!
Office of the Colored Colonization Society
Topeka, Kansas
Your brethren and friends throughout the North have observed with painful solicitude the outrages heaped upon you by your rebel Masters, and are doing all they can to alleviate your miseries and provide for your future happiness and prosperity. President Hayes, by his iniquitous Southern policy, has deserted you, while the Democrats who now have control of Congress, will seek to enslave you if you remain in the South, and to protect you from their designs, the Colonization Society has been organized by the Government to provide land by each of a family, which will be given in bodies of one hundred and sixty acres gratuitiously. This land is located in the best portion of Kansas, in close proximity to Topeka and is very productive. Here there are no class distinctions in society; all are on equality. Leave the land of oppression and come to free Kansas.

Lycurgus P. Jones, president of the Colored Colonization Society, Topeka, Kansas, Announcement of April 19, 1879, in the Daily Picayune *(New Orleans).*

I am reliably informed, from a trustworthy source, that a colony of 1,200 persons are being formed at different points in Kansas, notably of Kansas City and Coffeyville, to invade the Indian Territory.

They are to meet at the latter place May 5, fully armed for all emergencies, thence to proceed to the unoccupied lands west of the Creek, Pottawatomie, and Chickasaw Reservations, for the purpose of taking possession of these lands, upon which they intend to settle colonies from the States other than Indians.

M.P. Roberts, editor of the Indian Journal, *to E.J. Brooks, Indian Affairs commissioner, letter of April 22, 1879, in the U.S. Senate's* Document 10, Operations to Control Squatters in Indian Territory *(1879).*

. . . for the purpose of properly protecting the interests of the Indian nations and tribes, as well as of the United States, in said Indian Territory, and of duly enforcing the laws governing the same, I, Rutherford B. Hayes, President of the United States, do admonish and warn all such persons so intending or preparing to remove upon said lands or said Territory, without permission of the proper agreement of the Indian Department, against any attempt to so remove or settle upon any lands of said Territory; and I do further warn and notify any and all such persons who may offend that they will be speedily and immediately removed therefrom by the agent according to the laws made and provided . . .

President Rutherford B. Hayes, proclamation of April 26, 1879, warning settlers not to intrude upon the Indian Territory (present-day Oklahoma), in Letters and Messages of Rutherford B. Hayes *(1881).*

It lies in a most beautiful and fertile country between the Cimarron and Canadian rivers, and has every advantage for a great city . . . There is no country in the world half so beautiful. Clearly running streams of water, and better than all, and something that Kansas never had, grand old forests of trees along the stream.

J.R. Boyd, Wichita, Kansas, settler, on the Indian Territory (present-day Oklahoma), April 28, 1879, in Rister's Land Hunger: David L. Payne and the Oklahoma Boomers *(1942).*

The officer at Wichita telegraphs: No excitement here; no organized body. Nearly every emigrant train passing through has been visited. Some few acknowledge that they were going into Territory, but are now disposed to obey proclamation. About twenty-five teams pass here daily, but a good many intend locating in Kansas. A few emigrants were met by Lieutenant Claggett coming out of the Territory. I think the proclamation will be respected.

General Philip Sheridan, to Adjutant General William Sherman, dispatch of May 9, 1879, in the U.S. Senate's Document 10, Operations to Control Squatters in Indian Territory *(1879).*

It seems as if the North is slow to wake up to the importance and magnitude of this movement of the colored people. No longer ago than last Saturday I had a call from a delegation of 100 leading colored men from the states of Mississippi and Alabama, who are here canvassing Kansas and other Northern states with a view of migrating this coming fall and spring. I had a talk with them for nearly an hour in the Senate chamber, in which I gave them a full and fair understanding of the condition of things in Kansas, and what they may and may not expect by coming here. They answered me that they had borne troubles until they had become so oppressive on them that they could bear them no longer and that they had rather die in the attempt to reach the land where they can be free than to live in the South anymore.

John P. St. John, governor of Kansas, June 17, 1879, in Dick's The Sod-House Frontier.

> Dis Dixie's land what I was born in;
> Tain't no place for raisin' corn in;
>   Away! Away! Away! Dixie land!
> Den I wished I was in Kansas
>   Away! Away!

> Wid Gideon's hand in Kansas land,
> To lib and die in Kansas—
>   Away! Away! Away up norf in Kansas.

Song sung by the Exodusters, black Southerners migrating to Kansas; in the Daily Picayune *(New Orleans), August 16, 1879.*

Cheyenne was a frontier town of perhaps 15,000 people. The capital of Wyoming Territory, it had two railroads, one leading south to Denver and the Union Pacific running east and west from Ogden, Utah, to Omaha, Nebraska. After five months of rough life on the trail, we Texas cowboys, deprived as we had been of all the conveniences and comforts of civilization, were a picturesque squad as we rode into Cheyenne. Our neglected and dilapidated clothes were worn and patched, our hair was uncut, and our faces unshaven. We presented no particularly novel sight to the natives, however, as they were accustomed to the arrival of travel-worn cowboys.

John Baylis Fletcher, Texas trail driver, August 1879, in Up the Trail in '79 *(1968).*

The Indians seem to consider the advance of the troops as a declaration of war. In this I am laboring to undeceive them, and at the same time to convince them they cannot do whatever they please. The first object now is to allay apprehension.

Nathan Meeker, Indian Agent, to Major Thomas Thornburgh, on the Ute uprising in Colorado, dispatch of September 27, 1879 in Sprague's Massacre: The Tragedy at White River *(1957).*

What you see here to-day is the result of five years battling of civilization against primitive nature . . . The war-whoop of the savage has been supplanted by the shrill whistle of the locomotive, and in place of the buffalo we have the Alderney, the Devon, the Durham and the Texas steer. Here, midway between the two oceans, and under the shadow of the greatest mountain range, every true Kansan expects to build up a civilization that shall at once be the surprise and wonder of the nineteenth century.

Henry Booth, Kansas settler, to President Rutherford B. Hayes and government officials, speech of October 2, 1879, in Miner's West of Wichita *(1986).*

It is too soon by half a century to repeat to these civilized Indians: "Go West." There is room in Nebraska for half a million farmers. There is a tract in Dakota about the size of Indiana, yet unappropriated, with a climate suitable for Northern people, and a most prolific soil. When these are filled, and our population really begins to feel crowded, it will be time enough to trouble the Indians. But with Kansas on one side and Texas on the other offering millions of acres of good land, it seems as if thousands are half crazy to get into the Indian Territory [present-day Oklahoma] just because it is forbidden.

J.H. Beadle, Cincinnati Commercial *correspondent, 1870s, in Morgan and Strickland's* Oklahoma Memories *(1981).*

These lands lie west of the five civilized tribes, so called, and their northern boundary is about ninety miles south of the Kansas line. These lands are among the richest in the world. Public attention is being called to them and my opinion is that, if Congress shall fail to make suitable provision for the opening of the Territory within a very short time, the people will take the matter into their own hands and go down there and occupy and cultivate those lands.

T.C. Sears, attorney for the Missouri, Kansas, and Texas Railroad Company, 1879, in Thoburn and Wright's Oklahoma, A History of the State and Its People *(1929).*

10. The Closing Frontier: 1880–1897

CATTLE COUNTRY

By 1880 the cattle industry was firmly established throughout the Great Plains. Herds of longhorns, grazing under the watchful eyes of hardy cowboys, could be seen in lower Texas; in the Panhandle country along the Pecos Valley of New Mexico; on the dry plains of the Indian Territory; among the rolling Prairie of western Kansas and Nebraska; scattered throughout the high grasslands of eastern Colorado and Wyoming; and across the northern Plains of Montana and Dakota. Adventurous cattlemen had created a new empire—the Cattle Kingdom of the West.

The potential for enormous profits attracted entrepreneurs from the East as well as from Europe. The land was free, millions of acres of it, and most of it was rich with prairie grass. Cattle to stock the range was cheap; longhorns could be purchased in Texas at $7 or $8 a head, then driven north to the nearest railroad junction to fetch a price of from $50 to $60 for each healthy steer. After a few years of working and living on the range any resourceful pioneer could turn a modest investment into a considerable fortune.

As more and more ranchers moved onto the Great Plains a system of frontier law and order was needed. How could each rancher keep his cattle separate from those of his neighbors? How could newcomers be prevented from overcrowding the range? The ranchers developed a system of rules that permitted the expansion to continue with relatively little disorder.

Even though the ranchers did not legally own all the land on their ranges, they worked out a system of "range rights" and imaginary "range lines." Cattle were permitted to drift from ranch to ranch in their search for better pastures, and eventually steers from several owners intermingled, until the "roundup." Each spring and fall, a roundup was held to separate mixed herds and identify newborn calves.

In the roundup, cowboys fanned out over the range, driving the cattle toward one camp, until a herd of several thousand was assembled.

271

Cow hands killing sheep. Courtesy of the New York Public Library.

Riders from the ranches then skillfully rode through the herd and singled out the animals bearing their employer's brand, thereby separating the herds.

The symbol of the Cattle Kingdom—the cowboy—actually had only a brief career. By the early 1880s the days of the open range were coming to an end. Markets for beef were expanding as the railroads pushed into the Great Plains and as steamships made it easier to ship beef to Europe. Exaggerated accounts of fortunes to be had by simply raising cattle on free government land began to circulate throughout the East, and eastern farmers and factory workers boarded jam-packed trains for the new El Dorado.

Investors formed corporations, hired a few experienced ranchers and began to raise cattle on government land. English and Scottish investors also poured their money into corporations to compete with American companies for range rights and cattle.

By 1885 experienced cattlemen realized that the prosperity could last only as long as favorable weather conditions continued. A hot and dry summer, with withering grass and dried up streams, could result in an insufficiently fattened herd; and a cold, blustery winter could destroy thousands of steer. In order to ensure themselves against hard times, some ranchers fenced their ranges to protect their own pastures from intruding cattle. The growing uncertainty among ranchers resulted in the stock-breeder associations, cooperative organizations that kept intruders out of the ranges, supervised roundups, pursued rustlers, battled prairie fires and protected the brands of members. Livestock associations had spread across the Great Plains by the mid-1880s, representing the cattlemen's interest in self-government and their fear of an overcrowded range.

The cattle boom was diminishing by the mid-1880s as profits were spent on fencing, dues to livestock associations and rising costs of young cattle. Some experienced ranchers sold their herds rather than risk wintering cattle on the overcrowded range. The resulting oversupply drove beef prices downward. Adding to the cowman's difficulties was a presidential order in August 1885 that forced stockmen who had leased lands in the Indian Territory to leave that region.

The open range was also being threatened by the appearance of two groups; the sheepherder and the pioneer farmer. During the 1870s, sheepherders from the Ohio Valley, seeking new gazing grounds where fodder was less expensive, moved into California, New Mexico and Wyoming. By 1881, they had invaded the Plains country. Cattle ranchers claimed that the sheep ruined the grass by close cropping, and thereby reduced the carrying capacity of the range. Open warfare erupted between cowboys and sheepherders along the western border of the cow country. Shootouts became commonplace, accounting for 20 deaths and 100 injuries along the Wyoming-Colorado range alone. Hundreds of thousands of sheep were either killed at gunpoint or driven over cliffs. But sheep raising became such a profitable business that force could not hold it back. Even some ranchers switched to raising bleating "woolies" after they learned that sheep could be raised with less effort and realize double the profit of steers.

The pioneer farmers posed an even greater threat than the sheepherders. Their advance onto the Great Plains narrowed down the area where the range cattle business could operate. For the farmer, the open range, where range rights and customs held sway, did not exist. The range was merely the public domain where a poor homesteader could have a quarter-section of land and a home. There was constant feuding between the gun-toting cowboy and the farmer, who began fencing the land with barbed wire, blocking trails and access to waterholes. The barbed wire fence was shrinking the open range and putting an end to the cowboy's way of life.

The Cattle Kingdom began to collapse in the winter of 1886–87. In November 1886, heavy snow blanketed the northern Plains, and starving animals were unable to paw down to the grass. In January 1887, the worst blizzard ever experienced by ranchers spread across the West from Dakota to Texas. As temperatures dipped down to 68 degrees below zero, thousands of cattle died. When the spring finally arrived cattlemen witnessed a sight they would never forget. In every ravine there was carcass piled upon carcass, dead steers along the fences, and trees stripped of their bark.

With the winter of 1886–87 the days of raising cattle on the open range came to a close. A few small ranchers struggled on, but the large livestock corporations were unable to overcome the difficulties. With creditors at their door, they dumped steers on the market so quickly that steers worth $30 a year before went begging at $8 or $10 each.

In the future, the size of the herds would have to be matched carefully to the available grass supply. As this was impossible on the open range, the solution was for each rancher to fence his lands, keep his herds at a reasonable size and ensure adequate winter fodder by growing hay. Instead of cowboys herding cattle across the Great Plains, they now spent their days digging postholes, repairing fences and haying. The romantic image of the open range was over. The West was becoming a land of fenced-in pastures, where cattle were carefully bred and raised.

By 1883 the Northern Pacific Railroad had completed its northern, transcontinental route between Duluth, Minnesota, and Portland, Oregon. With easy transportation available, settlers pushed across the northern plains into the Dakotas. During the height of the "Dakota Boom" of 1878–85 settlers came by the thousands from the Mississippi Valley and from Europe. Eager homesteaders arrived every week, jamming the government land offices. Settlement was so rapid that by 1885 all Dakota Territory east of the Missouri River was settled and the population reached 550,000—a 400% increase over 1880.

As the tracks of the Northern Pacific entered Montana Territory in 1881, settlers began to drift toward the region, laying out such towns as Glendive and Billings and starting farms across the Yellowstone Valley. They began arriving during the 1870s, attracted by the prospect of feeding the permanent mining population in Butte and other mountain towns. By the end of the 1880s Montana had gained 100,000 settlers.

THE OKLAHOMA LAND RUSH

As the frontier swept across the northwestern plains, another group of pioneers was moving into the Southwest. Early interest in opening the Indian Territory, present-day Oklahoma, was expressed by the railroads that crossed the region or planned to build there, such as the Atlantic and Pacific and the Atchison, Topeka and Santa Fe. In 1874, railroad officials petitioned Congress to open some of the Indian lands, but Washington would act only when the requests were supported by popular demand.

Elias C. Boudinot, a disgruntled Cherokee who had broken with his tribe and who was working as a clerk in the nation's capital, became the railroad's first spokesman for opening up the Indian Territory. After receiving several financial favors from the Missouri, Kansas and Texas Railroad, Boudinot published an article in the *Chicago Times* during spring 1879, declaring that the Indian country belonged to no particular tribe and was really part of the public domain. Although Boudinot's statements were exaggerated, there did exist 2,000,000 acres of good land that had been ceded to the United States by the Creeks and Seminole but was yet unassigned to any tribe.

During summer 1879, Kansas pioneers talked glowingly about the fertile lands in the "Oklahoma District." Small groups of eager homesteaders slipped across the borders of the Indian Territory and staked out their claims. Federal troops tried to slow the invasion by setting up barricades along the Kansas border, but the barrier was ineffective at keeping out determined frontiersmen who wanted to settle in this unclaimed territory.

In 1880, the "Boomers" found their leader, David L. Payne. Payne was an Indian fighter, an unsuccessful homesteader and a drifter who had been dismissed from his job as an assistant doorkeeper at the House of Representatives. In May 1880, Payne led a small party of "Boomers" into the district. When they were discovered by federal troops, they were escorted back to the border. Payne was not discouraged, and during the next two years he played a game of hide-and-seek along the Kansas border with the federal troops. By 1883 Payne had rallied 40,000 Kansas homeseekers into forming a compact society—the Oklahoma Colony. The organization included a set of officers, including Payne as president, and its members took an oath binding them to defy the government until the Oklahoma District was theirs.

The early invasions of the Indian Territory paved the way for an organized campaign to open the territory to settlement. In the spring of 1884, Payne led 500 to 600 heavily armed members across the Kansas border into the Indian Territory, publicly proclaiming that he and his followers intended to shoot it out with soldiers if they tried to remove them. Most of the invaders were soon persuaded to return to Kansas by federal troops. Only Payne and a few followers remained, and they were arrested and escorted to Fort Smith for trial.

Payne was charged with conspiring against the United States in an attempt to settle on public domain land. However, in November 1884, Judge C.G. Foster, ruled that the charges did not demonstrate a conspiracy against the government, and Payne was acquitted. Judge Foster's decision was a triumph for the Boomers. Payne returned to Kansas and was welcomed by a parade of Boomers carrying banners declaring "On to Oklahoma" and "We Go This Time to Stay."

When Payne died from diphtheria in late November he was succeeded by one of his lieutenants, W.L. Couch. In winter 1885, Couch led bands of "Boomers" into the Indian Territory. When their camps were discovered by federal troops, Couch refused to leave and told the commander that his followers were determined to fight for the land. A bloody confrontation was avoided, however, when the "Boomers," unable to get supplies from Kansas, were forced to give up their claims.

During the next three years Couch led group after group into present-day Oklahoma at every opportunity, while in Washington western congressmen, railroad lobbyists and Boomer representatives urged the Indian Office to open the two unoccupied portions of the Indian Territory—the Oklahoma District and the Cherokee Outlet. In January 1889, the Creeks and Seminole were forced to cede their rights to the Oklahoma District in return for a payment of $4,193,799. Two months later Congress officially opened the district to settlers under the Homestead Act. President Benjamin Harrison, on March 23, 1889, announced the Oklahoma District would be thrown open at noon on April 22.

Between March 23 and April 22, 1889, from all over the West the homeless, the speculators and the adventurous flocked toward the still forbidden land. On the morning of April 22 nearly 100,000 people surrounded the Oklahoma District. Horsemen, wagons, bicycles and even men pushing their possessions in wheelbarrows, stretched for miles around, awaiting the signal. Troops were stationed at regular intervals to hold back "Sooners" unwilling to wait for the deadline.

The minutes slowly ticked away toward the zero hour, as officers synchronized their watches and prepared to fire their pistols in the air as the signal for the official opening of the Oklahoma District. At long last the moment arrived, gunshots blasted from the revolvers and pandemonium broke out. Within a few hours the 1,920,000 acres of the Oklahoma District were settled. "Boomers" labored everywhere to erect shelters to establish their homestead claims, while less successful ones wandered around seeking some overlooked spot. By dusk Oklahoma City had a population of 10,000 tent dwellings and Guthrie nearly 15,000.

Under increasing pressure from the homesteaders, Congress created the Oklahoma Territory on May 2, 1890. Soon further demands were made to open still more Indian lands for settlement. The Dawes Commission negotiated with various tribes for dissolving their titles in return for grants in severalty of approximately 160 acres for each man, woman and child. Under the Dawes Severalty Act, also known as the General Allotment Act, the lands assigned to the Indians could be sold only after 25 years (in order to prevent them from immediately selling their holdings). However, reservation lands remaining after the division were to be sold by the government, with profits held by the Treasury as a trust fund for Indian development programs. Although the Dawes Act had good intentions, its ultimate goal was to appropriate the land from the Indians and absorb the whole Oklahoma Territory into one state. It opened up millions of acres for homesteading and resulted in the greatest "run" of its kind in history. In 1893, the Cherokee Strip in north-central Oklahoma was opened, along with the Tonkawa and Pawnee reservations, a total of six million acres. At noon on September 16, a dramatic rush by homeseekers occurred that paralleled the Boomer invasion of 1889.

THE POPULIST MOVEMENT

Between 1887 and 1893 farmers in Kansas, Nebraska and the Dakotas were hit with a devastating drought that drove down prices and caused many farmers to abandon their homesteads. Some joined the land rush in Oklahoma, while others packed up their covered wagons and retreated back East, proclaiming "In God We Trusted, in Kansas We Busted." Thousands of western Kansas farmers moved out between 1888 and 1892. Farmers with larger stakes in lands and improvements were unable to leave, and many remained on overmortgaged farms, going deeper into debt each year and ultimately rising up in the agrarian revolt of the 1890s, as we shall see below.

These hard times coincided with the shocking realization that the frontier had become populated more rapidly than anyone had predicted. With the settlement of the Indian Territory, every parcel of land between the Atlantic and the Pacific was organized into the federal system. The superintendent of the census reported in 1890 that his department could no longer draw a line marking the frontier. The only unsettled wilderness regions remained in Alaska.

Emigrants entering the Loup Valley, Custer County, Nebraska, 1886. Courtesy of the New York Public Library.

Reformers cried for solutions to the nation's economic troubles, especially throughout the farming frontier. The farmer realized his hard times were not, as he once believed, caused by the railroads or grain elevator operators, but by the nation's financial structure. He was encouraged to borrow money for expansion during boom times; now he desparately needed cash and none was forthcoming. A rousing Populist orator, Mary Elizabeth Lease, best represented the plight of the farmer in her speeches throughout the state of Kansas during the presidential election of 1890: "Let the bloodhounds of money who have dogged us thus far beware. What you farmers need is to raise less corn and more hell."

Eastern banks had closed their doors to western farmers as the nation was faced with a depressed economy, and farmers were forced to borrow from usurers at 20% to 40% interest, with their crops taken as payment. Many were unable to keep up the payments and were faced with foreclosure. There was also an alarming increase in farm tenancy. By 1890, one-quarter of the farmers of Kansas were either tenants or sharecroppers. Although the Westerner was unfamiliar with the complexities of finance, it was apparent that the root of the problem was in the nation's monetary system. More money was needed in circulation to raise the falling prices of farm goods and to relieve the mortgage load of western farmers.

In the 1890 elections, the People's Party, better known as the Populists, concentrated their efforts on freeing the farmers of their crushing debts and making money available to them. The new party did not win a single state, but in four—Kansas, Nebraska, South Dakota and Minnesota—it did show itself a powerful force to be reckoned with.

In 1892, the Populists held their first presidential convention in Omaha, Nebraska. Among the planks on the party's platform were demands for the unlimited coinage of silver, and the abolition of land holdings held by "railroads and other corporations in excess of their actual needs." The "Omaha Platform" promised to end the economic woes of the West and to usher in justice, equality and prosperity for common people throughout the nation.

The Populist presidential candidate, James B. Weaver, attracted about one million votes as compared with the approximately five million each for Grover Cleveland and Benjamin Harrison. Most of Weaver's support came as expected from the South and the West. The Populists had no expectation of winning the presidency, but a million votes represented a triumphant success for the new party. They expected their movement to continue to grow, and a national victory in 1896 seemed possible.

During the next four years the nation's economic condition continued to decline. A run to convert silver certificates into gold developed, and shortly after Grover Cleveland became president in 1893, the nation's gold reserve slipped below the $100,000,000 mark. A panic

Homesteaders in Custer County, Nebraska, 1888. Courtesy of the New York Public Library.

swept across the country. Banks closed their doors, railroads went into the hands of receivers, factories shut down and creditors foreclosed mortgages. For the farmer, the panic of 1893 meant prices would slide even lower.

Throughout the West there were calls for restoring the unlimited coinage of silver. Westerners declared that "silver was the money of the people and gold the money of the rich." Defenders of the gold standard were equally vehement. They contended that the government purchases and coining of silver (authorized by the Sherman Silver Purchase Act of 1890) had undermined the gold standard, and if bimetallism were allowed to continue, the United States would find itself isolated from the European financial centers. Although gold was the accepted international form of payment, the Sherman Act mandated that the government pay for silver in certificates that could be redeemed in either silver or gold. Advocates of the gold standard cried that the schemes of ignorant farmers and Populist politicians would destroy the credit of the United States and throw the nation's banks and businesses into further turmoil.

The silverites were convinced that they faced a conspiracy waged by the industrialists and bankers of the East. In Congress, "the battle of the standards" divided along sectional lines. President Cleveland, being a sound money man, felt if the government did not pay its obligations in gold, faith in its solvency would be shaken. He ignored the West, and in a special session of Congress he used his personal influence to win support for repealing the Sherman Silver Purchase Act. Consequently, Cleveland divided his party, the Democrats, along sectional lines. After 1893, western Democrats and Republicans rallied for free silver as much as the Populists, and Easterners from both parties supported the gold standard.

At the 1896 Democratic convention in Chicago, William Jennings Bryan, a young Populist leader from Nebraska, chastised the Republicans in his magnificent "Cross of Gold" speech: "If they dare to come out in the open field and defend the gold standard as a good thing, we will fight them to the uttermost. Having behind us the producing masses of the nation and the world, supported by the commercial interests, the laboring interests, and the toilers everywhere, we will answer their demand for a gold standard by saying to them: You shall not press down upon the brow of labor this crown of thorns, you shall not crucify mankind upon a cross of gold." The Democrats adopted the silver plank and enthusiastically nominated the "boy orator of the Platte" as their presidential candidate.

The "Battle of the Standards"—silver and gold—was one of the most bitterly contested elections in American history. Bryan crisscrossed the nation, traveling over 13,000 miles, visiting two-thirds of the states and delivering 400 rousing speeches. But Bryan's one-issue campaign faced insurmountable obstacles. There was confusion within his own party resulting from the nomination of separate vice presidential candidates by the Populists and Democrats. The Republicans had superior financial resources, and they skillfully used the nation's newspapers to win support for their candidate, William McKinley.

The Republicans won a decisive victory, with a majority of 600,000 popular votes, and 271 electoral votes versus 176 for Bryan. McKinley did well with the urban vote in the Northeast, previously Democratic, and among prosperous farmers in the Midwest. Bryan carried all of the West except Minnesota, Iowa, North Dakota, California and Oregon, and won most of the South.

With Bryan's defeat, the West was in despair. But two unexpected gold discoveries resulted in loosening currency restrictions and helped return the nation to prosperity. One find was in Colorado, at Cripple Creek, on the southwestern slopes of Pikes Peak; the other, on the Klondike River of Canada, near Alaska.

In 1897, when miners returned from the North to the docks of San Francisco and Seattle they told of spectacular finds: Some had returns of $100,000 or more each. During the next three years thousands of prospectors descended upon the Klondike area, but the vast majority, as in previous gold rushes, were greeted with hard work and few rewards. However, many who did not strike it rich chose to settle in Washington, the nation's most northwestern state. The Alaskan traffic also turned Seattle into the Pacific Northwest's most populous city.

DEFINING THE FRONTIER

As the frontier disappeared during the last years of the nineteenth century, historians began to consider the importance of the West in American history. At a meeting of the American Historical Association held at the Chicago World's Fair in July 1893, a young history professor from the University of Wisconsin, Frederick Jackson Turner, read a paper entitled "The Significance of the Frontier in American History." Turner declared that "the existence of an area of free land, its continuous recession, and the advance of American settlement westward, explain American development." He identified a series of successive kinds of frontiers: the trader's frontier, the miner's frontier, the rancher's frontier and, finally, the farmer's frontier—each paving the way for the one to follow.

Out of this wave of settlement emerged a unique American character and experiment in democracy, making it different from every other nation. Turner stated, "The true point of view in the history of this nation is not the Atlantic Coast, it is the Great West." He pointed to certain characteristics of the frontier: democracy, individualism, freedom, optimism, ingenuity and exuberance. Most of all the frontier promoted "the composite nationality" of the American people.

Turner's "frontier thesis" has received as much acclaim as it has criticism. Critics have pointed to his interchangeable use of "frontier" and "the West." At times Turner refers to the frontier as a line, an area, and at others, as a state of mind. Turner also focuses primarily on the pioneer farmer, neglecting the land speculator, the miner, the Indian and other Westerners. Turner describes the westward march as a desire for liberty, but most emigrants left the East for economic opportunities and merely to settle in less congested areas.

Turner's thesis continues to encourage debate among historians about the nature of the frontier experience and westward expansion. In some cases the criticism raises important doubts about generalizations once accepted without question. However, there is no disagreement that the nation's expansion over nearly 3,000 miles of wilderness has left an indelible mark on American history and on the American character.

CHRONICLE OF EVENTS

1880:

February 12: President Hayes issues a warning to illegal settlers who have been stealing lands in Indian Territory.

March 4: James A. Garfield is inaugurated as the 20th president of the United States.

March 8: A second transcontinental railroad line is completed when the Southern Pacific joins the Atchison, Topeka and Santa Fe Railroad at Deming in New Mexico Territory.

1881:

Helen Hunt Jackson publishes *A Century of Dishonor,* an account of the atrocities committed against Indian tribes in the West.

July 19: Sitting Bull, the Sioux chief, returns from Canada after a four-year exile. He surrenders at Fort Buford, Dakota Territory.

September 20: Vice President Chester A. Arthur is sworn in as the 21st president of the United States. James Garfield has died after being wounded by a deranged office-seeker on July 2.

1882–1883:

The Apaches of Arizona and New Mexico rebel at reservation life and go on the warpath. General George Crook persuades most of the Indians to return to their reservations, but one group, led by Chief Geronimo, flees into Mexico.

1883:

The Cherokee Strip Live Stock Association is formed by cattlemen at Caldwell, Kansas. A five-year lease at $100,000 per year is negotiated with the Cherokee Nation for exclusive use of 6,500,000 acres of the Cherokee Outlet in Indian Territory.

May: General Crook leads his forces into Mexico in pursuit of Geronimo. The Apaches and Geronimo surrender and are taken back to the reservation.

September 6: A northern transcontinental railroad line is completed between Duluth, Minnesota, and Portland, Oregon, with the Northern Pacific Railroad driving the traditional golden spike at Independence Creek, 60 miles west of Helena, Montana Territory.

1884:

The land boom in Dakota Territory reaches its height with 11,082,818 acres filed for claims under public land laws, representing 40% of all land disposed by the Federal Government in 1884.

1885:

January 30: Henry M. Teller, the secretary of the interior, recommends the opening of Indian lands in the Indian Territory to Homesteaders.

February 25: An act of Congress prohibits the fencing of public lands in the West.

March 4: Grover Cleveland is inaugurated the 22nd president of the United States.

May 17: One-hundred Apaches led by Geronimo flee their reservation at San Carlos in Arizona Territory and head for Mexico. Panic sweeps across the area and newspaper editorials and citizens call for the dispatch of federal troops.

1886:

April 12: General Nelson Miles succeeds General George Crook in commanding the Department of Arizona. Crook has resigned after the War Department refused to honor his promise to Geronimo that, upon the chief's surrender, he would be permitted to return to the reservation in Arizona.

September 4: Apaches led by Geronimo return from Mexico to Arizona Territory. Geronimo and the Apache leaders surrender to General Nelson Miles and are sent into exile at Fort Marion, Florida, where they will remain until 1894.

November: A devastating winter storm sweeps across the Great Plains from the Canadian bor-

Geronimo. Courtesy of the New York Public Library.

der to Texas. Snow continues to fall throughout the winter, freezing cattle and burying their grasslands. Entire herds die when temperatures plunge to 50° below zero. Some ranchers lose 75% of their livestock. The severe winter ends the cattle boom and the open-range method of raising cattle.

1887:

California experiences a deluge of immigrants as a result of a rate war between the Atchison, Topeka, and Santa Fe Railroad and the Southern Pacific Railroad. More than 200,000 people arrive in California by rail.

February 8: President Cleveland signs the Dawes Severalty Act. It gives the president the authority to divide the lands of any tribe, giving each head of a family 160 acres, 80 acres for single persons and 40 acres for minors. The plots are held in trust by the federal government for 25 years. After this period, full own-ership will be transferred and U.S. citizenship granted.

1889:

February 22: President Cleveland signs the Omnibus Bill, providing for the admission of North Dakota, South Dakota, Montana and Washington to the Union.

March 2: Congress authorizes transfer of the Unassigned Lands in Indian Territory to the public domain.

March 4: Benjamin Harrison is inaugurated as the 23rd president of the United States.

March 23: President Harrison announces that the part of Indian Territory known as Oklahoma will be opened for settlement on April 22.

April 22: Thousands of eager settlers crowd the borders of the Unassigned Lands in central Indian Territory, waiting for the 12 noon signal to rush in and stake their claims. The 1,920,000 acres had formerly belonged to the Seminole and Creek tribes, but have been purchased by the federal government for $4 million.

April 23: Every available homestead lot has been claimed in the newly opened Oklahoma Territory. Oklahoma City has an instant population of 10,000.

November 2: North Dakota and South Dakota are admitted to the Union as separate states.

November 8: Montana is admitted to the Union.

November 11: Washington is admitted to the Union.

November 17: The Union Pacific Railroad commences daily service to the Pacific Coast between Chicago and Portland, Oregon, and between Chicago and San Francisco.

1890:

February 11: President Harrison opens to white settlement about one-third of the Great Sioux Reservation of 22 million acres. The reservation stretches from the Missouri River on the east to the Black Hills on the west, and from the Nebraska border almost as far north as Bismarck, North Dakota.

May 2: Congress enacts the Oklahoma Organic Act, establishing territorial government for the area formerly known as Indian Territory. The so-called "No Man's Land" is also attached to the territory and becomes the Oklahoma panhandle.

July 3: Idaho is admitted to the Union.

July 10: President Harrison signs an act granting statehood to Wyoming. Women retain the right to vote, thus Wyoming becomes the first state in the nation to have women's suffrage.

October 1: Yosemite National Park in California is created by an act of Congress.

December 15: Sitting Bull is arrested and killed by army troops at his home in South Dakota. Federal officials had called for his arrest after he encouraged what they called the "Ghost Dance craze." In response to the killing of Sitting Bull, hundreds of Sioux flee their reservations in South Dakota.

December 29: In the battle of Wounded Knee Creek, South Dakota, 350 Sioux, led by Chief Big Foot, are ordered to surrender all of their weapons. When a shot is fired, the Seventh Cavalry opens fire upon the Sioux with rapid-firing Hotchkiss guns. Nearly 300 Sioux are killed, including Chief Big Foot, and 25 troops are dead and 39 wounded. This is the last major engagement between Indians and U.S. soldiers in American history.

1891:

January 14: General Nelson Miles, commander of the U.S. troops at the Wounded Knee massacre, announces that the Sioux are finally returning to their reservations.

January 28: Thousands of Oklahoma homesteaders illegally occupy sections of the so-called Cherokee Strip, land set aside for Indians, after a rumor circulates that the area is open for settlement.

May 19: The People's Party, which will become known as the Populist Party, is founded at a convention in Cincinnati, Ohio, by representatives of various farm, labor and reform groups.

September 22: President Harrison opens another 900,000 acres of Indian land in Oklahoma for settlement.

1892:

April 3–9: In Johnson County, Wyoming, a group of cattlemen raid small ranchers who they believe are stealing their cattle. Federal troops arrive to put an end to the Johnson County War.

October 15: President Harrison opens 1,800,000 acres of Crow Indian land in Montana for settlement.

1893:

Congress establishes the Dawes Commission to find ways of reorganizing the Indian Territory.

June 27: Silver hits an all-time low of 77 cents per ounce, plunging the stock market into a collapse, and resulting in a nationwide depression.

September 16: The greatest opening of Western Indian lands, the 6,500,000-acre Cherokee Strip, in north-central Oklahoma, and the Tonkawa and Pawnee reservations are opened to homesteaders. Nearly 50,000 people claim land on the first day.

November 7: Colorado adopts women's suffrage by popular vote.

1894:

June 21: William Jennings Bryan, a U.S. congressman from Nebraska, bursts on the national scene after delivering a speech to 1,000 delegates at a Democratic Silver convention in Omaha. His platform proposes a simple solution to the nation's economic problems—free coinage of silver.

August 18: Congress passes the Carey Land Act, calling for the federal government to give each state up to one million acres of public land if the state will irrigate them.

1895:

February 27: After experiencing a severe drought, Nebraska farmers are selling their horses for as little as 25 cents each, and hay is going for $2 a ton. The state of Nebraska requests a loan of $1,500,000 from the federal government to help 100,000 desperate farmers.

1896:

July 7: At the Democratic convention in Chicago, Populist William Jennings Bryan is nominated as the party's presidential candidate.
August 12: Gold is discovered near Klondike Creek in northwestern Canada, near Alaska.
November 3: William McKinley is elected president, with 7,104,799 votes to Bryan's 6,502,925.

1897:

April 28: The Dawes Commission reaches an agreement with the Choctaw and Chickasaw nations, dissolving tribal government and dividing common lands into 40-acre homesteads.
June 16: The Hawaiian government and U.S. Secretary of State John Sherman sign a Treaty of Annexation. Submitted to the U.S. Senate, the treaty does not get enough votes to go into effect.
July 14: The gold find in the Klondike is confirmed with the arrival in San Francisco of *Excelsior,* carrying $750,000 worth of gold aboard. It triggers a "gold rush" that results in 100,000 immigrants to Alaska during the next few years.

EYEWITNESS TESTIMONY

Whoopee ti yi yo, git along little dogies,
It's your misfortune, and none of my own,
Whoopee ti yi yo, git along little dogies,
For you know Wyoming will be your new home.
Cattle trail song, 1880s, in Lomax's Cowboy
Songs *(1922).*

I saw men already swarming into the land. I knew the derby hat, the smoking chimneys, the cord-binder, and the thirty-day note were upon us in a restless surge. I knew the wild riders and the vacant land were about to vanish forever . . .
Frederic Remington, illustrator and painter, on visiting the Montana range in 1880, in "A Few Words from Mr. Remington" (1905).

Although I rode sidesaddle like a lady, the double standard did not exist on the ranch. Up to the point of my actual physical limitations, I worked side by side with the men, receiving the same praise or same censure for like undertakings. I can still hear Bowlegs scoffing at me because a "longear" got away from me in the brush. What kind of brush rider was I that I couldn't keep close enough to a yearling to see which way it went?
Agnes Morley Cleaveland, cattle rancher in New Mexico Territory, 1880s, in No Life For a Lady *(1977).*

Please say to any that may wish to know that the public lands in the Indian Territory are not only open to settlement, but settled. We are here to stay; are building houses and making homes. Brought with me 153 men, all of them with good teams. Will have one thousand people here in thirty days.
David L. Payne, Oklahoma Boomer leader, to the Kansas City Times, *letter of May 3, 1880.*

It is not surprising that politicians got a military post established here, so this wonderful country could be opened and settled, for the country itself is not only beautiful, but it has an amount of game every place that is almost beyond belief. Deer are frequently seen to come down from the mountains to the creek

Wyoming cattle roundup, ca. 1891. Courtesy of the New York Public Library.

for water, an prairie chicken would come to our very tents, I fancy, if left to follow their inclinations.

Frances M.A. Roe, wife of U.S. Army officer, to her mother, from Fort Maginnis, Montana Territory, letter of October 1880, in Army Letters from an Officer's Wife *(1909).*

I, D.L. Payne, with thirteen others whose names are herewith attached, do most earnestly and solemnly protest against being removed from these lands belonging to the United States Government and thereby to the people of said government.

We protest because the lands from which we are about to be removed are free from Indian title and belong solely and exclusively to the government of the United States and in our opinion subject to settlement by the people of the United States and that they have legitimate and legal right to occupy the same. And we further protest because we made known to the officials of the United States our desire and wish and stated to them that we would at a certain time and on a certain day proceed to and move upon the said public lands; that they could at the time have made arrest, if necessary, and granted our request for a test case in which the title to the lands in question could be tested in the Federal Courts . . . And lastly we protest against being removed . . . because we are doing what our fathers have done before us—to settle upon and occupy the Public Domain.

David L. Payne, petition of May 1880, in Rister's Land Hunger: David L. Payne and the Oklahoma Boomers.

Let it be recorded that I am the last man of my people to lay down my gun.

Sitting Bull, Sioux chief, surrender speech at Fort Buford, Dakota Territory, July 19, 1881, in Vestal's Sitting Bull: Champion of the Sioux *(1957).*

Language cannot exaggerate the rapidity with which these communities are built up. You may stand ankle deep in the short grass of the uninhabited wilderness; next month a mixed train will glide over the waste and stop at some point where the railroad has decided to locate a town. Men, women, and children will jump out of the cars and their chattels will be tumbled out after them. From that moment the building begins.

Anonymous North Dakota pioneer, 1880s, in Robinson's History of North Dakota *(1966).*

Roundup No. 1 shall begin at Fort Laramie on May 23, shall proceed up the south side of Laramie river to the mouth of Sabile creek, up the Sabile to the Black hills divide, thence to the head of the Chugwater; down the Chugwater to Kelley's ranches; thence to the head of Richard's creek; down said creek to its mouth; thence to Houston's creek; thence to the Bear creeks, up said Bear creeks to their head, thence to the telegraph road, where it intersects Horse creek; thence up said Horse creek to Horse creek lakes; thence to the head of Pole creek, and down Pole creek to the telegraph road; thence across the country to Big Crow springs; thence up Big Crow creek to its head; thence across to the bend of Lone Tree creek; thence down Lone Tree creek to Charles Terry's ranch; thence to Jack Springs; thence to Box Elder.

Wyoming Stock-Growers' Association, circular of 1881, in Webb's The Great Plains *(1931).*

On the whole it seems to be a good deal easier to make a living but there are many hardships connected with the life of a pioneer, especially at first. I should like to see you and others come over, yet consider the matter twice before you leave the Fatherland and the place where your cradle stood. It is not a small matter.

Anonymous Dakota Territory immigrant, to a friend in Norway, letter of 1881, in Robinson's History of North Dakota.

It will very soon be cheaper to fence than to herd stock. The time, I believe, is not far distant when the West will supply the people of the East with beef for their tables; wool for their clothing; horses for their carriages, busses, and street railways; and gold and silver for their purses. Horse-raising and sheep-growing have proved to be successful enterprises in Wyoming and Montana, and the profits are enormous.

James S. Brisbin, cattle rancher, 1881, in The Beef Bonanza; or How to Get Rich on the Plains *(1959).*

. . . it is absolutely necessary to own a large part of your range, especially the waterfront, so as to keep out sheepmen, settlers, and other cattle owners. Sheep and cattle cannot be grazed together, and the interests should be entirely separate. Government lands, where watering places exist, are fast becoming occupied by settlers and colonies, and very soon the opportunity for locating large ranches will entirely

Harvesting on a bonanza farm. Drawing by W.A. Rogers, Harper's Weekly, *August 29, 1891. Courtesy of the Library of Congress.*

disappear. In a few years at most it will not be possible—it is scarcely so now in Colorado—to obtain a range where the cattle business can be conducted on a large scale.
David W. Sherwood, Colorado rancher, 1881, in Brisbin's The Beef Bonanza *(1959).*

The women of Denver and the state at large are earnestly urged to attend to discuss the social and political status of women with a view to organizing a society through which they may help themselves and each other to self culture and self government.
Rocky Mountain News *(Colorado Territory), notice of January 15, 1881.*

The next day the Indians submitted and pledged themselves to go quietly and at once. Mackenzie being satisfied of their good faith returned them to the charge of the Indian Commissioners, and they moved off in a day or two thereafter peaceably, but

manifesting the great grief and regret at being obliged to abandon, in this manner, the home of their tribe for so many years. The whites who had collected, in view of their removal, were so eager and so unrestrained by common decency that it was absolutely necessary to use military force to keep them off the reservation until the Indians were fairly gone.
General John Pope, on the removal of the Utes from Colorado to reservations in Utah, report of August 1881, in Hafen's Colorado and Its People *(1948).*

The steers and strong cows in the lead would string out about a mile, with the "drags" always bringing up the rear. In a few days, as we were passing north of Boise City, the capital of Idaho, the boss went with the wagon into town to load it with grub. This was, as I remember it, the only town we were near enough from which to get provisions, until we arrived at South Pass City, on the continental divide, in western Wyoming. We did not see a house of any sort for weeks at a time, although occasionally we could see dust from trail herds several miles in front or behind us.

Frank Abbott, Wyoming trail driver, 1882, in Rollinson's Wyoming Cattle Trails *(1948).*

Harvesting [of wheat] begins about the middle of July, and with it everything takes on new life. Villages, which a month before were almost devoid of activity, are transformed almost by magic. The whir of the harvester and binder is heard on every side. Strangers come in such numbers that the hotels are incapable of providing sleeping rooms. I never saw such a mixture of laborers. A man who has outrun the sheriff of his county is pretty sure to be safe while the harvest lasts. The lumbermen from the camps of Minnesota and Wisconsin are enticed by the prospects for fair wages, and prospectors who failed to make their "stake" in the mines of the far west stop to earn enough to carry them back home. Hundreds come from the cities, others from colleges, and perhaps most important of all, hundreds of small farmers and homesteaders and others who would hire out for the season in order to get a small amount of cash to start farming for themselves a little further out, but within range of a market.

Anonymous North Dakota settler, January 19, 1882, in Briggs' Frontiers of the Northwest *(1940).*

The king of motors—steam—has been utilized successfully until now in every direction may be seen the ascending columns of coal smoke until our vast farming region has more the appearance of an enormous manufacturing center than a quiet, unobtrusive, unparalleled grain raising community.

Anonymous Kansas farmer, 1882, in Miner's West of Wichita *(1986).*

Less than twenty years ago it was generally supposed that only those counties bordering the Missouri in the eastern part of Nebraska, were fit for agricultural purposes, and those of the earlier settlers who took land and opened out farms west of these counties were regarded as foolhardy and unwise men. But still settlers continued to push farther west and engage in farming contrary to the gratuitous advice of those who thought they knew all about the capabilities of the state. At the present time farming has reached Lincoln county, and reports from there

are to the effect that the finest kinds of crops of wheat, oats, etc., will be harvested. As the sturdy farmer takes possession of and cultivates the soil the Great American Desert moves still farther west, and soon we may look for it to entirely disappear, and in its place—as has already occurred for hundreds of miles—find the most fertile and productive grain fields in the country.

Plum Creek Pioneer *(Nebraska), 1883, in Dick's* Conquering the Great American Desert: Nebraska *(1975).*

An Indian in his mode of warfare is more than the equal of the white man, and it would be practically impossible with white soldiers to subdue the Chiricahuas in their own haunts. The country they inhabit is larger than New England, and the roughest on the continent, and though affording no food upon which soldiers can subsist, provides the Indian with everything necessary for sustaining his life indefinitely. The agave grows luxuriantly in all their mountains, and upon this plant alone the Indians can live. They have no property . . . nor settled habitations of any kind, but roam about like coyotes, and their temporary resting places are chosen with all the experience gained by generations of warfare. The Indian knows every foot of his territory; can endure fatigue and fasting, and can live without food or water for periods that would kill the hardiest mountaineer. In fighting them we must of necessity be the pursuers, and unless surprised by sudden and unexpected attack, the advantages are all in their favor.

General George Crook, annual report of 1883, in Thrapp's General Crook and the Sierra Madre Adventure *(1972).*

I want to talk first of the causes which led me to leave the reservation . . . I was behaving well. I hadn't killed a horse or man, American or Indian . . . and I learned from the American and Apache soldiers . . . that the Americans were going to arrest me and hang me, and so I left . . . I was praying to the light and to the darkness, to God and to the sun, to let me live quietly there with my family . . . I never do wrong without cause . . . Every day I am thinking how am I to talk to you to make you believe what I say.

Geronimo, Apache chief, to General George Crook, meeting of March 1883 at Canyon de los Embudos, New Mexico, in Davis' The Truth About Geronimo *(1976).*

In 1885 cattlemen often fenced public lands and water; then homesteaders, like these Nebraskans masked against recognition, retaliated with wire cutters. Courtesy of the New York Public Library.

Everything you did on the reservation is known. There is no use for you to try and talk nonsense. I am no child. You must make up your own mind whether you will stay out on the warpath or surrender unconditionally. If you stay out, I'll keep after you and kill the last one, if it takes fifty years.

General George Crook, to Geronimo, meeting of March 26, 1883, in Britton's The Truth About Geronimo.

Cattle was never so high before. There never was a time when capital was so crazy for investment in cattle growing.

Boulder Country News and Courier (Colorado), 1883, in Peake's The Colorado Range Cattle Industry *(1937).*

The large cattleman owns no lands and makes no improvements, is opposed to the settling up of the country, is in fact a bitter enemy to the homesteader

. . . Every foot of the territory is now claimed by the large cattle companies.

Robert Walker, Wyoming Territory farmer, to Henry M. Teller, secretary of the interior, letter of March 9, 1883, in Pelzer's The Cattlemen's Frontier *(1936).*

It was now time to close the gap between the East and West. Two loaded cars, one from the East and one from the West, bore the material for the track. Each car was manned by a crew of well-trained workmen. Two well-trained horses, one at each car, drew their rails into place, bringing the West and East closer and closer until in less time than it takes to tell it the gap was closed. Villard appeared, holding aloft an old rusty spike that had been drawn from the road at the terminal near the Great Lakes. "This," he said, "is the Golden Spike! We will proceed to drive it here to commemorate the extension of the Northern Pacific from the Great Lakes to the Pacific Coast—the union of the East with the West." There was a mad scramble to "hit the spike a lick." Miss Villard, General Grant, and others tried. Rod Leggat, one of the Butte delegation, had a hammer in his hand all the time and was hitting the spikes as they were driven by the workmen. "Let General Grant drive it!" he cried, but no one will ever know who drove the Golden Spike. The engines hissed, and all was over.

George A. Bruffey, Montana farmer, at Gold Creek, Montana, September 8, 1883, in Eighty-One Years in the West *(1925).*

The West was very tolerant toward the lesser faults of human conduct. It was even willing to overlook the greater if they were not repeated. A man's past was not questioned, nor a woman's either; the present was what counted. A man could even be known as wanted by the law elsewhere, yet this was not held against him here so long as he showed a willingness to walk the straight path. Half the charm of the country for me was its broad-mindedness. I loved it from the first.

Nannie T. Alderson, Montana homesteader, 1880s, in Howard's Montana Margins *(1946).*

I hadn't needed to come to Montana to find out that a new country offered greater personal liberty than an old and settled one. I had learned this while visiting my aunt in Kansas, and it was one of the reasons why I so enjoyed my visits there. I always thought that people should be judged for their human qualities alone. However, I didn't like everybody I met out here by any means. I was struck by the number of people who thought it necessary to apologize for being in the West. With the first breath they would explain that they were, of course, out here for their health, and with the next they would tell you all about *who* they were, and how rich and important and aristocratic their connections were back East. I never had any patience with that kind of thing. I've always said there were two things you never needed to talk about—your blue blood and your religion; if you had a speck of either, it was bound to show in some other way.

Nannie Tiffany Alderson, Montana pioneer, 1880s, in A Bride Goes West *(1942).*

The matter of irrigation is an all-important one with us. Our rainfall is practically limited to one season of the year, although it may surprise us at other seasons. In amount it cannot be depended upon; it may rain too little, or, again, it may even rain too much—quien sabe?

Edith M. Nicholl, New Mexico rancher, 1880s, in Observations of a Ranchwoman in New Mexico *(1898).*

The money and lands are clutched by foul hands,
    Thus kept from the poor and the needy,
While Liberty stands in fetters and bands,
    Being outraged by officers greedy.
The Senators come—at will they may roam
    O'er a hundred square miles of plantation,
While the homeless may come, be denied a small
        home
    On the free public lands of the Nation.

William F. Gordon, Oklahoma Boomer, author of "Give Us a Home" (1884), a song dedicated to the Oklahoma Boomer cause, in Rister's Land Hunger: David L. Payne and the Oklahoma Boomers.

This is the first time I got a chance to write or to mail a letter since I got your letter at Fort Boise some five weeks back. We lay over here for two days camped on a creek a short ways from Eagle Rock so that we could get a blacksmith to shrink our tires and to make some repairs and I have been washing shirts and other clothes all morning as we did not have a chance to wash clothes so far on the trip until today.

Nate Rush, cowboy, to Josh Deane, a friend, while leading a herd across a trail in Idaho Territory, letter of August 21, 1884, in Rollinson's Wyoming Cattle Trails.

When the roundup herd was gathered, there might be several thousand, perhaps 5,000, head of all kinds of cattle. Some of the wagon bosses or their top men would then ride slowly into the herd on their best cutting horses and begin the process of separating each owner's cattle from the mixed herd. They worked easily and without talking or exciting the cattle, for to chouse up the wild cattle might start a stampede. In cutting out, the calves and their mothers were always taken first, then the steers. After the various smaller herds of different brands had been made up, they would be moved farther away from the big herd by each ranch owners' hands. Each outfit would take its "cut" back to its home range and there pick a suitable spot to brand the calves and castrate the bull calves. They would look their own cattle over at this time for ticks, screwworm, blackleg, pleuro-pneumonia, or any other disease.

Jim Heron, cowboy, 1884, on a cattle round-up in the Cherokee Outlet ("No Man's Land"), 1884, in Fifty Years on the Owl Hoot Trail *(1969).*

On the 24th [1884], we were approached by Lieut. Day, and a company of soldiers, and ordered to surrender at once, declaring he would open fire upon us if we refused. I asked by what authority he ordered us to surrender, to which he replied: "Military authority." I refused to surrender to anything but civil process. He said he didn't propose to discuss the matter but would form his line and give us five minutes to surrender or be shot down. We said we would return the fire. He then detailed five men to seize and tie me, but as the detail advanced we halted them, and after I made a little speech, he ordered his men back into line and ordered them to fire. Seeing we were determined to protect ourselves, he made the excuse that his men were freezing to death there, and that he would go to camp and allow us until morning to make up our minds.

William L. Couch, Oklahoma Boomer leader, speech of February 3, 1885, in Chapman's The Founding of Stillwater *(1948).*

The homestead and pre-emption laws, designed to secure to the actual settler lands at a reasonable price, have become agencies by which the capitalist secures large and valuable areas of public lands.

Secretary of the Interior Henry M. Teller, report of 1885, in Ellis' Henry Moore Teller: Defender of the West *(1941).*

The cowmen looks upon us the same as the Indians do the white man, driving them off their hunting grounds.

Anonymous Kansas farmer, 1885, in Miner's West of Wichita.

Cattle properly handled on the trail are kept headed toward their destination, just grazing along, not driven much. These are men at the "lead" who point them in the right direction, but hold them back so they won't get too far ahead. Then men at the "swing" or "flank" aim to keep the center moving. This makes it easier for the men at the rear or "drag," who drive the slow ones. Men generally prefer the lead because it is easily handled, but a cowhand is supposed to fit

himself in where he is needed most. On this drive it seemed that the whole bunch would stay in the lead close together. I was working the drag. Sometimes the cattle would string out three miles, and when they turned off to graze I would be an hour behind.

Oliver Nelson, cowboy, on driving a herd across the Texas Panhandle, 1885, in The Cowman's Southwest *(1953).*

To a very considerable extent foreigners of large means, and who indicate no intention whatever of becoming citizens of the United States, have purchased lands within the great range and ranch cattle area, and embarked in the cattle business. Titles to such lands have been secured, not only by individuals, but also by foreign corporations. Certain of the foreigners are titled noblemen of Europe. Some of them have brought over from Europe considerable numbers, herdsmen and other employees who sustain to them the dependent relationships which characterize the condition of peasantry on the larged landed estates of Europe. The public sentiment of this country appears to be opposed to allowing foreigners to acquire title to large tracts of land in this country.

Joseph Nimmo, chief of the Bureau of Statistics, Treasury Department, May 16, 1885, in Report in Regard to the Range and Cattle Business of the United States *(1972).*

Every step taken, every move made, every suggestion offered, everything done with reference to the Indians should be with a view of impressing upon them that this is the policy which has been permanently determined upon the Government in reference to their management. They must abandon tribal relations; they must give up their superstition; they must forsake their savage habits and learn the arts of civilization; they must learn to labor, and must learn to rear their families as white people do, and to know more of their obligations to the Government and to society.

Commissioner of Indian Affairs John D.C. Atkins, annual report of 1885, in Kinney's A Continent Lost—A Civilization Won *(1937).*

I feel just this; that every dollar of money, and every hour of effort that can be applied to each individual Indian, day and night, in season and out of season, with patience and perseverance, with kindness and charity, is not only due him in atonement for what we have inflicted upon him in the past, but is our own obligation towards him in order that we may not have him a vagabond and a pauper, without home or occupation among us in this land.

Henry L. Dawes, politician, and Indian reformer, speech to an Indian commissioners' conference, 1885, in Kinney's A Continent Lost—A Civilization Won.

I was living peacefully with my family, having plenty to eat, sleeping well, taking care of my people, and perfectly contented. I don't know where those bad stories first came from. There we were doing well and my people well. I was behaving well. I hadn't killed a horse or man, American or Indian. I don't know what was the matter with the people in charge of us. They knew this to be so, and yet they said I was a bad man and the worst man there; but what had I done? I was living peacefully there with my family under the shade of the trees, doing just what General Crook had told me I must do and trying to follow his advice. I want to know now who it was ordered me to be arrested.

Geronimo, Apache chief, 1885, in Brown's Bury My Heart at Wounded Knee *(1971).*

Early the next morning a body of irregular Mexican troops began firing into the camp, apparently under the impression that they had encountered hostile Apaches. The first attack ceased after a time, apparently the result of shouts and explanations from the American side, although the Mexicans would not reply or give any indication that they understood. Perhaps they were astonished to find they were dealing with American Government scouts instead of Geronimo's band.

Anton Mazzanovich, soldier, Sixth U.S. Cavalry, on a skirmish with Mexican troops while in pursuit of Geronimo, 1885, in Trailing Geronimo *(1926).*

. . . that the poor men who assembled on the border of the Indian Territory, with a view of locating their families on lands in that Territory, were lawless men. They were from the States of Kansas, Missouri, Arkansas, and Iowa, and to my personal knowledge a large majority of them were just as law-abiding men as this country affords. When the President of the United States ordered them to leave the Territory they left. Not only that, but I protest against this assault upon those poor people when it is known that the cattle syndicates of this country are occupying that Territory in violation of law.

Congressman James B. Weaver (Iowa) to Congress, speech of March 11, 1886, in Haynes' James Baird Weaver *(1919).*

I do not see what you can now do except to concentrate your troops at the best points and give protection to the people. Geronimo will undoubtedly enter upon other raids of murder and robbery, and as the offensive campaign against him with scouts has failed, would it not be best to take up defensive and give protection to the people and business interests of Arizona and New Mexico? The infantry might be stationed by companies on certain points requiring protection, and the cavalry patrol between them. You have in your department forty-six companies of infantry and forty companies of cavalry, and ought to be able to do a good deal with such a force.

General Philip Sheridan, to General George Crook, dispatch of April 1, 1886, in Davis' The Truth About Geronimo.

The chief object of the troops will be to capture or destroy any band of Apache Indians found in this section of the country; and to this end the most vigorous and persistent efforts will be required of all officers and soldiers until the object is accomplished.

General Nelson Miles, Fort Bowie, Arizona Territory, orders of April 20, 1886, in Personal Recollections and Observations of General Nelson A. Miles *(1896).*

By squads the hostiles came in, unsaddled and turned out their ponies to graze. Among the last to arrive was Geronimo. He laid his rifle down twenty feet away and came and shook hands, remarking my apparent bad health and asking what was the matter. The tobacco having been passed around, of which I had brought fifteen pounds on my saddle, he took a seat alongside as near as he could get, the others in a semi-circle, and announced that the whole party was there to listen to General Miles' message.

It took but a minute to say "Surrender, and you will be sent with your families to Florida, there to await the decision of the President as to your final disposition. Accept these terms or fight it out to the bitter end."

A silence of weeks seemed to fall on the party. They sat there with never a movement, regarding me intently. Finally Geronimo passed a hand across his eyes, made his hands tremble, and asked me for a drink.

Charles B. Gatewood, at Skeleton Canyon in
Arizona Territory, September 1886, in The
Truth About Geronimo.

These lands will never pass into the possession or occupancy of the Creeks and Seminoles. There is only one possible way in which this could be done, and that possible way we all know will never be accomplished. That way would be for the Creeks and Seminoles to pay to the United States the money with interest which the United States paid them in 1866. The Creeks and Seminoles have not the money which they can use for that purpose, and the United States would not receive it if they had. Looking at the matter in commonsense light, it seems that if the Creeks and Seminoles negotiate it will result in over-running the whole territory in a few years with white settlers; and if they refuse to negotiate the irrepressible conflict between the boomers and cattlemen and army will go on, to end at last in the triumph of the boomers and the settlement of the lands without the Indians having any voice in their valuation.

Elias Boudinot, Cherokee Indian and attorney,
on the opening of the Cherokee Strip, 1886, in
Thoburn and Wright's Oklahoma, A History
of the State and Its People (1929).

About the middle of November the storms began. Day after day the snow came down, thawing and then freezing and piling itself higher and higher. By January the drifts had filled the ravines and coulées almost level. The snow lay in great masses on the plateaus and river bottoms; and this lasted until the end of February. The preceding summer we had been visited by a prolonged drought, so that the short, scanty grass was already well cropped down; the snow covered what pasturage there was to the depth of several feet, and the cattle could not get at it at all, and could hardly move round. It was all but impossible to travel on horseback—except on a few well-beaten trails. It was dangerous to attempt to penetrate the Bad Lands, whose shape had been completely altered by the great white mounds and drifts. The starving cattle died by scores of thousands before their helpless owners' eyes. The bulls, the cows who were suckling calves, or who were heavy with calf, the weak cattle that had just been driven up on the trail, and the late calves suffered most; the old range animals did better, and the steers best of all; but the best was bad enough.

"Buffalo Bill" Cody. Courtesy of the New York Public Library.

Theodore Roosevelt, politician, 1886, on the
Bad Lands of Montana, in Ranch Life and
The Hunting Trail (1888).

The livestock market is at the lowest ebb and most stockmen are adverse to shipping until it shows some improvement, but the condition of the ranges does not encourage this desire to hold their cattle. The dry season has resulted in very short grass, which though exceedingly rich and nutritious, is not abundant. The fires have devastated a large amount of grazing and, as is usual, the very best of that . . .

Glendive Times (Montana), 1886, in Kennedy's Cowboys and Cattlemen (1964).

. . . more people have frozen to death this winter than for a quarter century. The cold has been intense.

Reports are coming in from the ranges of Dakota, Montana and Wyoming of the large losses of cattle owing to the scarcity of feed and insufficient protection from the severe weather. Losses already reach eight to twenty percent and it is not overdoing it to say that in event of the snow lying on the ground for four weeks longer the losses will reach from fifty to seventy-five percent.

Dakota and Burleigh Settler *(newspaper),*
February 11, 1887.

It is extremely probable that the experiences of the stockmen of western Dakota and Montana this winter will bring about a radical change in the present system of stock raising. . . The experiences from the financial stand point should teach stockmen to keep smaller herds and care for them well.

The Bismarck Weekly *(Dakota Territory),*
February 26, 1887.

The effects of this storm following the other so closely and with such severely cold weather intervening, cannot be otherwise than extremely disastrous to the livestock interests of this locality. It is useless to speculate on the percentage of loss that must occur, but it is certain that the mortality in sheep, where no provision has been made to feed them, will be very large and all but the robust and well-conditioned cattle must succumb to it . . .

The Weekly Yellowstone Journal and Live
Stock Reporter, *March 5, 1887.*

It was impossible to tell just what losses were for a long time as the cattle drifted in the big January storm. We did not get some of ours back for a year. Our entire losses were sixty-six per cent of the herd.

Granville Stuart, cattle rancher, on the severe
winter in Montana, March 19, 1887, in Kenne-
dy's Cowboys and Cattlemen.

In the territories throughout, it is safe to say that 75 per cent is not too high an estimate of losses. It is not pleasant to say that the losses are known to be large, much larger in fact than we have been willing to admit until forced by known facts.

The Daily Pioneer *(Mandan, Dakota Terri-*
tory), July 23, 1887, on cattle losses on the
range as a result of the severe winter storms.

"Oh, bury me not on the lone prair-ee"—
   These words came low and mournfully

From the pallid lips of a youth who lay
   On his dying bed at the close of day.

   "Oh, bury me not on the lone prair-ee,
   Where the wild coyotes will howl over me,
   Where the rattlesnakes hiss and the crow flies
      free;
   Oh, bury me not on the lone prair-ee."

"Oh, bury me not—" And his voice failed there;
But we took no heed of his dying prayer.
In a narrow grave just six by three
We buried him there on the lone prair-ee.

"The Dying Cowboy," popular song of the
1880s, in Lomax's Cowboy Songs *(1922).*

There must have been a great many "sooners" in the country. We saw new faces all the time. They would come and go. No one knew where they were from or their ultimate destination.

Detachments of Cavalry from Fort Reno scoured the country to round up and deport the "sooners." We at the station generally knew about when a detachment was expected. We could tell by the scramble in getting to the depot. As many as a hundred tickets to Purcell for one train was sold. Purcell was the closest place of exit from the forbidden districts. When the raid was over they filtered back.

Arthur W. Dunham, railroad agent in the Un-
assigned Lands, 1888, in the Oklahoma Histori-
cal Society's Chronicles of Oklahoma *(1924).*

Some are poor, indeed, and their garments show the effect of sun, storms and rough usage. Their unkempt hair and rough beards show a most reckless disregard of conventionalities. Their rattling old rigs and rattling piles of bones that draw them are well in keeping with their appearance. Such, however, are not all of them, for many have fine times and outfits. Some have their homes upon wheels ready to move at the word. One man camped on the South Canadian has a sawmill which he will move upon his claim.

Wichita Eagle, *on eager homesteaders ready to*
settle on the Unassigned Lands in central In-
dian Territory, present-day Oklahoma, March
22, 1889.

Not far from the depot at Oklahoma Station, two gamblers operated a Faro game in a tent. The word

was out that boomer Tom War had lost his all there—his entire sixty-five cents.
Wichita Eagle, March 22, 1889.

Boomers, boomers everywhere. The white tops of their wagons or tents appear upon every available camping ground. On all the highways leading southward are seen their wagons. Yesterday the actual number of wagons that passed down one street of Arkansas City alone was 247 and today as the time for the opening approaches the number increases. From Winfield down to Arkansas City the road lies near the railroad and salutations are almost continuously exchanged between the boomers aboard the train and the boomers in their wagons.
Wichita Eagle, on homesteaders bound for the Oklahoma Territory, April 19, 1889.

All along the line to the west as far as the eye can reach the boomers with their fast horses are ready. In the hands of most are long sticks that look like fishing rods or lances. They are peeled willow rods, pointed at one end, with the owner's name, and the words on most are "Soldier's claim." The intention is to rush their horses at their highest possible speed and as they reach the border of their land to stake their claim pole in the ground while going at full jump by a quick motion of the hand. The desirable claims will be dotted with sticks.
Chicago Tribune, April 19, 1889.

Monday, April 22d, 1889! A never to be forgotten day! More than forty thousand human beings waited in feverish anxiety on the borders of the promised land for the watchman's cry of "Noon! Twelve O'clock!" From far and near they had traveled on foot, in wagons, on horseback, and by railways. Their wanderings in the wilderness were over. Caanan lay before them resplendent and enticing. The sun rushed along his way till the center station in the heavens was reached. A wild shout ascended from forty thousand throats and it was greater by far than the glad cry that echoed across the Red Sea when the children of Israel were delivered from the hosts of Pharoh. The halted forces broke and rushed over into the land so long waited and hoped for—and lo, when the sun went down, the elysian fields, the high hills, the happy valleys, and the sylvan shades of Oklahoma—The Beautiful Land—teemed with a joyous, civilized people—who were there to build homes, carve out fortunes, achieve fame, raise families and mingle together in the sorrows and joys and vanities of this life.
Irving Geffs, itinerant preacher, April 22, 1889, in The First Eight Months of Oklahoma City *(1890).*

When the hour of noon approached, we were too far from the crowd to hear any bugle calls, nor did we have a rollicking cavalryman on one of Uncle Sam's big bays, to yank a carbine from a scabbard under his leg and fire into the air, as at the later Cherokee Strip opening, but we did stroll down to a stone having numerous notches on its four corners and one man for long years since prominent in our county, (A. Jack Hartenbower), leaned over the stone and set a stake, beyond it, saying as he did so, "Gentlemen, I take this claim for mine." The rest of us started south, not at a furious gallop, for there was little speed left in our mounts. At twenty-five minutes past one o'clock, I set my stake in a creek bottom place some miles below and the great opening for me, was over. Two of us got onto the same quarter section, but is was so plain that I was there first, that there was no trouble. My bay cow pony was soon staked out and fell to on the lush grass all about my camp fire.
James K. Hastings, Oklahoma homesteader, April 22, 1889, in the Oklahoma Historical Society's Chronicles of Oklahoma *(1949).*

After running eight or ten miles I came to a pretty valley that just suited me, and stopped by a spring under some great big trees. I had a nice, hand-painted claim stake that I put down by the spring and four little stakes, with blue flags and the edges marked with woosted, to put on the corners. My directions said to pace eight hundred paces on each side but I was afraid I could not step far enough so I only counted once in a while. In this way I got a rose bush on one corner of my claim. I had to go around a cow to stake the other corner but I staked him in on the ground too. I put the other two corners in places where I knew it would be nice to have picnics and then went back to my pony. You see by a little foresight, a person can made a farm real nice. Another claimer from Arkansas says my stakes are stuck in a semi-circle; if they are, won't it be real pretty when I have flowers set out all along the line?
Anonymous Oklahoma homesteader, April 1889, in Geffs' The First Eight Months of Oklahoma City.

People, people everywhere and the inexhaustable subject was Oklahoma, town site, Guthrie. No one thought of anything else, no one talked of anything else.

Wichita Eagle, *April 26, 1889.*

Just taking a claim did not hold it. We had to let many others, who claimed they had done the same thing, know we were first ones on the claim. Hundreds of people were passing, and we kept busy riding like the devil seeing to it that others did not stop our claims.

The creek ran through the claim I took and men came from the west side of the creek and claimed they settled there. I stopped on the east side of the claim, which was all prairie; the west side was timber. It was necessary to outtalk the other man, and if we thought he was a sooner, we told him so, and stayed with it.

Evan G. Barnard, Oklahoma homesteader, 1889, in Morgan and Strickland's Oklahoma Memories *(1981).*

The rights of citizens of the state of Wyoming to vote and hold office shall not be denied or abridged on account of sex. Both male and female citizens of this state shall equally enjoy all civil, political, and religious rights and privileges.

State of Wyoming, constitution, article IV, section I, 1889, in Hebard's The History and Government of Wyoming *(1919).*

The bill provides for capitalizing the remainder of the land for the benefit of the Indian, but the greed of the land-grabber is such to press the application of this bill to the utmost . . . There is no danger but this will come most rapidly,—too rapidly, I think,—the greed and hunger and thirst of the white man for the Indian's land is almost equal to his hunger and thirst for righteousness.

Henry L. Dawes, report of 1889 on the Dawes Severalty Act, in Otis' The Dawes Act and the Allotment of Indian Lands *(1973).*

It was a dark cold Monday morning that found us all assembled in the narrow north end of Deadwood Gulch to meet the first through train from Chicago. We gathered early on the scant platform of the little station that later grew into a freight depot. Deadwood in December is dark at eight o'clock in the morning. There was not a glint of light on the pinnacle of White Rocks rising high above the town on

the east. But people were everywhere. They crowded the platform. They lined the uneven board sidewalks and filled the rough frozen street. They covered the house tops and clambered up the side of the hill on the west. No inch of room anywhere that could command a view of the waiting track's new shining rails, but was crammed with crowds—a heterogeneous, hilarious multitude, some of whom never had seen a railroad train before. They came from Lead, Central City, Terraville, Spearfish—places that knew nothing of railroads; and from the train-wise towns of Chadron, Rapid City, and Whitewood. They came in carriages, on horseback, and on foot. The entire population of the northern Hills was there.

Estelline Bennett, pioneer, on the arrival of the Union Pacific Railroad at Deadwood, South Dakota, 1890, in Old Deadwood Days *(1928).*

Our land here is the dearest thing on earth to us. Men take up land and get rich on it, and it is very important for us Indians to keep it.

White Thunder, Sioux chief, 1890, in Brown's Bury My Heart at Wounded Knee.

The Indian of to-day is not the Indian who was in this country when the present policy was inaugurated . . . The Indian as an Indian has already disappeared in this country. He has partaken of the spirit of change. He begins himself to be uneasy. He is discontented; he is determined he will no longer stay in the places and ways of the Indian of ten years ago. He has caught the idea of selling his land. He has caught it of the white man. It has been found that the easiest way to negotiate with the Indians for a portion of their reservation is to propose to pay a part, if not all, of the purchase-money by distribution per capita among the Indians . . . It might as well have been thrown into the Pacific Ocean, for any permanent good it would bring the Indian . . .

Twenty-five years ago the Indians could not understand the idea of allotment. Now they are crazy to have allotment, because along with it comes the provision that they may sell to the government the balance of their land.

Henry L. Dawes, to an Indian commissioners' conference, on the Dawes Severalty Act, speech of 1890, in Otis' The Dawes Act and the Allotment of Indian Lands.

It has been reported here a few days ago that there was an Indian visitor up at White Swan from Rosebud agency who has been telling or teaching the doctrines of the new messiah, and has made some agitation among the people up there. According to the request of Captain Conrad, United States Army, of Fort Randall, South Dakota, and by your order of the 21st instant. I went up to White Swan and have arrested the wanted man (Kuwapi, or One they chased after).

William T. Selwyn, U.S. Indian agent, to General E.W. Foster, South Dakota, dispatch of November 22, 1890, in Mooney's The Ghost Dance Religion and the Sioux Outbreak of 1890 *(1976).*

I look upon the policy which has been pursued by the administration of Indian affairs as a crime revolting to man and God. I look upon the present outbreak or threatened outbreak—which will bring not merely the destruction of the Indians, but will bathe the snows of the Northwest crimson with the blood of our own brave soldiers and officers—as something revolting in the extreme, and that instead of sitting here debating Election bills and Force bills, and providing for the issuance of arms to the States in the Northwest, we should be hurrying, anxiously and eagerly, to provide for the feeding of these starving people.

Senator Daniel Voorhees (Indiana), to Congress, on sending troops to Pine Ridge Agency, Sioux reservation, South Dakota, speech of December 3, 1890, in Utley's The Last Days of the Sioux Nation *(1963).*

The Indians are better armed now than they ever were and their supply of horses is all that could be desired. Every buck has a Winchester rifle, and he knows how to use it. In the matter of subsistence they are taking but little risk. They can live on cattle just as well as they used to on buffalo, and the numerous horse ranches will furnish them with fresh stock, when cold and starvation ruin their mounts. The Northern Indian is hardy and can suffer a great deal. These hostiles have been starved into fighting, and they will prefer to die fighting rather than starve peaceably.

I hope the problem may be solved without bloodshed, but such a happy ending to the trouble seems impossible. An outbreak would cost the lives of a great many brave men, and the destruction of hundreds of homes in the Northwest. If peace is possible we will have it.

General Nelson Miles, on the Ghost Dance uprising at the Sioux reservation in South Dakota, dispatch of December 1, 1890, in Boyd's Recent Indian Wars *(1891).*

When we gave up the Black Hills you told us in that treaty that a man would get three pounds of beef a day. The meaning was three pounds for one man. Besides, you said we could get food just like soldiers, you did not, however, give it to us at that rate.

Great Father, we are starving, and beg you therefore, to give us just so, as you have promised.

Sioux Indians, Pine Ridge Agency, South Dakota, to President Benjamin Harrison, message of December 4, 1890, in Boyd's Recent Indian Wars.

The fight of Monday was a most desperate one, about six hundred being engaged upon both sides and a little over two hundred being wounded or killed. The terrible character of the wounds and the large number of killed is accounted for easily. Most of the troops that did the firing when the Indians broke were within twenty-five feet of them. It was expected the Indians would run, but they stood their ground, never flinching until at least fifty of their number lay upon the ground. Their courage continues to be the one topic discussed. Not since 1859 has such an Indian fight been known, fighting when it was certain death to do so. This closeness accounts for the gaping and awful wounds. These shots had almost the effect of a cannon ball.

William Fitch Kelly, correspondent of the Nebraska State Journal, on the massacre at Wounded Knee Creek, South Dakota, December 29, 1890, in Kelly's Pine Ridge, 1890 *(1971).*

Wall street owns the country. It is no longer a government of the people, for the people, by the people, but a government of Wall street, for Wall street, and by Wall street. The great common people of the country are slaves, and monopoly is the master. The West and the South are bound and prostrate before the manufacturing East.

Mary Elizabeth Lease, Populist leader, to Kansas City convention, speech of March 1891, in Clanton's Kansas Populism *(1969).*

The cattle business looked like a good one to me in 1891. Everybody you talked to was thinking about doing the same thing. It figured good on paper.

Nineteen days after U.S. troops fired into an encampment of Sioux at Wounded Knee, South Dakota, General Nelson Miles and his staff inspect the defeated tribe—January 16, 1891. The surrender of the Sioux marks the end of the American Indian wars. Courtesy of the National Archives.

Mary Elizabeth Lease. Courtesy of the Kansas State Historical Society.

Borrow money at 10 per cent, buy a few cows, and the herd will double every three years. Start with 100, three years later you have 200, then 400, 800, 1,600, 3,200, 6,400, and so on. There was lots of grass in that 11,000,000-acre pasture taken from the Sioux in 1889, and there were very few settlers. Of course, it was a hard life, with cold winters and hot summers, alkali water, and danger of Indian uprisings, but it looked mighty good to me.

Bruce Siberts, South Dakota cattle rancher,
1891, in Wyman's Nothing But Prairie and
Sky *(1970).*

I had a mortgage on my team, like all my brother farmers, of $64.50. I was given to understand that this must be paid. To borrow money was out of the question. Nothing was left for me to do but haul off corn, hogs, etc., and pay it. I went to work, hauled off my corn and hogs and sold my hay and paid it. I had made calculations and found I would have no feed, seed, or even bread and meat . . . I did not know what to do. I received a letter from my uncle in Oklahoma, stating there was plenty of work here at good wages. There was no work, as you all know, in Custer county. After taking all things in careful consideration I concluded I would come to Oklahoma where I could get work. Before reaching this conclusion it cost me many a bitter tear and sleepless night.

M.F. Blankenship, Nebraska farmer, to Custer City [Nebraska] Beacon, *letter of March 24, 1892.*

The long row towing this line is bending forward, panting with excitement, and looking with greedy eyes toward the new Canaan, the women with their dresses tucked up to their knees, the men stripped of coats and waistcoats for the race to follow. And then a trumpet call, answered by a thousand hungry yells from all along the line, and hundreds of men and women on foot and on horseback break away across the prairie.

Harper's Weekly, *on Boomers awaiting the opening of the Indian Territory, April 23, 1892.*

These pilgrims do not drop on one knee to give thanks decorously, as did Columbus according to the twenty-dollar bills, but fall on both knees and hammer stakes into the ground and pull them up again, and drive them down somewhere else at a place they hope will eventually become a corner lot facing the post-office, and drag up the next man's stake, and threaten him with a Winchester because he is on their land, which they have owned for the last three minutes.

Harper's Weekly, *on Boomers settling in the Oklahoma Territory, April 23, 1892.*

The Land, including all the natural resources of wealth, is the heritage of the people, and should not be monopolized for speculative purposes, and alien ownership of land should be prohibited. All land now held by the railroads and other corporations in excess of their actual needs, and all lands now owned by aliens, should be reclaimed by the government and held for actual settlers only.

People's Party, campaign platform, July 4, 1892, in Fine's Labor and Farm Parties in the United States: 1828–1928 *(1928).*

In God we trusted.
In Texas we busted
But let 'er rip'
We'll make 'er in the strip.

Motto on ''Boomer'' wagons, during the opening of the Cherokee Strip, August 11, 1893, in the Oklahoma Historical Society's Chronicles of Oklahoma *(1931).*

At one minute before twelve o'clock my brother and I, noticing that the soldier out in front was squinting upward along his rifle barrel and intent on the coming signal, slipped out fifty feet in front of the line, along the railroad embankment. It was the best possible place from which to view the start. It has been estimated that there were somewhere around one hundred thousand men in line on the Kansas border. Within the two-mile range of vision that we had from our point of vantage there were at least five thousand and probably nearly eight.

Viewed from out in front the waiting line was a breath-taking sight. We had seen it only from within the crowd or from the rear. The back of the line was ragged, incoherent; the front was even, smooth, solid. It *looked* like the line-up that it was. I thought I had sensed the immensity of the spectacle, but that one minute out in front gave me the unmatched thrill of an impending race with six thousand starters in sight.

Seth K. Humphry, author, on the opening of the Cherokee Strip, August 11, 1893, in Following the Prairie Frontier *(1931).*

Thousands were disappointed after all the lots had been taken, and thousands went right on through the district without stopping. That the land was totally inadequate to the demand was made evident this evening, when the northbound train went through. Every train was almost as heavily loaded as when it came in this morning, and thousands of persons who returned brought tales of as many more persons wandering around aimlessly all over the Strip, looking for what was not there. The station platforms all along the line were crowded with people who had rushed in and who were now hoping for a chance to rush out. The opening is over, the Indian land is given away, and still there are thousands of men and women in this part of the country without homes.

Anonymous correspondent, New York Tribune, *on the opening of the Cherokee Strip, September 17, 1893.*

First in regard their lands, they complain that for years the whites have been closing in on them from all sides and now although their lands are small they are pressed further and further. The whites pasture cattle and horses on their lands and the Indian can get no redress. They feel that although they are citizens they do not obtain the same rights as white citizens. Again, they are hungry and half naked.

Soon after the opening of the Cherokee Strip in Oklahoma Territory—the new town of Guthrie, 1893. Courtesy of the National Archives.

They do not get their full ration and what they do get is of inferior quality and often times not fit for dogs to eat. The issue of blankets and clothing heretofore has not been made at the beginning of the winter when needed, but in the spring. They feel they are unjustly treated in these and other ways.

Lieutenant Kirby Walker, to post adjutant, Fort Supply, on complaints by Cheyenne Indians over intruding settlers in the Oklahoma District, letter of December 6, 1893, in Carriker's Fort Supply: Indian Territory *(1970).*

Cattle and sheep ranges are held by suffrage and custom. There is now a law in the territory which prevents trespassing upon unoccupied ranges near settlements, but away from settlements the shot-gun is the only law; and sheep and cattlemen are engaged in constant warfare.

Edward D. Smith, Wyoming cattle rancher, 1893, in Briggs' Frontiers of the Northwest.

Up to and including 1880 the country had a frontier or settlement, but at present the settled area has been so broken into by isolated bodies of settlement, that there can hardly be said to be a frontier line.

Robert D. Porter, Superintendent of the Census Bureau, 1893, in Turner's The Significance of the Frontier in American History *(1894).*

. . . any woman who can stand her own company, can see the beauty of the sunset, loves growing things, and is willing to put in as much time at careful labor as she does over the washtub, will certainly succeed; will have independence, plenty to eat all the time, and a home of her own in the end.

Elinore Pruitt Stewart, homesteader, on establishing a homestead in the Cherokee Strip, 1894, in Letters of a Woman Homesteader *(1961).*

The sheepmen on the Wyoming line are talking of again attempting to range their flocks in Routt County. It is quite probable that the cattlemen of this country are as determined a set of men as are the woolgrowers, and it is not at all likely that they will permit the devastation of their ranges to proceed without interruption.

Craig Courier (Colorado), on the conflict between sheepherders and cattle ranchers, July 27, 1895.

There are two ideas of government. There are those who believe that, if you will only legislate to make the well-to-do prosperous, their prosperity will leak through on those below. The Democratic idea, however, has been that if you legislate to make the masses

William Jennings Bryan. Courtesy of the New York Public Library.

prosperous, their prosperity will find its way up through every class which rests upon them.

You come to us and tell us that the great cities are in favor of the gold standard; we reply that the great cities rest upon our broad and fertile prairies. Burn down your cities and leave our farms, and your cities will spring up again as if by magic; but destroy our farms and the grass will grow in the streets of every city in the country.

William Jennings Bryan, Populist presidential candidate, to the Chicago Democratic convention, speech of June 30, 1896, in The First Battle *(1896).*

The news that the telegraph is bringing the past few days of the wonderful things of Klondike in the land of the midnight sun has opened the flood gates, and a stream of humanity is pouring through Seattle and on to the golden Mecca of the North. It is a crowd at once strange, weird, and picturesque. Some say it eclipses anything in the days of '49. The good ship *Portland*, which recently brought a million and a half of treasure to this port, sails for Alaska tomorrow at noon. She will carry every passenger and every pound of cargo that she has the ability to transport. The *Portland* has booked for this passage fifty first class and ninety-eight second class passengers. The names of an ex-governor and a general are on the list. Fifteen hundred passengers are booked for Alaska on the overland passage. Every available streamer is full.

The Post-Intelligencer *(Seattle), August 1896, in Quiett's* They Built the West *(1965).*

The granger and the sheepmen are gradually, but no less surely, surrounding the open country. As the red man was driven to his reservation, as the buffalo disappeared, so the days of open ranging—that life of rollicking work in summer and loafing in winter—is fast approaching dissolution. The southern part of the state, outside of Custer county, has no large herds left. The farmer has taken up much of the best valley lands, and is prospering. The large and small cattlemen are getting together land so that it is now a pasture and hay proposition in winter, while there is yet a good deal of summer grazing in the open . . .

John Clay, Montana cattle rancher, in Montana Stockman and Farmer *(January 1898).*

Appendix A
List of Documents

1. Leaden Plate Setting Forth French Claims in North America, 1749

2. The Proclamation of 1763, October 7, 1763

3. Petition by Officers of the Continental Army for Western Lands, June 16, 1783

4. The Northwest Ordinance, July 13, 1787

5. Treaty of Greenville, August 3, 1795

6. Land Act of 1800, May 10, 1800

7. Treaty of Louisiana Purchase, April 30, 1803

8. The Missouri Compromise, 1819–1821

9. Land Law of 1820, April 24, 1820

10. Removal Act, May 28, 1830

11. Compromise of 1850, September 9–20, 1850

12. Treaty of Fort Laramie, September 17, 1851

13. Homestead Act, May 20, 1862

14. The Timber Culture Act, March 3, 1873

15. Opening of the Great Sioux Reservation, February 10, 1890

1. Leaden Plate Setting Forth French Claims in North America

1749

IN THE YEAR 1749 DURING THE REIGN OF LOUIS XV KING OF FRANCE WE CÉLERON COMMANDER OF A DETACHMENT SENT BY MONSIEUR THE MARQUIS DE LA GALISSONIÈRE COMMANDER IN CHIEF OF NEW FRANCE FOR THE RESTORATION OF TRANQUILLITY IN SOME VILLAGES OF INDIANS OF THESE DISTRICTS HAVE BURIED THIS PLATE AT THE CONFLUENCE OF THE OHIO AND TCHADAKOIN THIS 29 JULY NEAR THE RIVER OYO OTHERWISE BEAUTIFUL RIVER AS A MONUMENT OF THE RENEWAL OF POSSESSION WHICH WE HAVE TAKEN OF THE SAID RIVER OYO AND OF ALL THOSE THAT THEREIN FALL AND OF ALL THE LANDS ON BOTH SIDES AS FAR AS THE SOURCES OF THE SAID RIVERS IN THE SAME MANNER AS THE PRECEDING KINGS OF FRANCE ENJOYED OR HAD A RIGHT TO ENJOY THEM AND AS THEY THEREIN HAVE MAINTAINED THEMSELVES BY ARMS AND BY TREATIES ESPECIALLY BY THOSE OF RISWICK OF UTRECHT AND OF AIX-LA-CHA-PELLE

2. The Proclamation of 1763

October 7, 1763

Whereas we have taken into our royal consideration the extensive and valuable acquisitions in America secured to our Crown by the late definitive treaty of peace concluded at Paris the 10th day of February last; and being desirous that all our loving subjects, as well of our kingdom as of our colonies in America, may avail themselves, with all convenient speed, of the great benefits and advantages which must accrue therefrom to their commerce, manufactures, and navigation; we have thought fit, with the advice of our Privy Council, to issue this our Royal Proclamation, hereby to publish and declare to all our loving subjects that we have, with the advice of our said Privy Council, granted our letters patent under our Great Seal of Great Britain, to erect within the countries and islands ceded and confirmed to us by the said treaty, four distinct and separate governments, styled and called by the names of Quebec, East Florida, West Florida, and Grenada, and limited and bounded as follows, viz:

First, the government of Quebec, bounded on the Labrador coast by the river St. John, and from thence by a line drawn from the head of that river, through the lake St. John, to the South end of the lake Nipissim; from whence the said line, crossing the river St. Lawrence and the Lake Champlain in 45 degrees of North latitude, passes along the High Lands, which divide the rivers that empty themselves into the said river St. Lawrence, from those which fall into the sea; and also along the North coast of the Bayes des Chaleurs, and the coast of the Gulph of St. Lawrence to Cape Rosieres, and from thence crossing the mouth of the river St. Lawrence by the West end of the island of Anticosti, terminates at the aforesaid river St. John.

Secondly, The government of East Florida, bounded to the Westward by the Gulph of Mexico and the Apalachicola river; to the Northward, by a line drawn from that part of the said river where the Catahoochee and Flint rivers meet, to the source of St. Mary's river, and by the course of the said river to the Atlantic Ocean; and to the East and South by the Atlantic Ocean, and the Gulph of Florida, including all islands within six leagues of the sea coast.

Thirdly, The government of West Florida, bounded to the Southward by the Gulph of Mexico, including all islands within six leagues of the coast from the river Apalachicola to lake Pontchartrain; to the Westward by the said lake, the lake Maurepas, and the river Mississippi; to the Northward, by a line drawn due East from that part of the river Mississippi which lies in thirty-one degrees North latitude, to the river Apalachicola, or Catahoochee; and to the Eastward by the said river.

Fourthly, The government of Grenada, comprehending the island of that name, together with the Grenadines, and the islands of Dominico, St. Vincent, and Tobago.

And to the end that the open and free fishery of our subjects may be extended to, and carried on upon the coast of Labrador and the adjacent islands, we have thought fit . . . to put all that coast, from the river St. John's to Hudson's Streights, together with the islands of Anticosti and Madelane, and all other smaller islands lying upon the said coast, under the care and inspection of our governor of Newfoundland.

We have also . . . thought fit to annex the islands of St. John and Cape Breton, or Isle Royale, with the lesser islands adjacent thereto, to our government of Nova Scotia.

We have also . . . annexed to our province of

Georgia, all the lands lying between the rivers Atamaha and St. Mary's.

And . . . we have . . . given express power and direction to our governors of our said colonies respectively, that so soon as the state and circumstances of the said colonies will admit thereof, they shall, with the advice and consent of the members of our council, summon and call general assemblies within the said governments respectively, in such manner and form as is used and directed in those colonies and provinces in America, which are under our immediate government; and we have also given power to the said governors, with the consent of our said councils, and the representatives of the people, so to be summoned as aforesaid, to make, constitute, and ordain laws, statutes, and ordinances for the public peace, welfare, and good government of our said colonies, and of the people and inhabitants thereof, as near as may be, agreeable to the laws of England, and under such regulations and restrictions as are used in other colonies; and in the mean time, and until such assemblies can be called as aforesaid, all persons inhabiting in, or resorting to, our said colonies, may confide in our royal protection for the enjoyment of the benefit of the laws of our realm of England: for which purpose we have given power under our great seal to the governors of our said colonies respectively, to erect and constitute, with the advice of our said councils respectively, courts of judicature and public justice within our said colonies, for the hearing and determining all causes as well criminal as civil, according to law and equity, and as near as may be, agreeable to the laws of England, with liberty to all persons who may think themselves aggrieved by the sentence of such courts, in all civil cases, to appeal, under the usual limitations and restrictions, to us, in our privy council.

And whereas it is just and reasonable, and essential to our interest and the security of our colonies, that the several nations or tribes of Indians with whom we are connected, and who live under our protection, should not be molested or disturbed in the possession of such parts of our dominions and territories as, not having been ceded to or purchased by us, are reserved to them, or any of them, as their hunting-grounds; we do therefore, with the advice of our Privy Council, declare it to be our royal will and pleasure, that no Governor or commander in chief, in any of our colonies of Quebec, East Florida, or West Florida, do presume, upon any pretence whatever, to grant warrants of survey, or pass any patents for lands beyond the bounds of their respective governments, as described in their commissions; as also that no Governor or commander in chief of our other colonies or plantations in America do presume for the present, and until our further pleasure be known, to grant warrants of survey or pass patents for any lands beyond the heads or sources of any of the rivers which fall into the Atlantic Ocean from the west or northwest; or upon any lands whatever, which, not having been ceded to or purchased by us, as aforesaid, are reserved to the said Indians, or any of them.

And we do further declare it to be our royal will and pleasure, for the present as aforesaid, to reserve under our sovereignty, protection, and dominion, for the use of the said Indians, all the land and territories not included within the limits of our said three new governments, or within the limits of the territory granted to the Hudson's Bay Company; as also all the land and territories lying to the westward of the sources of the rivers which fall into the sea from the west and northwest as aforesaid; and we do hereby strictly forbid, on pain of our displeasure, all our loving subjects from making any purchases or settlements whatever, or taking possession of any of the lands above reserved, without our special leave and license for that purpose first obtained.

And we do further strictly enjoin and require all persons whatever, who have either wilfully or inadvertently seated themselves upon any lands within the countries above described, or upon any other lands which, not having been ceded to or purchased by us, are still reserved to the said Indians as aforesaid, forthwith to remove themselves from such settlements.

And whereas great frauds and abuses have been committed in the purchasing lands of the Indians, to the great prejudice of our interests, and to the great dissatisfaction of the said Indians; in order, therefore, to prevent such irregularities for the future, and to the end that the Indians may be convinced of our justice and determined resolution to remove all reasonable cause of discontent, we do, with the advice of our Privy Council, strictly enjoin and require, that no private person do presume to make any purchase from the said Indians of any lands reserved to the said Indians within those parts of our colonies where we have thought proper to allow settlement; but that if at any time any of the said Indians should be inclined to dispose of the said lands, the same shall be purchased only for us, in our name, at some public meeting or assembly of the said Indians, to be held for that purpose by the Governor or commander in chief of our colony respectively within which they shall lie: and in case they shall lie within the limits of any proprietary government, they shall be purchased only for the use and in the name of such proprietaries, conformable to such directions and instructions as we or they shall think proper to give for that purpose. And we do, by the advice of our Privy Council, declare and enjoin, that the trade with the said Indians shall be free and open to all our subjects whatever, provided that every person who may incline to trade with the said Indians do take out a license for carrying on such trade, from the Governor or commander in chief of any of our colonies respectively where such person shall reside, and also give security to observe such regulations as we shall at any time think fit, by ourselves or commissaries to be appointed for this purpose, to direct and appoint for the benefit of the said trade. And we do hereby authorize, enjoin, and require the Governors and commanders in chief of all our colonies respectively, as well those under our immediate government as those under the government and direction of proprietaries, to grant such licenses without fee or reward, taking especial care to insert therein a condition that such license shall be void, and the security forfeited, in case the person to whom the same is granted shall refuse or neglect to observe such regulations as we shall think proper to prescribe as aforesaid.

And we do further expressly enjoin and require all officers whatever, as well military as those employed in the management and direction of Indian affairs within the territories reserved as aforesaid, for the use of the said Indians, to seize and apprehend all persons whatever who, standing charged with treasons, misprisions of treasons, murders, or other felonies or misdemeanors, shall fly from justice and take refuge in the said-territory, and to send them under a proper guard to the colony where the crime was committed of which they shall stand accused, in order to take their trial for the same.

Given at our Court at St. James's, the 7th day of October 1763, in the third year of our reign.

3. Petition by Officers of the Continental Army for Western Lands

June 16, 1783
TO HIS EXCELLENCY, THE PRESIDENT AND HONORABLE DELEGATES OF THE UNITED STATES OF AMERICA, IN CONGRESS ASSEMBLED.

The Petition of the Subscribers, Officers in the Continental Line of the Army, humbly showeth:

That, by a Resolution of the Honorable Congress, passed September 20, 1776, and other subsequent resolves, the officers (and soldiers engaged for the War) of the American Army who shall continue in service till the establishment of *Peace*, or, in case of their dying in service, their heirs are entitled to receive certain Grants of Lands, according to their several grades, to be procured for them at the expense of the United States.

That your petitioners are informed that that tract of country, bounded north on Lake *Erie*, east on *Pennsylvania*, southeast and south on the river *Ohio*, west on a line beginning at that part of the *Ohio* which lies twenty-four miles west of the river *Scioto*, thence running north on a meridian line till it intersects with the river *Miami*, which falls into Lake *Erie*, thence down the middle of that river to the lake, is a tract of country not claimed as the property of or in jurisdiction of any particular state in the Union.

That this country is of sufficient extent, the land of such quality, and situation such as may induce Congress to assign and mark it out as a Tract or Territory suitable to form a distinct Government (or Colony of the United States) in time to be admitted *one* of the confederated States of America.

Wherefore your petitioners pray that, whenever the Honorable Congress shall be pleased to procure the aforesaid Lands of the natives, they will make provision for the location and survey of the lands to which we are entitled within the aforesaid District, and also for all Officers and Soldiers who wish to take up their lands in that quarter.

That provision also be made for a further grant of lands, to such of the Army as wish to become adventurers in the new Government, in such quantities and on such conditions of settlement and purchase, for public securities, as Congress shall judge most for the interest of the intended government, and rendering it of lasting consequence to the American Empire.

And your petitioners, as in duty bound, shall ever pray.
[Signed by some 288 officers of the Continental Army at Newburgh, New York.]

4. The Northwest Ordinance

July 13, 1787

An Ordinance for the government of the Territory of the United States northwest of the River Ohio.

Be it ordained by the United States in Congress assembled, That the said territory, for the purposes of temporary government, be one district, subject, however, to be divided into two districts, as future circumstances may, in the opinion of Congress, make it expedient.

Be it ordained by the authority aforesaid, That the estates, both of resident and nonresident proprietors in the said territory, dying intestate, shall descend to, and be distributed among their children, and the descendants of a deceased child, in equal parts; the descendants of a deceased child or grandchild to take the share of their deceased parent in equal parts among them: And where there shall be no children or descendants, then in equal parts to the next of kin in equal degree; and among collaterals, the children of a deceased brother or sister of the intestate shall have, in equal parts among them, their deceased parents' share; and there shall in no case be a distinction between kindred of the whole and half-blood; saving, in all cases, to the widow of the intestate her third part of the real estate for life, and one-third part of the personal estate; and this law relative to descents and dower, shall remain in full force until altered by the legislature of the district. And until the governor and judges shall adopt laws as hereinafter mentioned, estates in the said territory may be devised or bequeathed by wills in writing, signed and sealed by him or her in whom the estate may be (being of full age), and attested by three witnesses; and real estates may be conveyed by lease and release, or bargain and sale, signed sealed and delivered by the person, being of full age, in whom the estate may be, and attested by two witnesses, provided such wills be duly proved, and such conveyances be acknowledged, or the execution thereof duly proved, and be recorded within one year after proper magistrates, courts, and registers shall be appointed for that purpose; and personal property may be transferred by delivery; saving, however to the French and Canadian inhabitants, and other settlers of the Kaskaskies, St. Vincents and the neighboring villages who have heretofore professed themselves citizens of Virginia, their laws and customs now in force among them, relative to the descent and conveyance, of property.

Be it ordained by the authority aforesaid, That there shall be appointed from time to time by Congress, a governor, whose commission shall continue in force for the term of three years, unless sooner revoked by Congress; he shall reside in the district, and have a freehold estate therein in 1,000 acres of land, while in the exercise of his office.

There shall be appointed from time to time by Congress, a secretary, whose commission shall continue in force for four years unless sooner revoked; he shall reside in the district, and have a freehold estate therein in 500 acres of land, while in the exercise of his office. It shall be his duty to keep and preserve the acts and laws passed by the legislature, and the public records of the district, and the proceedings of the governor in his executive department, and transmit authentic copies of such acts and proceedings, every six months, to the Secretary of Congress: There shall also be appointed a court to consist of three judges, any two of whom to form a court, who shall have a common law jurisdiction, and reside in the district, and have each therein a freehold estate in 500 acres of land while in the exercise of their offices; and their commissions shall continue in force during good behavior.

The governor and judges, or a majority of them, shall adopt and publish in the district such laws of the original States, criminal and civil, as may be necessary and best suited to the circumstances of the district, and report them to Congress from time to time: which laws shall be in force in the district until the organization of the General Assembly therein, unless disapproved of by Congress; but afterwards the Legislature shall have authority to alter them as they shall think fit.

The governor, for the time being, shall be commander-in-chief of the militia, appoint and commission all officers in the same below the rank of general officers; all general officers shall be appointed and commissioned by Congress.

Previous to the organization of the general assembly, the governor shall appoint such magistrates and other civil officers in each county or township, as he shall find necessary for the preservation of the peace and good order in the same: After the general assembly shall be organized, the powers and duties of the magistrates and other civil officers shall be regulated and defined by the said assembly; but all magistrates and other civil officers not herein otherwise directed, shall, during the continuance of this temporary government, be appointed by the governor.

For the prevention of crimes and injuries, the laws

to be adopted or made shall have force in all parts of the district, and for the execution of process, criminal and civil, the governor shall make proper divisions thereof; and he shall proceed from time to time as circumstances may require, to lay out the parts of the district in which the Indian titles shall have been extinguished, into counties and townships, subject however to such alterations as may thereafter be made by the legislature.

So soon as there shall be five thousand free male inhabitants of full age in the district, upon giving proof thereof to the governor, they shall receive authority, with time and place, to elect representatives from their counties or townships to represent them in the general assembly: *Provided,* That, for every five hundred free male inhabitants, there shall be one representative, and so on progressively with the number of free male inhabitants shall the right of representation increase, until the number of representatives shall amount to twenty-five; after which, the number and proportion of representatives shall be regulated by the legislature: *Provided,* That no person be eligible or qualified to act as a representative unless he shall have been a citizen of one of the United States three years, and be a resident in the district, or unless he shall have resided in the district three years; and, in either case, shall likewise hold in his own right, in fee simple, two hundred acres of land within the same: *Provided, also,* That a freehold in fifty acres of land in the district, having been a citizen of one of the states, and being resident in the district, or the like freehold and two years residence in the district, shall be necessary to qualify a man as an elector of a representative.

The representatives thus elected, shall serve for the term of two years; and, in case of the death of a representative, or removal from office, the governor shall issue a writ to the country or township for which he was a member, to elect another in his stead, to serve for the residue of the term.

The general assembly or legislature shall consist of the governor, legislative council, and a house of representatives. The Legislative Council shall consist of five members, to continue in office five years, unless sooner removed by Congress; and three of whom to be a quorum: and the members of the Council shall be nominated and appointed in the following manner, to wit: As soon as representatives shall be elected, the Governor shall appoint a time and place for them to meet together; and, when met, they shall nominate ten persons, residents in the district, and each possessed of a freehold in five hundred acres of land, and return their names to Congress; five of whom Congress shall appoint and commission to serve as aforesaid: and, whenever a vacancy shall happen in the council, by death or removal from office, the house of representatives shall nominate two persons, qualified as aforesaid, for each vacancy, and return their names to Congress; one of whom Congress shall appoint and commission for the residue of the term. And every five years, four months at least before the expiration of the time of service of the members of council, the said house shall nominate ten persons, qualified as aforesaid, and return their names to Congress; five of whom Congress shall appoint and commission to serve as members of the council five years, unless sooner removed. And the governor, legislative council, and house of representatives, shall have authority to make laws in all cases, for the good government of the district, not repugnant to the principles and articles in this ordinance established and declared. And all bills, having passed by a majority in the house, and by a majority in the council, shall be referred to the governor for his assent; but no bill, or legislative act whatever, shall be of any force without his assent. The governor shall have power to convene, prorogue, and dissolve the general assembly, when, in his opinion, it shall be expedient.

The governor, judges, legislative council, secretary, and such other officers as Congress shall appoint in the district, shall take an oath or affirmation of fidelity and of office; the governor before the president of congress, and all other officers before the Governor. As soon as a legislature shall be formed in the district, the council and house assembled in one room, shall have authority, by joint ballot, to elect a delegate to Congress, who shall have a seat in Congress, with a right of debating but not of voting during this temporary government.

And, for extending the fundamental principles of civil and religious liberty, which form the basis whereon these republics, their laws and constitutions are erected; to fix and establish those principles as the basis of all laws, constitutions, and governments, which forever hereafter shall be formed in the said territory: to provide also for the establishment of States, and permanent government therein, and for their admission to a share in the federal councils on an equal footing with the original States, at as early periods as may be consistent with the general interest:

It is hereby ordained and declared by the authority aforesaid, That the following articles shall be considered as articles of compact between the original States and the people and States in the said territory and forever remain unalterable, unless by common consent, to wit:

ART. 1. No person, demeaning himself in a peaceable and orderly manner, shall ever be molested on account of his mode of worship or religious sentiments, in the said territory.

ART. 2. The inhabitants of the said territory shall always be entitled to the benefits of the writ of *habeas corpus*, and of the trial by jury; of a proportionate representation of the people in the legislature; and of judicial proceedings according to the course of the common law. All persons shall be bailable, unless for capital offences, where the proof shall be evident or the presumption great. All fines shall be moderate; and no cruel or unusual punishments shall be inflicted. No man shall be deprived of his liberty or property, but by the judgment of his peers or the law of the land; and, should the public exigencies make it necessary, for the common preservation, to take any person's property, or to demand his particular services, full compensation shall be made for the same. And, in the just preservation of rights and property, it is understood and declared, that no law ought ever to be made, or have force in the said territory, that shall, in any manner whatever, interfere with or affect private contracts or engagements, *bona fide*, and without fraud, previously formed.

ART. 3. Religion, morality, and knowledge, being necessary to good government and the happiness of mankind, schools and the means of education shall forever be encouraged. The utmost good faith shall always be observed towards the Indians; their lands and property shall never be taken from them without their consent; and, in their property, rights, and liberty, they shall never be invaded or disturbed, unless in just and lawful wars authorized by Congress; but laws founded in justice and humanity; shall from time to time be made for preventing wrongs being done to them, and for preserving peace and friendship with them.

ART. 4. The said territory, and the States which may be formed therein, shall forever remain a part of this Confederacy of the United States of America, subject to the Articles of Confederation, and to such alterations therein as shall be constitutionally made; and to all the acts and ordinances of the United States in Congress assembled, conformable thereto. The inhabitants and settlers in the said territory shall be subject to pay a part of the federal debts contracted or to be contracted, and a proportional part of the expenses of government, to be apportioned on them by Congress according to the same common rule and measure by which apportionments thereof shall be made on the other States; and the taxes for paying their proportion shall be laid and levied by the authority and direction of the legislatures of the district

or districts, or new States, as in the original States, within the time agreed upon by the United States in Congress assembled. The legislatures of those districts or new States, shall never interfere with the primary disposal of the soil by the United States in Congress assembled, nor with any regulations Congress may find necessary for securing the title in such soil to the *bona fide* purchasers. No tax shall be imposed on lands the property of the United States; and, in no case, shall non-resident proprietors be taxed higher then residents. The navigable waters leading into the Mississippi and St. Lawrence, and the carrying places between the same, shall be common highways and forever free, as well to the inhabitants of the said territory as to the citizens of the United States, and those of any other States that may be admitted into the confederacy, without any tax, impost, or duty therefor.

ART. 5. There shall be formed in the said territory, not less than three nor more than five States; and the boundaries of the States, as soon as Virginia shall alter her act of cession, and consent to the same, shall become fixed and established as follows, to wit: The western State in the said territory, shall be bounded by the Mississippi, the Ohio, and Wabash Rivers; a direct line drawn from the Wabash and Post Vincents, due North, to the territorial line between the United States and Canada; and, by the said territorial line, to the Lake of the Woods and Mississippi. The middle State shall be bounded by the said direct line, the Wabash from Post Vincents to the Ohio, by the Ohio, by a direct line, drawn due north from the mouth of the Great Miami, to the said territorial line, and by the said territorial line. The eastern State shall be bounded by the last mentioned direct line, the Ohio, Pennsylvania, and the said territorial line: *Provided, however*, and it is further understood and declared, that the boundaries of these three States shall be subject so far to be altered, that, if Congress shall hereafter find it expedient, they shall have authority to form one or two States in that part of the said territory which lies north of an east and west line drawn through the southerly bend or extreme of lake Michigan. And, whenever any of the said States shall have sixty thousand free inhabitants therein, such State shall be admitted, by its delegates, into the Congress of the United States, on an equal footing with the original States in all respects whatever, and shall be at liberty to form a permanent constitution and State government: *Provided*, the constitution and government so to be formed, shall be republican, and in conformity to the principles contained in these articles; and, so far as it can be consistent with the general interest of the confederacy, such admission shall be allowed at an earlier period, and when there may be a less number of free inhabitants in the State than sixty thousand.

ART. 6. There shall be neither slavery nor involuntary servitude in the said territory, otherwise than in the punishment of crimes whereof the party shall have been duly convicted: *Provided, always,* That any person escaping into the same, from whom labor or service is lawfully claimed in any one of the original States, such fugitive may be lawfully reclaimed and conveyed to the person claiming his or her labor or service as aforesaid.

Be it ordained by the authority aforesaid, That the resolutions of the 23rd of April 1784, relative to the subject of this ordinance, be, and the same are hereby repealed and declared null and void.

5. Treaty of Greenville

August 3, 1795

BETWEEN THE UNITED STATES OF AMERICA AND THE TRIBES OF INDIANS, CALLED THE WYANDOTS, DELAWARES, SHAWANEES, OTTAWAS, CHIPPEWAS, POTTAWATAMIES, MIAMIS, EEL-RIVER, WEEA'S, KICKAPOOS, PIANKESHAWS, AND KASKASKIAS.

TO PUT AN END to a destructive war, to settle all controversies, and to restore harmony and a friendly intercourse between the said United States, and Indian tribes; Anthony Wayne, major-general, commanding the army of the United States, and sole commissioner for the good purposes abovementioned, and the said tribes of Indians, by their Sachems, chiefs, and warriors, met together at Greenville, the head quarters of the said army, have agreed on the following articles, which, when ratified by the President, with the advice and consent of the Senate of the United States, shall be binding on them and the said Indian tribes.

ARTICLE I

Henceforth all hostilities shall cease; peace is hereby established, and shall be perpetual; and a friendly intercourse shall take place, between the said United States and Indian tribes.

ARTICLE II

All prisoners shall on both sides be restored. The Indians, prisoners to the United States, shall be immediately set at liberty. The people of the United States, still remaining prisoners among the Indians, shall be delivered up in ninety days from the date hereof, to the general or commanding officer at Greenville, Fort Wayne or Fort Defiance; and ten chiefs of the said tribes shall remain at Greenville as hostages, until the delivery of the prisoners shall be effected.

ARTICLE III

The general boundary line between the lands of the United States, and the lands of the said Indian tribes, shall begin at the mouth of Cayahoga river, and run thence up the same to the portage between that and the Tuscarawas branch of the Muskingum; thence down that branch to the crossing place above Fort Lawrence; thence westerly to a fork of that branch of the great Miami river running into the Ohio, at or near which fork stood Loromie's store, and where commences the portage between the Miami of the Ohio, and St. Mary's river, which is a branch of the Miami, which runs into Lake Erie; thence a westerly course to Fort Recovery, which stands on a branch of the Wabash; then south-westerly in a direct line to the Ohio, so as to intersect that river opposite the mouth of Kentucky or Cuttawa river. And in consideration of the peace now established; of the goods formerly received from the United States; of those now to be delivered, and of the yearly delivery of goods now stipulated to be made hereafter, and to indemnify the United States for the injuries and expenses they have sustained during the war; the said Indian tribes do hereby cede and relinquish forever, all their claims to the lands lying eastwardly and southwardly of the general boundary line now described; and these lands, or any part of them, shall never hereafter be made cause or pretence, on the part of the said tribes or any of them, of war or injury to the United States, or any of the people thereof.

And for the same considerations, and as an evidence of the returning friendship of the said Indian tribes, of their confidence in the United States, and desire to provide for their accommodation, and for that convenient intercourse, which will be beneficial to both parties, the said Indian tribes do also cede to the United States the following pieces of land; to wit. (1.) One piece of land six miles square at or near Loromie's store before mentioned. (2.) One piece two miles square at the head of the navigable water or landing on the St. Mary's river, near Girty's town. (3.) One piece six miles square at the head of the navigable water of the Au-Glaize river. (4.) One piece six miles square at the confluence of the Au-Glaize and Miami rivers, where Fort Defiance now stands. (5.) One piece six miles square at or near the confluence of the rivers St. Mary's and St. Joseph's, where Fort Wayne now stands, or near it. (6.) One piece two miles square on the Wabash river at the end of the portage from the Miami of the lake, and about eight miles westward from Fort Wayne. (7.) One piece six miles square at the Ouatanon or old Weea towns on the Wabash river. (8.) One piece twelve miles square at the British fort on the Miami of the lake at the foot of the rapids. (9.) One piece six miles square at the mouth of the said river where it empties into the Lake. (10.) One piece six miles square upon Sandusky lake, where a fort formerly stood. (11.) One piece two miles square at the lower rapids of Sandusky river. (12.) The post of Detroit and all the land to the north, the west and the south of it, of which the Indian title has been extinguished by gifts or grants to the French or English governments; and so much more land to be annexed to the district of Detroit as shall be comprehended between the river Rosine on the south, lake St. Clair on the north, and a line, the general course whereof shall be six miles distant from the west end of lake Erie, and Detroit river. (13.) The post of Michillimackinac, and all the land on the island, on which that post stands, and the main land adjacent, of which the Indian title has been extinguished by gifts or grants to the French or English governments; and a piece of land on the main to the north of the island, to measure six miles on lake Huron, or the strait between lakes Huron and Michigan, and to extend three miles back from the water of the lake or strait, and also the island De Bois Blanc, being an extra and voluntary gift of the Chippewa nation. (14.) One piece of land six miles square at the mouth of Chikago river emptying into the south-west end of lake Michigan, where a fort formerly stood. (15.) One piece twelve miles square at or near the mouth of the Illinois river, emptying into the Mississippi. (16.) One piece six miles square at the old Piorias fort and village, near the south end of the Illinois lake on said Illinois river: And whenever the United States shall think proper to survey and mark the boundaries of the lands hereby ceded to them, they shall give timely notice thereof to the said tribes of Indians, that they may appoint some of their wise chiefs to attend and see that the lines are run according to the terms of this treaty.

And the said Indians tribes will allow to the people of the United States a free passage by land and by water, as one and the other shall be found convenient, through their country, along the chain of posts herein before mentioned; that is to say, from the commencement of the portage aforesaid at or near Loromie's store, thence along said portage to the St. Mary's, and down the same to Fort Wayne, and then down the Miami to lake Erie: again from the commencement of the portage at or near Loromie's store along the portage from thence to the river Au-Glaize, and down the same to its junction with the Miami at Fort Defiance: again from the commencement of the portage aforesaid, to Sandusky river, and down the same to Sandusky bay and lake Erie, and from Sandusky to the post which shall be taken at or near the foot of the rapids of the Miami of the lake: and from thence to Detroit. Again from the mouth of Chikago, to the commencement of the portage, between that river and the Illinois, and down the Illinois river to the Mississippi, also from Fort Wayne along the portage aforesaid which leads to the Wabash, and then down the Wabash to the Ohio. And the said Indian tribes will also allow to the people of the United States the free use of the harbours and mouths of rivers along the lakes adjoining the Indian lands, for sheltering vessels and boats, and liberty to land their cargoes where necessary for their safety.

In consideration of the peace now established and of the cessions and relinquishments of lands made in the preceding article by the said tribes of Indians, and to manifest the liberality of the United States, as the great means of rendering this peace strong and perpetual; the United States relinquish their claims to all other Indian lands northward of the river Ohio, eastward of the Mississippi, and westward and southward of the Great Lakes and the waters uniting them, according to the boundary line agreed on by the United States and the king of Great-Britain, in the treaty of peace made between them in the year 1783. But from this relinquishment by the United States, the following tracts of land, are explicitly expected. 1st. The tract of one hundred and fifty thousand acres near the rapids of the river Ohio, which has been assigned to General Clark, for the use of himself and his warriors. 2d. The post of St. Vincennes on the river Wabash, and the lands at all other places in possession of the French people and other white settlers among them, of which the Indian title has been extinguished as mentioned in the 3d article; and 4th. The post of fort Massac towards the mouth of the Ohio. To which several parcels of land so expected, the said tribes relinquish all the title and claim which they or any of them may have.

And for the same considerations and with the same views as above mentioned, the United States now deliver to the said Indian tribes a quantity of goods to the value of twenty thousand dollars, the receipt whereof they do hereby acknowledge; and henceforward every year forever the United States will deliver at some convenient place northward of the river Ohio, like useful goods, suited to the circumstances of the Indians, of the value of nine thousand five hundred dollars; reckoning that value at the first cost of the goods in the city or place in the United States, where they shall be procured. The tribes to which those goods are to be annually delivered, and the proportions in which they are to be delivered, are the following.

1st. To the Wyandots, the amount of one thousand dollars. 2d. To the Delawares, the amount of one thousand dollars. 3d. To the Shawanese, the amount of one thousand dollars. 4th. To the Miamis, the amount of one thousand dollars. 5th. To the Ottawas, the amount of one thousand dollars. 6th. To the Chippewas, the amount of one thousand dollars. 7th. To the Pottawatamies, the amount of one thousand dollars. 8th. And to the Kickapoo, Weea, Eel-river, Piankeshaw and Kaskaskias tribes, the amount of five hundred dollars each.

Provided, That if either of the said tribes shall hereafter at an annual delivery of their share of the goods aforesaid, desire that a part of their annuity should be furnished in domestic animals, implements of husbandry, and other utensils convenient for them, and in compensation to useful artificers who may reside with or near them, and be employed for their benefit, the same shall at the subsequent annual deliveries be furnished accordingly.

To prevent any misunderstanding about the Indian lands relinquished by the United States in the fourth article, it is now explicitly declared, that the meaning of that relinquishment is this: The Indian tribes who have a right to those lands, are quietly to enjoy them, hunting, planting, and dwelling thereon so long as they please, without any molestation from the United States; but when those tribes, or any of them, shall be disposed to sell their lands, or any part of them, they are to be sold only to the United States; and until such sale, the United States will protect all the said Indian tribes in the quiet enjoyment of their lands against all citizens of the United States, and against all other white persons who intrude upon the same. And the said Indian tribes again acknowledge themselves to be under the protection of the said United States and no other power whatever.

ARTICLE VI

If any citizen of the United States, or any other white person or persons, shall presume to settle upon the lands now relinquished by the United States, such citizen or other person shall be out of the protection of the United States; and the Indian tribe, on whose land the settlement shall be made, may drive off the settler, or punish him in such manner as they shall think fit; and because such settlements made without the consent of the United States, will be injurious to them as well as to the Indians, the United States shall be at liberty to break them up, and remove and punish the settlers as they shall think proper, and so effect that protection of the Indian lands herein before stipulated.

ARTICLE VII

The said tribes of Indians, parties to this treaty, shall be at liberty to hunt within the territory and lands which they have now ceded to the United States, without hindrance or molestation, so long as they demean themselves peaceably, and offer no injury to the people of the United States.

ARTICLE VIII

Trade shall be opened with the said Indian tribes; and they do hereby respectively engage to afford protection to such persons, with their property, as shall be duly licenced to reside among them for the purpose of trade, and to their agents and servants; but no person shall be permitted to reside at any of their towns or hunting camps as a trader, who is not furnished with a licence for that purpose, under the hand and seal of the superintendent of the department northwest of the Ohio, or such other person as the President of the United States shall authorise to grant such licences; to the end, that the said Indians may not be imposed on in their trade. And if any licenced trader shall abuse his privilege by unfair dealing, upon complaint and proof thereof, his licence shall be taken from him, and he shall be further punished according to the laws of the United States. And if any person shall intrude himself as a trader, without such licence, the said Indians shall take and bring him before the superintendent or his deputy, to be dealt with according to law. And to prevent impositions by forged licences, the said Indians shall at least once a year give information to the superintendent or his deputies, of the names of the traders residing among them.

ARTICLE IX

Lest the firm peace and friendship now established should be interrupted by the misconduct of individuals, the United States, and the said Indian tribes agree, that for injuries done by individuals on either side, no private revenge or retaliation shall take place; but instead thereof, complaint shall be made by the party injured, to the other: By the said Indian tribes, or any of them, to the President of the United States, or the superintendent by him appointed; and by the superintendent or other person appointed by the President, to the principal chiefs of the said Indian tribes, or of the tribe to which the offender belongs; and such prudent measures shall then be pursued as shall be necessary to preserve the said peace and friendship unbroken, until the Legislature (or Great Council) of the United States, shall make other equitable provision in the case, to the satisfaction of both parties. Should any Indian tribes meditate a war against the United States or either of them, and the same shall come to the knowledge of the before-mentioned tribes, or either of them, they do hereby engage to give immediate notice thereof to the general or officer commanding the troops of the United States, at the nearest post. And should any tribe, with hostile intentions against the United States, or either of them, attempt to pass through their country, they will endeavor to prevent the same, and in like manner give information of such attempt, to the general or officer commanding, as soon as possible, that all causes of mistrust and suspicion may be avoided between them and the United States. In like manner the United States shall give notice to the said Indian tribes of any harm that may be meditated against them, or either of them, that shall come to their knowledge; and do all in their power to hinder and prevent the same, that the friendship between them may be uninterrupted.

ARTICLE X

All other treaties heretofore made between the United States and the said Indian tribes, or any of them, since the treaty of 1783, between the United States and Great Britain, that come within the purview of this treaty, shall henceforth cease and become void.

In Testimony whereof, the said Anthony Wayne, and the Sachems and War-Chiefs of the before-mentioned Nations and Tribes of Indians, have hereunto set their Hands, and affixed their seals. Done at Greenville, in the Territory of the United States, northwest of the river Ohio, on the third Day of August, one thousand seven hundred and ninety-five.

ANTHONY WAYNE.

Wyandots.
TAR-HÉ, (OR CRANE)
J. WILLIAMS, JUN.,
TEY-YAGH-TAW,
HA-RO-EN-YOU, (OR HALF KING'S SON)
TE-HAAW-TO-RENS,
AW-ME-YEE-RAY,
STAYÉ-TAH,
SHA-TEY-YA-RON-YAH, (OR LEATHER LIPS)
DAUGH-SHUT-TAY-AH,
SHA-AW-RUN-THE.

Delawares.
TETA-BOKSH-KE, (OR GRAND GLAIZE KING)
LE-MAN-TAN-QUIS, (OR BLACK KING)
WA-BAT-THOE,
MAGH-PI-WAY, (OR RED FEATHER)
KIK-THA-WE-NUND, (OR ANDERSON)
BU-KON-GE-HE-LAS,
PEE-KEE-LUND,
WELLE-BAW-KEE-LUND,
PEE-KEÉ-TÉLÉ-MUND, (OR THOMAS ADAMS)
KISH-KO-PE-KUND, (OR CAPTAIN BUFFALOE)
AME-NA-HE-HAN, (OR CAPTAIN CROW)
QUE-SHAWK-SEY, (OR GEORGE WASHINGTON)
WEY WIN-QUIS, (OR BILLY SISCOMB)
MOSES.

Shawanees.
MIS-QUA-COO-NA-CAW, (OR RED POLE)
CUT-THE-WE-KA-SAW, (OR BLACK HOOF)
KAY-SE-WA-E-SE-KAH,
WEY-THA-PA-MAT-THA,
NIA-NYM-SE-KA,
WAY-THE-AH, (OR LONG SHANKS)
WEY-A-PIER-SEN-WAW, (OR BLUE JACKET)
NE-QUE, TAUGH-AW,
HAH-GOO-SEE-KAW. (OR CAPTAIN REED)

Ottawas.
AU-GOOSH-AWAY,
KEE-NO-SHA-MEEK,
LA MALICE,
MA-CHI-WE-TAH,
THO-WO-NA-WA,
SE-CAW.

Chippewas.
MASH-I-PI-NASH-I-WISH, (OR BAD BIRD)

NAH-SHO-GA-SHE, (FROM LAKE SUPERIOR)
KA-THA-WA-SUNG,
MA-SASS,
NE-ME-KASS, (OR LITTLE THUNDER)
PE-SHAW-KAY, (OR YOUNG OX)
NAN-GUEY,
MEE-NE-DOG-GEE-SOGH,
PEE-WAN-SHE-ME-NOGH,
WEY-ME-GWAS,
GOB-MO-A-TICK.

Ottawa.
CHE-GO-NICKSKA. *(an Ottawa from Sandusky)*

Pottawatamies of the River Saint Joseph.
THU-PE-NE-BU,
NAW-AC, *(for himself and brother A-SI-ME-THE)*
NE-NAN-SE-KA,
KEE-SASS, (OR SUN)
KA-BA-MA-SAW, *(for himself and brother CHI-SAU-GAN)*
SUG-GA-NUNK,
WAP-ME-ME, (OR WHITE PIGEON)
WA-CHE-NESS, *(for himself and brother PE-DA-GO-SHOK)*
WAB-SHI-CAW-NAW,
LA-CHASSE,
ME-SHE-GE-THE-NOGH, *(for himself and brother WA-WA-SEK)*
HIN-GO-SWASH,
A-NE-WA-SAW,
NAW-BUDGH,
MIS-SE-NO-GO-MAW,
WA-WE-EG-SHE,
THAW-ME, (OR LE BLANC)
GEE-QUE. *(for himself and brother SHE-WIN-SE)*

Pottawatamies of Huron.
O-KI-A,
CHA-MUNG,
SE-GA-GE-WAN,
NA-NAW-ME, *(for himself and brother A-GIN)*
MAR-CHAND,
WE-NA-ME-AC.

Miamis.
NA-GOH-QUAN-GOGH, (OR LE GRIS)
ME-SHE-KUN-NOGH-QUOH. (OR LITTLE TURTLE)

Miamis and Eel-River.
PEE-JEE-WA, (OR RICHARD VILLE)
COCH-KE-POGH-TOGH.

Eel-River Tribe.
SHA-ME-KUN-NE-SA. (OR SOL-
    DIER)

Miamis.
WA-PA-MAN-GWA. (OR THE
    WHITE LOON)

*Weea's, for Themselves and the
    Piankeshaws.*
A-MA-CUN-SA, (OR LITTLE BEA-
    VER)
A-COO-LA-THA, (OR LITTLE FOX)
FRANCIS.

Kickapoos and Kaskaskias.
KEE-AW-HAH,
NE-MIGH-KA, (OR JOSEY RENARD)
PAI-KEE-KA-NOGH.

Delawares of Sandusky.
HAW-KIN-PUM-IS-KA,
PEY-A-MAWK-SEY,
REYN-TUE-CO. (*of the Six Nations,
    living at Sandusky*)

IN PRESENCE OF

H. DE BUTTS, *first A.D.C. and Sec'y to Maj. Gen. Wayne.* WM. H. HARRISON, *Aide-de-camp to Maj. Gen. Wayne.* T. LEWIS, *Aide-de-camp to Maj. Gen. Wayne.* JAMES O'HARA, *Quarter-Master Genl.* JOHN MILLS, *Major of Infantry, and Adj. Genl.* CALEB SWAN, *P.M.T.U.S.* GEO. DEMTER, *Lieut. Artillery,* VIGO, P. FRIS LA FONTAINE. ANT. LASELLE. JN. BEAU BIEN. DAVID JONES, *Chaplain U.S.L.* LEWIS BEUFAIT. R. LACHAMBRE. JAS. PEPEN. BATIES COUTIEN. P. NAVARRE.

SWORN INTERPRETERS

WM. WELLS. JACQUES LASELLE. M. MORINS. BT. SANS CRAINTE. CHRISTOPHER MILLER. ROBERT WILSON. ABRAHAM X WILLIAMS. ISAAC X ZANE.

6. Land Act of 1800

May 10, 1800

An Act to amend the act intituled "An act for providing for the sale of the lands of the United States, in the territory northwest of the Ohio, and above the mouth of the Kentucky River."

Sec. 1. *Be it enacted,* That for the disposal of the lands of the United States, directed to be sold by the act, intituled "An act providing for the sale of the lands of the United States, in the territory northwest of the Ohio, and above the mouth of Kentucky river," there shall be four land offices established in the said territory: one at Cincinnati . . . one at Chilicothe . . . one at Marietta . . . and one at Steubenville. . . . Each of the said offices shall be under the direction of an officer, . . . who shall be appointed by the President of the United States, by and with the advice and consent of the Senate, . . .

Sec. 3. That the surveyor-general shall cause the townships west of the Muskingum, which by the above-mentioned act are directed to be sold in quarter townships, to be subdivided into half sections of three hundred and twenty acres each. . . .

Sec. 4. That the lands thus subdivided . . . shall be offered for sale in sections and half sections, subdivided as before directed at the following places and times, . . . All lands, remaining unsold, at the closing of either of the public sales, may be disposed of at private sale by the registers of these respective land offices, in the manner herein after prescribed; . . .

Sec. 5. That no lands shall be sold by virtue of this act, at either public or private sale, for less than two dollars per acre, and payment may be made for the same by all purchasers, either in specie, or in evidences of the public debt of the United States, . . . and shall be made in the following manner, and under the following conditions, to wit:

1. At the time of purchase, every purchaser shall, exclusively of the fees hereafter mentioned, pay six dollars for every section, and three dollars for every half section, he may have purchased, for surveying expenses, and deposit one twentieth part of the amount of purchase money, to be forfeited, if within forty days one fourth part of the purchase money, including the said twentieth part, is not paid.

2. One fourth part of the purchase money shall be paid within forty days after the day of sale as aforesaid; another fourth part shall be paid within two years; another fourth part within three years; and another fourth part within four years after the day of sale.

3. Interest, at the rate of six per cent. a year from the day of sale shall be charged upon each of the three last payments, . . .

4. A discount at the rate of eight per cent., a year, shall be allowed on any of the three last payments, which shall be paid before the same shall become due, . . .

5. If the first payment of one fourth part of the purchase money shall not be made within forty days after the sale, the deposit payment and fees, paid and made by the purchaser, shall be forfeited, and the lands shall . . . be disposed of at private sale on the same terms and conditions, and in the same manner as the other lands directed by this act to be disposed of at private sale: *Provided,* that the lands which shall have been sold at public sale, and which shall, on account of such failure of payment, revert to the United States, shall not be sold at private sale, for a price less than the price that shall have been offered for the same at public sale. . . .

Sec. 16. That each person who, before the passing of this act, shall have erected . . . a grist-mill or saw-mill upon any of the lands herein directed to be sold, shall be entitled to the pre-emption of the section . . . at the rate of two dollars per acre. . . .

7. Treaty of Louisiana Purchase

April 30, 1803

Treaty of Purchase between the United States and the French Republic

The President of the United States of America, and the First Consul of the French Republic, in the name of the French people, desiring to remove all sources of misunderstanding relative to objects of discussion mentioned in the second and fifth articles of the Convention of (the 8th Vendémiaire, an 9,) September 30, 1800, relative to the rights claimed by the United States in virtue of the Treaty concluded at Madrid, the 27th October, 1795, between His Catholic Majesty and the said United States, and willing to strengthen the union and friendship, which at the time of the said Convention was happily re-established between the two nations, have respectively named their Plenipotentiaries, to wit: The President of the United States of America, by and with the advice and consent of the Senate of the said States, Robert R. Livingston, Minister Plenipotentiary of the United States, and James Monroe, Minister Plenipotentiary and Envoy Extraordinary of the said States, near the Government of the French Republic; and the First Consul, in the name of the French people, the French citizen Barbé Marbois, Minister of the Public Treasury, who, after having respectively exchanged their full powers, have agreed to the following articles:

ART. 1. Whereas, by the article the third of the Treaty concluded at St. Ildefonso, (the 9th Vendémiaire, an 9,) October 1, 1800, between the First Consul of the French Republic and His Catholic Majesty, it was agreed as follows: His Catholic Majesty promises and engages on his part to cede to the French Republic, six months after the full and entire execution of the conditions and stipulations herein, relative to his Royal Highness the Duke of Parma, the Colony or Province of Louisiana, with the same extent that it now has in the hands of Spain, and that it had when France possessed it; and such as it should be after the treaties subsequently entered into between Spain and other States: And whereas, in pursuance of the Treaty, particularly of the third article, the French Republic has an incontestable title to the domain and to the possession of the said territory, the First Consul of the French Republic, desiring to give to the United States a strong proof of friendship, doth hereby cede to the said United

States, in the name of the French Republic, for ever and in full sovereignty, the said territory, with all its rights and appurtenances, as fully and in the same manner as they might have been acquired by the French Republic, in value of the above-mentioned treaty, concluded with His Catholic Majesty.

ART. 2. In the cession made by the preceding article, are included the adjacent islands belonging to Louisiana, all public lots and squares, vacant lands, and all public buildings, fortifications, barracks, and other edifices, which are not private property. The archives, papers, and documents, relative to the domain and sovereignty of Louisiana and its dependencies, will be left in the possession of the Commissaries of the United States, and copies will be afterwards given in due form to the magistrates and municipal officers, of such of the said papers and documents as may be necessary to them.

ART. 3. The inhabitants of the ceded territory shall be incorporated in the Union of the United States, and admitted as soon as possible, according to the principles of the Federal Constitution, to the enjoyment of all the rights, advantages, and immunities, of citizens of the United States; and, in the mean time, they shall be maintained and protected in the free enjoyment of their liberty, property, and the religion which they profess.

ART. 4. There shall be sent by the Government of France a Commissary to Louisiana, to the end that he do every act necessary, as well to receive from the officers of His Catholic Majesty the said country and its dependencies in the name of the French Republic, if it has not been already done, as to transmit it, in the name of the French Republic, to the Commissary or agent of the United States.

ART. 5. Immediately after the ratification of the present treaty by the President of the United States, and in case that of the First Consul shall have been previously obtained, the Commissary of the French Republic shall remit all the military posts of New Orleans, and other parts of the ceded territory, to the Commissary or Commissaries named by the President to take possession; the troops, whether of France or Spain, who may be there, shall cease to occupy any military post from the time of taking possession, and shall be embarked as soon as possible in the course of three months after the ratification of this treaty.

ART. 6. The United States promise to execute such treaties and articles as may have been agreed between Spain and the tribes and nations of Indians, until, by mutual consent of the United States and the said tribes or nations, other suitable articles shall have been agreed upon.

ART. 7. As it is reciprocally advantageous to the commerce of France and the United States, to encourage the communication of both nations, for a limited time, in the country ceded by the present treaty, until general arrangements relative to the commerce of both nations may be agreed on, it has been agreed between the contracting parties, that the French ships coming directly from France or any of her Colonies, loaded only with the produce or manufactures of France or her said Colonies, and the ships of Spain coming directly from Spain or any of her Colonies, loaded only with the produce or manufactures of Spain or her Colonies, shall be admitted during the space of twelve years in the port of New Orleans, and in all other legal ports of entry within the ceded territory, in the same manner as the ships of the United States coming directly from France or Spain, or any of their Colonies, without being subject to any other or greater duty on the merchandise, or other or greater tonnage than those paid by the citizens of the United States.

During the space of time above-mentioned, no other nation shall have a right to the same privileges in the ports of the ceded territory. The twelve years shall commence three months after the exchange of ratifications, if it shall take place in France, or three months after it shall have been notified at Paris to the French Government, if it shall take place in the United States; it is, however, well understood, that the object of the above article is to favor the manufactures, commerce, freight, and navigation of France and Spain, so far as relates to the importations that the French and Spanish shall make into the said ports of the United States, without in any sort affecting the regulations that the United States may make concerning the exportation of the produce and merchandise of the United States, or any right they may have to such regulations.

ART. 8. In future and forever, after the expiration of the twelve years, the ships of France shall be treated upon the footing of the most favored nations in the ports above-mentioned.

ART. 9. The particular convention signed this day by the respective Ministers, having for its objects to provide the payment of debts due to the citizens of the United States by the French Republic, prior to the 30th of September, 1800, (8th Vendémiaire, an 9,) is approved, and to have its execution in the same manner as if it had been inserted in the present treaty; and it shall be ratified in the same form and in the same time, so that the one shall not be ratified distinct from the other. Another particular conven-

tion, signed at the same date as the present treaty, relative to a definitive rule between the contracting parties is, in the like manner, approved, and will be ratified in the same form and in the same time, and jointly.

ART. 10. The present treaty shall be ratified in good and due form, and the ratification shall be exchanged in the space of six months after the date of the signature by the Ministers Plenipotentiary, or sooner if possible.

In faith whereof, the respective Plenipotentiaries have signed these articles in the French and English languages, declaring, nevertheless, that the present treaty was originally agreed to in the French language, and have thereunto put their seals.

Done at Paris, the 10th day of Floréal, in the 11th year of the French Republic, and the 30th April, 1803.

R.R. LIVINGSTON,
JAMES MONROE,
BARBÉ MARBOIS.

This treaty, which has been often reprinted, was officially published in the annals of Congress, 1802–1803, pp. 1006–1008, which give an official current history of the negotiations.

8. The Missouri Compromise

1819–1821

1. THE TALLMADGE AMENDMENT
February 13, 1819
(*Journal of the House of Representatives*, 15th Congress, 2nd. Sess. p. 272)

And provided also, That the further introduction of slavery or involuntary servitude be prohibited, except for the punishment of crimes, whereof the party shall be duly convicted; and that all children of slaves, born within the said state, after the admission thereof into the Union, shall be free but may be held to service until the age of twenty-five years.

2. THE TAYLOR AMENDMENT
January 26, 1820
(*Annals of the Congress of the United States*, 16th Cong. 1st. Sess. Vol. I, p. 947)

The reading of the bill proceeded as far as the fourth section; when

MR. TAYLOR, of New York, proposed to amend the bill by incorporating in that section the following provision:

Section 4, line 25 insert the following after the

word "States"; "And shall ordain and establish, that there shall be neither slavery nor involuntary servitude in the said State, otherwise than in the punishment of crimes, whereof the party shall have been duly convicted: *Provided, always,* That any person escaping into the same, from whom labor or service is lawfully claimed in any other State, such fugitive may be lawfully reclaimed, and conveyed to the person claiming his or her labor or service as aforesaid: *And provided, also,* That the said provision shall not be construed to alter the condition or civil rights of any person now held to service or labor in the said Territory."

3. THE THOMAS AMENDMENT
February 17, 1820
(Annals of the Congress of the United States, 16th Cong. 1st. Sess. Vol. I, p. 427)

And it be further enacted, That, in all that territory ceded by France to the United States, under the name of Louisiana, which lies north of thirty-six degrees and thirty minutes north latitude, excepting only such part thereof as is included within the limits of the State contemplated by this act, slavery and involuntary servitude, otherwise than in the punishment of crimes whereof the party shall have been duly convicted, shall be and is hereby forever prohibited: *Provided always,* That any person escaping into the same, from whom labor or service is lawfully claimed in any State or Territory of the United States, such fugitive may be lawfully reclaimed, and conveyed to the person claiming his or her labor or service, as aforesaid.

4. MISSOURI ENABLING ACT
March 6, 1820
(U.S. Statutes at Large, Vol. III, p. 545 ff.)

An Act to authorize the people of the Missouri territory to form a constitution and state government, and for the admission of such state into the Union on an equal footing with the original states, and to prohibit slavery in certain territories.

Be it enacted That the inhabitants of that portion of the Missouri territory included within the boundaries hereinafter designated, be, and they are hereby, authorized to form for themselves a constitution and state government, and to assume such name as they shall deem proper; and the said state, when formed shall be admitted into the Union, upon an equal footing with the original states, in all respects whatsoever.

SEC. 2. That the said state shall consist of all the territory included within the following boundaries, to wit: Beginning in the middle of the Mississippi river, on the parallel of thirty-six degrees of north latitude; thence west, along that parallel of latitude, to the St. Francois river; thence up, and following the course of that river, in the middle of the main channel thereof, to the parallel of latitude of thirty-six degrees and thirty minutes; thence west, along the same, to a point where the said parallel is intersected by a meridian line passing through the middle of the mouth of the Kansas river, where the same empties into the Missouri river, thence, from the point aforesaid north, along the said meridian line, to the intersection of the parallel of latitude which passes through the rapids of the river Des Moines, making the said line to correspond with the Indian boundary line; thence east, from the point of intersection last aforesaid, along the said parallel of latitude, to the middle of the channel of the main fork of the said river Des Moines; thence down and along the middle of the main channel of the said river Des Moines, to the mouth of the main channel of the Mississippi river; thence down, and following the course of the Mississippi river, in the middle of the main channel thereof, to the place of beginning: . . .

SEC. 3. That all free white male citizens of the United States, who shall have arrived at the age of twenty-one years, and have resided in said territory three months previous to the day of election, and all other persons qualified to vote for representatives to the general assembly of the said territory, shall be qualified to be elected, and they are hereby qualified and authorized to vote, and choose representatives to form a convention. . . .

SEC. 8. That in all that territory ceded by France to the United States, under the name of Louisiana, which lies north of thirty-six degrees and thirty minutes north latitude, not included within the limits of the state, contemplated by this act, slavery and involuntary servitude, otherwise than in the punishment of crimes, whereof the parties shall have been duly convicted, shall be, and is hereby, forever prohibited: *Provided always,* That any person escaping into the same, from whom labour or service is lawfully claimed, in any state or territory of the United States, such fugitive may be lawfully reclaimed and conveyed to the person claiming his or her labour or service as aforesaid.

5. THE CONSTITUTION OF MISSOURI
July 19, 1820
(Poore, ed., *Federal and State Constitutions,* Vol. II, p. 1107–8)

SEC. 26. The general assembly shall not have power to pass laws—

1. For the emancipation of slaves without the con-

sent of their owners; or without paying them, before such emancipation, a full equivalent for such slaves so emancipated; and,

2. To prevent *bona-fide* immigrants to this State, or actual settlers therein, from bringing from any of the United States, or from any of their Territories, such persons as may there be deemed to be slaves, so long as any persons of the same description are allowed to be held as slaves by the laws of this State.

They shall have power to pass laws—

1. To prevent *bona-fide* immigrants to this State of any slaves who may have committed any high crime in any other State or Territory;

2. To prohibit the introduction of any slave for the purpose of speculation, or as an article of trade or merchandise;

3. To prohibit the introduction of any slave, or the offspring of any slave, who heretofore may have been, or who hereafter may be, imported from any foreign country into the United States, or any Territory thereof, in contravention of any existing statute of the United States; and,

4. To permit the owners of slaves to emancipate them, saving the right of creditors, where the person so emancipating will give security that the slave so emancipated shall not become a public charge.

It shall be their duty, as soon as may be, to pass such laws as may be necessary—

1. To prevent free negroes end [and] mulattoes from coming to and settling in this State, under any pretext whatsoever; and,

2. To oblige the owners of slaves to treat them with humanity, and to abstain from all injuries to them extending to life or limb.

6. RESOLUTION FOR THE ADMISSION OF MISSOURI
March 2, 1821
(*U. S. Statutes at Large,* Vol. III, p. 645)

Resolution *providing for the admission of the State of Missouri into the Union, on a certain condition.*

Resolved, That Missouri shall be admitted into this union on an equal footing with the original states, in all respects whatever, upon the fundamental condition, that the fourth clause of the twenty-sixth section of the third article of the constitution submitted on the part of said state to Congress, shall never be construed to authorize the passage of any law, and that no law shall be passed in conformity thereto, by which any citizen, of either of the states in this Union, shall be excluded from the enjoyment of any of the privileges and immunities to which such citizen is entitled under the constitution of the United States: *Provided,* That the legislature of the said state,

by a solemn public act, shall declare the assent of the said state to the said fundamental condition, and shall transmit to the President of the United States, on or before the fourth Monday in November next, an authentic copy of the said act; upon the receipt whereof, the President, by proclamation, shall announce the fact; whereupon, and without any further proceeding on the part of Congress, the admission of the said state into this Union shall be considered as complete.

9. Land Law of 1820

April 24, 1820
An act making further provision for the sale of the public lands.

Be it enacted, That from and after the first day of July next, all the public lands of the United States, the sale of which is, or may be authorized by law, shall, when offered at public sale, to the highest bidder, be offered in half quarter sections; and when offered at private sale, may be purchased, at the option of the purchaser, either in entire sections, half sections, quarter sections, or half quarter sections; . . .

SEC. 2. That credit shall not be allowed for the purchase money on the sale of any of the public lands which shall be sold after the first day of July next, but every purchaser of land sold at public sale thereafter, shall, on the day of purchase, make complete payment therefor; . . .

SEC. 3. That from and after the first day of July next, the price at which the public lands shall be offered for sale, shall be one dollar and twenty-five cents an acre; and at every public sale, the highest bidder, who shall make payment as aforesaid, shall be the purchaser; but no land shall be sold, either at public or private sale, for a less price than one dollar and twenty-five cents an acre; and all the public lands which shall have been offered at public sale before the first day of July next, and which shall then remain unsold, as well as the lands that shall thereafter be offered at public sale, according to law, and remain unsold at the close of such public sales, shall be subject to be sold at private sale, by entry at the land office, at one dollar and twenty-five cents an acre, to be paid at the time of making such entry as aforesaid; . . .

10. Removal Act

May 28, 1830

AN ACT TO PROVIDE FOR AN EXCHANGE OF LANDS WITH THE INDIANS RESIDING IN ANY OF THE STATES OR TERRITORIES, AND FOR THEIR REMOVAL WEST OF THE RIVER MISSISSIPPI

BE IT ENACTED *by the Senate and House of Representatives of the United States of America, in Congress assembled,* That it shall and may be lawful for the President of the United States to cause so much of any territory belonging to the United States, west of the river Mississippi, not included in any state or organized territory, and to which the Indian title has been extinguished, as he may judge necessary, to be divided into a suitable number of districts, for the reception of such tribes or nations of Indians as may choose to exchange the lands where they now reside, and remove there; and to cause each of said districts to be so described by natural or artificial marks, as to be easily distinguished from every other.

SECTION II

And be it further enacted, That it shall and may be lawful for the President to exchange any or all of such districts, so to be laid off and described, with any tribe or nation of Indians now residing within the limits of any of the states or territories, and with which the United States have existing treaties, for the whole or any part or portion of the territory claimed and occupied by such tribe or nation, within the bounds of any one or more of the states or territories, where the land claimed and occupied by the Indians, is owned by the United States, or the United States are bound to the state within which it lies to extinguish the Indian claim thereto.

SECTION III

And be it further enacted, That in the making of any such exchange or exchanges, it shall and may be lawful for the President solemnly to assure the tribe or nation with which the exchange is made, that the United States will forever secure and guaranty to them, and their heirs or successors, the country so exchanged with them; and if they prefer it, that the United States will cause a patent or grant to be made and executed to them for the same: *Provided always,* That such lands shall revert to the United States, if the Indians become extinct, or abandon the same.

SECTION IV

And be it further enacted, That if, upon any of the lands now occupied by the Indians, and to be exchanged for, there should be such improvements as add value to the land claimed by any individual or individuals of such tribes or nations, it shall and may be lawful for the President to cause such value to be ascertained by appraisement or otherwise, and to cause such ascertained value to be paid to the person or persons rightfully claiming such improvements. And upon the payment of such valuation, the improvements so valued and paid for, shall pass to the United States, and possession shall not afterwards be permitted to any of the same tribe.

SECTION V

And be it further enacted, That upon the making of any such exchange as is contemplated by this act, it shall and may be lawful for the President to cause such aid and assistance to be furnished to the emigrants as may be necessary and proper to enable them to remove to, and settle in, the country for which they may have exchanged; and also, to give them such aid and assistance as may be necessary for their support and subsistence for the first year after their removal.

SECTION VI

And be it further enacted, That it shall and may be lawful for the President to cause such tribe or nation to be protected, at their new residence, against all interruption or disturbance from any other tribe or nation of Indians, or from any other person or persons whatever.

SECTION VII

And be it further enacted, That it shall and may be lawful for the President to have the same superintendence and care over any tribe or nation in the country to which they may remove, as contemplated by this act, that he is now authorized to have over them at their present places of residence: *Provided,* That nothing in this act contained shall be construed as authorizing or directing the violation of any existing treaty between the United States and any of the Indian tribes.

And be it further enacted, That for the purpose of giving effect to the provisions of this act, the sum of five hundred thousand dollars is hereby appropriated, to be paid out of any money in the treasury, not otherwise appropriated.

Approved, May 28, 1830.

11. Compromise of 1850

September 9–20, 1850

I. Setting the Texas Boundaries, adjusting Texas claims, and establishing a Territorial government for New Mexico, September 9, 1850

Be it enacted by the Senate and House of Representatives of the United States of America in Congress assembled, That the following propositions shall be, and the same hereby are, offered to the State of Texas, which, when agreed to by the said State, in an act passed by the general assembly, shall be binding and obligatory upon the United States, and upon the said State of Texas: Provided, The said agreement by the said general assembly shall be given on or before the first day of December, eighteen hundred and fifty:

FIRST. The State of Texas will agree that her boundary on the north shall commence at the point at which the meridian of one hundred degrees west from Greenwich is intersected by the parallel of thirty-six degrees thirty minutes north latitude, and shall run from said point due west to the meridian of one hundred and three degrees west from Greenwich; thence her boundary shall run due south to the thirty-second degree of north latitude; thence on the said parallel of thirty-two degrees of north latitude to the Rio Bravo del Norte, and thence with the channel of said river to the Gulf of Mexico.

SECOND. The State of Texas cedes to the United States all her claim to territory exterior to the limits and boundaries which she agrees to establish by the first article of this agreement.

THIRD. The State of Texas relinquishes all claim upon the United States for liability of the debts of Texas, and for compensation or indemnity for the surrender to the United States of her ships, forts, arsenals, custom-houses, custom-house revenue, arms and munitions of war, and public buildings with their

sites, which became the property of the United States at the time of the annexation.

FOURTH. The United States, in consideration of said establishment of boundaries, cession of claim to territory, and relinquishment of claims, will pay to the State of Texas the sum of ten millions of dollars in a stock bearing five per cent. interest, and redeemable at the end of fourteen years, the interest payable half-yearly at the treasury of the United States.

SEC. 2. And be it further enacted. That all that portion of the Territory of the United States bounded as follows: Beginning at a point in the Colorado River where the boundary line with the republic of Mexico crosses the same; thence eastwardly with the said boundary line to the Rio Grande; thence following the main channel of said river to the parallel of the thirty-second degree of north latitude; thence east with said degree to its intersection with the one hundred and third degree of longitude west of Greenwich; thence north with said degree of longitude to the parallel of thirty-eighth degree of north latitude; thence west with said parallel to the summit of the Sierra Madre; thence south with the crest of said mountains to the thirty-seventh parallel of north latitude; thence west with said parallel to its intersection with the boundary line of the State of California; thence with said boundary line to the place of beginning—be, and the same is hereby, erected into a temporary government, by the name of the Territory of New Mexico: Provided, That nothing in this act contained shall be construed to inhibit the government of the United States from dividing said Territory into two or more Territories, in such manner and at such times as Congress shall deem convenient and proper, or from attaching any portion thereof to any other Territory or State: And provided, further That, when admitted as a State, the said Territory, or any portion of the same, shall be received into the Union, with or without slavery, as their constitution may prescribe at the time of their admission.

SEC. 3. And be it further enacted, That the executive power and authority in and over said Territory of New Mexico shall be vested in a governor, who shall hold his office for four years, and until his successor shall be appointed and qualified, unless sooner removed by the President of the United States . . .

II. The Admission of California, September 9, 1850

Whereas the people of California have presented a constitution and ask admission into the Union, which constitution was submitted to Congress by the President of the United States, by message dated February thirteenth, eighteen hundred and fifty, and which, on due examination, is found to be republican in its form of government.

Be it enacted by the Senate and House of Representatives of the United States of America in Congress assembled, That the State of California shall be one, and is hereby declared to be one, of the United States of America, and admitted into the Union on an equal footing with the original States in all respects whatever.

SEC. 2. And be it further enacted, That, until the representatives of Congress shall be apportioned according to an actual enumeration of the inhabitants of the United States, the State of California shall be entitled to two representatives in Congress.

SEC. 3. And be it further enacted, That the said State of California is admitted into the Union upon the express condition that the people of said State, through their legislature or otherwise, shall never interfere with the primary disposal of the public lands within its limits, and shall pass no law and do no act whereby the title of the United States to, and right to dispose of, the same shall be impaired or questioned and that they shall never lay any tax or assessment of any description whatsoever upon the public domain of the United States, and in no sense shall non-resident proprietors, who are citizens of the United States be taxed higher than residents; and that all navigable waters within the said State shall be common highways, and forever free, as well to the inhabitants of said State as to the citizens of the United States, without any tax, impost, or duty therefor: Provided, That nothing herein contained shall be construed as recognizing or rejecting the propositions tendered by the people of California as articles of compact in the ordinance adopted by the convention which formed the constitution of that State.

Approved, September 9, 1850.

III. Territorial government for Utah, September 9, 1850

Be it enacted by the Senate and House of Representatives of the United States of America in Congress assembled, That all that part of the territory of the United States included within the following limits, to wit: bounded on the west by the State of California, on the north by the Territory of Oregon, and on the east by the summit of the Rocky Mountains, and on the south by the thirty-seventh parallel of north latitude, be, and the same is hereby, created into a temporary government, by the name of the Territory of Utah; and, when admitted as a State, the said Territory, or any portion of the same, shall be received into the Union, with or without slavery, as their constitution may prescribe at the time of their admission: Provided, That nothing in this act contained shall be construed to inhibit the government of the United States from dividing said Territory into two or more Territories, in such manner and at such times as Congress shall deem convenient and proper, or from attaching any portion of said Territory to any other State or Territory of the United States.

IV. An amended Fugitive Slave Act, September 18, 1850

Be it enacted by the Senate and House of Representatives of the United States of America in congress assembled, That the persons who have been, or may hereafter be, appointed commissioners, in virtue of any act of Congress, by the Circuit Courts of the United States, and who, in consequence of such appointment, are authorized to exercise the powers that any justice of the peace, or other magistrate of any of the United States, may exercise in respect to offenders for any crime or offence against the United States, by arresting, imprisoning, or bailing the same under and by virtue of the thirty-third section of the act of the twenty-fourth of September seventeen hundred and eighty-nine, entitled "An Act to establishing the judicial courts of the United States," shall be, and are hereby, authorized and required to exercise and discharge all the powers and duties conferred by this act.

SEC. 2. And be it further enacted, That the Superior Court of each organized Territory of the United States shall have the same power to appoint commissioners to take acknowledgements of bail and affidavits, and to take depositions of witnesses in civil causes, which is now possessed by the Circuit Court of the United States; and all commissioners who shall thereafter be appointed for such purposes by the Superior Court of any organized Territory of the United States, shall possess all the powers, and exercise all the duties, conferred by law upon the commissioners appointed by the Circuit Courts of the United States for similar purposes, and shall moreover exercise and discharge all the powers and duties conferred by this act.

SEC. 3. And be it further enacted, That the Circuit Courts of the United States, and the Superior Courts of each organized Territory of the United States, shall from time to time enlarge the number of commissioners, with a view to afford reasonable facilities to reclaim fugitives from labor, and to the prompt discharge of the duties imposed by this act.

SEC. 4. And be it further enacted, That the commissioners above named shall have concurrent jurisdiction with the judges of the Circuit and District Courts of the United States, in their respective circuits and districts within the several States, and the judges of the Superior Courts of the Territories, severally and collectively, term-time and vacation; and shall grant certificates to such claimants, upon satisfactory proof being made, with authority to take and remove such fugitives from service or labor, under the restrictions herein contained, to the State or Territory from which such persons may have escaped or fled.

SEC. 5. And be it further enacted, That it shall be the duty of all marshals and deputy marshals to obey and execute all warrants and precepts issued under the provisions of this act, when to them directed; and should any marshal or deputy marshal refuse to receive such warrant, or other process, when tendered, or to use all proper means diligently to execute the same, he shall, on conviction thereof, be fined in the sum of one thousand dollars, to the use of such claimant, on the motion of such claimant, by the Circuit or District Court for the district of such marshal; and after arrest of such fugitive, by such marshal or his deputy, or whilst at any time in his custody under the provisions of this act, should such fugitive escape, whether with or without the assent of such marshal or his deputy, such marshal shall be liable, on his official bond, to be prosecuted for the benefit of such claimant, for the full value of the service or labor of said fugitive in the State, Territory, or District whence he escaped: and the better to enable the said commissioners, when thus appointed, to execute their duties faithfully and efficiently, in conformity with the requirements of the Constitution of the United States and of this act, they are hereby authorized and empowered, within their counties respectively, to appoint, in writing under their hands, any one or more suitable persons, from time to time, to execute all such warrants and other process as may be issued by them in the lawful performance of their respective duties; with authority to such commissioners, or the persons to be appointed by them, to execute process as aforesaid, to summon and call to their aid the bystanders, or posse comitatus of the proper county, when necessary to ensure a faithful observance of the clause of the Constitution referred to, in conformity with the pro-

visions of this act; and all good citizens are hereby commanded to aid and assist in the prompt and efficient execution of this law, whenever their services may be required, as aforesaid, for that purpose; and said warrants shall run, and be executed by said officers, any where in the State within which they are issued.

SEC. 6. And be it further enacted, That when a person held to service or labor in any State or Territory of the United States, has heretofore or shall hereafter escape into another State or Territory of the United States, the person to whom such service or labor may be due, or his, her, or their agent or attorney, duly authorized, by power of attorney, in writing, acknowledged and certified under the seal of some legal officer or court of the State or Territory in which the same may be executed, may pursue and reclaim such fugitive person, either by procurring a warrant from some one of the courts, judges, or commissioners aforesaid, of the proper circuit, district, or county, for the apprehension of such fugitive from service or labor, or by seizing and arresting such fugitive, where the same can be done without process, and by taking, or causing such person to be taken, forthwith before such court, judge, or commissioner, whose duty it shall be to hear and determine the case of such claimant in a summary manner; and upon satisfactory proof being made, by deposition or affidavit, in writing, to be taken and certified by such court, judge, or commissioner, or by other satisfactory testimony, duly taken and certified by some court, magistrate, justice of the peace, or other legal officer authorized to administer an oath and take depositions under the laws of the State or Territory from which such person owing service or labor may have escaped, with a certificate of such magistracy or other authority, as aforesaid, with the seal of the proper court or officer thereto attached, which seal shall be sufficient to establish the competency of the proof, and with proof, also by affidavit, of the identity of the person whose service or labor is claimed to be due as aforesaid, that the person so arrested does in fact owe service or labor to the person or persons claiming him or her, in the State or Territory from which such fugitive may have escaped as aforesaid, and that said person escaped, to make out and deliver to such claimant, his or her agent or attorney, a certificate setting forth the substantial facts as to the service or labor due from such fugitive to the claimant, and of his or her escape from the State or Territory in which such service or labor was due, to the State or Territory in which he or she was arrested, with authority to such claimant, or his or her agent or attorney, to use such reasonable force and restraint as may be necessary, under the circumstances of the case, to take and remove such fugitive person back to the State or Territory whence he or she may have escaped as aforesaid. In no trial or hearing under this act shall the testimony of such alleged fugitive be admitted in evidence; and the certificates in this and the first (fourth) section mentioned, shall be conclusive of the right of the person or persons in whose favor granted, to remove such fugitive to the State or Territory from which he escaped, and shall prevent all molestation of such person or persons by any process issued by any court, judge, magistrate, or other person whomsoever.

SEC. 7. And be it further enacted, That any person who shall knowingly and willingly obstruct, hinder, or prevent such claimant, his agent or attorney, or any person or persons lawfully assisting him, her, or them, from arresting such a fugitive from service or labor, either with or without process as aforesaid, when so arrested, pursuant to the authority herein given and declared; or shall aid, abet, or assist such person so owing service or labor as aforesaid, directly or indirectly, to escape from such claimant, his agent or attorney, or other person or persons legally authorized as aforesaid; or shall harbor or conceal such fugitive, so as to prevent the discovery and arrest of such person, after notice or knowledge of the fact that such person was a fugitive from service or labor as aforesaid, shall, for either of said offences, be subject to a fine not exceeding one thousand dollars, and imprisonment not exceeding six months, by indictment and conviction before the District Court of the United States for the district in which such offense may have been committed, or before the proper court of criminal jurisdiction, if committed within any one of the organized Territories of the United States; and shall moreover forfeit and pay, by way of civil damages to the party injured by such illegal conduct, the sum of one thousand dollars, for each fugitive so lost as aforesaid, to be recovered by action of debt, in any of the District or Territorial Courts aforesaid, within whose jurisdiction the said offence may have been committed. . . .

V. Slave Trade Prohibited in the District of Columbia, September 20, 1850

Be it enacted by the Senate and House of Representatives of the United States of America in Congress assembled, That from and after the first day of January, eighteen hundred and fifty-one, it shall not be lawful to bring into the District of Columbia any slave whatever, for the purpose of being sold, or for the purpose of being placed in depot, to be subsequently transferred to any other State or place to be sold as merchandize. And if any slave shall be brought into the said District by its owner, or by the authority or consent of its owner, contrary to the provisions of this act, such slave shall thereupon become liberated and free.

SEC. 2. And be it further enacted, That it shall and may be lawful for each of the corporations of the cities of Washington and Georgetown, from time to time, and as often as may be necessary, to abate, break up, and abolish any depot or place of confinement of slaves brought into the said District as merchandize, contrary to the provisions of this act, by such appropriate means as may appear to either of the said corporations expedient and proper. And the same power is hereby vested in the Levy Court of Washington county, if any attempt shall be made, within its jurisdictional limits, to establish a depot or place of confinement for slaves brought into the said District as merchandize for sale contrary to this act.

12. Treaty of Fort Laramie

September 17, 1851

ARTICLES OF A TREATY MADE AND CONCLUDED AT FORT LARAMIE, IN THE INDIAN TERRITORY, BETWEEN D.D. MITCHELL, SUPERINTENDENT OF INDIAN AFFAIRS, AND THOMAS FITZPATRICK, INDIAN AGENT, COMMISSIONERS SPECIALLY APPOINTED AND AUTHORIZED BY THE PRESIDENT OF THE UNITED STATES, OF THE FIRST PART, AND THE CHIEFS, HEADMEN, AND BRAVES OF THE FOLLOWING INDIAN NATIONS, RESIDING SOUTH OF THE MISSOURI RIVER, EAST OF THE ROCKY MOUNTAINS, AND NORTH OF THE LINES OF TEXAS AND NEW MEXICO, VIZ, THE SIOUX OR DAHCOTAHS, CHEYENNES, ARRAPAHOES, CROWS, ASSINABOINES, GROS VENTRE MANDANS, AND ARRICKARAS. PARTIES OF THE SECOND PART.

ARTICLE I

THE AFORESAID NATIONS, parties to this treaty, having assembled for the purpose of establishing and confirming peaceful relations amongst themselves, do hereby covenant and agree to abstain in future from all hostilities whatever against each other, to maintain good faith and friendship in all their mutual intercourse, and to make an effective and lasting peace.

ARTICLE II

The aforesaid nations do hereby recognize the right of the United States Government to establish roads, military and other posts, within their respective territories.

ARTICLE III

In consideration of the rights and privileges acknowledged in the preceding article, the United States bind themselves to protect the aforesaid Indian nations against the commission of all depredations by the people of the said United States, after the ratification of this treaty.

ARTICLE IV

The aforesaid Indian nations do hereby agree and bind themselves to make restitution or satisfaction for any wrongs committed, after the ratification of this treaty, by any band or individual of their people, on the people of the United States, whilst lawfully residing in or passing through their respective territories.

ARTICLE V

The aforesaid Indian nations do hereby recognize and acknowledge the following tracts of country, included within the metes and boundaries hereinafter designated, as their respective territories, viz:

The territory of the Sioux or Dahcotah Nation, commencing the mouth of the White Earth River, on the Missouri River; thence in a southwesterly direction to the forks of the Platte River; thence up the north fork of the Platte River to a point known as the Red Bute, or where the road leaves the river; thence along the range of mountains known as the Black Hills, to the head-waters of Heart River; thence down Heart River to its mouth; and thence down the Missouri River to the place of beginning.

The territory of the Gros Ventre, Mandans, and Arrickaras Nations, commencing at the mouth of Heart River; thence up the Missouri River to the mouth of the Yellowstone River; thence up the Yellowstone River to the mouth of Powder River in a southeasterly direction, to the head-waters of the Little Missouri River; thence along the Black Hills to the head of Heart River, and thence down Heart River to the place of beginning.

The territory of the Assinaboin Nation, commencing at the mouth of Yellowstone River; thence up the Missouri River to the mouth of the Muscle-shell River;

thence from the mouth of the Muscle-shell River in a southeasterly direction until it strikes the head-waters of Big Dry Creek; thence down that creek to where it empties into the Yellowstone River, nearly opposite the mouth of Powder River, and thence down the Yellowstone River to the place of beginning.

The territory of the Blackfoot Nation, commencing at the mouth of Muscle-shell River; thence up the Missouri River to its source; thence along the main range of the Rocky Mountains, in a southerly direction, to the head-waters of the northern source of the Yellowstone River; thence down the Yellowstone River to the mouth of Twenty-five Yard Creek; thence across to the head-waters of the Muscle-shell River, and thence down the Muscle-shell River to the place of beginning.

The territory of the Crow Nation, commencing at the mouth of Powder River on the Yellowstone; thence up Powder River to its source; thence along the main range of the Black Hills and Wind River Mountains to the head-waters of the Yellowstone River; thence down the Yellowstone River to the mouth of Twenty-five Yard Creek; thence to the head-waters of the Muscle-shell River; thence down the Muscle-shell River to its mouth; thence to the head-waters of Big Dry Creek, and thence to its mouth.

The territory of the Cheyennes and Arrapahoes, commencing at the Red Bute, or the place where the road leaves the north fork of the Platte River; thence up the north fork of the Platte River to its source; thence along the main range of the Rocky Mountains to the head-waters of the Arkansas River; thence down the Arkansas River to the crossing of the Santa Fé road; thence in a northwesterly direction to the forks of the Platte River, and thence up the Platte River to the place of beginning.

It is, however, understood that, in making this recognition and acknowledgement, the aforesaid Indian nations do not hereby abandon or prejudice any rights or claims they may have to other lands; and further, that they do not surrender the privilege of hunting, fishing, or passing over any of the tracts of country heretofore described.

ARTICLE VI

The parties to the second part of this treaty having selected principals or head-chiefs for their respective nations, through whom all national business will hereafter be conducted, do hereby bind themselves to sustain said chiefs and their successors during good behavior.

ARTICLE VII

In consideration of the treaty stipulations, and for the damages which have or may occur by reason thereof to the Indian nations, parties hereto, and for their maintenance and the improvement of their moral and social customs, the United States bind themselves to deliver to the said Indian nations the sum of fifty thousand dollars per annum for the term of ten years, with the right to continue the same at the discretion of the President of the United States for a period not exceeding five years thereafter, in provisions, merchandise, domestic animals, and agricultural implements, in such proportions as may be deemed best adapted to their condition by the President of the United States, to be distributed in proportion to the population of the aforesaid Indian nations.

ARTICLE VIII

It is understood and agreed that should any of the Indian nations, parties to this treaty, violate any of the provisions thereof, the United States may withhold the whole or a portion of the annuities mentioned in the preceding article from the nation so offending, until, in the opinion of the President of the United States, proper satisfaction shall have been made.

13. Homestead Act

May 20, 1862

AN ACT to secure homesteads to actual settlers on the public domain.

Be it enacted, That any person who is the head of a family, or who has arrived at the age of twenty-one years, and is a citizen of the United States, or who shall have filed his declaration of intention to become such, as required by the naturalization laws of the United States, and who has never borne arms against the United States Government or given aid and comfort to its enemies, shall, from and after the first of January, eighteen hundred and sixty-three, be entitled to enter one quarter-section or a less quantity of unappropriated public lands, upon which said person may have filed a pre-emption claim, or which may, at the time the application is made, be subject to pre-emption at one dollar and twenty-five cents, or less, per acre; or eighty acres or less of such unappropriated lands, at two dollars and fifty cents per acre, to be located in a body, in conformity to the legal subdivisions of the public lands, and after the same shall have been surveyed:

Provided, That any person owing or residing on land may, under the provisions of this act, enter other land lying contiguous to his or her said land, which shall not, with the land so already owned and occupied, exceed in the aggregate one hundred and sixty acres.

Sec. 2. That the person applying for the benefit of this act shall, upon application to the register of the land office in which he or she is about to make such entry, make affidavit before the said register or receiver that he or she is the head of a family, or is twenty-one or more years of age, or shall have performed service in the Army or Navy of the United States, and that he has never borne arms against the Government of the United States or given aid and comfort to its enemies, and that such application is made for his or her exclusive use and benefit, and that said entry is made for the purpose of actual settlement and cultivation, and not, either directly or indirectly, for the use or benefit of any other person or persons whomsoever, and upon filing the said affidavit with the register or receiver, and on payment of ten dollars, he or she shall thereupon be permitted to enter the quantity of land specified: *Provided, however,* That no certificate shall be given or patent issued therefor until the expiration of five years from the date of such entry; and if, at the expiration of such time or at any time within two years thereafter, the person making such entry—or if he be dead, his widow; or in case of her death, his heirs or devisee; or in case of a widow making such entry, her heirs or devisee, in case of her death—shall prove by two credible witnesses that he, she, or they have resided upon or cultivated the same for the term of five years immediately succeeding the time of filing the affidavit aforesaid, and shall make affidavit that no part of said land has been alienated, and that he has borne true allegiance to the Government of the United States; then, in such case, he, she, or they, if at that time a citizen of the United States, shall be entitled to a patent, as in other cases provided for by law: *And provided, further,* That in case of the death of both father and mother, leaving an infant child or children under twenty-one years of age, the right and fee shall inure to the benefit of said infant child or children; and the executor, administrator, or guardian may, at any time within two years after the death of the surviving parent, and in accordance with the laws of the State in which such children for the time being have their domicile, sell said land for the benefit of said infants, but for no other purpose; and the purchaser shall acquire the absolute title by the purchase, and be entitled to a patent from the United States, on payment of the office fees and sum of money herein specified. . . .

14. The Timber Culture Act

March 3, 1873
—An act to encourage the growth of Timber on Western Prairies.

Be it enacted by the Senate and House of Representatives of the United States of America in Congress assembled, That any person who shall plant, protect, and keep in a healthy, growing condition for ten years forty acres of timber, the trees thereon not being more than twelve feet apart each way on any quarter section of the public lands of the United States shall be entitled to a patent for the whole of said quarter section at the expiration of said ten years, on making proof of such fact by not less than two credible witnesses: *Provided,* That only one quarter in any section shall be thus granted.

Sec. 2. That the person applying for the benefit of this act shall, upon application to the register of the land office in which he or she is about to make such entry, make affidavit before said register or receiver that said entry is made for the cultivation of timber, and upon filing said affidavit with said register and receiver, and on payment of ten dollars, he or she shall thereupon be permitted to enter the quantity of land specified: *Provided, however,* That no certificate shall be given or patent issue therefor until the expiration of at least ten years from the date of such entry; and if at the expiration of such time, or at any time within three years thereafter, the person making such entry, or if he or she be dead, his or her heirs or legal representatives, shall prove by two credible witnesses that he, she, or they have planted, and for not less than ten years have cultivated and protected such quantity and character of timber as aforesaid, they shall receive the patent for such quarter section of land.

Sec. 3. That if at any time after the filing of said affidavit, and prior to the issuing of the patent for said land, it shall be proven after due notice to the party making such entry and claiming to cultivate such timber, to the satisfaction of the register of the land office that such person has abandoned or failed to cultivate, protect and keep in good condition such timber, then, and in that event, said land shall revert to the United States.

Sec. 4. That each and every person who, under the provisions of an act entitled "An act to secure homesteads to actual settlers on the public domain" approved May twentieth, eighteen hundred and sixty-two, or any amendment thereto, having a homestead on said public domain, who, at the end of the third year of his or her residence thereon, shall have had under cultivation, for two years, one acre of timber, the trees thereon not being more than twelve feet apart each way, and in a good, thrifty condition, for each and every sixteen acres of said homestead, shall upon due proof of said fact by two credible witnesses receive his or her patent for said homestead.

Sec. 5. That no land acquired under provisions of this act shall, in any event, become contracted prior to the issuing of patent therefore.

Sec. 6. That the Commissioner of the General Land Office is hereby required to prepare and issue such rules and regulations, consistent with this act, as shall be necessary and proper to carry its provisions into effect; and that the registers and the receivers of the several land offices shall be entitled to receive the same compensation for any lands entered under the provisions of this that they are now entitled to receive when the same quantity of land is entered with money.

Sec. 7. That the fifth section of the act entitled "An act in addition to an act to punish crimes against the United States, and for other purposes" approved March third, eighteen hundred and fifty-seven, shall extend to all oaths, affirmations, and affidavits required or authorized by this act.

Approved, March 3, 1873.

15. Opening of The Great Sioux Reservation

February 10, 1890
By the President of the United States of America.

A PROCLAMATION.

Whereas, it is provided in the Act of Congress, approved March second, eighteen hundred and eighty-nine, entitled "An Act to divide a portion of the reservation of the Sioux Nation of Indians in Dakota into separate reservations and to secure the relinquishment of the Indian title to the remainder, and for other purposes"—

That this act shall take effect, only, upon the acceptance thereof and consent thereto by the different bands of the Sioux Nation of Indians, in manner and form prescribed by the twelfth article of the treaty between the United States and said Sioux Indians concluded April twenty-ninth, eighteen hundred and sixty-eight, which said acceptance and consent shall be made known by proclamation by the President of the United States, upon satisfactory proof presented to him, that the same has been obtained in the manner and form required, by said twelfth article of said treaty; which proof shall be presented to him within one year from the passage of this act; and upon failure of such proof and proclamation this act becomes of no effect and null and void.

And,

Whereas satisfactory proof has been presented to me that the acceptance of and consent to the provisions of the said act by the different bands of the Sioux Nation of Indians have been obtained in manner and form as therein required;

Now, therefore, I, Benjamin Harrison, President of the United States, by virtue of the power in me vested, do hereby make known and proclaim the acceptance of said act by the different bands of the Sioux Nation of Indians, and the consent thereto by them as required by the act, and said act is hereby declared to be in full force and effect, subject to all the provisions, conditions, limitations and restrictions, therein contained.

All persons will take notice of the provisions of said act, and of the conditions, limitations and restrictions therein contained, and be governed accordingly.

I furthermore notify all persons to particularly observe that by said act certain tracts or portions of the Great Reservation of the Sioux Nation in the Territory of Dakota, as described by metes and bounds, are set apart as separate and permanent reservations for the Indians receiving rations and annuities at the respective agencies therein named;

That any Indian receiving and entitled to rations and annuities at either of the agencies mentioned in this act at the time the same shall take effect, but residing upon any portion of said Great Reservation not included in either of the separate reservations herein established, may, at his option, within one year from the time when this act shall take effect, and within one year after he has been notified of his said right of option in such manner as the Secretary of the Interior shall direct by recording his election with the proper agent at the agency to which he belongs, have the allotment to which he would be

otherwise entitled on one of said separate reservations upon the land where such Indian may then reside.

That each member of the Ponca tribe of Indians now occupying a part of the old Ponca Reservation, within the limits of the said Great Sioux Reservation, shall be entitled to allotments upon said old Ponca Reservation, in quantities as therein set forth, and that when allotments to the Ponca tribe of Indians, and to such other Indians as allotments are provided for by this act, shall have been made upon that portion of said reservation which is described in the act entitled "an act to extend the northern boundary of the State of Nebraska," approved March twenty-eighth, eighteen hundred and eighty-two, the President shall, in pursuance of said act, declare that the Indian title is extinguished to all lands described in said act not so allotted hereunder, and thereupon all of said land not so allotted and included in said act of March twenty-eighth, eighteen hundred and eighty-two, shall be open to settlement as provided in this act;

That protection is guaranteed to such Indians as may have taken allotments either within or without the said separate reservations under the provisions of the treaty with the Great Sioux Nation, concluded April twenty-ninth, eighteen hundred and sixty-eight; and that provision is made in said act for the release of all title on the part of said Indians receiving rations and annuities on each separate reservation, to the lands described in each of the other separate reservations, and to confirm the Indians entitled to receive rations at each of said separate reservations, respectively, to their separate and exclusive use and benefit, all the title and interest of every name and nature secured to the different bands of the Sioux Nation by said treaty of April twenty-ninth, eighteen hundred and sixty-eight; and that said release shall not affect the title of any individual Indian to his separate allotment of land not included in any of said separate reservations, nor any agreement heretofore made with the Chicago, Milwaukee and Saint Paul Railroad Company or the Dakota Central Railroad Company respecting certain lands for right of way, station grounds, etc., regarding which certain prior rights and privileges are reserved to and for the use of said railroad companies, respectively, upon the terms and conditions set forth in said act:

That it is therein provided that if any land in said Great Sioux Reservation is occupied and used by any religious society at the date of said act for the purpose of missionary or educational work among the Indians, whether situate outside of or within the limits of any of the separate reservations, the same, not exceeding one hundred and sixty acres in any one tract, shall be granted to said society for the purposes and upon the terms and conditions therein named, and

Subject to all the conditions and limitations in said act contained, it is therein provided that all the lands in the Great Sioux Reservation outside of the separate reservations described in said act, except American Island, Farm Island, and Niobrara Island, regarding which Islands special provisions are therein made, and sections sixteen and thirty-six in each township thereof (which are reserved for school purposes) shall be disposed of by the United States, upon the terms, at the price and in the manner therein set forth, to actual settlers only, under the provisions of the homestead law (except section two thousand three hundred and one thereof) and under the law relating to town-sites.

That section twenty-three of said act provides—

That all persons who, between the twenty-seventh day of February, eighteen hundred and eighty-five, and the seventeenth day of April, eighteen hundred and eighty-five, in good faith, entered upon or made settlement with intent to enter the same under the homestead or pre-emption laws of the United States upon any part of the Great Sioux Reservation lying east of the Missouri River, and known as the Crow Creek and Winnebago Reservation, which, by the President's proclamation of date February twenty-seventh, eighteen hundred and eighty-five, was declared to be open to settlement, and not included in the new reservation established by section six of this act, and who, being otherwise legally entitled to make such entries, located or attempted to locate thereon homestead, pre-emption, or town-site claims by actual settlement and improvement of any portion of such lands, shall, for a period of ninety days after the proclamation of the President required to be made by this act, have a right to re-enter upon said claims and procure title thereto under the homestead or pre-emption laws of the United States, and complete the same as required therein, and their said claims shall, for such time, have a preference over later entries; and when they shall have in other respects shown themselves entitled and shall have complied with the law regulating such entries, and, as to homesteads, with the special provisions of this act, they shall be entitled to have said lands, and patents therefor shall be issued as in like cases: *Provided*, That pre-emption claimants shall reside on their lands the same length of time before procuring title as homestead claimants under this act. The price to be paid for town-site entries shall be such as is required by law in other cases, and shall be paid into the general fund provided for by this act.

It is, furthermore, hereby made known that there has been and is hereby reserved from entry or settlement that tract of land now occupied by the agency and school buildings at the Lower Brule Agency, to wit:

The west half of the southwest quarter of section twenty-four; the east half of the southeast quarter of section twenty-three; the west half of the northwest quarter of section twenty-five; the east half of the northeast quarter of section twenty-six, and the northwest fractional quarter of the southeast quarter of section twenty-six; all in township one hundred and four, north of range seventy-two, west of the fifth principal meridian;

That there is also reserved as aforesaid the following described tract within which the Cheyenne River Agency, school and certain other buildings are located, to wit: Commencing at a point in the center of the main channel of the Missouri River opposite Deep Creek, about three miles south of Cheyenne River; thence due west five and one half miles; thence due north to the Cheyenne River; thence down said river to the center of the main channel thereof to a point in the center of the Missouri River due east or opposite the mouth of said Cheyenne River; thence down the center of the main channel of the Missouri River to the place of beginning:

That in pursuance of the provisions contained in section one of said act, the tract of land situate in the State of Nebraska and described in said act as follows; to wit: "Beginning at a point on the boundary-line between the State of Nebraska and the Territory of Dakota, where the range line between ranges forty-four and forty-five west of the sixth principal meridian, in the Territory of Dakota, intersects said boundary-line; thence east along said boundary-line five miles; thence due south five miles; thence due west ten miles; thence due north to said boundary-line; thence due east along said boundary-line to the place of beginning," same is continued in a state of reservation so long as it may be needed for the use and protection of the Indians receiving rations and annuities at the Pine Ridge Agency.

Warning is hereby also expressly given to all persons not to enter or make settlement upon any of the tracts of land specially reserved by the terms of said act, or by this proclamation, or any portion of any tracts of land to which any individual member of either of the bands of the great Sioux Nation, or the Ponca tribe of Indians, shall have a preference right under the provisions of said act; and further, to in no wise interfere with the occupancy of any of said tracts by any of said Indians, or in any manner to disturb, molest or prevent the peaceful possession of said tracts by them.

The surveys required to be made of the lands to be restored to the public domain under the provisions of the said act, and as in this proclamation set fourth will be commenced and executed as early as possible.

In witness whereof, I have hereunto set my hand and caused the seal of the United States to be affixed.

Done at the city of Washington this tenth day of February in the year of our Lord one thousand eight hundred and ninety, and of the

[SEAL.] Independence of the United States the one hundred and fourteenth.

BENJ. HARRISON.

By the President:
JAMES G. BLAINE,
Secretary of State.

S. Doc. 319, 58-2, pt 1——60

Appendix B
Biographies of Major Personalities

Abercomby, James (1706–1781): British army general. Supreme commander of British forces in America in the French and Indian War. After his defeat at Fort Ticonderoga in 1758, he was recalled to England and replaced by General Jeffrey Amherst.

Adams, John (1735–1826): Diplomat and second U.S. president (1797–1801); born in Braintree (Quincy), Massachusetts. He was a delegate to the first Continental Congress and signed the Declaration of Independence. In 1782, he joined Benjamin Franklin and John Jay as a delegate at the Paris peace conference. He followed Jay's leadership in negotiating only with the British, and not the French, helping to secure the vast trans-Appalachian West for the United States.

Adams, John Quincy (1767–1848): Statesman and sixth U.S. president (1825–1829); son of President John Adams. As a peace commissioner at the Ghent conference (1814), maintained a strongly national attitude and refused, along with his fellow commissioners, to sign a peace treaty that would diminish the territory of the United States. As president, he obtained from Great Britain an agreement to jointly occupy the Oregon country. As a congressman (1831–1848) he opposed the extension of slavery but favored the admission of Texas to the Union.

Amherst, Jeffrey Lord (1717–1797): British army officer who played a major role in the French and Indian War. In July 1758, a force under his command captured the stronghold of Louisbourg on Cape Breton Island, guarding the ocean gateway to Canada. Along with Generals John Forbes and James Wolfe, he won North America for Great Britain. He also controlled Indian affairs during Pontiac's Rebellion

(1763) and defeated the uprising by sending an expedition to relieve the besieged Fort Pitt, near present-day Pittsburgh.

Applegate, Jesse (1811–1888): Oregon pioneer; born in Kentucky and immigrated with his parents to Missouri in 1821. Attracted by "Oregon fever" he joined the Great Migration of 1843. Departing from Independence, Missouri, he captained the first wagon train, including a large herd of cattle, to the Columbia River, and settled with his family near present-day The Dalles, Oregon. He drafted a memorial to Congress for granting territorial government to Oregon and opened a southern route to the Willamette Valley in 1846, from Fort Hall, Idaho, via Nevada and northern California. From his experiences he wrote a classic description of early overland travel, *A Day with the Cow Column in 1843*, first published in 1868.

Armijo, Manuel (1792?–1853): Governor, soldier and trader. He ruled as Mexico's governor of New Mexico three times (1827–1829, 1837–1844 and 1845–1846) in the period prior to the Mexican War. In 1841, he directed operations resulting in the capture of members of the Texan-Santa Fe expedition, who had sought to annex New Mexico to the Republic of Texas. When the American army arrived in 1846, he fled south with his troops without firing a shot. Charged with treason by the Mexican government, he was acquitted. After the war, he returned to New Mexico, where he engaged in trading and ranching.

Arista, Mariano (1802–1855): Mexican general and politician. He participated in Mexico's attempt to quell the Texas Revolution in 1836. A decade later, a force under his command crossed the Rio Grande, on April 25, 1846, and ambushed an American patrol, helping to precipitate the Mexican War. Arista served as minister of war and marine under President Herrera (1848–1851) and as president of Mexico from 1851 to 1853.

Ashley, William Henry (1778–1838): Fur trader and politician. Organized the brigade-rendezvous system that established the United States fur trade in the Rockies and revolutionized the fur business by instituting an annual meeting of trappers, traders, Indians and representatives of his company, the Rocky Mountain Fur Company. Ashley explored the Great Salt Lake region. He sold out to Smith, Jackson and Sublette and returned to St. Louis in 1826 to pursue mercantile interests and politics, but continued to provide expeditions with supplies and to market their furs. Elected to Congress for three terms (1831–1837), where he defended western interests.

Astor, John Jacob (1763–1848): Fur trader and financier; born in Germany and migrated to the United States in 1784. By 1800 he had developed one of the nation's leading fur businesses, and then formed the American Fur Company and the Pacific Fur Company, which challenged Britain's Hudson's Bay Company and other rivals. Astor founded Astoria, a post for the China trade at the mouth of the Columbia River, the first permanent American settlement in the Pacific Northwest. He withdrew from the fur business in 1834 and concentrated on real estate and other investments, becoming one of the wealthiest men of his time.

Atchison, David Rice (1807–1886): Missouri politician. As a U.S. senator he worked for the protection of Oregon settlers and was one of the leaders of the unsuccessful movement to declare 54°40′ as the border between the United States and Canada. Atchison supported the upholding of treaty rights for various tribes as chairman of the Committee on Indian Affairs and played a major role in the repeal of the Missouri Compromise through the Kansas-Nebraska Act, then led the struggle by Missourians to make Kansas a slave state. When this proved unsuccessful, he retired from the Senate, giving his support to the Confederacy.

Atkinson, Henry (1782–1842): U.S. army officer and explorer. Under authorization by Congress, he led an expedition to the mouth of the Yellowstone (1824) and negotiated treaties with several Indian tribes he encountered on the journey. During the Black Hawk War of 1832 he was in general command of the troops and led the fighting at Bad Axe River, where the Sauk forces were almost annihilated. In 1840, he

oversaw the removal of the Winnebego tribe from Wisconsin to Iowa.

Austin, Moses (1761–1821): Merchant, mine owner and colonizer. After suffering financial ruin in Missouri, he moved to San Antonio, Texas, in 1820, where he successfully applied to the Spanish government for permission to bring 300 families into Texas. He received a grant of 200,000 acres of Texas land on which to establish a colony, but ill health prevented him from carrying out his plans, and he died soon after. Before dying, he received the promise of his son Stephen to carry out his plans for establishing an American settlement in Texas.

Austin, Stephen Fuller (1793–1836): American colonizer and Texas political leader. The son of American businessman Moses Austin, Stephen was raised in Missouri and inherited a Texas land grant on the death of his father. In 1822, he settled 300 families at San Felipe de Austin on the Gulf Coast. By 1834 his successful colony had attracted another 750 American families to the settlement, and tensions between Mexicans and Americans were close to outright war. Austin traveled to Mexico City in 1835 to petition for the establishment of Texas as a separate Mexican state; he was then imprisoned on suspicion of trying to incite insurrection. Upon his release, finding the colonists on the verge of revolt, he abandoned his hope for an Anglo-American state within the boundaries of Mexico and became commander of the Texas Revolutionary Army. Defeated in 1836 by Sam Houston in an election for the presidency of the Texas Republic, he served briefly as the Republic of Texas' secretary of state until his death.

Baylor, John Robert (1822–1894): Texas soldier. As a delegate to the Texas secession convention in January 1861, he voted to remove Texas from the Union, then accepted a commission as a lieutenant colonel in the Texas Mounted Volunteers. Baylor defeated Union soldiers at Fort Fillmore and proclaimed the Confederate Territory of Arizona, then fought Union soldiers and Apache Indians until he was forced out of the territory by the California Volunteers in 1862.

Becknell, William (ca. 1790–1865): Explorer and Missouri Indian trader. He opened the Santa Fe trade in 1821 when his expedition, bound for the southern Rockies, met a group of Mexican soldiers who indicated that independent Mexico would welcome American goods. Becknell became the first American to arrive in Santa Fe after Mexico's independence and gained the distinction of opening the Santa Fe trade. On his second expedition in 1822 he added three wagons to his pack train, marking the first time wagons had been used on the Santa Fe trail.

Beckwourth, Jim [James Pierson] (ca. 1800–ca. 1866): Fur trader, explorer and member of William Henry Ashley's trading expeditions into the Rocky Mountains (1824–1825). He worked with various Rocky Mountain Fur Company partners until 1828, when he went to live with the Crow Indians, taking advantage of his mulatto background and dark skin to convince them that he was actually part-Indian. During the California gold rush he operated a ranch, trading post and hotel for immigrants at the summit of Beckwourth Pass, a new and easier route through the rugged Sierra Mountains.

Bent, Charles (1799–1847): Fur trader and government official. Born in Charleston, Virginia, he joined the Missouri Fur Company in 1822 and became a partner of Joshua Pilcher. He formed the trading firm of Bent and St. Vrain in 1830, and built Bent's Fort, near present-day La Junta, Colorado, which became the trading center for the entire mountain and Plains region. He moved to Taos sometime during the 1830s, and after the Mexican War was appointed the first American governor of New Mexico. During a brief rebellion he was killed and scalped.

Bent, William (1809–1869): Trader, scout and Indian agent. He was a partner in his older brother Charles' firm, Bent, St. Vrain & Company, and managed the firm's Indian trade center at Bent's Fort in Colorado. In 1857, he built a stockade at the mouth of the Purgatoire River, gathered settlers and founded the first Anglo-American settlement in Colorado. He established friendly relations with many Indian tribes. In 1864, Colorado militiamen forcibly restrained him from warning Black Kettle and his Cheyenne people of an impending military action against their encampment at Sand Creek.

Benton, Thomas Hart (1782–1858): Politician. Gained national attention as a spokesman for the West when he was elected to the U.S. Senate from the new state of Missouri in 1821. During his 30 years in the Senate he was a supporter of the Rocky Mountain fur trade; urged the building of a toll-free wagon road to Oregon; campaigned for cheap public land in the West; and as chairman on Indian affairs was instrumental in obtaining land cessions from the Creeks in Georgia. Although he was a slave-owning aristocrat, he turned against slavery during the debate over the Compromise of 1850, believing that the institution hindered westward expansion. His stand against slavery led to his defeat for another Senate term. Still popular, he ran successfully for the House of Representatives (1852–1854), but was defeated in his 1856 campaign for governor of Missouri.

Bidwell, John (1819–1900): California pioneer and politician. Organized the Western Emigration Society in 1840 and led an overland expedition of 69 pioneers from Missouri to California. Aided by guide Thomas Fitzpatrick, the party reached the Bear River in Idaho, where about half the emigrants turned toward Oregon, while the remainder, including Bidwell, continued on to California. After trekking across vast stretches of desert and struggling over icy mountain trails, Bidwell's party reached California on November 4, 1841, the first emigrant train to make the journey from the Missouri River over the California Trail. In 1849, he acquired a 22,000-acre ranch in northern California and became the most famous agriculturalist in California. Bidwell was elected to the U.S. House of Representatives in 1864 and ran unsuccessfully for governor of California three times.

Birkbeck, Morris (1764–1825): Pioneer and author. Born in England, he immigrated to the United States in 1817 and sought to create an English settlement in Illinois, where he established a settlement consisting of thousands of acres and founded present-day Albion, Illinois. His *Letters from Illinois* (1818) motivated scores of European settlers to immigrate to the prairies of the middle West.

Black Hawk [Ma-ka-tai-me-she-kia-kiak] (1767–1838): Sauk chief; born near the mouth of the Rock River (Illinois). His band joined the British in the War of 1812; after the war he became disenchanted with the Sac and Fox Treaty of 1804 whereby the Sauk and Fox Indians ceded their territory east of the Mississippi River to the United States. As settlers moved closer to his village, a peaceful group of the Sauk led by chief Keokuk moved to the west side of the Mississippi in 1829. But Black Hawk refused to leave, and in 1832 they raided nearby settlements. The result was the Black Hawk War, which ended in tragedy for the Indians and Black Hawk's own capture. After a brief incarceration, he returned to Iowa, where he was forced to live on a reservation.

Black Kettle (ca. 1803–1868): Cheyenne chief. In 1864, he attempted to make peace with the whites in Colorado, but was rebuffed by the Colorado militia. He survived the massacre at Sand Creek (November 29, 1864), where about half his people were killed by a force under the command of Colonel John M. Chivington. Black Kettle attended the Medicine Lodge Treaty council of 1867, where the Cheyennes and

Arapaho were assigned to a reserve along the upper Washita River. In 1868, he led bands of Cheyenne, Arapaho, Kiowa and Comanche warriors in a general uprising throughout the Southwest. He was killed during the fierce fighting at the battle of Washita.

Boone, Daniel (1734–1820): Frontiersman and explorer; symbol of American pioneering. Boone opened the Wilderness Road from the Cumberland Gap to the south bank of the Kentucky River for the Transylvania Company in 1775. He founded the Kentucky settlement of Boonesboro. Involved in Indian conflicts between 1775 and 1778, he was taken prisoner by the Shawnee for three months, but he escaped to successfully defend Boonesboro from Indian and British attacks. Disgusted with legal land titles, he moved with his family in 1799 to the Spanish territory of Missouri, then in 1814 was granted 850 acres by Congress in deference to his service to the country. He has been a popular figure in American folklore ever since the publication of John Filson's account of Boone's exploits in *The Discovery, Settlement, and Present State of Kentucke* (1784).

Bouquet, Henry (1719–1765): British army officer. Bouquet came to North America with his regiment in 1756 and was second in command to General John Forbes in the expedition against the French Fort Duquesne (Pittsburgh). Following the outbreak of Pontiac's Rebellion, he led British troops to victory at the battle of Bushy Run, near Pittsburgh, in 1763, defeating the Delaware and Shawnee Indians. Bouquet introduced to wilderness warfare the fighting technique of combining rapid troop movements with massive firepower. Though little appreciated by his fellow officers, these methods gained him the fearful respect of his Indian enemies.

Bozeman, John (1835–1867): Frontier trail blazer. In the winter of 1862–63, he established a new and shorter route from Colorado to the rich mining regions of Montana. Although the Bozeman Trail passed through Sioux territory, it was used regularly by gold miners, wagon trains and cattle drivers. The increase in travelers passing through Sioux lands led to a full-scale Indian conflict, known as Red Cloud's War (1866–68). Bozeman was killed in an Indian attack in 1867, and the trail that bears his name was partially abandoned following the Fort Laramie Treaty of 1868.

Brackenridge, Henry Marie (1786–1871): Traveler, author and jurist. He was born in Pittsburgh and as a young man migrated to St. Louis, where he practiced law and wrote sketches about the new territory. In 1811, he accompanied fur trader Manuel Lisa on a voyage up the Missouri. From 1822 to 1832 he served as a judge of the western district of Florida.

Braddock, Edward (1695–1755): British army officer, commander in-chief of British forces in America during the French and Indian War. He was decisively defeated at the battle of the Wilderness (near Fort Duquesne) by a joint force of French soldiers and Indians. He was killed in the course of battle.

Brant, Joseph (Thayendanega) (1742–1807): Mohawk chief and military leader. Like most of his tribe, he was strongly influenced by the British and became a convert to the Anglican Church. He attended an Indian school in Connecticut and was loyal to the British during the American Revolution, leading numerous raids on frontier settlements. After the American victory, he and his followers fled to Canada, settling on lands allotted to them by the British government.

Bridger, James (1804–1881): Frontiersman, fur trader and scout; one of the most famed western mountain men. While working as a blacksmith in St. Louis he joined the William Ashley expedition in 1822. Bridger was perhaps the first white to visit the Great Salt Lake. He and several partners established the Rocky Mountain Fur Company in 1822. To serve travelers on the Oregon Trail he established Fort Bridger in 1843. He guided Jedediah Smith and the Marcus Whitman parties, among many others, and became a symbol of the mountain man—illiterate but intelligent, spinner of tall tales and intimately knowledgeable about the West.

Brock, Sir Isaac (1769–1812): British army officer; commanded all British troops in Upper Canada in the War of 1812. He joined forces with Tecumseh and forced General William Hull to surrender Fort Detroit along with his 1,400 men, gaining control of the Upper Lakes region. He was killed while leading a charge at the battle of Queenston Heights (Ontario).

Brown, John (1800–1859): Abolitionist; born in Connecticut and as a young boy moved with his family to Ohio, near Cleveland. In 1854, five of his sons established claims near Lawrence, Kansas. After receiving reports of a conspiracy to make Kansas a slave state, he went to Kansas to wage an armed campaign against proslavery advocates. He spent about 20 months in the territory and participated in the Pottawatomie massacre (May 24, 1856), murdering five proslavery men. Brown was sought but only his sons were apprehended. In 1859, he tried to foment a slave uprising by raiding the federal arsenal at Harper's Ferry, Virginia, for which he was found guilty of treason and hanged.

Bryan, William Jennings (1860–1925): Politician and statesman. He was elected Nebraska's first Democratic congressman in 1890, serving two terms. Defeated when he ran for the Senate in 1894, he became the editor of the *Omaha World Herald*. After his famous "Cross of Gold" speech at the 1896 Democratic convention, he received the party's presidential nomination. Although popular in the West and the South, he could not attract voters in the Northeast and industrial Middle West, and he was defeated by Republican William McKinley. He ran for president in 1900 and 1908 with similar results, but remained a force in his party until his death.

Buchanan, James (1791–1868): Fifteenth U.S. president (1857–1861). As President Polk's secretary of state (1845–1849), he ended the Oregon dispute with Great Britain and supported the Mexican War and the annexation of Texas. Nominated by the Democrats, he was elected president in 1856, over Republican candidate John C. Fremont. On slavery he favored popular sovereignty; he accepted the pro-slavery Dred Scott decision as binding. He denied the right of states to secede.

Bull Bear (fl. 1860s–1870s): Cheyenne chief. He was one of the chiefs of the Cheyenne military clan known as the Dog Soldiers and often took a militant stance against the whites. He participated, along with Black Kettle, in the talks with Colorado's governor John Evans at Camp Weld in 1864. He joined the Comanches and Kiowas in the Red River War (1874–1875), and afterward accepted life on the reservation.

Burnet, David Gouverneur (1788–1870): Texas politician. Burnet promoted independence from Mexico and drew up a declaration of independence; made interim president of the republic, he served eight months in 1836. Refusing to be a candidate, he called an election in which Sam Houston was elected president of the Republic of Texas. He served as secretary of state for the new U.S. state of Texas in 1846 and opposed the 1861 secession of Texas from the United States. He was elected in 1866 to the Senate but was never allowed to serve because of Texas' status as an unreconstructed former slave state.

Butler, Richard (1743–1791): Indian commissioner and U.S. Army officer. He participated in treaty negotiations with the Six Nations and other tribes. In 1791, he was killed while leading troops in a campaign waged by General Arthur St. Clair against the Indians in the Ohio country.

Butterfield, John (1801–1869): Businessman. Butterfield founded and organized the Overland Mail Company in 1857 and traveled on the stagecoach carrying the first mailbags as far as Fort Smith, Arkansas. He operated a stagecoach line that ran from St. Louis and Memphis across the Southwest to Los Angeles and San Francisco. He proposed the establishment of the Pony Express, a daily overland mail service. After experiencing large financial losses from operating the Pony Express, he was removed from the presidency of the Overland Mail Company and returned to New York City to engage in various business enterprises.

Calhoun, John C. (1782–1850): Statesman. As secretary of war during President Monroe's administration (1817–1825), Calhoun organized the War Department into an efficient bureau, created a substantial standing army and removed the possibility of further collusion between the British and the Northwest Indians. The Yellowstone expedition of 1819 and Major Stephen H. Long's expedition to the Rocky Mountains were products of his policy. He used the army to build roads and open up the frontier. While in the Senate, representing South Carolina, he championed state sovereignty and the annexation of additional territory, especially if it was likely to develop into a slave state. He favored the annexation of Texas, and as secretary of state under President Tyler (1844) he helped develop a joint resolution to Congress whereby Texas was admitted to the Union. During the debate over the Compromise of 1850, he vehemently opposed any agreement that would exclude slavery from the new territories acquired from Mexico.

Canby, Edward Richard Sprigg (1817–1873): U.S. Army officer in the Seminole War and in the Mexican War. In the Civil War he commanded the Department of New Mexico, where he repelled the Confederate invasion in 1862. After the war, he was assigned to the Department of the Columbia on the Pacific Coast, where he was killed during a peace conference with the Modoc Indians.

Carleton, James Henry (1814–1873): U.S. Army officer. During the Civil War he was a brigadier general with the California Volunteers. He recaptured federal forts and frontier settlements from the invading Confederate army in the Southwest. As departmental commander in New Mexico (1862) he sent Kit Carson on an expedition against the Mescalero Apaches and later the Navajos. He forced the Mescalero to live on a reservation at Bosque Redondo in the Pecos Valley and oversaw an invasion of the Navaho country, resulting in their surrender and the Long Walk by 8,000 Navaho to Bosque Redondo.

Carrington, Henry Beebee (1824–1912): U.S. Army officer; adjutant general of the Ohio State Militia at the outbreak of the Civil War. At the end of the war his regiment was dispatched to the Great Plains to fight the Sioux. Carrington built and garrisoned Forts Reno, Phil Kearny and C.F. Smith to protect travelers over the Bozeman Trail. When a wagon convoy returning with wood for the construction of Fort Phil Kearny was attacked by bands of Sioux warriors in December 1866, Carrington permitted Captain William Fetterman to lead a relief column to repel the attackers. Fetterman and his small command were annihilated by about 2,000 Sioux, Cheyenne and Arapahos. Carrington was accused of being partly responsible for the disaster and he was relieved of his command. The "Fetterman Massacre" effectively ended his military career, and he was never again given an important command.

Carson, Christopher "Kit" (1809–1868): Mountain man, scout, soldier and Indian agent. Carson gained his earliest experience in the West as a fur trapper from 1829 to 1841. On three separate expeditions he guided John C. Fremont through the central Rockies, the Great Basin, Oregon and California. It was Carson's service with Fremont that first brought him public attention. During the Mexican War he guided General Stephen Kearny's troops from New Mexico to California. He served as an Indian agent from 1853 to 1861; he organized the First New Mexican Volunteer Infantry and served as its colonel during the Civil War. Carson fought the Confederates in a battle at Valverde, New Mexico, in 1862 and in 1864 led troops against the Navajos in the Southwest, forcing 8,000 Indians to accept life on a reservation. Carson fought the Comanche and Kiowa at the battle of Adobe Walls, an abandoned trading post in Texas. He resigned from the military in 1867, then settled with his family in Colorado.

Cass, Lewis (1782–1866): U.S. Army officer and politician. Cass commanded the Third Ohio Regiment during the War of 1812 and participated in General William Hull's unsuccessful campaign against Detroit. He fought with distinction at the battle of the Thames. As governor of Michigan Territory (1813–1831), he solved the territorial problems of land settlement and Indian affairs. As secretary of war under President Jackson (1831–1836), he drove the Indians beyond the Mississippi River, prosecuting the Black Hawk War (1832). In the Senate (1845–1848, 1849–1857), he demanded that the United States acquire the Oregon country and pressed for the occupation of Mexico. Cass received the Democratic nomination for president in 1848 but was defeated by Whig candidate Zachary Taylor. Cass developed the doctrine of popular sovereignty, the concept that territorial residents could decide whether to permit slavery in their territory.

Catlin, George (1796–1872): Painter and writer. Born in Wilkes-Barre, Pennsylvania, he studied law but abandoned that career to paint. Catlin was the first major artist to document the culture of the American Indian in pictorial terms. In 1832, he traveled with the American Fur Company to the upper Missouri, and in 1834, he accompanied a company of mounted dragoons out of Fort Gibson, Indian Territory, on an expedition into Pawnee and Comanche country. Following his western adventures, he exhibited his work in the East.

Chief Joseph (Hin-mah-too-yah-lat-kekt) (1840–1904): Nez Perce leader who opposed settlers seeking to drive his band from their extensive grazing lands and settle them on a reservation in Idaho. In 1877, General Oliver Howard ordered him to lead his followers to a reservation or face attack by the Cavalry. He was accused of commanding a hostile faction that started the Nez Perce War of 1877, when actually they were led by his brother, Olikut. Joseph opposed many of the plans adopted by the war councils, but he was overruled by his fellow chiefs. After months of fighting, he was the only leader left alive to surrender the remnants of the Nez Perce bands to General Nelson Miles at the Bear Paw battlefield in northern Montana.

Chisholm, Jesse (1805–1868): Trader. Chisholm is known for blazing the Chisholm Trail, one of the West's most-used cattle trails, which linked the railroad in Kansas with ranches in Texas. He engaged in frontier trade in the Indian Territory with the Osage, Wichita, Kiowa and Comanche tribes and operated several trading posts in the area, including one in Council Grove on the North Canadian River near present-day Oklahoma City. He served as an interpreter and negotiator in councils held between tribal chiefs and federal officials, resulting in the release of prisoners held by the Indians, and guided several important expeditions into the Southwest, including the Dodge-Leavenworth expedition in 1834. He operated a trading post near Wichita during the Civil War and later opened a wagon trail south to the Red River.

Chisum, John Simpson (1824–1884): Cattle rancher. During the Civil War, Chisum furnished cattle to the Confederacy. He was one of the earliest Texas ranchers to establish operations in New Mexico, and he drove herds of cattle into New Mexico before they were sold in Wyoming and Colorado. Chisum was the largest cattle owner in the United States by the 1870s, when he was known as the Cow King of New Mexico.

Chivington, John M. (1821–1894): Minister and Colorado militia officer. Chivington worked as a preacher in Ohio, Illinois, Missouri, Kansas and Nebraska before arriving in Denver, Colorado, in 1860. During the Civil War he fought with the First Regiment, participated in the battle at La Glorietta Pass, New Mexico, then spent the remainder of his military career fighting the Indians of the Colorado plains. He led a campaign against a Cheyenne camp on Sand Creek in 1864; it became known as the Sand Creek Massacre when 200 to 450 Indians were killed, including many women and children. Investigated by Congress and condemned for his actions, he resigned his commission in 1865, escaping military prosecution.

Clagett, William Horace (1838–1901): Northwest lawyer and politician. Clagett was elected to Congress in 1870, representing Montana Territory. He was instrumental in establishing Yellowstone Park. After settling in Idaho, he became president of the constitutional convention there in 1889. He also was an attorney for Idaho's largest lead-silver mining corporation, Bunker Hill and Sullivan. Like most westerners, he supported the silver standard, but as a Populist rather than as a Silver Republican.

Claiborne, William Charles Coles (1775–1817): Territorial politician. With the acquisition of Louisiana, he and Major General James Wilkenson were appointed commissioners to receive the new land from Spanish officials. Claiborne served as second governor of Mississippi Territory and the only governor of Orleans Territory (1804–1812). He was elected first governor of the state of Louisiana in 1812.

Clark, George Rogers (1752–1818): In the American Revolution, Clark commanded the American forces created to defend the frontier against British-supported Indian raids. He conquered Illinois, capturing Kaskaskia and Cahokia, and secured Vincennes, Indiana. He also engaged in several battles to protect the Northwest Territory, including conflict with the Shawnees, and successfully defended St. Louis against the British. Asked by President Jefferson to explore the land west of the Mississippi River, he refused, and the task was later carried out by his brother, William. He was involved in several questionable ventures supposedly aimed at French and Spanish colonization of the Mississippi Valley. Clark died in poverty.

Clark, William (1770–1838): Explorer and politician, younger brother of George Rogers Clark, hero of the American Revolution. Clark was raised on the frontier and became an Indian fighter. He fought under General Anthony Wayne in the battle of Fallen Timbers. Later he was coleader of the Lewis and Clark Expedition (1803–1806). On the journey, he was the principal cartographer and a skillful Indian negotiator. He served as Indian agent for the Louisiana Territory (1807–1813), governor of Missouri Territory (1813–1820), and superintendent of Indian affairs (1822–1838).

Clay, Henry (1777–1851): Statesman. Elected to Congress in 1810, Clay was a zealous advocate of the needs of his Kentucky constituents and the West. He supported a declaration of war against Great Britain, convinced that the British in Canada were inciting the Indians to attack the American frontier. Member of the peace commission to Ghent in 1814, he played a role in forcing Britain to abandon her right to navigate the Mississippi River. As speaker of the House of Representatives, he played a decisive role in achieving the Missouri Compromise that resolved the dispute over slavery in 1820, earning him the title of the "Great Pacificator." He was Whig candidate for the presidency in 1844; although favoring the annexation of Texas, he opposed acquiring it by waging war against Mexico. He was defeated by Democratic candidate James Polk. He returned to Congress as a senator in 1849, and with Daniel Webster ushered in the Compromise of 1850, preserving the Union for another decade.

Clay, John (1851–1934): Cattle rancher. Born in Scotland, Clay moved to Chicago in 1882 as an agent for Scottish companies with cattle investments in the West. He was president of the Wyoming Stock Growers Association from 1890 to 1896.

Clemens, Samuel Langhorne [Mark Twain] (1835–1910): Author. Twain was born in Florida, Missouri, and from 1839 to 1853 lived in Hannibal, Missouri, which he was later to depict in much of his fiction. He worked as a pilot on Mississippi River steamers from 1857 to 1861. When the Civil War disrupted river traffic, he traveled west to Nevada in 1862, where he became a newspaper reporter in Virginia City. Achieved his first fame with the short story

"The Celebrated Jumping Frog of Calaveras County" in 1865. He humorously described the West through eastern eyes in the travel book *Roughing It* (1872).

Clyman, James (1792–1881): Trader, trapper and guide. A member of William Ashley's fur trading company, in 1824–25, Clyman participated in the first trappers' rendezvous on the Green River in Wyoming, and from 1825 to 1827 he explored the Great Salt Lake region. He settled in Milwaukee, Wisconsin, in 1834 and set his sights west again in 1844, when he traveled to Oregon and California by wagon train from Missouri. Three years later, in 1848, he guided an emigrant wagon party from Wisconsin to California, where he settled in the Napa Valley.

Cody, William Frederick ["Buffalo Bill"] (1846–1917): Scout, soldier and showman. Born in Iowa, Cody moved with his family to Kansas in 1854, settling near Fort Leavenworth. He served as a Pony Express rider (1860–1861) and as a scout and trooper during the Civil War. He gained great fame in the West for killing huge numbers of buffalo to feed the workers on the Kansas Pacific Railroad. As a scout for the Fifth United States Cavalry (1868–1872), he participated in several Indian fights. Ned Buntline, a prolific writer of dime novels, made Cody the hero in many of his tales. He then went into show business, and in 1883 organized Buffalo Bill's Wild West Show, featuring bands of Indians, cowboys, roughriders, bucking broncos and buffalos.

Colter, John (ca. 1774–1813): Member of the Lewis and Clark Expedition; employed by fur trader Manuel Lisa and later by Andrew Henry. Colter is credited with being the first white to explore "Colter's Hell," present-day Yellowstone Park. In 1808, he escaped from the Blackfoot Indians, who had stripped him of his clothes and weapons, by outrunning the tribe's fastest braves. He returned to St. Louis in 1810, married and settled down to farming.

Comstock, Henry Tompkins Paige (1820–1870): Prospector and putative discoverer of the Comstock Lode, at Virginia City, Nevada, one of the richest mineral deposits in the world. Comstock founded the Ophir Mine, which produced hundreds of thousands of dollars in silver. After spending the $10,000 he had received for the Comstock Mine, he traveled to Montana and later took his own life at Bozeman.

Cooke, Jay (1821–1905): Financier. He founded Jay Cooke and Company, which marketed government bonds for financing the Civil War. In 1870, he financed construction of western railroads, including the Northern Pacific. The financial structure proved unsound, and in 1873 his bank collapsed, plunging the nation into the Panic of 1873.

Cornplanter (John O'Bail or Abeel) (ca. 1732–1836): Seneca chief. He joined the French during the French and Indian War and fought with the Iroquois against the Americans during the American Revolution. Cornplanter played a major role at the treaty councils at Fort Stanwix (1784) and Fort Harmar (1789). He advocated rapid assimilation of white ways and undertook peace missions to hostile tribes for the federal government. He made private agreements that brought him large amounts of land and money. In later years he became convinced that the "Great Spirit" had told him to break all his ties with the whites, and he repudiated the idea of assimilation.

Crazy Horse (Tashunca-utco) (ca. 1842–1877): Oglala Sioux chief and warrior. He participated in the "Fetterman Massacre" (1866), the Hayfield Fight (1867) and the Wagon-Box Fight (1867). Leader of the Southern Sioux and Northern Cheyenne who refused to stay on their reservations. He defeated General George Crook at the battle of Rosebud (June 17, 1876) and wiped out Lieutenant Colonel George Armstrong Custer and his command at the battle of Little Big Horn eight days later. He was defeated, along with an estimated 800 warriors, by General Nelson Miles in 1877. Crazy Horse surrendered to American troops in Nebraska and was later killed under mysterious circumstances.

Crocker, Charles (1822–1888): Railroad builder and businessman. After failing at prospecting during the California gold rush, he started a retailing business that prospered, and within a few years he became one of the richest men in San Francisco. Along with Collis P. Huntington, Leland Stanford and Mark Hopkins, he formed the Central Pacific Railroad in 1861, the western segment of the transcontinental line. He supervised the actual work, living with his crews and sharing their hardships, and completing the line seven years ahead of the government deadline. He organized the Southern Pacific and was involved in other railroads and various businesses.

Crockett, Davy (David) (1786–1836): Frontiersman, soldier and politician. He was a scout for General Andrew Jackson during the Creek War (1813–1815), then was elected to the Tennessee legislature in 1820 and served in the House of Representatives (1827–1831 and 1833–1835). Defeated in the 1835 election, he moved to Texas and joined the revolutionary movement there. He died at the Alamo when the Mexican army overran the fort, killing all of its defenders. His witty stories, expert marksmanship and his valiant death contributed to making him a legend.

Croghan, George (1722?–1782): Frontiersman and Indian diplomat. Immigrating to America in 1741 from Ireland, Croghan traded with the Indians on the colonial frontier, learned Indian languages and built up a trading empire. He was secretary of Indian affairs under Sir William Johnson. During the French and Indian War he was successful in winning many tribes away from the French cause, and he brought about the treaty ending Pontiac's Rebellion (1763–1766). Unable to clear himself from staggering debts incurred by Indian trading and land speculation, he died in poverty.

Crook, George (1828–1890): U.S. Army officer. He began his military career with the Fourth Infantry, stationed on the Pacific Coast and during the Civil War was colonel of the Ohio Volunteer Infantry, participating in the Second Battle of Bull Run. After the Civil War, he returned to the western frontier, commanding posts in Idaho and the Oregon country. He commanded the Department of the Platte in 1875, clearing the Black Hills of trespassing prospectors. He also participated in the Sioux War of 1876, fighting the Indians at the indecisive battle of Powder River, Montana, and the battle of Rosebud, where he was forced to retreat. He fought against the Apaches from 1882 to 1886, and was relieved of his command after Geronimo fled to Mexico. During his remaining years he supported Indian rights organizations and tried to improve the conditions of the Sioux by persuading them to accept a policy of land allotment.

Custer, Elizabeth (1842–1933): Author. Wife of Lieutenant Colonel George Armstrong Custer. She devoted much of her life to upholding his memory, and she wrote several books based upon her frontier experiences, including *Boots and Saddles* (1885), *Tenting in the Plains* (1887) and *Following the Guidon* (1890).

Custer, George Armstrong (1839–1876): U.S. Army officer. During the Civil War his gallant service led to his promotion to the rank of brevet brigadier general at the age of 23, the youngest in the Union Army. Lieutenant colonel in command of the Seventh U.S. Cavalry Regiment, he later fought Indians in the Southwest, Montana and the Dakota Territory. In 1868, he led his regiment to victory at the battle of Washita River in present-day Oklahoma. In 1874, he commanded an expedition to the Black Hills, an area that was guaranteed to the Sioux by treaty, and his confirmation of gold triggered a stampede of miners into the area. The conflict with the Sioux

culminated in the battle of Little Big Horn in 1876, in which Custer and his troops were annihilated.

Cutler, Manasseh (1742–1823): Clergyman, Revolutionary War veteran and land speculator; born in Killingsly, Connecticut. Cutler was an organizer of the Ohio Company. He promoted the Ordinance of 1787, which provided for the establishment of a territorial government in the Ohio valley, and obtained from Congress a grant of 1.5 million acres on the Ohio River. He served in the House of Representatives from 1801 to 1805.

Dana, Richard Henry, Jr. (1815–1882): Author. Born in Massachusetts, Dana traveled around Cape Horn to California in 1834 as a common sailor, and returned to Boston in 1836. He graduated from Harvard Law School in 1837. Dana described his voyage to California in the famed *Two Years Before the Mast*, published in 1840. The book was popular for its vivid description of life at sea and for its eyewitness report on life in California.

Davis, Jefferson (1808–1889): Politician and president of the Confederacy. As a senator from Mississippi (1847–1851), Davis opposed the Compromise of 1850. As secretary of war under President Pierce (1853–1856), he commissioned engineering surveys to mark possible routes for the first transcontinental railroad. He returned to the Senate in 1857, where he became an ardent defender of the South. In 1861 he withdrew from the Senate and became the first and only president of the Confederate States of America.

Dawes, Henry Laurens (1816–1903): Politician, Indian reformer, Massachusetts Republican congressman and senator (1857–1893). As chairman of the Senate Committee on Indian Affairs, he ushered in the Dawes Severalty Act (1887), an Indian land allotment policy. In 1893, he served as chairman of the Dawes Commission to place the Five Civilized Tribes in Oklahoma under the provisions of the Dawes Act.

Dearborn, Henry (1751–1829): Public official and U.S. Army officer. As secretary of war (1801–1809) under President Jefferson he helped form the plan for Indian removal beyond the Mississippi River. In the War of 1812, he was major general of the army and commander of the northern border. After the British seized Fort Detroit and Fort Dearborn, he was relieved of his command.

Deere, John (1804–1886): Inventor and manufacturer. A Vermont-born blacksmith, Deere developed the first plow with steel moldboard in 1837. This improvement upon cast-iron blades revolutionized prairie farming. Deere started a manufacturing company in Moline, Illinois, and by 1857 was producing 10,000 plows annually. The business was incorporated as Deere and Company in 1868, and he remained the president of the company for the rest of his life.

De Smet, Pierre Jean (1801–1873): Missionary and peace commissioner. Born in Belgium, De Smet immigrated to the United States in 1821. In 1840, he traveled to Montana with an American Fur Company expedition. He established a series of missions in present-day Montana, Idaho and Oregon and won the friendship of various tribes in the Pacific Northwest. He was a frequent mediator of Indian and settler disputes and served as a government peace commissioner at the Fort Laramie councils in 1851 and 1868. He wrote prolifically about his work and experiences on the Northern Plains.

Dinwiddie, Robert (1693–1770): British official; surveyor general of America (1738–1751); governor of Virginia (1751–1758). In 1753, he commissioned George Washington to lead a small party into the Ohio territory to warn the French that they were on Virginia soil. After receiving notice that the French intended to remain in the Ohio Valley, he ordered the construction of a fort at the confluence of the Allegheny and Monongahela rivers, present-day Pittsburgh.

Dodge, Grenville Mellen (1831–1916): Railroad builder. During the Civil War Dodge, as major general of the Fourth Iowa Regiment, constructed and rebuilt several southern railroads for the Union army. After the war, he was chief engineer for the Union Pacific Railroad, the eastern segment of the first transcontinental railroad; he supervised the building of the railroad until it was completed in 1870, setting construction records. He was chief engineer for the Texas and Pacific Railroad until its failure in the depression of 1873. He directed the construction of 9,000 miles of track for the Denver, Texas and Fort Worth and the Denver, Texas and Gulf railroads. During his career it is estimated he surveyed approximately 60,000 miles of railroad line in the Midwest, the West and Cuba.

Doniphan, Alexander William (1808–1887): U.S. Army officer. As a brigadier general he successfully negotiated with Joseph Smith for the disarming and removal of the Mormon colony in Missouri. Doniphan was commanding officer in New Mexico during the Mexican War. He defeated Mexican troops at the battle of Brazito and led the First Missouri Volunteers, known as "Doniphan's Thousand," a ragged and individualistic group of soldiers, from Valverde, New Mexico, to Chihuahua, Mexico, to reinforce American forces in Mexico, in what is considered one of the longest and most brilliant marches ever made.

Douglas, Stephen Arnold (1813–1861): Politician. Born in Vermont, he became a congressman and then senator from Illinois, and a Democratic presidential candidate in 1860. A vigorous exponent of westward expansion and development, Douglas successfully secured land grants for the Chicago Illinois Railroad, which was to run from Chicago to the Gulf of Mexico; he also advocated a homestead act. He was author of the Kansas-Nebraska Act, the most controversial and divisive issue of the 1850s. In his famous debates with Abraham Lincoln in 1858, he spoke in favor of popular sovereignty, despite the Dred Scott decision. After his defeat in the 1860 election, he supported Lincoln and worked tirelessly for the Union. His health suffered, and he died of typhoid fever.

Dragging-Canoe (Tsiyu-gunsini) (ca. 1730–1792): Cherokee chief. A leader of those Cherokee who were hostile to Americans during the Revolutionary War. After the war, he aided General Andrew Jackson in the Creek War and participated in the battle at Horseshoe Bend.

Dunbar, William (1749–1810): Botanist. Born in Scotland and came to the United States in 1771; Dunbar was later commissioned by President Jefferson to explore the Ouachita and Red River areas. He undertook the first meteorological observations in the Southwest; studied the rise and fall of the Mississippi River; and published his findings on these subjects and on the plants, animals and Indians of the region.

Dunmore, Lord (John Murray) (1732–1809): Fourth earl of Dunmore, Scotland. He was British administrator in America; governor of New York (1770–1771); and governor of Virginia (1771–1776). In 1774, he led Virginians in a campaign against the Shawnees of the Ohio country, usually known as Lord Dunmore's War. He defeated the Shawnees at Point Pleasant (October 10, 1774) and then negotiated the Treaty of Camp Charlotte, which opened up Kentucky to settlement.

Evans, John (1814–1897): Colorado businessman and politician. Evans was appointed the second governor of Colorado Territory in 1862 and, serving as the ex-officio superintendent of Indian affairs, played a controversial role in the investigation of the Sand Creek Massacre (1864). He resigned his post as governor in 1865. Remaining in Denver, he became a prominent figure in business circles, organizing the

Denver Pacific Railroad to connect Denver with the Union Pacific line at Cheyenne.

Fargo, William George (1818–1881): Businessman; partner in a number of transportation companies and banks. Best known of his operations was Wells, Fargo and Company, founded in 1852, a gold-rush express firm that provided the most reliable and the cheapest transportation over the major routes from Missouri to the West Coast in the mid-1800s. One of the founders of the American Express Company, he became its president in 1873, and held that position until his death.

Farnham, Thomas Jefferson (1804–1888): Author. In 1839, he led a small group of overland travelers across the continent to the Pacific coast via the Santa Fe Trail. Farnham published the account of his journey as *Travels in the Great Western Prairies* (1841) and supplemented it with *Life and Adventures in California* (1846), both of which described a partially new route to the West.

Fetterman, William Judd (ca. 1833–1866): U.S. Army officer. Fetterman served in the Union Army during the Civil War and was twice brevetted for gallant conduct. In December 1866, while at Fort Phil Kearny, Wyoming, he volunteered to lead an expedition of 80 soldiers on supply escort duty to relieve a wagon train carrying wood that had come under Sioux attack near the fort; he ignored orders not to leave the trail, and was ambushed by about 2,000 Sioux and Cheyenne warriors under the leadership of Red Cloud. He and his entire party were killed in the attack known as the "Fetterman Massacre" or the "Fetterman Fight."

Fillmore, Millard (1800–1874): Thirteenth U.S. president (1850–1853). As a congressman (1833–1835 and 1837–1843) Fillmore opposed the admission of Texas as a slave state. In 1848, he was elected vice president and succeeded as president on July 10, 1850, upon Zachary Taylor's death. He favored the Compromise of 1850 and signed the Fugitive Slave Law, but his policies pleased neither expansionists nor slaveholders and he was not nominated in 1852.

Finerty, John Frederick (1846–1908): Journalist. As correspondent for the *Chicago Times,* he covered more Indian wars than any other reporter: the Sioux War of 1876; Colonel Nelson Miles's operations against the Sioux in 1881, during which he visited Sitting Bull's camp in Canada; the Ute campaign of 1879; and an Apache uprising in 1881. He recounted his war experiences in *War-Path and Bivouac* (1890), which closely follows his dispatches.

Fitzpatrick, Thomas (1799–1854): Fur trader, mountain man, guide and Indian agent. Born in Ireland, Fitzpatrick immigrated to America while a young man. He led the expedition of William H. Ashley up the Missouri River (1824–1826); he was present at the fur trappers' rendezvous in 1825; was employed by Jedediah Smith, David Jackson and William Sublette's company; and in 1830 formed the Rocky Mountain Fur Company with James Bridger. Fitzpatrick also accompanied John C. Fremont on his second expedition (1843–1844). As Indian agent to the tribes of the upper Platte and Arkansas rivers (1845–1854), he convened the Fort Laramie council in 1851 to settle boundary disputes among warring Plains tribes.

Flint, Timothy (1780–1840): Minister, social historian and author. Born near North Reading, Massachusetts, in 1815 Flint moved west to Cincinnati, Ohio, and later to Alexandria, Louisiana. The trip formed the basis for much of the narrative of his first book, *Recollections of the Last Ten Years* (1826). Flint edited the *Western Monthly Review* (1827–1830), which he turned into the first successful literary periodical to be printed west of the Allegheny Mountains. He was best known to his contemporaries as the author of the extremely popular *Biographical Memoir of Daniel Boone* (1833).

Flower, George (1780–1862): Pioneer and author; born in England and immigrated to the United States in 1816. He and Morris Birkbeck, a fellow Englishman, established the "English Settlement" of Albion, Illinois.

Floyd, John (1783–1837): Virginia congressman (1817–1829) and advocate for the annexation of Oregon. Through his friendship with William Clark, the explorer, and his acquaintance with several members of the Astorian expedition, he developed an enthusiasm for Oregon, which made him known as "The Father of the Oregon Country."

Forbes, John (1710–1759): British army officer. Commanded expedition that captured the French stronghold of Fort Duquesne (November 25, 1758) and renamed it Pittsburgh. After the French and Indian War, the crude road his army cleared was referred to as Forbes' Road, and throngs of settlers used it as their route to the Ohio Valley.

Fowler, Jacob (1765–1850): Frontiersman and trader. Born in New York, as a young man Fowler immigrated to Kentucky and worked as a surveyor. For the federal government, his surveying extended to the Great Plains and the mountains of the Far West.

In 1821–1822, he undertook a trading expedition through the Southwest, from Arkansas to the Rio Grande. He played a major role in opening the Santa Fe trade.

Franchere, Gabriel (1786–1863): Fur trader. Born in Montreal, Canada, Franchere was a clerk at John Jacob Astor's Astoria post in the Oregon country (1810–1814). In 1820 his journal describing the founding of Astoria was published. He was also an agent for the American Fur Company (1815–1842) and Pierre Chouteau, Jr. & Company (1842–1857).

Fremont, Jessie Benton (1824–1902): Author; daughter of Thomas Hart Benton and wife of John C. Fremont. She helped her husband write his reports and encouraged his explorations. When their fortune was lost, she helped support the household by her writing. Among her books are *A Year of American Travel* (1878), *Far West Sketches* (1890) and *The Will and the Way Stories* (1891).

Fremont, John C. "The Pathfinder" (1813–1890): Explorer, politician and soldier. Fremont explored the Rocky Mountains and the Far West and made these expeditions known to the public through his voluminous reports. He began his career as a lieutenant of topography for the Army Corps of Engineers (1834–1841); mapped the Missouri River region (1838–1839); led an expedition to the South Pass of the Continental Divide (1842); and explored the Rockies, Great Salt Lake and Oregon country (1843). Expelled from California by Mexican authorities on his third expedition (1845–1846), he led the Bear Flag Rebellion against Mexico in California (1846). He served as U.S. senator from California (1850–1851) and presidential nominee of the Republican Party (1856); he briefly held two military commands during the Civil War (1862–1863).

Gadsden, James (1788–1858): Diplomat, railroad developer and Indian commissioner. In 1853, while minister to Mexico under Franklin Pierce, he negotiated the purchase of a wedge of territory between Texas and California (including parts of present-day southern New Mexico and Arizona), known as the Gadsden Purchase. He viewed the land cession as an important element in building a southern transcontinental railroad route.

Gaines, Edmund Pendleton (1777–1849): Soldier. In the War of 1812, he commanded the department of Fort Erie. He served under Andrew Jackson in the Creek and Seminole campaigns and participated in the Black Hawk War and Mexican War.

Gallatin, Abraham Alfonse Albert (1761–1849): Financier and public official. Born in Geneva, Switzerland, Gallatin immigrated to the United States in 1780, settling in Pennsylvania. He was a member of the House of Representatives (1795–1801) and secretary of the treasury (1801–1814), and he played a major role in negotiating the Treaty of Ghent (1814), ending the War of 1812. After the war, he served as president of the National Bank of New York from 1832 to 1839.

Gass, Patrick (1771–1870): Explorer. A member of the Lewis and Clark expedition, Gass was the first to publish a journal of the expedition, in 1807, seven years before the official Lewis and Clark journals were finally printed. He later fought under General Andrew Jackson against the Creeks in the War of 1812.

Geronimo (ca. 1825–1909): Medicine man and leader of the southernmost band of Chiricahua Apaches. Last American Indian to surrender formally to the United States (1886). After Mexicans killed his wife and children in 1858, he sought revenge by leading raids on encroaching settlers, on both sides of the border. In 1877, he was arrested by federal forces in New Mexico and was taken to Arizona, where he lived on a reservation until 1881, when he mounted a campaign against white settlers in New Mexico and Arizona. Geronimo surrendered in March 1886, escaped, later surrendered to General Nelson A. Miles and was sent into exile and prison in Florida. Released in 1894, he returned to Fort Sill, Oklahoma, took up farming, adopted Christianity and became a major attraction at expositions and public occasions.

Gilpin, William (1815–1894): Politician, lawyer, soldier and entrepreneur. In 1843 he visited the Columbia River region with John C. Fremont but left the expedition to aid the Willamette Valley settlers in forming a government and drafting a petition requesting congressional support. In 1845, he delivered the petition to Washington, and was commissioned to prepare a report on the Oregon country. His report, published in 1846, emphasized the need for western settlement and improved overland communication facilities. He also described the potential for trade between the Pacific Coast and Chinese ports. During the Mexican War he served as a major in Colonel Doniphan's regiment of Mounted Volunteers. After the war, he returned to Independence, Missouri, to practice law and pursue his interest in politics. In 1861, Gilpin was appointed by President Lincoln as the first governor of the newly created territory of Colorado.

Gist, Christopher (1706–1759): Frontiersman; born in Baltimore County, Maryland. Gist was commissioned by the Ohio Land Company to explore their western lands in 1750, and his journal of the expedition above the Ohio River and back across Kentucky in 1751 is one of the best accounts of the early frontier. He accompanied George Washington in 1753 on his expedition up the Allegheny River to French posts there. During the French and Indian War he was active in frontier trading, Indian diplomacy and frontier scouting.

Glidden, Joseph Farewell (1813–1906): Inventor; born in Charleston, New Hampshire. In 1844, Glidden settled in Illinois as a farmer, and he invented the first commercially successful barbed wire, with Isaac L. Ellwood, in 1874. He established Barb Fence and Company of De Kalb, Illinois, but sold his interest in the company in 1876.

Goodnight, Charlie (1836–1929): Texas cattle rancher and Indian scout. After a distinguished career as a Texas Ranger and a guide for a frontier regiment during the Civil War, Goodnight and Oliver Loving in 1866 pioneered a trail from Fort Belknap, Texas, to Fort Sumner, New Mexico. Known as the Goodnight-Loving Trail, it later became one of the most heavily used cattle trails in the Southwest. Goodnight was one of the first cattle ranchers in New Mexico and Colorado, and in 1877, he formed a partnership with John G. Adair in the JA Ranch, running 100,000 cattle on one million acres of land. He organized the Panhandle Stockmen's Association (1880) to improve breeding methods and curb rustling.

Gray, William H. (1810–1889): Oregon missionary and politician. Born in New York City, he first went to Oregon with Marcus Whitman and Henry Spalding in 1830 as a member of the first missionary group sent by the American Board of Commissioners. Hoping to get his own mission, he returned East in 1837. The following year he returned to Oregon with his new wife, Mary Augusta Dix of Ithaca, and a group of other missionaries, and he was influential in the formation of the provisional government there in 1843. As a member of the legislative committee he assisted in drafting the "First Organic Law," which governed the region until the United States established the Oregon Territory in 1848.

Greeley, Horace (1811–1872): Journalist and politician. Greeley founded the influential *New York Tribune*. He deplored the Mexican War, supported the idea of free land for settlers, and was credited with coining the phrase "Go West, young man, go West!"

After breaking with the Whigs in 1854, he became a founding member of the Republican Party. An ardent abolitionist, he opposed the Kansas-Nebraska Act and the Fugitive Slave Law and supplied arms to the Free-Soilers in Kansas. He was defeated by Ulysses S. Grant in the presidential election of 1872.

Gregg, Josiah (1806–1850): Trader and historian, born and raised on a Missouri farm. From 1831 to 1840 Gregg was active in the New Mexico trade. In his classic account, *Commerce of the Prairies* (1844), he vividly described how to organize caravans and handle mule trains, and he lauded the spirit of those who braved the Santa Fe Trail. He served with the Arkansas Volunteers during the Mexican War, and in 1848, he was a member of a botanical expedition to western Mexico and California. He died shortly after discovering Humboldt Bay, in northeast California.

Hancock, Winfield Scott (1824–1886): U.S. Army general. In the wake of the Fetterman Massacre of 1866, he was assigned to lead a strong military presence into Kansas to demonstrate the government's willingness to use military force to protect workers of the Kansas Pacific Railroad and travelers along the Santa Fe Trail. When he was unable to subdue Indian raiding parties in western Kansas and eastern Colorado in 1867, he was replaced as commander of the Department of the Missouri by General Philip H. Sheridan.

Harney, William Selby (1800–1889): U.S. Army officer. Harney began his military career with the First Infantry in 1818, participated in several expeditions against the Indians in Florida, and by the end of the Seminole campaign in 1840 had earned the rank of brevet colonel. During the Mexican War he was colonel of the Second Dragoons under General Winfield Scott. In the 1850s he commanded at Fort Leavenworth and Fort Laramie and held councils with bands of Sioux along the Oregon-California Trail. He served as commander of the Department of the West until 1861, and retired in 1863 after he came under suspicion as a Southern sympathizer.

Harrison, Benjamin (1833–1901): Twenty-third U.S. president (1889–1893). Grandson of William Henry Harrison, he was prominent in Indiana Republican politics. He was elected U.S. senator from Indiana in 1881 and in 1888 defeated Grover Cleveland, although he had 90,000 fewer popular votes, Harrison had won the presidency by an electoral count of 233 to Cleveland's 168. As president, Harrison signed the Sherman Silver Purchase Act and opened the Indian

Territory, present-day Oklahoma, for settlement. More states were admitted to the Union during his presidency than in that of any other president. He was defeated for reelection by William McKinley in 1892.

Harrison, William Henry (1773–1841): U.S. Army officer and 9th U.S. president (1841). Harrison commanded several campaigns against Indians in the Old Northwest Territory, including the decisive battle of Fallen Timbers (1794). He drafted a report that resulted in the formulation of the Harrison Land Law of 1800. As governor of Indiana Territory (1800–1812) he negotiated a series of treaties with various tribes that resulted in the cession of large blocks of land to settlers. He gained national fame with his modest victory against the Indians at the battle of Tippecanoe. During the War of 1812, he led American forces to victory at the battle of the Thames in Ontario. His popularity and his reputation as a hero in the West gained him the presidency in 1840, but he died only six weeks after taking office.

Hastings, Lansford Warren (1818–1868): Writer, lawyer and emigrant guide. In 1842, he and Elijah White led the first overland wagon migration to Oregon. He wrote one of the early overland guidebooks, *The Emigrants' Guide to Oregon and California* (1845), which was used by the ill-fated Donner Party. In 1846, he led the first California emigrants west of Fort Bridger across the Salt Desert cutoff that now bears his name.

Heap, Gwinn Harris (1817–1887): As a journalist on the railroad survey expedition of the Central Route to the Pacific, Heap kept a day-by-day account of the expedition, which was led by Lieutenant Edward F. Beale. His journal, *The Central Route to the Pacific, From the Valley of the Mississippi to California,* was first published in 1854.

Heckewelder, John Gottlieb Ernestus (1743–1823): Moravian missionary. Born in England, Heckewelder immigrated with his parents to the United States in 1754, settling in Bethlehem, Pennsylvania. He later aided the United States in negotiating treaties with Indians in the Ohio Valley.

Henderson, Richard (1735–1785): Land speculator and lawyer. Henderson was born in Virginia and moved with his family in 1742 to North Carolina. It is presumed that he employed Daniel Boone to explore central Kentucky. He organized the Transylvania Company in 1774 for land speculation in that territory. The company negotiated the Treaty of Sycamore Shoals in 1775, by which the Cherokee Indians surrendered their claims beyond the Cumberland

Gap. In 1776, the Continental Congress denied Henderson's petition to accept Transylvania as the 14th state. Following the failure of the Transylvania Colony, he returned to North Carolina.

Henry, Patrick (1736–1799): American statesman. Henry was a leading figure in several pre-Revolutionary land companies in the Ohio Valley. As governor of Virginia during the American Revolution, he dispatched Colonel George Rogers Clark to the Illinois country to reestablish Virginia's long-standing claim to the region. He believed the Mississippi River was crucial to western settlement, and in 1786 he condemned John Jay's proposed Spanish alliance, which would have surrendered navigation rights on the river for several years.

Hill, James Jerome (1838–1916): Railroad builder. Born in Ontario, Canada, Hill moved to the Minnesota Territory in 1852 and found work on Mississippi River steamboats. He later operated a lucrative steamboat service down the Red River to Winnipeg. He formed a partnership to buy up the bonds from the bankrupt St. Paul and Pacific Railroad, and by 1879 he had supervised its construction to the Canadian border. Renamed the Great Northern Railway, it reached Puget Sound in 1893, without the aid of any land grants or other government aid. Along with Huntington's Southern Pacific, it was the only transcontinental railroad to avoid bankruptcy during the depression of the 1890s.

Hitchcock, Ethan Allen (1798–1870): U.S. Army officer. He was attached to the staff of General Edmund P. Gaines in 1836 as acting inspector general, serving in the Seminole War in Florida. In the Mexican War he was an inspector general with General Zachary Taylor's staff, and was promoted to brigadier general for his gallant service at the battle of Molino del Rey.

Holladay, Ben (1819–1887): Entrepreneur. In 1858, Holladay became associated with Russell, Majors and Waddell when he bought large quantities of livestock for them in connection with their freighting operations. In 1860, he made loans to assist the Central Overland California and Pikes Peak Express Company, owned by Russell, Majors and Waddell, in establishing the Pony Express. He assumed the partnership at a foreclosure sale in 1862. Holladay organized the Overland Stage Line, which operated the eastern section of the trans-Mississippi mail until 1864. He was awarded a four-year government contract to carry the mail eastward of Salt Lake City and on branches in Montana, Washington, Idaho and Oregon. Financial setbacks from Indian attacks forced him to sell out to Wells, Fargo and Company in 1865.

Hopkins, Mark (1813–1878): Merchant and railroad builder, Hopkins was one of the ''Big Four'' who built the Central Pacific and Southern Pacific railroads. He moved to California in 1849, opened a miners' supply store and became a partner with Collis Huntington in 1856. He and Huntington formed the Central Pacific Railroad in 1861 with Charles Crocker and Leland Stanford. He was treasurer of the transcontinental railroad venture, and held the post until his death.

Houston, Sam[uel] (1793–1863): Military officer and politician. Born in Virginia, Houston moved as a child to Tennessee, where he spent several years living among the Cherokee Indians. He distinguished himself at the battle of Horseshoe Bend against the Creeks in 1814. He was elected governor of Tennessee in 1827 and became a spokesman for the Indians in 1829. After several trips to Texas on Indian affairs, he decided to remain in Nacogdoches in 1833. Houston was named commander-in-chief of the Texas revolutionary troops in 1836, then was elected first president of the Republic of Texas (1836–1838), U.S. senator from Texas (1846–1859) and governor of Texas (1859–1861). He broke with Southern ideology by voting for antislavery provisions and for the Compromise of 1850. He resigned as governor in 1861 and refused to swear allegiance to the Confederacy.

Howard, Oliver Otis (1830–1909): U.S. Army general; commander of the Department of the Columbia (Oregon, Washington, Idaho) during the Nez Perce War (1877). He met with Nez Perce leaders, including Chief Joseph, and ordered the tribe to leave the Wallowa Valley and relocate on the Lapwai Reservation. The Nez Perce failed to move, resulting in the Nez Perce War. Howard participated in campaigns against the Nez Perce, including the battle of White Bird Canyon and the battle of the Clearwater.

Hull, William (1753–1825): U.S. Army officer and governor of Michigan Territory (1805–1812). As commander of the western army in the War of 1812, Hull led an attack from Detroit into Canada (July 1812). He was defeated by British General Isaac Brock at Detroit (August 16, 1812) and surrendered the fort and his 1,400 men without firing a shot, allowing the British to gain control of the Upper Lakes region.

Hunt, Wilson Price (1783–1842): Fur trader and explorer. In 1810, he led the overland Astoria expedition to the mouth of the Columbia River, tracing the route between the Snake and Columbia rivers that later became an important part of the western Oregon Trail. After the sale of Astoria to the British in 1814, he returned to St. Louis, where he prospered as a landowner and merchant.

Huntington, Collis Potter (1821–1900): Railroad builder. Huntington was one of the ''Big Four'' who built the Central and Southern Pacific railroads. Attracted to California in 1849 by the Gold Rush, he soon gave up mining and opened a miners' supply store in Sacramento in partnership with Mark Hopkins. He contributed part of the cost of a survey over the Sierras for Theodore Judah's transcontinental project. He organized in 1861 the Central Pacific along with Hopkins, Charles Crocker and Leland Stanford. He was the eastern agent in Washington, lobbying for federal assistance, and was influential in Congress' passage of the generous Pacific Railroad Act of 1864.

Iliff, John Wesley (1831–1878): Colorado cattle rancher. Born in McLuney, Ohio, Iliff attended Ohio Wesleyan University. In 1859, he traveled to the Cherry Creek settlements in Colorado, and in 1861, he invested in a small herd of cattle, beginning a successful career as a cattleman. At one time he reportedly had more than 50,000 herd of cattle grazing the Plains. He was called the ''cattle king of the Plains,'' and at his death he dominated a range of 150 miles along the South Platte.

Jackson, Andrew (1767–1845): Army officer and seventh U.S. president (1829–1837). Born at the Waxhaw frontier settlement along the South Carolina–North Carolina border, at age 13 he joined the Revolutionary militia and was captured by the British. He defeated the Creeks at the battle of Horseshoe Bend (1814) and led American troops to victory against the British at the battle of New Orleans (1815). In 1818, he briefly invaded Spanish Florida to quell Seminoles and outlaws harassing frontier settlers. He defeated John Quincy Adams in the presidential election of 1828, carrying the West and South. His Removal Act of 1830 cleared Indians from several frontier areas and opened large blocks of public land to settlement. His Indian policies and his advocacy of graduated land prices and preemption made him a favorite candidate in the West. During Jackson's two terms as president, 94 treaties were signed with the Indians of the Old Northwest and the Southeast to further the expansion of United States territory. Remaining tribal lands east of the Mississippi were ceded to the government and opened to settlement.

Jackson, Helen (Maria Fiske) Hunt (1830–1885): Author and Indian reformer. Born in Amherst, Massachusetts, she moved to California in 1872. Her most famous nonfiction work, *A Century of Dishonor* (1881), alerted the public to the plight of the American Indian by describing the atrocities committed against Indian tribes and thus indicting the nation's reservation policy; her case may have been stated even more effectively in her immensely popular romance, *Ramona* (1884).

Jackson, William Henry (1843–1942): Photographer and painter. Best known for his photographs of the West, Jackson accompanied a wagon train to California in 1866 and later was employed as the official photographer for the U.S. Geological Survey from 1870 to 1878. He was the first to take photographs of the Yellowstone Park region. He settled in Denver, where he set up a photographic studio.

Jay, John (1745–1829): Diplomat and jurist, born in New York City. Jay was a member of the Continental Congress (1774–1779), American minister to Spain (1779), and a member of the commission negotiating peace with Great Britain (1782). He negotiated Jay's Treaty with Great Britain (1794), which mandated the withdrawal of British forces from forts in the Northwest Territory in return for repayment of debts owed to British subjects before the Revolution, but also guaranteed Canadian traders the right to operate south of the boundary and guaranteed not to tax the furs they carried back to Montreal. Because of these provisions the treaty was unpopular in the West.

Jefferson, Thomas (1743–1826): Statesman and third U.S. president (1801–1809). As a member of the committee to draw up a "Declaration of Independence," he wrote the basic draft. While in the Continental Congress, he drew up an ordinance for the Old Northwest Territory, creating 10 states and forbidding slavery after 1800; its terms were put into the Northwest Ordinance. As president, he made the Louisiana Purchase (1803), reduced the land-purchase requirements imposed on settlers in the Northwest Territory and ordered the Lewis and Clark Expedition.

Johnson, Sir William (1715–1774): British army officer and diplomat. Born in Ireland, Johnson immigrated to America in 1737 or 1738 and settled on a family estate in the Mohawk Valley. As Indian commissioner in King George's War (1745–1748), he secured the loyalty of the Six Nations and performed valuable service against the French. As a major general during the French and Indian War, he commanded a mixed force of colonial militia and Indians that captured Fort Niagara in 1759 and in 1760 participated in the successful attack on Montreal. As superintendent of Indian affairs (1761–1774), he pro-

moted the idea of fixed boundaries between Indian and white lands.

Judah, Theodore Dehone (1826–1863): Engineer and railroad builder. Judah studied engineering at Rennselaer Polytechnic Institute, in Troy, New York, worked on the New York and New Haven and Connecticut Valley railroads, and planned and built the Niagara George Railroad. He moved to California in 1854 to supervise the building of the Sacramento Valley Railroad. In 1860, he discovered a practical route through the Sierras. His plan encouraged the "Big Four"—Collis P. Huntington, Leland Stanford, Charles Crocker and Mark Hopkins—to invest in a transcontinental railroad project.

Kearny, Stephen Watts (1794–1848): U.S. Army officer. Kearny was a member of General Henry Atkinson's expedition to the mouth of the Yellowstone River in 1825. In 1846, he commanded the Army of the West and with 1,700 troops conquered New Mexico during the Mexican War. He then joined forces with Commodore Robert F. Stockton and captured San Diego and Los Angeles. In 1847, he was briefly military governor of California, and in 1848, he served as governor-general at Veracruz and Mexico City.

Kelley, Hall Jackson (1790–1874): Promoter of Oregon settlement. In his early years he taught school in Massachusetts and wrote school books. In 1818, Kelley became the leading advocate of migration to the Oregon country. Although he knew Oregon only secondhand, he extolled its virtues in speeches, pamphlets, circulars and petitions. In 1829, he organized the American Society for Encouraging the Settlement of the Oregon Territory. When he was unable to win federal aid, his plan to lead settlers to Oregon collapsed. However, he continued to campaign for American settlement in the Oregon country. He visited Oregon only once, in 1832.

Kenton, Simon (1755–1836): Frontiersman, scout and soldier. Born in Fauquier County, Virginia, in 1777, Kenton settled at Boonesborough, on the Kentucky frontier, where he fought against the Shawnees with Daniel Boone. In the Revolutionary War, he was a member of George Rogers Clark's expedition from the Falls of the Ohio to the Illinois country, where he participated in attacks against the British and their Indian allies.

Keokuk (ca. 1790–1848): Sauk tribal leader. As war chief and member of the Sauk council during the War of 1812, Keokuk challenged the leadership of the veteran Black Hawk, placing himself at the head of a faction of the Sauk and Fox tribes that sought to accommodate American demands. The rivalry between him and Black Hawk culminated in the Black Hawk War of 1832. Keokuk led the peace party and was given charge of Black Hawk after his imprisonment. Keokuk signed land cession treaties and presided over the tribes' removal to Kansas.

Knox, Henry (1750–1806): Secretary of war. In 1783, he succeeded George Washington as commander of the army and in 1785 he became secretary of war. He was strongly opposed to acquiring Indian lands by force, and in 1789 he promulgated the Fort Harmar Treaties, under which various tribes ceded their claims to western lands in exchange for payment in goods by the federal government. During his term, federal laws were enacted to regulate the purchase of Indian lands. All cessions had to be acquired by federal treaties, and the military was assigned the role of protecting the Indians from the unlawful encroachment of white settlers into their territory.

Langford, Nathaniel Pitt (1832–1911): Explorer, naturalist and first superintendent of Yellowstone National Park. In 1870, he organized an official expedition into the Yellowstone Park region, accompanied by a military escort. He explored parts of Idaho, Wyoming and Montana that now comprise the national park. After the 1870 expedition, he embarked on a campaign that urged the preservation of the region as a national wilderness treasure. He was the chief force behind an act of Congress in 1872 that created the Yellowstone National Park.

Larkin, Thomas Oliver (1802–1858): United States consul in Mexican California. Larkin settled in California in 1832 and became an important merchant in Monterey. He became consul in 1844, and in 1845 Secretary of State James Buchanan appointed him a "confidential agent" with instructions to work for a peaceful secession of California from Mexico; however, the plan collapsed with the Bear Flag Rebellion and the outbreak of the Mexican War.

Lease, Mary Elizabeth [Clynes] (1853–1933): Populist orator. Born in Pennsylvania, she went to Osage Mission, Kansas, in 1870 to teach school. After experiencing hard times as a homesteader, she and her family moved to Wichita, where she took in laundry, began reading law and was admitted to the bar. She delivered speeches on behalf of the Farmers' Alliance movement and the People's Party in the early 1890s. In the campaign of 1890, she gave 160 speeches throughout Kansas. She campaigned nationally for the Populist candidates, but in 1896 she opposed

Populist-fusion leadership and refused to support William Jennings Bryan's candidacy for president.

Lee, Jason (1803–1845): Oregon missionary and pioneer. Lee was the leader of the first American settlement in the Oregon country and was the first missionary to bring Christianity to the Indians of the Pacific Coast. In 1834, he traveled overland with Nathaniel Wyeth's second expedition and settled on the banks of the Willamette River, 10 miles north of present-day Salem. He returned East in 1838 in search of more financial support and to recruit more settlers, and in 1840, he returned to Oregon with 51 settlers. Three years later the mission board in New York dismissed him on the grounds that his mission had grown too secular. After his followers deserted him, he returned to his home in New England.

Leonard, Zenas (1809–1857): Fur trader and explorer. He was a member of Captain Benjamin Bonneville's expedition of 1833–1834, and was a clerk on Joseph Reddeford Walker's expedition to California via the Humboldt River, which explored Utah and Nevada. He described his adventures with Bonneville and others in the Rocky Mountain fur trade in his book *Adventures of Zenas Leonard:* (1839).

Lewis, Meriwether (1774–1809): Explorer, military officer and politician. In 1794, Lewis enlisted in the Virginia militia to help suppress the Whiskey Rebellion in western Pennsylvania. By 1800 he was a captain in the First United States Infantry Regiment. He learned much about the wilderness and its aboriginal inhabitants through his service on the western frontier. In 1801, he became President Jefferson's private secretary, and began planning a transcontinental expedition. Appointed official commander of the expedition in 1803, he invited William Clark, whom he had served with in the Army, to become its coleader. Upon Lewis's return from the Pacific in 1807, President Jefferson appointed him governor of the Louisiana Territory. While en route to Washington in 1809 he died under mysterious circumstances; it is still unclear whether he was murdered or committed suicide.

Lincoln, Abraham (1809–1865): Sixteenth U.S. president (1861–1865). Born in a log cabin in Hodgenville, Kentucky, the young Lincoln moved with his family to Indiana, then to Illinois. He was captain of a local volunteer company during the Black Hawk War of 1832. While in Congress (1847–1849), he opposed the Mexican War. He argued against the Kansas-Nebraska Act of 1854 during his campaign for the Senate in 1855. He rose to national prominence after the famed Lincoln-Douglas debates of 1858, and in 1860 was elected the first Republican president. In 1862, he signed into law a bill prohibiting slavery in all the territorial possessions of the United States. He organized the remaining West into territories, passed the Homestead Act and provided for the building of a transcontinental railroad, as well as leading the nation through the Civil War.

Linn, Lewis Fields (1795–1843): Missouri politician. While representing Missouri in the U.S. Senate he staunchly supported the expansionist interests of his frontier constituents. He chaired the committee on territories and sought the protection of developing American interests in Oregon.

Lisa, Manuel (1772–1820): Fur trader. Born in New Orleans or Cuba of Spanish parents, Lisa was raised in Louisiana and settled in St. Louis about 1790. In 1807, he established Fort Manuel at the mouth of the Big Horn River, the first trading post on the upper Missouri. Lisa was one of the founders of the Missouri Fur Company in 1808, and he established Fort Lisa in 1812, a fur post on the Missouri River north of present-day Omaha. From 1814 to 1820, he served as the United States sub-agent for Indian tribes on the Missouri River around the mouth of the Kansas River.

Little Crow (ca. 1803–1863): Mdewakanton Sioux chief who led the Santee Sioux in the Minnesota Sioux Uprising of 1862, in which nearly 400 white settlers were killed. On September 23, 1862, his rebellion was crushed by Colonel Henry H. Sibley, who seized 1,400 Sioux prisoners. Little Crow escaped but was later killed by a settler in northern Minnesota.

Little Robe (1828–1886): Cheyenne chief. Following the Sand Creek Massacre (1864) he briefly engaged in hostilities against the whites in the Cheyenne-Arapaho War. After deciding that warfare against the whites was hopeless, he joined Black Kettle and George Bent in trying to convince the militant Cheyenne Indians to sign the Medicine Lodge Treaty (1867). During the Red River War (1874–1875) he participated in peace counsels between the federal government and the Comanches and the Kiowas.

Little Turtle (1752–1812): Miami war chief. Little Turtle first gained fame as the leader of the Miami tribe that defeated General Josiah Harmar's expedition at the Miami River in 1790. Little Turtle commanded the confederated Indian army that crushed General Arthur St. Clair's troops at the battle of Mississinewa in 1791. He also directed warriors against

General Anthony Wayne's army in 1793–94. After the battle of Fallen Timbers, he concluded that further Indian resistance was doomed to failure. He became an advocate of peace and played a major role in negotiating the Treaty of Greenville (1795).

Livingston, Robert R. (1746–1813): American Revolutionary War leader and diplomat; born in New York City. Livingston was a member of the Continental Congress (1775–77 and 1779–81) and one of the committee of five who drew up the Declaration of Independence; he was also the nation's first secretary of foreign affairs (1781–1783). In 1803, while minister to France, he conducted the negotiations that led to the Louisiana Purchase, acquiring 828,000 square miles of land for $15 million.

Long, Stephen Harriman (1784–1864): U.S. Army officer and explorer. Long is best known for his western expedition of 1820. His report on which he described the region east of the Rockies as "the Great American Desert," thus discouraging settlement there. As a major with the Army Topographical Engineers he explored the upper Mississippi and the lower Arkansas rivers. In 1823, he undertook another government expedition to determine the source of the Minnesota River, journeying up the Red River to Lake Winnipeg in Manitoba. He also surveyed the border region between the United States and Canada.

Loving, Oliver (1812–1867): Trail driver and cattle rancher. Born in Kentucky, Loving settled in Texas in 1845. In 1858, he made the first recorded movement of Texas cattle to the Chicago yards. During the Civil War he supplied the Confederate army with beef, and after the war he became associated with Charles Goodnight in filling contracts for Army and Indian beef. In 1866, they drove a herd from Fort Belknap, Texas, to Fort Sumner, New Mexico. The trail, known as the Goodnight-Loving trail, later became one of the most used cattle trails in the Southwest.

MacKenzie, Donald (1783–1851): Fur trader and explorer. Born in Scotland, MacKenzie immigrated to Montreal as a young man. He began his career in the fur trade as a clerk for the North West Company, then joined John Jacob Astor's Fur Company in 1809 and spent the fall of 1811 exploring a long stretch of the Snake River on his way to Astoria. After the failure of Astor's enterprise during the War of 1812, he returned to the North West Company in 1816. In 1822, he joined the Hudson's Bay Company, managing its operations around Winnipeg.

Magoffin, James Wiley (1799–1868): Businessman and diplomat. Born in Harrodsburgh, Kentucky. As early as 1825 Magoffin began developing a profitable mercantile business in northern Mexico while serving as American consul at Saltillo. In 1836, he moved to Chihuahua, where he entered the Santa Fe trade, and in 1844, he settled with his family in Independence, Missouri. Dispatched to New Mexico by President Polk during the Mexican War, he held a secret conference with Governor Manuel Armijo, helping to pave the way for a peaceful occupation of New Mexico by American forces.

Magoffin, Susan Shelby (1828–1855): In 1846, she accompanied her husband, James Magoffin, a Santa Fe trader, on a trek from Independence, Missouri, through New Mexico and south to Chihuahua. She kept a travel journal during the crucial period when the Mexican War was beginning and when New Mexico was occupied by Stephen Watts Kearny and the Army of the West. *The Diary of Susan Shelby Magoffin* has become a classic account of life on the Santa Fe Trail.

Marshall, James Wilson (1810–1885): Pioneer and discoverer of gold in California. Born in New Jersey, Marshall immigrated to California for health reasons. He arrived at Sutter's Fort in 1845, and in 1849, while supervising the digging for a mill, he discovered gold on Sutter's estate. He and John Augustus Sutter's claims were never recognized, and he spent his remaining years working as a gardener.

Marshall, John (1775–1835): Jurist and statesman; born in Midland, Virginia. Marshall was first chief justice of the Supreme Court (1801–1833). In *Worcester v. Georgia* (1832) he held that the Cherokee Indians possessed the status of a "domestic dependent nation" under the protection of the federal government, and that Georgia had no right to molest them. His opinion was not recognized by Georgia, and President Jackson did not enforce it.

Martineau, Harriet (1802–1876): English author who visited the United States from 1834 to 1836. She became an advocate for the abolition of slavery and criticized the American way of life in *Society in America* (1837) and *Retrospect of Western Travel* (1838).

Mason, George (1725–1792): American Revolutionary War statesman; born in Fairfax County, Virginia. Mason was a member of the Ohio Company (1752–1773) and a member of the Virginia House of Delegates (1776–1788). He outlined the plan by which Virginia ceded her western claims to the United States.

McCormick, Cyrus Hall (1809–1884): Inventor. McCormick developed the first mechanical reaper (1831), which became the basis of all grain harvesting machines that followed. He established his factory in Chicago in 1847.

McCoy, Joseph G. (1837–1915): Entrepreneur and cattle rancher. Born in Illinois, McCoy was a man of diverse pursuits, including grocer, real estate agent, stockman, speculator, wrought-iron fence salesman, cattle inspector, livestock broker and author. He gained prominence in the late 1860s when he made Abilene, Kansas, the principal railhead for Texas cattle bound for the packaging houses in the East and Midwest. He laid out the Chisholm Trail, along which great trail drives moved thousands of cattle to the town's railway station. In 1873, he moved to Kansas City, Missouri, where he organized his own livestock company.

McIntosh, William (ca. 1775–1825): Creek chief; born in Georgia, the son of a British army officer and a Creek woman. In the War of 1812, he led the lower Creeks against the British and was made brigadier general. He also fought with Andrew Jackson against the Seminoles. In 1825, he signed a treaty ceding Creek land east of the Chattahoochee River to Georgia, and shortly thereafter he was slain by the upper Creeks, who opposed the cession.

McLoughlin, John (1784–1857): Fur trader. Born in Quebec, Canada, he entered the fur trade in 1814 after gaining a medical degree. In 1821, he and Peter Ogden became directors of the Hudson's Bay Company's activities in the Columbia River Department, which ranged down into Washington and Oregon territories. He played a major role in erecting Fort Vancouver in 1825, and for 20 years he successfully commanded the post located in territory jointly occupied by the United States and Great Britain. Though he had difficulty with both sides from time to time, he managed to get along with American settlers and kept the furs flowing to Canada.

Meeker, Nathan Cook (1817–1879): Journalist, colonist and Indian agent. Supported by Horace Greeley, publisher of the *New York Tribune*, he founded the Union colony near present-day Denver, Colorado, in 1870. This cooperative farming community covered 20,000 acres and had its own schools and churches. In 1876, he was appointed a Ute Indian reservation agent, charged with transforming the Indians into small farmers. His inability to deal with the Utes led to the Meeker massacre, in which he was killed along with several of the workers at the agency.

Michaux, André (1746–1802): French scientist who visited the United States from 1785 to 1796. He traveled extensively beyond the Alleghenies and along the Atlantic Coast, studying the region's plant life.

Miles, Nelson Appleton (1839–1925): U.S. Army officer. Primary field commander in the Red River War (1874–1875) against the Kiowas, Comanche and Southern Cheyenne. His campaigns on the Northern Plains in 1876–1877 led to the capture of many Sioux. He also led troops in the battle of Bear's Paw (1877), defeating the Nez Perce. Miles replaced General George Crook in 1886 as commander of the Department of Arizona and succeeded in capturing Geronimo and his small band, whom he sent into confinement on a Florida reservation. In 1890, he ordered troops to confront the Ghost Dance participants at South Dakota's Pine Ridge and Rose Bud reservations, which precipitated the tragic battle of Wounded Knee.

Monroe, James (1758–1831): Fifth U.S. president (1817–1825). Monroe was a member of the Virginia House of Delegates and of Congress (1783–1786); U.S. senator (1790); minister to France (1794–1796); and governor of Virginia (1799–1802 and 1811). He helped Robert Livingston negotiate the Louisiana Purchase in 1803. As president, he acquired Florida from Spain; settled boundaries with Canada; and supported the antislavery position that led to the Missouri Compromise. He formulated the Monroe Doctrine, which opposed any European colonization or intervention in the sovereign states of the Western Hemisphere.

Morse, Samuel Finley Beese (1791–1872): Inventor; born in Charles, Massachusetts. In 1837, he invented the Morse code for transmitting messages over the telegraph. In 1843, Congress awarded him a grant of $30,000 for an experimental line between Washington and Baltimore. On May 24, 1844, he transmitted over the line the famous first message, "What hath God wrought!"

Muir, John (1838–1914): Writer and naturalist. A Scot by birth, he grew up on the central Wisconsin frontier in the 1850s. In 1868, he hiked to California's Sierra Nevada. He called the Sierra the "range of light," and it became the focal point of his exploration, writing and conservation activities. In 1892, he founded the Sierra Club, dedicated to exploring and conserving the mountain regions of the Pacific Coast and protecting Yosemite National Park. Muir is con-

sidered the founder of the wilderness preservation movement.

Ogden, Peter Skene (1794–1854): Fur trapper and explorer. Born in Quebec, Canada, Ogden entered the fur trade before he was 20 and joined the Hudson's Bay Company in 1821. He explored much of the West, including the Snake River region, the Oregon country, the Great Salt Lake and most of northern California. In 1828, he discovered the Humboldt River and traced its entire course. Throughout his career he had cordial relationships with the Indians. After the Whitman Massacre at Walla Walla in 1847, he successfully negotiated the return of nearly 50 white captives held by the Indians. He was an administrator of Fort Vancouver from 1845 until 1852.

Opothleyoholo (ca. 1798–1862): Upper Creek chief. In 1825, he led a Creek delegation to Washington to protest the land cession treaty negotiated by the lower Creeks. When the Creeks chose to support the Confederacy in the Civil War, he and several followers withdrew from the Creek Nation, and endorsed the cause of the Union.

Paredes y Arrilaga, Mariano (1797–1849): Mexican army general and president. He helped install Santa Anna in the presidency in 1841 but soon came to oppose him. In 1845, he led a successful revolt against President Herrera, charging that he was compromising the honor of Mexico by negotiating with the United States concerning California. He served as president of Mexico from January to July 1846.

Parker, Samuel (1779–1866): Missionary. In 1835, he joined fellow missionary Dr. Marcus Whitman in an overland expedition to Oregon. At the Green River rendezvous, Whitman returned to New York for reinforcements, while Parker pushed on, with a band of Nez Perce Indians as his sole companions. He arrived at Fort Walla Walla in October 1836. He remained in Oregon for one year and then returned East to make his report to the American Board of Commissioners for Foreign Missions.

Parkman, Francis (1823–1893): Author and historian. Born in Boston, Parkman graduated from Harvard College, where he studied history and law. He traveled to the Plains in 1846 with mountain man Henri Chatillon to study the Sioux. He described his visit to the Great Plains Indian country in his book *The Oregon Trail* (1849). Most of his other works focus on the history of New France, such as *The Conspiracy of Pontiac* (1851) and *Montcalm and Wolfe* (1884). Parkman is considered a preeminent historian, an imaginative writer who demonstrated that history can be both captivating and informative.

Pattie, James Ohio (ca. 1804–1851): Fur trapper. Born in Kentucky, in 1812, Pattie moved with his family to Missouri. In 1824, he began trading along the Missouri River and later that year traveled to Taos and Santa Fe. In 1828, he trapped on the Gila and eventually went down the Colorado River to its mouth and overland to San Diego, where he was jailed by the Mexican governor. Upon his release, he returned to the United States in 1830. His colorful reminiscences were made into a book by writer Timothy Flint, *The Personal Narrative of James O. Pattie of Kentucky, During an Expedition From St. Louis, Through the Vast Regions Between That Place and the Pacific Ocean* (1831). He became a 49er, and he disappeared in the Sierra Nevada in the winter of 1850–1851.

Payne, David L. (1836–1884): Oklahoma ''boomer'' leader. Born in Indiana, Payne immigrated to Kansas in 1880 and formed a homesteading society called the *Oklahoma Colony*. In 1884, he led the first organized group past the Kansas line and into the Oklahoma District. Although he was arrested and returned to Kansas, his invasion triggered a campaign in Congress for opening the Indian Territory to homesteaders.

Pierce, Franklin (1804–1869): Fourteenth U.S. president (1850–1853); born in Hillsboro, New Hampshire. Pierce served in Congress (1833–1837) and in the Senate (1837–1842) and was a brigadier general during the Mexican War under General Winfield Scott, whom he defeated in the 1852 presidential election. As president he approved the Gadsden Purchase from Mexico in 1853, and, although he opposed slavery, he signed the Kansas-Nebraska Act of 1854. Denied renomination by the Democrats, he spent his remaining years in Concord, New Hampshire.

Pike, Zebulon Montgomery (1779–1813): U.S. Army officer and explorer. Pike enlisted in the Army at the age of 15 and saw service in the Old Northwest with General Anthony Wayne. In 1799, he was made a lieutenant and in the following years was assigned to various frontier river posts. He commanded an expedition to explore the source of the Mississippi River, starting from St. Louis in 1805; he reached what he mistakenly thought was the source before turning back in 1806. In that same year he explored the headwaters of the Arkansas, which took him into Colorado, where he unsuccessfully tried to climb the mountain that ultimately came to bear his name, Pikes Peak. Pike was suspected of complicity in James Wilkenson and Aaron Burr's scheme to create a

Southwest empire, but he managed to clear himself and wrote a valuable report on the New Mexico territory. Commissioned a brigadier general during the War of 1812, he was killed while leading an attack on the British in Canada.

Pilcher, Joshua (1790–1843): Fur trader and superintendent of Indian affairs. A partner in the Missouri Fur Company, Pilcher became head of the company after Manuel Lisa's death in 1819. After the Missouri Fur Company failed in 1825, he organized his own company and between 1828 and 1830 penetrated the Northwest all the way to Fort Vancouver. He wrote a report in 1831 extolling the attractions of the Oregon country to American settlers. He also served as Indian agent on the upper Missouri (1834–1838) and became superintendent of Indian affairs for two years (1839–1841).

Polk, James Knox (1795–1849): Eleventh U.S. president (1845–1849). Born in North Carolina, Polk represented Tennessee in Congress (1825–1839) and as speaker (1835–1839). He was governor of Tennessee from 1839 to 1841, but was defeated for reelection in 1841 and 1843. As the Democratic candidate for president in 1844 he championed an expansionist platform, the occupation of Oregon and the annexation of Texas. As president, he sent troops under General Zachary Taylor to the Mexican border; when the Mexicans attacked, he declared war. The Mexican War ended with the annexation of California and much of the Southwest. He compromised on the Oregon boundary (''54-40 or fight!'') by accepting the 49th parallel as boundary and granting Vancouver to the British.

Pontiac (ca. 1720–1769): Ottawa chief. It is unclear whether Pontiac was actually a great warrior and leader or simply an eloquent spokesman whom writers mythologized. Nevertheless, the uprising given his name, Pontiac's Rebellion, was one of the most successful rebuffs against white encroachment on Indian lands. He was probably among the opponents of General Braddock at Fort Duquesne in 1755. It is believed that he organized an alliance of various tribes to oppose the opening of Western lands. In 1763, his alliance laid siege to the British fort at Detroit for 175 days, the longest siege in the history of Indian warfare. He finally signed a peace treaty with the British in 1766 and thereafter honored it despite French efforts to turn him against the British.

Pope, John (1822–1892): U.S. Army officer. Born into a prominent Illinois family, Pope graduated from West Point in 1842. In the Civil War he won a victory at New Madrid and commanded the Army of Virginia until his defeat at Second Bull Run. In 1862, he took command of the new Department of the Northwest and directed the campaigns against the Santee Sioux, organizing the successful Powder River campaign of 1865 against the Sioux and Cheyenne. From 1870 to 1883 he commanded the Department of the Missouri and sought to control the tribes of the southern Plains. He directed troop movements against the Utes (1879–1881) and attempted to keep the "Boomers" out of Indian Territory.

Powell, John Wesley (1834–1902): Explorer and conservationist. Born at Mount Morris near Palmyra, New York, Powell left home at the age of 16 for Wisconsin, where he became an elementary school teacher. Under congressional authorization, he made an expedition to the Grand Canyon in 1869, and in 1871 he surveyed the Colorado Plateau region. His 1878 *Arid Lands Report* to Congress described how land reform and irrigation could open the arid Southwest to agricultural settlement. Although Congress did not share his vision, he continued his scientific work through the Bureau of American Ethnology. His vision of ordered western development was finally implemented in 1902 with the New Lands Reclamation Act.

Proctor, Henry (ca. 1763–1822): British army general. In the War of 1812, at the battle of the Thames, he led 400 troops in a joint operation with Tecumseh, who commanded 600 Indian warriors, against General William Henry Harrison's forces. After a few minutes of furious fighting, the entire English force was either killed or captured, and Tecumseh was killed. Proctor fled to eastern Ontario and rejoined the British command.

Prophet, The [Tenskwatawa] (ca. 1778–1837): Spiritual leader of several Midwestern tribes. Known as the "man with the loud voice," the Prophet urged a return to a simple life by preaching against drunkenness and all forms of white "civilization." His brother, Tecumseh, planned an Indian confederacy to include all tribes between the Great Lakes, the Gulf, the Allegheny Mountains and the Rockies. During the battle of Tippecanoe in 1811, their headquarters, known as Prophetstown, was destroyed. After this defeat the Prophet lost much of his influence among his people.

Red Cloud (Makhpiya-luta) (ca. 1822–1909): Ogalala Sioux warrior. Born into the Ogalala Sioux of Nebraska, Red Cloud gained fame as a young warrior and became chief of his tribe in the 1860s. He led Sioux and Cheyenne resistance to the army's forts and to white emigration on the Bozeman Trail for nearly three years. He was a principal architect of Sioux tactics, including the trap that annihilated Captain Fetterman's command outside of Fort Phil Kearny. Such victories led to the Fort Laramie Treaty of 1868, where he agreed to peace in exchange for the closing of the Bozeman Trail and the Army's abandonment of the Powder River forts. Thereafter, he went off the warpath and lived for some time at the reservation named for him in Nebraska.

Red Jacket (Sagoyewatha) (ca. 1758–1830): Seneca chief. Red Jacket gained public attention in 1777 as a spokesman for the Seneca policy of neutrality during the American Revolution. When this policy was rejected by the warriors of the Six Nations, he followed the Iroquois war chiefs and joined the British against the Americans. After the American Revolution he became the official spokesman for the Seneca council and, on occasion, was the speaker for the Six Nations. From 1801 until his death he was the leader of the anti-Christian "pagan party" among the New York Iroquois. Until his death, he urged the right of his people to maintain their separate beliefs and forms of worship.

Remington, Frederic (1861–1909): Illustrator, writer, painter and sculptor; born in Canton, New York. Among the first to enroll at the Yale School of Fine Arts in 1878, Remington became widely known as a reporter of life in the West, where he went in 1880 for health reasons. He sold his first folio of western sketches in Kansas City in 1884. For the next two years he visited frontier military posts and traveled with the cavalry on several southwestern campaigns. He gained national fame in 1886 when one of his pictures appeared on the cover of *Harper's Weekly*.

Reno, Marcus Albert (1834–1889): U.S. Army officer. As a major in the Seventh Cavalry under Lieutenant Colonel George Custer he participated in the campaign against the Sioux Indians in 1876. He was later charged with cowardice for having failed to support his fellow soldiers in action on the Little Big Horn, where Custer and nearly all his regiment were killed. He was dismissed from the service in 1880.

Richardson, Albert Deane (1833–1869): Journalist. In 1859, he joined Horace Greeley and Henry Villard in an expedition to the gold fields of Pikes Peak in Colorado. In that same year he toured on horseback the western territories, visiting the Cherokee and Choctaw reservations and sending descriptive stories of his travels to newspapers in the East. In 1860, he returned to Pikes Peak as a special correspondent for the *New York Tribune*.

Roosevelt, Theodore (1858–1919): Author, conservationist and 26th U.S. president (1901–1909). Born in New York City, Roosevelt graduated from Harvard in 1880; attended Columbia Law School briefly; and was a member of the New York State Assembly from 1881 to 1884. In 1883, he moved to Dakota Territory, hoping to restore his spirits after his wife had died in childbirth. For three years he lived what he called the "strenuous life" on two ranches in the Badlands. His interest in the outdoors later influenced his policies while he was president, such as the conservation congresses he convened in 1901 and 1909. He wrote several books and articles on the West, including a multi-volume frontier history, *The Winning of the West* (1889–1896).

Ross, Alexander (1783–1856): Fur trader. Born in Scotland, Ross migrated to Canada in 1804 and served as a clerk on the Astor maritime expedition to the Pacific Coast in 1810. After Astor sold Fort Astoria to the British, Ross joined the North West Company as a trader in 1814. In 1818, he made an expedition up the Columbia River as far as the Snake River and established Fort Perce. For the Hudson's Bay Company he led an expedition up the Snake River in 1823–1824, exploring into present-day southern Idaho. He was replaced by Peter Skene Ogden in 1825 when Hudson's Bay officials became concerned that he was becoming too tolerant of American trappers in the region.

Ross, John (1790–1866): Cherokee chief. Ross was born near Lookout Mountain, Tennessee; his father was a Scotsman who had lived among the Cherokees, his mother was part Cherokee. After completing his education among the whites, he became an agent to the Arkansas Cherokee. In the War of 1812, he fought for Andrew Jackson in the battle of Horseshoe Bend, against the Creeks. He was elected leader of the eastern Cherokees in 1828. Despite years of effort, he was unable to prevent the government's forced removal of his tribe from Tennessee. In 1838, he accompanied them to Arkansas on the tragic "Trail of Tears" to what is now Oklahoma. He helped draft a constitution for the united Eastern and Western Cherokees and served as their chief until his death.

Russell, Charles Marion (1864–1926): Painter, sculptor and illustrator. He worked for some time as a cowboy in the West, spending his summers on the open range and his winters in various frontier towns, where he often painted pictures in exchange for room and board. Most of his work documents his early life as a cowboy, although in later years he turned to portraying the American Indian and depicting the historical events related to the exploration and settlement of the western frontier.

Russell, Osborne (1814–1892): Mountain man and pioneer judge. Born in Bowdoinham, Maine, at the age of 16 he joined the North West Trapping and Trading Company, which operated in the area of present-day Wisconsin and Minnesota. In 1834, he joined Nathaniel Wyeth's second expedition to Oregon as an employee of Wyeth's Columbia River Fishing and Trading Company. From 1835 until 1838 he worked for the Rocky Mountain Fur Company, then worked as a free trapper in the Fort Hall vicinity until 1842. When Oregon became a territory in 1848, he was elected to the legislative assembly. His *Journal of a Trapper: or, Nine Years in the Rocky Mountains, 1834–1843* is considered one of the most valuable accounts of the mountain man.

Russell, William Hepburn (1812–1872): Freighter and promoter of the Pony Express. Born in Burlington, Vermont, at the age of 16 he was employed as a store clerk in Liberty, Missouri. After failing in his own retail business, he formed a partnership in 1852 with William B. Waddell to transport military supplies to Santa Fe. His freighting operations rapidly expanded, and in 1854 he, Waddell and a new partner, Alexander Majors, entered the stagecoach business. In 1860, he persuaded his partners to support his speedy, horseback mail delivery service, the Pony Express. However, his days of glory were brief. Unable to win government assistance, he became involved in a financial scandal, and his transportation empire collapsed in 1862, leaving him bankrupt.

Sacajawea (ca. 1784–ca. 1812 or ca. 1884): Shoshone interpreter and guide for the Lewis and Clark Expedition. As a child she was abducted by the Minnetares, who gambled her away to a French Canadian, Toussaint Charbonneau, who married her. Lewis and Clark met her at Fort Mandan in 1804 and hired her as their guide. She was the only woman on the expedition, and with her two-month-old son strapped to her back, she guided the explorers across the Rockies and convinced the Shoshones to sell them horses and supplies. On the return journey, she joined Charbonneau at Minnetare country. Thereafter her story is uncertain: By one account she died along the Missouri in 1812; by another she was identified at the Shoshone agency at the age of 100.

Saint Clair, Arthur (1737–1818): U.S. Army officer and politician. Born in Caithness County, Scotland, Saint Clair came to North America as an ensign in Lord Jeffrey Amherst's army in 1758. During the American Revolution he was commissioned by Congress as a colonel in the Continental Army, and he served with Washington in the battles of Trenton and Princeton in 1776–1777. He attended the Continental Congress from 1785 to 1787 and served as its president in 1787. He was the first governor of the Northwest Territory, from 1787 to 1802, and in 1791 he led an army against Indians in Ohio and suffered a major defeat at the headwaters of the Wabash River. He opposed statehood for the territory, and in 1802 President Jefferson removed him from office.

Santa Anna, Antonio Lopez de (1794–1876): Mexican general, president of Mexico from 1833 to 1836. Attempting to crush the Texas Revolution, he seized the Alamo in 1836 and was later defeated by General Sam Houston at San Jacinto (April 21, 1836). He commanded an army against the United States in the Mexican War, was defeated at Buena Vista, Cerro Gordo and Puebla and was driven out of Mexico City by General Winfield Scott. He went into exile in 1848, and in 1853 was recalled and made president. In 1855, he was exiled again, and until 1874 he lived in Cuba, Venezuela, St. Thomas and the United States. He returned to Mexico City in 1874, and died in poverty and neglect.

Satanta (Set-Tain-te) (1830–1878): Kiowa chief. He joined forces in 1871 with the Comanches and participated in the raid on Adobe Walls in Texas. He was later arrested for murdering a white settler and imprisoned in the Texas State Penitentiary, where he committed suicide.

Schoolcraft, Henry Rowe (1793–1864): Explorer, scientist and Indian agent; born in Albany County, New York. At Union and Middlebury colleges he studied chemistry and mineralogy. In 1820 he accompanied the expedition commissioned by Governor Lewis Cass to explore the Lake Superior copper region. In 1832, he discovered that Lake Itasca was the source of the Mississippi River. Schoolcraft served as superintendent of Indian affairs for Michigan from 1836 to 1841 and negotiated a cession of 16 million acres from the tribes of the upper Great Lakes region. He was commissioned by Congress in 1847 to compile a study of Indian tribes, which became his greatest work, the six-volume *Historical and Statistical Information Respecting the History, Condition and Prospects of the Indian Tribes of the United States* (1851–1857).

Scott, Winfield (1786–1866): U.S. Army officer and presidential candidate. During the War of 1812, he attained the rank of brigadier general and won fame in the battles of Chippewa and Lundy's Lane. Later he prosecuted the Second Seminole War (1835–1842) in Florida and supervised the removal of the Cherokee Indians from the South. In 1841, he became commanding general of the Army. During the Mexican War he landed an army at Veracruz and captured Mexico City. Acclaimed a national hero, in 1852 he ran unsuccessfully on the Whig ticket for president, and was defeated by Democrat Franklin Pierce. During the early months of the Civil War he organized the defense of Washington, D.C., then retired from military service in 1861 and settled at West Point.

Sheridan, Philip Henry (1831–1888): U.S. military officer. Sheridan served in Texas, California and the Northwest, then gained rapid advancement during the Civil War with his victories in Tennessee and Virginia, and his role at Chattanooga, Cedar Run and Petersburg. After the war, he was commander of the Fifth Military District (Texas and Louisiana). In 1867, he was assigned to the Department of the Missouri. He added the innovation of a winter campaign to Plains warfare in the battle of Washita (1868). He commanded large campaigns against the southern Plains tribes in 1874–1875 and against the Sioux in 1876–1877. Sheridan was appointed commander-in-chief of the Army in 1883 and was promoted to the Army's highest rank in 1888, general of the Army.

Sherman, William Tecumseh (1820–1891) U.S. Army officer. Renowned for his Atlanta campaign and march through Georgia during the Civil War. From 1866 to 1869, he commanded the Division of the Missouri, embracing the Plains country, protecting the lines of travel, especially railroads then under construction. Critical of the Bureau of Indian Affairs, he favored the transfer of Indian management to the Department of War and the permanent placement of Indians on reservations. In 1869, he became commander of the entire U.S. Army. During the Red River War (1874–1875) he ordered aggressive campaigns against the Kiowas and Comanches. He retired from the military in 1884.

Sibley, Henry Hastings (1811–1891): Minnesota politician and military officer. In 1848, elected congressional delegate by Minnesota settlers, he traveled to Washington to secure the organization of the territory. He was later instrumental in bringing about the land-ceding treaties of 1851 with the Sioux. In 1862, as governor, he commanded the state militia during the Minnesota Sioux Uprising. His forces defeated those of Little Crow at Wood Lake, thus ending the Sioux war in Minnesota. During 1863 and 1864 he led military expeditions into Dakota Territory to put down the remaining Sioux.

Sibley, Henry Hopkins (1816–1886): Confederate Army officer. He defeated Union Colonel E.R.S. Canby at Valverde and captured Albuquerque and Santa Fe in 1861. After losing his provisions and ammunition train at the battle of La Glorietta Pass (March 26–28, 1862), he was forced to give up the captured southwestern posts and retreat to Texas. For the duration of the war he was assigned to minor commands in Louisiana.

Sitting Bull (Tatanka Yotanka) (ca. 1831–1890): Sioux medicine man and chief. Born to a sub-chief of the Sioux in present-day South Dakota; a warrior in his early years, Sitting Bull became chief of the Sioux in 1866. When the discovery of gold in the Black Hills brought miners onto the Sioux reservation, he and Crazy Horse assembled a confederation of Sioux, Cheyenne and Arapaho warriors and went on the warpath in 1876. Although he participated in the planning, he took no part in the actual fighting at the battle of Little Big Horn. Fearing massive retaliation, he and his followers fled to Canada, where he remained until he surrendered to the United States in 1881. Imprisoned for two years, he turned to reservation life and even toured with Buffalo Bill Cody's Wild West Show for a year. Although he had little to do with the Indian Ghost Dance agitation of 1890, he was arrested by Indian police and fatally shot when he resisted.

Smith, Jedediah S. (1799–1831): Fur trader and explorer. Born in Bainbridge, New York, he gravitated to the adventurous life of the Rocky Mountain fur trade in the early 1820s. In 1822, he participated in William H. Ashley's first expedition up the Missouri. He became a partner with Ashley in the Rocky Mountain Fur Company in 1825. He led an expedition across the Great Basin region in 1826, becoming the first white to explore this formidable desert. After spending a difficult winter in the Sacramento Valley, he led a party up the coast toward Oregon in 1828, but they were attacked by Umpquas Indians, and only Smith and a few others managed to escape. He returned to the supposedly safer fur trade in Santa Fe and was killed by Comanches along the Cimarron River.

Smith, Joseph, Jr. (1805–1844): Founder of the Mormon Church; born in Sharon, Vermont, Smith claimed that in 1823 he was visited by the angel Moroni, who assigned him the task of translating an ancient history written on metal plates by pre-Columbian inhabitants of the Western Hemisphere. In 1830, he published the *Book of Mormon*, based on ancient records he said he had received, and in that same year he organized the Church of Jesus Christ of Latter-Day Saints, designating himself a prophet and apostle of Jesus Christ. He introduced to his followers the doctrine of plural marriage. After his church was driven from Missouri Territory, he moved it to Nauvoo, Illinois, in 1838. By the time he was killed by an angry mob in 1844, there were approximately 35,000 Latter-Day Saints. His successor, Brigham Young, led the Mormons to Utah.

Spalding, Eliza Hart (1807–1851): Missionary; born in Berlin, Connecticut. In 1836, she joined her husband, Henry Spalding, Dr. Marcus and Narcissa Prentiss and William Gray in an overland expedition to Oregon, where they planned to establish a mission. She and Narcissa Prentiss were the first white women to cross the North American continent. The Spaldings set up a mission at Lapwai near present-day Idaho, in the heart of Nez Perce country. After the Whitman massacre in 1847 at Waiilatpu, she moved with her husband to the Willamette Valley.

Spalding, Henry Harmon (1803–1874): Oregon missionary and pioneer; born in Wheeler, New York. In 1836, he traveled overland with his wife, Eliza Hart, and the Whitmans and William Gray, to the Oregon country, where they established a mission at Lapwai, near present-day Lewiston, Idaho. After his fellow missionaries complained to the board about his irascibility, he was dismissed in 1840. He returned East, and two years later he secured a reversal of the board's decision. Shortly after the Whitman massacre at the Walla Walla mission in 1847, he and his wife moved to Oregon's Willamette Valley, where he took up farming and became an Indian agent.

Spotted Tail (Sinte Galeshka) (ca. 1833–1881): Teton Sioux chief. He joined Red Cloud in the Sioux War of 1876–1877 and negotiated the settlement by which Crazy Horse surrendered to American forces.

Stanford, Leland (1824–1893): Railroad builder and politician. He was one of the "Big Four" (the others were Charles Crocker, Mark Hopkins and Collis P. Huntington) who built the Central Pacific and Southern Pacific. Born in Watervliet, New York; Stanford studied law as a young man. After a few years of practice in Wisconsin, he moved to California in 1852, where he began selling supplies to gold miners. He rose to prominence and was elected governor in 1861. While in office he played a key role in keeping California in the Union, and he lobbied for several laws that smoothed the way for the transcontinental railroad. He was president of the Central Pacific from 1863 until his death.

Stanley, Henry Morton (1841–1904): Journalist. Born in Wales, Stanley immigrated to the United States in 1858. After fighting on both sides of the Civil War, he began his career in journalism. As a correspondent for the *Missouri Democrat*, he covered the Medicine Lodge Creek council in southwestern Kansas, where some 7,000 Plains Indians gathered to conclude a series of peace treaties with members of the new Peace Commission established by Congress. He later gained prominence by trekking through Africa to find Dr. David Livingstone.

Stockton, Robert Field (1795–1866): U.S. Navy officer. With the outbreak of the Mexican War in 1846 he arrived at Monterey, California, and succeeded Commodore John D. Sloat as commander of the American forces. He commanded an army, along with John C. Fremont, that captured Los Angeles, and he proclaimed California a United States territory and himself governor. After the Mexicans pushed the American forces out of Los Angeles, he retook the city with General Stephen Watts Kearny.

Sublette, William Lewis (1799–1845): Fur trader. In 1823, he joined a small party of William Ashley's trappers, led by Jedediah Smith, on an untried overland trek to the Rockies. The expedition blazed new trails and opened up the northern Rockies to the fur trade. In 1830, he was the first trader to take wagons to the northern Rockies, and in that same year he sold out to the Rocky Mountain Fur Company. He began a profitable fur trading operation in the Santa Fe trade in 1831. In partnership with Robert Campbell, he built Fort Laramie in 1834. He left the mountains in 1836 to enter the mercantile business in St. Louis, and later became an important figure in Missouri politics.

Sumner, Edwin Vose (1797–1863): U.S. Army officer. Born in Boston, Massachusetts, Sumner entered the army as a second lieutenant in 1819 and spent most of his career as a cavalry officer on the frontier. During the Mexican War he served with General Winfield Scott and was at the battle of Cerro Gordo. He was commander of Fort Leavenworth during the civil disturbances of the 1850s in Kansas. He commanded the Department of the West in 1858, and during the Civil War he fought at Antietam, Fair Oaks and Fredericksburg.

Sutter, John Augustus (1803–1880): Colonizer of the Sacramento Valley. Born in Baden, Germany, Sutter immigrated to the United States at the age of 31. Arriving in Mexican California in 1839, he managed to receive a grant of nearly 50,000 acres from the Mexican governor. He built an estate, complete with a fort, livestock, fields and a small army of workers. From 1841 to 1848 his fort was a focal point for the increasing flow of settlers coming over the Sierras. The discovery of gold at Sutter's Mill triggered the great Gold Rush of 1849. Hordes of prospectors overran his property. American authorities did not recognize his land title, and by 1852 he was bankrupt. He spent his remaining years in an unsuccessful struggle with the government for compensation.

Symmes, John Cleves (1742–1814): American Revolutionary War soldier and land speculator. In 1788, Congress awarded him a grant of land between the Miami and Little Miami rivers. He founded a colony centered around present-day Cincinnati, Ohio.

Taney, Roger Brooke (1777–1864): Chief justice of the Supreme Court (1836–1864). He clearly expressed his support of the slavery laws in his opinion in *Dred Scott v. Sanford* (1857), which held that slaves were not citizens and could not sue in federal courts. The Court declared that Congress has no right to deprive persons of their property without due process of law according to the Fifth Amendment of the Constitution. In effect, the decision repealed the Missouri Compromise of 1820 and declared all laws banning slavery in the territories as unconstitutional.

Taylor, Bayard (1825–1878): Journalist. He covered the California Gold Rush of 1849 for Horace Greeley's *Chicago Tribune*. Arriving in San Francisco in August 1849, he sent back reports of that bustling city, gold-rush towns, the diggings and the constitutional convention. After he returned East, he revised the reports of his five-month visit and published them in 1850 as *Eldorado, or Adventures in the Path of Empire*. It was an immediate success that increased public interest in California.

Taylor, Zachary ["Old Rough and Ready"] (1784–1850): U.S. Army officer and 12th U.S. president (1849–1850); born in Montebello, Virginia. Taylor fought in the War of 1812; the Black Hawk War, 1832; and the Second Seminole War, 1837. In 1845, President Polk sent him with an army to the Rio Grande; when the Mexicans attacked him, Polk declared war. He occupied Monterrey and defeated General Santa Anna at Buena Vista. Taylor emerged from the war a national hero and in 1848 was elected president. As president, he urged immediate statehood for California and New Mexico as a solution to the crisis over the Mexican cession.

Tecumseh (ca. 1768–1813): Shawnee leader and warrior. Older brother of Tenskwatawa, the Prophet. He and the Prophet tried to establish a confederacy that would protect Indian lands from encroaching settlers. He traveled among the tribes of the Old Northwest and into the Deep South, pleading his case for Indian unity and his opposition to any further land cessions. During the War of 1812, he was allied with the British, and held the rank of brigadier general, in command of Indian troops. At the battle of the Thames he was killed while leading his forces against American soldiers.

Teller, Henry Moore (1830–1914): Colorado politician; born in Allegany County, New York. After practicing law in Illinois, he settled in Colorado in 1861, where he was active in mining law and territorial politics. In 1876, he was elected to the U.S. Senate, then appointed secretary of the interior in 1882, a post from which he spoke out for the needs of the West. Returning to the Senate in 1885, he fought the repeal of the Sherman Silver Purchase Act of 1893. He left the Republican Party in 1896 when it endorsed the gold standard. Teller was author of the Teller Amendment, which pledged the United States to an independent Cuba in 1898.

Terry, Alfred Howe (1827–1890): U.S. Army officer. In 1876, he directed the campaign against the Sioux and personally led a column converging on Indians from Dakota. The cavalry under Lieutenant Colonel George Armstrong Custer, massacred at the Little Big Horn in 1876, was a part of his force.

Thayer, Eli (1819–1899): Abolitionist; born in Massachusetts. Thayer was a Free-Soiler in the Massachusetts legislature from 1853 to 1854. In 1854, he organized the New England Emigration Aid Company to send antislavery settlers to Kansas. Despite his claims of having 20,000 antislavery settlers ready to immigrate to Kansas, only 4,208 pioneers moved there from New England during the late 1850s. He was a Republican member of the House of Representatives from 1857 to 1861.

Tocqueville, Alexis de (1805–1859): French statesman and historian. Traveling through the United States and the western territories in 1831 and 1832, he was one of the first foreign visitors to comment extensively on the frontier experience and its significance for American society. He visited the upper Great Lakes region and the Ohio Valley and traveled down the Mississippi River to New Orleans. He believed that the open lands of the West would decentralize the government and draw off excess population from the cities. His ideas about the frontier had a lasting impact on American thought and foreshadowed the theories of Frederick Jackson Turner.

Travis, William Barrett (1809–1836): Texas militia officer. Born near Red Banks, South Carolina, in 1831 he moved to Texas, where he became involved in the 1836 fight for independence. He led troops at Anahuac and San Antonio before he was appointed commander of the Texas militia. His forces defended the Alamo against Santa Anna's Mexican troops in March 1836. He refused to surrender the fort and was killed there with his men.

Trent, William (1715–?): Indian trader and agent. He served the colony of Virginia as an Indian agent and was a member of the Indiana Company, a land speculation firm. He also participated in the Fort Stanwix Treaty of 1768, which secured from the Iroquois much of southwestern New York for Great Britain. At the outbreak of the American Revolution, he joined the rebel cause and was commissioned a major.

Trist, Nicholas Philip (1800–1874): Diplomat. In 1847, he was sent by President Polk to Mexico as a special agent to negotiate an end to the Mexican War. Although recalled, he remained and signed the Treaty of Guadalupe Hidalgo (February 2, 1848).

Turner, Frederick Jackson (1861–1932): Historian and educator. Born in Portage, Wisconsin, Turner graduated from the University of Wisconsin at Madison, then received his doctorate from Johns Hopkins University. His dissertation, *The Character and Influence of the Indian Trade in Wisconsin* (1891), portrayed the fur-trading post as an historic institution on the frontier of Anglo-American civilization. In 1893, he introduced his influential frontier theory by reading his essay, *The Significance of the Frontier in American History,* at the meeting of the American Historical Association in Chicago. He emphasized the powerful influence that the availability of land and other frontier conditions had on the growth of American society. Turner taught at Wisconsin and Harvard University, and in 1932 won the Pulitzer Prize for *The Significance of Sections in American History.*

Two Moon (Ishaynishus) (fl. 1860s): Cheyenne chief. He participated in the war for the Bozeman Trail (1866–1868). Two Moon was an ally of Red Cloud, and was present at the Fetterman Massacre in Wyoming in 1866.

Tyler, John (1790–1862): Tenth U.S. president (1841–1845); born in Greenway, Virginia. Tyler served in Congress, 1816–1821; in the Virginia legislature, 1823–1825; as governor of Virginia, 1825–1826; and as U.S. senator, 1827–1836. In 1840, he was elected vice president, and on William Henry Harrison's death he succeeded him. As president, he favored the Preemption Act, which permitted settlers to stake a claim of 160 acres and after about one year's residence purchase the land from the federal government for as little as $1.25 an acre, before it was offered for public sale. Tyler supported the joint resolution to annex Texas and had the satisfaction of seeing it accepted by Texas just before he left office in 1845.

Upsher, Abel Parker (1790–1844): Public official. An ardent advocate of slavery, he reopened negotiations with Texas for its admission to the Union as a slave state. On Daniel Webster's resignation, he became secretary of state (1843–1844), and he played an important role in the movement for the annexation of Texas. He was killed by an explosion of a cannon on the battleship *Princeton.*

Villard, Henry (1835–1900): Journalist and railroad builder. He covered the Pikes Peak gold rush in Colorado for various eastern and midwestern newspapers. After reporting on the presidential campaign of 1861 and working as a war correspondent, he began operating his own news bureau in the United States and Europe. In 1871, he reorganized the interests of railroad investors, and was appointed the receiver of the Kansas Pacific Railroad. He bought control of the Northern Pacific Railroad in 1879. Failing to control construction costs in building the last sections of the transcontinental line, he was forced to resign from the board during the depression of the 1890s.

Walker, Felix (1753–1828): Frontiersman and soldier. In 1769 he accompanied Daniel Boone on his trail-blazing expedition through the Cumberland Gap to the Kentucky River, where he helped build Fort Boonesborough. In the Revolutionary War he fought the Cherokees on the frontier. He represented the western district of North Carolina in Congress from 1817 to 1823.

Walker, Joseph Reddeford (1798–1876): Fur trader and explorer; born in Virginia and raised in Tennessee. He commanded Captain Benjamin Booneville's expedition of 1833–1834, which crossed the Great Salt Lake, Wyoming and Nevada, and became the first white to traverse the Sierra Nevada. His expedition marked out the trail to California for later emigrants and helped establish American interest in the Pacific Coast. He guided emigrant parties to California and guided John C. Fremont's third expedition there in 1845–1846. For nearly two decades he traded in California. On an expedition to Arizona in 1861–1862, he discovered gold near present-day Prescott. He spent his remaining years in Contra Costa County, California.

Washington, George (1732–1799): Surveyor, American Revolutionary War Army officer and first U.S. president (1789–1797). Born in Westmoreland County, Virginia, at the age of 16 he worked as a surveyor in the Shenandoah Valley. Commissioned a major in the Virginia Militia in 1753, he carried a message from Governor Robert Dinwiddie to the French commander at Fort Le Boeuf, warning the French to stop building forts and settlements around the headwaters of the Ohio. He was an aide to General Edward Braddock during the ensuing French and Indian War. Washington served as commander-in-chief during the Revolution. Later, as president, he made the Old Northwest frontier reasonably safe from Indian attack; supported the highly unpopular Jay Treaty (1794); and signed the Treaty of San Lorenzo (1795). Jay's Treaty mandated the withdrawal of British forces from their posts in the Northwest Territory, while the Treaty of San Lorenzo stipulated that Spain relinquish its claim north of the 31st parallel and open the Mississippi to navigation. Washington was a major figure in the development of the early western frontier.

Wayne, Anthony (1745–1796): U.S. Army officer. He was known as "Mad Anthony" because of his boldness as a military leader in the American Revolution. In 1792, President Washington chose him to command an expedition against hostile Indians in the Northwest Territory; he defeated them decisively at the battle of Fallen Timbers (1794). The following year he dictated the terms of the Treaty of Greenville, which opened a large portion of the Northwest Territory to settlement.

Weaver, James Baird (1833–1912): Populist Party leader; born in Ohio. Weaver was elected to Congress as a Greenbacker in 1878, where he spoke out for financial reform. He was unsuccessful as the presidential nominee of the Populist Party in 1892. After his defeat, he advocated the fusion of the Populists with the Democratic Party, on the basis that both parties favored the free coinage of silver. He remained active in the Democratic Party until his death.

Webster, Daniel (1782–1852): Statesman; born in Salisbury, New Hampshire. In the Senate (1827–1841 and 1845–1850) he opposed the Mexican War and the annexation of Texas, and supported the compromise measures on slavery proposed by Henry Clay. In one of his most eloquent speeches, he placed the preservation of the Union above his own popularity, and supported the Compromise of 1850. He was denounced by antislavery groups in the North and by members of his own party, but he and Clay managed to hold the Union together for another decade.

White Antelope (1796–1864): Cheyenne warrior. In 1864, he was a spokesman for the Southern Cheyennes at the Camp Weld Council near Denver, Colorado, with Colonel John Chivington and Indian agent Edward Wynkoop. He was with Black Kettle at Sand Creek, and, when Chivington's troops approached, he walked out to meet them unarmed, but was fatally shot by the soldiers, who ignored his peaceful gestures.

Whitman, Marcus (1802–1847): Oregon missionary, pioneer and physician; born in Rushville, New York. After years of practicing medicine, he decided to become a missionary to the Indians of the Northwest. He and his wife, Narcissa, also a missionary, traveled overland to Oregon with a party that reached the Walla Walla River in 1836. Establishing mission stations in Oregon and in present-day Idaho, he tried to convert the Indians. His mission at Waiilatpu in the Walla Walla Valley became an important way station for Oregon pioneers during the early 1840s. When a measles epidemic broke out in 1847, the Cayuse tribe massacred Whitman and 12 others, believing that they were responsible for the disease that was killing their people.

Whitman, Narcissa Prentiss (1808–1847): Missionary; born in Grafton, Massachusetts. In 1836, she joined her husband, Dr. Marcus Whitman, and Henry and Eliza Spalding and William Gray in an overland expedition to Oregon, where they planned to establish a mission. She and Eliza Spalding became the first white women to cross the North American continent. The Whitmans set up a mission at Waiilatpu in the Walla Walla Valley. In 1847, they were killed by Cayuse Indians who believed they were responsible for a measles epidemic.

Whitney, Asa (1797–1872): Merchant and railroad promoter. Born in North Groton, Connecticut, in 1817, he moved to New York, where he learned the dry-goods business and eventually formed his own firm. After being wiped out by the Panic of 1837, he went to China for 15 months as an agent for several firms. He returned a wealthy man, and then spent the rest of his life promoting a transcontinental railroad, which he believed would open the United States to the lucrative China trade. In 1844, he lobbied in Congress for the construction of a road through the South Pass of the Rocky Mountains, but was met with indifference. He spent seven years in promoting the project, but was unable to interest Congress or Great Britain, which he approached on Canada's behalf.

Wilkenson, James (1757–1825): U.S. Army officer and politician. As commander of the U.S. Army in 1797, he was in charge of administering the enforcement of the terms of the Treaty of San Lorenzo. He was appointed governor of Upper Louisiana in 1805. Wilkenson became involved in the Burr Conspiracy to establish an independent empire in the Southwest, and he informed President Jefferson of the scheme in 1806. He negotiated the Neutral Ground Treaty between the United States and Mexico, pertaining to the territory along the Sabine River.

Wilkes, Charles (1798–1877): Explorer and naval officer. While commanding the government's South Sea Surveying and Exploring Expedition of 1838–1842, he visited the Pacific Northwest coast. His reports publicized the settlements in the Willamette Valley and strengthened the arguments for the American occupation of the Oregon country.

Wilmot, David (1814–1868): Politician; represented Pennsylvania in the House of Representatives from 1845 to 1851. In 1846, he introduced the Wilmot Proviso, attached to a bill for purchasing territory from Mexico, which would have prohibited slavery in any such territory acquired. The proviso was adopted in the House but defeated in the Senate.

Wolfe, James (1727–1759): British army officer. Second in command to General Jeffrey Amherst in the French and Indian War, he played a major role in winning North America for England. In 1759, he led an expedition of 9,000 men up the Saint Lawrence River and forced the French to surrender Quebec. At the battle of Quebec (September 1759) both he and French General Montcalm were killed.

Wooden Leg (Kummok'quivokta) (1858–1940): Cheyenne chief. He was a leader in the war for the Black Hills (1876–1877). He fought alongside the Sioux against George Armstrong Custer's troops at the battle of Little Big Horn (1876). After surrendering to federal troops, he was assigned to the Indian Territory with most of the Northern Cheyenne. His autobiography, *Wooden Leg: A Warrior Who Fought Custer*, is an important source for the Indian interpretation of Little Big Horn.

Wyeth, Nathaniel J. (1802–1856): Fur trader; born near Cambridge, Massachusetts. Wyeth planned to start a trading company in the Oregon country, but his first overland expedition in 1833 was beset by difficulties, including desertions by some of his men and the wreckage of his cargo ship, the *Sultana*, in the South Pacific. After returning to Boston, he organized a trading company that would send wares back East by ship rather than overland. Upon arriving at Fort Vancouver in 1835, he discovered that his ship, the *May Dare*, had been damaged and would arrive three months late. The venture failed, and he returned to Boston in 1836. Although he was unable to establish a trading post in the Oregon country, he did stir public interest in the region.

Wynkoop, Edward (1836–1891): Indian agent, reformer and Army officer. In July 1864, he and Colonel John Chivington met with Cheyenne Chief Black Kettle at the Camp Weld Council near Denver, Colorado. After the Sand Creek Massacre (November 1864), he was an outspoken critic of Chivington's actions. In 1868, he appeared before the United States Indian Commission and decried the unnecessary attack on Cheyennes by troops under George Armstrong Custer in the battle of the Washita, which resulted in the death of his friend Black Kettle.

Young, Brigham (1801–1877): Mormon leader. Born in Whittingham, Vermont, Young moved as a child to western New York state. He became a house painter and glazier by the age of 16. After encountering *The Book of Mormon* soon after its publication, he studied it for two years before joining the Church of Jesus Christ of Latter-Day Saints. He soon became a senior member of the Mormon Church. After Joseph Smith was murdered by an angry mob in Illinois, he led an exodus of Mormons to Nebraska, and, in 1847 proclaimed their "promised land" at the Great Salt Lake in Utah. During the next 30 years he brought in new settlers by the thousands, organized farms and businesses, irrigated the desert and paved the way for permanent settlement in the Great Basin region.

Appendix C
Maps

North America, 1783

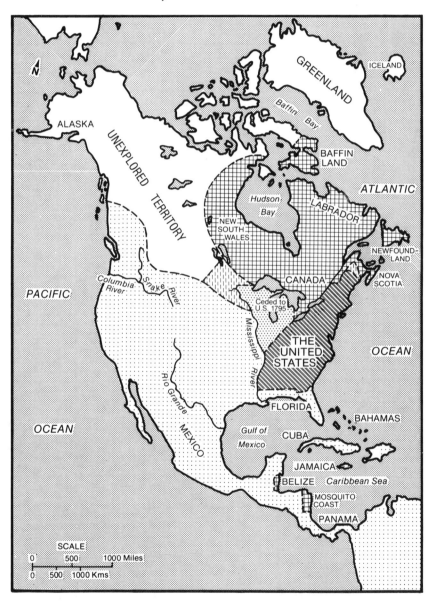

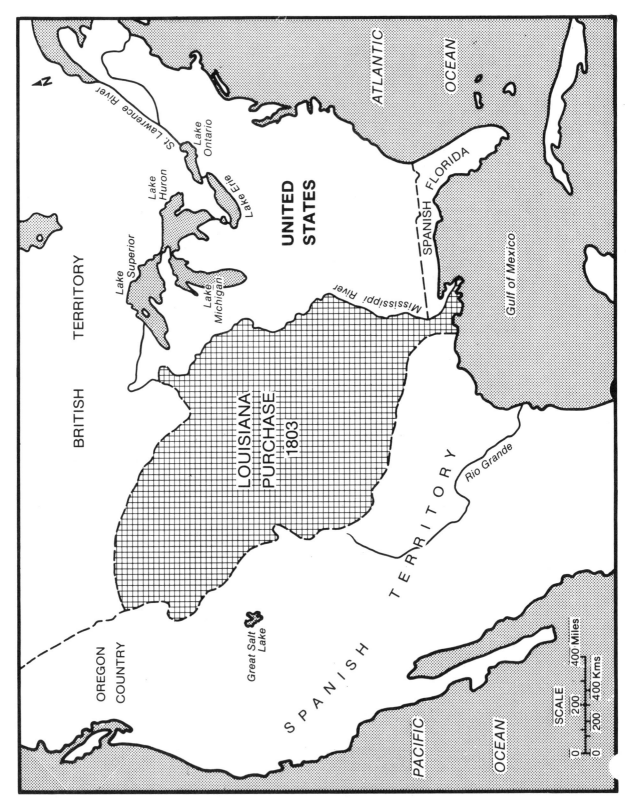

U.S. in 1803

BRITISH TERRITORY

OREGON COUNTRY

SPANISH TERRITORY

Great Salt Lake

Rio Grande

PACIFIC OCEAN

LOUISIANA PURCHASE 1803

Mississippi River

UNITED STATES

Lake Superior

Lake Michigan

Lake Huron

Lake Erie

Lake Ontario

St. Lawrence River

ATLANTIC OCEAN

SPANISH FLORIDA

Gulf of Mexico

N

SCALE
0 200 400 Miles
0 200 400 Kms

United States in 1860

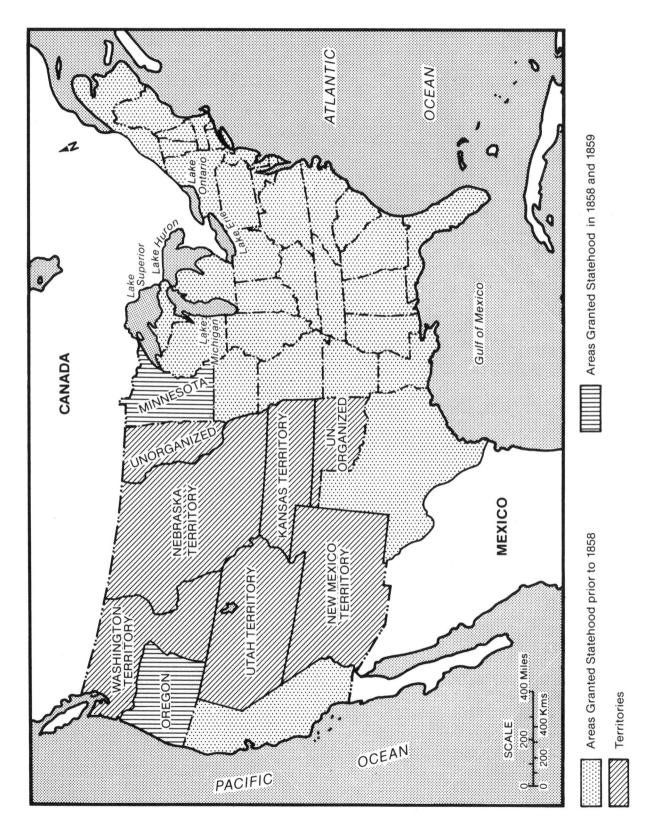

CANADA

MEXICO

ATLANTIC OCEAN

Gulf of Mexico

PACIFIC OCEAN

Lake Ontario
Lake Erie
Lake Huron
Lake Superior
Lake Michigan

MINNESOTA

UNORGANIZED

WASHINGTON TERRITORY

OREGON

UTAH TERRITORY

NEBRASKA TERRITORY

KANSAS TERRITORY

NEW MEXICO TERRITORY

UN-ORGANIZED

N

SCALE
0   200   400 Miles
0   200   400 Kms

Areas Granted Statehood in 1858 and 1859

Areas Granted Statehood prior to 1858

Territories

The National Pike and Other Main Roads to the West in the Early 19th Century

NATIONAL PIKE (CUMBERLAND ROAD)

------- UNCOMPLETED

----- WILDERNESS ROAD

-----· PHILADELPHIA-LANCASTER TURNPIKE

-·-·- MICHIGAN ROAD

········· MOHAWK TRAIL AND CHICAGO TURNPIKE

------- MAIN CONNECTING ROADS

-··-··- NATCHEZ TRACE (CHICKASAW TRAIL) AND ZANE'S TRACE

Major Roads and Trails, 1780–1860

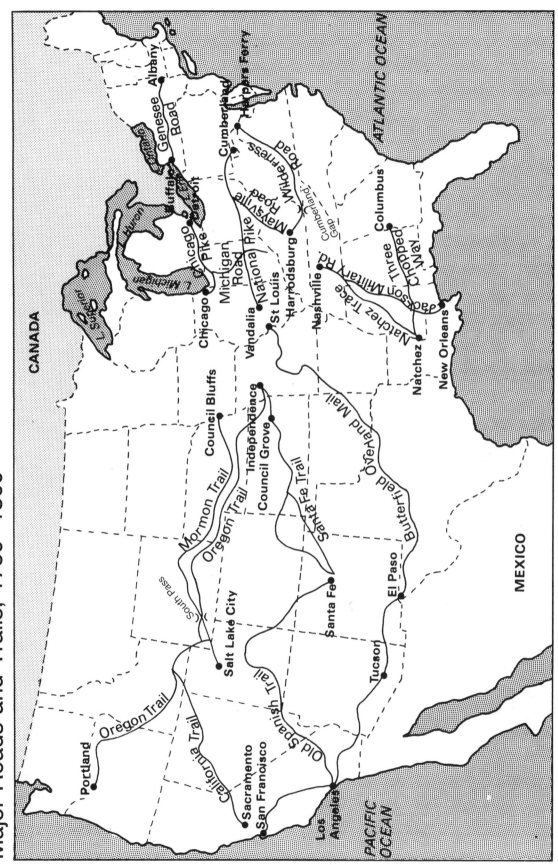

Roads or trails

Early Pacific Railroad Lines

Major Indian Wars and Battles, 1637–1890

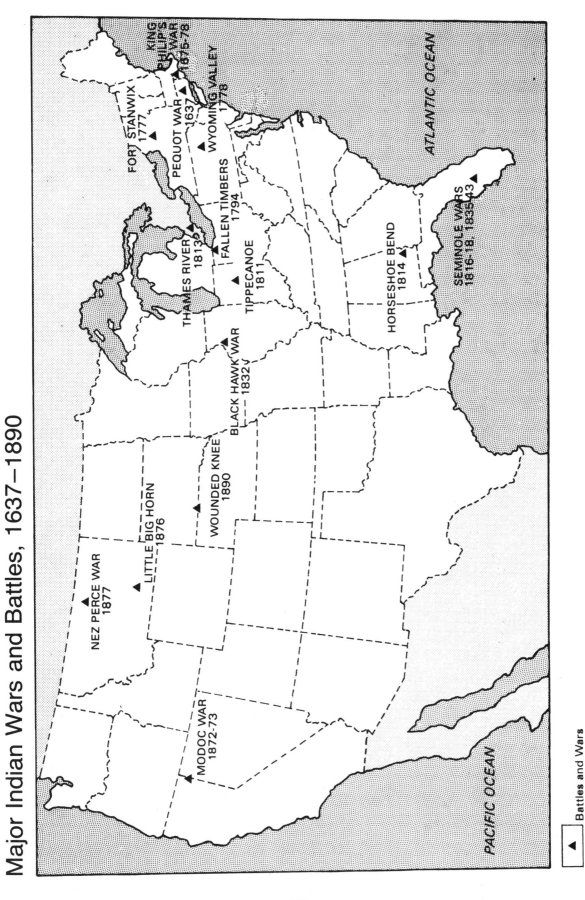

KING PHILIP'S WAR 1675-78

FORT STANWIX 1777

PEQUOT WAR 1637

WYOMING VALLEY 1778

FALLEN TIMBERS 1794

THAMES RIVER 1813

TIPPECANOE 1811

HORSESHOE BEND 1814

SEMINOLE WARS 1816-18 1835-43

BLACK HAWK WAR 1832

WOUNDED KNEE 1890

LITTLE BIG HORN 1876

NEZ PERCE WAR 1877

MODOC WAR 1872-73

ATLANTIC OCEAN

PACIFIC OCEAN

▲ Battles and Wars

Major Battles of the Mexican War, 1846–1848

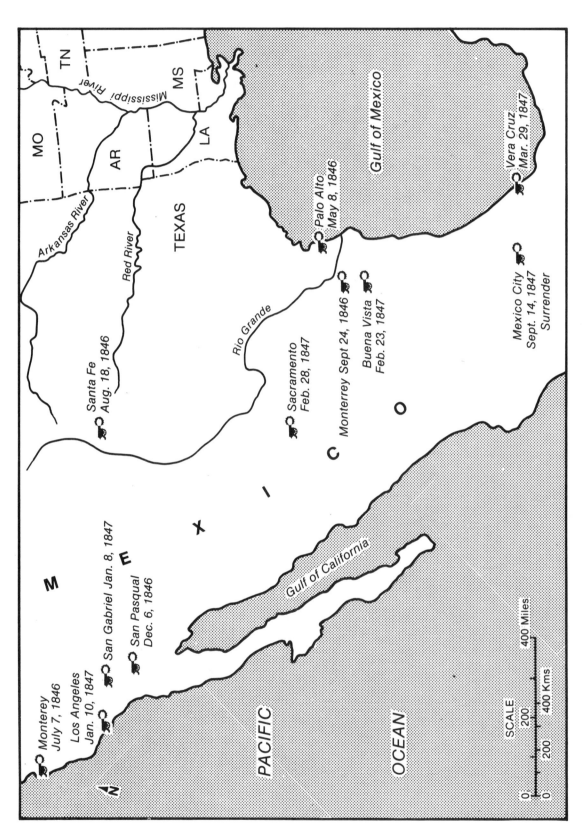

United States Acquisitions from Mexico, 1848

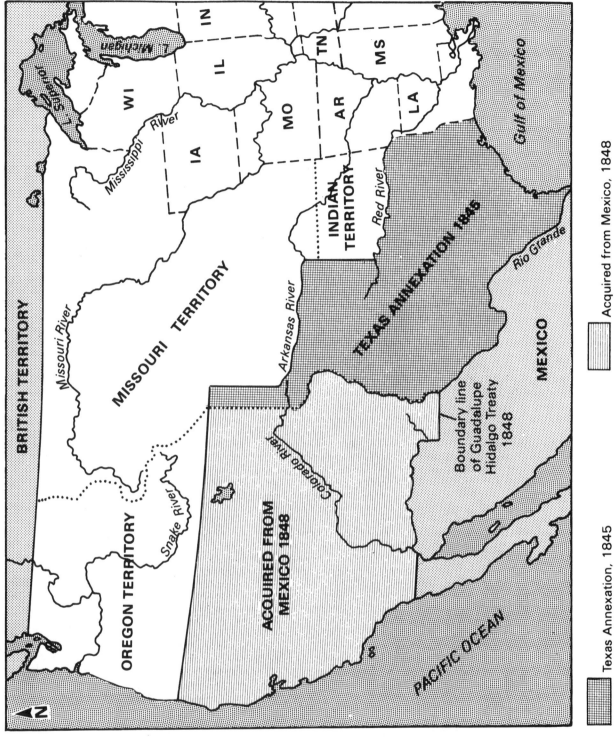

BRITISH TERRITORY

OREGON TERRITORY

MISSOURI TERRITORY

Snake River

Missouri River

Mississippi River

L. Superior

L. Michigan

WI

IA

IL

IN

MO

TN

MS

AR

LA

INDIAN TERRITORY

Arkansas River

Red River

Colorado River

ACQUIRED FROM MEXICO 1848

TEXAS ANNEXATION 1845

Boundary line of Guadalupe Hidalgo Treaty 1848

Rio Grande

MEXICO

Gulf of Mexico

PACIFIC OCEAN

N

Texas Annexation, 1845

Acquired from Mexico, 1848

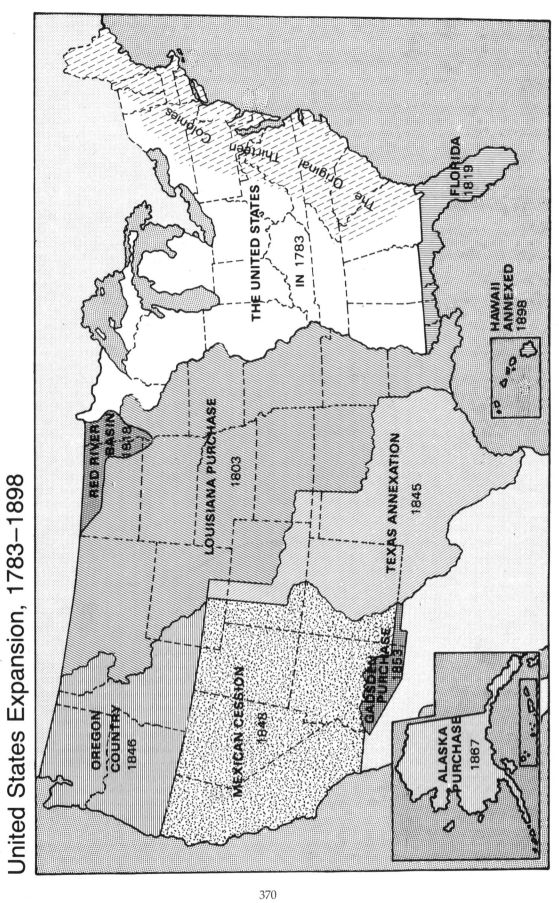

United States Expansion, 1783–1898

Year of Admission to the Union

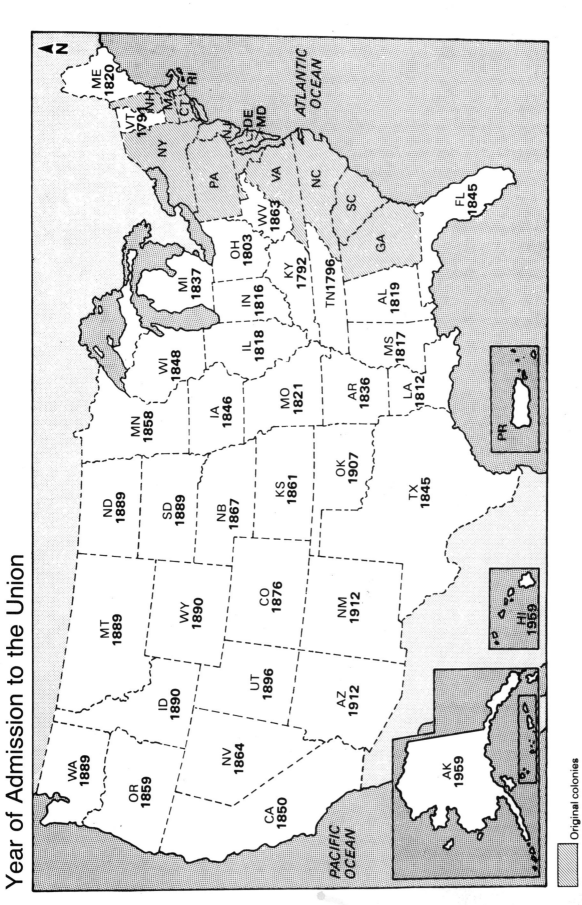

Bibliography

Abbott, E.C. and Smith, Helena Hunt, *We Pointed Them North*. Norman: University of Oklahoma Press, 1955; first published, 1939.

Abernethy, Thomas P., *The Burr Conspiracy*. New York: Oxford University Press, 1954.

————, *Western Lands and the American Revolution*. New York: Appleton-Century, 1937.

Adams, Alexander, *Sitting Bull: An Epic of the Plains*. New York: Putnam, 1973.

Adams, Henry, *History of the United States of America from 1801 to 1817*. Chicago: Chicago University Press, 1967; first published 1889–1891.

Adams, John, *Diary and Autobiography*, ed. L.H. Butterfield. Cambridge: Belknap Press of Harvard University Press, 1961; first published, 1850–1856.

Alderson, Nannie T., *A Bride Goes West*. New York: Farrar and Rinehart, 1942.

Alter, Cecil J., *James Bridger, A Historical Narrative*. Salt Lake City: Shepard Book Company, 1925.

Anderson, Gary Clayton and Woolworth, Alan R (eds.), *Through Dakota Eyes: Narrative Accounts of the Minnesota Indian War of 1862*. St. Paul: Minnesota Historical Society, 1988.

Anderson, William Marshall, *The Rocky Mountain Journals of William Marshall Anderson*, eds. Dale L. Morgan and Eleanor Tonles Harris. San Marino: Huntington Library, 1967; first published, 1938.

Angle, Paul M., *Prairie State, Impressions of Illinois, 1673–1967, By Travelers and Observers*. Chicago: University of Chicago Press, 1968.

Applegate, Jesse, *A Day with the Cow Column in 1843*, ed. Joseph Scafer. Chicago: Caxton Club, 1937; first published, 1868.

Armitage, Susan and Jameson, Elizabeth (eds.), *The Women's West*. Norman: University of Oklahoma Press, 1987.

Armstrong, Moses K., *The Early Empire Builders of the Great West*. St. Paul: E.W. Porter, 1901.

Athearn, Robert G. and Riegel, Robert E. (eds.), *America Moves West*. New York: Holt, Rinehart and Winston, 1964.

Austin, Stephen J., *The Austin Papers*, ed. Eugene C. Barker. Washington, D.C.: U.S. Government Printing Office, 1924.

Baily, Francis, *Journal of a Tour in Unsettled Parts of North America in 1796 and 1797*, ed. Jack D.L. Holmes. Edwardsville: Southern Illinois University Press, 1969; first published, 1856.

Baird, Robert, *View of the Valley of the Mississippi: or the Emigrant's and Traveller's Guide to the West*. Philadelphia: H.S. Tanner, 1832.

Baker, T. Lindsay and Harrison, Billy R., *Adobe Walls: The History and Archeology of the 1874 Trading Post*. College Station: Texas A&M University Press, 1986.

Ballou, Mary B., *A Woman's View of the Gold Rush*. New Haven: Yale University Press, 1962.

Bancroft, Hubert Howe, *The Works of Hubert Howe Bancroft*. San Francisco: A.L. Bancroft and Company, 1882–1890.

Banta, R.E., *The Ohio*. New York: Rinehart, 1949.

Barker, Eugene C., *The Life of Stephen F. Austin, Founder of Texas, 1793–1836*. Dallas: Cokesbury Press, 1925.

———, *Mexico and Texas, 1821–1835*. Dallas: P.L. Turner, 1928.

Bassett, J.S., *The Life of Andrew Jackson*. New York: Macmillan, 1911.

Beadle, J.H., *The Underdeveloped West; or Five Years in the Territories*. Philadelphia: National Publishing Company, 1873.

Beal, Merrill D., *I Will Fight No More Forever: Chief Joseph and the Nez Perce War*. Seattle: University of Washington Press, 1966.

Beauregard, Pierre Gustav, *With Beauregard in Mexico, The Mexican War Reminiscences of P.G.T. Beauregard*, ed. T. Harry Williams. New York: De Capo Press, 1969; first published, 1956.

Beckwourth, James P., *The Life and Adventures of James P. Beckwourth as Told to Thomas D. Bonner*. New York: Macmillan, 1926; first published, 1856.

Bell, William A., *New Tracks in North America, A Journey of Travel and Adventure whilst Engaged in the Survey for a Southern Railroad to the Pacific Ocean during 1867–8*. London: Chapman and Hall, 1869.

Bennett, Estelline, *Old Deadwood Days*. New York: J.H. Sears, 1928.

Benton, Thomas Hart, *Abridgement of the Debates of Congress, from 1789 to 1856*. New York: D. Appleton, 1857–1861.

———, *Thirty Years' View; or, A History of the Working of the American Government for Thirty Years, From 1820 to 1850*. New York: D. Appleton, 1856.

Bidwell, John, *Echoes of the Past About California*, ed. Milo Milton Quaife. Chicago: R.R. Donnelly & Sons, 1928.

———, *A Journey to California with Observations About the Country, Climate and the Route to this Country*. San Francisco: J.H. Nash, 1937; first published, 1842.

Billington, Ray Allen and Ridge, Martin, *Westward Expansion: A History of the American Frontier*. New York: Macmillan, 1982; first published, 1949.

Bird, Isabella, *A Lady's Life in the Rocky Mountains*. Norman: University of Oklahoma Press, 1966.

Birkbeck, Morris, *Letters from Illinois*. New York: A.M. Kelly, 1971; first published, 1818.

———, *Notes on a Journey in America from the Coast of Virginia to the Territory of Illinois*. New York: A.M. Kelly, 1971; first published, 1818.

Black Hawk, *Autobiography of Ma-ka-tai-me-she-kia-kiak, or, Black Hawk*. St. Louis: Press of Continental Printing, 1882.

Blegen, Theodore C., *Land of Their Choice: The Immigrants Write Home*. Minneapolis: University of Minnesota Press, 1955.

Bodley, Temple, *George Rogers Clark*. Boston: Houghton Mifflin, 1926.

Bouquet, Henry Col., *The Papers of Henry Bouquet: The Forbes Expedition*, eds. S.K. Stevens, D.H. Kent and A.L. Leonard. Harrisburg: The Pennsylvania Historical and Museum Commission, 1951.

Boyd, James P., *Recent Indian Wars*. Philadelphia: Franklin News Company, 1891.

Brackenridge, Henry Marie, *Journal of a Voyage Up the River Missouri; Performed in Eighteen Hundred and Eleven*. Baltimore: Coale and Maxwell, 1854.

Bradbury, John, *Travels in the Interior of America in the Years 1809, 1810, and 1811; including a Description of Upper Louisiana, Together with the States of Ohio, Kentucky, Indiana, and Tennessee, with the Illinois and Western Territories, and Containing Remarks and Observations Useful to Persons Emigrating to those Countries*. London: Sherwood, Neely, and Jones, 1818.

Bradley, Glen D., *The Story of the Pony Express*. Chicago: A.C. McClurg, 1920.

Brannan, John (ed.), *Official Letters of the Military and Naval Officers of the United States during the War with Great Britain in the Years 1812, 13, 14 & 15*. Washington, D.C.: Way & Gideon, 1823.

Breen, Patrick, *Diary of Patrick Breen, One of the Donner Party*, ed. Frederick J. Teggart. Berkeley: University of California Press, 1910.

Breihan, Carl W., *Quantrill and His Civil War Guerrillas*. Denver: Sage Books, 1959.

Briggs, Harold E., *Frontiers of the Northwest*. New York: D. Appleton-Century, 1940.

Brininstool, Earl Alonzo and Hebard, Grace Raymond, *The Bozeman Trail: Historical Accounts of the Blazing of the Overland Routes into the Northwest, and the Fights with Red Cloud's Warriors*. Cleveland: Arthur H. Clark, 1922.

Brinkley, William C. (ed.), *The Official Correspondence of the Texas Revolution*. New York: D. Appleton-Century, 1936.

Brisbin, James S., *The Beef Bonanza; or, How to Get Rich on the Plains*. Norman: University of Oklahoma Press, 1959; first published, 1881.

Brown, Dee Alexander, *Bury My Heart at Wounded Knee*. New York: Holt, Rinehart and Winston, 1971.

Brown, John Henry, *History of Texas, From 1685 to 1892*. St. Louis: L.E. Daniell, 1892.

Brown, Mark H., *The Flight of the Nez Perce*. New York: Putnam, 1967.

Brown, Uris, *Journal of a Journey from the City of Baltimore to the States of Pennsylvania, Virginia, and Ohio*. Baltimore: Maryland Historical Magazine, 1916.

Bruffey, George A., *Eighty-One Years in the West*. Butte: Butte Miner Company, 1925.

Bryan, William Jennings, *The First Battle*. Chicago: W.B. Conkey, 1896.

Bryant, Charles S. and Murch, Abel B., *History of the Great Massacre By the Sioux Indians in Minnesota*. Cincinnati: Rickey & Carroll, 1864.

Bryant, Edwin, *What I Saw in California; being the journal of a Tour, by the emigrant route, across the continent of North America, the Great Basin, and through California, in the years 1846–47*. Lincoln: University of Nebraska Press, 1985; first published, 1848.

Bryce, James B., *The American Commonwealth*. London and New York: Macmillan, 1888.

Buck, Solon J., *Illinois in 1818*. Chicago: University of Illinois Press, 1967; first published, 1917.

Buley, R. Carlyle, *The Old Northwest: Pioneer Period: 1815–1840*. Indianapolis: Indiana Historical Society, 1950.

Burnet, Jacobs, *Notes on the Early Settlements of the Northwest Territory*. New York: Arno Press, 1975; first published, 1847.

Cabell, James A., *The Trial of Aaron Burr*. Albany: Argus Company, 1900.

Calhoun, John C, *The Papers of John C. Calhoun*, ed. Robert L. Meriwether. Columbia: University of South Carolina Press, 1959; first published, 1851–1856.

Carley, Kenneth, *The Sioux Uprising of 1862*. St. Paul: Minnesota Historical Society, 1976.

Carriker, Robert C., *Fort Supply: Indian Territory*. Norman: University of Oklahoma Press, 1970.

Carrington, Frances, *My Army Life and the Fort Phil Kearney Massacre with an Account of the Celebration of "Wyoming Opened."* New York: Books for Libraries Press, 1971; first published, 1910.

Carson, Kit, *Kit Carson's Autobiography*, ed. Milo Milton Quaife. Chicago: Lakeside Press, 1935.

Caruso, John A., *The Great Lakes Frontier*. New York: Bobbs-Merrill, 1961.

Chapman, Berlin B., *The Founding of Stillwater*. Oklahoma City: Times Journal Publishing Company, 1948.

Chevalier, Michael, "Letters on America," Cincinnati, *Western Monthly Magazine*, IV(1835).

Chittenden, Hiram Martin, *The American Fur Trade of the far West; a history of the pioneer trading posts and early fur companies of the Missouri Valley and Rocky Mountains and of the overland commerce with Sante Fe*. New York: F.P. Harper, 1902.

Clanton, O. Gene, *Kansas Populism*. Lawrence: University of Kansas, 1969.

Clark, George Rogers, *George Rogers Clark Papers*, ed. J.A. James. Springfield: Illinois State Historical Society, 1912.

Clark, George T., *Leland Stanford*. Stanford: Stanford University Press, 1931.

Clay, Henry, *The Papers of Henry Clay*, ed. James F. Hopkins. Lexington: University of Kentucky Press, 1959; first published, 1853.

———, *The Works of Henry Clay*, ed. Calvin Colton. New York: Putnam, 1904; first published, 1857.

Clay, John, *My Life on the Range*. Chicago: Private Printing, 1924.

Clayton, William, *William Clayton's Journal*. Salt Lake City: Deseret News, 1921.

Cleaveland, Agnes (Morley), *No Life For A Lady*. Lincoln: University of Nebraska Press, 1977; first published, 1941.

Cleaves, Freeman, *Old Tippecanoe*. Port Washington: Kennikat Press, 1969; first published, 1939.

Clyman, James C., *Journal of a Mountain Man*, ed. Linda M. Hasselstrom. Missoula: Mountain Press Publishing Company, 1984; first published, 1928.

Cobbett, William, *A Year's Residence in the United States of America*. London: Sherwood, Neely and Jones, 1818.

Cochran, Thomas C., *The New American State Papers: Indian Affairs*. Wilmington: Scholarly Resources, 1972.

Cody, William F., *The Life of Honorable William F. Cody known as Buffalo Bill, the Famous Hunter, Scout and Guide: an Autobiography*. Hartford: Frank E. Bliss, 1879.

Collinson, Frank, *Life in the Saddle*, ed. Mary Whatley Clarke. Norman: University of Oklahoma, 1964.

Colton, Calvin, *The Life and Times of Henry Clay*. New York: A.S. Barnes, 1846.

Colton, Calvin (ed.), *The Works of Henry Clay*. New York: Putnam, 1904; first published, 1857.

Commager, Henry Steele (ed.), *The Blue and the Gray: The Story of the Civil War as Told by Participants*. New York: Bobbs-Merrill, 1950.

———, *Documents of American History*. New York: F.S. Crofts, 1934.

Connelley, William, *Quantrill and the Border Wars*. Cedar Rapids: Torch Press, 1910.

Cook, James H., *Fifty Years on the Old Frontier: As Cowboy, Hunter, Guide, Scout, and Ranchman*. New Haven: Yale University Press, 1923.

Cook, John R., *The Border and the Buffalo,* ed. Milo Milton Quaife. Chicago: Lakeside Press, 1938; first published, 1907.

Cortes, Carlos E. (ed.), *The Mexican Side of the Texas Revolution*. New York: Arno Press, 1976.

Cox, Sanford C., *Recollections of the Early Settlement of the Wabash Valley*. Lafayette: Courier Steam Book & Job Printing House, 1860.

Cox, Thomas C., *Blacks in Topeka Kansas: 1865–1915*. Baton Rouge: Louisiana State University Press, 1982.

Crane, William Carey, *Life and Select Literary Remains of Sam Houston of Texas*. Freeport: Books for Libraries Press, 1972; first published, 1884.

Crook, George, *General George Crook, His Autobiography*, ed. Martin F. Schmitt. Norman: University of Oklahoma Press, 1946.

Curley, Edwin A., *Nebraska; Its Advantages, Resources, and Drawbacks*. New York: American and Foreign Publishing, 1875.

Custer, Elizabeth R., *Boots and Saddles; or Life in Dakota with General Custer*. New York: Harper and Brothers, 1885.

Custer, George A., *My Life on the Plains, or Personal Experiences with Indians*. Norman: University of Oklahoma Press, 1962; first published, 1874.

Cutler, Manasseh, *Life, Journals and Correspondence of Rev. Mannasseh Cutler*, eds. William Cutler and Julia Cutler. Cincinnati: R. Clarke, 1888.

Dain, Floyd R., *Every House A Frontier*. Detroit: Wayne University Press, 1956.

Dale, Harrison Clifford, *The Ashley-Smith Explorations and the Discovery of A Central Route to the Pacific*. Glendale: Arthur H. Clark, 1941.

Dana, Richard Henry, *Two Years Before the Mast; A Personal Narrative of Life at Sea*. New York: Harper and Brothers, 1846.

Darlington, Mary C. (ed.), *History of Colonel Henry Bouquet: 1747–1764*. New York: Arno Press and The New York Times, 1971.

Davis, Britton, *The Truth about Geronimo*, ed. Milo M. Quaife. Lincoln: University of Nebraska Press, 1976; first published; 1929.

Davis, Jefferson, *Jefferson Davis: Constitutionalist, His Letters, Papers and Speeches*, ed. Rowland Dunbar. Jackson: Mississippi Department of Archives and History, 1923.

Dawson, Moses, *Historical Narrative of the Civil and Military Services of Major-General Harrison*. Cincinnati: M. Dawson, 1824.

Dellenbaugh, Frederick S., *Fremont and '49*. New York: Putnam, 1914.

Derleth, August, *Vincennes: Portal to the West*. Englewood Cliffs, N.J.: Prentice Hall, 1968.

De Smet, Pierre-Jean, *Life, Letters and Travels of Father De Smet Among the North American Indians*, ed. Hiram Martin Chittenden and Alfred Talbot Richardson. New York: Francis P. Harper, 1905.

DeVoto, Bernard (ed.), *Journals of Lewis and Clark*. Boston: Houghton Mifflin, 1953.

Dewees, Mary, *Journal from Philadelphia to Kentucky, 1787–1788*. Philadelphia: Pennsylvania Magazine of History and Biography, 1904.

Dick, Everett, *Conquering the Great American Desert: Nebraska*. Lincoln: Nebraska State Historical Society, 1975.

———, *The Sod-House Frontier*. New York: D. Appleton-Century, 1937.

———, *The Vanguards of the Frontier*. New York: D. Appleton, 1941.

Dickens, Charles, *American Notes for General Circulation*. London: Chapman and Hall, 1842.

Dinwiddie, Robert, *The Official Records of Robert Dinwiddie, lieutenant-governor of the colony of Virginia, 1751–1758*, ed. R.A. Brock. Richmond: Virginia Historical Society, 1883–84.

Dippie, Brian W. (ed.), *Nomad: George A. Custer in Turf, Field and Farm.* Austin: University of Texas, 1980.

Doddridge, Joseph, *Notes on the Settlement and Indian Wars of the Western Parts of Virginia and Pennsylvania from 1763 to 1783*, ed. Alfred Williams. Albany: Joel Munsell, 1876; first published, 1824.

Dodge, Grenville M., *How We Built the Union Pacific Railway.* Washington, D.C.: Government Printing Office, 1910.

Dondore, Dorothy A., *The Prairie and the Making of Middle America: Four Centuries of Description.* Cedar Rapids: Torch Press, 1926.

Drake, Benjamin, *The Life of Tecumseh.* New York: Kraus Reprints, 1969; first published, 1841.

Drumm, Stella M. (ed.), *The Journal of A Fur Trading Expedition on the Upper Missouri, 1812–13.* New York: Argosy-Antiquarian, 1964.

Drury, Clifford Merrill, *First White Women Over the Rockies.* Glendale: Arthur H. Clarke, 1963.

Dunbar, William, *The Life, Letters and Papers of William Dunbar*, ed. Mrs. Rowland Dunbar (Eron Rowland). Jackson: Press of the Mississippi Historical Society, 1930.

Ebbutt, Percy G., *Emigrant Life in Kansas.* New York: Arno Press, 1975; first published, 1886.

Edmonds, David, *Tecumseh and the Quest for Indian Leadership.* Boston: Little Brown, 1984.

Ellis, Elmer, *Henry Moore Teller: Defender of the West.* Caldwell: Caxton Printers, 1941.

Evans, Estwick, *A Pedestrious Tour of Four Thousand Miles Through the Western States and Territories, during the Winter and Spring of 1818. Interspersed with Brief Reflections Upon a Great Variety of Topics: Religious, Moral, Political, Sentimental.* Concord, N.H.: Joseph C. Spear, 1819.

Every, Dale Van, *The Final Challenge.* New York: William Morrow, 1964.

Farnham, Thomas J., *Travels in the Great Western Prairies, The Anahuac and Rocky Mountains, and in the Oregon Territory.* Poughkeepsie: Killey and Lossing, 1841.

Faux, William, *Memorable Days in America: Being a Journal of a Tour to the United States, Principally Undertaken to Ascertain, by Positive Evidence, the Condition and Probable Prospects of British Emigrants; including Accounts of Mr. Birkbeck's Settlement in the Illinois: and Intended to Show Men and Things as they Are in America.* London: W. Simpkin & R. Marshall, 1823.

Ferris, Benjamin G., *Utah and the Mormons.* New York: Harper and Brothers, 1854.

Filson, John, *The Discovery, Settlement, and Present State of Kentucke, and an Essay towards the Topography, and Natural History of that Important Country.* Wilmington: James Adams, 1784.

Fine, Nathan, *Labor and Farm Parties in the United States: 1828–1928.* New York: Rand School of Social Science, 1928.

Finerty, John Frederick, *War-Path and Bivouac; or The Conquest of the Sioux.* Chicago: Donohue and Henneberry, 1890.

Finley, James B., *Life Among the Indians; or, Personal Reminiscenses and Historical Incidents Illustrative of Indian Life and Character*, ed. D.W. Clark. Cincinnati: Methodist Book Concern, 1857.

Fite, Gilbert C., *The Farmers' Frontier: 1865–1900.* New York: Holt, Rinehart and Winston, 1966.

Fletcher, John Baylis, *Up The Trail in '79.*, ed. Wayne Gard. Norman: University of Oklahoma Press, 1968.

Flint, Timothy, *The History and Geography of the Mississippi Valley.* Cincinnati: E.H. Flint and L.R. Lincoln, 1832.

———, *Recollections of the Last Ten Years in the Valley of the Mississippi.* Boston: Cummings, Hilliard & Co., 1826.

Flower, George, *History of the English Settlement in Edwards County, Illinois, founded in 1817 and 1818 by Moris Birkbeck and George Flower.* Chicago: Chicago Historical Society, 1882.

Folwell, William W., *History of Minnesota*. St. Paul: Minnesota Historical Society, 1921–1930.

Forbes, John, *Writings of General John Forbes Relating to His Service in North America*. New York: Arno Press and The New York Times, 1971.

Foster, James S., *Outlines of History of the Territory of Dakota and Emigrant's Guide to the Free Lands of the Northwest*. Yankton, S.D.: M'Intyre & Foster, 1870.

Fowler, Elaine M. and Wright, Louis B. (eds.), *The Moving Frontier*. New York: Dell, 1972.

Fowler, Jacob, *Journal of Jacob Fowler, Narrating an Adventure from Arkansas through the Indian territory, Oklahoma, Kansas, Colorado, and New Mexico, to the sources of the Rio Grande del Norte, 1821–22*, ed. Elliot Couses. Lincoln: University of Nebraska Press, 1970; first published, 1898.

Franchere, Gabriel, *A Narrative of a Voyage to the Northwest Coast of America in the Years 1811, 1812, 1813, and 1814, or the First American Settlement of the Pacific*. New York: Bedfield, 1854.

Franklin, Benjamin, *Observations Concerning the Increase of Mankind, Peopling of Countries*. Boston: S. Kneeland, 1775.

Frederick, J.V., *Ben Holladay: The Stagecoach King*. Glendale: Arthur H. Clark, 1940.

Freeman, Henry B., *The Freeman Journal: The Infantry in the Sioux Camp of 1876*, ed. George A. Schneider. San Rafael: Presidio Press, 1977; first published, 1893.

Fremont, Jessie Benton, *A Year of American Travel*. New York: Harper and Brothers, 1877.

——, "The Origins of the Fremont Expedition," *The Century Magazine*, March 1891.

Fremont, John C., *Geographical Memoir Upon Upper California (1849)*. Philadelphia: William McCarty, 1849.

——, *Memoirs of My Life*. Chicago: Clarke and Company, 1887.

————, *A Report of an Exploration of the Country Lying Between the Missouri River and the Rocky Mountains on the Line and Great Platte Rivers.* Washington, D.C.: Government Printing Office, 1843.

————, *Report of the Exploring Expedition to the Rocky Mountains in the Year 1842 and to Oregon and North California in the Years 1843–1844.* Washington: Gales & Seaton, 1845.

Fulton, Alexander, *The Red Men of Iowa.* Des Moines: Mills and Company, 1882.

Gaboury, William J., *Dissension in the Rockies: A History of Idaho Populism.* New York: Garland, 1988.

Galland, Isaac, *Iowa Emigrant.* Chillicothe: Wm.C. Jones, 1840.

Gallatin, Albert, *Peace with Mexico.* New York: Bartlett and Welford, 1847.

Gard, Wayne, *The Chisholm Trail.* Norman: University of Oklahoma Press, 1954.

Gass, Patrick, *A Journal of the Voyages and Travels of a Corps of Discovery Under the Command of Captain Lewis and Captain Clarke.* Pittsburgh: David M'Keehan, 1807.

Geffs, Irving, *The First Eight Months of Oklahoma City.* Oklahoma City: McMaster Printing Company, 1890.

George, Isaac, *Heroes and Incidents of the Mexican War, Containing Doniphan's Expedition.* Hollywood, Calif.: Sun Dance Press, 1971; first published, 1903.

Gillett, James B., *Six Years With The Texas Rangers, 1875–1881*, ed. Milo Milton Quaife. Chicago: Lakeside Press, 1943; first published, 1921.

Gilpin, William, *Settlement of Oregon—Emigrants of 1843; 29th Congress, 1st Session, Senate Document 306; Report of the Commission on the Post Office and Post Roads.* Washington, D.C.: Government Printing Office, April 20, 1846.

Gist, Christopher, *Journals with historical, geographical and ethnological notes and biographies of his contemporaries*, ed. William H. Darlington. Pittsburgh: J.R. Weldin, 1893.

Going, Charles Buxton, *David Wilmot Free-Soiler: A Biography of the Great Advocate of the Wilmot Proviso*. New York: D. Appleton, 1924.

Golder, Frank Alfred, *The March of the Mormon Battalion*. New York: Century, 1928.

Goodnight, Charlie, *Pioneer Days in the Southwest from 1850 to 1879, thrilling descriptions of buffalo hunting, Indian fighting and massacres, cowboy life and home building*. Guthrie, Oklahoma: State Capital Company, 1909.

Goodwin, Cardinal L., *The Trans-Mississippi West (1803–1835): A History of its Acquisition and Settlement*. New York: D. Appleton, 1922.

Gordon, Mary McDougall (ed.), *Overland to California with the Pioneer Line, The Gold Rush Diary of Bernard J. Reid*. Stanford: Stanford University Press, 1983.

Gove, Jesse A., *The Utah Expedition, 1857–1858; Letters of Captain Jesse A. Gove, 10th Infantry, U.S.A. to Mrs. Gove, and Special Correspondence of the New York Herald*, ed. Otis G. Hammond. Concord: New Hampshire Historical Society, 1928.

Graham, William A., *The Custer Myth*. Harrisburg, Pa.: Stackpole Company, 1953.

Gray, John S., *Centennial Campaign: The Sioux War of 1876*. Fort Collins, Colorado: Old Army Press, 1976.

Greeley, Horace, *Hints Toward Reform: Lectures, Addresses, and Other Writings*. New York: Fowlers and Wells, 1857.

———, *An Overland Journey from New York to San Francisco, in the Summer of 1859*. New York: C.M. Saxton, Barker & Co., 1860.

Green, Michael D., *The Politics of Indian Removal*. Lincoln: University of Nebraska Press, 1982.

Gregg, Josiah, *Commerce of the Prairies; or the Journal of a Santa Fe Trader during Eight Expeditions Across the Great Western Prairies*. Ann Arbor: University Microfilms, 1966; first published, 1844.

Griffith, Jr., Benjamin W., *McIntosh and Weatherford, Creek Indian Leaders*. Tuscaloosa: University of Alabama Press, 1988.

Grinnell, George Bird, *The Fighting Cheyennes*. Norman: University of Oklahoma Press, 1966.

Grinnell, Josiah, *Home of the Badgers*. Milwaukee: Wilshire and Company, 1845.

Hafen, Leroy R., *Colorado and Its People*. New York: Lewis Historical Publishing Company, 1948.

——, *The Overland Mail, 1849–1869*. Cleveland: Arthur H. Clark, 1926.

Hafen, Leroy R. (ed.), *Colorado Gold Rush, Contemporary Letters and Reports*. Glendale: Arthur H. Clark, 1941.

——, *Pike's Peak Gold Rush Guidebooks of 1859*. Glendale: Arthur H. Clark, 1941.

——, *Powder River Campaigns and Swayers Expedition of 1865*. Glendale: Arthur H. Clark, 1961.

——, *The Utah Expedition, 1857–1858, A Documentary Account of the United States Military Movement under Colonel Albert Sidney Johnston, and The Resistance by Brigham Young and the Mormon Mauvoo Legion*. Glendale: Arthur H. Clark, 1958.

Hafen, Leroy R. and Ann W., *Handcarts to Zion: The Story of A Unique Western Migration, 1856–1860*. Glendale: Arthur H. Clarke, 1960.

——, *Old Spanish Trail*. Glendale: Arthur H. Clark, 1954.

——, *To The Rockies and Oregon, 1839–1842*. Glendale: Arthur H. Clark, 1955.

Hafen, Leroy R. and Ann W. (eds.), *Relations with the Indians of the Plains, 1857–1861*. Glendale: Arthur H. Clark, 1959.

Hale, Frederick, *Danes in North America*. Seattle: University of Washington Press, 1984.

Haley, James L., *The Buffalo War: The History of the Red River Indian Uprising of 1874*. New York: Doubleday, 1976.

Hall, James, *Letters from the West*. London: Henry Colburn, 1828.

Hamilton, William (ed.), *Anglo-American Law on the Frontier*. Ann Arbor: Books on Demand, University Microfilms International, 1953.

Hansen, Klaus J., *Quest for Empire: The Political Kingdom of Good and the Council of Fifty in Mormon History*. Ann Arbor: Michigan State University, 1967.

Harpster, John W. (ed.), *Crossroads: Descriptions of Western Pennsylvania 1720–1829*. Pittsburgh: University of Pittsburgh Press, 1938.

Harris, William Tell, *Remarks Made During a Tour Through the United States of America in the Years 1817, 1818, and 1819*. London: Sherwood, Neely & Jones, 1821.

Hastings, Lansford W., *The Emigrants' Guide to Oregon and California, containing scenes and incidents of a party of California emigrants; and a description of California; with a description of the different routes to those countries; and all necessary information relative to the equipment, supplies, and the method of traveling*. Princeton: University Press, 1932; first published, 1845.

Havighurst, Walter, *Wilderness for Sale*. New York: Hastings House, 1956.

Hayden, F.V., *U.S. Geological Survey of Wyoming and Adjacent Territories*. Washington, D.C.: Government Printing Office, 1871.

Hayes, Rutherford B., *Letters and Messages of Rutherford B. Hayes, Together with Letter of Acceptance and Inaugural Address*. Washington, D.C.: Government Printing Office, 1881.

Haynes, Frederick E., *James Baird Weaver*. Iowa City: State Historical Society of Iowa, 1919.

Heap, Gwinn Harris, *Central Route to the Pacific*. Glendale: Arthur H. Clarke, 1957; first published, 1854.

Hebard, G.R., *The History and Government of Wyoming*. San Francisco: C.F. Weber, 1919.

Hecht, Marie B., *John Quincy Adams: A Personal History of An Independent Man*. New York: Macmillan, 1972.

Heckewelder, John Gottlieb, *History, Manners, and Customs of the Indian Nations who once inhabited Pennsylvania and the Neighboring States,* ed. Rev. William C. Reichel. Philadelphia: Historical Society of Pennsylvania, 1876; first published, 1818.

Heron, Jim, *Fifty Years on the Owl Hoot Trail: The First Sheriff of No Man's Land,* ed. Harry E. Chrisman. Chicago: Sage Books, 1969.

Hildreth, Samuel P., *Pioneer History of the Ohio Valley.* Cincinnati: H.W. Derby, 1848.

Hitchcock, Ethan Allen, *Fifty Years in Camp and Field: Diary of E.A.H., U.S.A.,* ed. W.A. Croffut. New York: Putnam, 1969; first published, 1909.

Hoffman, Charles Fenno, *A Winter in the West, By a New Yorker.* Ann Arbor: University Microfilms, 1966; first published, 1835.

Hoig, Stan, *The Oklahoma Land Rush of 1889.* Oklahoma City: Oklahoma Historical Society, 1984.

———, *The Peace Chiefs of the Cheyennes.* Norman: University of Oklahoma Press, 1980.

———, *The Sand Creek Massacre.* Norman: University of Oklahoma Press, 1961.

Holley, Mary Austin, *Texas: Observations, Historical, Geographic, and Descriptive.* Lexington, Kentucky: J. Clark, 1836.

Hollister, Ovando J., *Boldly They Rode: A History of the First Colorado Regiment of Volunteers.* Lakewood, Colorado: The Golden Press, 1949; first published, 1863.

Holmes, Kenneth L. (ed.), *Covered Wagon Women: Diaries and Letters From the Western Trails.* Glendale: Arthur H. Clarke, 1983.

Hoopes, Alban W., *Indians Affairs and Their Administration.* Philadelphia: University of Pennsylvania Press, 1932.

Horsman, Reginald, *Expansion and American Indian Policy, 1783–1812.* East Lansing: Michigan State University Press, 1967.

Houston, Sam, *The Writings of Sam Houston*, eds. Amelia W. Williams and Eugene C. Barker. Austin: University of Texas Press, 1938–43.

Howard, James H. (ed.), *The Warrior Who Killed Custer: The Personal Narrative of Chief Joseph White Bull*. Lincoln: University of Nebraska, 1968.

Howard, Joseph Kinsey (ed.), *Montana Margins*. New Haven: Yale University Press, 1946.

Howard, Oliver O., *Nez Perce Joseph*. Boston: Lee and Shepard, 1881.

Howells, William Cooper, *Recollections of Life in Ohio from 1813 to 1840*. Cincinnati: Robert Clarke, 1895.

Hulbert, Archer Butler (ed.), *Forty-Niners: The Chronicle of the California Trial*. Boston: Little Brown, 1949.

———, *The Call of the Columbia: Iron Men and Saints Take the Oregon Trail*. Denver: Stewart Commission of Colorado College and Denver Public Library, 1934.

———, *Ohio in the Time of the Confederation*. Marietta, Ohio: Marietta Historical Commission, 1918.

———, *The Oregon Crusade: Across Land and Sea to Oregon*. Denver: Stewart Commission of Colorado College and Denver Public Library, 1935.

———, *Southwest on the Turquoise Trail: The First Diaries on the Road to Sante Fe*. Denver: Stewart Commission of Colorado College and Denver Public Library, 1933.

———, *Where Rolls Oregon: Prophet and Pessimist Look Northwest*. Denver: Stewart Commission of Colorado College and Denver Public Library, 1933.

Humphry, Seth K., *Following the Prarie Frontier*. St. Paul: University of Minnesota Press, 1931.

Hunt, Robert (ed.), *I Fought With Custer*. Lincoln: University of Nebraska Press, 1987.

Hunter, Marvin J. (ed.), *The Trial Drivers of Texas*. New York: Argosy-Antiquarian Ltd., 1963; first published, 1925.

Hyde, George E., *Red Cloud's Folk: A History of the Oglala Sioux*. Norman: University of Oklahoma Press, 1937.

Ingersoll, L.D., *The Life of Horace Greeley*. Philadelphia: Keystone, 1890.

Inman, Henry, *The Old Santa Fe Trail*. New York: Macmillan, 1899; first published, 1897.

Irving, Washington, *A Tour on the Prairies*. New York: John W. Lovell, 1883; first published as part of *The Crayon Miscellany*, 1835.

Jackson, Andrew, *The Correspondence of Andrew Jackson*, ed. John Spencer Bassett. Washington, D.C.: Carnegie Institute of Washington, 1926.

Jackson, Donald, *Thomas Jefferson and the Stony Mountains*. Chicago: University of Illinois, 1981.

Jackson, Donald (ed.), *The Letters of the Lewis and Clark Expedition, with Related Documents*. Chicago: University of Illinois, 1962.

Jackson, William Henry, *The Diaries of William Henry Jackson*, eds. Leroy and Ann Hafen. Glendale: Arthur H. Clarke, 1959.

James, James Alton, *The Life of George Rogers Clark*. Chicago: University of Chicago Press, 1928.

James, Thomas, *Three Years Among the Indians and Mexicans*, ed. Milo M. Quaife. New York: Citadel Press, 1966; first published, 1916.

Jay, John, *The Correspondence and Public Papers of John Jay*, ed. H.P. Johnston. New York: Putnam, 1891.

Jefferson, Thomas, *Letters and Addresses of Thomas Jefferson*, eds. W.B. Parker and J. Villes. New York: A. Wessel, 1907; first published, 1903.

————, *The Papers of Thomas Jefferson*, ed. Julian P. Boyd. Princeton: Princeton University Press, 1950.

————, *The Writings of Thomas Jefferson*, ed. P.L. Ford. New York: Putnam, 1891; first published, 1854–1857.

Jenkins, Jefferson, *The Northern Tier; or Life Among the Homestead Settlers*. Topeka: Geo. W. Kansas Publishing House, 1880.

Johannsen, Robert W., *Stephen A. Douglas*. New York: Oxford University Press, 1973.

Johnson, Harvey, *Tending the Talking Wire A Buck Soldier's View of Indian Country*, ed. William E. Unrau. Salt Lake City: University of Utah Press, 1979.

Johnson, Overton and Winter, Wm. H., *Route Across the Rocky Mountains with a Description of Oregon and California*. Lafayette: John B. Semans, 1846.

Johnson, Robert Underwood and Buel, Clarence Cough (eds.), *Battles and Leaders of the Civil War*. New York: Thomas Yoseloff, 1956; first published, 1887.

Judson, Phoebe Goodell, *A Pioneer's Search for an Ideal Home, by Phoebe Goodell Judson, who crossed the Plains in 1853 and Became a Resident on Puget Sound Before the Organization of Washington Territory*. Lincoln: University of Nebraska Press, 1984; first published, 1925.

Keith, Alice Barnwell (ed.), *The John Gray Blount Papers*. Raleigh: North Carolina State Department of Archives and History, 1952.

Kelly, William Fitch, *Pine Ridge, 1890: An Eye Witness Account of the Events Surrounding the Fighting at Wounded Knee*, ed. Alexander Kelly and Pierre Bovis. San Francisco: Pierre Books, 1971.

Kennedy, Michael S. (ed.,), *Cowboys and Cattlemen*. New York: Hastings House, 1964.

Kincaid, Robert L., *The Wilderness Road*. New York: Bobbs-Merrill, 1947.

Kinney, J.P., *A Continent Lost—A Civilization Won*. Baltimore: Johns Hopkins Press, 1937.

Kirsch, Robert and Murphy, William S., *West of the West, Witness to the California Expedition, 1542–1906*. New York: Dutton, 1967.

Klinck, Carl F., *Tecumseh: Fact and Fiction in Early Records*. Englewood Cliffs, N.J.: Prentice-Hall, 1961.

Knight, John, *The Emigrants Best Instructor, or, the most Recent and Important Information respecting the United States of America, selected from the Works of the latest Travellers in that Country.* Manchester: M. Wilson, 1818.

Knight, John (ed.), *Important Extracts from Original and Recent Letters, written by Englishmen, in the United States of America to their friends in England.* Manchester: Thomas Wilkenson, 1818.

Lamar, Howard Roberts, *Dakota Territory: 1861–1889, A Study of Frontier Politics.* New Haven: Yale University Press, 1956.

Langford, Nathaniel Pitt, *The Discovery of Yellowstone Park: Journal of the Washburn Expedition to the Yellowstone and Firehole Rivers in the Year 1870.* Lincoln: University of Nebraska Press, 1972; first published, 1923.

Lapsley, Arthur Broods (ed.), *The Writings of Abraham Lincoln.* New York: Putnam, 1905.

Larkin, Thomas Oliver, *The Larkin Papers: Personal, Business, and Official Correspondence of Thomas Oliver Larkin, Merchant and United States Consul in California,* ed. George P. Hammond. Berkeley: University of California Press, 1963; first published, 1951.

Larson, Gustave O., *Prelude to the Kingdom: Mormon Desert Conquest.* Westport: Greenwood Press, 1947.

Larson, Henrietta M., *Jay Cooke, Private Banker.* Cambridge: Harvard University Press, 1936.

Lavender, David, *The Fist in the Wilderness.* New York: Doubleday, 1964.

———, *The Great West.* New York: American Heritage Press, 1985; first published, 1965.

Lemmon, Ed, *Boss Cowman: Recollections of Ed Lemmon, 1857–1946,* ed. Wellie Snyder Yost. Lincoln: University of Nebraska Press, 1969.

Leonard, Zenas, *Narrative, Adventures of Zenas Leonard: Fur Trader and Trapper, 1831–1836,* ed. W.F. Wagner, M.D. Cleveland: Burrows Brothers Company, 1904; first published, 1839.

Lincecum, Gideon, *Autobiography*. Oxford: Publications of the Mississippi Historical Society, 1904.

Lincoln, Abraham, *Abraham Lincoln, Complete Works: Comprising His Speeches, Letters, State Papers and Miscellaneous Writings*, ed. John G. Nicolay and John Hay. New York: Century, 1920; first published, 1886–1906.

Linn, William Alexander, *The Story of the Mormons*. New York: Macmillan, 1923.

Lockley, Fred, *Oregon Trail Blazers*. New York: Knickerbocker Press, 1929.

Lomax, John A., *Cowboy Songs and Other Frontier Ballads*. New York: Macmillan, 1922.

McAfee, William and Robinson, Cordell J., *Origins of the Mexican War: A Documentary Source Book*. Salisbury: Documentary Publications, 1982.

McClellan, George B., *The Mexican War Diary of General George B. McClellan*, ed. William Starr Myers. New York: Da Capo Press, 1972; first published, 1917.

McClure, David, *Diary*. New York: Knickerbocker, 1899.

McCoy, Joseph G., *Historic Sketches of the Cattle Trade of the West and Southwest*. Glendale: Arthur H. Clark, 1940; first published, 1874.

McCracken, Harold, *Frederic Remington, Artist of the Old West*. Philadelphia: J.B. Lippincott, 1947.

McEllroy, Robert McNutt, *Kentucky in the Nation's History*. New York: Moffat, Yard, 1909.

McPherson, James M., *Battle Cry of Freedom: The Civil War Era*. New York: Oxford University Press, 1988.

McWhorter, Lucullus Virgil, *Hear Me, My Chiefs*. Caldwell: Caxton Printers, 1952.

Madison, James, *Letters and Other Writings of James Madison*. New York: R. Worthington, 1884.

———, *The Writings of James Madison*, ed. Gaillard Hunt. New York: Putnam, 1908.

Magoffin, Susan Shelby, *Down the Santa Fe Trail and Into Mexico: The Diary of Susan Shelby Magoffin*, ed. Stella M. Drumm. Lincoln: University of Nebraska Press, 1962; first published, 1926.

Maguire, Henry N., *Guide to the Black Hills*. Chicago: Rand, McNally, 1878.

Manning, William, *Diplomatic Correspondence of the United States: Inter-American Affairs, 1831–1860*. Washington, D.C.: Carnegie Endowment for International Peace, 1923–1939.

Marcy, Randolph B., *The Prairie Traveler: A Handbook For Overland Expeditions*. New York: Harper and Brothers, 1859.

Marmaduke, Meredith Miles, "Journal of M.M. Marmaduke of a Trip from Franklin, Missouri, to Santa Fe, New Mexico, in 1824," ed. F.A. Sampson, *Missouri Historical Review*, 6:1 (October 1911).

Marshall, James, "Interview with James Marshall," *The Century Magazine*, February 1891.

Martineau, Harriet, *Society in America*. London: Saunders and Otley, 1837.

Mazzanovich, Anton, *Trailing Geronimo*, ed. E.A. Brininstool. Los Angeles: Gem Publishing Company, 1926.

Melish, John, *Travels in the United States of America, in the Years 1806 & 1807, and 1809*. New York: Johnson Reprint Corporation, 1970; first published, 1818.

Merk, Frederick, *Albert Gallatin and the Oregon Problem*. Cambridge: Harvard University Press, 1950.

———, *Slavery and the Annexation of Texas*. New York: Alfred A. Knopf, 1972.

Michaux, Andre F., *Travels to the West of the Allegheny Mountains, in the States of Ohio, Kentucky, and Tennessee, and Back to Charleston, By the Upper Carolines; Comprising the Most Interesting Details on the Present State of Agriculture, and the Natural Produce of those Countries; Together with Par-*

ticulars Relative to the Commerce that Exists between the above-mentioned States, and those situated East of the Mountains and Low Louisiana, undertaken, in the Year 1802. London: B. Crosby and Company, 1805.

Miles, Nelson A., *Personal Recollections and Observations of General Nelson A. Miles.* Chicago: Werner, 1896.

Miller, Hunter, *Treaties and Other International Acts.* Washington, D.C.: Government Printing Office, 1933.

Miller, Loren, *The Petitioners: The Story of the Negro and the United States Supreme Court.* New York: Pantheon Books, 1966.

Miner, Craig, *West of Wichita: Settling the High Plains of Kansas, 1865–1890.* Lawrence: University Press of Kansas, 1986.

———, *Wichita: The Early Years, 1865–1880.* Lincoln: University of Nebraska, 1982.

Mitchell, Samuel Augustus, *Illinois in 1837.* Philadelphia: S.A. Mitchell, 1837.

Monaghan, Jay, *The Overland Trail.* Indianapolis: Bobbs-Merrill, 1947.

Monroe, James, *The Writings of James Monroe,* ed. Stanislaus Murray Hamilton. New York: Putnam, 1902; first published, 1898.

Mooney, James, *The Ghost Dance Religion and the Sioux Outbreak of 1890.* Chicago: University of Chicago Press, 1976.

Moore, Frank (ed.), *The Rebellion Record, A Diary of American Events.* New York: Arno Press, 1977.

Morgan, Anne Hodges and Strickland, Rennard (eds.), *Oklahoma Memories.* Norman: University of Oklahoma Press, 1981.

Morgan, Dale L., *Jedediah Smith and the Opening of the West.* Lincoln: University of Nebraska Press, 1969.

Morris, Richard B. (ed.), *John Jay, The Winning of the Peace, Unpublished Papers, 1780–1784.* New York: Harper and Row, 1980.

Muir, John, *Steep Trails,* ed. William Frederic Bade. Boston: Houghton Mifflin, 1918.

Mullen, Robert, *The Latter-day Saints: The Mormons Yesterday and Today*. New York: Doubleday, 1966.

Neff, Andrew L., *History of Utah*. Salt Lake City: Deseret News Press, 1940.

Nelson, Oliver, *The Cowman's Southwest*, ed. Angie Debo. Glendale: Arthur H. Clark, 1953.

Nevins, Allan, *Fremont: Pathmaker of the West*. New York: D. Appleton-Century, 1939.

————, *Ordeal of the Union*. New York: Scribner, 1947.

Nicoll, Edith M., *Observations of a Ranchwoman in New Mexico*. London: Macmillan, 1898.

Nimmo, Joseph, *Report in Regard to the Range and Cattle Business of the United States*. New York: Arno Press, 1972; first published, 1885.

Ogden, Peter Skene, *Peter Skene Ogden's Snake Country Journal, 1826–27*, ed. K.G. Davies. London: Hudson's Bay Record Society, 1961; first published, 1950.

Oklahoma Historical Society, *Chronicles of Oklahoma*. Oklahoma City: Oklahoma Historical Society, March 1924, December 1931, Spring 1949.

Olmstead, Frederick A., *A Journey Through Texas; or a Saddle-Trip on the Southwestern Frontier*. New York: Mason Brothers, 1860.

Olson, James C., *History of Nebraska*. Lincoln: University of Nebraska Press, 1966; first published, 1955.

O'Meara, Walter, *Guns at the Forks*. Englewood Cliffs, N.J.: Prentice-Hall, 1965.

Ormsby, Waterman L., *The Butterfield Overland Mail, Only Through Passenger on the First Westbound Stage*, eds. Lyle H. Wright and Josephine M. Byrum. San Marino: Huntington Library, 1942.

Osgood, Ernest Staples, *The Day of the Cattleman*. Chicago: University of Chicago Press, 1929.

Oskison, John M., *Tecumseh and His Times*. New York: Putnam, 1938.

Otis, Delos S., *The Dawes Act and the Allotment of Indian Lands*. Norman: University of Oklahoma Press, 1973.

Owsley, Frank L., *Plain Folks of the Old South*. Baton Rouge: Louisiana State University Press, 1949.

Painter, Irwin Nell, *Exodusters: Black Migration to Kansas after Reconstruction*. Lawrence: University Press of Kansas, 1986.

Palmer, Joel, *Journal of Travels Over the Rocky Mountains, to the Mouth of the Columbia River. . . . 1845 and 1846, Containing Descriptions of the Valleys of the Willamette, Umpqua, and Clamet; a General Description of Oregon Territory. . . . A List of Necessary Outfits for Emigrants; and a Table of Distances from Camp to Camp on the Route*. Cincinnati: J.A. & U.P. James, 1847.

Parker, Samuel, *Journal of an Exploring Tour Beyond the Rocky Mountains*. Ithaca, NY: Mack, Andrus & Woodruff, 1842.

Parkman, Francis, *The Conspiracy of Pontiac and the Indian War After the Conquest of Canada*. New York: E.P. Dutton, 1908; first published, 1851.

————, *Montcalm and Wolfe*. Boston: Little Brown, 1937; first published, 1884.

————, *The Oregon Trail: Being Sketches of Prairie and Rocky Mountain Life*. Madison: University of Wisconsin Press, 1969; first published, 1849.

Parsons, Samuel Holden, *Life and Letters of Samuel Holden Parsons*, ed. Charles Hall. Binghamton, NY: Otseningo Publishing Company, 1905.

Parton, James, *Life of Andrew Jackson*. New York: Mason Brothers, 1860.

Patterson, Lawson B., *Twelve Years in the Mines of California*. Cambridge: Miles & Dillingham, 1862.

Pattie, James Ohio, *The Personal Narrative of James O. Pattie*, ed. Timothy Flint. Ann Arbor: University Microfilms, 1966; first published, 1833.

Peake, Ora Brooks, *The Colorado Range Cattle Industry*. Glendale: Arthur H. Clark, 1937.

Peck, John Mason, *Guide for Emigrants: Containing Sketches of Illinois, Missouri, and the Adjacent Parts*. New York: Arno Press, 1975; first published, 1831.

Pelzer, Louis, *The Cattlemen's Frontier: A Record of the Trans-Mississippi Cattle Industry*. New York: Russell and Russell, 1969; first published, 1936.

Perkins, Elisha Douglass, *Gold Rush Diary: Being the Journal of Elisha Douglass Perkins on the Overland Trail in the Spring and Summer of 1849*, ed. Thomas D. Clark. Lexington: University of Kentucky, 1967.

Perkins, Jacob R., *Trails, Rails, and War: The Life of Grenville M. Dodge*. Indianapolis: Bobbs-Merrill, 1929.

Pike, Zebulon M., *The Journals of Zebulon Montgomery Pike, with Letters and Related Documents*, ed. Donald Jackson. Norman: University of Oklahoma Press, 1966; first published, 1807.

Polk, James, *Diary of James Polk During His Presidency 1845–1849*, ed. Milton Milo Quaife. Chicago: A.C. McClurg, 1910.

Pollack, Norman (ed.), *The Populist Mind*. New York: Bobbs-Merrill, 1967.

Pooley, William Vipond, *The Settlement of Illinois From 1830–1850*. Madison: University of Wisconsin, 1908.

Powell, John Wesley, *Report on the Lands of the Arid Region of the United States*, ed. Wallace Stegner. Cambridge: Belknap Press of Harvard University Press, 1962; first published 1878.

Powers, Mary Rockwood, *A Woman's Overland Journey to California*, ed. W.B. Thorson. Fairfield, Washington: Ye Galleon Press, 1985; first published, 1951.

Pratt, Julius N., *Expansionists of 1812*. New York: Macmillan, 1925.

Prucha, Francis P., *American Indian Policy in the Formative Years*. Cambridge: Harvard University Press, 1962.

Quiett, Glenn C., *They Built the West*. New York: Cooper Square Publishers, 1965.

Quille, Dan De (William Wright), *The Big Bonanza: An Authentic Account of the Discovery, History, and Working of the World Renowned Comstock Lode of Nevada*. New York: Alfred A. Knopf, 1947; first published, 1876.

Ranck, George W., *Boonesborough*. New York: Arno Press and The New York Times, 1971; first published, 1901.

Ray, Orman P., *The Repeal of the Missouri Compromise*. Cleveland: Arthur H. Clark, 1909.

Read, Georgia Willis (ed.), *A Pioneer of 1850*. Boston: Little, Brown, 1927.

Reid, Bernard J., *Overland to California with the Pioneer Line*, ed. Mary McDougall Gordon. Stanford, CA: Stanford University Press, 1983; first published, 1937.

Remington, Frederic, "A Few Words From Mr. Remington," *Collier's Weekly*, March 18, 1905.

Rhodes, James Ford, *History of the United States from the Compromise of 1850*. New York: Harper and Brothers, 1893.

Richardson, Albert D., *Beyond the Mississippi: From the Great River to the Great Ocean, Life and Adventures on the Prairies, Mountains, and Pacific Coast*. New York: Bliss and Company, 1867.

Richardson, James D. (ed.), *Messages and Papers of the Presidents*. Washington, D.C.: United States Government Printing Office, 1896.

Richardson, Rupert N. and Rister, Carl C., *The Greater Southwest*. Glendale: Arthur H. Clark, 1934.

Richmond, Robert W. and Mardock, Robert W. (eds.), *A Nation Moving West*. Lincoln: University of Nebraska Press, 1966.

Ridings, Sam P., *The Chisholm Trail; a history of the world's greatest cattle trail together with a description of the persons, a narrative of the events, and reminiscences associated with the same*. Guthrie, Oklahoma: Co-operative Publishing Company, 1936.

Riegel, Robert E. and Athearn, Robert G., *America Moves West*. New York: Holt, Rinehart and Winston, 1964.

Ripley, Roswell S., *The War with Mexico*. New York: Harper and Brothers, 1849.

Rister, Carl Coke, *Land Hunger: David L. Payne and the Oklahoma Boomers*. Norman: University of Oklahoma Press, 1942.

Rives, George Lockhart, *The United States and Mexico: 1821–1848*. New York: Scribner, 1913.

Rives, John C. (ed.), *The Congressional Globe, Containing Sketches of the Debates and Proceedings of the First Session of the Thirty-First Congress*, (Vol. XXI, Pt. 1). Washington, D.C.: John C. Rives, 1850.

Robbins, Robin M., *Our Landed Heritage: The Public Domain, 1776–1936*. Lincoln: University of Nebraska, 1962.

Roberts, O.M., *Confederate Military History*. New York: Thomas Yoseloff, 1962.

Robertson, James Alexander, *Louisiana Under the Rule of Spain, France, and the United States, 1785–1807*. Freeport, NY: Books for Libraries Press, 1969; first published, 1910–1911.

Robinson, Charles, *The Kansas Conflict*. Freeport, NY: Books For Libraries Press, 1972.

Robinson, Elwyn B., *History of North Dakota*. Lincoln: University of Nebraska Press, 1966.

Robinson, Jacob S. (ed.) *A Journal of The Santa Fe Expedition under Colonel Doniphan*. Princeton: Princeton University Press, 1932.

Rodman, Paul W., *The California Gold Discovery: Sources, Documents, Accounts & Memoirs Relating to the Discovery of Gold at Sutter's Mill*. Georgetown, Calif.: Talisman Press, 1967.

Roe, Frances M.A., *Army Letters from an Officer's Wife*. New York: D. Appleton and Company, 1909.

Roenigk, Adolph (ed.), *Pioneer History of Kansas*. Lincoln, Nebraska: Adolph Roenigk, 1933.

Rohrbough, Malcolm J., *Land-Office Business, The Settlement and Administration of American Public Lands, 1789–1837*. New York: Oxford University Press, 1968.

————, *The Trans-Appalachian Frontier*. New York: Oxford University Press, 1978.

Rollinson, John K., *Wyoming Cattle Trails*. Caldwell: Caxton Printers Ltd., 1948.

Roosevelt, Theodore, *Ranch Life and the Hunting Trail*. Lincoln: University of Nebraska Press, 1983; first published, 1888.

Root, Frank A. and Connelley, William E., *The Overland Stage to California: Personal Reminiscences and Authentic History of the Great Overland Stage Line and Pony Express From the Missouri River to the Pacific Ocean*. Columbus, Ohio: Long's College Book Company, 1950; first published, 1901.

Ross, Alexander, *The Adventures of the First Settlers on the Oregon or Columbia River*, ed. M.M. Quaife. Chicago: Lakeside Press, 1923; first published, 1849.

Royce, Sarah, *A Frontier Lady, Recollections of the Gold Rush and Early California*, ed. Ralph Henry Gabriel. New Haven: Yale University Press, 1932.

Ruede, Howard, *Sod-Hod House Days: Letters From A Kansas Homesteader, 1877–1878*, ed. John Ise. New York: Columbia University Press, 1937.

Rusling, James F., *Across America; or, The Great West and the Pacific Coast*. New York: Sheldon and Company, 1875.

Russell, Osborne, *Journal of a Trapper: or Nine Years Residence in the Rocky Mountains, 1834–1843; being a General Description of the Country, Climate, Rivers, Lakes, Mountains, etc. and a View of the Life Led by a Hunter in Those Regions*. Lincoln: University of Nebraska Press, 1955; first published, 1914.

Sabin, Edwin L., *Kit Carson Days*. New York: Press of Pioneers, 1935; first published, 1914.

Sage, Rufus B., *His Letters and Papers, 1836–1847*, eds. Leroy R. Hafen and Ann W. Hafen. Glendale: Arthur H. Clark, 1956.

Sanford, Mollie Dorsey, *Mollie: The Journal of Mollie Dorsey Sanford in Nebraska and Colorado Territories, 1857–1866*, ed. Donald F. Danker. Lincoln: University of Nebraska Press, 1959.

Sargent, Winthrop (ed.), *The History of an Expedition Against Fort Du Quesne in 1755*. Philadelphia: Historical Society of Pennsylvania, 1855.

Scharmann, Hermann B., *Overland Journey to California*. Freeport: Books for Libraries Press, 1969; first published, 1918.

Schultz, Christian, *Travels on an Inland Voyage through the States of New York, Pennsylvania, Virginia, Ohio, Kentucky and Tennessee, and through the Territories of Indiana, Louisiana, Mississippi and New Orleans; Performed in the Years 1807 and 1808*. New York: Isaac Riley, 1810.

Schlissel, Lillian (ed.), *Women's Diaries of the Westward Journey*. New York: Schocken Books, 1982.

Schmeekebier, Laurence F., *The Office of Indian Affairs*. Baltimore: Johns Hopkins Press, 1927.

Schoolcraft, Henry Rowe, *Travels in the Central Portions of the Mississippi Valley*. New York: Collins and Hannay, 1825.

Seineke, Katherine W., *The George Rogers Clark Adventure in the Illinois*. New Orleans: Polyanthos, 1981.

Semmes, Raphael, *Service Afloat and Ashore during the Mexican War*. Cincinnati: W.H. Moore, 1851.

Shoemaker, Floyd C., *Missouri's Struggle for Statehood, 1804–1821*. Jefferson City, Missouri: The Hugh Stephens Printing Company, 1916.

Simpson, Sir George, *Narrative of a Journey Round the World*. London: H. Colburn, 1847.

Smith, Alice E. (ed.), *Wisconsin's First Railroad*. Madison: Wisconsin Magazine of History, March 1947.

Smith, George Winston and Judah, Charles (eds.), *Chronicles of the Gringos: The U.S. Army in the Mexican War, 1846–1848: Accounts of Eye-*

witnesses and Combatants. Albuquerque: University of New Mexico Press, 1968.

Smith, Henry Nash, *Virgin Land: The American West as Symbol and Myth.* Cambridge: Harvard University Press, 1950.

Smith, James, *An Account of the Remarkable Occurrence's in the Life and Travels of Colonel James Smith, During his Captivity with the Indians, in the Years 1755, '56, '57, '58 & '59,* ed. William M. Darlington. Cincinnati: Robert Clarke & Company, 1907; first published, 1799.

Smith, Jedediah, *The Travels of Jedediah Smith: A Documentary Outline Including the Journal of the Great American Pathfinder,* ed. Maurice S. Sullivan. Santa Anna, California: Fine Arts Press, 1934.

Smith, Justin H., *The Annexation of Texas.* New York: AMS Press, 1971; first published, 1911.

Sosin, Jack M. (ed.), *The Opening of the West.* New York: Harper and Row, 1969.

Speed, Thomas, *The Wilderness Road.* New York: Lenox Hill, 1971; first published, 1886.

Sprague, Marshall, *Massacre: The Tragedy at White River.* Boston: Little Brown, 1957.

Sprague, William Forest, *Women and the West.* New York: Arno Press, 1972; first published, 1940.

Spring, Agnes Wright, *When Grass Was King.* Boulder: University of Colorado Press, 1956.

Stanley, Henry M., *My Early Travels and Adventures in America and Asia.* Lincoln: University of Nebraska Press, 1982; first published, 1895.

Stanley, Reva, *A Biography of Parley P. Pratt: The Archer of Paradise.* Caldwell, Idaho: Caxton Printers, 1937.

Stevens, Walter B., *Centennial History of Missouri.* St. Louis: S.J. Clarke Publishing Company, 1921.

Stewart, Edgar I., *Penny-An-Acre Empire in the West.* Norman: University of Oklahoma Press, 1968.

Stewart, Elinore Pruitt, *Letters of A Woman Homesteader*. Lincoln: University of Nebraska Press, 1961; first published, 1914.

Stewart, George R., *The California Trail*. New York: McGraw-Hill, 1962.

———, *Ordeal By Hunger: The Story of the Donner Party*. Lincoln: University of Nebraska, 1960; first published, 1936.

Still, Bayard (ed.), *The West; Contemporary Records of America's Expansion Across the Continent, 1607–1890*. New York: Capricorn, 1961.

Stokes, George W., *Deadwood Gold: A Story of the Black Hills*. New York: World, 1926.

Stone, William, *The Life of Joseph Brant*. New York: Alexander V. Blake, 1838.

Stourzh, Gerard, *Benjamin Franklin and American Policy*. Chicago: University of Chicago Press, 1954.

Strahorn, Robert E., *The Hand-book of Wyoming and Guide to the Black Hills and Big Horn Regions*. Chicago: Knight & Leonard, 1877.

———, *To The Rockies and Beyond, or A Summer on the Union Pacific Railway and Branches*. Omaha: Omaha Republic Print, 1878.

Sutter, John, *Captain Sutter's Account of the First Discovery of Gold*. San Francisco: Britton and Rey, 1854.

Symmes, John Cleves, *The Correspondence of John Cleves Symmes*, ed. Beverly W. Bond. New York: Macmillan, 1926.

Taylor, Bayard, *Eldorado, or Adventures in the Path of Empire; comprising a voyage to California via Panama; Life in San Francisco and Monterey; Pictures of the Gold Region, and Experiences of Mexican Travel*. New York: Putnam, 1868; first published, 1850.

Taylor, Zachary, *Letters of Zachary Taylor: From the Battlefields of the Mexican War*. Rochester: Kraus Reprint Company, 1970; first published, 1908.

Thayer, Eli, *A History of the Kansas Crusade*. Freeport, NY: Books For Libraries Press, 1971; first published, 1889.

Thoburn, Joseph B. and Wright, Muriel H., *Oklahoma, A History of the State and Its People.* New York: Lewis Historical Publishing Company, 1929.

Thrapp, Dan L., *General Crook and the Sierra Madre Adventure.* Norman: University of Oklahoma Press, 1972.

Thwaites, Reuben Gold, *Cyrus Hall McCormick and the Reaper.* Madison: Historical Society of Wisconsin, 1969; first published, 1909.

———, *Documentary History of Lord Dunmore's War.* Madison: Wisconsin Historical Society, 1905.

Thwaites, Reuben Gold (ed.), *Early Western Travels, 1748–1846,* 32 vols. Cleveland: Arthur H. Clark, 1904–07.

Townsend, Edward Davis, *The California Diary of General E.D. Townsend* ed. Malcolm Edwards. Los Angeles: Ward Ritchie Press, 1970; first published, 1884.

Townsend, John, *A Narrative of a Journey Across the Rocky Mountains, to the Columbia River; and A Visit to the Sandwich Islands, Chile, &, with a Scientific Appendix.* Philadelphia: H. Perkins, 1839.

Trafzer, Clifford E., *The Kit Carson Campaign.* Norman: University of Oklahoma Press, 1982.

Trent, William, "Journal at Fort Pitt," *Mississippi Historical Review,* 11:390–413 (1914).

Triggs, J.H., *History of Cheyenne and Northern Wyoming.* Omaha: Herald Printing House, 1876.

Trollope, Frances, *Domestic Manners of the Americans.* London: Whittaker, Treacher and Company, 1832.

Tryon, Warren S. (ed.), *A Mirror for Americans.* Chicago: University of Chicago Press, 1952.

Tucker, Glenn, *Tecumseh: Vision of Glory.* New York: Russell and Russell, 1973.

Tullidge, Edward W., *Life of Brigham Young; or Utah and her founders.* Washington, D.C.: Library of Congress, 1876.

Tupper, Ferdinand Brock, *The Life and Correspondence of Major-General Sir Isaac Brock.* London: Simpkin, Marshal and Company, 1847.

Turner, Frederic Jackson, *The Frontier in American History.* New York: Henry Holt, 1920.

————, *The Significance of the Frontier in American History.* Madison: State Historical Society of Wisconsin, 1894.

————, *The Significance of Sections in American History.* New York: Henry Holt, 1932.

Turner, John, *Pioneers of the West, A True Narrative.* Cincinnati: Jennings & Pye, 1963.

Twain, Mark, *Roughing It.* New York: Harper and Brothers, 1899; first published 1872.

U.S. Congress, *American State Papers: Documents, Legislative and Executive of the Congress of the United States; Indian Affairs.* Washington, D.C.: Government Printing Office, 1832–61.

U.S. Senate, *Document 10, 46th Congress, 2d Session, Operations to Control Squaters in Indian Territory.* Washington, D.C.: Government Printing Office, 1879.

U.S. Senate, *Document 512, 23d Congress, 1st Session, Correspondence on Removal of Indians West of the Mississippi River, 1831–1833, and Accounts of Disbursing Agents.* Washington, D.C.: Government Printing Office, 1833.

United States War Department, *The War of Rebellion: A Compilation of the Official Records of the Union and Confederate Armies.* Washington, D.C.: Government Printing Office, 1880–1901.

Utley, Robert M., *The Last Days of the Sioux Nation.* New Haven: Yale University Press, 1963.

Varnum, Charles A., *Custer's Chief of Scouts: The Reminiscences of Charles A. Varnum*, ed. John M. Carroll. Lincoln: University of Nebraska Press, 1982.

Vestal, Stanley, *Sitting Bull: Champion of the Sioux.* Norman: University of Oklahoma Press, 1957; first published, 1932.

Veterans of Foreign Wars of the United States, *Great Crises in Our History Told by Its Makers*. Chicago: Veterans of Foreign Wars of the United States, 1925.

Waldman, Carl, *Who Was Who in Native American History: Indians and Non-Indians From Early Contacts Through 1900*. New York: Facts On File, 1990.

Ware, Joseph, *The Emigrants' Guide to California, Containing Every Point of Information for the Emigrant—including Routes, Distances, Water, Grass . . . with a Large Map of Routes, and Profile of Country, &—with Full Directions for Testing and Essaying Gold and Other Ores*. New York: Da Capo Press, 1972; first published, 1849.

Warren, Charles, *The Supreme Court in United States History*. Boston: Little, Brown, 1935.

Washburn, Wilcomb E. (ed.), *The American Indian and the United States, A Documentary History*. New York: Random House, 1973.

Washington, George, *The Diaries of George Washington*, ed. John C. Fitzpatrick. Boston and New York: Houghton Mifflin, 1925.

——, *Journal of Major George Washington*. Williamsburg, Va.: Colonial Williamsburg, 1959; first published, 1756.

——, *The Papers of George Washington*, ed. W.W. Abbot. Charlottesville: University Press of Virginia, 1983; first published, 1833–39.

——, *The Writings of George Washington*, 39 Vols., ed. John C. Fitzpatrick. Washington, D.C.: Government Printing Office, 1939; first published, 1833–1839.

Water, L.L., *Steel Trails to Santa Fe*. Lawrence: University of Kansas Press, 1950.

Wayne, Anthony, *Anthony Wayne, A Name in Arms: Soldier, Diplomat, defender of expansion westward of a nation; the Wayne-Knox-Pickering-McHenry Correspondence*, ed. Richard C. Knopf. Pittsburgh: University of Pittsburgh Press, 1959.

Weaver, James B., *A Call to Action*. Des Moines: Iowa Printing Company, 1892.

Webb, Walter Prescott, *The Great Plains.* Boston: Ginn and Company, 1931.

Webster, Daniel, *The Works of Daniel Webster.* Boston: Little, Brown, 1872.

Weems, John Edward, *To Conquer A Peace: The War Between the United States and Mexico.* New York: Doubleday, 1974.

Welch, Murlin G., *Border Warfare in Southeast Kansas, 1856–1859.* Pleasonton, KS: Linn County Publishers, 1977.

Wentworth, Edward N., *America's Sheep Trails.* Ames: Iowa State College Press, 1948.

Westermeier, Clifford P. (ed.), *Trailing the Cowboy.* Caldwell, Idaho: Caxton Printers, Ltd., 1955.

Whitney, Ellen M. (ed.), *The Black Hawk War: 1831–1832.* Springfield: Illinois State Historical Society, 1970.

Wilkes, Charles, *Narrative of the United States Exploring Expedition During the Years 1838, 1839, 1840, 1841, 1842.* Philadelphia: Lea and Blanchard, 1845.

Williams, R.H., *With the Border Ruffians, 1852–1868, Memories of the Far West,* ed. E.W. Williams. Lincoln: University of Nebraska Press, 1982; first published, 1907.

Winther, Oscar Osburn, *Express and Stagecoach Days in California, From the Gold Rush to the Civil War.* Stanford: Stanford University Press, 1936.

Woods, Daniel B., *Sixteen Months at the Gold Diggings.* New York: Arno Press, 1973; first published, 1851.

Worth, Gorham A., *Recollections of Cincinnati.* Cincinnati: Abingdon Press, 1916; first published, 1851.

Wright, John Stillman, *Letters from the West; or A Caution to Emigrants.* Ann Arbor: University Microfilms, 1966; first published, 1819.

Wright, Robert M., *Dodge City: The Cowboy Capital.* Wichita: Wichita Eagle Press, 1913.

Wyeth, John B., *Oregon; or A Short History from the Atlantic Ocean to the Region of the Pacific, by land; drawn up from the notes and oral information of John B. Wyeth, one of the party who left Mr. Nathaniel J. Wyeth, July 28, 1832, four days march beyond the ridge of the Rocky Mountains, and the only one who has returned to New England.* Cambridge: J.B. Wyeth, 1833.

Wyeth, Nathaniel J., *The Correspondence and Journals of Captain Nathaniel J. Wyeth, 1831–6; A Record of two Expeditions for the Occupation of the Oregon Country, with maps, introduction and index.* ed. F.G. Young. Eugene, Oregon: University Press, 1899.

Wyman, Walker D. (ed.), *Nothing But Prairie and Sky: Life on the Dakota Range in the Early Days.* Norman: University of Oklahoma Press, 1970.

Young, Ann Eliza, *Life in Mormon Bondage.* Philadelphia: Aldine Press, 1908.

Young, Calvin M., *Little Turtle (Me-She-Kin-No-Quah), The Great Chief of the Miami Indian Nation.* Indianapolis: Sentinel Printing, 1917.

INDEX

Page numbers in bold refer to biographical entries in Appendix B;
numbers in italics refer to illustrations, captions and maps.